An Encyclopaedia

of

Buddhist
Deities, Demigods, Godlings, Saints and Demons

Emerging Perceptions in Buddhist Studies, no. 2

An Encyclopaedia of Buddhist Deities, Demigods, Godlings, Saints and Demons

With Special Focus on Iconographic Attributes

Volume 2

By

Fredrick W. Bunce, Ph.D.
Professor of Art
Indiana State University

Illustrations by
G.X. Capdi, M.F.A.

D.K. Printworld (P) Ltd.
NEW DELHI-110015

Cataloging in Publication Data — DK

Bunce, Fredrick W. (Fredrick William), 1935-
An encyclopaedia of Buddhist deities, demigods, godlings, saints, and demons.
(Emerging perceptions in Buddhist studies; nos. 1-2).
Includes bibliographical references (P.).

1. Buddhism — Dictionaries. 2. Gods, Buddhist — Dictionaries. 3. Buddhsit saints — Dictionaries. 4. Demonology, Buddhist — Dictionaries. 5. Art, Budhist — Dictionaries. I. Title. II. Series: Emerging perceptions in Buddhist studies; nos. 1-2.

ISBN 81-246-0018-X (vol. 1)
ISBN 81-246-0019-8 (vol. 2)
ISBN 81-246-0020-1 (set)

First Published, 1994
Second Impression, 1995
Third Impression, 1998

Published in India by:
D.K. Printworld (P) Ltd.
Regd. office: Sri Kunj, F-52, Bali Nagar
NEW DELHI - 110015
Phones : (011) 545 3975, 546 6019; *Fax:* (011) 546 5926
E-mail: dkprint@4mis.com

Printed at :DP's Impressive Impressions, New Delhi. Ph. 5642897

Contents

Volume 1

Volume 2

List of Figures

Figure

List of Plates

User's Guide

1. General

Since this iconographic encyclopaedia is a compilation, the information is as it appears within the sources. In many instances not all descriptive material is included--e.g., Rene de Nebesky-Wojkowitz merely noted the mountain-deity *Me-tog-spungs-sems* and the region O-rgyan within a list of *gzhi-bdag*-type deities of the Bon. Also, the photographic reproductions of the Pao Hsiang Lou of the Forbidden City, Beijing, and the reproductions of the xylographs of the three hundred and sixty figures of the *Chu Fo P'u-sa Sheng Hsiang Tsan* (by anonymous Chang Chia Hutuktu)(WEC), and the reproductions of the xylographs of the three hundred figures of the *Chang Chia Hutuktu Lalita-vajra* (by Rolpa Dorje [Rol-pahi rDo-rje], 1717-1778)(WEC) are such that not all of the iconographic details can be identified, nor is color always indicated. This is noted by a (?) following a questionable identification or by (?) following a reproduction in which the details are such that not even a possible identification can be made.

2. Individual Entries/Headwords

2.1 Word order

The individual entries are alphabetical, according to the Roman/English alphabet.

2.2 Transliteral equivalent variations

The Chinese transliteration is that of Wade-Giles, rather than the Pinyin, since the sources cited utilize the former transliteration rather than the latter; whereas the Tibetan transliteration is, for the most part, from A. von Staël-Holstein and S.C. Das. Even when the Wade-Giles or A. von Staël-Holstein transliteration is used by different authors, certain personal variations appear--e.g. W.E. Clark uses the spelling *rDo-rje-dbyins* (*Vajradhatu*) while B.C. Olschak employs *rDor-dByings*. Spelling variations will be noted and each will receive its own entry.

The Tibetan prefix letters appear under the alphabetized Roman/English transliteral equivalent--e.g., *dPal-ldan-lha-mo* is alphabetized under "D" rather than "Pa."

While these practices may seem "unscholarly" to the specialist, they are undertaken primarily for the ease of the non-specialist. When noted within the source, the phonetic English equivalent of the Tibetan is included in the compilation.

2.3 Diacritical Marks

Diacritical marks that are frequently used in the Roman/English transliteration of the Sanskrit, Mongolian, etc. are omitted. Again this is has been done primarily for the ease of the non-specialist .

2.4 Transliteral Variations

In addition, the inter-changeable use of the letters "v" and "w" within the Sanskrit are presented as found with the particular source--e.g., *deva* /*dewa*.

3. Language Origin(s) and Variation(s)

3.1 Headword

A deity's primary entry (headword) and description, within this compilation, will be found generally in the Sanskrit form. However, if there is no Sanskrit transliteral equivalent, it will appear as found in the text cited. The language origin will be found within the parenthesis directly following each primary entry (headword).

Within the parenthesis they will be noted as--Anam. (Annamese, Viet Namese), Chin. (Chinese), Jap. (Japanese), Jav. (Javanese), Mon. (Mongolian), Pali, Skt. (Sanskrit), Tib. (Tibetan) as applicable.

3.2 Headword variations

One scholar may present Avalokitesvara's Tibetan spelling as *sPyan-ras-gzigz*, whereas another may use *sPyan-ras-cigs*. Generally, the first consulted source's spelling has been used. If there are variations in spelling found in the language of the headword, they will be noted in within the parenthesis, following the language origin notation. In addition, deities like Chamunda (RG) and Chamunda (devi) (WEC), or Candrakanti(?)-Tara (LC) and Candtrakanti(?)-Tara (fo-mu) (WEC), etc., are merely different forms of the same deity. They are, however, given separate primary entries (headword).

3.3 Headword: other language source

Following the headword's language-source-and-variations parentheses may appear a second set of parentheses in which will be found other language sources and their variations. The deity (headword) entries within this parentheses will be italicized and each appear as a separate entry at the appropriate location.

4. Descriptive name

Frequently the English translation of the deity's name, or a 'common name' by which the deity is commonly known is given and this will appear in parentheses after the other-language-source parentheses.

5. Description

Following the above forms, there will appear a descriptive passage relating to the specific deity. In some cases this passage is lengthy, in others it is quite cursory due to the information gleaned from the various sources and, of course, to the status of the particular deity. Within this description, italicized deity names appear elsewhere in this iconographic encyclopaedia as primary entries (headwords).

6. Attributes/iconography

6.1 Form

The color, number of faces (heads), arms, iconographic attributes vary in bewildering combinations. A blue faced, three eyed, fierce dharmapala may be one of many forms of *mGon-po*. Therefore, in dealing with the individual deities, whenever possible, the following form will be used:

6.2 Face

A description including number of faces or heads, number of eyes if more than two per face, hair, whether angry or fierce (if there is no notation, it is to be assumed to be calm), and any special ornaments worn on the head and color variations will appear. See: 8. Example Entry, below.

6.3 Arms/hand

An enumeration including number and objects held.[1] Within the attribute/iconographic entries, the Sanskrit generally appears first, followed by the Tibetan--e.g., "thunderbolt (*vajra, rdo-rje*)" or "alms bowl (*patra, lhung-bzed*) " or "mongoose (*ichneumon* or *nakula, nehu-li*)." If the transliteral equivalent presented is not Sanskrit, or if the Sanskrit equivalent is not included, the language source of the term will be noted--e.g., "divination arrow (Tib.: *mda'-dar*)." Also, since diacritical marks are not being used the English phonetic spelling will be used for the attributes/iconography--e.g., *chakra* rather than *cakra* and *shara* rather than *sara*. See: 8. Example Entry, below.

6.4 Mudra

The mudra or ritual hand position will be noted only in the cases where the hands do not hold any objects. See: 8. Example Entry, below.

6.5 Body

A description of the body including garments worn and any specific attribute included

[1] In the case of a staff/stick, there are over twelve different types. In many written descriptions, they are not noted as to type, also in many of the xylographic representations the specific type is not identifiable. In those cases the term staff/stick is used without the Sanskrit/Tibetan terms.

will appear. See: **8. Example Entry**, below.

6.6 Legs

A description of the legs including number and covering will appear. See: **8. Example Entry**, below.

6.7 Asana

A description of the seated or standing position will appear. See: **8. Example Entry**, below.

6.8 Color

The specific, main color of the deity will appear. In many of the sources the color is not noted. However, especially in the calm deities, if the deity is an emanation of one of the major deities--e.g., Aksobhya, Amitabha, etc.-- the color of the kulesa will be noted. See: **8. Example Entry**, below.

6.9 Ornaments

Only in rare cases is a deity depicted nude, generally they wear specific ornaments whether they are Buddha-like, bodhisattvas, dharmapalas, etc. These generic ornaments and specific ornaments appropriate to a deity will we listed. See: **8. Example Entry**, below.

6.10 Vahana

The description of the seat, foot rest or vehicle of the deity will appear. See: **8. Example Entry**, below.

6.11 Shakti

Whether the deity is shakti to another deity or the name of the primary entry's shakti will be noted. See: **8. Example Entry**, below.

6.12 Companion

The companions of the primary entry (headword) and of whom the entry is a companion will be noted. See: **8. Example Entry**, below.

6.13 Emanation

The name of the deity from which the primary entry (headword) emanated or was derived will appear. See: **8. Example Entry**, below.

6.14 Form

The various forms or emanations of major deities will appear. See: **8. Example Entry**, below.

6.15 Source(s)

The source(s) will appear within parentheses as initials which are also found below under Abbreviations and the complete entry will be found in the Bibliography See: **8. Example Entry**, and **9. Abbreviations**, below..

7. Variations in Headword Entry

When a deity appears with symbols, colors, asanas, etc., that are at variance with the headword entry, they will appear following the primary entry preceded by an appropriate number--e.g., **-- (2) --**. See: **8. Example Entry**, below.

8. Example Entry

Note: the superscript numbers refer to the numbers above and their proper heading--e.g., (Skt.)3.1, 3.2 , refers to **3.1 Headword** and and **3.2 Headword Variations**.

Amitabha[2] -- (Skt.)[3.1, 3.2](Chin.: *A-mi-to* or *A-mi-to fo, O-mi-to, Wu-liang-kuang fo*; Jap.; *Amida*; Mon.: *Caghlasi ugei gereltu* aka *Abida* and *Ąmindev-a*; Tib.: *'Od-dpag-med, hOd-dpag-med , Snang-va-mthah-yas*, [phon. Eng.] *Opagme*)[3.3]("immeasurable light" or "infinite light")[4.] A *Dhyani Buddha* oriented in the West. His recognition symbol is the lotus (*padma*). Water and the night are his associations. He is the lord of the heavenly Sukhavati (Dewa Chen). The personification of the five Buddha energies, and represents the lotus energy which changes passion into spiritual purity. He may be portrayed sitting on a peacock throne.[5.] Face: one, usnisa, urna, long ear lobs;[6.2] arms/hands: two, *dhyana* with bowl (*patra, lhung-bzed*);[6.3] mudra: *dhyana*;[6.4] body: mature;[6.5] legs: two;[6.6] asana: *dhyanasana*;[6.7] color: red;[6.8] vahana: pair of peacocks.[6.10] Amitabha's various forms/emanations are: *Acala-Amitayus, Amida,*

Amida Nyorai, Amindev-a, Amitabha (Bodhisattva), Amitayus, Amitayus, Amitayus (Buddha), Amitayus Jina, A-mi-to, A-mi-to fo, Ayusi, Ba-ri-lugs-Amitayus, Bhagavan Amitabha, Caryatantra Amitayus, Caturbhuja-Amitayus, (Caturbhuja)-Sita-Amitayus, Dharma-Vasita, Guna-Amitayus, Hayagriva, Jina-Amitabha, Jnana-Amitayus, Jnana-Vasita, Karma-Amitayus, Karma-Vasita, Mahasitavati, Mitra-krama-Sita-Amitayus, Nirmanakaya-Amitayus, O-mi-to-fo, Padma-Amitayus, Pariskara-Vasita, Ratna-Amitayus, Tathatavasita, Upapatti-Vasita, Vajra-Amitayus. [6.14] (RG, AKG, AG, WEC, WE-W, ML, LC)[6.15]

-- **(2)**[7.] -- One of the deities pictured in the "Three-hundred Icons" (Tib.: *sKu-brnan-brgya-phrag-gsum* or *sKu-brnan-sum-brgya*) with preface by Lcan-skya Qutugtu Rol-pahi-rdo-rje (1736-1795). The *yi-dam* form of the *Dhyani Buddha*. Face: one, crowned; arms/hands: two, *dhyana* with bowl (*patra, lhung-bzed*) and bell (*ghanta, dril-bu*) embracing *Pandara*; mudra: *dhyana*; body: in *yab-yum* position; legs: two; asana: *dhyanasana*; color: red; ornaments: five leafed crown, earring, tight necklace, armlet, wristlet, bracelet, anklet, a wrap for the lower body and one for the upper, a garland to the thigh and one to the navel, a girdle (wide belt) and a sash;[6.9] vahana: pair of peacocks; *shakti*: *Pandara* in *yab-yum* position, holds skull-cup (*kapala, thod-pa*) and ritual chopper (*karttrika, grig-gug*). [6.11] (AKG, BO, LC)

-- **(3)** -- (Chin.: *Wu-liang-kuang fo*) A tantric form of the *Dhyani Buddha Amitabha* and one of the *Buddha-bodhisattva* images found in the Pao Hsiang Lou temple of the Forbidden City, Beijing. Face: three; arms/hands: six, right hands hold thunderbolt (*vajra, rdo-rje*), wheel (*chakra, hkhor-lo*) and in *vitarka mudra*, left hands hold bell (*ghanta, dril-bu*), sword (*khadga, ral-gri*) and (?); mudra: *vitarka*; legs: two; asana: *vajrasana*; ornaments: five leafed crown, earring, tight necklace, armlet, wristlet, bracelet, anklet, a wrap for the lower body and one for the upper, a garland to the thigh and one to the navel, a girdle (wide belt) and a sash; vahana: lotus throne. (WEC)

-- **(4)** -- (Skt.: aka *Bhagavan Amitabha*)(Tib.: *Snang-va-mthah-yas*) He personifies life eternal and is the embodiment of all-discerning wisdom. A Tantric manifestation, a deity of the second state of the Bardo-Thodol ("Liberation by hearing on the After Death Plane") known as the Chonyid Bardo ("Transitional State of the Experiencing of Reality"), the deity of the fourth day, known as *Bhagavan Amitabha*, the *Dhyani Buddha* of the Western Realm. Face: one; arms/hands: two, holding an lotus (*padma*); body: human-form, in *yab-yum* position; legs: two; asana: *vajrasana* ; ornaments: five leafed crown, earring, tight necklace, armlet, wristlet, bracelet, anklet, a wrap for the lower body and one for the upper, a garland to the thigh and one to the navel, a girdle (wide belt) and a sash; color: red; shakti:, Divine Mother *Gos-dkar-mo* in *yab-yum* position. (WE-W)

9. Abbreviations

Source abbreviations, following the User's Guide, are the identifying initials which appear in parentheses after each deity-entry, where applicable. Full bibliographic information is to be found in the Bibliography.

10. Deity Identification Tables

The second volume begins with the "Deity Identification Tables." The major deities are listed in a readily accessible table form. They are set up to provide easy access/identification on a nine-step separation/distinction basis: color, calm or wrathful, head/eyes, hands, objects held, body, feet, asana, and other attributes.

11. Appendices

11.1 Classes, Groups and Hierarchies

A hierarchic table of deities is followed by an alphabetical list of various classes and groups. A number of the major classes and groups, due to their importance, have separate listings with this iconographic encyclopaedia.

11.2 Tibetan Alphabet

The Roman/English transliteral equivalent of the Tibetan alphabet.

11.3 Tibetan Vajrayana Orders

A listing and brief description of the major Vajrayana sects in Tibet.

12. Glossaries

The glossaries, due to their specific nature, appear in three sections:

12.1 Asana

Asana (the ritual position of the legs),

12.2 Mudra

Mudra or hasta (the ritual position of the hands), and

12.3 Attributes

Attributes or iconography, which includes both articles held in the hands or arms and the vahanas (the seat, vehicle or animal upon which the deity stands or sits).

13. Deity List

An alphabetized list of all the entries in the encyclopaedia.

14. Figures

The "Figures" were drawn and are presented to show basic iconographic features--i.e., number of faces, hands and feet, mudra, asana, ornaments, and objects held in hands. They are not purported to adhere to Vajrayana Iconometric Theory or Practices.[2]

[2] For a thorough explanation of Tibetan Vajrayana Iconometric theory, refer to: David P. Jackson and Janice A. Jackson, Tibetan Thangka Painting: Methods and Materials, London: 1984, pp. 45-75.

Abbreviations

The following identifying initials which appear in parentheses after each deity-entry, where applicable. Full bibliographic information is to be found in the Bibliography.

AC A. Chattopadhyay, *Catalogue of Kanjur and Tanjur.*
AD-N A. David-Neel, *Magic and Mystery in Tibet.*
AG Alice Getty, *The Gods of Northern Buddhism, Their History, Iconography, and Progressive Evolution through the Northern Buddhist Countries.*
AGr Albert Grünwedel, *bSa-mbha-la I lan yig: Der Weg nach bSambhala.*
AKG Antoinette K. Gordon, *The Iconography of Tibetan Lamaism.*
AM Ajit Mookerjee, *Tantra Art.*
ASH A. F. von Sta(h)el-Holstein, (ed.), *Der Karmapradeipa.*
BB Benoytosh Bhattacharyya, ed., *Guhyasa-meaja tantra or Tatheagataguhyaka.*
BB I __________, *The Indian Buddhist Iconography Mainly Based on the Seadhanamealea and other Cognate Tantric Texts of Rituals.*
BB II __________, ed., *Two Vajrayana Works.*
BHH Brian H. Hodgson, *Essays on the Languages, Literature and Religion Nepal and Tibet.*
BNG B.N. Goswamy and A.L. Dahmen-Dallapiccola. *An Early Document of Indian Art.*
BO Blanche C. Olschak and Gesche Thupten Wangyal, *Mystic Art of Ancient Tibet.*
BP P. Banerjee et al, *Buddhist Iconography.*
CAW C.A.S. Williams, *Outlines of Chinese Symbolism and Art Motives.*
CB C. Bell, *The Religion of Tibet.*
CH Christmas Humphreys, *A Popular Dictionary of Buddhism.*
DB Dipak Chandra Bhattacharyya, *Studies in Buddhist Iconography.*
DB I __________, *Tantric Buddhist Iconographic Sources.*
DIG David I. Gredzens, *Visions from the Top of the World.*
DIL Detlef Ingo Lauf, *Tibetan Sacred Art; The Heritage of Tantra.*
DLS David L. Snellgrove, *Indo-Tibetan Buddhism.*
DLS I __________, *Four Lamas of Dolpo.*
DLS II __________, *The Image of the Buddha.*
DPJ David P. Jackson and Janice A. Jackson, *Tibetan Thangka Painting.*
EDS E. Dale Saunders, *Mudra: A study of Symbolic Gestures in Japanese Buddhist Sculpture.*
EP Eugene Pander, *Das Pantheon dTschangtscha Hutuktu.*
ES Emil Schlagintweit, *Le bouddhisme au Tibet.*
ES I __________, *Buddhism in Tibet.*
FL Ferdinamd D. Lessing, *Yung-Ho-Kung: An Iconography of the Lamaist Cathedral in Peking.*
GB G. Beguin, *Forty-one Thang-kas from the Collection of His Holiness the Dalai Lama.*
GK Kelsang Gyatso, *Buddhism in the Tibetan Tradition.*
GKG Geshe Kelsang Gyatso. *Buddhism in the Tibetan Tradition.*
GR George Roerich, *Tibetan Paintings.*
GT Giuseppi Tucci, *The Religions of Tibet.*
GT I __________, *The Theory and Practice of the Mandala.*
GT II __________, *Tibetan Painted Scrolls.*
GT III __________, *Indo Tibetica.*
HD Har Dayal, *The Doctrine in Buddhist Sanskrit Literature.*
HH H. Hoffman, *The Religion of Tibet.*
HK H. Karmay, *Early Sino-Tibetan Art.*
HPS Hera Prasad Shastri, *A Descriptive Catalogue of Sanskrit Manuscripts in the Government Collection under the care of the Asiatic Society of Bengal.*
HVG H.V. Guenther, *Tibetan Buddhism without Mystification.*
RJ Richard Josephson, *Swayambu.*

JL J. Lowry, *Tibetan Art.*
KSC Kenneth K.S. Ch'en, *Buddhism in China.*
KV ·Kapila Vatsyayan, *Buddhist Iconography.*
Lal M. Lalou, *Iconographie des etoffes peintes d'apres le Manjusrimulakalpa.*
Lal I __________, *Repertoire du Tanjur d'apres le Catalogue de P. Cordier.*
LAW L.A. Waddell, *The Buddhism of Tibet or Lamaism.*
LC Lokesh Chandra, *Buddhist Iconography.*
LJ Lumir Jisl, *Tibetan Art.*
MacD A. MacDonald, and A.V. Stahl, *Newar Art.*
ML Manfred Lurker, *Dictionary of Gods and Goddesses, Devils and Demons.*
MM M.T. Mallmann, *Introduction a l'iconographie du tantrisme bouddhidtique.*
MWV M. W. de Visser, *Ancient Buddhism in Japan.*
NMA Newark Museum Association, *Catalogue of the Tibetan Collection and other Lamist Art.*
NMA I __________, *Tibet, A Lost World.*
PP Pratapaditya Pal, et al. *Light of Asia: Buddha Sakyamuni in Asian Art.*
PP I __________, *Art of the Himalayas: Treasures from Nepal and Tibet.*
PP II __________, *The Arts of Nepal.*
PP III __________, *The Arts of Tibet.*
PP IV __________, *Tibetan Paintings.*
PR Philip Rawson, *The Art of Tantra.*
RAP R.A. Paul, *The Tibetan Symbolic World.*
RFG Richard Francis Gombrich, *Precept and Practice: Traditional Buddhism in the Rural Highlands of Ceylon.*
RG Ramesh S. Gupte, *Iconography of the Hindus, Buddhists and Jains.*
RHG V. Reynolds, A. Heller and J. Gyats*Catalogue of the Newark Museum Tibetan Collection, III, Sculpture and Painting.*
R/L Raghuvira and Lokeshchandra (Lokesh Chandra), *A New Tibeto-Mongol Pantheon.*
RN-W Réne de Nebesky-Wojkowitz, *Oracles and Demons of Tibet: The Cult and Iconography of the Tibetan Protective Deities.*
RT Marylin M.Rhie and Robert A.F. Thurman, *Wisdom and Compassion: The Sacred Art of Tibet.*
SCD Sarat Chandra Das, *A Tibetan-English Dictionary.*
SB Stephen Batchelor, *The Tibet Guide.*
SG S. Gyatsho, *Tibetan Mandalas: the Ngor Collection.*
SH Siegbert Hummel, *Geschichte der Tibetischen Kunst.*
SK S. Kramrisch, *The Art of Nepal.*
SO S. d'Oldenburg, 'Materiaux pour l'iconographie bouddhique de Kharakhoto I,' *Materiaux pour l'ethnographie de la Russie.*
TT T. Tulku, *Sacred Art of Tibet.*
VR Valrae Reynolds, *Tibet, A Lost World.*
WEC Walter Eugene Clark, *Two Lamaistic Pantheons.*
WE-W W.Y. Evans-Wentz, *The Tibetan Book of the Dead.*
WHF Willy H. Fischle, *The Way to the Center.*

Deity Identification Tables

User's Guide
Deity Indentification Tables

On the following pages appear the "Deity Identification Tables." They are set up to provide easy access/identification on a nine-step separation/distinction basis.

I. **Color** -- The first major separation/distinction is by color. The Dhyani Buddhas each have their specific color and generally this color is borne by their various forms and/or emanations--e.g., Vairocana (white), Amitabha (red), Aksobhya (blue), Amoghasiddhi (green), and Ratnasambhava (yellow). Wrathful forms frequently bear dark colors (dark green, black, dark red or blue). The color separation/distinctions are:

A. white (Skt.: sita; Tib.: dkar),
B. red (Skt.: rakta; Tib.: dmar),
C. blue (Skt.: nila; Tib.: snon-[can], snong),
D. green or "dark" (Skt.: syama; Tib.: ljan, ljang),
E. yellow (Skt.: pita; Tib.: ser-[po]),
F. black (Skt.: krsna; Tib.: nag-[po]),
G. brown (Skt.: babhru), dark (Skt.: syama), purple, "smoke (grey) color" (Skt.: dhumavarna; Tib.: dud-kha),
I. Natural color, and
H. Colors not designated or noted in the sources.

II. **Calm or Wrathful** -- The second separation/distinction is whether a deity is calm or wrathful. This distinction is made within each color separation--e.g., White, Calm or White, Wrathful, etc.

III. **Head/Eyes** -- The third separation/distinction is by the number of head(s) and eye(s) of a particular deity--e.g., one/two or three/nine indicates that a deity has one head and two eyes or three heads and nine eyes (three per head), respectively.

IV. **Hands** -- The fourth separation/distinction is by the number of hands a particular deity possesses.

V. **Objects Held** -- The fifth separation/distinction lists the objects held in the hands of the deity.

VI. **Body** -- The sixth separation/distinction describes the body-type of a particular deity--e.g., whether youthful, mature, corpulent or aged, and whether nude.

VII. **Feet** -- The seventh separation/distinction enumerates the number of feet of a particular deity.

VIII. **Asana** -- The eighth separation/distinction describes the asana of the particular deity.

IX. **Other Attributes** -- The final separation/distinction lists other pertinent attributes of a particular deity, such as:

A. ornaments (bodhisattva-like or dharmapala-like),
B. vahana,
C. color variations,

D. facial variations, etc.

Therefore, if one finds a white deity, with a calm single face with two eyes, four hands (the principle ones holding a stringed instrument, the right in *abhaya mudra* and the left holding a serpent /snake), two feet, *dhyanasana*, and seated upon a lotus throne; one would follow the procedures below:

1. turn to the "white, clam" deity table,
2. find the single headed/two eye deities,
3. locate the four handed deities,
4. search through those deities until a deity with principle hands holding a stringed instrument, the other right in *abhaya mudra* and the left holding a serpent /snake is found,
5. check the body type,
6. note the number of feet,
7. note the *asana*, and
8. verify the "Other Attributes."

If all has been done correctly one may assume that the deity in question is in all probability *Arya-Janguli*, a white *Tara* deity.

In many of the sources the color has not been noted, consequently, there is a rather lengthy section of deities for which color has not been noted--e.g., "Colors not designated or noted in the sources." In addition there are deities for which color has not been noted but for which color has been tentatively assigned through either the deity's *kulesa* or form. This has been noted in the written entries and with a double asterisk (**) following the deity's name in the chart.

Also, in a number of cases different forms of the same deity may have identical iconography--e.g., both *Sadyonubhava-Arapacana* and *Sadyonubhava-Manjusri* are described thus: "Face: one, calm; arms/hands: two, right hand holds the sword (*khadga, ral-gri*), left hand holds *Prajna Paramita* book/manuscript (*pustaka, sher-phyin*) against the chest; legs: two; asana: *vajrasana*; ornaments: five leafed crown, earring, tight necklace, armlet, wristlet, bracelet, anklet, a wrap for the lower body and one for the upper, a garland to the thigh and one to the navel, a girdle (wide belt) and a sash; color: red." In order to identify both deity forms, it is important to refer to the written entry where the attendant deities may help in identifying each separate deity.

White (Skt.: sita; Tib.: dkar-po), Calm Deities

Abbreviations:

as. = asana	bk. = black	bl. = blue	bodh. = bodhisattva
bn. = brown	corp. = corpulent	dhar. = dharmapala	gn. = green
lt. = left	mu. = mudra	pu. = purple	rd. = red
rt. = right	sc. = smokey	va. = vahana	wh. = white
yw. = yellow			

(*) special variations or attributes noted within the entry.

(**) following deity's name indicates that the color is not noted in the source, kulesa's color is applied to the entry.

(eyes: 2-3, 6-9, etc.) in sources the deity's faces are noted, but the number of the eyes are not noted.

Head/Eyes	Hands	Objects Held	Body	Feet	Asana	Other Attributes	Deity Name
one/two	two	rt.: thunderbolt lt.: bell; vajrahumkara mu.	mature	two	vajra	bodh. ornaments, va.: lotus throne	Adi-Buddha (Vajradhara)
one/two	two	rt. thunderbolt on point at chest level lt.: bell on thigh	mature	two	sama-bhanga or vajra	bodh. ornaments, va.: lotus throne	Adi-Buddha (Vajrasattva)
							Dhyani Buddha Vairocana
one/two	two	rt.: rosary lt.: pink lotus	youth	two	dhyana	bodh. ornaments, va: lotus throne	Avalokitesvara[1]
one/two	two	dharmachakra mu. with lotus bud	youth	two	sattva	bodh. ornaments,	Avalokitesvara va: lotus throne
one/two	two	dharmachakra mu. with lotus bud	youth	two	sama-bhanga	bodh. ornaments, va: lotus throne	Avalokitesvara
one/two	two	rt.: abhaya mu. conch-topped staff/ stick on rt. shoulder lt.: alms bowl	youth	two	sama-bhanga	bodh. ornaments, va.: lotus throne	Acalaketu-Lokesvara**[2]
one/two	two	rt.: varada tl.: sword	youth	two	vajra	bodh. ornaments, va.: lotus throne	Akasagarbha-Lokesvara
one/ two	two	rt.: rosary lt.: lotus on a vase/vessel against chest	youth	two	vajra	bodh. ornaments, va.: lotus throne	Aksayamati-Lokesvara

[1] Avalokitesvara and his various forms' colors are generally red (as an emanation of Amitabha) except in Nepal where his color is white

[2] The astrisks (**) after the deities' name denote that the color was not designated or shown in the source, and that the deities' color-placement is assigned via the kulesa, the emanant deity or of whose form the deity is derived. If the emanant deity has a number of colors, the deity will be placed in the "Color not designated" section at the end of the Identification Charts.

one/two	two	rt.: conch shell-topped staff/stick lt.: wheel at shoulder	youth	two	sama- bhanga	bodh. ornaments, va.: lotus throne	Amitabha-Lokesvara
one/two	two	rt.: goad/hook lt.: noose/snare	youth	two	sama- bhanga	bodh. ornament, va.: lotus throne	Amoghankusa-Avalokitesvara
one/two	two	dharmacakra mu. with lotus	youth	two	vajra	bodh. ornaments, va.: lotus throne	Amoghapasa-isvara(=Lokesvara)- Avalokitesvara (Bodhisattva)
one/ two	two	rt.: crossed thunderbolts lt.: lotus on a water vase/vessel	youth	two	sama- bhanga	bodh. ornaments, va.: lotus throne	Amrtaprabha-Lokesvara
one/ two	two	rt.: stem of lotus lt.: varada mu.	youth	two	sama- bhanga	bodh. ornaments, va.: lotus throne	Anandadi-Lokesvara
one/two	two	rt.: bhumisparsa mu. lt.: stem of lotus	youth	two	sopasraya	bodh. ornaments, va.: lotus throne	Anucara-Avalokitesvara
one*/two	two	rt.: abhaya mu. lt.: vitarka mu. with stem of lotus	youth	two	vajra	*hair in toupet bodh. ornaments, va.: lotus throne	Ardhacaturth-aksara- Avalokitesvara
one/two	two	dhyana mu	youth	two	vajra	red monastic robes va.: lotus throne	Avalokita
one/two	two	rt.: sword tlt.: stem of lotus against chest	youth	two	vajra	bodh. ornaments, va.: lotus throne	Avalokita-Lokesvara
one/two	two	upper raised in anjali mu. with small image others hold tantric symbols	youth	two	dhyana	bodh. ornaments, va.: lotus throne	Avalokitesvara
one/two	two	rt.: varada mu. lt.: stem of lotus	youth	two	vamalalita	bodh. ornaments, va.: lotus throne	Avalokitesvara
one/two	two	rt.: thunderbolt lt.: thunderbolt	mature	two	vajra	bodh. ornaments, va.: lotus throne	Achala
one/two	two	rt.: lotus lt.: priyangu flower two	mature	two	(?)	bodh. ornaments, va.: lotus throne	Adhimuktivasita
one/two	two	rt.: varada mu. lt.: kataka mu. against chest	mature	two	dhyana	bodh. ornaments, va.: lotus throne	Aksayamati
one/two	two	rt.: sword lt.: abhaya mu. with lotus	mature	two	dhyana	bodh. ornaments, va.: lotus throne	Aksayamati

one/two	two	dhyana mu. with bowl filled with the elixir of life	mature	two	dhyana	bodh. ornaments, va.: lotus throne	Aksayamati
one/two	two	two rt.: crossed thunderbolts lt.: dhyana mu.	mature	two	dhyana	bodh. ornaments, va.: lotus throne	Aksayamati
one/two	two	two holding dhyana mu.	youth	two	vajra-paryanka	bodh. ornaments, va.: lotus throne	Amitabha-Manjusri
one/two	two	rt.: vase/vessel with elixir of life lt.: clenched fist on hip	mature	two	dhyana	bodh. ornaments, va.: lotus throne	Amitaprabha
one/two	two	both hold vase/vessel with elixir of life in dhyana mu.	mature	two	dhyana	bodh. ornaments, va.: lotus throne	Amitaprabha
one/two	two	rt.: double lotus lt.: vase/vessel with elixir of life on lotus	mature	two	dhyana	bodh. ornaments, va.: lotus throne	Amitaprabha
one/two	two	holding a vase/vessel	youth	two	sama-bhanga	long flowing garments	Anoku Kwan-non
one/two	two	rt.: thunderbolt lt.: noose/snare	youth	two	vamalalita	bodh. ornaments va.: lotus throne	Aparajita
one/two	two	rt.: sword lt.: *Prajna Paramita* book/manuscript	youth	two	vajra	bodh. ornaments, va.: lotus throne	Arapacana
one/two	two	rt.: sword lt.: *Prajna Paramita* book/manuscript	youth	two	vajra	bodh. ornaments, va.: lotus throne	Arapacana-Manjughosa
one/two	two	rt.: lotus lt.: lotus with book/manuscript	youth	two	sama-bhanga	bodh. ornaments, va.: lotus throne	Arya-Sarasvati
one/two	two	rt.: varada mu. lt.: jewel	mature	two	dhyana	bodh. ornaments, va.: lotus throne	Bhadrapala
one/two	two	rt.: jewel lt.: clenched at hip	mature	two	dhyana	bodh. ornaments, va.: lotus throne	Bhadrapala
one/two	two	dhyana mu.	mature	two	dhyana	bodh. ornaments, va.: lotus throne	Bhadrapala
one/two	two	rt.: varada mu. lt.: stem of lotus in karana mu.	youth	two	vamalalita	bodh. ornaments, va.: lotus throne	Ba-ri-lugs-Pacatmaka-Amoghapasa**
one/two	two	rt.: varada mu.	youth	two	dhyana	bodh. ornaments,	Bhadrapala

		lt.: jewel				va.: lotus throne	
one/two	two	rt.: jewel lt.: clenched at hip	youth	two	dhyana	bodh. ornaments, va.: lotus throne	Bhadrapala
one/two	two	dhyana mu.	youth	two	dhyana	bodh. ornaments, va.: lotus throne	Bhadrapala
one/two	two	rt.: thunderbolt lt.: abhaya mu.	youth	two	vamalalita	bodh, ornaments, va.: lotus throne	Buddha-Locana (fo-mu)**
one/two	two	moon disc on lotus	youth	two		bodh. ornaments, va.: swan	Candra
one/two	two	rt.: flaming jewels lt.: rests on thigh	youth	two	sattva	bodh. ornaments, va.: lotus throne	Candra (deva)**
one/two	two	rt.: vase/vessel lt.: lotus	youth	two	sattva	bodh. ornaments, va.: lotus throne	Candra (deva)**
one/two	two	rt.: vitarka mu. lt.: stem of lotus to chest	youth	two	vajra	bodh. ornaments, va.: lotus throne	Candraprabha-Lokesvara
one/two	two	rt.: lotus(?) lt.: harina mu.	youth	two	vamalalita	bodh. ornaments, va.: lotus throne	Candravairocana (Bodhisattva)
one/two	two	rt.: crossed thunderbolts lt.: rosary and vase/vessel	youth	two	vamalalita	bodh. ornaments, va.: lotus throne	Cunda
one/two	two	rt.: varada mu. lt.: lotus with moon disc	youth	two	dhyana	bodh. ornaments, va.: lotus throne	Chandraprabha
one/two	two	rt.: wheel marked with thunderbolt lt.: lotus with moon disc	youth	two	dhyana	bodh. ornaments, va.: lotus throne	Chandraprabha
one/two	two	rt.: lotus with moon disc lt.: clenched fist at hip	youth	two	dhyana	bodh. ornaments, va.: lotus throne	Chandraprabha
one/two	two	holding parasol	youth	two		bodh. ornaments, va.: lotus throne	Chatrosnisa
one/two	two	rt.: jewel lt.: wheel in dhyana mu.	youth	two	vajra	bodh. ornaments, va.: lotus throne	Cintamanichakra-Avalokitesvara**
one/two	two	rt.: varada mu. lt.: stem of lotus in karana mu.	youth	two	vajra	bodh. ornaments, va.: lotus throne	Cintamanichakra-sita-Tara

one/two	two	rt.: shrine lt.: held at waist	youth	two	sama-bhanga	bodh. ornaments, va.: lotus throne	Cintamani-Lokesvara**
one/two	two	rt.: image of *Dhyani Buddha Amitabha* lt.: abhaya mu.	youth	two	sama-bhanga	bodh. ornaments, va.: lotus throne	Cittadhatu-Lokesvara**
one/two	two	rt.: abhaya mu. lt.: bhumisparsa mu.	youth	two	sattva	bodh. ornaments, va.: lotus throne	Cittavisramana-Avalokitesvara**
one/two	two	rt.: lotus lt.: thunderbolt	youth	two		bodh. ornaments, va.: lotus throne	Citta-Vasita
one/two	two	rt.: stem of lotus lt.: (?)	youth	two	vamalalita	bodh. ornaments, va.: lotus throne	Citta-Vasita
one*/two	two	rt.: goad/hook lt.: leads elephant by trunk	youth	two	sama-bhanga	*angry bodh. ornaments, va.: lotus throne	Dasa-kundali
one/two	two	rt.: goad/hook lt.: tarjani mu.	youth	two	sama-bhanga	bodh. ornaments, va.: lotus throne	Dasa-kundali
one/two	two	rt.: thunderbolt lt.: axe	youth	two	sama-bhanga	bodh. ornaments, va.: lotus throne	Dharmacakra-Lokesvara
one/two	two	water vase/vessel at waist	youth	two	sama-bhanga	bodh. ornaments, va.: lotus throne	Dharmacakra-Lokesvara
one*/two	two	dhyana mu.	mature	two	vajra	*white or "whitish-red," bodh. ornaments, va.: lotus throne	Dharmadhatu-Vagisvara
one/two	two	dhyana mu.	mature	two	vajra	bodh. ornaments, blue lotus at shoulder level, va.: lotus throne	Dharmasanka-samadhi Manjusri
one/two	two	dhyana mu.	youth	two	vajra-paryanka	bodh. ornaments, va.: lotus throne	Dharmasanka-samadhi Manjusri
one/two	two	rt.: lotus lt.: alms bowl on lotus	youth	two		bodh. ornaments, va.: lotus throne	Dharma-Vasita
one/two	two	rt.: stem of lotus with blossom at shoulder lt.: vase/vessel	youth	two	vamalalita	bodh. ornaments, va.: lotus throne	Dharma-Vasita

one/two	two	rt.: ritual chopper lt.: human skull-cup	mature	two	ardha- paryanka	bodh. ornaments, realm: South, va.: lotus throne	Durjaya
one/two	two	rt.: short staff/stick lt.: chain	corp.	two	sopasraya	bodh. ornaments, fancy boots, realm: South, va.: raised throne	Durjaya
one/two	two	embraces his shakti	youth	two	sukha	bodh. ornaments, va.: lotus throne	Dvibhuja-Padmanartesvara- Avalokitesvara**
one/two	two	holding book/manuscript	youth	two	vajra	bodh. ornaments, va.: lotus throne	Dvibhuja-Prajnaparamita**
one/two	two	rt.: crossed thunderbolts lt.: alms bowl	youth	two	vajra	bodh. ornaments, va.: lotus throne	Dvibhuja-Usnisa-vijaya
one/two	two	rt.: vitarka mu. lt.: book/manuscript	youth	two	vajra	bodh. ornaments, va.: lotus throne	Gaganaganja-Lokesvara
one/two	two	rt.: thunderbolt lt.: rests at hip	youth	two	vajra	bodh. ornaments va.: lotus throne	Ghantapani
one/two	two	rt.: varada mu. lt.: stem of lotus in karana mu.	youth	two	vajra	bodh. ornaments, va.: lotus throne	gNan-lugs Sita Tara
one/two	two	rt.: goad/hook human skull-cup	youth	two		bodh. ornaments, va.: lotus throne	gShin-rje'i-sring-mo-mtshan-byed
one/two	two	rt.: divination arrow lt.: mirror	mature	two		silk garments, bejeweled, va.: deer	g.Yu-sgron-dkar-mo
one/two	two	vyakhyana mudra	youth	two	sama- bhanga	bodh. ornaments, va.: lotus throne	Harihara-Lokesvara**
one/two	two	rt.: vasae/vessel lt.: conch shell	youth	two	sama- bhanga	bodh. ornaments, lotus throne	Harivahana-Lokesvara**
one/two	two	rt.: flaming sun disc lt.: casque	youth	two	vamalalita	bodh. ornaments, va.: lotus throne	hGro-bzan-ma
one/two	two	uttarabodhi mu.	mature	two	vajra	bodh. ornaments, va.: lotus throne	Hung-kuang Vairocana (Buddha)**
one/two	two	rt.: abhaya mu.	youth	two	vamalalita	bodh. ornaments,	Isvara(=Lokesvara)-Avalokitesvara

		lt.: stem of lotus				va.: lotus throne	(Bodhisattva)**
one/two	two	rt.: sword on lotus lt.: stem of lotus with blossom at shoulder level	youth	two	vajra	bodh. ornaments va.: lotus throne	Ialiniprabha-Lokesvara**
one/two	two	rt.: fly-whisk lt.: serpent/snake	youth	two	vajra	bodh. ornaments, va.: lotus throne	Ianguli
one/two	two	dharmachakra mu. embracing shakti	youth	two	alidha, yab-yum	bodh. ornaments, va.: lotus throne	Jinasagara-Avalokitesvara**
one/two	two	vajrahumkara mu. embracing shakti	youth	two	vajra, yab-yum	bodh. ornaments, va.: lotus throne	Jinasagara-Avalokitesvara**
one/two	two	embraces shakti rt.: rosary lt.: (?)	youth	two	alidha, yab-yum	bodh. ornaments, va.: lotus throne	Jinasagara-Avalokitesvara (Buddha)**
one/two	two	rt.: banner/flag wish fulfilling jewel lt.: bodhi tree	mature	two		bodh. ornaments va.: lotus throne	Inana-Paramita
one/two	two	rt.: (?) lt.: book/manuscript	youth	two	vamalalita	bodh. ornaments va.: lotus throne	Inana-Paramita
one/two	two	rt.: vitarka mu. lt.: vitarka mu. at chest	youth	two	sama- bhanga	bodh. ornaments, va.: lotus throne	Kamalacandra-Lokesvara
one/two	two	rt.: thunderbolt lt.: book/manuscript against chest	youth	two	vajra	bodh. ornaments, va.: lotus throne	Karandavyuha-Lokesvara**
one/two	two	rt.: abhaya mu. lt.: stem of lotus in karana mu.	mature	two	sopasraya	bodh. ornaments, va.: lotus throne	Karunesvara-Avalokitesvara
one/two	two	rt.: varada mu. lt.: stem of lotus in karana mu. with book/manuscript	youth	two	vajra	bodh. ornaments, va.: lotus throne	Kasmira-mahapandita-krama-Sita-Manjughosa
one/two	two	rt.: varada mu. lt.: stem of lotus in karana mu.	youth	two	vajra	bodh. ornaments, va.: lotus throne	Kasmira-mahapandita-krama-Sita-Tara
one/two	two	rt.: varada mu. lt.: stem of lotus	youth	two	vamalalita	bodh. ornaments, va.: lotus throne	Khasarpana**
one/two	two	rt.: abhaya mu. lt.: stem of lotus	youth	two	vajra	bodh. ornaments, va.: lotus throne	Khasarpana-Avalokitesvara**

one/two	two	rt.: abhaya mu. lt.: stem of lotus	youth	two	vajra	bodh. ornaments, va.: lotus throne	Khasarpana-Avalokitesvara ** (Bodhisattva)
one/two	two	rt.: varada mu. lt.: stem of lotus	youth	two	lalita	bodh. ornaments, va.: lotus throne	Khasarpana-Lokesvara **
one/two	two	rt.: varada mu. lt.: stem of lotus	youth	two	ardha- paryanka	bodh. ornaments, va.: lotus throne	Khasarpana-Lokesvara **
one/two	two	rt.: varada mu. lt.: stem of lotus	youth	two	vamalalita	bodh. ornaments, va.: lotus throne	Khasarpana-Lokesvara **
one/two	two	karana mu.	youth	two	sattva	bodh. ornaments, va.: lotus throne	Krodhaparajita (devi)**
one/two	two	rt.: lotus lt.: abhaya mu.	youth	two	sattva	bodh. ornaments, va.: lotus throne	Krodhaparajitavajra**
one/two	two	namaskara mu.	youth	two	sama- bhanga	bodh. ornaments, va.: lotus throne	Krtanjali-Lokesvara**
one/two	two	namaskara mu.	youth	two	vajra	bodh. ornaments, va.: lotus throne	Krtanjali-Lokesvara**
one/two	two	rt.: shallow bowls of jewels lt.: varada mu.	youth	two	vajra	bodh. ornaments, va.: lotus throne	Ksitigarbha-Lokesvara**
one/two	two	flaming jewel	youth	two	sama- bhanga	draped garment, va.: lotus throne	Kuan-shih-yin p'u-sa
one/two	two	dhyana mu. with flaming jewel	youth	two	dhyana	draped garment, va.: lotus throne	Kuan-shih-yin p'u-sa
one/two	two	vase/vessel with willow	youth	two	maha- rajalila	draped garment, va.: lotus throne	Kuan-shih-yin p'u-sa
one/two	two	rt.: varada mu. lt.: abhaya mu.	youth	two	vajra	bodh. ornaments, flowing garments, vase/vessel at side, va.: lion	Kuan-yin
one/two	two	holds child	youth	two	sama- bhanga	bodh. ornaments, flowing garments, va.: lotus throne	Kuan-yin
oen/two	two	rt.: stem of lotus with jewel in varada mu. lt.: stem of lotus with triangle in	youth	two	vamalalita	bodh. ornaments, va:. lotus throne	Locana

kartari mu.

one/two	two	rt.: varada mu. lt.: in lap holding stem of lotus	youth	two	lalita	bodh. ornaments, va.: lotus throne	Lokanatha-raktaryy-Avalokitesvara**
one/two	two	rt.: varada mu. lt.: lotus	youth	two	sama-bhanga	bodh. ornaments, va.: lotus throne	Mahabhumika-Avalokitesvara (Bodhisattva)**
one/two	two	rt.: abhaya mu. lt.: stem of lotus	youth	two	sama-bhanga	bodh. ornaments, va.: lotus throne	Mahabhumika(?)-rakta-Avalokitesvara**
one/two	two	rt.: sword lt.: varada mu.	youth	two	sama-bhanga	bodh. ornaments, va.: lotus throne	Mahasahasrabhuja-Lokesvara**
one/two	two	rt.: varada mu. lt.: six lotus	youth	two	dhyana	bodh. ornaments, va.: lotus throne	Mahasthamaprata
one/two	two	rt.: sword lt.: lotus	youth	two	dhyana	bodh. ornaments, va.: lotus throne	Mahasthamaprata
one/two	two	rt.: sword lt.: lotus in vitarka mu.	youth	two	sattva	bodh. ornaments, va.: lotus throne	Mahasthamaprata
one/two	two	rt.: varada mu. lt.: stem of a white lotus	youth	two	sama-bhanga	bodh. ornaments, va.: lotus throne	Mahasarasvati
one/two	two	rt.: varada mu. lt.: stem of lotus	youth	two	sama-bhanga	bodh. ornaments, va.: lotus throne	Mahasthamaprapta-Lokesvara**
one/two	two	rt.: rosary lt.: rests on knee	corp	two	sattva	smiling, monastic robed, va.: antelope skin	Maitreya [pot-bellied]
one/two	two	rt.: rosary lt.: sack	corp.	two	sattva	smiling, monastic robed, dancing children companions, va.: antelope skin	Maitreya [pot-bellied]
one/two	two	rt.: rosary in vitarka mu. lt.: holds corner of robe	corp.	two	sattva	smiling, monastic robed, hemp bag at side, va.: lotus throne	Maitreya [pot-bellied]
one/two	two	rt.: varada mu. with stem of lotus lt.: vitarka mu. with stem of lotus and sword	youth	two	dhyana	bodh. ornaments, va.: lotus throne	Manjughosa

one/two	two	rt.: rosary lt.: book/manuscript	youth	two	sama- bhanga	bodh. ornaments, va.: lotus throne	Manjunatha-Lokesvara**
one/two	two	dhyana mu.	youth	two	vajra- paryanka	bodh. ornaments, va.: lotus throne	Manjusri-Bhattaraka
one/two	two	rt.: shallow bowl lt.: vase/vessel	youth	two	ardha- paryanka	bodh. ornaments, va.: lotus throne	Naivedya
one/two	two	rt.: rosary lt.: book/manuscript	youth	two	sama- bhanga	bodh. ornaments, va.: lotus throne	Nityanatha-Lokesvara
one/two	two	rt.: vitarka mu. with lotus lt.: varada mu. with lotus and vase/vessel	youth	two	lalita	bodh. ornaments, va.: lotus throne	Padmapani-Lokesvara**
one/two	two	rt.: vitarka mu. lt.: varada mu. with vase/vessel	youth	two	sama- bhanga	bodh. ornaments, va.: lotus throne	Padmapani-Lokesvara**
one/two	two	rt.: vitarka mu. with lotus stem lt.: abhaya mu. with lotus stem	youth	two	rajalila	bodh. ornaments, va.: lotus throne	Padmapani-Lokesvara**
one*/two	two	hanging at sides	youth	two	sama- bhanga	* nine images of Buddha/Bodhisattvas surround figure, bodh. ornaments, va.: lotus throne	Padmapani-Lokesvara**
one*/two	two	rt.: harina mu. with blue lotus lt.: varada mu. with blue lotus	youth	two	vamalalita	*rose-color, bodh. ornaments, va.: lotus throne	Pandara**
one*/two	two	rt.: unopened blue lotus lt.: unopened blue lotus	youth	two	vamalalita	*rose-color, bodh. ornaments, va.: lotus throne	Pandara**
one/two	two	rt.: held palm down at chest level lt.: lotus	youth	two	vajra	bodh. ornaments, va.: lotus throne	Pandaravasini-Devi
one/two	two	alms bowl	youth	two	sama- bhanga	bodh. ornaments, va.: lotus throne	Pindapatra-Lokesvara**
one/two	two	namaskara mu. with stem of lotus	youth	two	vamalalita	bodh. ornaments, va.: lotus throne	Pandaravasini (fo-mu)**

one/two	two	rt.: flaming sword lt.: book/manuscript	youth	two	vajra	*"red-yellow" color, bodh. ornaments, va.: lotus throne	Prajnachakra-Sita-Manjughosa
one/two	two	rt.: staff/stick lt.: human skull-cup with magic stick in crook of arm	youth	two	alidha	bodh. ornaments, va.: lotus throne	Prajnalokakrtya-sita-Vajravarahi
one/two	two	rt.: red lotus lt.: Prajna Paramita book	youth	two	vajra	bodh. ornaments, va.: lotus throne	Prajna-Paramita
one/two	two	rt.: flaming jewel lt.: blue lotus	youth	two	vamalalita	bodh. ornaments, va.: lotus throne	Prajna-Paramita
one/two	two	rt.: crossed thunderbolts lt.: sword	youth	two		bodh. ornaments, va.: lotus throne	Prajnavardhani
one/two	two	rt.: noose/snare lt.: bowl filled with jewels	youth	two	vajra	bodh. ornaments, va.: lotus throne	Pratibhanakakuta-Lokesvara**
one/two	two	1st pr.: varada mu. 2nd pr.: jewel, book/manuscript	youth	two		bodh. ornaments, va.: lotus throne	Pretasantarpita-Lokesvara**
one/two	two	rt.: varada mu. lt.: vase/vessel filled with nectar of life	youth	two	sattva	bodh. ornaments, va.: lotus throne	Prithivi
one/two	two	holding vase/vessel	youth	two	vamalalita	bodh. ornaments, va.: lotus throne	Prithivi (devi)**
one/two	two	rt.: Mount Sumeru lt.: vase/vessel with elixir of life	youth	two		robe and train of white silk, bodh. ornaments, va.: lotus throne	Rab-brtan-ma
one/two	two	rt.: varada mu. lt.: rests on shoulder	youth	two	sama-bhanga	bodh. ornaments, va.: lotus throne	Ratnadala-Lokesvara**
one/two	two	rt.: sword lt.: varada mu.	youth	two	vajra	bodh. ornaments, va.: lotus throne	Ratnapani-Lokesvara**
one/two	two	rt.: divination arrow lt.: mirror	youth	two		bodh. ornaments, va.: wild yak	rDo-rje-khyung-lung-ma
one/two	two	hold silver mirror	youth	two		bodh. ornaments, va.: lotus throne	rGyal-po'i-bu-mo-dkar-sham
one/two	two	rt.: club/cudgel	youth	two		bodh. ornaments,	rGyal-po-skye-'gro'i-dpal

		lt.: banner/flag of victory				va.: lotus throne	
one/two	two	rt.: thunderbolt lt.: sword on lotus	youth	two		bodh. ornaments, va.: lotus throne	Sadhumati
one/two	two	rt.: thunderbolt lt.: sword on lotus	youth	two	vamalalita	bodh. ornaments, va.: lotus throne	Sadhumati (fo-mu)**
one/two	two	rt.: crossed thunderbolt lt.: stem of lotus against chest	youth	two	sama-bhanga	bodh. ornaments, va.: lotus throne	Sagaramati-Lokesvara**
one/two	two	both outstretched and fingers depicting waves	youth	two	dhyana	bodh. ornaments, va.: lotus throne	Sagarmati
one/two	two	rt.: conch shell lt.: sword marked with thunderbolt	youth	two	dhyana	bodh. ornaments, va.: lotus throne	Sagarmati
one/two	two	holding wheel	youth	two	kneeling	bodh. ornaments, va.: lotus throne	Sahampati-Brahma**
one/two	two	rt.: thunderbolt lt.: at waist	youth	two	sama-bhanga	bodh. ornaments, va.: lotus throne	Sakyabuddha-Lokesvara**
one/two	two	rt.: varada mu. lt.: lotus, against chest	youth	two	vajra	bodh. ornaments, va.: lotus throne	Samantabhadra-Lokesvara**
one/two	two	rt.: conch shell lt.: lotus	youth	two	sama-bhanga	bodh. ornaments, va.: lotus throne	Sankhanatha-Lokesvara**
one/two	two	rt.: varada mu. lt.: asoka (?) branch	youth	two	sama-bhanga	bodh. ornaments, va.: lotus throne	Santamati-Lokesvara**
one/two	two	rt.: trident lt.: lotus	youth	two	sama-bhanga	bodh. ornaments, va.: lotus throne	Sarasiri(?)-Lokesvara**
one/two	two	rt.: varada mu. lt.: begging bowl	youth	two	sama-bhanga	bodh. ornaments, va.: lotus throne	Sarthavaha-Lokesvara**
one/two	two	rt.: stem of lotus with sword lt.: thunderbolt against chest	youth	two	vajra	bodh. ornaments, va.: lotus throne	Sarvanivaranaviskambhi-Lokesvara**
one/two	two	rt.: thumb and index finger join together with the rest of the fingers clenched lt.: bhumisparsa mu.	youth	two	dhyana	bodh. ornaments, va.: lotus throne	Sarvanivaranaviskambhi
one/two	two	rt.: varada mu. with jewel	youth	two	dhyana	bodh. ornaments,	Sarvanivaranaviskambhi

		lt.: varada mu. with jewel				va.: lotus throne	
one/two	two	rt.: varada mu. lt.: vitarka mu. holding moon disc & manuscript	youth	two	dhyana	bodh. ornaments, va.: lotus throne	Sarvanivaranaviskambhi
one/two	two	rt.: elephant goad/hook lt.: elephant goad/hook	youth	two	dhyana	bodh. ornaments, va.: lotus throne	Sarvapayanjaha
one/two	two	holds vandana mu. at chest	youth	two	sopasraya	bodh. ornaments, va.: lotus throne	Sarvapayanjaha
one/two	two	rt.: varada mu. lt.: stringed instrument	youth	two		bodh. ornaments, va.: lotus throne	Sarasvati
one/two	two	holds stringed instrument	mature	two	ardha- paryanka	bodh. ornaments, va.: lotus throne	Sarasvati
one/two	two	rt.: lotus lt.: varada mu.	mature	two		bodh. ornaments, va.: lotus throne	Sarasvati
one/two	two	holds bell	youth	two	vajra	bodh. ornaments, va.: lotus throne	sGeg-mo-ma
one/two	two	holds conch shell	youth	two	lalita	bodh. ornaments, va.: lotus throne	Shankha
one/two	two	rt.: varada mu. lt.: blue lotus	youth	two	vajra	bodh. ornaments, va.: lotus throne	Siddhaikavira
one/two	two	rt.: banner/flag with wish fulfilling jewel lt.: flowery wheel	youth	two	vamalalita	bodh. ornaments, va.: lotus throne	Sila-Paramita
one/two	two	rt.: wish fulfilling jewel lt.: branch	youth	two	vamalalita	bodh. ornaments, va.: lotus throne	Sila-Paramita
one/two	two	rt.: sword on lotus lt.: trident entwined with serpent/snake	youth	two	maha- rajalila	bodh. ornaments, va.: roaring lion	Simhanada-Avalokitesvara**
one/two	two	rt.: (?) lt.: stem of lotus with sword in bowl.	youth	two	vamalalita	bodh. ornaments, va.: lion	Simhanada-Avalokitesvara**
one/two	two	rt.: chowrie lt.: held at waist	youth	two	sama- bhanga	bodh. ornaments, va.: lotus throne	Simhanada-Lokesvara**
one/two	two	rt.: sword lt.: noose/snare	youth	two	sama- bhanga	bodh. ornaments, va.: lotus throne	Sirisara(?)-Lokesvara**

one/two	two	rt.: goad/hook lt.: jewels	youth	two	lalita	bodh. ornaments, va.: lion	Sita-Ayurvardhana-Vaisravana
one*/two	two	rt.: crystal sword lt.: jewel filled pan & noose/snare of lightning, lance with red banner/flag in crook of arm	youth	two		*conch-shell toupet, bodh. ornaments, va.: lotus throne	Sitabrahma
one*/two	two	rt.: crystal sword lt.: battle lance & blue noose/snare, mongoose in the crook of arm	youth	two	astride	*conch-shell toupet, gr., rd. & wh. cloak, circular breast plate, bodh. ornaments, va.: white horse	Sitabrahma
one*/two	two	rt.: ritual chopper lt.: circular banner	youth	two	astride	*conch-shell toupet, bodh. ornaments, va.: lotus throne	Sitabrahma
one*/two	two	rt.: ritual chopper lt.: circular banner	youth	two	astride	*wh. turban, bodh. ornaments, va.: white horse	Sitabrahma
one/two	two	holding stems of lotus in dharmachakra mu.	youth	two	vajra	bodh. ornaments, va.: lotus throne	Sita-Candra
one/two	two	rt.: vitarka mu. lt.: alms bowl in dhyana mu	mature	two	dhyana	Buddha-like, monastic robe, va.: lotus throne	
one/two	two	rt.: karana mu. lt.: throwing staff/stick	youth	two	vamalalita	bare breasted, bodh. ornaments, va.: lotus throne	Sita (deva)
one/two	two	rt.: stem of lotus in tarjani mu. lt.: stem of lotus in karana mu.	youth	two	vajra	bodh. ornaments, va.: lotus throne	Sita-Manjughosa
one/two	two	rt.: rosary lt.: trident	youth	two	vajra	bodh. ornaments, va.: lotus throne	Sita-Manjusri (Bodhisattva)
one/two	two	holds cloud	youth*	two		*snake-like lower body, bodh. ornaments, va.: lotus throne	Sita-Nagaraja
one/two	two	holds cloud	youth*	two		*snake-like lower body, bodh. ornaments, va.: lotus throne	Sita-Nagi

one/two	two	rt.: red lotus lt.: Prajna Paramita book	youth	two	vajra	bodh. ornaments, va.: lotus throne	Sitaprajnaparamita
one/two	two	in vajrahumkara mu. holding vases/vessels and embraces shakti	youth	two	vajra, yab-yum	bodh. ornaments, va.: lotus throne	Sita-Samvararaja (Buddha)
one/two	two	playing a lute	youth	two	sattva	bodh. ornaments, va.: lotus throne	Sita Sarasvati
one*/two	two	rt.: abhaya mu. lt.: white umbrella	youth	two	lalita	*angry, body. ornaments, va.: lotus throne	Sitatapatra-Aparajita
one*/two	two	rt.: abhaya mu. lt.: white umbrella	youth	two	lalita	*angry, bodh. ornaments, va.: lotus throne	Sitatapatra
one/two	two	holds parasol	youth	two	sopasraya	bodh. ornaments, va.: lotus throne	Sitatapatra (Avalokitesvara)
one/two	two	holds a parasol	youth	two	vamalalita	bodh. ornaments, va.: lotus throne	Sitatapatra (Bodhisattva)
one/two	two	rt.: abhaya mu. lt.: parasol	youth	two	vajra	bodh. ornaments, va.: lotus throne	Sitatapatra (fo-mu)
one/two	two	rt.: wheel lt.: rests behind left thigh	youth	two	vajra	bodh. ornaments, va.: lotus throne	Sitatapatrosnisa (Buddha)
one/two	two	rt.: kartari mu. lt.: stem of lotus	youth	two	vajra	bodh. ornaments, va.: lotus throne	Sita-Tara (fo-mu)
one/two	two	rt.: vitatrka mu. resting on knee holding stem of lotus lt.: vitatrka mu. holding stem of lotus	youth	two	vajra	bodh. ornaments, va.: lotus throne	Sita-Tara (fo-mu)
one/two	two	holds serpent snake	youth	two	vamalalita	bodh. ornaments, va.: serpent/snake	Sita-Varuna
one/two	two	rt.: abhaya mu. lt.: stem of lotus	youth	two	vajra	bodh. ornaments, va.: lotus throne	Sita-Visva (fo-mu)
one/two	two	rt.: thunderbolt lt.: stem of lotus near waist	youth	two	sama- bhanga	bodh. ornaments, va.: lotus throne	Srimadaryavalokitesvara**
one/two	two	rt.: varada mu.	youth*	two	sama-	15 Buddha-like images	Srstikanta-Lokesvara**

		lt.: held at waist			bhanga	in mandalas surround the body with lines to various parts of the body bodh. ornaments, va.: lotus throne	
one/two	two	rt.: varada mu. lt.: sword	youth	two	vajra	bodh. ornaments, va.: lotus throne	Sthiracakra
one/two	two	rt.: varada mu. lt.: stem of lotus topped with sword	youth	two	sukha	bodh. ornaments, shakti behind lt. leg, va.: lotus throne	Sthiracakra
one/two	two	rt.: rosary lt.: lotus cup with nectar of life	youth	two	vajra	bodh. ornaments, va.: animal	Sukla-Kurukulla
one/two	two	rt.: rosary lt.: vase/vessel	youth	two		bodh. ornaments, va.: lotus throne	Sukra
one/two	two	rt.: sword lt.: rests on hip clenched	youth	two	dhyana	bodh. ornaments, va.: lotus throne	Surangama
one/two	two	rt.: jewel lt.: dhyana	youth	two	sattva	bodh. ornaments, va.: lotus throne	Surangama
one/two	two	holds sun disc	youth	two		bodh. ornaments, va.: lotus throne	Suryahasta
one/two	two	rt.: lotus lt.: jewels	youth	two		bodh. ornaments, va.: lotus throne	Tathatavasita
one/two	two	rt.: noose/snare lt.: goad/hook	youth	two	vajra	bodh. ornaments, va.: lotus throne	Trailokyavasamkara-Avalokitesvara**
one/two	two	rt.: noose/snare lt.: goad/hook	youth	two	vajra	bodh. ornaments, va.: lotus throne	Trailokyavasamkara-Avalokitesvara (Bodhisattva)**
one/two	two	rt.: crossed thunderbolts lt.: container of moonstones	youth	two		bodh. ornaments, va.: lotus throne	Usnisavijaya
one/two	two	rt.: dhyana mu. with crossed thunderbolts lt.: varada mu. holds a vase/vessel	youth	two		bodh. ornaments, va.: lotus throne	Usnisavijaya
one/two	two	rt.: wheel lt.: tarjani mu.	youth	two		bodh. ornaments, va.: lotus throne	Usnisavijaya

one/two	two	dharmachakra mu.	youth	two	ardha-paryanka	bodh. ornaments, va.: tiger	Vadirat
one/two	two	dharmachakra mu.	youth	two	dhyana	bodh. ornaments, va.: pair of dragons	Vairocana
one/two	two	dhyana mu. hokds wheel	youth	two	dhyana	bodh. ornaments, va.: pair of dragons	Vairocana
one/two	two	dharmachakra mu. with bell and wheel	youth	two	dhyana, yab-yum	bodh. ornaments, va.: pair of dragons	Vairocana
one/two	two	hokds eight spoked wheel	youth	two	vajra	bodh. ornaments, va.: lion throne	Vairocana
one/two	two	dhyana mu. holding (?)	youth	two	vajra	bodh. ornaments, va.: lotus throne	Vairocanabhisambodhi
one/two	two	holds dhyana mu.	youth	two	vajra	bodh. ornaments, va.: lotus throne	Vairocanabhisambodhi (Buddha)
one/two	two	hokds dharmachakra mu	youth	two	alidha	bodh. ornaments, va.: lotus throne	Vairocana-Sakyasimha
one/two	two	rt.: blooming lotus against chest lt.: lotus with 16 petals	youth	two	vajra	bodh. ornaments, va.: peacock	Vajradharma
one/two	two	rt.: abhaya mu. lt.: dhyana mu. with lotus	youth	two	vajra	bodh. ornaments, va.: lotus throne	Vajradharma (Bodhisattva)**
one/two	two	rt.: abhaya mu. lt.: lotus with book/manuscript	youth	two	sattva	bodh. ornaments, va.: lotus throne	Vajradharma (Bodhisattva)**
one/two	two	rt.: abhaya mu. lt.: stem of blue lotus	youth	two	vajra	bodh. ornaments, va.: lotus throne	Vajradharma-Lokesvarat**
one/two	two	rt.: varada mu. lt.: lotus	youth	two	sama-bhanga	bodh. ornaments, va.: lotus throne	Vajradhatu-Lokesvara**
one/two	two	rt.:vitarka mu. with stem of lotus with wish-fulfilling jewel lt.: varada mu. stem of lotus with triangle	youth	two	lalita	bodh. ornaments, va.: lotus throne	Vajradhatvisvari
one/two	two	rt.: thunderbolt lt.: stem of lotus	youth	two	vajra	bodh. ornaments, va.: lotus throne	Vajragarbha-Lokesvara**

one/two	two	rt.: lotus bud lt.: book/manuscript	youth	two	sama-bhanga	bodh. ornaments, va.: lotus throne	Vajrakhanda-Lokesvara**
one/two	two	rt.: thunderbolt lt.: lotus	youth	two	ardha-paryanka	bodh. ornaments, va.: lotus throne	Vajranatha-Lokesvara**
one/two	two	rt.: goad/hook lt.: tarjani mu.	youth	two		bodh. ornaments, va.: lotus throne	Vajrankusi
one/two	two	rt.: abhaya mu. lt.: thunderbolt	youth	two	dhyana	bodh. ornaments, va.: lotus throne	Vajrapani
one/two	two	rt.: varada mu. lt.: vitarka mu. with thunderbolt	youth	two	dhyana	bodh. ornaments, va.: lotus throne	Vajrapani
one/two	two	holds dhyana mu. with thunderbolt on point in palm	youth	two	dhyana	bodh. ornaments, va.: lotus throne	Vajrapani
one/two	two	rt.: thunderbolt at breast lt.: varada mu.	youth	two	lalita	bodh. ornaments, va.: lotus throne	Vajrapani
one/two	two	rt.: vase/vessel lt.: rosary	youth	two	vamalalita	bodh. ornaments, va.: lotus throne	Vajrapani
one/two	two	rt.: thunderbolt on head lt.: held at waist	youth	two	ardha-paryanka	bodh. ornaments, va.: lotus throne	Vajrapani-Lokesvara**
one/two	two	hold dhyana mu.	youth	two	vajra-paryanka	bodh. ornaments, va.: lotus throne	Vajraraga
one/two	two	rt.: sword(?) lt.: karana mu.	youth	two	vajra	bodh. ornaments, va.: lotus throne	Vajraraga (Bodhisattva)
one/two	two	rt.: bow lt.: arrow	youth	two	sattva	bodh. ornaments, va.: lotus throne	Vajraraga (Bodhisattva)
one/two	two	Prajna Paramita book/manuscript on a lotus	youth	two		bodh. ornaments, va.: lotus throne	Vajrasarasvati
one/two	two	rt.: varada mu. with thunderbolt lt.: varada mu. with thunderbolt	youth	two	seated	bodh. ornaments, va.: lotus throne	Vajrasarasvati
one/two	two	rt.: lotus lt.: book/manuscript	youth	two	sama-bhanga	bodh. ornaments, va.: lotus throne	Vajrasarada
one/two	two	rt.: thunderbolt balanced on tip lt.: bell on his left hip	youth	two	dhyana	Buddha-like, va.: lotus throne	Vajrasattva

one/two	two	rt.: thunderbolt balanced on tip lt.: bell on his left hip	youth	two	sama- bhanga	bodh. ornaments, va.: lotus throne	Vajrasattva
one/two	two	rt.: varada mu. lt.: vitarka mu.	youth	two	lalita	bodh. ornaments, va.: lotus throne	Vajrasattva
one/two	two	rt.: thunderbolt lt.: bell	youth	two	vajra	Buddha-like, va.: lotus throne	Vajrasattva
one/two	two	rt.: wheel lt.: conch shell	youth	two	sama- bhanga	bodh. ornaments, va.: lotus throne	Vajrasattvadhatu-Lokesvara**
one/two	two	rt.: harina mu. at knee holding stem of lotus with thunderbolt lt.: harina mu. at chest level holding stem of lotus with bell	youth	two		bodh. ornaments, va.: lotus throne	Vajrasattvatmika
one/two	two	rt.: conch shell lt.: lotus	youth	two	sama- bhanga	bodh. ornaments, va.: lotus throne	Vajrasrsta-Lokesvara**
one/two	two	holds lute	youth	two	sama- bhanga	bodh. ornaments, va.: lotus throne	Vajravina Sarasvati
one/two	two	holds dhyana mu.	youth	two	vajra- paryanka	bodh. ornaments, va.: lotus throne	Vak
one/two	two	holds alms bowl in dhyana mu.	youth	two	vajra	bodh. ornaments, va.: lotus throne	Vasyadhikara-Lokesvara**
one/two	two	rt.: held against chest lt.: lotus	youth	two	sama- bhanga	bodh. ornaments, va.: lotus throne	Vidyapati-Lokesvara**
one/two	two	rt.: thunderbolt lt.: white lotus	youth	two		bodh. ornaments, va.: lotus throne	Vimala
one/two	two	rt.: wheel lt.: tantric staff/stick	youth	two	sama- bhanga	bodh. ornaments, va.: lotus throne	Visnucakra-Lokesvara**
one/two	two	rt.: varada mu. lt.: book/manuscript	youth	two	sama- bhanga	bodh. ornaments, va.: lotus throne	Visnukanta-Lokesvara**
one/two	two	rt.: trident lt.: bud of a lotus	youth	two	sama- bhanga	bodh. ornaments, va.: lotus throne	Visnupani-Lokesvara**
one/two	two	rt.: rosary lt.: lotus	youth	two	sama- bhanga	bodh. ornaments, va.: lotus throne	Vishvabhuta-Lokesvara**

one/two	two	rt.: abhaya mu. lt.: white lotus	youth	two	vajra	bodh. ornaments, va.: lotus throne	Vishvamata Tara
one/two	two	rt.: varada mu. lt.: serpent/snake	youth	two	sama- bhanga	bodh. ornaments, va.: lotus throne	Vishvavajra-Lokesvara**
one/two	two	rt.: white, silver mirror lt.: white, six-handled silver vase/vessel	youth	two	sattva	bodh. ornaments, attribute: white syllable "bhyo", va.: lotus throne	Zhi-ba'i-lha-mo
one/two	two	rt.: rosary lt.: vase/vessel	youth	two		bodh. ornaments, realm: East and Monday, va.: lotus throne	Zla-ba
one/two	four	principle hands vina rt.:abhaya mu lt.: serpent/snake	mature	two	dhyana	bodh. ornaments, va.: lotus throne	Arya-Ianguli
one/two	four	rt.: noose/snare in abhaya mu., lt.: trident	mature	two	vajra	bodh. ornaments, va.: lotus throne	Amoghapasa
one/two	four	rt.: sword, trident lt.: lotus, (?)	youth	two	vajra	bodh. ornaments, va.: lotus throne, flanked by two deities	Amoghapujamanmi- Avalokitesvara
one/two	four	prin. anjali mu. rt.: rosary lt.: lotus	youth	two	vajra	bodh. ornaments, va.: lotus throne	Arya-(Atisa)-krama-Sadaksara- Avalokitesvara
one/two	four	rt.: noose/snare, thunderbolt lt.: rosary, goad/hook	youth	two	alidha	bodh. ornaments, va.: lotus throne	Anucara-Rakta-Amoghapasa
one*/two	four	rt.: radish, rosary lt.: axe, mongoose	mature	two	lalita	*elephant form, bodh. ornaments, va.: rat	Arya-(Atisa)-krama-Caturbhuja- Sita-Ganapati
one/two	four	prin. plays stringed instrument rt.: abhaya mu. lt.: serpent/snake	youth	two	dhyana	bodh, ornaments, va.: lotus throne	Arya-Ianguli
one/two	four	prin.: namaskara mu. rt.: rosary, lt.: lotus	youth	two	dhyana	bodh. ornaments, va.: lotus throne	Avalokitesvara (sPyan-ras-gZigs- Phyan-bZhi-pa)

one/two	four	prin. anjali mu. at chest rt.: rosary lt.: lotus	youth	two	vajra	bodh. ornaments, va.: lotus throne	Bkah-gdams-Avalokitesvara
one/two	four	rt.: trident and varada mu. lt.: vase/vessel of jewels and karana mu.	youth	two	lalita	bodh. ornament, shakti on lt. knee,	Brahmadanda-Lokesvara
one/two	four	rt.: rosary and karana mu. lt.: flower in dhyana mu.	youth	two	vamalalita	bodh. ornaments, va.: lotus throne	Brahma (deva)
one/two	four	prin.: namaskara mu. rt.: rosary lt.: lotus	youth	two	vajra	bodh. ornaments, va.: lotus throne	Caturbhuja-Avalokitesvara**
one/two	four	prin.: namaskara mu. rt.: rosary lt.: lotus	youth	two	vajra	bodh. ornaments, va.: lotus throne	Caturbhuja-Avalokitesvara (Bhodisattva)**
one/two	four	rt.: clun/cudgel, knife lt.: lotus, short staff/stick	youth	two	vamalalita	bodh. ornaments, va.: lotus throne	Cunda
one/two	four	prin.: abhaya mu. at chest level rt.: abhaya mu. lt.: lotus with book/manuscript	youth	two	vajra	bodh. ornaments, va.: lotus throne	Caturbhuja-Prajnaparamita (fo-mu)**
one/two	four	prin.: vase/vessel in dhyana mu. embracing shakti rt.: thunderbolt lt.: rosary	youth	two	vajra, yab-yum	bodh. ornaments, va.: lotus throne	(Caturbhuja)-Sita-Amitayus
one/two	four	prin.: play lute rt.: sword lt.: lotus	youth	two	vajra	bodh. ornaments, va.: lotus throne	Caturbhuja-Sita-Sarasvati
one/two	four	prin.: uttarabodhi mu. rt.: varada mu. lt.: varada mu.	youth	two		bodh. ornaments, va.: lotus throne	Chaturbhuja-Sitatara
one*/two	four	rt.: ritual chopper, rosary lt.: human skull-cup, radish	corp.	two	vamalalita	*elephant head, bodh. ornaments, va.: mouse on lotus throne	Ganapati
one*/two	four	rt.: trident, ball of sweetmeat lt.: battle axe, radish	corp.	two	vamalalita	*elephant head, bodh. ornaments, va.: rat on lotus throne	Ganapati

one/two	four	prin.: namaskara mu. embracing shakti rt.: rosary lt.: lotus	mature	two	vajra, yab-yum	bodh. ornaments, va.: lotus throne	Guhyasadhana-Avalokitesvara**
one/two	four	prin.: vykhyana mu. rt.: rosary lt.: lotus	youth	two	vajra	bodh. ornaments, va.: lotus throne	Hayagriva-Lokesvara
one/two	four	prin.: plays lute rt.: abhaya mu. lt.: white serpent/snake	mature	two	vamalalita	bodh. ornaments, va.: animal	Ianguli
one/two	four	prin.: plays lute rt.: abhaya mu. lt.: serpent/snake	youth	two		bodh. ornaments, va.; lotus throne	Ianguli-Tara
one/two	four	rt.: rosary, varada lt.: lotus, vase/vessel	youth	two	sama-bhanga	bodh. ornaments, va.: lotus throne	Iatamukuta-Lokesvara
one/two	four	prin.: anjali mu. over head rt.: trident lt.: human skull-cup	youth	two	lalita	bodh. ornaments, va.: bull	Mahesvara
one/two	four	rt.: (?), thunderbolt lt.: human skull-cup, trident	youth	two		bodh. ornaments, va.: bull	Mahesvara (deva)
one/two	four	prin.: namaskara mu. against chest rt.: rosary lt.: lotus	youth	two	vajra	bodh. ornaments, va.: lotus throne	Manipadma-Lokesvara**
one/two	four	prin.: dhyana mu. rt.: abhaya mu. **lt.: lotus**	youth	two	vajra	bodh. ornaments, va.: lotus throne	Padmavikasana-Avalolitesvara**
one/two	four	prin.: namaskara mu. rt.: rosary lt.: noose/snare	youth	two	vajra	bodh. ornaments, va.: lotus throne	Potapada-Lokesvara**
one/two	four	prin.: dharmachakra mu. rt.: rosary lt.: Prajna Paramita book	youth	two		bodh. ornaments, va.: lotus throne	Prajna-Paramita
one/two	four	rt.: rosary, thunderbolt lt.: dhyana mu, (?)	youth	two	vajra	bodh. ornaments, va.: lotus throne	Prajnaparamita (fo-mu)**
one/two	four	rt.: rosary, abhaya mu.	youth	two	vajra	bodh. ornaments,	Pupala-Lokesvara**

		lt.: book/manuscript, karana mu.				va.: lotus throne	
one/two	four	prin.: namaskara mu. rt.: rosary lt.: lotus	youth	two	sopasraya	bodh. ornaments, va.: lotus throne	Sadaksari**
one/two	four	prin.: namaskara mu. rt.: rosary lt.: lotus	youth	two	vajra	bodh. ornaments, va.: lotus throne	Sadaksari-Lokesvara**
one/two	four	prin.: namaskara mu. rt.: rosary lt.: lotus	youth	two	dhyana	bodh. ornaments, va.: lotus throne	Sadaksari-Lokesvara**
one/two	four	rt.: prayer roll, rosary lt.: conch shell, lotus	youth	two	dhyana	bodh. ornaments, va.: lotus throne	Sadaksari-Lokesvara**
one/two	four	prin.: namaskara mu. 2nd pr.: dhyana mu. holding bowl	youth	two	sama- bhanga	bodh. ornaments, va.: lotus throne	Sadaksari-Lokesvara**
one/two	four	prin.: abhaya mu against chest rt.: rosary lt.: blue lotus	youth	two	sama- bhanga	bodh. ornaments, va.: lotus throne	Sarvasokatamonirghata- Lokesvara**
one/two	four	rt.: arrow, magic notched staff/stick lt.: bow, tarjani mu.	youth	two	sama- bhanga	bodh. ornaments, va.: lotus throne	Sakyabuddha-Lokesvara**
one/two	four	prin.: stringed instrument rt.: lotus lt.: book/manuscript	mature	two		bodh. ornaments, va.: lotus throne	Sarasvati
one/two	four	rt.: sword, jewel lt.: book/manuscript, noose/snare	youth	two	sama- bhanga	bodh. ornaments, va.: lotus throne	Simhanatha-Lokesvara**
one*/two	four	rt.: ritual chopper, rosary (?) lt.: human skull-cup, plant	youth	two	vamalalita	*elephant-head, bodh. ornaments, va.: mouse	Sita-Ganapati
one/two	four*	rt.: blue lotus, varada mu. with wish fulfilling jewel lt.: blue lotus, lotus bud	youth	two	vajra	*eye in the palm of each hand, bodh. ornaments, va.: lotus throne	Sita-Tara
one/two	four	rt.: noose/snare, abhaya mu. lt.: goad/hook, (?)	youth	two	vajra	bodh. ornaments, va.: lotus throne	Sitavati (fo-mu)
one/two	four	rt.: rosary, abhaya mu.	youth	two	vajra	bodh. ornaments,	Sitavati (fo-mu)

		lt.: book/manuscript, end of sash				va.: lotus throne	
one/two	four	rt.: goad/hook, abhaya mu. lt.: karana mu., abhaya mu.	youth	two	vajra	bodh. ornaments, va.: lotus throne	Sita-Vijaya-Tara
one/two	four	rt.: sword, jewel lt.: book/manuscript, noose/snare	youth	two	vajra	bodh. ornaments, va.: lotus throne	Trilokasandarsana-Lokesvara**
one/two	six	rt.: sword, arrow, varada mu. lt.: ritual chopper, bow, abhaya mu	youth	two	lalita	bodh. ornaments, va.: lotus throne	Acata(?)-Lokesvara
one/ two	six	holding noose/snare, rosary, trident, ewer, lotus, conch	mature	two	vajra	bodh. ornaments, va.: lotus throne	Amoghapasa
one/two	six	rt.: thunderbolt, arrow, fist on thigh lt.: noose/snare, bow, (?)	youth	two	lalita	bodh, ornaments, va.: lotus throne	Arya-Ianguli
one/two	six	prin.: buddhasramana mu. rt.: rosary, abhaya mu. lt.: (?), dhyana mu.	youth	two	sattva	bodh. ornaments, va.: lion	Ch'i-hou Isvara (= Lokesvara)-Avalokitesvara (Bodhisattva)**
one/two	six	rt.: Buddha image, rosary, abhaya mu. lt.: staff/stick, deer skin, vase/vessel	youth	two	*astride	*lion on the bottom, then eagle or garuda, then Vishnu, and on Vishnu's shoulders rides Avalokitesvara	Harihariharivahanobdhava-Lokesvara**
one/two	six	rt.: varada mu., rosary, abhaya mu. lt.: trident, black deer skin, spouted vase/vessel	youth	two	*astride	*lion on the bottom, then eagle or garuda, then Narayana, and on Narayana's shoulders rides Avalokitesvara	Harihariharivahanobdhava-Lokesvara**
one/two	six	rt.: abhaya mu., rosary, varada mu. lt.: black deer-skin, noose/snare, vase/vessel	youth	two	sattva	bodh. ornaments, va.: lion on lotus throne	Harihariyahana-Lokesvara
one/two	six	rt.: sword, lotus, thunderbolt lt.: myrobalan fruit(?), bowl, karana mu.	youth	two	vajra	bodh. ornaments va.: lotus throne	Iamadanda-Lokesvara**
one/two	six	prin.: draws bow and arrow rt.: thunderbolt, wheel lt.: bell, vase/vessel	youth	two	sama-bhanga	bodh. ornaments, va.: lotus throne	Kamandalu-Lokesvara**
one/two	six	rt.: sword, arrow, varada mu. lt.: bow, noose/snare, battle axe	youth	two	vajra	bodh. ornaments in variegated colors, va.: lotus throne	Mahasahasrapramardani

one/two	six	rt.: sword, arrow, abhaya mu. lt.: bow, noose/snare, trident	youth	two	lalita	bodh. ornaments in variegated colors, va.: lotus throne	Mahasahasrapramardani
one/two	six	rt.: sword, arrow, varada mu. lt.: bow, karana mu., dhyana mu.	youth	two	vajra	bodh. ornaments in variegated colors, va.: lotus throne	Mahasahasrapramardani
one/two	six	prin.: dharmachakra mu. rt.: rosary, varada mu. lt.: book/manuscript, abhaya mu.	youth	two	sama-bhanga	bodh. ornaments, va.: lotus throne	Santasi-Lokesvara**
one/two	six	rt.: varada mu., abhaya mu., rosary lt.: lotus, waterpot, short staff/stick	youth	two		bodh. ornaments, va.: lotus throne	Sugatisandarsana**
one/two	six	rt.: rosary, varada mu., abhaya mu. lt.: trident, blue lotus, vase/vessel	youth	two	sama-bhanga	bodh. ornaments, va.: lotus throne	Sugatisandarsana-Lokesvara**
one/two	six	rt.: abhaya mu., rosary, three jewels lt.: lotus, vase/vessel, embraces shakti	youth	two	lalita, yab-yum	bodh. ornaments, va.: lotus throne	Sukhavati-Avalokitesvara**
one/two	six	prin.: kanjo-in mu. rt.: arrow, noose/snare(?) lt.: bow, flaming jewels	youth	two	vajra	bodh. ornaments, va.: lotus throne	Vajradhatu-Vairocana (Buddha)
one/two	six	rt.: rosary, trident, abhaya mu. lt.: book/manuscript, noose/snare, varada mu.	youth	two	sama-bhanga	bodh. ornaments, va.: lotus throne	Vajronisa-Lokesvara**
one/two	six	prin.: namaskara mu. rt.: rosary, varada mu. lt.: book/manuscript, karana mu.	youth	two	sama-bhanga	bodh. ornaments, va.: lotus throne	Varadayaka-Lokesvara**
one/two	six	rt.: sword, arrow, wheel lt.: noose/snare, bow, abhaya mu.	youth	two	vajra	bodh. ornaments, va.: lotus throne	Vishvahana-Lokesvara**
one/two	six	rt.: blue lotus, arrow, varada mu. lt.: book/manuscript, bow, abhaya mu.	youth	two	lalita	bodh. ornaments, va.: lotus throne	Vrsnacana-Lokesvara**
one/two	eight	prin. namaskara mu., others alarm staff/stick, lotus, rosary, noose/snare, varada mu.	mature	two	vajra	bodh. ornaments, va.: lotus throne	Amoghapasa
one/two	eight	rt.: lion, elephant, serpent/snake, (?) lt. : (?), chain, Buddha image	youth	two	ardha-paryanka	bodh. ornaments, va.: lotus throne	Asta-bhaya-trana-Avalokitesvara

one/two	eight	prin.: namaskara mu. 2nd pair: ksepana mu. rt.: rosary, trident lt.: book/manuscript, noose/snare	youth	two	sama-bhanga	bodh. ornaments, va.: lotus throne	Inanadhatu-Lokesvara
one/two	eight	rt.: abhaya mu., rosary, noose/snare, buddhasramana mu. lt.: trident, book/manuscript, lotus, vase/vessel	youth	two	sama-bhanga	bodh. ornaments, va.: lotus throne	Kasmira-mahapandita-krama-Amoghapasa**
one/two	eight	rt.: sword, rosary, wheel, abhaya mu. lt.: noose/snare, trident, conch shell, bowl of jewels	youth	two	vajra	bodh. ornaments, va.: lotus throne	Mahavajrasattva-Lokesvara**
one/two	12	prin.: dhyana mu. rt.: rose wreath, thunderbolt, jewel, wheel, magic notched stick lt.: book/manuscript, vase/vessel, bell, leafed branch, ewer	youth	two	sama-bhanga	bodh. ornaments, va.: lotus throne	Candrakanti(?)-Gauri-Tara
one/two	12	prin.: dhyana mu. rt.: rose wreath, thunderbolt, jewel, wheel, magic notched stick lt.: book/manuscript, vase/vessel, bell, leafed branch, ewer	youth	two	vajra	bodh. ornaments, va.: lotus throne	Candrakanti(?)-Tara (fo-mu)
one*/two	12	prin.: ritual chopper, human skull-cup rt.: axe, arrow, (?), sword, (?) lt.: thunderbolt, bow, jewel(?), (?), lance	mature	two	lalita	*elephant-head, bodh. ornaments, va.: rat or mouse	Maharakta-Ganapati**
one*/two	12	prin.: ritual chopper, human skull-cup rt.: vajra-topped goad/hook, arrow, vajra-topped axe, sword, arrow lt.: pestle, bow, magic notched staff/stick, human skull-cup, lance	youth	two	ardha-paryankha	*elephant-head, bodh. ornaments, va.: rat or mouse	Maharakta-Ganapati**
one/two	12	rt.: abhaya mu., anjali mu., sword on crossed thunderbolts, tarpana mu., ksepana mu., dhyana mu. lt.: abhaya mu., anjali mu., magic notched stick, tarpana mu., ksepana mu., dhyana mu.	youth	two	vajra	bodh. ornaments, va.: lotus throne	Namasangiti
one/two	12	prin.: abhaya mu. 2nd pr.: vitarka mu. 3rd pr.: "lotus mudra"mu. 4th pr.: ksepana mu.	youth	two	vajra	bodh. ornaments, va.: lotus throne	Namasangiti-Avalokitesvara**

		5th pr.: tarpana mu. 6th pr.: dhyana mu. holding a vase/vessel					
one/two	12	prin.: in kanjo-in mu. 2nd: dhyana mu. rt.: sword, cylindrical banner, lotus, (?), (?), (?) lt.: thunderbolt, branch, book/manuscript, (?), (?), (?)	youth	two	vajra	bodh. ornaments, va.: lotus throne	Sodasabhuja-Avalokitesvara (Bodhisattva)**
one/two	12	all carry blue lotus	youth	two	ardha-paryanka	bodh. ornaments, va.: lotus throne	Vajrahuntika-Lokesvara**
one/two	16	rt.: varada mu., thunderbolt, wheel, club/cudgel, ritual dagger, (?), rosary, (?) lt.: vase/vessel, axe, trident, bow, dagger, (?), scepter, (?)	youth	two	vamalalita	bodh. ornaments, va.: lotus throne	Cunda
one/two	18	each holds a lotus	youth	two	vajra	bodh. ornaments, va.: lotus throne	Padmanartesvara-Avalokitesvara (Bodhisattva)**
one/two	18	each holds double lotus	youth	two	ardha-paryanka	bodh. ornaments, va.: lotus throne	Padmanartesvara-Avalokitesvara (Bodhisattva)**
one/two	20	prin. in namaskara mu., two lay in lap with noose/snare and rosary, two hold cymbols, two hold lotus, two hold thunderbolt and bell, the other five pair hold various symbols	mature	two	vajra	bodh. ornaments, va.: lotus throne	Amoghapasa
one/ three	two	rt.: varada mu. lt.: stem of lotus in karana mu.	youth	two	vajra	bodh. ornaments, va.: lotus throne	Arya-(Atisa)-krama Sita Tara
one/ three	two	rt.: varada mu. lt.: stem of lotus in karana mu.	youth	two	vajra	bodh. ornaments, va.: lotus throne	Bari-lugs Sita Tara Tara
one/three	two	rt.: varada mu. lt.: stem of lotus in karana mu.	youth	two	vajra	bodh. ornaments, va.: lotus throne	Bari-lugs Sita Tara
one/three	two	rt.: wish-fulfilling jewel lt.: divination arrow	youth	two		silk turban, white silk garment, peacock feather cloak, va.: white lioness	bKra-shis-tshe-ring-ma
one/three	two	rt.: divination arrow and thunderbolt lt.: vase/vessel with elixir of life	youth	two		silk turban, white silk garment,	bKra-shis-tshe-ring-ma

						peacock feather cloak, va.: white lioness	
one/three	two	hold skull-cup, ritual chopper and embraces shakti	youth	two	yab-yum	bodh. ornaments, va.: lotus throne	Sarvanivaranaviskambhi
one/three	two	holds namaskara mu., rosary on lotus at rt. shoulder	youth	two	maha-rajalila	bodh. ornaments, va.: roaring lion	Simhanada-Avalokitesvara**
one/three	two	rt.: varada mu. lt.: stem of lotus in kartari mu.	youth	two	vajra	bodh. ornaments, va.: lotus throne	Sita-Visvamatr
one/three	two	rt.: noose/snare lt.: goad/hook	youth	two	vajra	bodh. ornaments, va.: red lotus	Trailokyavasankara-Lokesvara**
one/three	two	rt.: varada mu. lt.: stem of lotus in karana mu.	youth	two	vajra	bodh. ornaments, va.: lotus throne	Vanaratna-krama Sita Tara
one/three	four	rt.: abhaya mu., jewels lt.: flowering branch, wheel	corp.	two	alidha	bodh. ornaments, va.: lotus throne	Jala-bhayatrana-(Avalokitesvara)
one*/three	eight		mature, bare to waist	two	sama-bhanga	*each curl a Buddha, Buddhas cover chest, Buddha on each toe	Lokesvara (Irradiant)
one/three	18	prin.: uttarabodhi (renge-no-in) mu. upper two: sword, cylindrical banner/flag other hands: tantric symbols	mature	two		white flowing robes, bodh. ornaments, va.: lotus throne	Jun-tei Kwan-non
three/six	two	rt.: wish fulfilling jewel lt.: wheel	youth	two	sama-bhanga	bodh. ornaments, va.: lotus throne	Cintamani-Avalokitesvara
three/six	two	rt.: sword, crossed vajra, wheel lt.: bell, lotus, (?)	youth	two	vajra	bodh. ornaments, va.: lotus throne	Sarvanivaranaviskambhi
three/six	two	holds flaming wheel in dhyana mu.	youth	two		bodh. ornaments, va.: lotus throne	Sarvavid-Vairocana (Buddha)**
three/six	four	rt.: varada mu. with lotus, abhaya lt.: trident, tarjani mu.	youth	two	vajra	bodh. ornaments, va.: lotus throne	Amoghapasa-Lokesvara
three*/six	four	rt.: bow, arrow lt.: book/manuscript, sword	youth	two	vajra-paryanka	*reddish white, bodh. ornaments, va.: lotus throne	Namasangiti-Manjusri
three*/six	six	rt.: lotus, flaming jewels and sword	mature,	four	alidha	*rt. head: pig, cent.	Ajna-vinivarta-Ganapati**

		lt.: vase/vessel, axe and jewel	nude			head: elephant. lt. head: human, va.: goddess on lotus throne	
three/six	six	rt.: wheel, flower, arrow lt.: thunderbolt noose/snare, bow	youth	two	vajra	bodh. ornaments, va.: lotus throne	Arya-Sitatapatra
three/six	six	rt.: rosary, baton-like staff/stick, abhaya mu. lt.: baton-like staff/stick, noose/snare, rests behind left thigh	youth	two	vajra	bodh. ornaments, va.: lotus throne	Ch'i-hou Avalokitesvara (Bodhisattva)**
three/six	six	prin.: embrace shakti in vajrahumkara mu. rt.: wheel, sword lt.: (?). vitarka mu.	youth	two	vajra	bodh. ornaments va.: lotus throne	Guhya-isvara (=Lokesvara)-Avalokitesvara**
three*/six	six	rt.: *varada mudra*, rosary, arrow lt.: bow, lotus, touches shakti	youth	two	vajra	*bl., wh., rd., to right: trident with snake entwined, to the left a skull-cup on lotus, bodh. ornaments, shakti sits on left knee, va.: lion on lotus throne	Halahala-Lokesvara
three/six	six	rt.: sword, rosary, varada mu. lt.: lotus, noose/snare, blue lotus	youth	two	lalita	bodh. ornaments, shakti sits on left knee, va.: lotus throne	Halahala-Lokesvara**
three/six	six	prin.: book/manuscript against chest rt.: thunderbolt, rosary lt.: bell, trident	youth	two	sama-bhanga	bodh. ornaments, va.: lotus throne	Maha-abhayakari-Lokesvara**
three/six	six	rt.: thunderbolt, sword, blue lotus lt.: bell, book/manuscript, bell	youth	two	sama-bhanga	bodh. ornaments, va.: lotus throne	Maha-abhayaphalada-Lokesvara**
three/six	six	rt.: arrow,, blue lotus, myrobalan (?) fruit lt.: bow, thunderbolt, wheel	youth	two	sama-bhanga	bodh. ornaments, va.: lotus throne	Mahacandrabimba-Lokesvara**
three/six	six	rt.: sword, thunderbolt, vase/vessel lt.: rosary, blue lotus, bell	youth	two	sama-bhanga	bodh. ornaments, va.: lotus throne	Mahamanjubhuta-Lokesvara**
three/six	six	rt.: bell, sword, jewel lt.: thunderbolt, bell, blue lotus	youth	two	sama-bhanga	bodh. ornaments, va.: lotus throne	Mahamanjudatta-Lokesvara**
three/six	six	rt.: myrobalan(?) fruit, blue lotus,	youth	two	sama-	bodh. ornaments,	Maharatnakirti-Lokesvara**

		conch shell lt.: whip, namaskara mu., bow			bhanga	va.: lotus throne	
three/six	six	rt.: sword, blue lotus, rosary lt.· book/manuscript, lotus, blue lotus	youth	two	sama-bhanga	bodh. ornaments, va.: lotus throne	Maharatnakula-Lokesvara**
three/six	six	rt.: thunderbolt, abhaya mu., thunderbolt lt.: noose/snare, arrow, bell	youth	two	sama-bhanga	bodh. ornaments, va.: lotus throne	Mahasankhanatha-Lokesvara**
three/six	six	rt.: thunderbolt, wheel, thundetbolt lt.: blue lotus, bowl, blue lotus	youth	two	sama-bhanga	bodh. ornaments, va.: lotus throne	Mahasuryyabimba-Lokesvara**
three/six	six	rt.: sword, arrow, abhaya mu. lt.: book/manuscript, bow, flower	youth	two	vajra-paryanka	bodh. ornaments, va.: lotus throne	Namasangiti-Manjusri
three/six	six	rt.: arrow, rosary, varada mu. lt.: bow, lotus, rests on the thigh of Tara	youth	two	lalita	bodh. ornaments, Tara sits on thigh, va.: lotus throne	Sukhavati-Lokesvara**
three/six	six	rt.: rosary, arrow, abhaya mu. lt.: stem of lotus, bow, flower	youth	two	lalita	bodh. ornaments, va.: lotus throne	Trimukhasadbhuja-sita-Tara (fo-mu)
three/six	six	rt.: wheel, thunderbolt, (?) lt.: sword, bell, (?)	youth	two	vajra	bodh. ornaments, va.: lotus throne	Vajrapani
three/six	six	rt.: rosary, arrow, abhaya mu. lt.: lotus, (?) mudra, bow	youth	two	vajra	bodh. ornaments, va.: lotus throne	Vajradharma-Avalokitesvara**
three/six	six	rt.: abhaya mu., arrow, noose/snare(?) lt.: embraces shakti, flower, bow	youth	two	vajra, vab-yum	bodh. ornaments, va.: lotus throne	Vajradharma (Buddha)**
three/six	six	rt.: wish fulfilling jewel, thunderbolt, karana mu. lt.: bell, flaming jewels, sword	youth	two	vajra	bodh. ornaments, va.: lotus throne	Vairocana
three/six	eight	prin.: dharmachakra mu. rt.: sword, baton/mace, thunderbolt lt.: (?), bow, bell	mature	two	vajra	bodh. ornaments, va.: lotus throne	Dharmadhatuvagisvara (Buddha)
three/six	eight	rt.: rosary, noose/snare, abhaya mu., varada mu. lt.: book/manuscript, trident, lotus, resting at waist	youth	two	sama-bhanga	bodh. ornaments, va.: lotus throne	Mahavajranatha-Lokesvara**
three/six	eight	prin.: thunderbolt in dharmachakra mu. 2nd pr.: dhyana mu.	youth	two	vajra	bodh. ornaments, va.: pair of dragons	Vairocana

		rt.: rosary, arrow lt.: wheel, bow					
three/six	eight	prin.: crossed thunderbolts, noose/snare rt.: image of Buddha, arrow, varada mu. lt.: abhaya mu., bow, vase/vessel	youth	two	vajra	bodh. ornaments, va.: lotus throne	Vijaya (female)
three*/six	12	1st: dharmachakra mu. 2nd: dhyana mu. others: abhaya mu., varada mu., noose/snare, bow, arrow, wish fulfilling jewel, thunderbolt, lotus	youth	two	vajra	*rd., wh., gr., bodh. ornaments, va.: lotus throne	Mahamantranusarini
three/six	24	prin.: kanjo-in mu; 2nd prin.: dhyana mu. with thunderbolt other hands hold tantric symbols	youth	two	lalita	bodh. ornaments, va.: lotus throne	Bahubhuja-Cunda (devi)
three/6-9	six	rt.: wheel, thunderbolt, lotus lt.: bell, flaming jewel, sword	mature	two	vajra	bodh, ornaments, va.: lotus throne	Buddha-Locana (fo-mu)**
three/6-9	six	prin.: embrace shakti in vajrahumkara mu. rt.: thunderbolt, flaming jewel lt.: sword, lotus	youth	two	sattva, yab-yum	bodh. ornaments, va.: lotus throne	Guhyasamaja-Lokesvara (Buddha)**
three/6-9	eight	rt.: cylindrical banner, (?), arrow, thunderbolt lt.: parasol, (?), bow, karana mu.	youth	two	vajra	bodh. ornaments, va.: lotus throne	Sitatapatra (fo-mu)
three/6-9	26	prin.: anjali mu. other hands hold tantric symbols	youth	two	paryanka	bodh. ornaments, va.: lotus throne	Sita-Cunda-Devi
three/6-9	26	prin.: anjali mu. other hands hold tantric symbols	youth	two	paryanka	bodh. ornaments, va.: lotus throne	Sita-Cunda-Devi
three/nine	six	rt.: varada mu., rosary, arrow lt., bow, lotus, touches shakti	youth	two	vajra	bodh. ornaments, va.: lion on lotus throne	Halahala-Lokesvara
three*/nine	six	hands hold lotus, the moon disc, sword, axe, noose/snare and in the tarjani mu.				*smiling-bk., wh., rd., bodh. ornaments	bDud-rtsi-spyan-ma
three/nine	six	rt.: wheel, arrow, goad/hook lt.: tarjani mu., bow, sword	youth	two	lalita	bodh. ornaments, va.: lotus throne	Usnisasitatapatra

three*/nine	eight	prin.: hold white parasol rt.: wheel, bow lt.: arrow, book/manuscript	youth	two		*bl., wh., rd., dhar. ornaments, va.: lotus throne	Sitatapatra-Aparajita
three/nine	eight	rt.: crossed thunderbolt, Buddha on a lotus, arrow, varada mu. lt.: bow, tarjani mu. with noose/snare, abhaya mu., vase/vessel	youth	two	vajra	bodh. ornaments, va.: lotus throne	Usnisavijaya
three/nine	eight	prin.: crossed thunderbolt 2nd pr.: vase/vessel in dhyana mu. rt.: Buddha image, bow lt.: noose/snare, arrow	youth	two		bodh. ornaments, va.: lotus throne	Usnisavijaya
four/eight	two	holding wheel	mature	two	vajra	bodh. ornaments, va.: lotus throne	Brahma
four/eight	two	holds wheel in dhyana mu.	youth	two	vajra	bodh. ornaments, va.: lotus throne	Sarvavid-Vairocana**
four*/eight	six	prin.: dharmachakra mu., rt.: bow, arrow, lt.: noose/snare, goad/hook	mature	two	vajra	*white or "whitish-red," bodh. ornaments, va.: lotus throne	Dharmadhatu-Vagisvara
four/eight	eight	rt.: thunderbolt, sword, goad/hook bow lt.: bell, trident, noose/snare, arrow	youth	two	sama-bhanga	bodh. ornaments, va.: lotus throne	Amoghapasa-Lokesvara**
four/eight	eight	rt.: thunderbolt, bow, trident, sword lt.: bell, arrow,, jewel, noose/snare	youth	two	sama-bhanga	bodh. ornaments, va.: lotus throne	Devadevata-Lokesvara**
four/eight	eight	rt.: thunderbolt, bow, trident, sword lt.: bell, arrow, vase/vessel, noose/snare	youth	two	sama-bhanga	bodh. ornaments, va.: lotus throne	Mahavajradhatu-Lokesvara**
four/eight	eight	rt.: sword, thunderbolt, bow, vase/vessel lt.: blue lotus bell arrow, noose/snare	youth	two	sama-bhanga	bodh. ornaments, va.: lotus throne	Mahavajradhrk-Lokesvara**
four/eight	eight	rt.: sword, goad/hook, tantric baton, staff/stick, rosary lt.: wheel, noose/snare, blue lotus, book/manuscript	youth	two	sama-bhanga	bodh. ornaments, va.: lotus throne	Mahavajrapani-Lokesvara**
four/eight	eight	rt.: sword, banner/flag, thunderbolt, goad/hook lt.: bell, conch, blue lotus, lotus	youth	two	sama-bhanga	bodh. ornaments, va.: lotus throne	Mahavisvasuddha-Lokesvara**
four*/eight	eight	rt.: bow, arrow, noose/snare, goad/hook lt.: book/manuscrip, sword, bell,	mature	two	vamalalita	*white or "whitish-red," bodh. ornaments,	Dharmadhatu-Vagisvara

		thunderbolt				va.: lotus throne	
four*/eight	eight	prin.: abhaya mu. at chest level rt.: sword, arrow, thunderbolt lt.: book/manuscript, bow, bell	mature	two	vajra	*white or "whitish-red," bodh. ornaments, va.: lotus throne	Dharmadhatu-Vagisvara
four/eight	eight	prin.: anjali mu. 2nd pr.: dhyana mu. rt.: rosary, arrow lt.: wheel, bow	youth	two	vajra	bodh. ornaments, va.: lotus throne	Vajradhatu-Vairocana**
four/8-12	eight	prin.: hold white parasol rt.: wheel, bow lt.: arrow, book/manuscript	mature	two		*bl., wh., rd., bk., bodh. ornaments, va.: lotus throne	Sitatapatra-Aparajita
four/eight	24	upper raised in anjali mu. with small image others hold tantric symbols	youth	two	dhyana	bodh. ornaments, va.: lotus throne	Avalokitesvara
ten/20	12	prin.: anjali mudra rt.: rosary, arrow, (?), sword, trident lt.: lotus, bow, vase/vessel, (?), magic staff/stick	youth	two	sama-bhanga	bodh. ornaments, va.: lotus throne	Padmapani-Avalokitesvara**
11*/22	two	rt.: varada mudra with rosary lt.: vase/vessel	mature	two		*3-5-3 rows bodh. ornaments,	Ju-ichi-men Kwan-non
11*/22	two	rt.: varada mudra with alarm staff/stick lt.: vase/vessel	mature	two		*3-5-3 rows bodh. ornaments,	Ju-ichi-men Kwan-non
11/22	eight	prin.: jewel in namaskara mu. rt.: rosary, wheel, abhaya lt.: lotus, bow, arrow	youth	two	sama-bhanga	bodh. ornaments, va.: lotus throne	Ekadasamukha**
11/22	eight	prin.: jewel in namaskara mu. rt.: rosary, flaming jewels, varada mu. lt.: lotus, bow, vase/vessel	youth	two	sama-bhanga	bodh. ornaments, va.: lotus throne	Ekadasamukha-Avalokitesvara**
11/22	eight	prin.: jewel in namaskara mu. rt.: rosary, flaming jewels, varada mu. lt.: lotus, bow, vase/vessel	youth	two	sama-bhanga	bodh. ornaments, va.: lotus throne	Ekadasamukha-Avalokitesvara (Bodhisattva)**
11/22	eight	prin.: namaskara mu. rt.: rosary, wheel, varada mu. lotus, bow and arrow, vase/vessel	youth	two	sama-bhanga	bodh. ornaments, va.: lotus throne	Ekadasamukha-Mahakarunika**

11/22	eight	prin.: namaskara mu. rt.: rosary, wheel, varada mu. lt.:lotus, bow, arrow	youth	two	sama-bhanga	bodh. ornaments, va.: lotus throne	Laksmi-krama-Ekadasamukha-Avalokitesvara
11/22	eight	prin.: abhaya mudra against chest rt.: rosary, wheel, varada mu. lt.: blue lotus, bow and arrow, vase/vessel	youth	two	sama-bhanga	bodh. ornaments, va.: lotus throne	Mahasahasrasuryya-Lokesvara**
11/22	eight	prin.: hold jewel rt.: rosary, wheel, goad/hook lt.: lotus, bow, arrow	youth	two	sama-bhanga	bodh. ornaments, va.: lotus throne	Vajragarbhapramardin-Avalokitesvara**
11/22	ten	prin.: jewel in namaskara mu. rt.: karana mu., thunderbolt, abhaya mu., karana mu. lt.: karana mu., vase/vessel, (?), karana mu.	youth	two	sama-bhanga	bodh. ornaments, va.: lotus throne	Gaganaraja**
11/22	32	holds tantric symbols	youth	two	lalita	bodh. ornaments, va.: lotus throne	Visvesa-Avalokitesvara**
11/1,000	1,000	each hand has an eye in the palm, principle hands: anjali mu., rosary, lotus, disc, bow, arrow, varada mu. with jewel	youth	two	sama-bhanga	bodh. ornaments, va.: lotus throne	Ekadasamukha Astabhyatrana-(Arya-Avalokitesvara)
11/1,000	1,000	1st pr.: namaskara mu. 2nd pr.: rosary, lotus 3rd pr.: wheel, bow & arrow 4th pr.: abhaya mu., vase/vessel remaining in abhaya mu.	youth	two	sama-bhanga	eye in each palm, bodh. ornaments, va.: lotus throne	Sahasra-bhuja Avalokitesvara
1000/2000	1000*	prin.: wheel, parasol other hands: tantric and non-tantric symbols	youth	two	sama-bhanga	*eye in each palm, bodh. ornaments, va.: lotus throne	Usnisasitatapatra
1000/2000	1000*	prin.: abhaya mu., parasol rt.: abhaya mu. lt.: abhaya mu.	youth	scores	alidha	*eye in each palm, bodh. ornaments, va.: kneeling human figures	Usnisasitatapatra

White (Skt.: sita; Tib.: dkar-po), Wrathful, Angry or Haughty Deities

Abbreviations:

as. = asana
bn. = brown
lt. = left
rt. = right
yw. = yellow
bk. = black
corp. = corpulent
mu. = mudra
sc. = smokey
bl. = blue
dhar. = dharmapala
pu. = purple
va. = vahana
bodh. = bodhisattva
gn. = green
rd. = red
wh. = white

(*) special variations or attributes noted within the entry.
(**) following deity's name indicates that the color is not noted in the source, kulesa's color is applied to the entry.
(eyes: 2-3, 6-9, etc.) in sources the deity's faces are noted, but the number of the eyes are not noted.

Head/Eyes	Hands	Objects Held	Body	Feet	Asana	Other Attributes	Deity Name
one*/two	two	rt.: goad/hook or axe lt.: crystal vase/vessel with elixir of life	mature	two	rajalila	*angry, richly garbed, va.: lion on lotus throne	Ayurdhara-Sita-Vaisravana
one/two	two	holds a precious vase/vessel	mature	two		calm deity's dress, va.: six jewel throne	bKra-bzang-zhing-skyong
one*/two	two	holding treasure casque and crystal lance with banner/flag	mature	two		*angry, conch shell armor, va.: white lion	bsTan-bsrung-mdzad-gnod-sbyin-mched-lnga
one*/two	two	holding noose/snare of intestines	mature	two	alidha	*bear-head, dhar. ornaments	Ishvari, "White Bear-Headed Indra-Goddess"
one*/two	two	holding club/cudgel	mature	two	alidha	*eagle-head, dhar. ornaments	Ishvari, "White Eagle-Headed Mighty-Goddess"
one*/two	two	holding thunderbolt	mature	two	alidha	*kite-head, dhar. ornaments	Ishvari, "White Kite-Headed Moon-Goddess"
one*/two	two	rt.: iron goad/hook lt.: vase/vessel	corp.	two		*angry, richly dressed, fancy leather boots, va.: caprisoned horse	Jambhala
one*/two	two	plays stringed instrument (vina)	mature	two	rajalila	*haughty, richly armored, fancy boots	Dhritarastra

one*/two	two	playing stringed instrument	mature	two	sattva	*haughty richly armored, fancy boots, va.: lotus throne	Dhritarastra/Dhrtarastra
one*/two	two	playing stringed instrument	mature	two	sattva	*haughty richly armored, fancy boots, va.: red monkey and green demon	Dhritarastra/Dhrtarastra
one*/two	two	playing stringed instrument	mature	two	sattva	*haughty richly armored, fancy boots, attrib: syllable "nghri" va.: elephant	Dhritarastra/Dhrtarastra
one*/two	two	rt.: goad/hook lt.: human skull-cup	mature	two	praty-alidha	*tiger-head eastern quarter	White Tiger-headed Goad-Holding Goddess
one*/two	two	rt.: iron goad/hook lt.: vase/vessel	mature	two		*angry, bodh. ornaments, va.: lotus throne	Gang-ba-bzang-po
one*/two	two	rt.: iron goad/hook lt.: vase/vessel	mature	two	astride	*angry fancy leather boots, bodh. ornaments, va.: caprisoned horse	Kubera
one*/two	two	rt.: iron goad/hook with red lance in crook of arm lt.: vase/vessel	mature	two	astride	*angry fancy leather boots, bodh. ornaments, va.: caprisoned horse	Kubera
one*/two	two	rt.: goad/hook lt.: noose/snare	mature, nude	two		*angry, bone ornaments, va.: lotus throne	Mahadeva
one*/two	two	rt.: cylindrical banner/flag lt.: crystal sword	mature,	two		*angry, white silk cloak, va.: white *gnam-ru*	Mahadeva
one*/two	two	rt.: sword lt.: lance with banner/flag	mature,	two		*angry, dhar. ornaments, va.: white yak	Mahadeva
one*/two	two	rt.: jewel	mature	two	astride	*angry,	Manibhadra

		lt.: treasure producing mongoose				richly armored, dhar. ornaments, va.: caprisoned horse	
one*/two	two	rt.: iron goad/hook lt.: vase/vessel	mature	two	astride	*angry, richly armored, dhar. ornaments, va.: caprisoned horse	Manibhadra
one*/two	two	rt.: iron goad/hook, red lance in crook of arm lt.: vase/vessel	mature	two	astride	*angry, richly armored, dhar. ornaments, va.: caprisoned horse	Manibhadra
one*/two	two	rt.: lance with banner/flag lt.: wish granting jewel	mature	two	astride	*angry, golden armor, dhar. ornaments, va.: horse with jeweled saddle	Ma-zhing-khyung-rtse
one*/two	two	rt.: trident lt.: banner/flag	mature	two	lalita	*angry,, dhar. ornaments, va.: human corpse	mGon-po-Bram-zehi-gZugs-can
one*/two	four	rt.: iron goad/hook, red lance lt.: vase/vessel, iron goad/hook	corp.	two		*angry, richly dressed, fancy leather boots, va.: caprisoned horse	Iambhala
one*/two	four	rt. embraces shakti, human skull-cup lt.: **staff/stick**, ritual chopper	youth	two	standing, yab-yum	*angry, bodh. ornaments, va.: lotus throne	Sadaksari-Lokesvara**
one*/two	six	rt.: citron, sword, arrow lt.: mongoose, bow, embraces shakti	corp.	two	vamalalita, vab-yum	*angry, bodh. ornaments, va.: lotus throne	Iambhala
one*/two	two	holds blood-sack	mature	two	aseat	*angry, fancy dressed, attribute: syllable "la" va.: white stag	Vajralocani
one*/two	two	rt.: goad/hook lt.: blue lotus	mature	two	alidha	*angry, dhar. ornaments, realm: Eastern gate va.: lotus throne	Vajrankusi

one*/two	two	rt.: banner/flag and lance lt.: jewel	mature	two		*angry, richly dressed, fancy boots, va.: red yaksha and yellow yaksha	<u>Vaisravana</u>
one*/2-3	two	rt.: goad/hook lt.: vase/vessel	mature	two	astride	*angry, white garments, high fancy boots, va.: caprisoned horse	<u>'Brog-gnas</u>
one/2-3	two	rt.: thunderbolt on point in abhaya mu. lt.: dhyana mu.	mature, nude	two	alidha	dhar, ornaments, va.: lotus throne	<u>Buddha-Locana (fo-mu)</u>**
one*/2-3	two	rt.: conch shell lt.: white lance	mature	two		dhar. ornaments, va.: elephant	<u>Chos-bdag-bkra-shis-dpal</u>
one/2-3	two	rt.: white noose/snare lt.: white staff/stick	mature	two	astride	dhar. ornaments, va.: white horse with black heels	<u>Chos-gter-gyi-srung-ma</u>
one*/2-3	two	rt.: sword lt.: shield	mature	two	astride	*angry, richly armored, fancy boots, va.: caprisoned horse	<u>Dzam-po-'khyil-pa</u>
one*/2-3	two	rt.: iron goad/hook lt.: vase/vessel	mature	two	astride	*angry, richly armored, fancy boots, va.: caprisoned horse	<u>Dzam-po-'khyil-pa</u>
one*/2-3	two	rt.: iron goad/hook, red lance in crook of arm lt.: vase/vessel and iron goad/hook	mature	two	astride	*angry, richly armored, fancy boots, va.: caprisoned horse	<u>Dzam-po-'khyil-pa</u>
one*/2-3	two	rt.: noose/snare lt.: ritual chopper	mature	two		*angry, a yaksa, va.: elephant	<u>gNod-sbyin-nor-gyi-rgyal-po</u>
one*/2-3	two	rt.: iron goad/hook lt.: vase/vessel	mature	two	astride	*angry, bejeweled, richly armored, va.: caprisoned horse	<u>lNga-rten</u>
one*/2-3	two	rt.: iron goad/hook, red lance in crook of arm	mature	two	astride	*angry, bejeweled,	<u>lNga-rten</u>

		lt.: vase/vessel				richly armored, va.: caprisoned horse	
one*/2-3	four	rt.: goad/hook and red lance lt.: vase/vessel and goad/hook	mature	two	astride	*angry, white garments, high fancy boots, va.: caprisoned horse	'Brog-gnas
one/three	two	rt.: lance with red pennants lt.: noose/snare	mature	two	astride	toupet with conch shell, white silk garment, fancy boots, va.: white horse	Dung-skyong-dkar-po
one/three	two	rt.: club with skull finial lt.: human skull-cup	mature	two	yab-yum	bodh. ornaments, multicolored lower garment	Dur-khrod-bdag-po-lcam-dral
one/three	two	rt.: noose/snare lt. staff/stick of cane	mature	two		white-silk garment, bodh. ornaments, va.: red rooster	gTer-gyi-bsrung-ma
one/three	two	rt.: lance with banner/flag lt.: bowl with jewels	mature	two	astride	garment of vari-colored silk, dhar. ornaments, vahana: white horse	g.Ya'-spang-brgya-byin
one/three	two	rt.: thunderbolt lt.: karana mu.	corp.	two	alidha	dhar. ornaments, va.: lotus throne	Hsiao-Vajrapani**
one/three	two	rt.: trident lt.: bejeweled club	corp	two		silk garments, bodh. ornaments, va.: turquoise dragon	Iambhala-dkar-po-lha-lnga-jo-bo'i-lugs
one*/three	two	rt.: crystal lance lt.: flat bowl filled with gems	mature	two		*crystal color, white silk garments' dhar. ornaments	Io-bo-chen-po
one/three	two	rt.: club/cudgel lt.: basin filled with gems	mature	two		wh. and rd. silk garment	Kha-chu'i-gzhi-bdag-mNgon-dga'
one/three	two	rt.: vajra-topped staff/stick lt.: noose/snare, embraces shakti	corp	two	alidha, yab-yum	dhar. ornaments, va.: prostrate human figures	Krodhaparajita**
one/three	two	rt.: thunderbolt lt.: flame(?)	mature	two	alidha	dhar. ornaments, va.: lotus throne	Krodha-Vajrapani**

one/three	two	rt.: thunderbolt lt.: human skull-cup	corp.	two	alidha	dhar. ornaments, va.: prostrate human forms	<u>Kutagara-Vajrapani</u>
one/three	two	rt.: red lance with banner/flag lt.: red noose/snare	mature	two	astride	dhar. ornaments, fancy boots, va.: red horse	<u>lHa-btsan</u>
one/three	two	rt.: battle lance lt.: divination arrow	mature	two	astride	dhar. ornaments, fancy boots, va.: white horse	<u>lHa-chen-gnam-the-dkar-po</u>
one/three	two	holds crystal sword	mature	two	astride	dhar. ornaments, fancy boots, va.: white horse	<u>lHa-chen-gnam-the-dkar-po</u>
one/three	two	holds white noose/snare	mature	two		dhar. ornaments, va.: lotus throne	<u>lHa'i-srung-ma</u>
one/three	two	rt.: iron falcon lt.: sickle	mature	two		dhar. ornaments, va.: hind	<u>lHa-mo-dung-gha-bza'</u>
one/three	two	rt.: white noose/snare lt.: bridle and arrow	mature	two	astride	dhar. ornaments, va.: white horse	<u>lHa-rigs</u>
one/ three	two	rt.: white cylindrical banner lt.: book/manuscript	corp.	two	astride	dhar. ornaments, crystal cuirsaa, va.: horse	<u>lHa-yi-dge-bsnyen-drag-rtsal</u>
one/three	two	rt.: crystal sword lt.: battle lance	mature	two	astride	dhar. ornaments, va.: white horse	<u>Li-byin-ha-ra-dkar-po</u>
one/three	two	rt.: flaming crystal sword lt.: treasure producing mongoose	mature	two		garments of black and white silk, dhar. ornaments, va.: lotus throne	<u>Mahakali-Remati</u>
one/three	two	rt.: lance with white banner/flag lt.: mongoose	mature	two	astride	richly armored, dhar. ornaments, va.: white horse	<u>mGon-po-mgron-lha</u>
one/three	two	rt.: abhaya mu., cylindrical banner/flag lt.: lotus, vase/vessel	mature	two	alidha	dhar. ornaments, va.: lotus throne	<u>Naga-bhayatrana (Avalokitesvara)</u>**
one*/three	two	rt.: fruit (?) lt.: serpent/snake	mature	two	astride	*angry, dhar. ornaments, va.: horse	<u>Nagarajavajra</u>

one*/three	two	rt.: human corpse-club lt.:	mature	two	astride	*angry, dhar. ornaments, attribute: syllable "*le*" va.: black boar	Nagarajavajra
one/three	two	rt.: crystal spear lt.: basin filled with jewels	mature	two	astride	white felt hat, dhar. ornaments, va.: white horse	Ne-ser-jo-bo-chen-po
one/three	two	rt.: lance lt.: riding stick	mature	two	astride	helmeted, armored, dhar. ornaments, va.: white horse	Ngom-rgyal-mtsho-bkra
one/three	two	rt.: jewel lt.: casque filled with jewels	mature	two		dhar. ornaments, va.: lotus throne	Nor-lha
one/three	two	rt.: crystal thunderbolt lt.: alms bowl	mature	two		dhar. ornaments, va.: tiger	Nyi-sang-pad
one/three	two	rt.: human corpse club/cudgel lt.: human skull-cup	mature	two		bone ornaments, human skin cape	Kermina
one/three	two	rt.: abhaya mu. lt.: (?)	mature, nude	two	alidha	dhar. ornaments, va.: prostrate human form	Pandaravasini (fo-mu)**
one/three	two	rt.: golden staff/stick lt.: vase/vessel of silver	mature	two	alidha	bamboo hat, red garments, dhar. ornaments, va.: lotus throne	Pe-har
one/three	two	rt.: golden staff/stick lt.: vase/vessel of silver filled with blood	mature	two	alidha	brown hat, dhar. ornaments, va.: lotus throne	Pe-har
one*/three	two	rt.: treasure casque lt.: lance with banner/flag	mature	two		*angry, armor of conch shells, dhar. ornaments, va.: lotus throne	Phu-yi-gzhi-bdag-mdzod-lnga-spun-lnga
one/three	two	rt.: white lance with silk banner/flag lt.: wish fulfilling jewel	mature	two	astride	white felt hat, white silk garment with wide sleeves, dhar. ornaments,	Phying-dkar-ba

						va.: white horse	
one/three	two	holding garland of flowers	mature	two	alidha	dhar. ornaments, va.: lotus throne	Puspa
one/three	two	holding garland of flowers	mature, nude	two	alidha	dhar. ornaments, va.: prostrate human figure	Puspa (fo-mu)**
one/three	two	rt.: lance lt.: jewel	mature	two		dhar. ornaments, va.: white horse	rDo-rje-brag-btsan-rDo-rje-dbang-drag-rtsal
one*/three	two	holds five pointed thunderbolt	mature	two		*angry, dhar. ornaments, syllable "ma", va.: lion	rDo-rje-kun-tu-bzang
one*/three	two	rt.: banner/flag of victory lt.: thunderbolt	mature	two		*angry, armor of crystal, va.: tan horse with turquoise mane	rGyam-rgyal-rdo-ti-gangs-dkar
one/three	two	rt.: lance lt.: shallow bowl filled with jewels	mature	two	astride	red turban, varicolored cloak, dhar. ornaments, va.: white horse	Rung-ma'i-yul-lha-g.Ya'-spang-brgya-byin
one/three	two	embraces shakti & holds vase/vessel	mature	two	vajra, yab-yum	dhar. ornaments, va.: lotus throne	Sita-Chakrasamvara
one/three	two	rt.: sword lt.: noose/snare	mature	two	*	*left knee on ground, right foot flat, dhar. ornaments, va.: lotus throne	Sita-Acalavajra
one/three	two	rt.: sword lt.: tarjani mu.	corp.	two	alidha	dhar. ornaments, va.: lotus throne	Sita-Acala
one/three	two	rt.: flaming crystal sword lt.: treasure producing mongoose	mature	two	astride	dhar. ornaments, va.: mule	Shankhapali Devi
one/three	two	rt.: baton lt.: (?)	corp.	two	alidha	dhar. ornaments, va.: lotus throne	Shan-hsing Vajrapani (Buddha)**
one/three	two	rt.: thunderbolt lt.: (?)	corp.	two	alidha	dhar. ornaments, va.: lotus throne	Sa-(skya)-lugs-Vajrapani**

one/three	two	rt.: goad/hook lt.: alms bowl	mature	two	astride	dhar. ornaments, va.: water buffalo	sByi-ring-khrid
one*/three	two	holds banner/flag of victory with a cat's head finial	mature**	two		*deer-head, **leopard tail, dhar. ornaments, va.: lotus throne	Se-byi
one/three	two	rt. chapatedana mu. lt. : noose/snare	mature	two	alidha	dhar. ornaments, va.: Ganesa under foot on lotus throne	Aparajita
one/three	two	rt.: abhaya mu. lt.: noose/snare	mature	two	alidha	dhar. ornaments, va.: demons under foot on lotus throne	Aparajita
one*/three	two	rt.: goad/hook lt.: treasure casque	mature	two		*angry, white garments	Aparajita-yaksa
one*/three	two	rt.: goad/hook lt.: vase/vessel	mature	two	sama-bhanga	*angry, bodh. ornaments, va,: lotus throne	Aparajita-yaksa
one/ three	two	rt.: trident lt.: staff/stick	mature	two	alidha	dhar. ornaments, va.: lotus throne on back of dragon	Arya-(Atisa)-krama-Pancatmaka-Sita-Jambhala
one/three	two	vajrahumkara mu. embracing shakti	youth	two	alidha	dhar. ornaments, va.: human figures	Ayuhsadhana-Sita-Samvara
one/ three	two	rt.: mace lt.: vase/vessel	mature	two	lalita	richly garbed, va.: lion on lotus throne	Ayurdhara-Sita-Vaisravana
one/three	two	rt.: magic throwing staff/stick lt.: human skull-cup with a heart	mature	two		dhar. ornaments	bDud-mo-ro-langs-ma
one/three	two	rt.: thunderbolt lt.: bell	corp.	two	alidha	dhar. ornaments, va.: lotus throne	Bhutadamara-Vajrapani (Buddha)**
one*/three	two	rt.: nine-pointed thunderbolt lt.: vase/vessel with elixir of life	mature	two		*angry, , haughty, dhar. ornaments, syllable "mani", va.: white lioness	bKra-shis-tshe-ring-ma
one/three	two	rt.:wheel lt.: human skull-cup and magic	mature	two	ardha-paryanka	dhar. ornaments, va.: lotus throne	Buddha-Dakini

		staff/stick in crook of arm					
one/three	two	rt.: thunderbolt lt.: bell	corp.	two	alidha	dhar. ornaments, va.: snakes	Canda-Vajrapani (chun)**
one/three	two	rt.: thunderbolt lt.: (?)	corp.	two	alidha	dhar. ornaments, va.: prostrate human forms	Garudayuta-Vajrapani**
one/three	two	rt.: thunderbolt lt.: tarjani mu.	mature	two	alidha	dhar. ornaments, va.: prostrate human forms	Khra-thogs-Canda-Vajrapani
one/three	two	rt.: thunderbolt lt.: battle lance	mature	two	astride	white garment, dhar. ornaments, va.: white goat	rDo-rje-legs-pa
one/three	two*	rt.: vitarka mu. lt.: stem of lotus in varada mu.	mature	two	dhyana	*eye in the palm of hands, dhar. ornaments, va.: lotus throne	Sita-Tara
one/three	two	embrace shakti and holds vase/vessel	mature	two	vajra, yab-yum	dhar. ornaments, va.: lotus throne	Sita-Chakrasamvara
one/three	two	rt.: staff/stick lt.: noose/snare, embraces shakti	corp	two	alidha, yab-yum	dhar. ornaments, va.: prostrate human figures	Sita-Hayagriva
one/three	two	rt.: crossed thunderbolts lt.: crossed thunderbolts	corp.	two	alidha	dhar. ornaments, va.: lotus throne	Sita-Hayagrivavajra (Buddha)
one/three	two	rt.: trident lt.: tantric staff/stick	corp.	two	ardha-paryanka	dhar. ornaments, va.: dragon	Sita-Iambhala
one/three	two	rt.: trident lt.: jewel tipped baton/mace	corp.	two	lalita	dhar. ornaments, va.: dragon	Sita-nagavahana-Iambhala
one/three	two	embraces shakti in vajrahumkara mu. holding vase/vessel	mature	two	vajra, yab-yum	dhar. ornaments, va.: lotus throne	Sita-Samvara
one/three	two	rt.: sun disc lt.: moon disc	corp.	two	alidha	dhar. ornaments, va.: lotus throne	Sita-Surya-Candra
one/three	two	rt.: thunderbolt lt.: karana mu.	corp.	two	alidha	dhar. ornaments, va.: prostrate human	Sita-Vajrapani

						bodies	
one*/three	two	rt.: thunderbolt on end lt.: bell on thigh	youth	two	vamalalita	*angry, dhar. ornaments, va.: lotus throne	<u>Sita-Vajravidarana</u>
one*/three	two	rt.: thunderbolt lt.: human skull-cup, magic staff/stick in crook of arm	mature	two	ardha-paryanka	*pigs head on right of head, dhar. ornaments, va.: lotus throne	<u>Sita-Varahi</u>
one/three	two	rt.: noose/snare lt.: tarjani mu.	mature, nude	two	alidha	dhar. ornaments, va.: prostrate human figure	<u>Sita-Vetali (fo-mu)</u>
one*/three	two	rt.: sword lt.: cylindrical banner/flag	mature, nude	two	alidha	*bull-head, dhar. ornaments, va.: bull	<u>Sita Yamaraja</u>
one/three	two	rt.: short lance with banner/flag lt.: skull of a wolf	mature	two		crystal helmet, coat of white silk, va.: white horse	<u>sKu-la-mkha'-ri</u>
one/three	two	rt.: lance lt.: noose/snare	mature	two	astride	silver helmet, silver harness, cloak of bird feathers, va.: white horse	<u>sKu-sprul-stobs-rgyal</u>
one/three	two	rt.: cylindrical victory banner lt.: lance with banner/flag	mature	two	astride	harness of conch shells, va.: wild Asiatic ass	<u>sKyes-bu-(')phrag-lha</u>
one/three	two	rt.: lance with white flag lt.: jewel	mature	two	astride	crystal helmet, crystal harness, va.: white horse	<u>sMad-shod-rdo-rje-mu-nam</u>
one/three	two	rt.: noose/snare lt.: ritual chopper	mature	two		vulture feather cloak, va.: white lion	<u>Srog-bdag-tshangs-pa-dkar-po</u>
one/three	two	rt.: club lt.: basin of gems	mature	two		garment of white and red silk, va.: lotus throne	<u>sTag-lung-dge-bsnyen</u>
one/three	two	raises Mt. Sumeru	mature	two		1000 sun & moon necklace, dhar. ornaments, va.: lotus throne	<u>Surya-Candra-Gauri</u>

one/three	two	rt.: shrine lt.: bud (?)	corp.	two	alidha	pendulous breasts, dhar. ornaments, va.: lotus throne	<u>Surya-Candra-Gauri</u>
one/three	two	rt.: thunderbolt lt.: tarjani mu.	corp.	two	alidha	dhar. ornaments, va.: lotus throne	<u>Sutra-krama-Vajrapani</u>**
one/three	two	rt.: hammer with thunderbolt handle lt.: noose/snare	mature	two		dhar. ornaments, va.: lotus throne	<u>Tho-ba-'jigs-byed</u>
one*/three	two	holds sword	mature	two	alidha	*angry, dhar. ornaments, va.: monkey and demon	<u>Tseng-chang</u>
one*/three	two	rt.: staff/stick with jewel lt.: mongoose	mature	two	astride	*elephant-head, dhar. ornaments, harness of conch shells, va.: wild Asiatic ass	<u>Tshong-lha-tshogs-bdag-glang-sna</u>
one/three	two	holds bell surmounted by a thunderbolt	mature	two	alidha	dhar. ornaments, realm: Northern gate, va.: lotus throne	<u>Vajraghanta</u>
one/three	two	rt.: thunderbolt lt.: noose/snare	corp.	two	alidha	dhar. ornaments, va.: lotus throne	<u>Vajrapani(?)</u>
one/three	two	rt.: bhumisparsa mu. lt.: dhyana mu.	mature	two		dhar. ornaments, va.: human form	<u>Vajrosnisa</u>
one/three	two	rt.: ritual chopper, embraces shakti lt.: human skull-cup, embraces shakti	mature	two	alidha, yab-yum	dhar. ornaments, va.: lotus throne	<u>Vidya-Dhara</u>[3]
one/three	two	rt.: white crystal scepter lt.: white; club/cudgel	mature	two	astride	dhar. ornaments, white crystal scepter, va.: white horse	<u>Ya-bdud-tshogs-kyi-gtso-bo</u>
one*/three	two	rt.: human skull-drum lt.: divination arrow	mature	two	alidha	*bull-head, dhar. ornaments, va.: lotus throne	<u>Yama</u>
one/three	two	rt.: goad/hook lt.: human skull-cup	mature	two	alidha	dhar. ornaments, va.: lotus throne	<u>Yama dati</u>
one/three	two	rt.: flaming tooth lt.: human skull-cup	mature	two		dhar. ornaments, va.: lotus throne	<u>Yama-disti</u>

[3] The Vidya-Dhara , Knowledge Holding Deities who appear on the seventh day of the second state of the Bardo-Thodol. They are forms of the Dhyani Buddhas.

one*/three	two	rt.: scepter topped with skeleton lt.: noose/snare	corp.	two	alidha	*bull-head, dhar. ornaments, va.: bull standing on a woman	Yama (phyi-sgrub)
one*/three	two	rt.: human skull-cup lt.: human skull-cup	corp.	two	alidha	*bull-head, dhar. ornaments, va.: billy goat or copper mule	Yama tasti
one*/three	two	rt.: iron goad/hook lt.: vase/vessel	mature	two	astride	*angry, white garments and bejeweled, high fancy leather boots, va.: caprisoned horse	Yang-dag-shes
one/three	two	rt.: short lance with banner/flag lt.: crystal sword	mature	two		dhar. ornaments, white garments, va.: lotus throne	Yar-lha-sham-po
one/three	two	rt.: ritual chopper lt.: skull-cup filled with blood	mature	two		dhar. ornaments, va.: lotus throne	Ye-shes-mkha'-'gro-ma
one/three	two	rt.: thunderbolt lt.: human skull-cup, magic staff/stick in crook of arm	mature	two	ardha-paryanka	dhar. ornaments, va.: prostrate human figure	(Yig-rnin-lugs)Prajnalokakrtya Sita Vahari
one/three	two	rt.: divination arrow lt.: human skull-cup	mature	two		dhar. ornaments, va.: white elephant	Zhi-ba'i-rgyal-chen
one/three	four	rt.: abhaya mu. and staff/stick lt.: flowering branch and lotus	corp.	two	alidha	dhar. ornaments, va.: lotus throne	Agni-bhayatrana (Avalokitesvara)**
one/three	four	prin. in bhutadamara mu. rt.: thunderbolt lt.: noose/snare	corp.	two	pratyalidha	dhar. ornaments, va.: Ganesa	Bhutadamara-Vajrapani**
one/three	four	rt.: thunderbolt, abhaya mu. lt.: lotus, bell	corp.	two	alidha	dhar. ornaments, va.: lotus throne	Cora-bhayatrana (Avalokitesvara)**[4]
one/three	four	rt.: abhaya mu., trident lt.: lotus, staff/stick	corp.	two	alidha	dhar. ornaments, va.: lotus throne	Dakini-bhayatrana (Avalokitesvara)**
one/three	four	rt.: abhaya mu., goad/hook lt.: lotus, noose/snare	corp.	two	alidha	dhar. ornaments, va.: lotus throne	Danda-bhayatrana-(Avalokitesvara)**

[4] one of the few fierce forms of *Avalokitesvara.*

one*/three	four	rt.: iron goad/hook, red lance in crook of arm lt.: vase/vessel, iron goad/hook	mature	two	astride	*angry, bodh. ornaments, va.: caprisoned horse	Gang-ba-bzang-po
one/three	four	rt.: abhaya mu., flowering branch lt.: lotus, lotus bud	corp.	two	alidha	bodh. ornaments, va.: lotus throne	Hasti-bhayatrana (Avalokitesvara)**
one/three	four	prin.: bhutadamara mu. rt.: thunderbolt lt.: noose/snare	corp.	two	alidha	dhar. ornaments, va.: lotus throne	Iagaddama-Vajrapani**
one/three	four	prin.: vajrahumakra mu. with wheel rt.: human skull-drum lt.: magic notched staff/stick	youth	two	alidha	dhar. ornaments, va.: prostrate human form on lotus throne	Kavaca-Vairocana**
one/three	four	prin.: vajrahumakra mu. embraces shakti in yab-yum rt.: human skull-drum lt.: magic notched staff/stick	youth	two	alidha, yab-yum	dhar. ornaments, va.: prostrate human form on lotus throne	Kavaca-Vajrasattva**
one/three	four	rt.: thunderbolt, serpent/snake lt.: bell, other end of serpent/snake	corp.	two	alidha	dhar. ornaments, va.: lotus throne	Lohanadi(?)-Vajrapani
one/three	four	rt.: crystal vase/vessel with nectar of life, skull-cup lt.: ritual chopper, trident	mature	two	alidha	dhar. ornaments, va.: lotus throne	mGon-po-dkar-po
one/three	four	prin.: dharmachakra mu. (?) rt.: thunderbolt lt.: noose/snare	corp	two	alidha	dhar. ornaments, va.: prostrate human forms	Nava-Bhutadamara-Vajrapani**
one/three	four	rt.: abhaya mu., jewels lt.: flowering branch, book/manuscript	corp.	two	alidha	dhar. ornaments, va.: lotus throne	Simha-bhayatrana (Avalokitesvara)**
one*/three	four	rt.: shield, rosary lt.: mongoose, battle axw	mature	two		*elephant-head, tiger skin garment, va.: rat	Tshogs-bdag-dkar-po-phyag-bzhi-pa-jo-bi'i-lugs
one/three	four	prin.: bhutadamara mu. rt.: thunderbolt lt.: noose/snare	mature	two	alidha	dhar. ornaments, va.: lotus throne	Vairocanabhisambodhi
one/three	four	rt.: sword, thunderbolt lt.: skull-cup, (?)	mature, nude	two	alidha	dhar. ornaments, va.: prostrate human form	Vajraraga(?) (fo-mu)**

one/three	six	rt.: flaming jewel, human skull-drum, ritual chopper lt.: snare/noose, trident, vase/vessel	corp.	two	sama-bhanga	dhar. ornaments, va: prostrate Ganesa form	Cintamani-Sita-Mahakala
one/three	six	rt.: vitarka mu., ritual chopper, (?) lt.: wish-fulfilling jewel, trident, goad/hook	corp	two	alidha	dhar. ornaments, va.: snakes	Sita-chintamani-Mahakala
one/three	six	rt.: vitarka mu., ritual chopper, (?) lt.: wish-fulfilling jewel, trident, goad/hook(?)	corp	two	alidha	dhar. ornaments, va.: snakes	Sita-chintamani-Mahakala
one/three	six	rt.: ritual chopper, noose/snare, flaming jewels lt.: human skull-cup with vase/vessel, trident, goad/hook	corp.	two	sama-bhanga	dhar. ornaments, va.: prostrate elephants	Sita-Mahakala
one/three	six	rt.: wish fulfilling jewel, skull-cup, ritual chopper lt.: human skull-drum, goad/hook, trident	mature	two		dhar. ornaments, va.: two elephants	Gom-kar
one*/three	six	rt.: wish-fulfilling jewel, human skull-cup, ritual chopper lt.: small drum, trident, goad/hook	mature	two		may look like a bull, dhar. ornaments, va.: two elephants	Mahakala-mGon-dkar
one/three	six	rt.: flaming jewels, hold ritual chopper, human skull-drum lt.: skull-cup with crystal vase/vessel filled with nectar of life, trident, noose/snare	mature	two	alidha	dhar. ornaments, va.: lotus throne	mGon-po-dkar-po
one/three	six	rt.: flaming jewels, ritual chopper, human skull-drum lt.: human skull-cup, trident, goad/hook	mature	two	alidha	dhar. ornaments, va.: lotus throne	mGon-po-dkar-po
one/three	six	rt.: ritual chopper, wish granting jewel, human skull-drum lt.: skull-cup, full of nectar of life, trident, noose/snare	mature	two		cloak of variegated silk, dhar. ornaments, va.: lotus throne	mGon-po-yid-bzhin-nor-bu
one/three	six	rt.: flaming jewels, ritual chopper, human skull-drum lt.: vase/vessel in human skull-cup, trident, noose/snare	corp	two	sama-bhanga	loose garments, dhar. ornaments, va.: prostrate Ganesa form	Nikama-varsi-Sita-Mahakala

one/three	six	prin.: embrace shakti rt.: staff/stick marked with a thunderbolt, sword lt.: jewel, lotus	corp.	two	yab-yum	dhar. ornaments, va.: lotus throne	Prajnantaka
one/three	eight	prin. renge-no-in (Skt.: Uttarabodhi) mu. other hands hold wheel, sword, noose/snare, mace, thunderbolt, trident	mature	two	vajra	horse head in hair, white hair, flowing robe va.: lotus throne	Ba-to Kwan-non
one*/three	eight	prin.: renge-no-in (Skt.: Uttarabodhi) mu., lt. varada mu., wheel, noose/snare, mace, thunderbolt, trident or sword	mature	two	maharaja-lila	*angry bodh. ornaments, va.: lotus throne	Ba-to Kwan-non
one/three	ten	tantric symbols including: hunderbolt, goad/hook, arrow, needle, asoka branch, bow, thread, tarjani mu.	mature	two	alidha	dhar. ornaments, va.: Brahma, Vishnu and Siva on a sow	Marici
two*/four	two*	rt.: staff/stick with skull finial or flame lt.: human skull-cup	skeletal	two	ardha-paryanka	*two figures. rt. hands hold different objects, va,: lotus throne	Citipati
three*/6-9	six	prin.: embrace shakti rt.: mongoose, jewel lt.: citron, sword	corp	two	vajra, yab-yum	*angry, richly dressed, fancy leather boots, va.: lotus throne	Jambhala
three/nine	four	prin.: bhutadamara mu. rt.: thunderbolt lt.: noose/snare	corp.	two	alidha	dhar. ornaments, va.: prostrate human form on lotus throne	Bhutadamara-Anuttara-Vajrapani**
three/nine	four	prin.: embrace shakti with skull-cup, karana mu. rt.: magic staff/stick lt.: thunderbolt	mature	two	alidha	dhar. ornaments, va.: human form	Vajrosnisa
three*/nine	six	prin. embrace shakti rt.: sword, jewel lt.: wheel, lotus	mature	two	alidha	*wh., bk., rd., dhar. ornaments, va.: lotus throne	Aparajita
three*/nine	six	rt.: lotus, moon disc, sword lt.: axe, noose/snare, tarjani mu.	mature	two	alidha(?)	dhar. ornaments,	bDud-rtsi-spyan-ma
three/nine	six	prin.: abhaya mu. & dhyana mu. rt.: thunderbolt, wheel	mature	two	vajra	dhar. ornaments, va.: lotus throne	Pandaravasini (fo-mu)**

		lt.: sword, (?)					
three/nine	six	orin.: embraces shakti with ritual chopper, human skull-cup rt.: staff/stick with thunderbolt finial, sword lt.: flaming jewel, lotus	corp.	two	partyalidha, yab-yum	dhar. ornaments, va.: lotus throne	<u>Prajnantaka</u>
three*/nine	six	prin.: dharmachakra mu. rt.: blue lotus, thunderbolt lt.: bow, arrow	youth	two	vamalalita	*bl., wh., rd., dhar. ornaments, va.: lotus throne	<u>rJe-btsun-ma-Rig-ma-chen-mo</u>
three*/nine	six	prin. vajrahumkara mu. embraces shakti rt.: human-skin cape, human skull-drum lt.: human-skin cape, human skull-cup	youth	two	alidha	bejeweled, va.: human figures	<u>Saptaksara-Lokesvara</u>**
three/nine	six	rt.: varada mu., rosary, arrow lt.: blue lotus, bow, lotus in bowl	youth	two	ardha-paryanka	dhar. ornaments, va.: lotus throne	<u>Sadbhuja-Sitara</u>
three/nine	six	rt.: abhaya mu., rosary, arrow lt.: lotus, bow, varada mu.	youth	two	vamalalita	dhar. ornaments, va.: lotus throne	<u>Sadbhuja-Sitara</u>
three*/nine	six	rt.: wheel, goad/hook, arrow lt.: thunderbolt, arrow noose/snare	youth	two	sama-bhanga	*angry, bodh. ornaments,	<u>Sitatapatra-Aparajita</u>
three*/nine	six	rt.: chain, sword, axe lt.: pestle, thunderbolt, tarjani mu.	mature	two		*rd., wh., bk., dhar. ornaments, va.: lotus throne	<u>Vajrasrinkhala</u>
three*/nine	six	rt.: container of Tibetan beer, jewel, sword lt.: trident, battle axe, (?)	mature, nude	two	alidha, yab-yum	*monkey-head, elephant-head, cat-head, dhar. ornaments, va.: lotus throne	<u>'Zur-'gegs-sel-ba'i-tshogs-bdag-chags-pa-rdo-rje</u>
three/nine	12	tantric symbols	corp.	two	alidha	dhar. ornaments, va.: lotus throne	<u>Pancamukhadvadasabhuja-krsna-Avalokitesvara (Bodhisattva)</u>**
four/12	four	hands hold thunderbolt, noose/snare, sword, human skull-cup	mature	four	pratyalidha	dhar. ornaments, va.: demons under foot on lotus throne	<u>Acala-Vajrapani</u>
four*/12	four	rt.: vase/vessel of elixir of life, human skull-cup lt.: ritual chopper and trident	corp.	two	alidha	*rd., wh., & bl., dhar. ornaments va.: lotus throne	<u>Ayur-vardhana-Sita-Caturmukha-(Sri-Mahakala)</u>

four/12	four	rt.: thunderbole, vase/vessel lt.: human skull-cup and trident	corp.	two	alidha	dhar. ornaments, va.: lotus throne	Ayur-vardhana-Sita-Caturmukha-(Sri-Mahakala)
five*/15	ten	rt.: sun disc, blue thunderbolt, arrow, goad/hook, needle lt.: moon disc, bow, Asoka bough, noose/snare in tarjani mudra, string	mature	four		*haughty *rd., bl., wh., gr., yw., bodh. ornaments, va.: chariot drawn by seven pigs	Dasabhujasita Marici
six*/18	ten	tantric symbols including: hunderbolt, goad/hook, arrow, needle, asoka branch, bow, thread, tarjani mu.	mature	two	astride	*rd., bl., gr., yw., wh. & boarhead dhar. ornaments, va.: Brahma, Vishnu and Siva on a sow	Marici

Red (Skt.: rakta; Tib.: dmar-po), Calm Deities

Abbreviations:

as. = asana	bk. = black	bl. = blue	bodh. = bodhisattva
bn. = brown	corp. = corpulent	dhar. = dharmapala	gn. = green
lt. = left	mu. = mudra	pu. = purple	rd. = red
rt. = right	sc. = smokey	va. = vahana	wh. = white
yw. = yellow			

(*) special variations or attributes noted within the entry.

(**) following deity's name indicates that the color is not noted in the source, kulesa's color is applied to the entry.

(eyes: 2-3, 6-9, etc.) in sources the deity's faces are noted, but the number of the eyes are not noted.

Head/Eyes	Hands	Objects Held	Body	Feet	Asana	Other Attributes	Deity Name
one/two	two	rt. & lt.: dhyana mu. with begging bowl	youth	two	dyana	Buddha-like, monastic robe, va.: pair of peacocks	Dhyani Buddha Amitabha
one/two	two	holding lotus	mature	two	vajra, yab-yum	bodh. ornament, shakti: Gos-dkar-mo, va.: lotus throne	Amitabha
one/two	two	rt. & lt.: dhyana mu. with bowl, embarcing shakti	mature	two	dyana, yab-yum	bodh. ornament, va.: pair of peacocks, shakti: Pandara	Amitabha (yab-yum)
one/two	two	in dhyana mu.	mature	two	vajra	bodh. ornament, va.: lotus throne	Amitabha (Bodhisattva)
one/two	two	rt. & lt.: dhyana mu.	mature	two	dhyana	Buddha-like, monastic robe, color: light red, va.: lotus throne	Acokottamasri
one/two	two	rt. holds ritual dagger lt. in abhaya mu.	mature	two	lalita	hair swept back, loose robe	Abhimukha
one/two	two	rt.: flat staff/stick with sword tip lt.: ?	mature	two	sattva	bodh. ornament, va.: lotus throne	Abhimukha (Bodhisattva)
one/two	two	rt. & lt.: vase/vessel in dhyana mu.	mature	two	vajra	bodh. ornament, va.: lotus throne	Acala-Amitayus

one/two	two	rt.: thunderbolt lt.: red lotus	mature	two	vajra	bodh. ornament, va.: lotus throne	Adhimukticharya
one/two	two	dharmachakra mu. with lotus bud	youth	two	sattva	bodh. ornaments, va: lotus throne	Avalokitesvara[5]
one/two	two	dharmachakra mu. with lotus bud	youth	two	sama- bhanga	bodh. ornaments, va: lotus throne	Avalokitesvara
one/two	two	rt.: abhaya mu., conch-topped staff stick on rt. shoulder lt.: alms bowl	youth	two	sama- bhanga	bodh. ornament, va.: lotus throne	Acalaketu-Lokesvara
one/two	two	rt.: varada lt.: sword	youth	two	vajra	bodh. ornaments, va.: lotus throne	Akasagarbha-Lokesvara
one/ two	two	rt.: rosary lt.: lotus on a vase/vessel against chest	youth	two	vajra	bodh. ornaments, va.: lotus throne	Aksayamati-Lokesvara
one/two	two	rt.: conch shell-topped staff/stick lt.: wheel at shoulder	youth	two	sama- bhanga	bodh. ornaments, va.: lotus throne	Amitabha-Lokesvara
one/two	two	rt.: goad/hook lt.: noose/snare	youth	two	sama- bhanga	bodh. ornament, va.: lotus throne	Amoghankusa-Avalokitesvara
one/ two	two	rt.: crossed thunderbolts lt.: lotus on a water vase/vessel	youth	two	sama- bhanga	bodh. ornaments, va.: lotus throne	Amrtaprabha-Lokesvara
one/ two	two	rt.: stem of lotus lt.: varada mu.	youth	two	sama- bhanga	bodh. ornaments, va.: lotus throne	Anandadi-Lokesvara
one/two	two	rt.: bhumisparsa mu. lt.: stem of lotus	youth	two	sopasraya	bodh. ornaments, va.: lotus throne	Anucara-Avalokitesvara
one/two	two	dhyana mu	youth	two	vajra	red monastic robes va.: lotus throne	Avalokita
one/two	two	rt.: sword lt.: stem of lotus against chest	youth	two	vajra	bodh. ornaments, va.: lotus throne	Avalokita-Lokesvara
one/two	two	rt.: varada mu. lt.: stem of lotus	youth	two	vamalalita	bodh. ornaments, va.: lotus throne	Avalokitesvara
one/two	two	playing a lute-like instrumnet	mature	two	vajra	bodh. ornament, va.: lotus throne,	Aloka

[5] One of the few fierce forms of *Avalokitesvara*.

one/two	two	rt.: vase/vessel with elixir of life lt.: clenched fist on hip	mature	two	dhyana	bodh. ornaments, va.: lotus throne	Amitaprabha
one/two	two	both hold vase/vessel with elixir of life in dhyana mu.	mature	two	dhyana	bodh. ornaments, va.: lotus throne	Amitaprabha
one/two	two	rt.: double lotus lt.: vase/vessel with elixir of life on lotus	mature	two	dhyana	bodh. ornaments, va.: lotus throne	Amitaprabha
one/two	two	in dhyana mu. with vase/vessel with elixir of life	mature	two	vajra	bodh. ornament, va.: lotus throne	Amitayus
one/two	two	dhyana mu.	mature	two	vajra	Buddha-like, monastic robe, va. : lotus throne	Amitayus (Buddha)
one/ two	two	dhyana mu. with vase/vessel topped with peacock feathers	mature	two	vajra	bodh. ornament, va.: lotus throne	Amitayus Jina
one/two	two	rt.: sword lt.: *Prajna Paramita* book/manuscript	youth	two	vajra	bodh. ornaments, va.: lotus throne	Arapacana
one/two	two	rt.: sword lt.: *Prajna Paramita* book/manuscript	youth	two	vajra	bodh. ornaments, va.: lotus throne	Arapacana-Manjughosa
one*/two	two	rt.: lotus lt.: image of Buddha	mature	two	sattva	*color: pink, bodh. ornaments,, va.: lotus throne	Ayur-Vasita
one*/two	two	rt.: stem of lotus which is level with shoulder lt.: image of Buddha	mature	two	sattva	*color: pink, bodh. ornaments,, va.: lotus throne	Ayur-Vasita
one/two	two	rt.: banner/flag with wish fulfilling jewel lt.: book/manuscript	mature	two		bodh. ornaments, va.: lotus throne	Balaparamita
one/two	two	holding vase/vessel in dhyana mu.	youth	two	vajra	bodh. ornaments, va.: lotus throne	Ba-ri-lugs-Amitayus
one/two	two	rt.: varada mu. lt.: stem of lotus in karana mu.	youth	two	vamalalita	bodh. ornaments, va.: lotus throne	Ba-ri-lugs-Pacatmaka-Amoghapasa
one/two	two	rt.: varada mu. lt.: jewel	mature	two	dhyana	bodh. ornaments, va.: lotus throne	Bhadrapala

one/two	two	rt.: jewel lt.: clenched at hip	mature	two	dhyana	bodh. ornaments, va.: lotus throne	Bhadrapala
one/two	two	dhyana mu.	mature	two	dhyana	bodh. ornaments, va.: lotus throne	Bhadrapala
one/two	two	rt.: banner/flag with wish fulfilling jewel lt.: manuscript	mature	two		bodh. ornaments va.: lotus throne	Balaparamita
one/two	two	vase/vessel in dhyana mu.	youth	two	vajra	bodh. ornaments, va.: lotus throne	Ba-ri-lugs-Amitayus**
one/two	two	rt.: red copper lance with banner/flag lt.: bow and arrow	youth	two	astride	golden cuirass, high leather boots, va.: horse	Brag-btsan-dmar-po
one/two	two	dhyana mu. holds vase/vessel with peacock feathers	youth	two	vajra	bodh. ornaments, va.: lotus throne	Caryatantra Amitayus**
one/two	two	rt.: abhaya mu. lt.: human skull-cup	youth	two	sattva	bodh. ornaments, va.: lotus throne	Chamunda (devi)
one/two	two	rt.: jewel lt.: wheel in dhyana mu.	youth	two	vajra	bodh. ornaments, va.: lotus throne	Cintamanichakra-Avalokitesvara**
one/two	two	rt.: shrine lt.: held at waist	youth	two	sama-bhanga	bodh. ornaments, va.: lotus throne	Cintamani-Lokesvara**
one/two	two	rt.: image of *Dhyani Buddha Amitabha* lt.: abhaya mu.	youth	two	sama-bhanga	bodh. ornaments, va.: lotus throne	Cittadhatu-Lokesvara**
one/two	two	rt.: abhaya mu. lt.: bhumisparsa mu.	youth	two	sattva	bodh. ornaments, va.: lotus throne	Cittavisramana-Avalokitesvara**
one*/two	two	rt.: banner/flag with wish-fulfilling jewel lt.: ears of corn	youth	two		*pink body color, bodh. ornaments,	Dana-Paramita
one*/two	two	rt.: wish-fulfilling jewel lt.: branch	youth	two	vamalalita	*pink body color, bodh. ornaments, va.: lotus throne	Dana-Paramita
one*/two	two	playing a lute	mature	two	sama-bhanga	*reddish-gray, monastic robes,	Devaloka Buddha
one/two	two	rt.: thunderbolt lt.: axe	youth	two	sama-bhanga	bodh. ornaments, va.: lotus throne	Dharmacakra-Lokesvara

one/two	two	water vase/vessel at waist	youth	two	sama-bhanga	bodh. ornaments, va.: lotus throne	Dharmacakra-Lokesvara
one/two	two	dharmachakra mu.	mature	two	dhyana	Buddha-like, monastic robed, va.: lotus throne	Dharmakirtisagaraghosa
one*/two	two	rt.: goad/hook lt.: noose/snare	youth	two	vamalalita	*pink body color, bodh. ornaments, va.: lotus throne	Dharma Pratisamvita
one*/two	two	rt.: goad/hook lt.: varada mu.	youth	two	vamalalita	*pink body color, bodh. ornaments, va.: lotus throne	Dharma Pratisamvita**
one/two	two	rt.: lamp	mature	two	alidha	bodh. ornaments, va.: lotus throne	Dipa
one/two	two	rt.: tarpana mu. lt.: lamp	youth	two	ardha-paryanka	bodh. ornaments, va.: lotus throne	Dipa
one/two	two	embraces his shakti	youth	two	sukha	bodh. ornaments, va.: lotus throne	Dvibhuja-Padmanartesvara-Avalokitesvara**
one/two	two	rt.: scarf lt.: jewel	youth	teo	astride	bodh. ornaments, va.: horned, cloven-hoofed animal	Ekabhaisajyavajra
one/two	two	rt.: raised over head lt.: rests on hip	mature	two	dhyana	bodh. ornaments, va.: lotus throne	Gagananania
one/two	two	rt.: wish fulfilling jewel lt.: alms bowl with kalpa tree	mature	two	dhyana	bodh. ornaments, va.: lotus throne	Gagananania
one/two	two	rt.: blue lotus in varada mu. lt.: blue lotus in varada mu.	mature	two	dhyana	bodh. ornaments, va.: lotus throne	Gagananania
one/two	two	rt.: sword on lotus lt.: rests on hip	mature	two	dhyana	bodh. ornaments, va.: lotus throne	Gagananania
one/two	two	rt.: wish fulfilling jewel lt.: dhyana	mature	two	sattva	bodh. ornaments, va.: lotus throne	Gagananania
one*/two	two	rt.: palm towards chest lt.: harina mu.	youth	two	vamalalita	*elephant head bodh. ornaments, va.: rat	Ganapati (deva)**

one/two	two	rt.: harina mu. lt.: jnana mu.	mature	two	ardha-paryanka	bodh. ornaments, lotus throne	Ging-chen-sna-khrid
one/two	two	plays stringed instrument	youth	two	sattva	bodh. ornaments, va.: lotus throne	Gita (fo-mu)
one/two	two	vase/vessel in dhyana mu.	youth	two	vajra	bodh. ornaments, va.: lotus throne	Guna-Amitayus
one/two	two	vyakhyana mudra	youth	two	sama-bhanga	bodh. ornaments, va.: lotus throne	Harihara-Lokesvara**
one/two	two	rt.: vasae/vessel lt.: conch shell	youth	two	sama-bhanga	bodh. ornaments, lotus throne	Harivahana-Lokesvara**
one/two	two	rt.: abhaya mu. lt.: stem of lotus	youth	two	vamalalita	bodh. ornaments, va.: lotus throne	Isvara(=Lokesvara)-Avalokitesvara (Bodhisattva)**
one/two	two	rt.: varada mu. lt.: sun disc on lotus	mature	two	dhyana	bodh. ornaments, va.: lotus throne	Ialiniprabha
one/two	two	rt.: sword lt.: sun disc on moon lotus	mature	two	dhyana	bodh. ornaments, va.: lotus throne	Ialiniprabha
one/two	two	rt.: cage marked with thunderbolt lt.: clenched on hip	mature	two	dhyana	bodh. ornaments, va.: lotus throne	Ialiniprabha
one/two	two	holding dhyana mu.	mature	two	dhyana	bodh. ornaments, va.: lotus throne	Ialiniprabha
one/two	two	rt.: sword on lotus lt.: stem of lotus with blossom at shoulder level	youth	two	vajra	bodh. ornaments va.: lotus throne	Ialiniprabha-Lokesvara**
one/two	two	dhyana mu.	youth	two	vajra	Buddha-like, monastic robe, rt. shoulder uncovered, va.: lotus throne	Iina-Amitabha
one/two	two	holding vase/vessel in dhyana mu.	youth	two	vajra	bodh. ornaments, va.: lotus throne	Inana-Amitayus
one/two	two	holding stem of lotus	youth	two	ardha-paryanka	bodh. ornaments, va.: lotus throne	Kama
one/two	two	rt.: vitarka mu. lt.: vitarka mu. at chest	youth	two	sama-bhanga	bodh. ornaments, va.: lotus throne	Kamalacandra-Lokesvara

one/two	two	rt.: thunderbolt lt.: book/manuscript against chest	youth	two	vajra	bodh. ornaments, va.: lotus throne	Karandavyuha-Lokesvara**
one/two	two	holding vase/vessel in dhyana mu.	youth	two	vajra	bodh. ornaments, va.: lotus throne	Karma-Amitayus
one/two	two	rt.: abhaya mu. lt.: stem of lotus in karana mu.	mature	two	sopasraya	bodh. ornaments, va.: lotus throne	Karunesvara-Avalokitesvara
one/two	two	rt.: varada mu. lt.: stem of lotus	youth	two	vamalalita	bodh. ornaments, va.: lotus throne	Khasarpana**
one/two	two	rt.: abhaya mu. lt.: stem of lotus	youth	two	vajra	bodh. ornaments, va.: lotus throne	Khasarpana-Avalokitesvara**
one/two	two	rt.: abhaya mu. lt.: stem of lotus	youth	two	vajra	bodh. ornaments, va.: lotus throne	Khasarpana-Avalokitesvara ** (Bodhisattva)
one/two	two	rt.: varada mu. lt.: stem of lotus	youth	two	lalita	bodh. ornaments, va.: lotus throne	Khasarpana-Lokesvara **
one/two	two	rt.: varada mu. lt.: stem of lotus	youth	two	ardha- paryanka	bodh. ornaments, va.: lotus throne	Khasarpana-Lokesvara **
one/two	two	rt.: varada mu. lt.: stem of lotus	youth	two	vamalalita	bodh. ornaments, va.: lotus throne	Khasarpana-Lokesvara **
one/two	two	namaskara mu.	youth	two	sama- bhanga	bodh. ornaments, va.: lotus throne	Krtanjali-Lokesvara**
one/two	two	namaskara mu.	youth	two	vajra	bodh. ornaments, va.: lotus throne	Krtanjali-Lokesvara**
one/two	two	rt.: shallow bowls of jewels lt.: varada mu.	youth	two	vajra	bodh. ornaments, va.: lotus throne	Ksitigarbha-Lokesvara**
one/two	two	rt.: varada mu. lt.: in lap holding stem of lotus	youth	two	lalita	bodh. ornaments, va.: lotus throne	Lokanatha-raktaryy- Avalokitesvara**
one/two	two	each holding a crown(?)	youth	two	sattva	bodh. ornaments, va.: lotus throne	Lasya (fo-mu)
one/two	two	rt.: varada mu. lt.: in lap holding stem of lotus	youth	two	lalita	bodh. ornaments, va.: lotus throne	Lokanatha-raktaryy- Avalokitesvara**
one/two	two	rt.: varada mu.	youth	two	sama-	bodh. ornaments,	Mahabhumika-Avalokitesvara

		lt.: lotus			bhanga	va.: lotus throne	(Bodhisattva)**
one/two	two	rt.: abhaya mu. lt.: stem of lotus	youth	two	sama- bhanga	bodh. ornaments, va.: lotus throne	Mahabhumika(?)-rakta- Avalokitesvara**
one/two	two	rt.: sword lt.: varada mu.	youth	two	sama- bhanga	bodh. ornaments, va.: lotus throne	Mahasahasrabhuja-Lokesvara**
one/two	two	rt.: varada mu. lt.: stem of a white lotus	youth	two	sama- bhanga	bodh. ornaments, va.: lotus throne	Mahasarasvati
one/two	two	rt.: varada mu. lt.: stem of lotus	youth	two	sama- bhanga	bodh. ornaments, va.: lotus throne	Mahasthamaprapta-Lokesvara**
one/two	two	rt.: blue lotus lt.: graceful pose	mature	two	ardha- paryanka	bodh. ornaments, va.: lion	Maharajalila-Manjusri
one/two	two	rt.: bell lt.: graceful pose	mature	two	pralam- bapada	bodh. ornaments, va.: lion throne	Maharajalila-Manjusri
one/two	two	rt.: rosary lt.: book/manuscript	youth	two	sama- bhanga	bodh. ornaments, va.: lotus throne	Manjunatha-Lokesvara**
one/two	two	holds sword	youth	two	vajra	bodh. ornaments, va.: lotus throne	Manjusri
one*/two	two	rt.: crossed thunderbolts lt.: needle and string	mature	two		*pink color, bodh. ornaments, va.: lotus throne	Mara
one/two	two	rt.: abhaya mu. lt.: stem of lotus	corp.	two	sattva	bodh. ornaments, va.: lotus throne on back of pig	Marici (fo-mu)
one/two	two	dhyana mu. with vase/vessel	youth	two	vajra	bodh. ornaments, va.: lotus throne	Mitra-krama-Sita-Amitayus
one/two	two	rt.: rosary lt.: book/manuscript	youth	two	sama- bhanga	bodh. ornaments, va.: lotus throne	Nityanatha-Lokesvara
one/two	two	holding a chain	youth	two		bodh. ornaments, va.: lotus throne	Nirukti-Pratisamvita
one/two	two	rt.: holding a chain lt.: abhaya mu. on knee	mature	two	vamalalita	bodh. ornaments, va.: lotus throne	Nirukti-Pratisamvita

one/two	two	rt.: vitarka mu. with lotus lt.: varada mu. with lotus and vase/vessel	youth	two	lalita	bodh. ornaments, va.: lotus throne	Padmapani-Lokesvara**
one/two	two	rt.: vitarka mu. lt.: varada mu. with vase/vessel	youth	two	sama-bhanga	bodh. ornaments, va.: lotus throne	Padmapani-Lokesvara**
one/two	two	rt.: vitarka mu. with lotus stem lt.: abhaya mu. with lotus stem	youth	two	rajalila	bodh. ornaments, va.: lotus throne	Padmapani-Lokesvara**
one*/two	two	hanging at sides	youth	two	sama-bhanga	* nine images of Buddha/Bodhisattvas surround figure, bodh. ornaments, va.: lotus throne	Padmapani-Lokesvara**
one/two	two	alms bowl	youth	two	sama-bhanga	bodh. ornaments, va.: lotus throne	Pindapatra-Lokesvara**
one/two	two	dhyana mu. with vase/vessel	youth	two	vajra	bodh. ornaments, va.: lotus throne	Padma-Amitayus**
one/two	two	rt.: dancing gesture lt.: red lotus	youth	two	vajra	bodh. ornaments, va.: lotus throne	Padmanartesvara
one/two	two	rt.: noose/snare lt.: bowl filled with jewels	youth	two	vajra	bodh. ornaments, va.: lotus throne	Pratibhanakakuta-Lokesvara**
one/two	two	1st pr.: varada mu. 2nd pr.: jewel, book/manuscript	youth	two		bodh. ornaments, va.: lotus throne	Pretasantarpita-Lokesvara**
one/two	two	rt.: thunderbolt lt.: sun on lotus	mature	two		bodh. ornaments, va.: lotus throne	Prabhakari
one/two	two	rt.: thunderbolt lt.: jewel	mature	two		bodh. ornaments, va.: lotus throne	Pramudita
one/two	two	rt.: thunderbolt lt.: flaming jewel	mature	two	lalita	bodh. ornaments, va.: lotus throne	Pramudita (fo-mu)**
one*/two	two	rt.: flaming sword lt.: manuscript/book	youth	two	vajra	*red-yellow color bodh. ornaments, va.: lotus throne	Purnamati-stotrasadhana-kirtita-Manjughosa
one/two	two	rt.: varada mu. lt.: rests on shoulder	youth	two	sama-bhanga	bodh. ornaments, va.: lotus throne	Ratnadala-Lokesvara**

one/two	two	rt.: sword lt.: varada mu.	youth	two	vajra	bodh. ornaments, va.: lotus throne	Ratnapani-Lokesvara**
one/two	two	rt.: stem of lotus in karana mu. lt.: stem of lotus in dhyana mu.	youth	two	vajra	bodh. ornaments, va.: chariot pulled by seven horses	Rakta-Aditya
one/two	two	rt.: jewels lt.: mirror	youth	two	vamalalita	bodh. ornaments, va.: lotus throne	Rakta-Sarasvati
one/two	two	holds vase/vessel in dhyana mu.	mature	two	vajra	bodh. ornaments, va.: lotus throne	Ratna-Amitayus
one/two	two	rt.: banner/flag with wish fulfilling jewel lt.:disc of moon on lotus	mature	two		bodh. ornaments, va.: lotus throne	Ratnaparamita
one/two	two	rt.: (?) lt.: noose/snare	youth	two	astride	dhar. ornaments, va.: khyung	rDo-rje-g.ya'-mo-bsil
one/two	two	rt.: human skull-drum lt.: ritual chopper	mature	two		*red-brown, wreath of flowers, silk loin cloth with a thigh-bone trumpet, va.: white lion	rDo-rje-ne-ne-gnam-sman-sgron
one/two	two	rt.: thunderbolt lt.: at waist	youth	two	sama-bhanga	bodh. ornaments, va.: lotus throne	Sakyabuddha-Lokesvara**
one/two	two	rt.: varada mu. lt.: lotus, against chest	youth	two	vajra	bodh. ornaments, va.: lotus throne	Samantabhadra-Lokesvara**
one/two	two	rt.: conch shell lt.: lotus	youth	two	sama-bhanga	bodh. ornaments, va.: lotus throne	Sankhanatha-Lokesvara**
one/two	two	rt.: varada mu. lt.: asoka (?) branch	youth	two	sama-bhanga	bodh. ornaments, va.: lotus throne	Santamati-Lokesvara**
one/two	two	rt.: trident lt.: lotus	youth	two	sama-bhanga	bodh. ornaments, va.: lotus throne	Sarasiri(?)-Lokesvara**
one/two	two	rt.: varada mu. lt.: begging bowl	youth	two	sama-bhanga	bodh. ornaments, va.: lotus throne	Sarthavaha-Lokesvara**
one/two	two	rt.: stem of lotus with sword lt.: thunderbolt against chest	youth	two	vajra	bodh. ornaments, va.: lotus throne	Sarvanivaranaviskambhi-Lokesvara**

one/two	two	rt.: sword lt.: Prajna Paramita book/manuscript	mature	two	vajra	bodh. ornaments, va.: lotus throne	Sadyonubhava-Arapacana
one/two	two	rt.: sword lt.: Prajna Paramita book/manuscript	mature	two	vajra	bodh. ornaments, va.: lotus throne	Sadyonubhava-Manjusri
one/two	two	rt.: thunderbolt lt.: image of Dhyani Buddha Amitabha	mature	two		bodh. ornaments, va.: lotus throne	Samantaprabha
one/two	two	rt.: thunderbolt lt.: image of Dhyani Buddha Amitabha	mature	two	vamalalita	bodh. ornaments, va.: lotus throne	Samantaprabha (fo-mu)
one/two	two	rt.: sword on lotus lt.: trident entwined with serpent/snake	youth	two	maha- rajalila	bodh. ornaments, va.: roaring lion	Simhanada-Avalokitesvara**
one/two	two	rt.: (?) lt.: stem of lotus with sword in bowl	youth	two	vamalalita	bodh. ornaments, va.: lion	Simhanada-Avalokitesvara**
one/two	two	rt.: chowrie lt.: held at waist	youth	two	sama- bhanga	bodh. ornaments, va.: lotus throne	Simhanada-Lokesvara**
one/two	two	rt.: sword lt.: noose/snare	youth	two	sama- bhanga	bodh. ornaments, va.: lotus throne	Sirisara(?)-Lokesvara**
one*/two	two	rt.: flaming sword lt.: karana mu. with stem of lotus with manuscript/book	youth	two	vajra	*red-yellow, bodh. ornaments, va.: lotus throne	Sa-(skya)-lugs-Raktapita-Arapacana-Manjughosa
one/two	two	rt.: goad/hook lt.: stem of lotus in karana mu.	youth	two	sopasraya	bodh. ornaments, va.: lotus throne	Sa-skya-lugs-Rakta-Tara
one*/two	two	rt.: abhaya mu. lt.: dhyana mu.	mature	two	dhyana	*red-orange, Buddha-like, monastic robes, va.: lotus throne	Sikhin
one/two	two	rt.: thunderbolt lt.: stem of lotus near waist	youth	two	sama- bhanga	bodh. ornaments, va.: lotus throne	Srimadaryavalokitesvara**
one/two	two	rt.: varada mu. lt.: held at waist	youth*	two	sama- bhanga	15 Buddha-like images in mandalas surround the body with lines to various parts of the body, bodh. ornaments, va.: lotus throne	Srstikanta-Lokesvara**

one/two	two	rt.: noose/snare lt.: goad/hook	youth	two	vajra	bodh. ornaments, va.: lotus throne	Trailokyavasamkara-Avalokitesvara**
one/two	two	rt.: noose/snare lt.: goad/hook	youth	two	vajra	bodh. ornaments, va.: lotus throne	Trailokyavasamkara-Avalokitesvara (Bodhisattva)**
one/two	two	rt.: abhaya mu. lt.: stem of blue lotus	youth	two	vajra	bodh. ornaments, va.: lotus throne	Vajradharma-Lokesvarat**
one/two	two	rt.: varada mu. lt.: lotus	youth	two	sama-bhanga	bodh. ornaments, va.: lotus throne	Vajradhatu-Lokesvara**
one/two	two	rt.: thunderbolt lt.: stem of lotus	youth	two	vajra	bodh. ornaments, va.: lotus throne	Vajragarbha-Lokesvara**
one/two	two	rt.: lotus bud lt.: book/manuscript	youth	two	sama-bhanga	bodh. ornaments, va.: lotus throne	Vajrakhanda-Lokesvara**
one/two	two	rt.: thunderbolt lt.: lotus	youth	two	ardha-paryanka	bodh. ornaments, va.: lotus throne	Vajranatha-Lokesvara**
one/two	two	rt.: thunderbolt on head lt.: held at waist	youth	two	ardha-paryanka	bodh. ornaments, va.: lotus throne	Vajrapani-Lokesvara**
one/two	two	rt.: wheel lt.: conch shell	youth	two	sama-bhanga	bodh. ornaments, va.: lotus throne	Vajrasattvadhatu-Lokesvara**
one/two	two	rt.: conch shell lt.: lotus	youth	two	sama-bhanga	bodh. ornaments, va.: lotus throne	Vajrasrsta-Lokesvara**
one/two	two	rt.: blue lotus lt.: "graceful pose"	youth	two	ardha-paryanka	bodh. ornaments, va.: lion	Vagisvara
one/two	two	rt.: bell lt.: "graceful pose"	youth	two	pralam-bapada	bodh. ornaments, va.: lion throne	Vagisvara
one/two	two	vase/vessel in dhyana mu.	mature	two	vajra	bodh. ornaments, va.: lotus throne	Vajra-Amitayus**
one/two	two	rt.: chain lt.: chain	mature	two	sopasraya	bodh. ornaments, va.: lotus throne	Vajrasphota (fo-mu)
one/two	two	holds alms bowl in dhyana mu.	youth	two	vajra	bodh. ornaments, va.: lotus throne	Vasyadhikara-Lokesvara**
one/two	two	rt.: held against chest lt.: lotus	youth	two	sama-bhanga	bodh. ornaments, va.: lotus throne	Vidyapati-Lokesvara**

one/two	two	rt.: wheel lt.: tantric staff/stick	youth	two	sama-bhanga	bodh. ornaments, va.: lotus throne	Visnucakra-Lokesvara**
one/two	two	rt.: varada mu. lt.: book/manuscript	youth	two	sama-bhanga	bodh. ornaments, va.: lotus throne	Visnukanta-Lokesvara**
one/two	two	rt.: trident lt.: bud of a lotus	youth	two	sama-bhanga	bodh. ornaments, va.: lotus throne	Visnupani-Lokesvara**
one/two	two	rt.: rosary lt.: lotus	youth	two	sama-bhanga	bodh. ornaments, va.: lotus throne	Vishvabhuta-Lokesvara**
one/two	two	rt.: abhaya mu. lt.: white lotus	youth	two	vajra	bodh. ornaments, va.: lotus throne	Vishvamata Tara
one/two	two	rt.: varada mu. lt.: serpent/snake	youth	two	sama-bhanga	bodh. ornaments, va.: lotus throne	Vishvavajra-Lokesvara**
one/two	four	prin.: namaskara mu. rt.: rosary, lt.: lotus	youth	two	dhyana	bodh. ornaments, va.: lotus throne	Avalokitesvara (sPyan-ras-gZigs-Phyan-bZhi-pa)**
one/two	four	prin. anjali mu. at chest rt.: rosary lt.: lotus	youth	two	vajra	bodh. ornaments, va.: lotus throne	Bkah-gdams-Avalokitesvara**
one/two	four	rt.: trident and varada mu. lt.: vase/vessel of jewels and karana mu.	youth	two	lalita	bodh. ornament, shakti on lt. knee,	Brahmadanda-Lokesvara
one/two	four	prin.: namaskara mu. rt.: rosary lt.: lotus	youth	two	vajra	bodh. ornaments, va.: lotus throne	Caturbhuja-Avalokitesvara**
one/two	four	prin.: namaskara mu. rt.: rosary lt.: lotus	youth	two	vajra	bodh. ornaments, va.: lotus throne	Caturbhuja-Avalokitesvara (Bhodisattva)**
one/two	four	prin.: alms bowl in dhyana mu. rt.: varada mu. lt.: lotus	youth	two	vamalalita	bodh. ornaments, va.: lotus throne	Cunda
one/two	four	rt.: rosary, book/manuscript lt.: alms bowl, lotus	youth	two	vamalalita	bodh. ornaments, va.: lotus throne	Cunda

one/two	four	prin.: alms bowl with dhyana mu. rt.: varada mu. with lotus lt.: varada mu. with lotus	youth	two	sattva	bodh. ornaments, va.: lotus throne	Caturbhuja-Cunda (devi)**
one/two	four	prin.: dhyana mu. rt.: vitarka mu. on knee lt.: vitarka mu. on knee	youth	two	sattva	bodh. ornaments, va.: lotus throne	Caturbhuja-Cunda (fo-mu)**
one/two	four	rt.: noose/snare(?), goad/hook lt.: bow, arrow	youth	two	vajra	bodh. ornaments, va.: lotus throne	Caturbhuja-rakta-Avalokitesvara (Bodhisattva)
one*/two	four	rt.: shield, battle axe lt.: conch shell, rosary	mature	two	lalita	bodh. ornaments, va.: rat	Caturbhuja-Rakta-Ganapati
one*/two	four	rt.: radish, battle axe lt.: conch shell, rosary	mature	two	lalita	bodh. ornaments, va.: rat with jewel in mouth	Caturbhuja-Rakta-Ganapati
one/two	four	rt.: noose/snare, short staff/stick(?) lt.: bow, arrow	youth	two	vajra	bodh. ornaments, va.: lotus throne	Caturbhuja-rakta-Lokesvara
one/two	four	prin.: anjali mu. rt.: knife lt.: human skull-cup	mature	two		bodh. ornaments, va.: human corpse	Chamunda
one/two	four	prin.: namaskara mu. embracing shakti rt.: rosary lt.: lotus	mature	two	vajra, yab-yum	bodh. ornaments, va.: lotus throne	Guhyasadhana-Avalokitesvara**
one/two	four	prin.: vykhyana mu. rt.: rosary lt.: lotus	youth	two	vajra	bodh. ornaments, va.: lotus throne	Hayagriva-Lokesvara
one/two	four	rt.: rosary, varada lt.: lotus, vase/vessel	youth	two	sama- bhanga	bodh. ornaments, va.: lotus throne	Iatamukuta-Lokesvara
one/two	four	rt.: rosary, varada mu. lt.: thunderbolt, book/manuscript	mature	two	ardha- paryanka	bodh. ornaments, va.: lotus throne	Mahasitavati
one/two	four	prin.: namaskara mu. against chest rt.: rosary lt.: lotus	youth	two	vajra	bodh. ornaments, va.: lotus throne	Manipadma-Lokesvara**
one/two	four	prin.: dhyana mu. rt.: abhaya mu. lt.: lotus	youth	two	vajra	bodh. ornaments, va.: lotus throne	Padmavikasana-Avalolitesvara**

one/two	four	prin.: namaskara mu. rt.: rosary lt.: noose/snare	youth	two	vajra	bodh. ornaments, va.: lotus throne	Potapada-Lokesvara**
one/two	four	rt.: rosary, abhaya mu. lt.: book/manuscript, karana mu.	youth	two	vajra	bodh. ornaments, va.: lotus throne	Pupala-Lokesvara**
one/two	four	prin.: holds red lotus & opens petals with rt. rt.: noose/snare lt.: goad/hook	mature	two	sama-bhanga	asoka tree shades, bodh. ornaments, va.: lotus throne	Rakta-Lokesvara
one/two	four	prin.: holds red lotus & opens petals with rt. rt.: bow lt.: arrow	mature	two	sama-bhanga	asoka tree shades, bodh. ornaments, va.: lotus throne	Rakta-Lokesvara
one/two	four	prin.: namaskara mu. rt.: rosary lt.: lotus	youth	two	sopasraya	bodh. ornaments, va.: lotus throne	Sadaksari**
one/two	four	prin.: namaskara mu. rt.: rosary lt.: lotus	youth	two	vajra	bodh. ornaments, va.: lotus throne	Sadaksari-Lokesvara**
one/two	four	prin.: namaskara mu. rt.: rosary lt.: lotus	youth	two	dhyana	bodh. ornaments, va.: lotus throne	Sadaksari-Lokesvara**
one/two	four	rt.: prayer roll, rosary lt.: conch shell, lotus	youth	two	dhyana	bodh. ornaments, va.: lotus throne	Sadaksari-Lokesvara**
one/two	four	prin.: namaskara mu. 2nd pr.: dhyana mu. holding bowl	youth	two	sama-bhanga	bodh. ornaments, va.: lotus throne	Sadaksari-Lokesvara**
one/two	four	prin.: abhaya mu against chest rt.: rosary lt.: blue lotus	youth	two	sama-bhanga	bodh. ornaments, va.: lotus throne	Sarvasokatamonirghata-Lokesvara**
one/two	four	rt.: arrow, magic notched staff/stick lt.: bow, tarjani mu.	youth	two	sama-bhanga	bodh. ornaments, va.: lotus throne	Sakyabuddha-Lokesvara**
one/two	four	rt.: sword, jewel lt.: book/manuscript, noose/snare	youth	two	sama-bhanga	bodh. ornaments, va.: lotus throne	Simhanatha-Lokesvara**
one/two	four	rt.: sword, jewel	youth	two	vajra	bodh. ornaments,	Trilokasandarsana-Lokesvara**

		lt.: book/manuscript, noose/snare				va.: lotus throne	
one/two	four	rt.: bow, red lotus lt.: arrow, abhaya mu.	mature	two	vajra	bodh. ornaments, va.: Kamadeva and his wife Rati riding on Rahu	Tarodbhava-Kurukulla
one/two	four	rt.: thunderbolt, arrow lt.: bow, Asoka bough	mature	two		bodh. ornaments, va.: lotus throne	Varahamukhi
one/two	six	rt.: abhaya mu., rosary, varada mu. lt.: black deer-skin, noose/snare, vase/vessel	youth	two	sattva	bodh. ornaments, va.: lion on lotus throne	Harihariv ahana-Lokesvara
one/two	six	rt.: sword, arrow, varada mu. lt.: ritual chopper, bow, abhaya mu.	youth	two	lalita	bodh. ornament, va.: lotus throne	Acata(?)-Lokesvara
one/two	six	prin.: dhyana mu. holding vase/vessel and embracing shakti rt.; thunderbolt, vase/vessel lt.: sword, (?)	youth	two	sattva, yab-yum	bodh. ornaments, va.: lotus throne	Caturbhuja-Amitayus
one/two	six	rt.: Buddha image, rosary, abhaya mu. lt.: staff/stick, deer skin, vase/vessel	youth	two	*astride	*lion on the bottom, then eagle or garuda, then Vishnu, and on Vishnu's shoulders rides Avalokitesvara	Harihariharivahanobdhava-Lokesvara**
one/two	six	rt.: varada mu., rosary, abhaya mu. lt.: trident, black deer skin, spouted vase/vessel	youth	two	*astride	*lion on the bottom, then eagle or garuda, then Narayana, and on Narayana's shoulders rides Avalokitesvara	Harihariharivahanobdhava-Lokesvara**
one/two	six	rt.: sword, lotus, thunderbolt lt.: myrobalan fruit(?), bowl, karana mu.	youth	two	vajra	bodh. ornaments va.: lotus throne	Iamadanda-Lokesvara**
one/two	six	prin.: draws bow and arrow rt.: thunderbolt, wheel lt.: bell, vase/vessel	youth	two	sama-bhanga	bodh. ornaments, va.: lotus throne	Kamaṇdalu-Lokesvara**
one/two	six	rt.: varada mu., abhaya mu., rosary lt.: lotus, waterpot, short staff/stick	youth	two		bodh. ornaments, va.: lotus throne	Sugatisandarsana**
one/two	six	rt.: rosary, varada mu., abhaya mu. lt.: trident, blue lotus, vase/vessel	youth	two	sama-bhanga	bodh. ornaments, va.: lotus throne	Sugatisandarsana-Lokesvara**
one/two	six	rt.: abhaya mu., rosary, three jewels	youth	two	lalita,	bodh. ornaments,	Sukhavati-Avalokitesvara**

		lt.: lotus, vase/vessel, embraces shakti			yab-yum	va.: lotus throne	
one/two	six	rt.: rosary, trident, abhaya mu. lt.: book/manuscript, noose/snare, varada mu.	youth	two	sama-bhanga	bodh. ornaments, va.: lotus throne	Vajronisa-Lokesvara**
one/two	six	prin.: namaskara mu. rt.: rosary, varada mu. lt.: book/manuscript, karana mu.	youth	two	sama-bhanga	bodh. ornaments, va.: lotus throne	Varadayaka-Lokesvara**
one/two	six	rt.: sword, arrow, wheel lt.: noose/snare, bow, abhaya mu.	youth	two	vajra	bodh. ornaments, va.: lotus throne	Vishvahana-Lokesvara**
one/two	six	rt.: blue lotus, arrow, varada mu. lt.: book/manuscript, bow, abhaya mu.	youth	two	lalita	bodh. ornaments, va.: lotus throne	Vrsnacana-Lokesvara**
one/two	eight	rt.: lion, elephant, serpent/snake, (?) lt. : (?), chain, Buddha image	youth	two	ardha-paryanka	bodh. ornaments, va.: lotus throne	Asta-bhaya-trana-Avalokitesvara
one/two	eight	prin.: trailokyavijaya mu. rt.: goad/hook, arrow, varada mu. lt.: noose/snare, bow, lotus	mature	two	vajra	bodh. ornaments, va.: sun disc above red lotus	Astabhuja-Kurukulla
one/two	eight	rt.: sword, rosary, wheel, abhaya mu. lt.: noose/snare, trident, conch shell, bowl of jewels	youth	two	vajra	bodh. ornaments, va.: lotus throne	Mahavajrasattva-Lokesvara**
one/two	eight	1st.: dancing pose rt.: suci mu. at chest, staff/stick, rosary lt.: red lotus, trident, vase/vessel	mature	two	ardha-paryanka	bodh. ornaments, va.: lotus throne	Padmanartesvara
one/two	12	prin.: abhaya mu. 2nd pr.: vitarka mu. 3rd pr.: "lotus mudra"mu. 4th pr.: ksepana mu. 5th pr.: tarpana mu. 6th pr.: dhyana mu. holding a vase/vessel	youth	two	vajra	bodh. ornaments, va.: lotus throne	Namasangiti-Avalokitesvara**
one/two	12	prin.: in kanjo-in mu. 2nd: dhyana mu. rt.: sword, cylindrical banner, lotus, (?), (?), (?) lt.: thunderbolt, branch, book/manuscript, (?), (?), (?)	youth	two	vajra	bodh. ornaments, va.: lotus throne	Sodasabhuja-Avalokitesvara (Bodhisattva)**
one/two	12	all carry blue lotus	youth	two	ardha-	bodh. ornaments,	Vajrahuntika-Lokesvara**

					paryanka	va.: lotus throne	
one/two	18	all hands hold lotus	youth	two	vajra	bodh. ornaments, va.: lotus throne	Astadasabhuja-Padmanartesvara**
one/two	18	each holds a lotus	youth	two	vajra	bodh. ornaments, va.: lotus throne	Padmanartesvara-Avalokitesvara (Bodhisattva)
one/two	18	each holds double lotus	youth	two	ardha-paryanka	bodh. ornaments, va.: lotus throne	Padmanartesvara-Avalokitesvara (Bodhisattva)
one/two	18	each hand holds double lotus	youth	two	ardha-paryanka	bodh. ornaments, va.: lotus throne	Padmanartesvara
one/three	two	rt.: vajra-topped goad/hook lt.: noose/snare, embraces shakti	youth	two	alidha, yab-yum	bodh. ornaments, va.: lotus throne	Rakta-Kamaraja
one*/three	two	rt.: thunderbolt lt.: human skull-cup	mature	two		*pink, patched cape, bodh. ornaments, va.: elephant	Li-byin-ha-ra
one/three	two	holds namaskara mu., rosary on lotus at rt. shoulder	youth	two	maha-rajalila	bodh. ornaments, va.: roaring lion	Simhanada-Avalokitesvara**
one/three	four	rt.: abhaya mu., jewels lt.: flowering branch, wheel	corp.	two	alidha	bodh. ornaments, va.: lotus throne	Iala-bhayatrana-(Avalokitesvara)
one*/three	eight	not noted	mature, bare to waist	two	sama-bhanga	*each curl a Buddha, Buddhas cover chest, Buddha on each toe	Lokesvara (Irradiant)
one*/three	12	rt.: kuthara, arrow, goad/hook, thunderbolt, sword, sula lt.: pestle, bow, magic notched staff/stick, human skull-cup filled with blood, human skull-cup filled with flesh, tusk	corp.	two	ardha-paryanka	*elephant head, bodh. ornaments, va.: mouse on red lotus	Ganapati
three*/six	four	holding bow, arrow, book/manuscript and sword	youth	two	vajra-paryanka	*"reddish-white" bodh. ornaments, va.: lotus throne	Arya-Namasangiti
three*/six	six	rt.: lotus, flaming jewels and sword lt.: vase/vessel, axe and jewel	mature, nude	four	alidha	*rt. head: pig, cent. head: elephant. lt. head: human, va.: goddess on lotus throne	Ajna-vinivarta-Ganapati

three/six	six	rt.: thunderbolt, wheel, vitarka mu. lt.: bell, sword, (?)	mature	two	vajra	bodh. ornament, va.: lotus throne	Amitabha
three/six	six	prin.: embrace shakti in vajrahumkara mu. rt.: wheel, sword lt.: (?). vitarka mu.	youth	two	vajra	bodh. ornaments va.: lotus throne	Guhya-isvara (=Lokesvara)-Avalokitesvara**
three*/six	six	rt.: *varada mudra*, rosary, arrow lt.: bow, lotus, touches shakti	youth	two	vajra	*bl., wh., rd., to right: trident with snake entwined, to the left a skull-cup on lotus, bodh. ornaments, shakti sits on left knee, va.: lion on lotus throne	Halahala-Lokesvara
three/six	six	rt.: sword, rosary, varada mu. lt.: lotus, noose/snare, blue lotus	youth	two	lalita	bodh. ornaments, shakti sits on left knee, va.: lotus throne	Halahala-Lokesvara**
three/six	six	prin.: book/manuscript against chest rt.: thunderbolt, rosary lt.: bell, trident	youth	two	sama-bhanga	bodh. ornaments, va.: lotus throne	Maha-abhayakari-Lokesvara**
three/six	six	rt.: thunderbolt, sword, blue lotus lt.: bell, book/manuscript, bell	youth	two	sama-bhanga	bodh. ornaments, va.: lotus throne	Maha-abhayaphalada-Lokesvara**
three/six	six	rt.: arrow,, blue lotus, myrobalan (?) fruit lt.: bow, thunderbolt, wheel	youth	two	sama-bhanga	bodh. ornaments, va.: lotus throne	Mahacandrabimba-Lokesvara**
three/six	six	rt.: sword, thunderbolt, vase/vessel lt.: rosary, blue lotus, bell	youth	two	sama-bhanga	bodh. ornaments, va.: lotus throne	Mahamanjubhuta-Lokesvara**
three/six	six	rt.: bell, sword, jewel lt.: thunderbolt, bell, blue lotus	youth	two	sama-bhanga	bodh. ornaments, va.: lotus throne	Mahamanjudatta-Lokesvara**
three/six	six	rt.: myrobalan(?) fruit, blue lotus, conch shell lt.: whip, namaskara mu., bow	youth	two	sama-bhanga	bodh. ornaments, va.: lotus throne	Maharatnakirti-Lokesvara**
three/six	six	rt.: sword, blue lotus, rosary lt.: book/manuscript, lotus, blue lotus	youth	two	sama-bhanga	bodh. ornaments, va.: lotus throne	Maharatnakula-Lokesvara**
three/six	six	rt.: thunderbolt, abhaya mu., thunderbolt lt.: noose/snare, arrow, bell	youth	two	sama-bhanga	bodh. ornaments, va.: lotus throne	Mahasankhanatha-Lokesvara**

three/six	six	rt.: thunderbolt, wheel, thundetbolt lt.: blue lotus, bowl, blue lotus	youth	two	sama-bhanga	bodh. ornaments, va.: lotus throne	Mahasuryyabimba-Lokesvara**
three/six	six	rt.: sword, arrow, varada mu. lt.: book/manuscript, blue lotus, bow	youth	two	vajra	bodh. ornaments, va.: animal	Manjukumara
three/six	six	rt.: sword, varada mu., arrow lt.: book/manuscript, blue lotus, bow	youth	two	vajra, yab-yum	bodh. ornaments, va.: moon or lion	Manjuvajra
three/six	six	prin.: embrace shaktu rt.: sword, arrow lt.: bow, blue lotus	youth	two	vajra, yab-yum	bodh. ornaments, va.: moon or lion	Manjuvajra
three/six	six	rt.: arrow, rosary, varada mu. lt.: bow, lotus, rests on the thigh of Tara	youth	two	lalita	bodh. ornaments, Tara sits on thigh,	Sukhavati-Lokesvara**
three/six	six	rt.: rosary, arrow, abhaya mu. lt.: lotus, (?) mudra, bow	youth	two	vajra	bodh. ornaments, va.: lotus throne	Vajradharma-Avalokitesvara**
three*/six	six	rt.: book/manuscript on lotus, sword, ritual chopper lt.: head of Brahma, jewel, wheel	mature	two	pratyalidha	bodh. ornaments, va.: lotus throne	Vajrasarasvati
three/six	eight	rt.: rosary, noose/snare, abhaya mu., varada mu. lt.: book/manuscript, trident, lotus, resting at waist	youth	two	sama-bhanga	bodh. ornaments, va.: lotus throne	Mahavajranatha-Lokesvara**
three/six	eight	rt.: lotus in abhaya mu., arrow, thunderbolt, sword lt.: noose/snare in tarjani mu., bow, jewel, banner/flag, and book/manuscript in crook of arm against chest	mature	two	ardha-paryanka	bodh. ornaments, va.: lotus throne	Mahasitavati
three/six	24	prin.: kanjo-in mu. 2nd prin.: dhyana mu with vajra on end, other hands hold tantric symbols	youth	two	lalita	bodh. ornaments, va.: lotus throne	Bahubhuja-Cunda (devi)
three/6-9	six	prin.: embrace shakti in vajrahumkara mu. rt.: thunderbolt, flaming jewel lt.: sword, lotus	youth	two	sattva, yab-yum	bodh. ornaments, va.: lotus throne	Guhyasamaja-Lokesvara (Buddha)**
three/6-9	six	rt.: flower, sword, ritual chopper lt.: wheel, jewel (?), human skull-cup	youth	two	lalita	bodh. ornaments, va.: lotus throne	Rakta-Sarasvati (fo-mu)

three*/nine	six	rt.: lotus, pestle, sword lt.: axe, noose/snare, tarjani mu.	mature	two		*heads: yw., wh., rd. va.: lotus throne	bDe-sgrub-ma
four/eight	eight	rt.: thunderbolt, sword, goad/hook bow lt.: bell, trident, noose/snare, arrow	youth	two	sama-bhanga	bodh. ornaments, va.: lotus throne	Amoghapasa-Lokesvara**
four/eight	eight	rt.: thunderbolt, bow, trident, sword lt.: bell, arrow,, jewel, noose/snare	youth	two	sama-bhanga	bodh. ornaments, va.: lotus throne	Devadevata-Lokesvara**
four/eight	eight	rt.: thunderbolt, bow, trident, sword lt.: bell, arrow, vase/vessel, noose/snare	youth	two	sama-bhanga	bodh. ornaments, va.: lotus throne	Mahavajradhatu-Lokesvara**
four/eight	eight	rt.: sword, thunderbolt, bow, vase/vessel lt.: blue lotus bell arrow, noose/snare	youth	two	sama-bhanga	bodh. ornaments, va.: lotus throne	Mahavajradhrk-Lokesvara**
four/eight	eight	rt.: sword, goad/hook, tantric baton, staff/stick, rosary lt.: wheel, noose/snare, blue lotus, book/manuscript	youth	two	sama-bhanga	bodh. ornaments, va.: lotus throne	Mahavajrapani-Lokesvara**
four/eight	eight	rt.: sword, banner/flag, thunderbolt, goad/hook lt.: bell, conch, blue lotus, lotus	youth	two	sama-bhanga	bodh. ornaments, va.: lotus throne	Mahavisvasuddha-Lokesvara**
four*/eight	12	prin.: dharmachakra mu. 2nd pair: dhyana mudra with bowl with Buddha head others: thunderbolt, bow, crescent, peacock feather, book/manuscript, lotus, arrow, noose/snare	mature	two		*gr., rd., bl., wh., bodh. ornaments, va.: lotus throne	Mahamayuri
four/eight	24	upper raised in anjali mu. with small image others hold tantric symbols	youth	two	dhyana	bodh. ornaments, va.: lotus throne	Avalokitesvara
ten/20	12	prin.: anjali mudra rt.: rosary, arrow, (?), sword, trident lt.: lotus, bow, vase/vessel, (?), magic staff/stick	youth	two	sama-bhanga	bodh. ornaments, va.: lotus throne	Padmapani-Avalokitesvara**
11/22	eight	prin.: jewel in namaskara mu. rt.: rosary, wheel, abhaya lt.: lotus, bow, arrow	youth	two	sama-bhanga	bodh. ornaments, va.: lotus throne	Ekadasamukha**
11/22	eight	prin.: jewel in namaskara mu. rt.: rosary, flaming jewels, varada mu.	youth	two	sama-bhanga	bodh. ornaments, va.: lotus throne	Ekadasamukha-Avalokitesvara**

		lt.: lotus, bow, vase/vessel					
11/22	eight	prin.: jewel in namaskara mu. rt.: rosary, flaming jewels, varada mu. lt.: lotus, bow, vase/vessel	youth	two	sama-bhanga	bodh. ornaments, va.: lotus throne	Ekadasamukha-Avalokitesvara (Bodhisattva)**
11/22	eight	prin.: namaskara mu. rt.: rosary, wheel, varada mu. lotus, bow and arrow, vase/vessel	youth	two	sama-bhanga	bodh. ornaments, va.: lotus throne	Ekadasamukha-Mahakarunika**
11/22	eight	prin.: namaskara mu. rt.: rosary, wheel, varada mu. lt.:lotus, bow, arrow	youth	two	sama-bhanga	bodh. ornaments, va.: lotus throne	Laksmi-krama-Ekadasamukha-Avalokitesvara
11/22	eight	prin.: abhaya mudra against chest rt.: rosary, wheel, varada mu. lt.: blue lotus, bow and arrow, vase/vessel	youth	two	sama-bhanga	bodh. ornaments, va.: lotus throne	Mahasahasrasuryya-Lokesvara**
11/22	eight	prin.: hold jewel rt.: rosary, wheel, goad/hook lt.: lotus, bow, arrow	youth	two	sama-bhanga	bodh. ornaments, va.: lotus throne	Vajragarbhapramardin-Avalokitesvara**
11/22	ten	prin.: jewel in namaskara mu. rt.: karana mu., thunderbolt, abhaya mu., karana mu. lt.: karana mu., vase/vessel, (?), karana mu.	youth	two	sama-bhanga	bodh. ornaments, va.: lotus throne	Gaganaraja**
11/22	32	holds tantric symbols	youth	two	lalita	bodh. ornaments, va.: lotus throne	Visvesa-Avalokitesvara**

Red (Skt.: rakta; Tib.: dmar-po), Wrathful, Angry or Haughty Deities

Abbreviations:

as. = asana	bk. = black	bl. = blue	bodh. = bodhisattva
bn. = brown	corp. = corpulent	dhar. = dharmapala	gn. = green
lt. = left	mu. = mudra	pu. = purple	rd. = red
rt. = right	sc. = smokey	va. = vahana	wh. = white
yw. = yellow			

(*) special variations or attributes noted within the entry.
(**) following deity's name indicates that the color is not noted in the source, kulesa's color is applied to the entry.
(eyes: 2-3, 6-9, etc.) in sources the deity's faces are noted, but the number of the eyes are not noted.

Head/Eyes	Hands	Objects Held	Body	Feet	Asana	Other Attributes	Deity Name
one*/two	two	rt.: embraces shakta Jambhala-dmar-po-srog-sgrubs-sa-lugs lt.: human skull-cup with elixir of life	mature	two	yab-yum	*angry va.: lotus throne	bDe-gryas-byed-ma
one*/two	two	rt.: human skull-cup lt.: sword	mature, steel wings	two	kneeling	*raven head dhar. ornaments	bDud-mgon-bya-rog-gdong-can
one*/two	two	rt.: iron goad/hook lt.: fly whisk	mature	two		*angry dhar. ornaments,	Bharali
one*/two	two	holding treasure casque and coral lance with banner/flag	mature	two		*angry, iron shell armor, va.: horse	bsTan-bsrung-mdzad-gnod-sbyin-mched-lnga
one/two	two	rt.: banner/flag of victory and red lance lt.: mongoose and goad/hook	mature	two	lalitasana	richly armored, high fancy boots, va.: lion	Caturayudha-Atiguhya-Vaisravana
one/two	two	rt.: banner/flag of victory with tigerskin lt.: mongoose and goad/hook	mature	two	lalitasana	richly armored, high fancy boots, va.: lion	Caturayudha-Atiguhya-Vaisravana
one*/two	two	rt.: iron chain lt.: human skull-cup	mature	two	praty-alidha	*lion-head western quarter	Red Lion-headed Chain-Holding Goddess
one*/two	two	rt.: pomegranate(?) lt.: rests behind thigh	youth	two	sattva	*angry, bare breasts, bodh. ornaments, va.: lotus throne	Hariti (deva)**

one*/two	two	rt.: goad/hook ly.: mongoose	corp.	two	lalita	*angry, bodh. ornaments, va.: lotus throne	Hariti-Yaksini
one*/two	two	crossed downwards	mature	two	alidha	*tiger-head, dhar. ornaments	Htamenma, "Red Tiger-headed One"
one*/two	two	large corpse on the shoulder	mature	two	alidha	*bird-head, dhar. ornaments	Htamenma, "Dark-Red Cemetery-Bird-Headed One"
one*/two	two	holding trunk of corpses	mature	two	alidha	*horse-head, dhar. ornaments	Ishvari, "Red Horse-Headed Delight-Goddess"
one*/two	two	holding iron chain	mature	two	alidha	*lion-head, dhar. ornaments	Ishvari, "Red Lion-Headed Mystic Goddess"
one*/two	two	holding lotus	mature	two	alidha	*serpent-head, dhar. ornaments	Ishvari, "Reddish-Yellow Serpent-Headed Bahma-Goddess"
one*/two	two	holding short lance/spear	mature	two	alidha	*snowbear-head, dhar. ornaments	Ishvari, "Red Snow-Bear-Headed Virgin Goddess"
one*/two	two	holding lotus	mature	two	alidha	*scorpion-head, dhar. ornaments	Ishvari, "Red Scorpion-Headed Amrita-Goddess"
one*/two	two	rt.: bow lt.: arrow	mature	two	alidha	*hoopoo-head, dhar. ornaments	Ishvari, "Red Hoopoo-Headed Desire-Goddess"
one*/two	two	holding vase/vessel	mature	two	alidha	*makara-head, dhar. ornaments	Ishvari, "Red Makara-headed Peaceful-Goddess"
one*/two	two	holding pointed staff/stick	mature	two	alidha	*ibex-head, dhar. ornaments	Ishvari, "Red Ibex-Headed Woman-Goddess"
one*/two	two	holding infant corpse	mature	two	alidha	*crow-head, dhar. ornaments	Ishvari, "Red Crow-Headed Thunderbolt-Goddess"
one*/two	two	holds white conch shell	mature	two		*angry, richly garbed, fancy boots	Kubera-svarottama(?)-Vaisravana
one*/two	two	holds white conch shell	corp.	two	lalita	*angry, richly garbed, fancy boots, va.: lotus throne on lion throne	Kubera-svarottama(?)-Vaisravana

one*/two	two	wings	bird-like	two		*bird-head claws hold chain, realm: below the genitals	lCags-sgrog-gi-khyung
one*/two	two	rt.: red lance with silken streamers lt.: treasure producing mongoose	mature	two		*angry, richly armored, fancy leather boots, va.: blue horse	rNam-sras-mdung-dmar-rta-sngon-can
one*/two	two	rt.: banner/flag of victory & red lance lt.:treasure producing mongoose	mature	two		*angry, richly clothed, fancy leather boots, va.: lotus throne	rNam-sras-yang-gsang-phyag-mtshan-bzhi-pa
one/two	two	rt.: iron goad/hook lt.: fly whisk	mature	two		bodh. ornaments, va.: lotus throne	Sarasvati
one*/two	16	rt.: banner/flag of victory, club, sword, arrow, trident, hammer, citron, red lance lt.: mongoose, serpent/snake noose/snare, wheel, thunderbolt noose/snare, bow, vase/vessel, mountain, twig	mature	two		*angry, richly armored, dhar. ornaments, va.: lotus throne	Nartakavara-Rakta-Vaisravana
one*/2-3	two	rt.: skull-cup lt.: sword	mature	two	kneeling on one knee	raven head, wings of steel blades	bDud-mgon-bya-rog-gdong-can
one*/2-3	two	rt.: iron chain lt.: club/cudgel	raksasa-like	two		*bk. yak head, *dark red, dhar. ornaments	bDun-po-raksa'i-mgo-g.yag
one/2-3	two	rt.: banner/flag of victory lt.: dripping heart	mature	two	astride	red armor, high leather boots, va.: red horse	bKra-shis-'od-'bar
one*/2-3	two	rt.: sack of pestilence lt.: pair of dice	emaciated, pend. breasts	two		*dark rd., ugly, dhar. ornaments	bSod-byed-nag-mo
one*/2-3	two	rt.: noose/snare lt.: cane staff/stick	mature	two		*angry, red cuirass, va.: light br. horse with wh. heels	bTsan-gyi-dmag-dpon

one*/2-3	two	holding sickle and human heart	mature	two	kneeling	*raven head, wings of steel,	bTsan-mgon-bya-rog-gdong-can
one/2-3	two	iron magic dagger	youth	two		yak and sheep skin garment, iron toupet	Byang-'brog-'khor-'dul-ma
one*/ 2-3	two	rt.: ritual chopper lt.: human skull-cup	mature, nude	two		*vulture head, dhar. ornaments,	Bya-rgod-kyi-gdong-pa-can
one/2-3	two	rt.: lance with magic knife lt.: red noose/snare	mature	two	astride	leather harness dhar. ornaments, va.: horse	Chos-bdag-brag-btsan-Zangs-phur-can-pa
one*/2-3	two	rt.: trumpet lt.: ritual dagger	mature	two		*bird head, orange color, copper wings	Dus-'dzin-se-bya
one*/2-3	two	holding magic dagger	mature	two		dhar. ornaments, attribute: syllable "ta," va.: black mule with a yellow muzzle	Ekabhaisajyavajra
one/2-3	four	rt.: gold knife, lance with white banner/flag lt.: noose/snare, mongoose	mature	two		leather armor dhar. ornaments,	Chos-kyi-rgyal-po-gnod-sbyin-Yang-dag-shes
one/2-3	two	rt.: copper sword lt.: twists bowels	mature	two		*angry, dhar. ornaments, lotus throne	Ging-chen-sna-khrid
one/2-3	two	plays gong in tarjani mu.	mature	two	pratyalidha	*angry, *pink color, dhar. ornaments, lotus throne	Ging-chen-sna-khrid
one/2-3	two	plays lute	mature	two	pratyalidha	*angry, dhar. ornaments, lotus throne	Ging-chen-sna-khrid
one/2-3	two	rt.: thunderbolt lt.: bell	mature	two	vajra	*angry, dhar. ornaments, lotus throne	Ging-chen-sna-khrid
one*/2-3	two	rt.: human thigh-bone lt.: iron goad/hook	mature	two	kneeling	*raven head, steel-blade wings,	gNod-sbyin-bya-rog-gdong-can

						dhar. ornaments	
one/2-3	two	rt.: lance lt.: noose/snare	mature	two		copper helmet, cloak of bird feathers, va.: red horse	gSung-sprul-'bri-byed
one*-2-3	two	human skull-cup filled with blood and a corpse held above head	mature	two	kneeling on one knee	wings of steel blades, bone ornaments	Gying-mgon-bya-rog-gdong-can
one*/2-3	two	rt.: pomegranate lt.: child to her breast	mature	two		hair forms crown,	Hariti
one*/2-3	two	rt.: varada mu. with child to her breast lt.: mongoose	mature	two		hair forms crown,	Hariti
one/2-3	two	holding door planks	mature, nude	two	pratyalidha	va.: lotus throne	Kapata
one*/2-3	two	rt.: mirror of karma lt.: pair of dice	mature	two		*ugly, dhar. ornaments	Ka-ra-ra-tri
one*/2-3	two	rt.: ritual chopper lt.: human skull-cup	mature, nude	two		*crow-head, dhar. ornaments	Khva-ta'i-gdong-pa-can
one*/2-3	two	rt.: ritual chopper lt.: human skull-cup	mature, nude	two		*dog-head, dhar. ornaments	Khyi'i-gdong-pa-can
one/three	two	rt.: copper sword lt.: human skull-cup filled with brains and blood	mature, nude	two	alidha	erect phalus, bone/ ornaments va. lotus throne	Am-kri-mi-dmar
one/three	two	rt.: dagger/knife lt.: lifts (?) to his mouth	corp.	two	alidha	bone/ ornaments, human skin cape, va.: human fig. with partially severed head	Am-kri-mi-dmar
one/ three	two	rt.: thunderbolt-topped staff/stick lt.: tarjani mu.	corp.	two	alidha	dhar. ornaments, va.: human forms	Arya-(Atisa)-krama-Sahaja-Ekavira-Hayagriva
one*/three	two	rt.: sandal-wood club lt.: heart lungs and "life root" of evil doer	mature	two		*dark red dhar. ornaments,	Arya-(Atisa)-krama-Simha-vahana-Traksad-Mahakala
one*/three	two	rt.: thunderbolt-topped staff/stick lt.: heart lungs and "life root" of evil doer	corp	two	alidha	*dark red dhar. ornaments, va.: lion	Arya-(Atisa)-krama-Simha-vahana-Traksad-Mahakala

one*/three	two	rt.: sword lt.: tarjani mu.	corp	two	ardha- paryanka	* horse-head in hair dhar. ornaments, va.: human forms	Babhru-nila-Hayagriva
one*/three	two	rt.: goad/hook lt.: human skull-cup	aged, pendulous breasts	two	seated	*dark rd., va.: water buffalo	bDud-kun-gtso-remadzu
one*/three	two	rt.: goad/hook lt.: heart of enemy	mature	two	astride	*blood flows from mouth, dhar. ornaments, va.: black wild yak, syllable "sha"	bDud-mo-phung-khrol-ma
one/three	two	rt.: trident lt.: human heart	mature	two	alidha (?)	dhar. ornaments, shakti: to bDud-mgon- seng-gdong va.: lotus throne	bDud-mo-seng-gdong-ma
one/three	two	rt.: knife lt.: noose/snare	mature	two	astride	dhar. ornaments, va.: *bse-bya* bird	bDud-po-ma-ru-rtse
one/three	two	rt.: copper sword lt.: twisted bowels	mature	two	alidha(?)	dhar. ornaments,	bDud-po-sha-zan
one*/three	two	rt.: iron chain lt.: club/cudgel	mature, raksasa- like	two		*dark red ornaments of bone and skins	bDun-po-raksa'i-mgo-g.yag
one/three	two	rt.: embraces her yab lt.: skull-cup with the elixir of life	mature	two	yab-yum	shakti of Jambhala- dmar-po-srog-sgrubs- sa-lugs	bDe-gryas-byed-ma
one/three	two	rt.: goad/hook lt.: skull-cup	mature, pendulous breasts	two	astride	dark red, dhar. ornaments, va.: black water buffalo	bDud-kun-gtso-remadzu
one*/three	two	rt.: trident lt.: human heart	mature, nude	two		*lioness head, dhar. ornaments	bDud-mo-seng-gdong-ma
one/three	two	rt.: knife lt.: noose/snare	mature	two		dhar. ornaments, va.: bse-bya bird	bDud-po-ma-ru-rtse
one/three	two	rt.: copper sword lt.: twists bowels	mature	two		dhar. ornaments, human and ox-skin garments	bDud-po-sha-zan

one/three	two	rt.: bejeweled club lt.: heart of an enemy	mature	two	alidha	dhar. ornaments, tiger-skin loin-cloth, black silk cloak, va.: lotus throne	pKa'-srung-brag-lha-mgon-po
one/three	two	bow and arrow, and lance	mature	two		leather cloak, red horse	Brag-btsan-dmar-po
one/three	two	rt.: club/cudgel lt.: noose/snare in tarjani mu.	mature	two	astride	dhar. ornaments, red silk garment with cuirass, va.: light br. horse	
one/three	two	rt.: flaming sword lt.: heart of enemy in mouth	mature	two		dhar. otnaments, va.: rd. with wh. heels horse	bTsan-gyi-dmag-dpon
one/three	two	rt.: lance lt.: noose/snare	mature	two	astride	cuirass and helmet of leather, dhar. ornaments, syllable: "tsa," va.: red horse	bTsan-rgod
one/three	two	rt.: noose/snare lt.: red silk banner/flag	mature	two	astride	dhar. ornaments, red silk garment, va.: red horse	bTsan-rgod
one/three	two	rt.: red lance lt.: noose/snare	mature	two	astride	*red-brown color, dhar. ornaments, va.: "wind horse"	bTsan-rgod-rdo-rje
one/three	two	rt.:wheel lt.: human skull-cup and magic staff/stick in crook of arm	mature	two	ardha-paryanka	dhar. ornaments, va.: lotus throne	Buddha-Dakini
one/three	two	rt.: sandal wood club lt.: iron vessel filled with hearts of enemies	mature	two		dhar. ornaments, black silk cloak, high boots	Bu-ston-lugs-dpal-mgon-beng-dmar
one/three	two	rt.: ritual chopper lt.: human skull-cup	mature, nude	two	alidha	dhar. ornaments, va.: human corpse	Carcika
one/three	two	rt.: ritual chopper, lt.: human skull-cup and magic notched staff/stick in crook of left arm	mature, nude	two	alidha	dhar. ornaments, va.: prostrate human forms	Chinnamunda (Vajravarahi)**

one*/three	two	rt.: trident with human head impaled lt.: human heart	mature	two		*dog-like dhar. ornament, va.: lotus throne	<u>Dakamukha-Guhyasadhana-Traksad-Mahakala</u>
one*/three	two	rt.: trident lt.: human heart to mouth	mature	two		*lion-like dhar. ornament, va.: lotus throne	<u>Dakamukha-Guhyasadhana-Traksad-Mahakala</u>
one/three	two	rt.: goad/hook lt.: noose/snare	mature	two	astride	red silk garment with red sash, dhar. ornaments, va.: red mule	<u>dBang-gi-lha-mo</u>
one/three	two	rt.: trident lt.: human skull-cup	corp.	two		dhar. ornaments, a raksasa	<u>dBang-mo</u>
one/three	two	rt.: cane staff/stick lt.: sandal-wood club	mature	two	yab-yum	black silk garment dhar. ornaments, va.: black mule with white heels	<u>dGra-lha-skyes-gcig-bu</u>
one/three	two	rt.: copper sword lt.: twists bowels	mature	two		dhar. ornaments,	<u>Dung-gi-rdo-rje</u>
one*/three	two	rt.: trident lt.: heart	mature	two	vamalalita	*distorted with rage. one tooth, dhar. ornaments, va.: donkey	<u>Ekajata</u> (red)
one/three	two	rt.: ritual knife lt.: noose/snare	mature	two		dhar. ornaments, realm: North, va.: bse-bya bird	<u>gNod-sbyin-ma-ru-rtse</u>
one/three	two	rt.: flaming copper sword lt.: heart to mouth and holds bow and arrow, stick of coral and lance in crook of arm	mature	two	alidha	blood flows out of mouth, copper fangs, cuirass of copper, dhar. ornaments va.: corpse of a man and carcass of a horse	<u>gNod-sbyin-sgrol-gying-bshan-pa</u>
one/three	two	rt.: red lance with banner-flag lt.: red noose/snare	mature	two	astride	high leather boots, dhar. ornaments, va.: red horse	<u>Grib-btsan</u>
one/three	two	rt.: red lance with banner/flag lt.: red sword	mature	two	astride	dhar. ornaments, high leather boots va. red horse	<u>Gri-btsan</u>

one/three	two	rt.: flaming sword lt.: human skull-cup	mature, nude	two	astride	loose garments, dhar. ornaments, va.: blue yak	<u>Gri-gug-mgon-po</u>
one/three	two	rt.: goad/hook lt.: human skull-cup	mature, nude	two	astride	loose garments, dhar. ornaments, va.: blue yak	<u>Gri-gug-mgon-po</u>
one/three	two	rt.: goad/hook lt.: human skull-cup	mature, nude	two	astride	loose garments, dhar. ornaments, attribute: syllable "bhyo" va.: water buffalo	<u>Gri-gug-mgon-po</u>
one/three	two	rt.: saber lt.: noose/snare around a human form	mature	two	astride	red silk garment, dhar. ornaments, va.: red horse	<u>Gro-shod-bod-kyi-sgang-dmag-rje</u>
one*/three	two	rt.: ritual chopper lt.: human skull-cup	mature	two		*jackal face, dhar. ornaments	<u>gSang-ba'i-las-mgon</u>
one/three	two	rt.: snake noose/snare lt.: magic dagger	youth	two	astride	dhar. ornaments va.: yellow horse	<u>gSer-chen-mkh'-lding-klu-mo</u>
one/three	two	rt.: lance lt.: noose/snare	mature	two	astride	quiver & bow-case at belt, white turban, rhino-skin shield, va.: horse	<u>gTer-bsrung-rGyal-ba-thod-dkar</u>
one/three	two	rt.: copper sword lt.: human skull-cup filled with brains and blood	mature, nude	two		erect phallus, dhar. ornaments	<u>Ha-shang-mi-dmar</u>
one*/three	two	rt.: sword lt.: noose/snare	dwarfish	two	alidha	*horse-head in hair, dhar. ornaments, va.: lotus throne	<u>Hayagriva</u>
one*/three	two	embracing shakti	dwarfish	two	alidha	*horse-head in hair, dhar. ornaments, va.: lotus throne	<u>Hayagriva</u>
one*/three	two	rt.: baton/mace lt.: karana mu.	corp	two	alidha	*horse in hair, dhar. ornaments, va.: lotus throne	<u>Hayagrivavajra</u>
one*/three	two	rt.: abhaya mu.	corp	two	alidha	*horse in hair,	<u>Hayagrivavajra</u>

		lt.: club/cudgel				dhar. ornaments, va.: lotus throne	
one*/three	two	rt.: mace staff/stick lt.: noose/snare	corp	two	alidha	*horse in hair, dhar. ornaments, va.: lotus throne	Hayagrivavajra
one*/three	two	rt.: torch lt.: human skull-cup	mature	two		*orange color, dhar. ornaments	hBar-ma-gnod-sbyin-ba-glang-sna, hBar-ma-gnod-sbyin-khyung-thogs, hBar-ma-gshin-rje-skar-mda'-gdong, hBar-ma-khyer-glog-'phreng-ma, hBar-ma-klu-mo-lce-'bebs-ma, hBar-ma-nyi-zhags-thogs-ma, hBar-ma-rlung-bdag, hBar-ma-srin-mo-mdung-'phen-ma
one/three	two	rt.: copper sword lt.: twists bowels	mature	two		dhar. ornaments	hLigs-byed-rdo-rje
one/three	two	rt.: jewel lt.: mongoose and embraces shakti	corp.	two	yab-yum	silk garments, bodh. ornaments	Iambhala-dmar-po-srog-sgrubs-sa-lugs
one/three	two	rt.: human skull-drum lt.: human skull-cup filled with blood	corp.	two	alidha	dhar. ornaments, va.: human form	Iinamitra
one/three	two	rt.: human skull-drum lt.: human skull-cup filled with blood	corp.	two	ardha-paryanka	dhar. ornaments, va.: human form	Iinamitra
one/three	two	rt.: red lance lt.: noose/snare in tarjani mu.	mature	two	alidha	cuirass of leather, green cloak, fancy boots	Jing-gir-rgyal-po
one/three	two	rt.: thunderbolt lt.: vajra-topped staff/stick	corp.	two	alidha	dhar. ornaments, va.: prostrate human body	Kasmira-mahapandita-krama-Hayagriva**
one/three	two	rt.: red lance lt.: noose/snare encircling a demon's neck	mature	two	astride	richly armored, leather cuirass, va.: red horse with white spots	Kha-che-dmar-po
one/three	two	rt.: red lance with banner/flag lt.: red noose/snare	mature	two	astride	fancy boots, rich garments, va.: red horse	Khrag-btsan-dmar-po
one*/three	two	rt.: ritual chopper	mature,	two		* garuda-head,	Khyung-gi-gdong-pa-can

		lt.: human skull-cup	nude			dhar. ornaments	
one*/three	two	rt.: battle lance lt.: noose/snare	corp.	two	astride	*orange color, dhar. ornaments, va.: horse of the water spirits	kLu-bdud-nag-po-sog-pa-med
one/three	two	rt.: dagger/knife lt.: human skull-cup	corp.	two	ardha-paryanka	dhar. ornaments, va.: prostrate human figure	Kro-dhi-mi-dmar
one/three	two	rt.: human skull-drum lt.: tarjani mu.	mature	two		dhar. ornaments, va.: lotus throne	Ksetrapala
one/three	two	rt.: red lotus lt.: bow and arrow	mature	two	vajra	bodh. ornaments, va.: lotus throne	Kurukulla
one/three	two	hold leafy branches	mature	two	alidha	dhar. ornaments, va.: prostrate human figure	Kurukulla (fo-mu)
one/three	two	rt.: lance lt.: noose/snare	corp.	two	astride	loose garments, fancy boors, va.: horse-like animal with clawed feet	Las-mkhan-dmar-po
one/three	two	rt.: karana mu. lt.: abhaya mu.	youth	two	alidha	dhar. ornaments, va.: lotus throne	Lasya (fo-mu)
one/three	two	rt.: sword lt.: human heart both arms clasp to body bow and arrow and banner/flag				dhar. ornaments, Mongolian boots, va.: right foot stands on horse, left on a human form	lCam-sring
one/three	two	rt.: copper sword lt.: twists bowels	mature	two		dhar. ornaments	Legs-nyes-stangs-'dzin
one/three	two	holding iron goad/hook	mature	two	astride	richly armored, va.: red horse	lHa-chen-khang-kas
one/three	two	rt.: trident lt.: human skull-cup-hilt knife	mature	two		dhar. ornaments, va.: lotus throne	lHa-chen-ma
one/three	two	rt.: rosary lt.: lance	mature	two	astride	dhar. ornaments, va.: mule	lHa-mo-ma(m)-gha-bza'

one/three	two	rt.: flaming ritual chopper lt.: human skull-cup and noose/snare around neck of demon	mature	two		dhar. ornaments	lHo-nub-mgon-po-gri-gug-dmar-po
one/three	two	rt.: sword lt.: noose/snare	corp.	two	alidha	horse-head in hair dhar. ornaments, va.: lotus throne	Lohakhadga-Hayagriva
one/three	two	rt.: sword lt.: tarjani mu.	corp.	two	alidha	horse-head in hair dhar. ornaments, va.: prostrate human body	Lohakhadga-Hayagriva
one/three	two	rt.: staff/stick lt.: karana	mature	two	alidha	dhar. ornaments, va.: prostrate human figures	Mahabala
one*/three	two	both holds length of chain	corp.	two	pratyalidha	*horse-head in hair, dhar. ornaments, va.: lotus throne	Mahapadmesvara
one*/three	two	rt.: bell lt.: karana mu.	corp.	two	pratyalidha	*horse-head in hair dhar. ornaments, va.: lotus throne	Mahasiddharthesvara
one*/three	two	rt.: golden jewel lt.: bow and arrow	corp.	two	astride	*copper color dhar. ornaments, va.: white horse	mGon-po-zas-lha-dmar-po
one/three	two	rt.: copper sword lt.: twists bowels	corp	two		dhar. ornaments, va.: lotus throne	Mi-dmar-gshar-pa
one/three	two	rt.: copper sword lt.: skull-cup with brains and blood	cotp, nude	two		erect phallus, dhar. ornaments, va.: lotus throne	Mi-dmar-khra-ma
one/three	two	rt.: dagger/knife (churi, gri) carving the chest of a human lt.: rests on waist	corp	two	alidha	dhar. ornaments, va.: human, being carved	Mi-dmar-khra-ma-srog-bdag
one/three	two	holds red lotus	mature	two		*orange color, dhar. ornaments, realm: South and Tuesday, va.: lotus throne	Mig-dmar

one/three	two	rt.: serpent/snake lt.: noose/snare, stupa	mature	two		richly armored, attrib.: the syllable "bi" va.: "sea-elephant"	Mig-mi-bzang
one*/three	two	rt.: corpse as a club lt.: red corpse	mature	two		*heron-head, dhar. ornaments, va.: lotus throne	mNag-gzhung-ma
one/three	two	rt.: tarjani mu. lt.: asoka bough	mature	two	alidha	dhar. ornaments, va.: lotus throne on chariot supported by seven pigs	Marici (fo-mu)
one/three	two	rt.: abhaya mu., cylindrical banner/flag lt.: lotus, vase/vessel	mature	two	alidha	dhar. ornaments, va.: lotus throne	Naga-bhayatrana (Avalokitesvara)**
one/three	two	rt.: magic notched stick lt.: pair of dice	mature	two		dhar. ornaments, va.: lotus throne	Nam-gru-chen-mo
one/three	two	rt.: red lance lt.: noose/snare encircling a demons neck	mature	two		dhar. ornaments, leather cuirass, va.: lotus throne	Nam-mkha'-sbar-'dzin
one/three	two	rt.: iron goad/hook lt.: fly-whisk	mature	two		dhar. ornaments, va.: lotus throne	Nor-skyong-ma
one/three	two	rt.: sandal wood club lt.: human heart	corp.	two	alidha	dhar. ornaments, va.: corpse	Padatika-Traksad-Mahakala
one/three	two	rt.: trident lt.: human skull-cup	corp.	two	alidha	dhar. ornaments, va.: corpse	Padatika-Traksad-Mahakala
one/three	two	rt.: ritual chopper lt.: human skull-cup blood filled	mature, nude	two	ardha-paryanka	dhar. ornaments, va.: lotus throne	Padma-Dakini
one/three	two	human skull-cup blood filled & magic staff/stick in crook of left arm	mature, nude	two	ardha-paryanka	dhar. ornaments, va.: lotus throne	Padma-Dakini
one/three	two	rt.: lotus lt.: goad/hook	mature, nude	two	ardha-paryanka	dhar. ornaments, va.: lotus throne	Padma-Dakini
one/three	two	rt.: ritual chopper lt.: human skull-cup & magic staff/stick in crook of left arm	mature	two	ardha-paryanka	dhar. ornaments, va.: prostrate human figure	Padma-Dakini

one/three	two	dhyana mu. with alms bowl	mature	two	ardha-paryanka	dhar. ornaments, va.: lotus throne	Padma-Heruka
one/three	two	rt.: encircles yab's neck lt.: human skull-cup	mature	two	pratyalidha, yab-yum	dhar. ornaments, va.: lotus throne	Padma-Krotishaurima
one*/three	two	rt.: lotus lt.: serpent/snake	mature	two		*bird-head, serpent in beak, winged &bird claws, dhar. ornaments, va.: serpent/snake	Padma-Garuda
one*/three	two	rt.: ritual chopper lt.: human skull-cup	mature, nude	two		*pig-head, dhar. ornaments, va.: lotus throne	Phag-gi-gdong-pa-can
one/three	two	rt.: treasure casque lt.: lance with banner	mature	two	astride	dhar. ornaments, armored, va.: horse	Phu-yi-gzhi-bdag-mdzod-lnga-spun-lnga
one/three	two	rt.: jewel lt.: vase/vessel	mature	snake-like		*7 snakes in halo, legs are snake-coils, dhar. ornaments, va.: lotus throne	Pad-ma-gtsug-phud-ma
one/three	two	holding makara banner/flag	mature	two		dhar. ornaments, va.: lotus throne	Pramoha
one/three	two	both hands hold intestines wich she holds in mouth	mature	two		dhar. ornaments, va.: lotus throne	Pukkase
one/three	two	rt.: black iron lance lt.: noose/snare of poisonous snakes	mature	two	astride	bodh. ornaments, blue silk cloak, va.: yellow horse	Raja-gos-sngon-gyi-klu-btsan
one/three	two	holding weapons of a raksasa	mature	two		dhar. ornaments, va.: red horse	rDo-rje-brag-btsan-rDo-rje-dbang-drag-rtsal
one/three	two	rt.: goad/hook lt.: jewel	mature	two		red silk turban, red cloak, high boots, va.: tigress	rDo-rje-brag-btsan-rDo-rje-dbang-drag-rtsal
one/three	two	rt.: thunderbolt lt.: noose/snare	corp.	two	alidha	dhar. ornaments, va.: lotus throne	Rakta-Alpacanda-Vajrapani
one/three	two	rt.: an-i-in mu.	corp.	two	alidha,	dhar. ornaments,	Rakta-Bhairavavajra Buddha

		lt.: embraces shakti and human skull-cup			yab-yum	va.: human figure on back of bull	
one/three	two	rt.: sword lt.: mongoose	mature	two	lalita	long flowing garment, dhar. ornaments, va.: lotus throne	Raktadhusaravajra
one*/three	two	rt.: sword lt.: staff/stick	corp.	two	ardha-paryanka	*horse head in hair, dhar. ornaments, va.: lotus throne	Rakta-Hayagriva
one/three	two	rt.: sword lt.: flaming wind-wheel	corp.	two	alidha	dhar. ornaments, va.: buffalo	Rakta-Karma-Yama
one/three	two	rt.: sword lt.: disc	corp.	two	alidha	erect phallus, dhar. ornaments, va.: bull	Rakta-Karma-Yama
one/three	two	rt.: ritual chopper lt.: human skull-cup and noose/snare around the neck of a human figure	mature	two	alidha	dhar. ornaments, va.: prostrate human form	Rakta-Kartaridhara-Makahala-daksina-pascima
one/three	two	rt.: stem of lotus in karana mu. lt.: crossed thunderbolt	corp.	two	ardha-paryanka	dhar. ornaments, va.: lotus throne	Rakta-krsna-Hayagriva
one/three	two	rt.: human skull-cup lt.: thigh-bone trumpet	mature	two		dhar. ornaments, va.: lotus throne	Rakta-Mahakala
one/three	two	rt.: human thigh-bone trumpet, human skull-cup embracing shakti	corp.	two	pralam-bapada, yab-yum	dhar. ornaments, va.: triangle	Rakta-Mahakala
one/three	two	rt.: thunderbolt lt.: tarjani mu.	corp.	two	alidha	richly armored, va.: lotus throne	Rakta-Parnasabari
one*/two	two	rt.: red lance & cylindrical banner/flag lt.: treasure producing mongoose & axe	mature	two	vamalalita	richly armored, va.: lion	Raktashula-Vaishravana
one/three	two	rt.: cylindrical banner/flag & lance lt.: staff/stick & mongoose	corp.	two	pralam-bapada	richly armored, va.: lotus throne	Raktashula-Vaishravana
one*/three	two	rt.: skull topped staff/stick lt.: pestle (?)	mature	two	astride	*lion-head, loose garments, va.: horse	Rakta-Simhasya
one*/three	two	rt.: ritual chopper, magic staff/stick	mature	two	ardha-	*lion-head,	Rakta-Simhavaktra

		on shoulder lt.: skull-cup			paryanka	dhar. ornaments, va.: lotus throne	
one/three	two	rt.: thunderbolt lt.: human skull-cup	mature	two	ardha- paryanka	dhar. ornaments, va.: lotus throne	Rakta-Vahari
one/three	two	rt.: ear of rice lt.: human skull-cup	youth	two	alidha	dhar. ornaments, va.: lotus throne	Rakta-Vasudhara
one*/three	two	rt.: staff/stick with Buddha head finial lt.: human skull-cup and embraces shakti	mature, nude	two	pratyalidha	*bull-head, dhar. ornaments, va.: female figure on back of bull	Rakta-Yamantaka
one*/three	two	rt.: flaming jewels lt.: human skull-cup	mature	two		*bull-head, dhar. ornaments, va.: bull	Rakta Yamaraja
one/three	two	rt.: white staff/stick lt.: human skull-cup	corp.	two	pratyalidha, yab-yum	dhar. ornaments, va.: buffalo	Rakta-Yamari
one/three	two	rt.: red lance lt.: noose/snare	mature	two		*red-brown, dhar. ornaments, va.: airy horse (rlung rta)	rDo-gling-yul-gangs-chen
one/three	two	rt.: red lance lt.: noose/snare of bowels	mature	two	astriide	red turban , red silk cloak, dhar. ornaments, va.: red ass with white stomach	rDo-rings-dmar-po'i-gri-btsan
one/three	two	rt.: iron lance lt.: bowl of jewels	mature	two		black silk garments, dhar. ornaments, va.: lotus throne	rDo-rje-'bar-ba
one/three	two	rt.: iron chain lt.: magic dagger	mature	two		pendulous breasts, dhar. ornaments, va.: leopard	rDo-rje-bse-byin-chen-mo
one/three	two	rt.: jewel lt.: trident	mature	two		silk garments, dhar. ornaments, va.: elephant	rDo-rje-dpa'-rtsal
one/three	two	rt.: copper sword lt.: twists bowels	mature	two		human skins and ox-hides, va.: lotus throne	rDo-rje-ging-chen

one*/three	two	rt.: victory banner/flag lt.: mongoose	corp.	two		*red-brown color, armored, va.: horse of the gnyan	rDo-rje-gnod-sbyin-nor-bdag
one*/three	two	holds sacred dagger of sandal-wood	mature	two		*angry, cloak of black snakes, dhar. ornaments, syllable "te", va.: hind	rDo-rje-g.ya'-mo-bsil
one/three	two	rt.: red banner/flag lt.: flat pan of gems & noose/snare	mature	two		red armor, high red leather boots, va.: red horse	rDo-rje-khro-'bar
one/three	two	rt.: copper sword lt.: skull-cup filled with brains and blood	mature, nude	two		erect phallus, dhar. ornaments, va.: lotus throne	Ro-kri-mi-dmar
one/three	two	rt.: dagger/knife lt.: points at partially severed head of figure upon which he is kneeling	corp	two	kneeling	dhar. ornaments, va.: human figure with partially severed head	Ro-kri-mi-dmar
one/three	two	rt.: trident lt.: skull-cup filled with blood	mature	two		dhar. ornaments, va.: lotus throne	rTog-'dod-ma
one/three	two	rt.: red lance with black banner/flag lt.: copper sword	mature	two		red turban, red cuirass of copper, dhar. ornaments, va.: horse	rTsal-thog-rgyug-gi-gri-btsan
one/three	two	rt.: five pointed thunderbolt with a human heart lt.: tarjani mu. with noose/snare	corp.	two	alidha	tiger skin loin cloth, va.: lotus throne	Rudhira-varna-Rakta-Karma-Yama
one/three	two	rt.: lotus bud(?) lt.: noose/snare	corp.	two	alidha	dhar. ornaments, va.: sun disc on moon disc	Rudhira-varna-Rakta-Karma-Yama
one/three	two	rt.: nine point thunderbolt lt.: heart to mouth	mature	two	astride	purple and brown hat, garment of red silk, dhar. ornaments, va.: light brown billy-goat	rDo-rje-legs-pa
one/three	two	rt.: thunderbolt lt.: heart	mature	two	astride	garment of red silk, dhar. ornaments,	rDo-rje-legs-pa

					va.: white lion	
one/three	two	rt.: gold thunderbolt lt.: erect thumb at heart	mature	two	astride	white felt hat with pink skull, piebald garment, dhar. ornaments, va.: white lion	rDo-rje-legs-pa
one*/three	two	rt.: white circular banner/flag lt.: battle lance	mature	two	astride	*fire-like color, dres sed in white silk, dhar. ornaments, va.: white lion	rDo-rje-legs-pa
one/three	two	rt.: thunderbolt lt.: magic dagger	mature	two		dhar. ornaments, va.: lotus throne	rDo-rje-sgrol-ma-za-byed-ma
one/three	two	rt.: flaming sword lt.: human skull-cup with the organs of the five senses, crook of arm rests mongoose & golden goad/hook	mature	two		dhar. ornaments, va.: carpet of human skins on one hundred thousand thunderbolts on back of garuda-like bird	rDo-rje-shugs-ldan
one/three	two	rt.: thunderbolt lt.: magic dagger	mature	two		dhar. ornaments, va.: lotus throne	rDo-rje-ye-shes-chen-mo-ma
one/three	two	rt.: battle lance lt.: bow & arrow	mature	two		red turban, garment of human skin, dhar. ornaments, va.: lotus throne	rGyal-chen-bsod-nams-dpal
one/three	two	rt.: copper sword lt.: human skull-cup filled with brains and blood	mature, nude	two		erect phallus, dhar. ornaments, va.: lotus throne	Ri-tsi-mi-dmar
one/three	two	rt.: dagger/knife lt.: devours part of a human	corp.	two	kneeling	dhar. ornaments, va.: human being whose throat has been cut	Ri-tsi-mi-dmar
one/three	two	rt.: chain lt.: magic dagger	mature	two		dhar. ornaments, va.: lotus throne	Sa-bdag-klu'dul-chen-mo
one/three	two	rt.: basket of relics lt.: rosary	mature	two	alidha	dhar. ornaments, va.: lotus throne	Sa-ghan-er-khe-hong-si-can-tha'i-ji
one/three	two	rt.: ritual chopper lt.: lifts skull-cup to lips, magic stick of	mature	two	alidha	dhar. ornaments, va.: lotus throne	Sarvabuddha-Dakini

		Padmasambhava on shoulder					
one*/three	two	rt.: embraces shakti, flaming jewels lt.: mongoose	mature	two	alidha, yab-yum	*angry, dhar. ornaments, va.: lotus throne	Sa-(skya)-lugs-(Pranasadhana)-Rakta-Jambhala
one/three	two	rt.: skull-cup, magic stick of Padmasambhava over right shoulder lt.: ritual chopper	mature	two	ardha- paryanka	dhar. ornaments, va.: human form	Simhavaktra
one/three	two	namaskara mu. with sun disc & moon disc	mature	two		dhar. ornaments, realm: Northwest va.: lotus throne	sGra-gcan
one/three	two	rt.: iron goad/hook lt.: human skull-cup	mature	two		dhar. ornaments, short pants-like garment, va.: lotus throne	Shan-ti-ro-zan-ma
one*/three	two	rt.: ritual chopper lt.: human skull-cup	corp.	two		*jackal-head, dhar. ornaments, jackals issue from every hair of his body, va.: lotus throne	Sha-za-ce-spyang-gdong-can
one/three	two	rt.: copper sword lt.: twists bowels	mature	two		dhar. ornaments, garments of human skins and ox-hides, va.: lotus throne	Shug-sgrogs-mgyogs-byed
one/three	two	rt.: lance lt.: noose/snare	mature	two		leather helmet, leather harness, va.: red horse	sKu-rgyal-she-ne
one/three	two	rt.: trident lt.: human skull-cup filled with blood	corp.	two		dhar. ornaments, va.: lotus throne	sNa-chen-ma
one/three	two	rt.: copper sword lt.: twists bowels	mature	two		garments of human skins and ox-hides, va.: lotus throne	Sog-po-sha-zan
one*/three	two	rt.: ritual chopper lt.: skull-cup	mature, nude	two		*wolf-head, dhar. ornaments, va.: lotus throne	sPyang-ki'i-gdong-pa-can
one/three	two	rt.: knife	mature	two		dhar. ornaments,	Srin-po-ma-ru-rtse

		lt.: noose/snare				va.: bse-bya bird	
one/three	two	rt.: copper sword lt.: twists bowels	mature	two		garments of human skins and ox-hides, va.: lotus throne	Srin-po-mi-ring
one/three	two	rt.: copper sword lt.: twists bowels	mature	two		garments of human skins and ox-hides, va.: lotus throne	Srin-po-mi-zan
one/three	two	rt.: copper sword lt.: twists bowels	mature	two		garments of human skins and ox-hides, va.: lotus throne	Srog-bdag-bdud-kyi-bu
one/three	two	rt.: red lance lt.: red noose/snare	mature	two		eating flesh, coat of mail, va.: wolf, a mad jackal, or a billy-goat	Srog-bdag-dmar-po
one/three	two	rt.: copper sword lt.: skull-cup filled with brains and blood	mature, nude	two	alidha	erect phallus, va.: lotus throne	Srog-bdag-ko-'o-sha
one/three	two	rt.: copper sword lt.: twists bowels	mature	two		garments of human skins and ox-hides, va.: lotus throne	Srog-bdag-la-li-pa
one/three	two	rt.: copper sword lt.: skull-cup filled with brains and blood	mature, nude	two	alidha	erect phallus, va.: lotus throne	Srog-bdag-thal-ba
one/three	two	rt.: dagger/knife lt.: lifts (?) to mouth	corp.	two	alidha	cape of human skin, va.: prostrate human form	Srog-bdag-thal-ba
one/three	two	rt.: bow lt.: arrow	mature	two		leather helmet, red silk cloak, va.: red horse	Srong-zan-dmar-po
one*/three	two	rt.: ritual chopper lt.: skull-cup	mature, nude	two		*tiger-head, dhar. ornaments, va.: lotus throne	sTag-gi-gdong-pa-can
one/three	two	rt.: battle lance lt.: red noose/snare	mature	two		dhar. ornaments, va.: red horse	sTong-btsan-pa
one/three	two	rt.: jewel	mature	two		dhar. ornaments,	Sukanthi

		lt.: treasure casque				dress of silk, attribute: syllable "mam", va.: stag	
one*/three	two	rt.: noose/snare lt.: tarjani mu	mature	two		*dark red, dhar. ornaments, va.: lotus throne	Takkiraja
one/three	two	rt.: golden box lt.: iron staff/stick	mature	two		red fur coat, dhar. ornaments, va.: lotus throne	Te-so
one/three	two	rt.: copper sword lt.: twists bowels	mature	two		human skins and ox-hides, dhar. ornaments, va.: lotus throne	Theb-'mying-pa-rdeg
one/three	two	holds great khyung of copper	mature	two	raja-paryanka	red fur coat, dhar. ornaments, va.: lotus throne	The-se-rgyal-po
one/three	two	rt.: lance lt.: noose/snare	mature	two		armored, va.: horse	Thog-btsan-pa
one/three	two	rt.: red battle lance lt.: flat bowl filled with jewels	mature	two		red turban, dhar. ornaments, va.: horse	Thog-lha-me-'bar
one/three	two	rt.: lance lt.: noose/snare	mature	two	astride	dhar. ornaments, va.: blue dragon	Tho-ri-rgyal-ba
one/three	two	rt.: ritual chopper lt.: heart	mature	two		covered by a human skin, dhar. ornaments, va.: lotus throne	Tsa-mun-tri
one/three	two	rt.: trident lt.: skull-cup filled with blood	mature	two		dhar. ornaments, va.: lotus throne	Tshang-ma
one/three	two	rt.: noose/snare lt.: lance	mature	two		red silk turban, cloak of red silk, dhar. ornaments, va.: red horse	Tsi-dmar-ba
one/three	two	rt.: red silk banner/flag lt.: btsan noose/snare	mature	two	astride	aigrette and vulture feather helmet,	Tsi'u-dmar-po

						dhar. ornaments, va.: black horse with white heels	
one/three	two	rt.: red lance with banner/flag lt.: red noose/snare	mature	two	astride	dhar. ornaments, high leather boots, va.: red horse	Tsi'u-dmar-po
one*/three	two	rt.: ritual chopper lt.: human skull-cup	mature, nude	two		*owl-head, dhar. ornaments, realm: South, va.: lotus throne	'Ug-pa'i-gdong-pa-can
one/three	two	rt.: chain lt.: tarjani mu.	mature	two		dhar. ornaments, va.: lotus throne	Vajrasphota
one/three	two	holds chain	mature	two		dhar. ornaments, va.: lotus throne	Vajrasrinkhala
one*/three	two	rt.: thunderbolt in tarjani mu. lt.: human skull-cup	mature, nude	two	ardha-paryanka	*pig-head near right ear, dhar. ornaments, magic staff/stick at rt. shoulder, va.: lotus throne	Vajravarahi
one*/three	two	rt.: knife lt.: human skull-cup	mature	two	ardha-paryanka	*pig-head near right ear, dhar. ornaments, va.: human corpse	Vajravarahi
one*/three	two	rt.: human skull-cup lt.: ritual chopper	mature	two	ardha-paryanka	*pig-head near right ear, magic staff/stick at rt. shoulder, dhar. ornaments, va.: lotus throne	Vajravarahi
one/three	two	rt.: thunderbolt lt.: human skull-cup, magic staff/stick at shoulder	mature	two	alidha	dhar. ornaments, va.: human corpse	Vajrayogini
one/three	two	plays flute	mature	two	pratyalidha	dhar. ornaments, va.: lotus throne	Vamsa
one*/three	two	rt.: goad/hook lt.: rosary of skulls	mature	two	ardha-paryankha	*lion-head, dhar. ornaments, va.: lotus throne	Varahamukhi
one/three	two	rt.: iron goad/hook	mature	two		dhar. ornaments,	Vasudhara

		lt.: fly whisk				va.: lotus throne	
one/three	two	rt.: ritual chopper, embraces shakti lt.: human skull-cup, embraces shakti	mature	two	alidha, yab-yum	dhar. ornaments, va.: lotus throne	Vidya-Dhara[6]
one*/two	two	rt.: serpent/snake lt.: pearl	mature	two	sattva	*angry, helmeted & armored, dhar. ornaments, va.: lotus throne	Virupaksa
one*/three	two	rt.: shrine lt.: karana mu.	mature	two	sattva	*angry, helmeted & armored, dhar. ornaments, va.: lotus throne	Virupaksa
one*/three	two	rt.: shrine lt.: serpent/snake	mature	two	sama- bhanga	*angry, helmeted & armored, dhar. ornaments, va.: lotus throne	Virupaksa
one*/three	two	rt.: ritual chopper lt.: human skull-cup	mature	two	alidha	*tiger-head, dhar. ornaments, va.: lotus throne	Vyaghravaktra
one*/three	two	rt.: axe lt.: wheel	mature	two	ardha- paryankha	*leopard-head, dhar. ornaments, va.: lotus throne	Vyaghravaktra
one*/three	two	rt.: human skull-drum lt.: divination arrow	corp.	two		*bull-head, dhar. ornaments, va.: lotus throne	Yama
one*/three	two	rt.: jewel lt.: human skull-cup	corp.	two	alidha	*bull-head, dhar. ornaments, va.: bull	Yama (gsang sgrub)
one/three	two	rt.: command staff/stick lt.: human skull-cup, embraces shakti	corp.	two	alidha	dhar. ornaments, va.: buffalo copulating with woman	Yamantaka
one/three	two	rt.: red throwing lance lt.: red noose/snare and human heart	mature	two	astride	leather helmet, va.: red horse	Yam-shud-dmar-po
one/three	two	rt.: throwing lance lt.: thunderbolt	corp.	two	astride	diadem of red silk and thunderbolts, dhar. ornaments,	Yam-shud-dmar-po

[6] The Vidya-Dhara , Knowledge Holding Deities who appear on the seventh day of the second state of the Bardo-Thodol. They are forms of the Dhyani Buddhas.

						va.: red horse	
one*/three	two	rt.: iron goad/hook lt.: mongoose	mature	two		*angry, dhar. ornaments, va.: lotus throne	Yi-'phrog-nor-rgyun-ma
one/three	two	rt.: battle lance lt.: noose/snare	mature	two		dhar. ornaments, va.: lotus throne	Yul-lha-rgyal-po-gzhon-nu
one/three	two	rt.: mirror lt.: victory banner/flag	mature	two		dhar. ornaments, va.: vixen of iron	Zangs-phreng-ma
one/three	two	rt.: lance lt.: magic dagger	mature	two	astride	leather hat with silk brim, leather harness and cloak, va.: horse	Zangs-phur-can-pa
one/three	two	rt.: red lance lt.: heart of an enemy	mature	two	astride	copper helmet, cuirass of copper, va.: red horses	Zangs-ri-btsan-rgod-mthu-chen-mched-gnyis
one/three	two	rt.: divination arrow lt.: flat bowl	mature	two		helmeted, clothed in red armor, va.: red horse	Zla-btsan-gnyan-po-tshe-bdang-rtsal
one/three	four	rt.: abhaya mu. and staff/stick lt.: flowering branch and lotus	corp.	two	alidha	dhar. ornaments, va.: lotus throne	Agni-bhayatrana (Avalokitesvara)**
one/three	four	rt.: karana mu., staff/stick lt.: wheel, lotus	mature	two	alidha	dhar. ornaments, va.: lotus throne	Anucara-Rakta-Hayagriva
one*/three	four	rt.: thunderbolt, goad/hook lt.: human skull-cup, tarjani	corp.	two	alidha	*sow's head from right ear, dhar. ornaments, magic staff/stick on rt. shoulder, va.: human forms	Aryavajravarahi
one/three	four	rt.: thunderbolt, abhaya mu. lt.: lotus, bell	corp.	two	alidha	dhar. ornaments, va.: lotus throne	Cora-bhayatrana (Avalokitesvara)**[7]
one/three	four	rt.: abhaya mu., trident lt.: lotus, staff/stick	corp.	two	alidha	dhar. ornaments, va.: lotus throne	Dakini-bhayatrana (Avalokitesvara)**
one/three	four	rt.: abhaya mu., goad/hook	corp.	two	alidha	dhar. ornaments,	Danda-bhayatrana-

[7] Lessing describes this deity as "Guhya-samaja the Adibuddha is the Lord of the mantras and the personification of the Mantrayana."

		lt.: lotus, noose/snare				va.: lotus throne	(Avalokitesvara)**
one/three	four	rt.: heart of an enemy,, noose/snare lt.: ritual chopper, sword	mature*	two		fire-clod garment, va.: red copper khyung	gNod-sbyin-dmar-nag
one/three	four	all hold a thread of thunderbolts	youth	two	ardha- paryanka	dhar. ornaments, va.: prostrate human forms	Guhyasadhana-Kurukulla
one/three	four	rt.: abhaya mu., flowering branch lt.: lotus, lotus bud	corp.	two	alidha	bodh. ornaments, va.: lotus throne	Hasti-bhayatrana (Avalokitesvara)**
one*/three	four	rt.: mace, "mystic mudra" lt.: flower, wheel	dwarfish	two	alidha	*horse-head in hair, dhar. ornaments, va.: lotus throne	Hayagriva
one/three	four	rt.: human skull-cup, cow's head lt.: hammer, trident	mature	two	alidha	dhar. ornaments, va.: horse	Kaladuti
one/three	four	rt.: ace, karana mu. lt.: abhaya mu., noose/snare	corp.	two	alidha	dhar. ornaments, va.: lotus throne	Krodha-Mahabala
one/three	four	rt.: black silken banner/flag , sword lt.: sack of diseases, noose/snare	mature	two		*orange color, dhar. ornaments	Kun-gyi-'jigs-byed
one/three	four	prin.: draws draw leafed bow & arrow rt.: goad/hook lt.: lotus	mature, nude	two	ardhad- paryanka	bodh. ornaments, va.: prostrate human forms lotus throne	Kurukulla
one/three	four	prin.: draws draw leafed bow & arrow rt.: goad/hook lt.: noose/snare	mature	two	ardhad- paryanka	bodh. ornaments, va.: lotus throne	Kurukulla
one/three	four	rt.: staff/stick, fly-whisk lt.: varada mu., tarjani mu.	mature	two	pratyalidha	dhar. ornaments, va.: human figures	Mahabala
one/three	four	rt.: karana mu., wheel lt.: noose/snare, abhaya mu.	corp.	two	alidha	dhar. ornaments, va.: lotus throne	Mahabalavajra
one/three	four	rt.: goad/hook, flaming ritual chopper lt.: skull-cup, trident	corp	two	alidha	dhar. ornaments, va.: lotus throne	mGon-po-dmar-po
one/three	four	prin.: draw flowered bow & arrow rt.: goad/hook of flowers lt.: red lotus	corp.	two	ardha- paryanka	dhar. ornaments, va.: human corpse	Oddiyana-Kurukulla
one/three	four	rt.: human skull-drum, ritual chopper	mature	two	alidha	dhar. ornaments,	Sarvabuddha-Dakini

		lt.: trident, human skull-cup				va.: lotus throne	
one/three	four	rt.: abhaya mu., jewels lt.: flowering branch, book/manuscript	corp.	two	alidha	dhar. ornaments, va.: lotus throne	Simha-bhayatrana (Avalokitesvara)**
one/three	four	rt.: sword, human skull-cup lt.: bow, arrow	mature, nude	two		dhar. ornaments, va.: lotus throne	Tsandika
one/three	four	prin.: bow, arrow 2nd pr.: goad/hook of flowers, red lotus	mature	two	ardha-paryanka	dhar. ornaments, va.: corpse	Uddiyana-Kurukulla
one*/three	four	rt.: thunderbolt, goad/hook lt.: human skull-cup, noose/snare in tarjani mu.	mature	two	ardha-paryanka	*pig-head near right ear, dhar. ornaments, va.: human corpse	Vajravarahi
one*/three	four	rt.: skull-cup, noose/snare lt.: elephant goad/hook, ritual chopper	mature	two	ardha-paryanka	*pig-head near right ear, dhar. ornaments, va.: lotus throne	Vajravarahi
one*/three	four	rt.: ritual chopper, human skull-drum lt.: trident, magic staff/stick of Padmasambhava	mature	two	ardha-paryanka	*pig-head near right ear, dhar. ornaments, va.: lotus throne	Vajravarahi
one/three	four	rt.: tantric staff, curved knife lt.: thunderbolt, club	mature	two		dhar. ornaments, va.: lotus throne	Vajrayogini
one*/three	four	rt.: goad/hook, needle lt.: noose/snare, Asoka bough	mature	two		*sow-head, dhar. ornaments, va.: lotus throne	Varttali
one/three	six	prin.: embrace shakti, ritual chopper, human skull-cup rt.: human skull-drum, goad hook lt.: snare/noose, trident	corp.	two	alidha, yab-yum	dhar. ornaments, va.: prostrate Ganesa form	Cintamani-Rakta-Mahakala
one/three	six	prin.: dharmachakra mu. with ritual chopper rt.: severed human head, goad/hook lt.: magic notched staff/stick, noose/snare	youth, nude	two	alidha	dhar. ornaments, va.: prostrate human form on lotus throne	Kavaca-Vajravarahi
one/three	six	tantric symbols	mature	two	ardhad-paryanka	bodh. ornaments, va.: corpse on lotus throne	Kurukulla
one/three	six	prin.: embrace shakti rt.: trident, sword	mature	two	pratyalidha, yab-yum	dhar. ornaments, va.: human figures	Mahabala

		lt.: jewel, lotus					
one/three	six	rt.: short staff/stick, sword, wheel lt.: noose/snare, battle axe, lotus	corp.	two	alidha	dhar. ornaments, va.: lotus throne	Mahabalavajra
one/three	six	prin.: hold trailokyavijaya mu 2nd pr.: hold kunda flower and abhaya mu. 3rd pr.: rosary, vase/vessel	mature	two	vajra	dhar. ornaments, va.: serpent Taksaka	Mayajalakrama-Kurukulla
one/three	six	prin.: embrace shakti with ritual chopper, skull-cup rt.: small drum, trident lt.: iron goad/hook, noose/snare	corp.	two	alidha	dhar. ornaments, va.: lotus throne	mGon-dmar-dbang-gi-rgyal-po
one/three	six	rt.: axe, staff/stick, sword (?) lt.: noose/snare embracing shakti, human skull-cup, tarjani mu.	corp.	two	alidha, yab-yum	dhar. ornaments, va.: prostrate human figures	Rakta-Acala
one/three	six	rt.: thunderbolt, sword, wheel lt.: skull-cup, jewel, lotus	mature	two	ardha-paryanka	dhar. ornaments, va.: corpse	Vajracarcika
one*/three	ten	holds war-like attributes	mature	two		*angry, dhar. ornaments, va.: lotus throne	Marici
two/six	two	rt.: thunderbolt lt.: staff/stick	dwarfish	two		dhar. ornaments, va.: the world	Saptasatika-Hayagriva
three*/six	six	rt.: lotus, flaming jewels and sword lt.: vase/vessel, axe and jewel	mature, nude	four	alidha	*rt. head: pig, cent. head: elephant. lt. head: human, va.: goddess on lotus throne	Ajna-vinivarta-Ganapati
three/nine	four	prin. draw bow and arrow rt.: thunderbolt lt.: lotus	corp.	two	alidha	dhar. ornaments, va.: human forms	Arya-(Atisa)-krama-Caturdakini-parivara-Hayagriva
three/nine	four	prin.: hold bow and arrow rt.: thunderbolt lt.: lotus	corp	two	alidha	horsehead over brows dhar. ornaments, va.: lotus throne	Atisha-Hayagriva**
three*/nine	four	rt.: thunderbolt, flower lt.: bow, arrow	dwarfish	two	alidha	*horse-head in hair, dhar. ornaments, va.: demons on lotus throne	Hayagriva

three/nine	six	rt.: thunderbolt, noose/snare, short staff/stick lt.: human skull-cup, sword, tarjani mu.	corp.	two	alidha	dhar. ornaments, va.: human forms	Arya-(Atisa)-krama-Garudapaksavat-Hayagriva
three*/nine	six	holding lotus, pestle, sword, axe, noose/snare, tarjani mu.	mature	two		*yw., wh., & rd. dhar. ornaments, va.: lotus throne	bDe-sgrub-ma
three/nine	six	prin.: human skull-cup and ritual chopper and embrace shakti rt.: sword. (?) lt.: branch and flaming jewel	corp.	two	alidha, yab-yum	dhar. ornaments, lotus throne	Carcika (fo-mu)
three*/nine	six	rt.: thunderbolt in karana mudra, trident, sword lt.: karana mudra, lance, noose/snare	mature	two	alidha	dhar. ornaments, va.: lotus throne	Guhya-Sadhana Hayagriva**
three*/nine	six	rt.: thunderbolt, trident, mace, lt.: flower, wheel, "mystic mudra"	dwarfish	two or four	alidha	*wh., rd., gr., *3 horse-heads in hair, dhar. ornaments, va.: lotus throne	Hayagriva
three*/nine	six	rt.: thunderbolt, noose/snare, trident lt.: sword, banner/flag, flame	dwarfish	eight	alidha	*wh., rd., gr., *3 horse-heads in hair, dhar. ornaments, va.:nagas on lotus throne	Hayagriva
three*/nine	six	rt.: crossred thunderbolt, sword, mace lt.: magic staff/stick, human skull-cup, "mystic mudra"	dwarfish	eight	alidha yab-yum	*wh., rd., gr., *3 horse-heads in hair, dhar. ornaments, va.:nagas on lotus throne	Hayagriva
three*/nine	six	prin.: embrace shakti rt.: lotus, jewel lt.: sword, wheel	dwarfish	two	alidha	*horse-head missing dhar. ornaments, va.: lotus throne	Hayagriva
three*/nine	six	rt.: sword, thunderbolt, mace lt.: bell, axe, noose/snare	corp	two	alidha	*horse in hair, dhar. ornaments, va.: lotus throne	Hayagrivavajra
three/nine	six	prin.: embrace shakti with lotus, human skull-cup rt.: vajra-tipped goad/hook, mirror(?) lt.: noose/snare, sword	corp.	two	yab-yum	dhar. ornaments, va.: prostrate human forms on lotus throne	Kruddha-atiguhya-Hayagriva
three/nine	six	prin.: embrace shakti	mature	two	alidha,	dhar. ornaments,	Mahabala

		rt.: trident, jewel lt.: sword, lotus			yab-yum	va.: human figures	
three/nine	six	rt.: lotus, trident, club lt.: bell, human skull-cup, small drum	mature	two	pratyalidha, yab-yum	dhar. ornaments, va.: lotus throne	Padma-Heruka
three/nine	six	prin.: embrace shakti with ritual chopper & human skull-cup rt.: lotus, sword lt.: flaming jewel, lotus	corp.	two	partyalidha, yab-yum	dhar. ornaments, va.: lotus throne	Padmantaka
three/nine	six	prin.: embrace shakti with ritual chopper & human skull-cup rt.: red lotus, sword lt.: jewel, wheel	corp.	two	partyalidha, yab-yum	dhar. ornaments, va.: lotus throne	Padmantaka
three/nine	six	rt.: goad/hook, sword, thunderbolt lt.: pestle, axe, tarjani mu.	mature	two	alidha	*rd., wh., bk., dhar. ornaments, va.: lotus throne	rDo-rje-lcags-kyu-ma
three/nine	six	rt.: thunderbolt, trident, sword lt.: tarjani mu., lance, bowels (?)	corp.	eight	ardha- paryanka	dhar. ornaments, va.: serpent/snakes	Sadbhuja-Hayagriva
three/nine	six	rt.: book/manuscript, sword, ritual chopper lt.: Brahmakapala, prayer rolls, wheel	mature	two		bodh. ornaments, va.: lotus throne	Sarasvati
three*/nine	six	rt.: thunderbolt, magic staff/stick, sword lt.: (?), lance, noose/snare	corp.	two	alidha	horse head in hair, dhar. ornaments, va.: prostrate human body	sKyer-sgan-lugs-Hayagriva
three*/nine	eight	rt.: thunderbolt, lotus, bow, "mystic mudra" lt.: mace, arrow, flower, and "mystic mudra"	dwarfish	two	alidha	*horse-head in hair, *wh., rd., bl., dhar. ornaments, va.: lotus throne	Hayagriva
three*/nine	eight	prin.: embrace shakti rt.: wheel, axe, flower, lt.: sword, noose/snare, skull-cup	mature	four	alidha, yab-yum	*horse head in hair, dhar. ornaments, va.: human form	Krodha-Hayagriva
three/nine	eight	rt.: goad/hook, arrow, thunderbolt, (?) lt.: noose/snare, bow, karana mu., (?)	corp.	two	alidha	dhar. ornaments, va.: prostrate human bodies	Marici (fo-mu)
three/nine	eight	embrace sakti in vajrahumkara mu. rt. & lt. tantric symbols	corp.	two	alidha, yab-yum	dhar. ornaments, va.: lotus throne	Padmanartesvara-Hayagriva**

three/nine	eight	rt.: thunderbolt, noose/snare, severed human head, trident lt.: magic staff/stick, human skull-cup, human figure, rosary	mature	two	ardha-paryanka	dhar. ornaments, va.: lotus throne	Raktapa (=Heruka)
three/nine	eight	rt.: sword, staff/stick, (?), (?) lt.: lotus, bow, arrow, (?)	mature	two	alidha	dhar. ornaments, va.: prostrate human forms	Trimukhastabhuja-rakta-Hayagrivavajra
three/nine	12	tantric symbols	corp.	two	alidha	dhar. ornaments, va.: lotus throne	Pancamukhadvadasabhuja-krsna-Avalokitesvara (Bodhisattva)**
three*/nine	12	rt.: needle, goad/hook, lance, sword, knife, staff/stick lt.: tarjani mu., Asoka bough, vajra-topped goad/hook, skull-cup, head of Brahma, vase/vessel	mature	two	alidha	*two are sow-like, dhar. ornaments, va.: Hara, Hari and Brahma	Ubhayavarahanana-Marici
three*/nine	16	rt.: thunderbolt, wheel, jewel, lotus, sword, noose/snare, arrow, battle axe lt.: bell, trident, mongoose, flower ornament, circular banner, skull-cup, bow, whisk	mature	two		*yw., bl., wh., snakes and jewels, va.: lotus throne	Sras-gar-mkhan-mchog
three/nine	18	prin.: shallow bowl rt.: banner/flag of victory, club, sword, arrow, trident, hammer, citron, red lance lt.: mongoose, serpent/snake noose/snare, wheel, noose/snare bow, vase/vessel, mountain, twig	mature	two	astride	*angry richly armored, dhar. ornaments, va.: dragon	Nartakavara-Rakta-Vaisravana
four/12	two	rt.: goad/hook tearing heart from an enemy's body, noose/snare with enemy lt.: bone rosary, vessel of Tibetan beer	mature	two	alidha	dhar. ornaments, va.: human form	Vasamkara-Rakta-Caturmukha-(Sri-Mahakala)
four/12	four	rt.: sword, ritual chopper lt.: vase/vessel, human skull-cup	corp	two	alidha	dhar. ornaments, va.: lotus throne	Caturmukhastabhuja-Hayagrivavajra**
four/12	four	rt.: goad/hook, rosary lt.: vase/vessel, noose/snare	mature	two	alidha	dhar. ornaments, va.: lotus throne	Vasamkara-Rakta-Caturmukha-(Sri-Mahakala)
four/12	eight	rt.: thunderbolt, short staff/stick, vitarka mu., spiral short staff/stick,	corp.	two	alidha	dhar. ornaments, va.: lotus throne	Caturmukhastabhuja-Hayagrivavajra**

		lt.: karana mu., lotus, vitarka mu. noose/snare					
four*/12	eight	rt.: crossed thunderbolts, sword, arrow, tripataka mu. lt.: staff/stick with double lotus, dart, skull topped staff/stick, bow	mature	two	partyalidha	*one is horse-like, dhar. ornaments, va.: four Hindu gods & four Hindu goddesses	Paramasva
four/12	16	prin.: embrace shakti all hands hold human skull-cups	mature	two	alidha, yab-yum	dhar. ornaments, va.: lotus throne	Padma-Dakini (fo-mu)
five/15	six	prin.: casque of jewels 2nd pr.: wheel and fruit 3rd pr.: vase/vessel of medicine	mature	two	astride	richly armored, high fancy boots, va.: caprisoned horse (?)	'Brog-gnas
six/18	12	tantric symbols	mature	two		*rd., bl., gr., yw., wh., sow-head, dhar. ornaments, va.: seven pigs	Marici
nine*/27	two	prin.: staff/stick, lake of blood other hands hold tantric symbols	corp.	two	alidha	*1st row 3 dk. gr., 2nd row 3 pu., 3rd row gr, rd., wh., dhar. ornaments, va.: dragon	Rahu
nine/27	two	rt.: staff/stick lt.: lake of blood	mature	two		dhar. ornaments, va.: lotus throne	Yab-gcig-yaksa-dzva-la
nine/27	two	rt.: lake of blood lt.: snake noose/snare	mature	two		dhar. ornaments, realm: West, va.: lotus throne	Yum-rdo-rje-glog-'gyu(ma)
nine/27	four	rt.: arrow, cylindrical banner/flag lt.: bow, serpent/snake	corp.	two		body covered with eyes, dhar. ornaments, va.: ocean waves	Rahu

Blue (Skt.: nila; Tib.: sngon-po), Calm Deities

Abbreviations:

as. = asana | bk. = black | bl. = blue | bodh. = bodhisattva
bn. = brown | corp. = corpulent | dhar. = dharmapala | gn. = green
lt. = left | mu. = mudra | pu. = purple | rd. = red
rt. = right | sc. = smokey | va. = vahana | wh. = white
yw. = yellow

(*) special variations or attributes noted within the entry.
(**) following deity's name indicates that the color is not noted in the source, kulesa's color is applied to the entry.
(eyes: 2-3, 6-9, etc.) in sources the deity's faces are noted, but the number of the eyes are not noted.

Head/Eyes	Hands	Objects Held	Body	Feet	Asana	Other Attributes	Deity Name
one/two	two	vajrahumkara mudra embracing nude shakti	mature nude	two	vajra, yab-yum		Adi-Buddha (Samantabhadra)
one/two	two	rt.: crossed thunderbolt at chest lt.: bell at hip	mature	two	vajra	bodh. ornaments, va.: lotus throne	Adi-Buddha (Dharmavajra)**
one/two	two	rt.: bhumisparsa mu. lt.: dhyani mu. with thunderbolt	mature	two	vajra	Buddha-like, va.: pair of elephants	Dhyani Buddha Aksobhya
one/two	two	rt.: bhumisparsa mu. lt.: dhyani mu.	mature	two	vajra	bodh. ornaments, va.: lotus throne	Aksobhya
one/two	two	rt.: bell lt.: thunderbolt	mature	two	dhyana, yab-yum	bodh. ornaments, va.: pair of elephants shakti: Locana	Aksobhya
one/two	two	rt.: thunderbolt lt.: bell	mature	two	dhyana, yab-yum	bodh. ornaments, va.: pair of elephants shakti: Mamaki	Aksobhya
one/two	two	rt.: thunderbolt lt.: stem of lotus	mature	two	vamalalita	bodh. ornaments, va.: lotus throne	Acala (fo-mu)
one/two	two	rt.: sword lt.: noose/snare	mature	two	sattva	bodh. ornaments, va.: lotus throne	Aksobhyavajra
one/two	two	rt.: medicinal arura or myrobalam plant in varada mu. lt.: iron alms bowl with the plant	mature	two	dhyana	Buddha-like, monastic robes, va.: lotus throne	Bhaisajyaguru

one/two	two	rt.: medicinal arura or myrobalam plant in varada mu. lt.: iron alms bowl with the plant	mature	two	dhyana	bodh. ornaments, va.: lotus throne	Bhaisajyaguru
one/two	two	rt.: abhaya mu. with myrobalam lt.: dhyana mu. with alms bowl	mature	two	vajra	Buddha-like, monastic robes, va.: lotus throne	Bhaisajyagurutathagata Buddha**
one/two	two	dhyana mu.	mature	two	vajra	bodh. ornaments, va.: lotus throne	Bhutadamara
one/two	two	rt.: thunderbolt lt.: book/manuscript	youth	two	vamalalita	bodh. ornaments, va.: lotus throne	Dharmamegha
one/two	two	rt.: thunderbolt lt.: (?)	youth, bare breasted	two	vamalalita	bodh. ornaments, va.: lotus throne	Dharmamegha (fo-mu)**
one/two	two	rt.: banner/flag lt.: wish fulfilling jewel	mature	two		bodh. ornaments, va.: human form on lotus throne	Dhvajosnisa
one/two	two	rt.: banner/flag with wish fulfilling jewel lt.: white lotus	mature	two		bodh. ornaments, va.: lotus throne	Dhyanaparamita
one/two	two	rt.: (?) with lotus at right shoulder lt.: dhyana mu.	mature	two	vamalalita	bodh. ornaments, va.: lotus throne	Dhyanaparamita
one/two	two	rt.: light stick	mature	two	alidha	bodh. ornaments, va.: lotus throne	Dipa
one/two	two	rt.: ritual chopper lt.: human skull-cup	youth	two	lalita	bodh. ornaments, va.: lotus throne	Dvibhuja-Ekajata (fo-mu)
one/two	two	rt.: thunderbolt lt.: human skull-cup	youth	two	ardha- paryanka	bodh. ornaments, va.: prostrate human figure	Dvibhuja-Heruka
one/two	two	embraces shakti in vajrahumkara mu.	mature	two	alidha	dhar. ornaments, va.: prostrate human figures on lotus throne	Dvibhuja-Samvara**
one/two	two	rt.: stem of lotus with thunderbolt in vitarka mu. lt.: varada mu.	mature	two	lalita	bodh. ornaments, va.: lotus throne	Guhyapati-Vajradhara**
one/two	two	dharmachakra mu.	mature	two	sattva	bodh. ornaments,	Hastivahana-Samantabhadra

						va.: elephant on lotus throne	
one/two	two	holds bow in lap	mature	two	sattva	bodh. ornaments, va.: lotus throne	Jaya-(devi)
one*/two	two	rt.: lotus lt.: sword	youth	two		*pale blue, bodh. ornaments, va.: lotus throne	Inana-Vasita
one/two	two	rt.: vitarka mu. lt.: lotus	mature	two	vajra	bodh. ornaments, va.: lotus throne	Karmavajra
one/two	two	rt.: holds stem of lotus with thunderbolt lt.: holds stem of lotus with thunderbolt	mature	two	lalita	bodh. ornaments va.: lotus throne	Locana
one/two	two	vajrahumkara mu.	mature	two	vajra	bodh. ornaments, va.: lotus throne	Mahavajradhara
one/two	two	rt.: stem of lotus with human skull-cup lt.: stem of lotus with thunderbolt	youth	two	vamalalita	bodh. ornaments, va.: lotus throne	Mamaki
one/two	two	holding a crown	youth	two	vamalalita	bodh. ornaments, va.: lotus throne	Mamaki (fo-mu)
one/two	two	rt.: thunderbolt lt.: thunderbolt	youth	two	sattva	bodh. ornaments, va.: lotus throne	Mamaki (fo-mu)
one/two	two	holding gandaharan temborin-in mu.	youth	two	vamalalita	bodh. ornaments, va.: lotus throne	Nila-Tara (fo-mu)
one/two	two	holding lotus between the palms	youth	two	sattva	bodh. ornaments, va.: lotus throne	Nila-Tara (fo-mu)
one/two	two	holding a scarf	youth	two	ardha-paryanka	bodh. ornaments, va.: lotus throne	Nrtya
one/two	two	held above head holding thunderbolts	youth	two	sattva	bodh. ornaments, va.: lotus throne	Nrtya (fo-mu)
one/two	two	rt.: red lotus with Kamasastra lt.: Kamasastra book on bluelotus	youth	two	padma	bodh. ornaments, va.: lotus throne	Prajna-Paramita
one/two	two	rt.: banner/flagwith wish fulfilling jewel lt.: sword on lotus	mature	two		bodh. ornaments, va.: lotus throne	Pranidhana-Paramita
one/two	two	rt.: (?)	mature	two	vamalalita	bodh. ornaments,	Pranidhana-Paramita

		lt.: sword				va.: lotus throne	
one/two	two	holding cymbals over head	youth	two	astride	bejeweled, long loose robe, va.: stag	rDo-rje-g.ya'-ma-skyong
one/two	two	rt.: flaming jewels lt.: abhaya	youth	two	sopasraya	bodh. ornaments, va.: lotus throne	Sarvanivaranaviskambhi (devi)**
one/two	two	rt.: staff/stick with banner/flag lt.: large jewel filled bowl	youth	two	sopasraya	bodh. ornaments, va.: lotus throne	Sridevi
one/two	two	rt.: thunderbolt lt.: bell on thigh	youth	two	vajra	bodh. ornaments, va.: lotus throne	Syama-nila-Vajravidarana
one/two	two	rt.: divination arrow lt.: divination mirror	mature	two		bejeweled, dress of white silk, va.: Asiatic wild ass	Sumukhi
one/two	two	holds book/manuscript	mature	two	sama- bhanga	buddha-like, monastic robed, va.: lotus throne	Tiryagloka
one/two	two	holds buppatsu-in mu.	mature	two	sattva	bodh. ornaments, va.: lotus throne	Trailokyavijaya (Bodhisattva)**
one/two	two	rt.: goad/hook lt.: abhaya mu.	youth	two	sattva	bodh. ornaments, va.: lotus throne	Uma (devi)
one/two	two	holds vajrahumkara mu.	youth	two	dhyana	bodh. ornaments, va.: lotus throne	Vajradhara
one/two	two	rt.: thunderbolt lt.: bell	youth	two	dhyana	bodh. ornaments, va.: lotus throne	Vajradhara
one/two	two	embraces shakti in vajrahumkara mu.	youth	two	dhyana, yab-yum	bodh. ornaments, va.: lotus throne	Vajradhara
one/two	two	rt.: thunderbolt lt.: book/manuscript	youth	two	dhyana	bodh. ornaments, va.: lotus throne	Vajragarbha
one/two	two	rt.: blue lotus lt.: rests on hip with clenched fist	youth	two	dhyana	bodh. ornaments, va.: lotus throne	Vajragarbha
one/two	two	rt.: crossed thunderbolts lt.: dhyana mu.	youth	two	sattva	bodh. ornaments, va.: lotus throne	Vajragarbha

one/two	two	rt.: thunderbolt lt.: bell	youth	two	sattva	bodh. ornaments, va.: lotus throne	Vajrasadhu
one/two	two	rt.: vismaya mu. with thunderbolt lt.: thunderbolt	youth	two	vajra	bodh. ornaments, va.: lotus throne	Vajrasadhu (Bodhisattva)**
one/two	two	rt.: crossed thunderbolts lt.: bell	youth	two	vajra	bodh. ornaments, va.: lotus throne	Vajravidarani
one/two	two	holds goad/hook	youth	two	sattva	bodh. ornaments, va.: lotus throne	Varahi (devi)
one/two	two	rt.: sword lt.: skull-cup	youth, nude	two	astride	bodh. ornaments, va.: golden mule	Vasanta-devi
one/two	two	dharmachakra mu., embracves shakti	youth, nude	two	dhyana	Buddha-like, va.: lotus throne	Yogambara (Adi-Buddha)
one/two	four	rt.: thunderbolt, varada mu. lt.: battle axe, noose/snare	mature	two	vajra	bodh. ornaments, attribute: the syllable "hum," va.: lotus throne	Mahamantranusarini
one/two	eight	prin. hands embrace shakti rt.: thunderbolt, wheel and lotus lt.: bell, jewel and sword	mature	two	vajra-paryanka, yab-yum	bodh. ornaments, va.: pair of elephants shakti: Mamaki or Locana	Aksobhya
one/three	two	rt.: cylindrical banner/flag lt.: sun disc	mature	two	astride	long loose robe, bodh. ornaments, va.: dragon	rDo-rje-kun-grags-ma
one/three	two	rt.: thunderbolt lt.: abhaya	youth	two	vira	bodh. ornaments, va.: lotus throne	Santa-Vajrapani
one/three	four	rt.: sword, ritual chopper lt.: blue lotus, human skull-cup	mature	two	pratyalidha	all hands hold tiger-skin cape, bodh. ornaments, va.: corpse	Mahacina-Tara
one/three	six	rt.: sword, goad/hook, varada mu. lt.: tarjani mu. with noose/snare, red lotus, trident	mature	two	vajra	bodh. ornaments, va.: lotus throne	Mahapratyangira
one/three	six	rt.: sword, goad/hook, varada mu. lt.: wheel, red lotus, trident	mature	two	alidha	bodh. ornaments, va.: lotus throne	Mahapratyangira

three/six	two	holds flaming wheel in dhyana mu.	youth	two		bodh. ornaments, va.: lotus throne	Sarvavid-Vairocana (Buddha)**
three/six	six	prin.: vajrahumkara mu. embracing shakti rt.: lotus, wheel lt.: sword, flaming jewel	mature	two	vajra	bodh. ornaments, va.: lotus throne	Guhya-Aksobhyavajra Buddha
three/six	six	prin.: embrace shakti in vajrahumkara mu. rt.: wheel, lotus lt.: jewel, sword	mature	two	vajra, yab-yum	bodh. ornaments, va.: lotus throne	Guhyasamaja-Aksobhya**
three/six	six	prin.: embrace shakti in vajrahumkara mu. rt.: wheel, lotus lt.: jewel, sword	mature	two	vajra, yab-yum	bodh. ornaments, va.: lotus throne	Guhyasamaja-Aksobhyavajra (Buddha)**
three/six	six	prin.: embrace shakti in vajrahumakra mu. rt.: sword, arrow lt.: lotus, bow	mature	two	vajra, yab-yum	bodh. ornaments, va.: lotus throne	Sahaja-Guhyasamaja**
three/six	six	prin.: embrace shakti with vajrahumkara rt.: sword, goad/hook lt.: noose/snare, human skull-cup	youth	two	lalita, yab-yum	bodh. ornaments, va.: lotus throne	Vajrasattva-Samvara**
three*/six	six	prin.: thunderbolt, thunderbolt marked bell rt.: (?), arrow lt.: lotus bow[1], bow	mature	two	vajra	*haughty, bodh. ornaments, va.: lotus throne	Yogambara (Buddha)
three/six	12	prin.: dharmachakra mu. 2nd pair: dhyana mu. rt.: thunderbolt, arrow, varada mu., abhaya mu. lt.: noose/snare in tarjani mu., bow, jewel, jar	mature	two	vajra	bodh. ornaments, va.: lotus throne	Mahamantranusarini
three/6-9	six	prin.: embrace shakti in vajrahumkara mu. rt.: wheel, vitarka mu. lt.: sword, karana mu.	mature	two	vajra, yab-yum	bodh. ornaments va.: lotus throne	Guhya-Vajraksobhya Buddha**
three*/6-9	six	rt.: lotus, mirror, axe lt.: noose/snare, pestle, tarjani mu.	mature	two		*bl., wh., rd., bodh. ornaments,	rDo-rje-bdud-rtsi-ma

						va.: lotus throne	
three/nine	four	prin.: embrace shakti rt.: (?) lt.: magic notched staff/stick	mature	two	ardha-paryanka, yab-yum	bodh. ornaments, va.: lotus throne	<u>Mahamayavajra (Buddha)</u>
three*/nine	six	hands hold lotus, image of Buddha, sword, axe, noose/snare and tarjani mu.	mature	two		*smiling-bl., wh., rd., bodh. ornaments (?), va.: lotus throne	<u>bDud-rtsi-lus-can-ma</u>
three/nine	six	prin.: embrace shakti in vajrahumkara mu. rt.: wish fulfilling jewel, wheel lt.: sword, jewel	mature	two	yab-yum	bodh. ornaments va.: lotus throne	<u>Guhya-pati</u>
three/nine	six	prin.: vajrahumkara mu. embracing shakti rt.: wheel, lotus lt.: sword, jewel	mature	two	padma, yab-yum	bodh. ornaments, va.: lotus throne	<u>Guhya-samaja</u>
four/eight	two	holds wheel in dhyana mu.	youth	two	vajra	bodh. ornaments, va.: lotus throne	<u>Sarvavid-Vairocana</u>**
four/eight	four	prin.: embrace shakti with human skull-cups rt.: bow lt.: arrow	mature	two	yab-yum	bodh. ornaments, va.: lotus throne	<u>Mahamaya</u>
four/eight	eight	rt.: thunderbolt, sword, wheel, arrow lt.: bell, bow, noose/snare, magic staff/stick	youth	two	alidha	bodh. ornaments, va.: Vishnu and his wife	<u>Vajravalanalarka</u>

[8] Although "syama" is green, the term is also used to describe "dark" colored deities as well.

Blue (Skt.: nila; Tib.: sngon-po), Wrathful, Angry or Haughty Deities

Abbreviations:

as. = asana
bn. = brown
lt. = left
rt. = right
yw. = yellow
bk. = black
corp. = corpulent
mu. = mudra
sc. = smokey
bl. = blue
dhar. = dharmapala
pu. = purple
va. = vahana
bodh. = bodhisattva
gn. = green
rd. = red
wh. = white

(*) special variations or attributes noted within the entry.
(**) following deity's name indicates that the color is not noted in the source, kulesa's color is applied to the entry.
(eyes: 2-3, 6-9, etc.) in sources the deity's faces are noted, but the number of the eyes are not noted.

Head/Eyes	Hands	Objects Held	Body	Feet	Asana	Other Attributes	Deity Name
one*/one	two	rt.: heart of enemies lt.: turquoise falcon	mature	two		*one eye, one tooth, dhar. ornaments, va.: pedestal of earth	Ekajati-Devi
one/one	two	rt.: heart of enemy lt.: turquoise falcon	emaciat- ed	one		single tooth, va.: pedestal of earth	lHa-mo-ekajati-ral-gcig-ma
one*/one	two	no attributes noted	mature**	one		*one tooth, single tuft of hair, **one emaciated breast, dhar. ornaments, va.: brown flaming- triangular mandala	Ral-gCig-ma
one*/two	two	rt.: staff/stick with skull finial lt.: noose/snare	mature nude, erect phallus	two	pratyalidha	*bull's head, dhar. ornaments, va.: bull in intercourse with woman	Bahya-Sadhana Dharmaraja
one*/two	two	wing-form	bird-like	two		*horned, clawed feet holding censor, realm: left hip	bDug-spos-kyi-khyung
one*/two	two	rt.: magic throwing staff/stick lt.: human heart	mature	two		*dark blue dhar. ornaments,	Bhadra-nag-po
one*/two	two	holding treasure casque and iron	mature	two		*angry,	bsTan-bsrung-mdzad-gnod-sbyin-

		lance with banner/flag					thunderbolt shell armor, va.: khyung	mched-lnga
one*/two	two	playing stringed instrument	mature	two	sama-bhanga	*haughty richly armored, fancy boots, va.: lotus throne	Dhritarastra/Dhrtarastra
one*/two	two*	feet holds censor	bird-like	two, bird-like		*bird-head, wings, claws, realm: left hip	bDug-spos-kyi-khyung
one*/two	two	rt.: ritual dagger lt.: abhaya mu.	mature	two	lalita	*haughty, long swept-back hair, loose robe; va.: lotus throne	Durdharsha
one/two	two	embraces shakti in vajrahumkara mu.	mature	two	alidha	dhar. ornaments, va.: prostrate human figures on lotus throne	Dvibhuja-Samvara**
one*/two	two	tearing open a corpse	mature	two	alidha	*wolf-head, dhar. ornaments	Htamenma, "Dark Blue Wolf-headed One"
one*/two	two	rt.: thunderbolt lt.: sword	mature	two	alidha	*owl-head, dhar. ornaments	Htamenma, "Dark-Blue Owl-Headed One
one*/two	two	rt.: sword lt.: black banner/flag	mature	two		*angry, bodh. ornaments, va.: lotus throne	Gang-ba-bzang-po
one*/two	two	holding wheel	mature	two	alidha	*monkey-head, dhar. ornaments	Ishvari, "Blue Monkey-headed Goddess of Inquisitiveness"
one*/two	two	holding banner/flag	mature	two	alidha	*wolf-head, dhar. ornaments	Ishvari, "Blue Wolf-Headed Wind-Goddess"
one*/two	two	holding noose/snare	mature	two	alidha	*serpent-head, dhar. ornaments	Ishvari, "Blue Serpent-Headed Water-Goddess"
one*/ two	two	rt.: sword lt.: noose/snare around the neck of a human	mature	two	vamalalita	*angry, richly helmeted, loose agrments, va.: horse	Kayaraja
one*/ two	two	rt.: thunderbolt lt.: alarm staff/stick	mature	two	vamalalita	*angry, richly helmeted,	Kayaraja

						loose agrments, va.: yellow horse	
one*/ two	two	rt.: thunderbolt lt.: alarm staff/stick	mature	two	vamalalita	*angry, richly helmeted, loose agrments, va.: blue lion	Kayaraja
one*/two	two	rt.: flaming jewel lt.: sack of jewels	mature	two	astride	*angry, turquoise armor, va.: blue horse of water spirits	kLu-chen-rgyal-po
one*/two	two	rt.: ritual chopper lt.: heart of an enemy of religion	mature,	two		*angry, dark silk cloak, va.: lion	Mahadeva
one*/two	two	rt.: sword lt.: skin of an elephant head	mature	two	aseat	*angry, richly garbed, va.: elephant	Virudhaka
one*/two	two	rt.: sword lt.: vitarka mu.	mature	two	sattva	*angry, richly garbed, va.: lotus throne	Virudhaka
one*/two	two	rt.: sword lt.: karana mu.	mature	two	sama-bhanga	*angry, richly garbed, va.: lotus throne	Virudhaka
one/2-3	two	rt.: magic throwing staff/stick lt.: skull-cup	mature	two	(yab/yum as Pe-har's shakti)	dark blue fur cloak	bDud-gza'-smin-dkar-mo
one*/2-3	two	rt.: magic throwing staff/stick lt.: human heart	mature	two		*angry, breast-band of black silk and a tiger skin	Bhadra-nag-po
one*/2-3	two	holding *kha-tram* and human skull-cup	mature	two		*dark blue, black silk garment, va.: elephant	bTsun-mo-uma-devi
one*/2-3	two	rt.: ritual chopper lt.: human skull-cup	mature, nude	two	alidha	*head of a bull, erect phallus, dhar. ornaments, va.: bull	Chos-rGyal-gSang-sGrub**
one*/2-3	two	rt.: knife	mature	two		*angry,	Chos-skyon

		lt.: noose/snare				fancy boots, va.: white elephant	
one*/2-3	two	rt.: knife lt.: noose/snare	mature	two		*angry, fancy boots, va.: yellow lion	Chos-skyon
one/2-3	two	rt.: noose/snare lt.: reins of mule	mature	two	astride	dhar. ornaments, syllable "bhyo", va.: mule	Chu-srin-gdong-can
one/2-3	two	rt.: magic notched stick lt.: human skull-cup filled with blood	mature, nude	two		dhar. ornaments, attrib.: syllable "bhyo", va.: camel	dGun-gyi-rgyal-mo
one/2-3	two	rt.: baton-like staff/stick lt.: human skull-cup filled with blood	mature, nude	two	astride	dhar. ornaments, va.: camel	dGun-gyi-rgyal-mo
one*/2-3	two	rt.: ritual chopper human skull-cup	youth	two	lalita	*angry, bodh. ornaments, va.: lotus throne	Ekajata (devi)
one*/2-3	two	rt.: ritual chopper lt.: bowl	mature, winged	two		*head of a bird, va.: dying Naga	Garuda
one*/2-3	two	rt.: sword lt.: gourd-shaped bottle	mature, winged	two		*head of a bird, va.: dying Naga	Garuda
one*/2-3	two	in namaskara mu.	mature, winged	two		*head of a bird, va.: dying Naga	Garuda
one*/2-3	two	holding snake noose/snare	mature	two	astride	*snake-head, dhar. ornaments, va.: dragon	gCer-bu-lag-rdum
one*/2-3	two	rt.: sword lt.: noose/snare	youth	two		*angry, va.: kyang	Ha-ri-rdo-rje-ya-ma
one/2-3	two	rt.: ritual chopper lt.: human skull-cup	mature	two	ardha-paryanka	dhar. ornaments, va.: lotus throne	Kamini
one/2-3	two	rt.: ritual chopper lt.: human skull-cup	mature	two	ardha-paryanka	dhar. ornaments, va.: lotus throne	Karini
one/three	two	rt.: sword lt.: jnana mu.	corp.	two	kneeling	dhar. ornaments, va.: human forms	Acala

one/three	two	rt.: sword lt.: karana mu.	corp.	two	alidha	dhar. ornaments, va.: human forms	Acala
one/three	two	rt.: thunderbolt lt.: noose/snare	corp.	two	pratyalidha	dhar. ornaments, va.: lotus throne	Acarya-Vajrapani
one/three	two	rt.: ritual chopper lt.: human skull-cup	mature	two	ardha- paryanka	dhar. ornaments, va.: lotus throne, realm: North	Ajaya
one/three	two	rt.: ritual chopper lt.: human skull-cup, with tantric staff/stick in crook of arm	corp.	two	partyalidha	dhar. ornaments, va.: human forms	Ajita-Mahakala**
one/three	two	rt.: thunderbolt lt.: noose/snare	corp.	two	alidha	dhar. ornaments, va.: lotus throne	Alpacanda-Vajrapani**
one/three	two	rt.: thunderbolt lt.: bell	corp.	two	alidha	dhar. ornaments, va.: lotus throne	Amoghatrana(?)-Vajrapani**
one/three	two	rt.: sandal-wood club lt.: human skull-cup	corp	two	alidha	dhar. ornaments, va.: lotus throne	Anghora-Mahakala
one/three	two	rt.: sandal-wood staff/stick lt.: human skull-cup	corp	two	alidha	dhar. ornaments, va.: human forms	Anghora-Mahakala
one/three	two	rt.: ritual chopper lt.: human skull-cup	corp	two	alidha	dhar. ornaments, va.: human form	Antara-Sadhana Dharmaraja**
one/three	two	rt.: ritual chopper lt.: human skull-cup	youth	two	vamalalita	dhar. ornaments, va.: lotus throne	Anucara-Ekajata
one*/three	two	rt.: ritual chopper lt.: human skull-cup	mature, nude			8color: pale blue, dhar, jewelry, va.: lotus throne	A-wa-glang-mgo
one/three	two	rt.: sword lt.: tarjani mu.	corp.	two	ardha- paryanka	dark blue, dhar. ornaments, va.: human forms	Babhru-nila-Hayagriva
one*/three	two	rt.: staff/stick with skull finial lt.: noose/snare	mature, nude,	two	alidha	*bull-head, dhar. ornaments, erect phallus, va.: bull on female form	Bahya-Sadhana Dharmaraja
one/three	two	hands hold sandal-wood club	corp	two	alidha	dhar. ornaments,	Bhagavat-Mahakala-bhratr-traya

						black silk garment with golden girdle, va.: lotus throne	
one/three	two	hands hold staff/stick with skull finial	corp.	two	alidha	dhar. ornaments, loose garment va.: prostrate human form	Bhagavat-Mahakala-bhratr-traya
one/three	two	rt.: skull-topped staff/stick lt.: human skull-cup and shakti	corp.	two	alidha, yab-yum	dhar. ornaments, va.: lotus throne	Bhayada(?)-Mahakala**
one*/three	two	embrace shakti rt.: wheel lt.: tarjani mu.	youth	two	alidha, yab-yum	*angry, dhar. ornaments, va.: lotus throne	Bhaya-nasana-Krodha-Samvara**
one/three	two	rt.: ritual chopper lt.: human skull-cup	mature	two	ardha-paryanka	dhar. ornaments, va.: lotus throne	Bhimadarsana
one/three	two	rt.: thunderbolt lt.: bell	corp.	two	alidha	dhar. ornaments, va.: lotus throne	Bhutadamara-Vajrapani (Buddha)**
one/three	two	rt.: human thigh-bone trumpet lt.: cylindrical banner/flag	corp.	two	sukha	dhar. ornaments, va.: human forms on lotus throne	Brahmana-Rupadhara-Mahakala**
one/three	two	rt.: noose/snare lt.: razor	mature	two	yab-yum	dhar. ornaments, va.: lotus throne	brGya-byin
one/three	two	rt.: thunderbolt lt.: bell	corp.	two	alidha	dhar. ornaments, va.: snakes	Canda-Vajrapani (chun)**
one/three	two	rt.: sword lt.: human skull-cup	corp.	two	alidha, "grounded-knee"	dhar. ornaments, va.: human form	Catuspada-Acala**
one/three	two	rt.: ritual chopper lt.: human skull-cup with staff stick across the crook of both arms	corp.	two	alidha	dhar. ornaments, va.: human corpse on lotus throne	Danda-Mahakala
one/three	two	rt.: staff/stick lt.: lance	corp.	two	alidha	dhar. ornaments, va.: lotus throne	Danda(dhara)-Mahakala
one*/three	two	iron pan	mature	two		*dragon-like, dhar. ornaments,	dBus-kyi-'brug-lha-ga-pa
one*/three	two	holding club	corp.	two	alidha	*bull head,	Dharmaraja

						dhar. ornaments, va.: bull	
one*/three	two	rt.: noose/snare lt.: (?)	corp.	two	alidha	*bull head, dhar. ornaments, va.: lotus throne	Dharmaraja
one*/three	two	rt.: sword lt.: human skull-drum	corp.	two	sukha, yab-yum	*bull head, dhar. ornaments, va.: bull in intercourse with prostrate female	Dharmaraja
one*/three	two	rt.: ritual chopper lt.: human skull-cup	corp., nude	two		*bull head, pale plue body color, dhar. ornaments,	Dharmaraja
one/three	two	rt.: ritual chopper lt.: human skull-cup	mature	two		dhar. ornaments, va.: stands on corpse	Digambara-Devi
one/three	two	rt.: ritual chopper lt.: human skull-cup	corp., pendulous breasts	two	alidha	dhar. ornaments, va.: human form	Digambara-Devi
one/three	two	rt.: bejeweled sandal-wood club lt.: iron container filled with a number of liquids	mature	two		dhar. ornaments, va.: lotus throne	dKah-ma(?)-Dandadhara-Mahakala
one/three	two	rt.: sandal-wood staff/stick lt.: ihuman skull-cup(?)	mature	two		dhar. ornaments, va.: tiger on lotus throne	dKah-ma(?)-Dandadhara-Mahakala
one/three	two	rt.: club/cudgel lt.: human skull-cup filled with blood	mature	two	astride	dhar. ornaments, peacock feather canopy, human skin cape, va.: mule	dPal-ldan-lha-mo
one*/three	two	rt.: staff/stick lt.: shallow bowls filled with jewels	mature	two	sattva	*haughty, loose, flowing garments, fancy boots, bejeweled, va.: lotus throne	dPal-ldan-lha-mo
one/three	two	rt.: ritual chopper lt.: human skull-cup full of blood	mature	two		human skin garment, va.: mule	dPyid-kyi-rgyal-mo
one*/three	two*	claws hold bell	bird-like	two		*bird-like head, *wing-arms, realm: anus	Dri-chab-ma

one/three	two	rt.:ritual chopper lt.: human skull-cup, skull-topped staff/stick in crook of arm	mature	two	ardha-paryanka	dhar. ornaments, va.: disc on prostrate human figure on lotus throne	Dvibhuja-Vajra-Nairatma**
one*/three	two	rt.: serrated knife lt.: skulls	mature	two	vamalalita	*distorted with rage. one tooth, dhar. ornaments, va.: lotus throne	Ekajata
one/three	two	both vase/vessel with elixir of life at chest level	mature*	two	vamalalita	*blood gushes from vagina, bound hair hanging to left, dhar. ornaments, va.: donkey	Ekajata
one*/three	two	rt.: ritual chopper lt.: human skull-cup	mature	two	rajalila	*distorted with rage. one tooth, dhar. ornaments, va.: human form	Ekajata
one/three	two	rt.: trident lt.: noose/snare	corp.	two	alidha	dhar. ornaments, va.: lotus throne	Ekajati-Devi
one/three	two	rt.: ritual chopper lt.: human skull-cup	corp.	two	sama-bhanga	winged, dhar. ornaments, prostrate human form on triangle	Garudapaksavat-Kilapada-Panjara-Mahakala
one/three	two	rt.: ritual chopper lt.: human skull-cup, magic staff/stick across crooked arms	mature	two, bird-like		flaming thunderbolt wings, dhar. ornaments, va.: lotus throne	Garudapaksavat-Kilapada-Panjara-Mahakala
one/three	two	rt.: thunderbolt lt.: (?)	corp.	two	alidha	dhar. ornaments, va.: prostrate human forms	Garudayuta-Vajrapani**
one/three	two	rt.: thunderbolt lt.: karana mu.	corp.	two	alidha	dhar. ornaments, va.: lotus throne	Guhyaka-kruddha-Vajradhara**
one*/three	two	rt.: ritual chopper lt.: human skull-cup filled with blood	mature, nude	two	alidha	*bull-head, erect phallus, va.: bull	Guhya-Sadhana Dharmaraja

one*/three	two	rt.: trident lt.: human skull-cup	mature	two		*angry, dhar. ornaments, va.: lion	Gu-lang-raksa
one*/three	two	rt.: trident lt.: kha-ti	mature	two		*angry, dhar. ornaments, va.: buffalo	Gu-lang-raksa
one/three	two	rt.: hammer lt.: human skull-cup	mature	two	astride	*angry, dhar. ornaments, va.: bactrian camel	Hemanta-devi
one/three	two	rt.: baton staff/stick lt.: human skull-cup	mature	two	alidha	*angry, dhar. ornaments, va.: goat	Hemanta-devi
one/three	two	rt.: staff/stick lt.: human skull-cup	mature, nude	two	astride	pendulous breast, dhar. ornaments, va.: camel	Hemanta Rajni
one/three	two	rt.: thunderbolt lt.: human skull-cup full of blood, magic notched staff/stick with a flowing banner/flag against shoulder	mature	two	ardha- paryanka	dhar. ornaments, va.: corpse on lotus throne	Heruka
one/three	two	rt.: thunderbolt lt.: human skull-cup full of blood, magic notched staff/stick with a flowing banner/flag against shoulder	mature	two	ardha- paryanka, yab-yum	dhar. ornaments, va.: corpse on lotus throne	Heruka
one/three	two	prin.: embrace shakti rt.: thunderbolt lt.: human skull-cup marked with thunderbolt	mature	two	alidha, yab-yum	dhar. ornaments,	Hevajra
one/three	two	rt.: thunderbolt lt.: tarjani mu.	corp.	two	alidha	dhar. ornaments, va.: lotus throne	hGro-bzan-lugs-Nilambaradhara- Vajrapani**
one/three	two	holding sword	mature	two		armor covered, attribute: syllable "be," va.: buffalo	hPhags-skyes-po
one/three	two	rt.: thunderbolt lt.: karana mu.	corp.	two	alidha	dhar. ornaments, va.: lotus throne	Hsiao-Vajrapani**
one/three	two	rt.: ritual chopper lt.: human skull-cup	mature	two	ardha- paryanka	dhar. ornaments, va.: lotus throne	Jaya

one/three	two	rt.: ritual chopper lt.: human skull-cup	mature	two	ardha-paryanka	dhar. ornaments, va.: prostrate human	Kakasya-Karma-Mahakala**
one/three	two	rt.: ritual chopper lt.: human skull-cup	corp.	two	alidha	dhar. ornaments, va.: lotus throne	Kakasya-Karmanatha
one*/three	two	rt.: knife lt.: human skull-cup	corp.	two	alidha	dhar. ornaments, va.: lotus throne	Kakasya-Karmanatha
one/three	two	rt.: human skull-cup lt.: ritual chopper	mature, nude	two	alidha	bone ornaments, va.: human corpse	Kalika
one/three	two	rt.: ritual chopper lt.: human skull-cup	corp.	two	praty-alidha	dhar. ornaments, va.: human form on lotus throne	Kartaridhara-Traksad-Mahakala**
one/three	two	rt.: ritual chopper lt.: human skull-cup	corp.	two	alidha,	dhar. ornaments, va.: lotus throne over two figures on horse-back	Kartaridhara-Traksad-Mahakala**
one/three	two	rt.: ritual chopper lt.: human skull-cup and embraces shakti	mature, nude	two	alidha, yab-yum	dhar. ornaments, va.: disc on human figures	Kaya-Hevajra**
one/three	two	rt.: thunderbolt lt.: tarjani mu.	mature	two	alidha	dhar. ornaments, va.: prostrate human forms	Khra-thogs-Canda-Vajrapani
one/three	two	rt.: sharp-weaponed wheel lt.: human skull-cup filled with blood	mature	two		dhar. ornaments, va.: lotus throne	Khro-chen-vajra-ging-ka-ra
one/three	two	rt.: sword lt.: noose/snare	corp.	two	"grounded knee:"	dhar. ornaments, va.: lotus throne	(Krodharaja-arya)-Avani-nihita-janu-Nila-Acala
one/three	two	rt.: thunderbolt lt.: flame(?)	mature	two	alidha	dhar. ornaments, va.: lotus throne	Krodha-Vajrapani**
one/three	two	rt.: short staff/stick marked with thunderbolt lt.: noose/snare in tarjani mu.	mature	two	pratyalidha	dhar. ornaments, va.: buffalo	Krsnayamari
one*/three	two	rt.: ritual chopper lt.: human skull-cup	mature	two		*dark-blue color, dhar. ornaments, va.: bear on lotus throne	Ksetrapala

one*/three	two	rt.: ritual chopper lt.: human skull-cup filled with blood	mature	two		*dark-blue color, dhar. ornaments, human skin cape, attribute: syllable "kse", va.:black bear on lotus throne	Ksetrapala
one/three	two	rt.: ritual chopper lt.: human skull-cup	corp.	two	sopasraya	dhar. ornaments, va.: bear on lotus throne	Ksetrapala
one*/three	two	rt,: staff/stick with a skull finial and thunderbolt hilt lt,: tarjani mu. with black noose/snare and embraces shakti	mature, nude	two	yab-yum	*bull-head erect phallus, bone ornaments, va,: buffalo	Las-gshin-dpa'-gcig
one*/three	two	rt.: club with skull finial and thunderbolt hilt lt.: tarjani mu. with black noose/snare	mature, nude	two	alidha	*bull-head, erect phallus, va.: buffalo	Las-gshin-lha-bcu-gsum
one*/three	two	rt.: knife lt.: human skull-cup	corp.	two		*raven-head, dhar. ornaments,	Las-mgon-bya-rog-gdong-can
one/three	two	rt.: sword lt.: severed head to breast	mature, nude	two		bone ornaments, attribute: syllable "bhyo." va.: large corpse	lHa-mo-remati-gsang-sgrub
one/three	two	holding shallow bowl with multi colored ribbons and precious objects	mature	two		bone ornaments, va.: yak bull	lHa-mo-shel-bza'-sman-gcig-ma
one/three	two	rt.: ritual chopper, human skull-cup lt.: flaming sword, trident	mature	two		dhar. ornaments, lotus throne	Lugs-gnyis-gcig-tu-bsgril-ba'i-ye-shes-mgon-po-phyag-bzhi-pa
one/three	two	rt.: club lt.: human skull-cup of blood	mature	two	astride	dhar. ornaments, va.: mule on lake of menstrual blood	Ma-gcig-dPal-ldan-lha-mo
one*/three	two	rt.: standard staff/stick adorned with ribbons lt.: bowl of jewels	mature	two	lalita	bodh. ornaments, va.: lotus throne	Ma-gcig-dPal-ldan-lha-mo
one/three	two	rt.: copper sword lt.: iron dagger	mature	two		dhar. ornaments, va.: man-eating black bear	Ma-gcig-srid-pa'i-lha-mo-gdong-dmar-ma
one/three	two	rt.: ritual chopper lt.: human skull-cup	corp	two	pratyalidha	dhar. ornaments, va.: two corpses	Mahakala

one/three	two	rt.: sword lt.: human skull-cup of blood	mature	two	astride	dhar. ornaments, black silk cape, va.: black donkey	Mahakali-Remati
one/three	two	rt.: thunderbolt lt.: staff/stick with skull finial	corp.	two	partyalidha	dhar. ornaments, va.: lotus throne	Mahavajresvara**
one*/three	two	rt.: skull-topped staff/stick lt.: noose/snare	corp.	two	alidha, yab-yum	*bull-head erect phallus, dhar. ornaments, va.: kneeling bull	Mahavrati-Dharmaraja
one/three	two	rt.: ritual chopper lt.: human skull-cup	mature	two	ardha- paryanka	dhar. ornaments, va.: lotus throne	Mahayasa
one/three	two	rt.: ritual chopper lt.: human skull-cup	mature	two	ardha- paryanka	dhar. ornaments, va.: lotus throne	Mahodadhi
one/three	two	rt.: (?) lt.: tarjani mu.	corp.	two	alidha	dhar. ornaments, va.: prostrate human figures	Mamaki-Devi
one/three	two	rt.: staff/stick with human torso finial lt.: horse(?)	corp.	two	alidha	penduloud breasts, dhar. ornaments, va.: prostrate human form on lotus throne	Mantrapala-Ekajati**
one/three	two	rt.: ritual chopper lt.: human skull-cup	mature	two	ardha- paryanka	dhar. ornaments, realm: South-east va.: lotus throne	Marini
one/three	two	rt.: flaming bronze hammer lt.: black bellows	mature	two	astride	black silk garment, dhar. ornaments, va.: brown billy-goat	mGar-ba'i-mtshan-can
one/three	two	rt.: ritual chopper lt.: human skull-cup	mature	two		snake & bone ornaments, va.: lotus throne	Mig-dmar
one/three	two	rt.: disc(?) lt.: red tablet	mature	two	astride	black silk and rough cloth, dhar. ornaments, va.: mule	Nad-kyi-bdag-mo
one/three	two	rt.: knife lt.: human skull-cup, in crook of arm	mature	two	ardha- paryanka	dhar. ornaments, va.: corpse lying on its	Nairatma

		magic notched stick				back	
one/three	two	rt.: ritual chopper lt.: human skull-cup	mature	two	ardha-paryanka	dhar. ornaments, va.: lotus throne realm: Southern gate	<u>Nairatma</u>
one*/three	two	rt.: ritual chopper lt.: human skull-cup	mature	two	alidha	*raksasa-head, dhar. ornaments, va.: corpse	<u>Nang-sgrub-srin-gi-gdong-can</u>
one/three	two	rt.: staff/stick with skull finial lt.: human skull-cup	corp.	two	alidha	dhar. ornaments, va.: prostrate human form	<u>Nidhi-Dandadhara-Mahakala</u>
one/three	two	rt.: magic notched staff/stick lt.: human skull-cup	mature, nude	two	ardha-paryanka	dhar. ornaments, va.: lotus throne	<u>Nilambara-Dakini</u>
one/three	two	rt.: ritual chopper lt.: human skull-cup	mature	two	partyalidha	long flowing robe, dhar. ornaments, va.: lotus throne	<u>Nilambaradhara</u>
one/three	two	rt.: ritual thunderbolt lt.: bell	mature	two	partyalidha	long flowing robe, dhar. ornaments, va.: prostrate human forms	<u>Nilambaradhara</u>
one/three	two	rt.: thunderbolt lt.: bell	corp.	two	alidha	dhar. ornaments, va.: lotus throne	<u>Nilambaradhara-Vajrapani</u>
one*/three	two	rt.: ritual chopper, on shoulder magic stick of Padmasambhava lt.: humna skull-cup	mature	two	ardha-paryanka	*lion-head, dhar. ornaments, va.: human body	<u>Nila-Simhavaktra</u>
one/three	two	rt.: sword lt.: noose/snare	corp.	two	alidha	dhar. ornaments, va.: lotus throne	<u>Nila-Acala</u>
one/three	two	rt.: sword lt.: noose/snare	corp.	two	alidha	dhar. ornaments, snake garlands, va.: Ganesa figure	<u>Nila-Acala</u>
one/three	two	rt.: sword lt.: karana mu.	corp	two	alidha	dhar. ornaments, va.: lotus throne	<u>Nila-Acalavajra</u>
one/three	two	rt.: staff-stick lt.: karana mu.	corp.	two	alidha	dhar. ornaments, va.: prostrate human figures	<u>Niladanda</u>

one*/three	two	rt.: staff/stick with skull finial lt.: tarjani mu. with black noose/snare	corp.	two	alidha, yab-yum	*bull-head, dhar. ornaments, va.: buffalo	Nila-Dharmaraja-Karma-Yama
one/three	two	rt.: skull-toppeds staff/stick lt.: noose/snare	corp.,	two	alidha	erect phallus, dhar. ornaments, va.: bull in intercourse with female	Nila-Dharmaraja-Karma-Yama
one*/three	two	rt.: lotus lt.: crossed thunderbolt	corp.	two	ardha-paryanka	*horse-head in hair, dhar. ornaments, va.: prostrate human forms	Nila-Hayagriva
one/three	two	rt.: thunderbolt lt.: bell on thigh	corp.	two	alidha	dhar. ornaments, va.: lotus throne	Nila-Vajravidarana
one/three	two	rt.: thunderbolt lt.: karana mu.	youth	two	sattva	dhar. ornaments, va.: lotus throne	Nila-Vajrapani
one/three	two	rt.: thunderbolt lt.: human skull-cup	mature	two	ardha-paryanka	dhar. ornaments, va.: lotus throne	Nila-Vahari
one*/three	two	rt.: staff/stick with skull finial lt.: noose/snare	corp., nude	two	alidha	dhar. ornaments, va.: bull	Nila Yamaraja
one/three	two	rt.: ritual chopper lt.: human skull-cup	mature	two	ardha-paryanka	dhar. ornaments, va.: lotus throne	Ostaraki
one/three	two	rt.: ritual chopper lt.: human skull-cup	mature	two	ardha-paryanka	dhar. ornaments, va.: prostrate human forms	Pe-har-nag-can (?)
one/three	two	rt.: sword lt.: noose/snare	mature	two	vamalalita	broad brimmed helmet, loose garment, dhar. ornaments, va.: elephant	Pe-har-rgyal-po
one/three	two	rt.: frog & black serpent/snake lt.: sack of diseases	mature	two	astride	dhar. ornaments, va.: blue horse of the water spirits	Pho-klu-bdud-thod-dkar
one/three	two	rt.: treasure casque lt.: lance with banner	mature	two		dhar. ornaments, armored, va.: khyung	Phu-yi-gzhi-bdag-mdzod-lnga-spun-lnga

one/three	two	rt.: ritual chopper lt.: human skull-cup	mature, nude	two		*pale-blue, dhar. ornaments, va.: lotus throne	Phyva-sangs
one/three	two	holding wheel	mature nude	two		*pale-blue, dhar. ornaments, va.: lotus throne	Phyva-sangs
one/three	two	holding wheel	mature nude	two		*dark-blue, dhar. ornaments, va.: lotus throne	Phyva-sangs
one/three	two	rt.: ritual chopper lt.: human skull-cup	mature	two	ardha-paryanka	dhar. ornaments, realm: Western gate va.: lotus throne	Priyadarsana
one/three	two	rt.: magic staff/stick lt.: snake noose/snare	mature	two		nine locks of iron, dhar. ornaments, va.: lotus throne	rDo-rje-brag-btsan-rDo-rje-dbang-drag-rtsal
one/three	two	rt.: ritual chopper lt.: skull-cup filled with blood	mature, nude	two		dhar. ornaments, va.: lotus throne	Ral-pa-tshar-dgu
one/three	two	rt.: thunderbolt lt.: bell	corp.	two	alidha	dhar. ornaments, va.: prostrate human forms	Ras-chun-lugs-bsrun-bahi-mkhar-Canda-maharosana-Vajrapani
one*/three	two	rt.: thunderbolt lt.: human skull-cup	corp.	two	alidha	*garuda and horse head in hair, dhar. ornaments, va.: human body	Raudra-Vajrapani
one/three	two	rt.: gem studded ritual chopper lt.: skull-cup filled with hearts	mature	two		dhar. ornaments, va.: black horse with white heels	rDo-rje-bdud-'dul (sman-gyi-lha)
one*/three	two	holds iron sacred dagger	mature	two		*angry, dhar. ornaments, syllable "ma", va.: golden hind	rDo-rje-bgegs-kyi-gtso
one*/three	two	holding small drum	mature	two		*angry, syllable "te", dhar. ornaments, va.: turquoise lion	rDo-rje-dril-bu-gzugs-legs-ma
one*/three	two	holding small drum	mature	two		*angry,	rDo-rje-gzugs-legs-ma

						syllable "te," dhar. ornaments, va.: turquoise lion	
one/three	two	holding sacred dagger	mature	two	astride	dhar. ornaments, syllable "ma", va.: three legged mule	rDo-rje-g.ya'-ma-skyong
one*/three	two	rt.: thunderbolt lt.: vase/vessel of life	youth	two		*angry, dhar. ornaments, va.: white lion	rDo-rje-kun-bzang
one*/three	two	rt.: makara banner/flag lt.: mirror	youth	two		*angry, dhar. ornaments,	rDo-rje-kun-grags
one*/three	two	holds sacred dagger	mature	two		*angry, cloak of thousand black snakes, va.: pale blue-green dragon	rDo-rje-kun-grags-ma
one/three	two	rt.: offers food to her sakta lt.: sack of diseases	mature	two		white silk, golden girdle, garland of human heads, va.: lotus throne	rDo-rje-kun-'grub-ma
one/three	two	rt.: thunderbolt lt.: gem filled vase/vessel	mature	two		dhar. ornaments, va.: lotus throne	rDo-rje-mkha'-'gro-ma
one/three	two	rt.: goad/hook lt.: magic dagger	mature	two		pendulous breasts, dhar. ornaments, va.: turquoise dragon	rDo-rje-ya-byin
one/three	two	rt.: thunderbolt lt.: heart	mature	two		multicolored turban, high silk boots, dhar. ornaments, va.: white lion	rDzogs-chen-pa'i-gter-bdag
one/three	two	rt.: trident lt.: human skull-cup filled with blood	mature	two		dhar. ornaments, va.: lotus throne	rGan-byang-ma
one/three	two	rt.: flaming sword lt.: mongoose	mature	two	astride	iron helmet, dhar. ornaments, va.: black horse with white heels	rNam-snang

one/three	two	rt.: ritual chopper lt.: skull-cup	mature	two		dhar. ornaments, va.: human corpse	rNog-lugs-Ekanta-Panjara-Mahakala
one/three	two	rt.: ritual chopper lt.: human skull-cup	mature	two	ardha-paryanka	dhar. ornaments, realm: North, va.: lotus throne	Rupini
one*/three	two	embracing shakti in vajrahumkara mu.	mature	two	alidha, yab-yum	*angry, five ;leaf crown, dhar. ornaments, va.: prostrate human bodies	Sahaja-Samvara
one/three	two	rt.: goad/hook lt.: magic dagger	mature	two		pendulous breasts, dhar. ornaments, va.: turquoise dragon	Sa-bdag-chen-mo-rDo-rje-ya-byin
one/three	two	rt.: rosary of the skulls of children lt.: human skull-cup	mature	two		flowing robe of black silk, dhar. ornaments, va.: lotus throne	Sa-bsen-gdug-byed
one/three	two	rt.: thunderbolt lt.: human skull-cup & embrace shakti, magic notched stickrests in crook of left arm	mature	two	ardha-paryanka	dhar. ornaments, va.: prostrate human figure	Sahaja-Hevajra**
one/three	two	embraces shakti and holds vase/vessel filled with nectar of life	mature	two	vajra, yab-yum	dhar. ornaments, va.: Kalaratri	Samvara
one/three	two	rt.: thunderbolt lt.: (?)	corp.	two	alidha	dhar. ornaments, va.: lotus throne	Sa-(skya)-lugs-Vajrapani**
one*/three	two	rt.: human skull-cup lt.: ritual chopper, magic staff/stick of Padmasambhava over shoulder	mature	two	ardha-paryanka	*lion-head, blue body & white face, dhar. ornaments, va.: human body	Simhavaktra
one/three	two	rt.: baton lt.: (?)	corp.	two	alidha	dhar. ornaments, va.: lotus throne	Shan-hsing Vajrapani (Buddha)**
one/three	two	holds noose/snare of snakes	mature	two		dhar. ornaments, va.: snake	Sa-sman
one/three	two	rt.: thunderbolt lt.: tarjani mu.	corp.	two	alidha	dhar. ornaments, va.: lotus throne	Sutra-krama-Vajrapani**

one/three	two	rt.: ritual chopper lt.: human skull-cup filled with hearts	mature	two		dhar. ornaments, black silk cloak, va.: black horse with white heels	sMan-bla'i-bka'-sdod
one/three	two	tearing apart and eating the head of a corpse	mature	two		dhar. ornaments, va.: lotus throne	Smasha
one/three	two	rt.: banner/flag lt.: mirror	mature	two		dhar. ornaments, va.: khyang	sNang-gsal-(s)pra-ston-ma
one/three	two	rt.: sword lt.: noose/snare	mature	two		toupet of turquoise dhar. ornaments, va.: tigress	So-bdar-ma
one/three	two	rt.: staff-stick lt.: tray of jewels in dhyana mu	youth	two	sopasraya	dhar. ornaments, loose garment. va.: lotus throne	Sridevi
one/three	two	rt.: sandalwood club lt.: skull-cup of a child born of an incestuous union and filled with blood	mature	two	lalita	canopy of peacock, feathers, covered in black silk, bone ornaments, va.: mule, riding on a sea of blood and fat	Srimati-Parvati-rajni
one/three	two	rt.: vajra-topped staff/stick lt.: human skull-cup	corp	two	lalita	pendulous breast, bone ornaments, va.: mule, riding on a sea of blood and fat	Srimati-Parvati-rajni
one/three	two	rt.: golden razor lt.: bowels	mature	two		dhar. ornaments, black silk and a tiger skin, va.: lotus throne	Srin-mo-ral-gcig-ma
one/three	two	rt.: ritual chopper lt.: human skull-cup	mature	two	ardha-paryanka	dhar. ornaments, va.: lotus throne	Subha
one/three	two	rt.: ritual chopper lt.: human skull-cup	mature	two	ardha-paryanka	dhar. ornaments, realm: Northern gate va.: lotus throne	Subhaga
one/three	two	rt.: ritual chopper lt.: human skull-cup	mature	two	ardha-paryanka	dhar. ornaments, realm: East va.: lotus throne	Subhamekhala

one/three	two	rt.: ritual chopper lt.: human skull-cup filled with blood	mature	two	ardha-paryanka	dhar. ornaments, realm: Northwest va.: lotus throne	<u>Suladhara</u>
one/three	two	rt.: tarjani mu. lt.: lotus blossom	corp.*	two	alidha	*face on abdomen, dhar. ornaments, va.: clouds	<u>Suladhara</u>
one/three	two	rt.: ritual chopper lt.: human skull-cup	mature	two	ardha-paryanka	dhar. ornaments, realm: East va.: lotus throne	<u>Sumalini</u>
one/three	two	rt.: noose/snare of a serpent/snake lt.: tarjani mu.	mature	two		dhar. ornaments, realm: "down", va.: lotus throne	<u>Sumbha</u>
one/three	two	rt.: ritual chopper lt.: human skull-cup	mature	two	ardha-paryanka	dhar. ornaments, realm: Eastern gate, va.: lotus throne	<u>Sundara</u>
one/three	two	rt.: ritual chopper lt.: human skull-cup	mature	two	ardha-paryanka	dhar. ornaments, realm: West, va.: lotus throne	<u>Sundari</u>
one/three	two	rt.: ritual chopper lt.: human skull-cup	mature	two	ardha-paryanka	dhar. ornaments, realm: North-east, va.: lotus throne	<u>Suraksini</u>
one/three	two	rt.: circular banner lt.: mirror	mature	two	aseat	dress of silk, attribute: syllable "mam", va.: Asiatic wild ass	<u>Sumukhi</u>
one/three	two	rt.: human skull-drum lt.: human skull-cup	corp.	two	pratyalidha	dhar. ornaments, va.: prostrate human form	<u>Takkiraja</u>
one/three	two	rt.: human skull-drum lt.: karana mu.	mature	two	alidha	dhar. ornaments, va.: prostrate human figure	<u>Takkiraja</u>
one/three	two	rt.: goad/hook lt.: karana mu.	mature	two	alidha	dhar. ornaments, va.: prostrate human figure	<u>Takkiraja</u>
one/three	two	rt.: ritual chopper	mature	two	alidha	dhar. ornaments,	<u>Tamra-Kartaridhara-krsna-cola-</u>

		lt.: human skull-cup				leather boots, va.: human corpse	Mahakala
one/three	two	rt.: ritual chopper lt.: human skull-cup	mature	two	alidha	dhar. ornaments, va.: prostrate human form	Tamra-Kartaridhara-Mahakala**
one/three	two	rt.: ritual chopper lt.: human skull-cup	mature	two	alidha	dhar. ornaments, high brown leather boots, va.: human corpse	Tamra-Kartaridhara-Nagna-Mahakala
one/three	two	rt.: ritual chopper lt.: human skull-cup	corp.	two	lalita	dhar. ornaments, loose garment, va.: tiger treading on a prostrate human figure	Tamra-Kartaridhara-Nagna-Mahakala
one/three	two	rt.: lance lt.: noose/snare	mature	two		iron helmet, iron armor and a cloak of bird feathers, va.: dark blue horse	Thugs-sprul-go-bo
one*/three	two	rt.: sword lt.: book/manuscript	mature	two		*blue-green, dhar. ornaments, va.: human being	Tiksnosnisa
one/three	two	holds vajrahumkara mu.	mature	two	pratyalidha	dhar. ornaments, va.: two humans	Trailokyavijaya
one/three	two	holds bhutadamara mu.	mature	two	alidha	dhar. ornaments, va.: prostrate human bodies	Trailokyavijaya (Buddha)**
one/three	two	rt.: human skull-cup lt.: mongoose	dwarfish, corp, nude	two	pratyalidha	dhar. ornaments, erect phallus, va.: Kubera vomiting jewels	Ucchusma-Jambhala
one/three	two	rt.: human skull-cup lt.: mongoose	corp, nude	two	pratyalidha	dhar. ornaments, va.: Kubera	Ucchuśma-Jambhala
one/three	two	rt.: kha-tram lt.: human skull-cup	mature	two	aseat	dhar. ornaments, black silk garment, va.: elephant	Uma-Devi
one/three	two	rt.: magic staff/stick lt.: émbraces shakti, skull-cup	mature	two	alidha	dhar. ornaments, va.: human figure on	Vairocana-Bhairavavajra**

						back of a bull	
one/three	two	rt.: thunderbolt lt.: human skull-cup, magic staff/stick in crook of arm	mature, nude	two	ardha-paryanka	dhar. ornaments, va.: lotus throne	Vajra-Dakini
one/three	two	rt.: thunderbolt lt.: vase/vessel	mature, nude	two	ardha-paryanka	dhar. ornaments, va.: lotus throne	Vajra-Dakini
one*/three	two	two wings	mature	two, claws	standing	*bird-like, legs hold thunderbolt, realm: heart va.: lotus throne	Vajra-Garuda
one*/three	two	to the side, palms out, fingers up	mature	two, claws	standing	*bird-like, dhar. ornaments, va.: lotus throne	Vajragaruda (sabala)**
one/three	two	rt.: bhumisparsa mu lt.: thunderbolt	mature	two	ardha-paryanka	dhar. ornaments, va.: lotus throne	Vajra-Heruka
one/three	two	rt.: bell lt.: thunderbolt	mature	two	alidha	dhar. ornaments, va.: Bhairava	Vajrahumkara
one/three	two	rt.: encircles yab's neck lt.: human skull-cup filled with blood	mature	two	pratyalidha, yab-yum	dhar. ornaments, va.: lotus throne	Vajra-Krotishaurima
one/three	two	rt.: thunderbolt lt.: heart	mature	two		cane hat with silk pennants, dhar. ornaments, va.: lotus throne	Vajrasadhu
one/three	two	rt.: vajra topped hammer lt.: triangular flag	mature	two		dhar. ornaments, fancy boots, va.: horse	Vajrasadhu
one/three	two	rt.: knife lt.: human skull-cup	mature	two	astride	dhar. ornaments, va.: mule	Vasanta-devi
one/three	two	rt.: ritual chopper lt.: human skull-cup	mature	two		dhar. ornaments, va.: lotus throne	Vetali
one/three	two	rt.: ritual chopper, embraces shakti lt.: human skull-cup, embraces shakti	mature	two	alidha, yab-yum	dhar. ornaments, va.: lotus throne	Vidya-Dhara[9]

[9] The Vidya-Dhara , Knowledge Holding Deities who appear on the seventh day of the second state of the Bardo-Thodol. They are forms of the Dhyani Buddhas.

one/three	two	rt.: thunderbolt lt.: tarjani mu. with noose/snare	mature	two	pratyalidha	dhar. ornaments, va.: form of Ganesa	Vighnantaka
one/three	two	rt.: thunderbolt lt.: karana mu.	mature	two	alidha	dhar. ornaments, va.: lotus throne	Vighnantakavajra
one/three	two	rt.: ritual chopper lt.: human skull-cup	mature	two	ardha-paryanka	dhar. ornaments, realm: North-west, va.: lotus throne	Vikalaratri
one/three	two	rt.: crossed thunderbolts lt.: skull-cup, magic staff/stick in the crook arm	mature	two		dhar. ornaments, va.: lotus throne	Vishva-Dakini
one/three	two	rt.: ritual chopper lt.: human skull-cup filled with blood	mature, nude	two		dhar. ornaments, va.: lotus throne	Ya-ba-ti
one/three	two	holds club/cudgel	mature, nude	two		dhar. ornaments, va.: lotus throne	Ya-ba-ti
one*/three	two	rt.: ritual chopper lt.: human skull-cup	corp.	two	alidha	*bull-head, dhar. ornaments, va.: bull copulating with a woman	Yama
one/three	two	rt.: ritual chopper lt.: human skull-cup filled with blood	mature, nude	two		dhar. ornaments, va.: lotus throne	Yama-daksad (?)
one/three	two	rt.: human skull-drum lt.: human skull-cup	mature	two	ardha-paryanka	pendulous breasts, dhar. ornaments, va.: lotus throne	Yamaduti
one*/three	two	rt.: human skull-cup lt.: ritual chopper	mature	two	alidha	*bull-head, dhar. ornaments, va.: bull	Yamantaka
one*/three	two	holds jewel	mature	two		*stag-head, dhar. ornaments, va.: lotus throne	Yang-dag-shes
one*/three	two	rt.: iron goad/hook, red lance in crook of arm lt.: iron goad/hook	mature	two		*angry, white garments, high fancy leather boots, va.: lotus throne	Yang-dag-shes
one/three	two	rt.: heart	mature	two	aseat	flat, pendulous breasts,	Za-byed-spyang-gryal-nag-mo

		lt.: tarjani mu.				dhar. ornaments, va.: nine headed wolf	
one*/three	two	holds noose/snare of snakes	mature	two		*snake-head, dhar. ornaments, va.: human-form	Zla-ba'i-sa-rgyal
one/three	four	prin. in bhutadamara mu. rt.: thunderbolt lt.: noose/snare	corp.	two	pratyalidha	dhar. ornaments, va.: Ganesa	Bhutadamara-Vajrapani**
one/three	four	rt.: ritual chopper, trident lt.: bow, arrow	corp.	two	alidha	dhar. ornaments, va.: lotus throne	Candika Devi**
one/three	four	rt.: human skull cup, sword lt.: bow and arrow, freshly severed head	corp.	two	astride	dhar. ornaments, va.: horse	Candika Devi**
one/three	four	rt.: sword, human skull-cup lt.: sun disc and vitarka mu.	mature	two	pratyalidha	dhar. ornaments, va.: lotus throne	Caturbhuja
one/three	four	rt.: magic notched staff/stick, black thunderbolt lt.: sword, jewel	mature	two	ardha-paryanka, yab-yum	dhar. ornaments, va.: lotus throne	Caturbhuja-Heruka
one/three	four	rt.: trident, ritual chopper lt.: bow and arrow, heart	corp.	two	ardha-paryanka	dhar. ornaments, pendulous breasts, va,: prostrate human form	Caturbhuja-(jnana)-Mahakalanucara-Candika-Devi
one/three	four	rt.: magic staff/stick, human skull-cup lt.: human skull-drum, ritual chopper	mature	two	praty-alidha	dhar. ornaments, va.: lotus throne	Dakini
one/three	four	rt.: flower(?) and disc or human skull-drum(?) lt.: goad/hook, human skull-cup	mature, nude	two	alidha	dhar. ornaments, va.: human forms on lotus throne	Dakini (fo-mu) **
one/three	four	rt.: sword, human skull-cup lt.: lance , trident	corp, pendulous breasts	two		dhar. ornaments, va.: mule	dPal-ldan-lha-mo-'dod-khams-dbang-phyug-ma
one/three	four	rt.: ritual chopper, skull-cup filled with blood lt.: flaming sword, trident	corp	two	alidha	dhar. ornaments, va.: prostrate human form	dPal-ye-shes-mgon-pa-mahakala-dpa'-bo-chen-po
one*/three	four	rt.: sword, arrow lt.: bow, skull	mature	two	vamalalita	*distorted with rage. one tooth, dhar. ornaments,	Ekajata

						va.: lotus throne	
one/three	four	rt.: thunderbolt lt.: human skull-cup marked with thunderbolt	mature	two	alidha, yab-yum	dhar. ornaments,	Hevajra
one/three	four	prin.: ritual chopper, human skull-cup rt.: seord lt.: trident	corp.	two	lalita	dhar. ornaments, va.: prostrate human forms on lotus throne on triangle	Htshal-lugs-Caturbhuja-(Inana)-Mahakala**
one/three	four	prin.: bhutadamara mu. rt.: thunderbolt lt.: noose/snare	corp.	two	alidha	dhar. ornaments, va.: lotus throne	Iagaddama-Vajrapani**
one/three	four	rt.: thunderbolt, serpent/snake lt.: bell, other end of serpent/snake	corp.	two	alidha	dhar. ornaments, va.: lotus throne	Lohanadi(?)-Vajrapani
one/three	four	rt.: thunderbolt, serpent/snake lt.: serpent/snake, bell	corp.	two	alidha	dhar. ornaments, serpent/snake in mouth va.: lotus throne	Lohanadi(?)-Vajrapani
one/three	four	rt.: sword, ritual chopper lt.: blue lotus, human skull-cup	corp	two	pratyalidha	dhar. ornaments, va.: corpse	Mahacina-Tara
one/three	four	rt.: ritual chopper ,human skull-cup lt.: sword, magic notched staff/stick	corp.	two	pratyalidha	dhar. ornaments, va.: two corpses	Mahakala
one/three	four	rt.: ritual chopper, hammer lt.: human skull-cup, human skull-drum	mature	two	alidha	dhar. ornaments, va.: lion	Mahamaya
one/three	four	prin.: dharmachakra mu. (?) rt.: thunderbolt lt.: noose/snare	corp	two	alidha	dhar. ornaments, va.: prostrate human forms	Nava-Bhutadamara-Vajrapani**
one/three	four	prin.: "mystic mu."	mature	two		dhar. ornaments, va.: crowned person on a bed of serpents	Nilambaradhara-Vajrapani
one/three	four	rt.: tarjani mu., battle axe lt.: noose/snare encircling human figure, fly whisk	corp.	two	alidha	dhar. ornaments, va.: lotus throne	Nila-Parnasabari
one/three	four	rt.: magic staff/stick, human skull-cup lt.: human skull-drum, ritual chopper	mature	two	pratyalidha	dhar. ornaments, va.: lotus throne	Rupini
one/three	four	rt.: magic staff/stick, black thunderbolt	mature	two	ardha-	dhar. ornaments,	Svabha-Prajna

		lt.: sword, jewel			paryanka, yab-yum	va.: lotus throne	
one/three	four	rt.: cocoa-nut, sword lt.: skull-cup, magic staff/stick of Padmasambhava	mature	two		dhar. ornaments, va.: lotus throne	'Tshal-lugs-kyi-ye-shes-mgon-po-phyag-bzhi-pa
one/three	four	rt.: sword, knife lt.: human skull-cup, blue lotus	mature	two	pratyalidha	dhar. ornaments, va.: lotus throne	Ugra-Tara
one/three	four	rt.: sword, knife lt.: human skull-cup, bow & arrow	mature	two	pratyalidha	dhar. ornaments, va.: lotus throne	Ugra-Tara
one/three	four	prin.: embrace shakti in vajrahumkara mu. rt.: ritual chopper lt.: human skull-cup	mature, nude	two	alidha, yab-yum	dhar. ornaments, va.: disc on prostrate human figures	Vag-Hevajra
one/three	four	rt.: lotus, sun disc lt.: axe, human skull-cup	mature	two	ardha-paryanka	dhar. ornaments, va.: lotus throne	Vajra-Dakini
one/three	four	prin.: anjali mu. rt.: fish lt.: human skull-cup	mature	two		dhar. ornaments, va.: owl	Varahi
one/three	four	rt.: ritual chopper, human skull-drum lt.: human skull-cup, trident	mature, nude	two	ardha-paryanka	dhar. ornaments, va.: human form	Varahi
one/three	four	rt.: ritual chopper, human skull-cup filled with blood lt.: flaming sword, victory banner/flag	mature	two		dhar. ornaments, va.: lotus throne	Ye-shes-mgon-po-phyag-bzhi-pa-rGva-lo'i-lugs
one/three	four	rt.: staff/stick of lotus, ritual chopper lt.: bowl of blood, fly whisk	mature	two	alidha	dhar. ornaments, realm: South, va.: buffalo	Yamaduti
one/ three	six	rt.: sword, thunderbolt, wheel lt.: karana mu., noose/snare and lotus	corp.	two	alidha	dhar. ornaments, va.: loyus throne	Aksobhyavajra
one/three	six	rt.: thunderbolt, arrow, trident lt.: bell, bow, human skull-cup	mature	two	alidha, yab-yum	dhar. ornaments,	Hevajra
one/three	six	rt.: magic staff/stick, axe, thunderbolt lt.: bell, skull-cup, sword	mature	two	lalita	dhar. ornaments, va.: lotus throne	Inanadakini
one/three	six	rt.: magic staff/stick, axe, thunderbolt lt.: bell, skull-cup, sword	mature	two	lalita	dhar. ornaments, va.: lion	Inanadakini

one/three	six	rt.: ritual chopper, rosary, human skull-drum lt.: human skull-cup, trident, noose/snare	corp.	two	pratyalidha	dhar. ornaments, va.: two corpses	Mahakala
one*/three	six	rt.: ritual chopper, skull-cup, rosary lt.: trident, noose/snare, wheel	corp.	two	alidha	dhar. ornaments, va.: Vinataka	Mahakala-mGon-po
one/three	six	rt.: sword, baton/mace, abhaya mu. lt.: wheel, trident, lotus	mature	two	alidha	dhar. ornaments, va.: lotus throne	Mahapratyangira (fo-mu)
one*/three	six	prin.: embrace shakti in semui-in mu. 2nd pr.: serpent/snake 3rd pr.: thunderbolt, karana mu.	mature	two	ardha-paryanka, yab-yum	*holds snake in mouth, dhar. ornaments, va.: prostrate human	Niladanda-Vajrapani
one/three	six	prin.: embrace shakti rt.: thunderbolt, sword lt.: jewel, lotus	mature	two	yab-yum	dhar. ornaments, va.: lotus throne	Sumbharaja
one/three	six	prin.: hold ritual chopper, human skull-cup rt.: human skull-drum, goad/hook lt.: trident, noose/snare in tarjani mu.	mature	two	pratyalidha	dhar. ornaments, va.: form of Ganesa	Vighnantaka
one/three	eight	rt.: noose/snare, lotus, arrow, sword lt.: staff/stick, wheel, bow, trident	corp.	two	alidha	dhar. ornaments, va.: lotus throne	Anucara-Ekajata
one*/three	eight	rt.: sword, arrow, thunderbolt, knife lt.: bow, lotus, battle axe, skull	mature	two	pratyalidha	*distorted with rage. one tooth, dhar. ornaments, va.: lotus throne	Ekajata
one/three	eight	rt.: sword, arrow, thunderbolt, knife lt.: human skull-cup, blue lotus, bow, axe	mature	two	pratyalidha	dhar. ornaments, va.: lotus throne	Ugra-Tara
one/three	12	prin.: embrace shakti in vajrahumkara mu. other hands hold tantric symbols	youth	two	alidha	bulls head in hair, dhar. ornaments, va.: lotus throne	Garuda-Samvara**
one*/three	12	prin.: embrace shakti in vajrahumkara mu. other hands hold tantric symbols	youth	two	alidha	*garuda head in hair, dhar. ornaments, va.: lotus throne	Garuda-Samvara (Buddha)**
one*/three	12	prin.: embrace shakti in vajrahumkara mu. other hands hold tantric symbols	youth	two	alidha	*garuda head in hair, dhar. ornaments, va.: lotus throne	Garuda-Samvaravajra (Buddha)**

one/three	16	prin.: embrace shakti in vajrahumkara mu. with skull-cup and vase/vessel rt.: human skull-cups lt.: vase/vessels	mature	two	alidha, yab-yum	dhar. ornaments, va.: bodies of subdued deities on lotus throne	Kapaladhara-Hevajra
three/nine	two	rt.: ritual chopper lt.: human skull-cup	corp.	two	alidha	dhar. ornaments, va.: prostrate human figure on lotus throne	Kartaridhara-Mahakala**
three/nine	two	rt.: abhaya mu. lt.: dhyana with thunderbolt on end	mature, nude	two	alidha	dhar. ornaments, va.: lotus throne	Mamaki (fo-mu)
three/nine	two	rt.: sandal-wood club lt.: raksasa thigh bone lance	corp.	two	alidha	cloak with gold belt dhar. ornaments, va.: lotus throne	Nidhi-Dandadhara-Mahakala
three*/nine	two	rt.: trident, club, sword lt.: skull-cup, noose/snare, goad/hook	mature	two		*bk., wh., rd., garment of black silk, va.: lotus throne	rDo-rje-bdud-'dul (gsang-sgrub)
three*/nine	two	rt.: trident, club, sword lt.: skull-cup, noose/snare, goad/hook	mature	two		*bk., wh., rd., garment of black silk, va.: lotus throne	rDo-rje-bdud-'dul (nang-sgrub)
three/nine	four	prin.: bhutadamara mu. rt.: thunderbolt lt.: noose/snare	corp.	two	alidha	dhar. ornaments, va.: prostrate human form on lotus throne	Bhutadamara-Anuttara-Vajrapani**
three/nine	four	rt.: sword, thunderbolt lt.: human skull-cup, noose/snare	youth	two	alidah	dhar. ornaments, va.: lotus throne	Caturbhuja-Acalavajra**
three/nine	four	rt.: sword, noose/snare lt.: magic notched staff/stick, wheel	corp.	two	praty-alidha	dhar. ornaments, va.: lotus throne	Dhvajagrakeyura
three/nine	four	rt.: hammer/mace, sword lt.: lotus, jewel	mature	two	pratyalidha, yab-yum	dhar. ornaments, va.: buffalo	Krsnayamari
three/nine	four	rt.: goad/hook, noose/snare lt.: sword, staff/stick	mature	two	alidha	dhar. ornaments, va.: lotus throne	Niladandavajra
three/nine	six	prin. embrace nude shakti, rt.: sword & jewel lt.: thunderbolt & lotus	mature	two	alidha, yab-yum	dhar. ornaments, va.: lotus throne	Acala
three/nine	six	rt.: thunderbolt, sword, wheel lt.: goad/hook, noose/snare, tarjani mu.	mature	two	alidha	bodh. ornaments va.: lotus throne	Astakapi-Acala**

three/nine	six	rt.: thunderbolt, sword, wheel lt.: goad/hook, noose/snare, karana mu.	mature	two	alidha	bodh. ornaments va.: lotus throne	<u>Astakapi-Acala</u>**
three*/nine	six	rt.: lotus, image of Buddha, axe lt.: sword ,noose/snare, tarjani mu.	mature	two	alidha(?)	*faces bl., wh., rd. dhar. ornaments,	<u>bDud-rtsi-lus-can-ma</u>
three*/nine	six	hands hold lotus, image of Buddha, sword, axe, noose/snare and tarjani mu.	mature	two		*smiling-bl., wh., rd., bodh. ornaments (?), va.: lotus throne	<u>bDud-rtsi-lus-can-ma</u>
three/nine	six	prin.: embrace shakti in vajrahumkara mu. rt.: thunderbolt, ritual chopper lt.: bell, trident	mature	two	alidha, yab-yum	dhar. ornaments, va.: human forms on lotus throne	<u>Citta-Hevajra</u>
three/nine	six	rt.: club/cudgel, human skull-cup, magic notched staff/stick lt.: noose/snare, mirror, magic dagger	mature	two		dhar. ornaments, va.: mule	<u>Drag-chen-srid-pa'i-rgyal-mo</u>
three/nine	six	prin.: embrace shakti, rt. in abhaya mu., lt. in varada mu. rt.: thunderbolt, sword lt.: jewel, flower (lotus?)	corp	two	alidha, yab-yum	dar. ornaments, va.: prostrate human forms	<u>(Guhyasamaja-uddhrta)-Krodha-Vighnantaka</u>**
three/nine	six	prin.: embrace shakti holding skull-cup and (?) rt.: wheel, sword lt.: karana mu, (?)	corp.	two	alidha, yab-yum	dhar. ornaments, va.: lotus throne	<u>Irsya-Bhairavavajra</u>
three/nine	six	rt.: sword, hammer/mace, thunderbolt lt.: pestle, thunderbolt, noose/snare	corp	two	pratyalidha	dhar. ornaments, va.: buffalo	<u>Krsnayamari</u>
three*/nine	six	prin.: embrace shakti rt.: thunderbolt, snake lt.: tarjani mu., snake	mature	two	alidha yab-yum	*wh., bl., rd., dhar. ornaments, va.: prostrate human forms	<u>Mahachakra-Vajrapani</u>
three*/nine	six	prin.: embrace shakti rt.: abhaya mu., thunderbolt lt.: abhaya mu , snake	mature	two	alidha, yab-yum	*wh., bl., rd., dhar. ornaments, va.: prostrate human forms	<u>Mahachakra-Vajrapani</u>
three*/nine	six	prin.: embrace shakti rt.: thunderbolt, serpent/snake lt.: karana mu., serpent/snake	mature	two	alidha, yab-yum	*wh., bl., rd., dhar. ornaments, va.: serpent	<u>Mahachakra-Vajrapani Buddha</u>

three/nine	six	prin.: embrace shakti rt.: short staff/stick, jewel lt.: sword, lotus	mature	two	alidha, yab-yum	dhar. ornaments, va.: lotus throne	Niladanda
three/nine	six	rt.: thunderbolt, wheel, lotus lt.: bell, flaming jewels(?), (?)	mature	two	vajra	dhar. ornaments, va.: lotus throne	Nairatma (fo-mu)
three/nine	six	rt.: iron goad/hook, arrow, sword lt.: knife, bow, staff/stick	mature	two		dhar. ornaments, va.: white lion	Pe-har
three/nine	six	rt.: human skull-cup, magic stick, trident lt.: thunderbolt, bell, human skin	mature	two	alidha	dhar. ornaments, va.: Kalaratri	Saptaksara
three/nine	six	prin.: embrace shakti, ritual chopper, human skull-cup rt.: thunderbolt, sword lt.: flaming jewel, lotus	corp.	two	partyalidha	dhar. ornaments, va.: lotus throne	Sumbharaja
three/nine	six	prin.: embrace shakti rt.: blue short staff/stick, sword lt.: jewel, lotus	mature	two		dhar. ornaments, va.: lotus throne	Takkiraja
three/nine	six	rt.: thunedrbolt, human skull-cup, battle axe lt.: bell, human skull-cup, plow-share	mature	two	pratyalidha	dhar. ornaments, va.: lotus throne	Vajra-Heruka
three/nine	six	prin.: vajrahumkara mu with thunderbolt, bell rt.: goad/hook, noose/snare lt.: skull-cup, magic stick rt. & lt.: hold tantric symbols	mature	two	alidha	dhar. ornaments, va.: Bhairava	Vajrahumkara
three/nine	six	prin.: embrace shakti with skull-cup, ritual chopper rt.: sword, wheel lt.: branch, flaming jewels	mature	two		dhar. ornaments, va.: lotus throne	Varahi
three/nine	six	prin.: embraces shakti with ritual chopper, human skull-cup rt.: thunderbolt, sword lt.: flaming jewel, lotus	mature	two	pratyalidha, yab-yum	dhar. ornaments, va.: form of Ganesa	Vighnantaka
three*/nine	six	prin.: embraces shakti rt.: hammer marked with thunderbolt, sword lt.: Jewel, lotus	corp.	two	alidha	*cent. bull-head, dhar. ornaments, va.: bull over a sun and lotus & tramples on Yama	Yamantaka

three/nine	six	prin.: thunderbolt, thunderbolt-marked bell, embraces shakti rt.: breast, arrow lt.: lotus bowl, bow	mature	two		dhar. ornaments, va.: lotus throne	Yogambara
three*/nine	12	prin.: (?) rt.: club, thunderbolt, goad/hook, dagger, bell lt.: skull-cup, rosary, club with skull finial, heart, snake-noose/snare	corp.	four	alidha	*wh., bl., rd., dhar. ornaments, va.: lotus throne	dPal-rdo-rje-nag-po-bstan-bsrung-yongs-rdzogs
three/nine	12	rt.: thunderbolt, bell, arrow, trident, sword,baton/mace lt.: tarjani mu., staff/stick, bow, (?), (?), noose/snare	mature	two	alidha	dhar. ornaments, va.: lotus throne	Vajragandhari (fo-mu)
three/nine	16	prin.: embrace shakti rt. & lt.: tantric symbols	mature	two	alidha, yab-yum	dhar. ornaments, va.: lotus throne	Garbha(?)-Hevajra
three/nine	16	prin.: embrace shakti rt. & lt.: skull-cups	mature	two	alidha, yab-yum	dhar. ornaments, va.: prostrate human form	Vajra-Dakini
four/12	two	rt.: thunderbolt lt.: bell	mature	two	alidha, yab-yum	dhar. ornaments, va.: Bhairava and Kalaratri	Samvara
four/12	four	hands hold thunderbolt, noose/snare, sword, human skull-cup	mature	four	pratyalidha	dhar. ornaments, va.: human forms on lotus throne	Acala-Vajrapani
four/12	four	prin.: karana mu with noose/snare(?) rt.: sword lt.: thunderbolt(?)	corp.	two	alidha	dhar. ornaments, va.: lotus throne	Caturbhuja-Acala
four/12	four	rt.: ritual chopper, human skull-cup lt.: flaming sword, golden vase/vessel	mature	two	alidha	dhar. ornaments, va.: lotus throne	Caturmukha-Karmayoga-Mahakala
four*/12	four	rt.: ritual chopper, skull-cup lt.: sword, trident	mature	two		*wh., bl., rd., gray, dhar. ornaments, va.: lotus throne	dPal-mgon-zhal-bzhi-pa-sngon-po-nyams-sgrol
four*/12	four	rt.: ritual chopper, human skull-cup lt.: sword, trident	mature	two		*wh., bl., rd., upper smoke, dhar. ornaments	Ksati-taraka-Nila-Caturmukha-(Sri-Mahakala)

four*/12	four	rt.: ritual chopper, sword lt.: human skull-cup, trident	corp.	two		*wh., bl., rd., upper smoke, dhar. ornaments, va.: lotus throne	Ksati-taraka-Nila-Caturmukha-(Sri-Mahakala)
four/12	four	rt.: human skull-cup, arrow lt.: magic notched staff/stick, bow	mature	two	ardha-paryanka	dhar. ornaments, va.: lotus throne	Mahamaya
four*/12	four	rt.: human skull-cup, bow lt.: magic notched staff/stick, arrow	mature	two	ardha-paryanka, yab-yum	dhar. ornaments, va.: lotus throne	Mahamaya
four/12	four	rt.: club, victory banner/flag lt.: sword, noose/snare	mature, nude	two		dhar. ornaments, va.: blue turquoise dragon	Raksa-mthu-bo-che
four*/12	eight	rt.: sword, short staff/stick, wheel, arrow lt.: trident, noose/snare, bow, tarjani mu.	corp.	two	alidha	dhar. ornaments, va.: prostrate human form	Dhvajagrakeyura**
four/12	eight	prin.: vajrahumkara mu. rt.: magic notched stick, goad/hook, arrow lt.: bow, noose/snare, thunderbolt	mature	two	pratyalidha	dhar. ornaments, va.: Gauri and Siva	Trailokyavijaya
four/12	ten	rt.: wheel on lotus, varada mu., goad/hook, arrow, sword lt.: thunderbolt, tarjani mu., noose/snare, bow, noose/snare	mature	two		*wh., bl., gr., yw. dhar. ornaments, va.: two yellow men	Mahasahasrapramardani
four/12	12	rt.: thunderbolt, thunderbolt marked bell, elephant skin, drum, axe, knife lt.: trident, left hands hold thunderbolt, thunderbolt marked bell, magic stick, skull-cup, noose/snare, Brahma's head	mature	two	alidha	dhar. ornaments, va.: Bhairava and Kalaratri	Samvara
four/12	12	prin.: embrace shakti other hands hold tantric symbols	mature	two	alidha, yab-yum	dhar. ornaments, va.: prostrate human figures	Vajra-garuda-Samvara
four/12	12	holding tantric symbols including: thunderbolt, goad/hook, magic staff/stick, sword, trident	mature	two	alidha	dhar. ornaments, va.: lotus throne	Vajragandhari
four*/12	24	prin.: embrace shakti rt.: thunderbolt, sword, trident, knife,	mature	two	alidha, yab-yum	*bl., rd., wt., yw. dhar. ornaments	Kalacakra

		fire, arrow, thunderbolt, goad/hook, wheel, knife, rod, axe lt.: bell, plate, ritual wand, skull-cup, bow, noose/snare, jewel, lotus, mirror, thunderbolt, chain, severed head of Brahma				va.: human forms	
five/15	10	rt.: goad/hook, sword, thunderbolt, varada mu., (?) lt.: noose/snare, shield, bow, banner/flag, abhaya mu.	mature	two	pratyalidha	dhar. ornaments, va.: lotus throne	Vajravidarani
five/15	12	rt.: drum, ritual wand, goad/hook, noose/snare, thunderbolt, arrow lt.: tarjani mu., skull-cup, red lotus, jewel, wheel, bow	mature	two	pratyalidha	dhar. ornaments, va.: lotus throne	Mayajalakrama-Avalokitesvara**
five/15	12	rt.: sword, thunderbolt, goad/hook, noose/snare, trident, arrow lt.: shield, wheel, jewel, deer skin, human skull-cup, tarjani mu.	mature	two	pratyalidha	dhar. ornaments, va.: lotus throne	Mayajalakramakrodha-Lokesvara**
six/18	12	rt.: thunderbolt, bell marked with thunderbolt, sword, trident, arrow, wheel lt.: magic notched staff/stick,, goad/hook, bow, battle axe, noose/snare, tarjani mu.	mature	two	pratyalidha	dhar. ornaments, va.: lotus throne	Vajragandhari
six*/18	12	rt.: sword, wooden pestle, arrow, crossed thunderbolt, thunderbolt, battle axe lt.: noose/snare, noose/snare, Asoka bough, head of Brahma, bow, trident	mature	two	alidha	*rd., bl., gr., yw., wh., & bl. sow-like, dhar. ornaments, va.: lotus throne	Vajravetali
eight/24	16	rt.: skull-cup with elephant, horse, mule, bill, camel, man, deer, cat lt.: skull-cup with Vishnu, vayu, Agni, Chandra, Surya, Yama, Vasudhara, terrestial deity	mature	two	alidha, yab-yum	dhar. ornaments, va.: lotus throne	Hevajra
eight*/24	16	prin.: embrace shakti holding human skull-cups with human figure and animal rt. & lt.: human skull-cup with either human figure or animal inside	mature	four	alidha, yab-yum	*7 with one above dhar. ornaments, va.: human figures	Kapala-Hevajra**

eight/24	16	prin.: embrace shakti rt.: ritual chopper, thunderbolt, elephant hide cape, hammer/mace,trident, sword, tantric staff/stick lt.: skull-cup, elephant hide cape, bell, goad/hook, chowrie, human skull-drum, human head	corp.	four	pratyalidha	dhar. ornaments, va.: two corpses	<u>Mahakala</u>
nine/27	34	prin.: embrace shakti with skull-cup, ritual chopper	mature	16	alidha, yab-yum	dhar. ornaments, va.: human bodies	<u>Vajrabhairava</u>**
12*/36	24	holding tantric symbols	mature	two	pratyalidha	*red chignon, dhar. ornaments va.: trampling on gods	<u>Ugra-Tara</u>

Green (Skt.: syama: Tib.: ljang-ku), Calm Deities

Abbreviations:

as. = asana
bk. = black
bl. = blue
bodh. = bodhisattva
bn. = brown
corp. = corpulent
dhar. = dharmapala
gn. = green
lt. = left
mu. = mudra
pu. = purple
rd. = red
rt. = right
sc. = smokey
va. = vahana
wh. = white
yw. = yellow

(*) special variations or attributes noted within the entry.

(**) following deity's name indicates that the color is not noted in the source, kulesa's color is applied to the entry.

(eyes: 2-3, 6-9, etc.) in sources the deity's faces are noted, but the number of the eyes are not noted.

Head/Eyes	Hands	Objects Held	Body	Feet	Asana	Other Attributes	Deity Name
one/ two	two	rt.: abhaya mu. lt.: dhyana mu. with crossed thunderbolts	mature	two	dhyana	Buddha-like, monastic robes, va.: lotus throne,	Dhyani Buddha Amoghasiddhi
one/ two	two	rt.: abhaya mu. lt.: dhyana mu.	mature	two	dhyana, yab-yum	bodh. ornaments, va.: lotus throne, shakti: Tara	Amoghasiddhi
one/two	two	rt.: bell lt.: crossed thunderbolts	mature	two	dhyana, yab-yum	bodh. ornaments, va.: lotus throne, shakti: Tara	Amoghasiddhi
one/ two	two	rt.: crossed thunderbolts lt.: dhyana mu.	mature	two	vajra	bodh. ornaments, va.: lotus throne	Amoghasiddhi
one/two	two	rt.: abhaya mu. lt.: dhyana mu.	mature	two	vajra	bodh. ornaments, va.: lotus throne	Amoghasiddhi
one/two	two	holding crossed thunderbolts	mature	two	vajra, yab-yum	bodh. ornaments, va.: harpy throne shakti: Sgrol-ma	Amoghasiddhi (Bhagavan)
one/two	two	rt.: noose/snare lt.: abhaya mu.	mature	two	vamalalita	bodh. ornaments, va.: lotus throne	Artha Pratisamvit
one/two	two	rt.: jewel lt.: noose/snare	mature	two		bodh. ornaments, va.: lotus throne	Artha Pratisamvita
one/two	two	rt.: abhaya mu.	youth	two	vamalalita	bodh. ornaments,	Arya-(Mula)-Syama-Tara

		lt.: karana mu.				va.: lotus throne	
one/two	two	rt.: varada mu. lt.: blue lotus	youth	two	ardha-paryanka	bodh. ornaments, va.: lotus throne	Arya-Tara
one/two	two	flaming sword	mature	two	sama-bhanga	monastic garm with coat of mail va.: lotus throne	Asuraloka
one/two	two	rt.: thunderbolt lt.: crossed thunderbolts on double lotus	mature	two		bodh. ornaments, va.: lotus throne	Durangama
one/two	two	rt.: thunderbolt lt.: (?)	youth	two	vamalalita	bodh. ornaments, va.: lotus throne	Durangama (fo-mu)**
one/two	two	rt.: abhaya mu, lt.: perfume bottle	youth	two	alidha	bodh. ornaments, va.: lotus throne	Gandha
one/two	two	rt.: conch shell lt.: rests on hip	youth	two	ardha-paryanka	bodh. ornaments, va.: lotus throne	Gandha
one*/two	two	rt.: varada mu. lt.: holds trunk of elephant	mature	two	dhyana	*"whitish-green" bodh. ornaments, va.: lotus throne	Gandhahasti
one/two	two	rt.: conch shell lt.: clenched on hip	mature	two	dhyana	bodh. ornaments, va.: lotus throne	Gandhahasti
one/two	two	rt.: jewel held on knee lt.: dhyana mu.	mature	two	sattva	bodh. ornaments, va.: lotus throne	Gandhahasti
one/two	two	rt.: abhaya mu. lt.: conch shell	youth	two	ardha-paryanka	bodh. ornaments, va.: lotus throne	Gandhavajra
one/two	two	rt.: divination arrow lt.: ladle of milk	mature	two		dress of white silk, bodh. ornaments, va.: dragon	gTal-dkar-'gro-bzang-ma
one/two	two	rt.: alarm staff/stick lt.: wish fulfilling jewel	mature	two	lalita	bodh. ornaments, lotus throne	Jizo
one/two	two	dharmachakra mu.	mature	two	sopasraya	bodh. ornaments, va.: lotus throne	Jnanakrama-Simhavahana-Syama-Vaisravana
one*/two	two	rt.: stem of lotus, blossom at shoulder lt.: sword	youth	two	vamalalita	*pale blue, bodh. ornaments,	Jnana-Vasita

						va.: lotus throne	
one/two	two	rt.: lotus lt.: crossed thunderbolts	mature	two		bodh. ornaments, va.: lotus throne	<u>Karma-Vasita</u>
one/two	two	rt.: stem of lotus lt.: crossed thunderbolts	mature	two	vajra	bodh. ornaments, va.: lotus throne	<u>Karma-Vasita</u>
one/two	two	rt.: varada mu. lt.: stem of blue lotus	youth	two	vamalalita	bodh. ornaments, va.: lotus throne	<u>Khadiravani-Tara</u>
one/two	two	rt.: abhaya mu. with stem of blue lotus lt.: vitarka mu. with stem of blue lotus	youth	two	vamalalita	bodh. ornaments, va.: lotus throne	<u>Khadiravani-Tara</u>
one/two	two	rt.: varada mu. lt.: kartari mu. stem of blue lotus with wheel	youth	two	lalita	bodh. ornaments, va.: lotus throne	<u>Khadiravani-Tara</u>
one/two	two	rt.: banner/flag with wish-fulfilling jewel lt.: white lotus	mature	two		bodh. ornaments, va.: lotus throne	<u>Ksanti-Paramita</u>
one/two	two	rt.: flaming jewel lt.: white lotus	mature	two	vamalalita	bodh. ornaments, va.: lotus throne	<u>Ksanti-Paramita</u>
one/two	two	rt.: bhumisparsa mu. lt.: lotus with wish-giving tree	mature	two		bodh. ornaments va.: winged lion	<u>Ksitigarbha</u>
one/two	two	rt.: stem of lotus in vitarka mu. with lotus and wish-fulfilling jewel lt.: stem of lotus in varada mu. with lotus and book/manuscript	mature	two	sama-bhanga	bodh. ornaments va.: winged lion	<u>Ksitigarbha</u>
one/two	two	rt.: alarm staff/stick lt.: flaming jewel	mature	two	vajra	bodh. ornaments va.: winged lion	<u>Ksitigarbha</u>
one/two	two	rt.: vitarka mu. withalarm staff/stick lt.: abhaya mu. with vase/vessel	mature	two	vajra	bodh. ornaments va.: winged lion	<u>Ksitigarbha</u>
one/two	two	rt.: alms bowl lt.: abhaya mu	mature	two	vajra	bodh. ornaments va.: winged lion	<u>Ksitigarbha</u>
one*/two	two	rt.: lotus covered with jewels lt.: abhaya mu.	mature	two		*smiling, haughty, bodh. ornaments, va.: lotus throne	<u>Mahalaksmi-Devi</u>
one*/two	two	rt.: vitarka mu. with stem of lotus	youth	two	lalita	*smiling, haughty,	<u>Mahalaksmi-Devi</u>

		lt.: abhaya mu.				bodh. ornaments, va.: lion	
one/two	two	rt.: peacock feather lt.: fly whisk	mature	two	ardha-paryaka	bodh. ornaments, va.: lotus throne	Mahamayuri
one/two	two	rt.: peacock feather lt.: varada mu.	mature	two		bodh. ornaments, va.: lotus throne	Mahamayuri
one/two	two	dharmachakra mu.	mature	two		bodh. ornaments, va.: lotus throne	Mahasri-Tara
one/two	two	rt.: whip lt.: clenched in lap	mature	two	dhyana	bodh. ornaments, va.: lotus throne	Pratibhanakuta
one/two	two	rt.: whip lt.: lotus topped with sword	mature	two	dhyana	bodh. ornaments, va.: lotus throne	Pratibhanakuta
one/two	two	rt.: lotus topped with crown lt.: clenched in lap	mature	two	dhyana	bodh. ornaments, va.: lotus throne	Pratibhanakuta
one/two	two	rt.: bell lt.: bell	mature	two		bodh. ornaments, va.: lotus throne	Pratibhana-Pratisamvita
one/two	two	rt.: bell lt.: abhaya mu. on knee	mature	two	vamalalita	bodh. ornaments, va.: lotus throne	Pratibhana-Pratisamvita
one/two	two	rt.: jewel lt.: moon disc	youth	two	dhyana	bodh. ornaments, va.: lotus throne	Ratnapani
one/two	two	rt.: varada mu. lt.: jewel	youth	two	vajra	bodh. ornaments, va.: lotus throne	Ratnapani
one/two	two	rt.: lotus lt.: sun disc & moon disc	mature	two		bodh. ornaments, va.: lotus throne	Riddhivasita
one/two	two	rt.: crossed thunderbolts lt.: thunderbolt	mature	two		bodh. ornaments, va.: lotus throne	Sarvakarmavaranavisodhani
one/two	two	rt.: varada mu. lt.: vitarka mu.	mature	two		bodh. ornaments, va.: lotus throne on roaring lion	Simhanada-Tara
one/two	two	rt.: three peacock feathers lt.: bowl of jewels	youth	two	vamalalita	bodh. ornaments, va.: bird	Syama-Parnasabari
one/two	two	rt.: vitarka mu.	mature	two	lalita	bodh. ornaments,	Syama-Tara

		lt.: varada mu. holding lotus				va.: lotus throne	
one/two	two	rt.: stem of lotus with crossed thunderbolts lt.: stem of lotus with crossed thunderbolts	mature	two	lalita	bodh. ornaments, va.: lotus throne	Syama-Tara
one/two	two	rt.: vitarka mu. lt.: vitarka mu. holding lotus	mature	two	vamalalita	bodh. ornaments, va.: lotus throne	Syama-Tara (fo-mu)
one/two	two	rt.: thunderbolt at chest level lt.: rests behind thigh	youth	two	lalita	bodh. ornaments, va.: lotus throne	Syama-Vajrapani
one/two	two	rt.: banner/flag with wish fulfilling jewel lt.: thunderbolt on lotus	mature	two		bodh. ornaments, va.: lotus throne	Upayaparamita
one/two	two	rt.: varada mu. lt.: lotus	mature	two	bhadra	bodh. ornaments, va.: lotus throne	Vasya-Tara
one/two	two	rt.: banner/flag with wish fulfilling jewel lt.: blue lotus	mature	two	lalita	bodh. ornaments, va.: lotus throne	Viryaparamita
one/two	two	rt.: triple jewel lt.: lotus in karana mu.	mature	two	vamalalita	bodh. ornaments, va.: lotus throne	Viryaparamita
one/two	four	prin.: vitarka and varada mu. rt.: rosary lt.: lotus with book/manuscript	mature	two		bodh. ornaments, va.: animal(?)	Dhanada-Tara
one/two	four	rt.: rosary, varada mu. lt.: blue lotus, book/manuscript	mature	two		bodh. ornaments, v.,: animal(?)	Dhanada-Tara
one/two	four	rt.: varada mu., rosary lt.: lotus, book/manuscript	youth	two	vajra	bodh. ornaments, va.: lotus throne	Dhanada-Tara (fo-mu)
one/two	four	rt.: varada mu., lotus lt.: noose/snare, goad/hook	mature	two		bodh. ornaments, va.: lotus throne	Durgottarini-Tara
one/two	four	rt.: varada mu., goad/hook lt.: stem of lotus, rings(?)	youth	two	vajra	bodh. ornaments, va.: lotus throne	Durgottarini-Tara
one/two	four	rt.: crossed thunderbolts, vitarka mu. lt.: stem of lotus, noose/snare	youth	two	sattva	bodh. ornaments, va.: lotus throne	Durgottarini-Tara (fo-mu)
one/two	four	rt.: abhaya mu, trident lt.: peacock feather, serpent/snake	youth	two	vamalalita	bodh. ornaments, va.: lotus throne	Ianguli

one/two	four	rt.: peacock feather, vase/vessel lt.: jewel, varada mu.	mature	two		bodh. ornaments, va.: lotus throne	Mahamayuri
one/two	four	rt.: flowering branch, flaming jewels lt.: vase/vessel, karitari	mature	two	sopasraya	bodh. ornaments, va.: makara	Varada-Tara
one/three	six	rt.: thunderbolt, axe, arrow lt.: noose/snare, three peacock(?) feathers, bow	youth	two	lalita	bodh. ornaments, va.: lotus throne	Sadbhuja-Parnasabari (fo-mu)**
three/six	six	rt.: sword, crossed thunderbolts, wheel lt.: bell, flower, (?)	mature	two	vajra	bodh. ornaments, va.: lotus throne	Amoghasiddhi
three/six	six	prin. in abhaya and dhyana with crossed thunderbolts,	mature	two	dhyana	bodh. ornaments, va.: eagles	Amoghasiddhi
three/six	six	rt.: wheel, thunderbolt, lotus lt.: sword, flaming jewel, bell	mature	two	vajra	bodh. ornaments va.: lotus throne	Ksitigarbha
three*/six	six	rt.: bow, arrow, noose/dnare lt.: circular banner/flag, thunderbolt, bell	mature	two	vajra	*rd., gr., wh., bodh. ornaments, va.: lotus throne	Mahamantranusarini
three/six	six	tantric symbols	mature	two		bodh. ornaments, va.: lotus throne	Parnasabari-Tara
three/six	six	rt.: thunderbolt, axe, arrow lt.: noose/snare, peacock feather, bow	mature	two	sattva	bodh. ornaments, va.: lotus throne	Sadbhuja-Parnasabari (fo-mu)**
three/six	six	prin.: embrace shakti with thunderbolt, bell rt.: wheel, sword lt.: noose/snare, goad/hook	mature	two		bodh. ornaments, va.: lotus throne	Vajramrita
three*/six	eight	rt.: abhaya mu., thunderbolt, chain, arrow lt.: skull-cup, noose/snare, tarjani mu., bow	mature	two	lalita	*central smiles, rt. & lt. contorted, bodh. ornaments, va.: lotus throne	Vajrasrinkhala
three/6-9	six	rt.: parasol, sword, wheel lt.: vase/vessel, peacock feather, Buddha in begging-bowl	mature	two	vajra	bodh. ornaments, va.: peacock	Mahamayuri
three/6-9	six	rt.: varada mu., arrow, sword lt.: peacock feather, bow, trident	youth	two	ardha- paryanka	bodh. ornaments, va.: lotus throne	Mahamayuri
three/6-9	six	rt.: peacock feather, arrow, abhaya mu.	youth	two	sattva	bodh. ornaments,	Mahamayuri (fo-mu)

		lt.: dhyana mu., bow, (?)				va.: lotus throne	
three/6-9	six	rt.: abhaya mu., thunderbolt, arrow lt.: noose/snare, bow, circular banner/flag	mature	two	ardha-paryanka	bodh. ornaments, va.: lotus throne	<u>Mahasitavati</u>
three/6-9	six	rt.: needle & thread, arrow, thunderbolt lt.: leafy branch, bow, noose/snare	mature	two	lalita	bodh. ornaments, va.: four wheeled-chariot drawn by seven horses	<u>Syamasva-Marici</u>
three/6-9	eight	rt.: jewel, arrow, varada mu., sword lt.: mendicant in a bowl, jewel showering vase/vessel, banner/flag with crossed thunderbolts, jewel	mature	two		bodh. ornaments, va.: lotus throne	<u>Mahamayuri</u>
three*/6-9	eight	rt.: vase/vessel, wheel, varada mu., sword lt.: Buddha in a bowl, axe, vase/vessel, banner/flag	youth	two	sattva	*bl., gr., wh., bodh. ornaments, va.: lotus throne	<u>Mahamayuri</u>
three/nine	six	rt.: varada mu., peacock feather, arrow lt.: vase/vessel, bow, jewel	youth	two	ardha-paryanka	bodh. ornaments, va.: lotus throne	<u>Mahamayuri</u>

Green (Skt.: syama; Tib.: ljang-ku), Wrathful, Angry or Haughty Deities

Abbreviations:

as. = asana	bk. = black	bl. = blue	bodh. = bodhisattva
bn. = brown	corp. = corpulent	dhar. = dharmapala	gn. = green
lt. = left	mu. = mudra	pu. = purple	rd. = red
rt. = right	sc. = smokey	va. = vahana	wh. = white
yw. = yellow			

(*) special variations or attributes noted within the entry.
(**) following deity's name indicates that the color is not noted in the source, kulesa's color is applied to the entry.
(eyes: 2-3, 6-9, etc.) in sources the deity's faces are noted, but the number of the eyes are not noted.

Head/Eyes	Hands	Objects Held	Body	Feet	Asana	Other Attributes	Deity Name
one*/two	two	holding treasure casque and turquoise lance with banner/flag	mature	two		*angry, copper shell armor, va.: dragon	bsTan-bsrung-mdzad-gnod-sbyin-mched-lnga
one*/two	two	rt.: bell lt.: human skull-cup	mature	two	praty-alidha	*serpent-head northern quarter	Green Serpent-headed Bell-Holding Goddess
one*/two	two	rt.: wavy-bladed knife lt.: human skull-cup filled with blood	mature	two		*angry, dhar. ornaments, realm: northern quarter va.: tiger	Drag-po'i-rgyal-chen
one/two	two	rt.: trident lt.: flower (lotus?)	emaci-ated	two	sattva	dhar. ornaments, va.: lotus throne	Dvibhuja-Parnasabari
one*/two	two	holding club/cudgel	mature	two	alidha	*fox-head, dhar. ornaments	Ishvari, "Dark-Green Fox-Headed baton-Goddess"
one*/two	two	holding vase/vessel	mature	two	alidha	*stag-head, dhar. ornaments	Ishvari, "Green Stag-Headed Wealth-Guardian Goddess"
one*/two	two	rt.: citron lt.: mongoose	corp.	two		*haughty, silk garments, bodh. ornaments	Iambhala-ljang-gu-dus-'khor-lugs
one/two	two	rt.: stem of lotus in varada mu. lt.: stem of lotus in karana mu.	youth	two	vamalalita	bodh. ornaments, va.: lotus throne	Kasmira-mahapandita-krama-Syama-Tara

one*/two	two	rt.: serpent/snake lt.: pill (pearl?)	mature	two	ardha-paryanka	*angry, antique armor, va.: white and yellow demons	Virupaksa
one*/two	two	rt.: noose/snare lt.: wish-fulfilling jewel	mature	two	ardha-paryanka	*angry, antique armor, va.: white and yellow demons	Virupaksa
one*/2-3	two	rt.: basket of grass lt.: noose/snare	mature	two		*angry, bejeweled, va.: dragon	gTad-dkar-'gro-bzang-ma
one*/2-3	two	rt.: jewel lt.: mongoose	mature	two	vamalalita, yab-yum	*angry, dhar. ornaments, va.: lotus throne	Kalacakra-krama-Syama-Jambhala
one/2-3	ten	rt.: magic notched staff/stick lt.: noose/snares with hearts and lungs	mature	two		human skin on torso bear skin on loins, syllable "bhyo", dhar. ornaments, va.: Asiatic wild ass with white muzzle	bDud-mo-gsod-byed-ma
one/two	four	rt.: trident, peacock feather lt.: abhaya mu., serpent/snake	mature	two		bodh. ornaments, va.; lotus throne	Janguli-Tara
one/three	two	holding vase/vessel	mature	two	alidha, yab-yum	dhar. ornaments, shakti; Dril-bu-ma, va.: lotus throne	Amritadhara
one/three	two	rt.: crossed thunderbolts-topped club lt.: noose/snare in tarjani mu.	mature	two	pratyalidha	dhar. ornaments, va.: sun lotus petal	Amritadhara
one/three	two	rt.: ritual chopper lt.: human skull-cup	mature	two	ardha-paryanka	dhar. ornaments, va.: lotus throne realm: West	Bhima
one/three	two	rt.: thunderbolt lt.: (?)	mature, nude	two	alidha	dhar. ornaments, va.: prostrate human forms	Candali (fo-mu)**
one/three	two	rt.: ritual chopper lt.: human skull-cup	mature	two	ardha-paryanka	dhar. ornaments, pendulous breasts, va.: lotus throne	Candali-Dakini**

one/three	two	rt.: red lance with banner/flag lt.: red noose/snare	mature	two	astride	dhar. ornaments, high leather boots, va.: red horse	
one*/three	two*	claws hold vase/vessel	bird-like	two		*bird-like head, *wing-arms, realm: lt. shoulder	Dri-chab-kyi-khyung
one*/three	two*	claws hold thunderbolt	bird-like	two		*bird-like head, *wing-arms, realm: lt. shoulder	Dri-chab-kyi-khyung
one/three	two	rt.: thunderbolt lt.: human skull-cup	mature	two		dhar. ornaments, ca.: lotus throne	Ghasmari
one/three	two	rt.: thunderbolt on thigh lt.: bell at shoulder level	mature, nude	two	alidha	dhar. ornaments, ca.: prostrate human form	Ghasmari (fo-mu)
one/three	two	rt.: serpent/snake lt.: human skull-cup	mature	two		dhar. ornaments, ca.: lotus throne	Ghasmari (fo-mu)
one*/three	two	rt.: ritual chopper lt.: human skull-cup	mature	two	alidha	*dark green, dhar. ornaments	gShin-rje-gsed
one*/three	two	rt.: club lt.: noose/snare	mature, nude	two		*lioness-head, dark-green, dhar. ornaments, va.: blue water bull	gShin-rje'i-rgyal
one/three	two	rt.: mace lt.: mongoose	corp.	two	maha- rajalila	dhar. ornaments, va.: lion	Inanakrama-Simhavahana-Syama-Vaisravana
one/three	two	rt.: lance with bk. banner/flag lt.: noose/snare	mature	two		dhar. ornaments, va.: brown horse with black muzzle	Kang-ka-thod-nag-bdud-btsan
one/three	two	rt.: sword lt.: human skull-cup with magic staff/stick in crook of arm	mature	two		dhar. ornaments, va.: lotus throne	Karma-Dakini
one/three	two	rt.: crossed thunderbolts lt.: mongoose	mature	two	ardha- paryanka	dhar. ornaments, va.: lotus throne	Karma-Dakini
one/three	two	rt.: ritual chopper lt.: human skull-cup with magic staff/stick in crook of arm	mature	two	ardha- paryanka	dhar. ornaments, va.: lotus throne	Karma-Dakini

one/three	two	rt.: abhaya mu. lt.: dhyana mu. with crossed thunderbolts	mature	two	ardha-paryanka, yab-yum	bodh. ornaments, va.: lotus throne	Karma-Heruka
one/three	two	rt.: encircles yab's neck lt.: red human skull-cup filled with blood	mature	two	pratyalidha, yab-yum	bodh. ornaments, va.: lotus throne, Karma-Heruka's yum	Karma-Krotishaurima
one*/three	two	wings	bird-like	two		claws hold sword, realm: genitals, bone ornaments	Las-kyi-khyung
one/three	two	rt.: crossed thunderbolts lt.: mongoose	mature	two		armored, va.: lotus throne	Las-kyi-mkha'-'gro-ma
one/three	two	rt.: ritual chopper lt.: human skull-cup	mature, nude	two		dhar. ornaments	Las-mdzad-gtum-mo
one/three	two	holding precious vase/vessel	mature	two		green garments, dhar. ornaments, va.: lotus throne	lHa-mo-dal-byad
one*/three	two	rt.: human skull-cup lt.: ritual chopper	mature	two	alidha	*sea-elephant-head dhar. ornaments, va.: lotus throne	Makaravaktra
one*/three	two	rt.: noose/snare lt.: chalice	mature	two	ardha-paryankha	*leopard-head dhar. ornaments, va.: lotus throne	Makaravaktra
one*/three	two	rt.: noose/snare lt.: chalice	mature, nude	two	ardha-paryankha	*elephant-head pendulous breasts, dhar. ornaments, va.: lotus throne	Makaravaktra
one/three	two	rt.: ritual chopper lt.: human skull-cup	mature	two	alidha	dhar. ornaments, va.: prostrate human form	Ljan-lugs-Saptadas-atmaka-Tamra-kartaridhara-Mahakala
one/three	two	rt.: club lt.: mongoose	mature	two		armored, dhar. ornaments, attrib.: syllable "be", va.: lion	Ngal-bsos-po
one/three	two	holding tarjani mudra and noose/snare	mature	two	pratyalidha	dhar. ornaments, va.: diseases in human	Parnasavari

					forms or Vighnas	
one/three	two	rt.: treasure casque lt.: lance with banner/flag	mature	two	dhar. ornaments, copper armor, va.: dragon	Phu-yi-gzhi-bdag-mdzod-lnga-spun-lnga
one*/three	two	holding sacred dagger	mature	two	*angry, dhar. ornaments, syllable "le", va.: yak with nine horns	rDo-rje-drag-mo-rgyal
one*/three	two	rt.: lance with banner/flag lt.: vase/vessel of gems	mature	two	*angry, cuirass of gold, white cloak, va.: horse	rMa-chen-spom-ra
one*/three	two	rt.: golden horse whip lt.: pan filled with jewels	mature	two	*angry, armored, va.: yellow horse treading on a yaksa and yaksi	rNam-sras
one/three	two	rt.: string of jewels lt.: treasure producing mongoose	mature	two	bejeweled diadem, clothed in silks, high fancy leather boots, va.: lion	rNam-sras-ljang-gu-seng-zhon-manyaja-na'i-lugs
one/three	two	rt.: bell lt.: magic dagger	mature	two	dhar. ornaments, va.: lotus throne	Sa-bdag-btsan-'dul-chen-mo
one/three	two	rt.: banner/flag lt.: abhaya mu.	mature	two	dhar. ornaments, realm: Southwest and Saturday, va.: lotus throne	sPen-pa
one/three	two	rt.: ritual chopper lt.: skull-cup	mature, nude	two	dhar. ornaments, va.: lotus throne	Srin-mo-chen-mo
one/three	two	holds axe	mature	two	richly helmeted, richly garbed, va.: black horse	Tha-hog-chos-rgyal-po
one/three	two	holds axe	mature	two	richly helmeted, richly garbed, va.: yellow deer	Tha-hog-chos-rgyal-po

one/three	two	rt.: bell lt.: tarjani mu.	mature	two		dhar. ornaments, va.: lotus throne	Vajraghanta
one/three	two	holding chain	mature	two	alidha	dhar. ornaments, va.: lotus throne	Vajrasrinkhala
one*/three	two	rt.: sword lt.: blade of sword	mature	two	ardha- paryanka	*angry, antique armor, va.: green and red demon	Virudhaka
one/three	two	rt.: lifts bowels to her mouth lt.: skull-cup filled with blood	mature	two		dhar. ornaments, va.: lotus throne	Vetali
one/three	two	rt.: bell lt.: varada mu.	mature, nude	two	ardha- paryanka	pendulous breasts, dhar. ornaments, va.: lotus throne	Vetali
one/three	two	rt.: ritual chopper, embraces shakti lt.: human skull-cup, embraces shakti	mature	two	alidha	dhar. ornaments, va.: lotus throne	Vidya-Dhara[10]
one/three	two	holds goad/hook, embraces shakti	mature	two	alidha, yab-yum	dhar. ornaments, va.: lotus throne	Vijaya (male)
one*/three	two	rt.: human skull-drum lt.: divination arrow	corp.	two	alidha	*bull-head, dhar. ornaments, va.: bull	Yama
one/three	four	rt.: sword, human skull-cup lt.: ritual chopper, trident	mature	two		dhar. ornaments, va.: lotus throne	mGon-po-ljang-khu
one/three	four	rt.: sword, tarjani mu. lt.: human skull-cup, magic staff/stick	corp.	two	ardha- paryanka	pendulous breasts, dhar. ornaments, va.: human form	Vetali-Devi
one/three	six	prin.: embraces shakti with ritual chopper, human skull-cup rt.: small drum, trident lt.: rosary of skulls and noose/snare	mature	two	yab-yum	dhar. ornaments, va.: lotus throne	mGon-ljang-tshe-bdag
one/three	six	rt.: thunderbolt, noose/snare, arrow lt.: karana mu., (?), bow	mature	two	alidha	dhar. ornaments, va.: lotus throne	Vajrasrinkhala
one*/three	ten	rt.: magic notched staff/sticks lt.: noose/snares with hearts and lungs	mature	two		*dark green, dhar. ornaments, va.: Asiatic wild ass,	bDud-mo-gsod-byed-ma

10 The Vidya-Dhara , Knowledge Holding Deities who appear on the seventh day of the second state of the Bardo-Thodol. They are forms of the Dhyani Buddhas.

						syllable "bhyo"	
three*/nine	two	rt.: crossed thunderbolts lt.: peacock feathers	mature	two	pratyalidha	*wh., yw., gr., dhar. ornaments, va.: diseases in human forms or Vighnas	Parnasavari
three*/nine	six	rt.: thunderbolt, battle axe, arrow lt.: bow, cluster of leaves, noose/snare	mature	two	pratyalidha	*wh., yw., gr., dhar. ornaments, va.: diseases in human forms or Vighnas	Parnasavari
three*/nine	six	rt.: sword, trident, club/cudgel lt.: bell, human skull-cup, plow-share	mature	two	pratyalidha, yab-yum	bodh. ornaments, va.: lotus throne	Karma-Heruka
three/nine	six	rt.: bell, sword, thunderbolt lt.: pestle, axe, tarjani mu.	mature	two		bodh. ornaments, va.: lotus throne	Kinkini-Dhari
three/nine	six	prin.: hold bhutadamara mu. rt.: thunderbolt, cane staff/stick lt.: bell, noose/snare	corp.	two	alidha	dhar. ornaments, va.: Ganesa figure	Syama-Krodha-Bhurkumkuta
three/nine	six	prin.: embrace shakti rt.: thunderbolt, sword lt.: jewel, lotus	mature	two	yab-yum	dhar. ornaments, va.: lotus throne	Vighnantaka
four/12	eight	rt.: thunderbolt, peacock feathers, battle axe, arrow lt.: bow, crossed thunderbolts, cluster of leaves, noose/snare in tarjani mu.	mature	two	alidha	dhar. ornaments, va.: diseases in human forms or Vighnas	Parnasavari

Yellow (Skt.: pita; Tib.: ser-po), Calm Deities

Abbreviations:

as. = asana	bk. = black	bl. = blue	bodh. = bodhisattva
bn. = brown	corp. = corpulent	dhar. = dharmapala	gn. = green
lt. = left	mu. = mudra	pu. = purple	rd. = red
rt. = right	sc. = smokey	va. = vahana	wh. = white
yw. = yellow			

(*) special variations or attributes noted within the entry.
(**) following deity's name indicates that the color is not noted in the source, kulesa's color is applied to the entry.
(eyes: 2-3, 6-9, etc.) in sources the deity's faces are noted, but the number of the eyes are not noted.

Head/Eyes	Hands	Objects Held	Body	Feet	Asana	Other Attributes	Deity Name
one/two	two	rt.: crossed thunderbolt at chest lt.: bell at hip	mature	two	vajra	bodh. ornaments, va.: lotus throne	Adi-Buddha (Dharmavajra)**
one/two	two	rt.: varada mu. lt.: wish fulfilling gem in dhyana mu.	mature	two	vajra	Buddha-like, monastic robes. va.: pair of lions or horses	Dhyani Buddha Ratnasambhava
one/two	two	rt.: bhumisparsa mu. lt.: dhyana mu	mature	two	vajra	urns, usnisa, long ear lobes, monastic robes, va.: lotus or lion throne	Gautama Buddha
one/two	two	holding dharmachakra mu.	mature	two	vajra	urns, usnisa, long ear lobes, monastic robes, va.: lotus or lion throne	Gautama Buddha
one/two	two	holding dhyana mu.	mature	two	vajra	urns, usnisa, long ear lobes, monastic robes, va.: lotus or lion throne	Gautama Buddha
one/two	two	rt.: bhumisparsa mu. lt.: dhyana mu	mature	two	virasena	urns, usnisa, long ear lobes, monastic robes, va.: lotus or lion throne	Gautama Buddha

one/two	two	rt.: thunderbolt lt.: book/manuscript	mature	two		bodh. ornaments, va.: lotus throne	Abhimukhi
one/two	two	rt.: thunderbolt, lt.: (?),	mature	two	vamalalita	bodh. ornaments, va.: lotus throne	Abhimukhi (fo-mu)
one/two	two	rt.: jewels lt.: wish-fulfilling jewel	mature	two	dhyana	bodh. ornaments, va.: lotus throne	Akasagarbha
one/two	two	rt.: vitarka mu. lt.: varada mu.	mature	two	dhyana	bodh. ornaments, va.: lotus throne	Akasagarbha
one/two	two	rt.: flower (lotus?) lt.: abhaya mu.	mature	two	dhyana	bodh. ornaments, va.: lotus throne	Akasagarbha
one/two	two	rt.: flower (lotus?) with sun disc lt.: varada mu.	mature	two	dhyana	bodh. ornaments, va.: lotus throne	Akasagarbha
one/two	two	rt.: vitarka mu. lt.: vitarka mu. with stem of lotus on which rests a sword on hilt	mature	two	dhyana	bodh. ornaments, va.: lotus throne	Akasagarbha
one/two	two	rt.: varada mu. lt.: kataka mu. against chest	mature	two	dhyana	bodh. ornaments, va.: lotus throne	Aksayamati
one/two	two	rt.: sword lt.: abhaya mu. with lotus	mature	two	dhyana	bodh. ornaments, va.: lotus throne	Aksayamati
one/two	two	dhyana mu. with bowl filled with the elixir of life	mature	two	dhyana	bodh. ornaments, va.: lotus throne	Aksayamati
one/two	two	rt.: crossed thunderbolts lt.: dhyana mu.	mature	two	dhyana	bodh. ornaments, va.: lotus throne	Aksayamati
one/two	two	rt.: lotus lt.: clenched on hip	mature	two	dhyana	bodh. ornaments, va.: lotus throne	Amoghadarsin (Bodhisattva)
one/two	two	rt.: bhumisparsa mu. lt.: dhyana mu.	mature	two	vajra	bodh. ornaments, va.: lotus throne	Amoghadarsin (Bodhisattva)
one/two	two	rt.: abhaya mu. lt.: dhyana mu.	mature	two	vajra	Buddha-like, monastic robes, va.: lotus throne	Amoghadarsin Buddha
one/two	two	rt.: flaming jewel at chest lt.: dhyana mu. with sun disc	mature	two	vajra	Buddha-like, monastic robes, va.: lotus throne	Amoghadarsin Buddha

one/two	two	holds shakti with sword and (?)	youth	two	vajra, yab-yum	bodh. ornaments, va.: lotus throne	Antarasadhana-Manjughosa
one/two	two	rt.: abhaya mu. lt.: vase/vessel	youth	two	sopasraya	bodh. ornaments, va.: lotus throne	Anucara-Maitreya
one/two	two	rt.: bhumisparsa mu. lt.: stem of lotus with sword	youth	two	sopasraya	bodh. ornaments, va.: lotus throne	Anucara-Manjusri
one/two	two	rt.: thunderbolt lt.: noose/snare	youth	two	vamalalita	bodh. ornaments va.: lotus throne	Aparajita
one/two	two	dharmacakra mu. with stem of lotus	youth	two	lalita	bodh. ornaments, va.: lotus throne, angry deity holds left foot	Arya-Manjughosa
one/two	two	rt.: heedle lt.: string	youth	two	vamalalita	bodh. ornaments, va.: golden pig	Arya-Marici
one/two	two	rt.: varada mu. lt.: asoka branch	youth	two	sama-bhanga	bodh. ornaments, va.: lotus throne	Asokakanta-Marici
one/two	two	rt.: staff/stick topped with a human, skull-cup lt.: snake noose/snare	mature	two		dhar. ornaments, realm: South	Bam-srin-dred-kyi-gdong-can
one/two	two	dhyana mu.	youth	two	vajra	bodh. ornaments, va.: lotus throne	Bhadrasvaresvara(?)raja-Manjughosa**
one/two	two	both in vitarka mu. holding rosary	youth	two	sattva	bodh. ornaments, va.: lotus throne	Bhrkuti (fo-mu)**
one/two	two	rt.: lotus lt.: banner/flag with wheel	youth	two		bodh. ornaments, va.: lotus throne	Buddhabodhiprabhavasita
one/two	two	rt.: bow lt.: arrow	mature	two		bodh. ornaments, va.: lotus throne	Budha
one/two	two	rt.: flaming jewel lt.: rests on thigh	youth	two	sattva	bodh. ornaments, va.: lotus throne	Budha (deva)**
one/two	two	rt.: abhaya mu. lt.: stem of lotus with wheel	mature	two	virasena	bodh. ornaments, va.: lotus throne	Dasa-bhumi-pati-Maitreya**
one/two	two	golden ladle	mature	two		white garments,	dGra-lha-thab-lha-gyu-mo

						bodh. ornaments, va.: three hearth stones	
one/two	two	rt.: varada mu. lt.: lotus	mature	two	vamalalita	bodh. ornaments, va.: chariot drawn by seven pigs	Dharani-vinirgata-Marici**
one/two	two	rt.: varada mu. lt.: stem of lotus in katari mu.	youth	two	vamalalita	bodh. ornaments, va.: lotus throne	Dharani-vinirgata-Vasudhara-Devi**
one/two	two	rt.: abhaya mu. lt.: incense burner	mature	two		bodh. ornaments, va.: lotus throne	Dhupa
one/two	two	holding shrine	mature	two	vajra	bodh. ornaments, va.: lotus throne	Dhupa
one/two	two	holding censor	mature	two	ardha-paryanka	bodh. ornaments, va.: lotus throne	Dhupa
one/two	two	rt.: smoking bundle of joss-stick or torch rt.: smoking bundle of joss-stick or torch	mature	two	ardha-paryanka	bodh. ornaments, va.: lotus throne	Dhupa
one/two	two	rt.: abhaya mu. lt.: holds edge of robe	mature	two	vajra	Buddha-like, monastic robed, right shoulder uncovered	Dipankara Buddha
one/two	two	dharmachakra mu.	youth	two	pralamba-pada	bodh. ornaments, va.: lotus throne	Dvibhuja-Maitreya**
one/two	two	rt.: varada mu. lt.: stem of lotus in karana mu.	youth	two	sattva	bodh. ornaments, va.: lotus throne on kneeling elephant	Dvibhuja-Marici**
one/two	two	rt.: flower (lotus?) lt.: book/manuscript	youth	two	vajra	bodh. ornaments, va.: lotus throne	Dvibhuja-Vajrasarasvati**
one/two	two	rt.: mace lt.: mongoose	coorp	two	lalita	bodh. ornaments, va.: lotus throne	Gadadhara-Syama-pita-Vaisravana
one/two	two	rt.: raised over head lt.: rests on hip	mature	two	dhyana	bodh. ornaments, va.: lotus throne	Gagananaanja

one/two	two	rt.: wish fulfilling jewel lt.: alms bowl with kalpa tree	mature	two	dhyana	bodh. ornaments, va.: lotus throne	Gagananania
one/two	two	rt.: blue lotus in varada mu. lt.: blue lotus in varada mu.	mature	two	dhyana	bodh. ornaments, va.: lotus throne	Gagananania
one/two	two	rt.: sword on lotus lt.: rests on hip	mature	two	dhyana	bodh. ornaments, va.: lotus throne	Gagananania
one/two	two	rt.: wish fulfilling jewel lt.: dhyana	mature	two	sattva	bodh. ornaments, va.: lotus throne	Gagananania
one/two	two	rt.: jewel lt.: stem of rice ear in katari mu.	youth	two	sama- bhanga	bodh. ornaments, va.: two vase/vessels	Gopala-Vasudhara
one/two	two	vajrahumkara mu. embracing shakti	mature	two	vajra, yab-yum	bodh. ornaments, va.: lotus throne	Guhya-Manjusri (Buddha)
one/two	two	vajrahumkara mu. embracing shakti	youth	two	vajra, yab-yum	bodh. ornaments, va.: lotus throne	Guhyasadhana-Manjughosa**
one/two	two	vajrahumkara mu. embracing shakti	youth	two	vajra, yab-yum	bodh. ornaments, va.: lotus throne	Guhya-Sadhana-Manjusri**
one/two	two	holding an apron of carved human bones	youth	two	ardha- paryanka	bodh. ornaments, va.: lotus throne	Hasya
one/two	two	rt.: jewel lt.: rice ear in katari mu.	youth	two	sama- bhanga	bodh. ornaments, va.: two vase/vessels	Jamaripada-krama-Vasudhara**
one/two	two	rt.: fly-whisk lt.: serpent/snake	youth	two	vajra	bodh. ornaments, va.: lotus throne	Janguli
one/two	two	rt.: crossed thunderbolts lt.: flowers	youth	two	vamalalita	bodh. ornaments, va.: snake or animal(?)	Janguli
one/two	two	rt.: banner/flag with wish fulfilling jewel lt.: varada mu.	mature	two	dhyana	bodh. ornaments va.: lotus throne	Jnanaketu
one/two	two	rt.: banner/flag with wish fulfilling jewel lt.: clenched at hip	mature	two	dhyana	bodh. ornaments va.: lotus throne	Jnanaketu
one/two	two	rt.: wish fulfilling jewel lt.: dhyana mu.	mature	two	sattva	bodh. ornaments va.: lotus throne	Jnanaketu
one/two	two	rt.: varada mu. lt.: vitarka mu. holding folds of garment	mature	two	dhyana	Buddha-like, monastic-robed,	Kasyapa

						va.: lotus throne	
one/two	two	rt.: karana mu. lt.: book/manuscript	mature	two	dhyana	Buddha-like, without usnisa, monastic-robed, rt. shoulder covered, va.: lotus throne	Kasyapa
one/two	two	rt.: karana mu. lt.: vase/vessel	youth	two	sattva	bodh. ornaments, va.: lotus throne	Kasyapadeva
one/two	two	rt.: lotus stem with varada mu. lt.: stem of blue lotus with vitarka mu.	youth	two	vamalalita	bodh. ornaments, va.: lotus throne	Khadiravani-Tara
one/two	two	karana mu.	youth	two	sattva	bodh. ornaments, va.: lotus throne	Krodhaparajita (devi)**
one/two	two	rt.: lotus lt.: abhaya mu.	youth	two	sattva	bodh. ornaments, va.: lotus throne	Krodhaparajitavajra**
one/two	two	rt.: bhumisparsa mu. lt.: lotus with wish-giving tree	mature	two		bodh. ornaments va.: winged lion	Ksitigarbha
one/two	two	rt.: stem of lotus in vitarka mu. with lotus and wish-fulfilling jewel lt.: stem of lotus in varada mu. with lotus and book/manuscript	mature	two	sama-bhanga	bodh. ornaments va.: winged lion	Ksitigarbha
one/two	two	rt.: alarm staff/stick lt.: flaming jewel	mature	two	vajra	bodh. ornaments va.: winged lion	Ksitigarbha
one/two	two	rt.: vitarka mu. withalarm staff/stick lt.: abhaya mu. with vase/vessel	mature	two	vajra	bodh. ornaments va.: winged lion	Ksitigarbha
one/two	two	rt.: alms bowl lt.: abhaya mu	mature	two	vajra	bodh. ornaments va.: winged lion	Ksitigarbha
one/two	two	rt.: sword lt.: book/manuscript	mature	two	vajra	bodh. ornaments, va.: lotus throne	Kumarabhuta-Manjusri**
one/two	two	holding a crown	youth	two	ardha-paryanka	bodh. ornaments, va.: lotus throne	Lasya
one/two	two	rt.: varada mu. lt.: ear of rice	mature	two		bejeweled	lHa'i-bud-med
one/two	two	rt.: varada mu.	youth	two	dhyana	bodh. ornaments,	Mahasthamaprata

		lt.: six lotus				va.: lotus throne	
one/two	two	rt.: sword lt.: lotus	youth	two	dhyana	bodh. ornaments, va.: lotus throne	Mahasthamaprata
one/two	two	rt.: sword lt.: lotus in vitarka mu.	youth	two	sattva	bodh. ornaments, va.: lotus throne	Mahasthamaprata
one/two	two	rt.: blue lotus lt.: graceful pose	mature	two	ardha- paryanka	dhar. ornaments, va.: lion	Maharajalila-Manjusri
one/two	two	rt.: bell lt.: graceful pose	mature	two	pralam- bapada	dhar. ornaments, va.: lion throne	Maharajalila-Manjusri
one/two	two	rt.: on knee lt.: blue lotus	mature	two	maha- rajalila	bodh. ornaments, va.: blue lion	Maharajalila-Manjusri
one/two	two	rt.: blue lotus lt.: graceful pose	mature	two	ardha- paryanka	bodh. ornaments, va.: lion	Maharajalila-Manjusri
one/two	two	rt.: bell lt.: graceful pose	mature	two	pralam- bapada	bodh. ornaments, va.: lion throne	Maharajalila-Manjusri
one/two	two	rt.: nagakesara flower lt.: alms bowl	youth	two	pralam- bapada	bodh. ornaments, va.: lotus throne	Maitreya
one/two	two	rt.: stem of lotus with wheel in vitarka mu. lt.: stem of lotus with vase/vessel in varada mu.	youth	two	pratyalidha	bodh. ornaments, va.: lotus throne	Maitreya
one/two	two	rt.: bhumisparsa mu. lt.: dhyana mu.	youth	two	sattva	bodh. ornaments, va.: lotus throne	Maitreya
one/two	two	rt.: vitarka mu. lt.: vase/vessel	youth	two	sama- bhanga	bodh. ornaments, va.: lotus throne	Maitreya
one/two	two	rt.: thunderbolt lt.: shrine	youth	two	vajra	bodh. ornaments, va.: lotus throne	Maitreya
one/two	two	rt.: stem of lotus with three peacock feathers lt.: stem of lotus with three peacock feathers	mature	two	lalita	bodh. ornaments, va.: lotus throne	Mamaki
one/two	two	dharmachakra mu. with lotus	youth	two	dhyana	bodh. ornaments, va.: lotus throne with	Manjughosa

						Yamari left and Sudhanakumara right	
one/two	two	rt.: flaming sword of wisdom lt.: blue lotus with book/manuscript	youth	two	dhyana	bodh. ornaments, va.: lion	Manjusri
one/two	two	rt.: dharmachakra mu. holding lotuses with sword, book/manuscript	youth	two	lalita	bodh. ornaments, va.: lion or lion throne	Manjusri
one/two	two	rt.: stem of lotus with sword atop book/manuscript lt.: vitarka mu.	youth	two	vamalalita	bodh. ornaments, va.: lotus throne	Manjusri
one/two	two	rt.: sword lt.: book/manuscript	youth	two	vajra	bodh. ornaments, va.: lotus throne	Manjusri-Manjughosa**
one/two	two	dharmachakra with stem of lotus & book/manuscript	youth	two	vamalalita	bodh. ornaments, va.: lion	Manjuvajra**
one/two	two	rt.: varada mu. lt.: bough of Asoka tree	mature	two	alidha	bodh. ornaments, va.: pig	Marici-Asokakanta
one/two	two	rt.: divination arrow lt.: basin of jewels	mature	two		white silk garment, bodh. ornaments, va.: tiger	Mi-g.yo-blo-bzang-ma
one/two	two	dhyana mu.	youth	two	vajra	bodh. ornaments, va.: lotus throne	Nilakantha-isvara (=Lokesvara)-Avalokitesvara (Bodhisattva)
one/two	two	rt.: bhumisparsa mu. lt.: tarjani mu.	youth	two	sattva	blue throat, bodh. ornaments, va.: lotus throne	Nilakantha-Lokesvara
one/two	two	holding flat bowl filled with jewels in samadhi mu.	youth	two	vajra	blue throat, bodh. ornaments, va.: lotus throne with skin of black deer	Nilakantha-Lokesvara
one/two	two	dhyana mu. holding skull-cup filled with gems	youth	two	dhyana	blue throat, bodh. ornaments, va.: antelope skin on red lotus	Nilakantharyavalokitesvara
one/two	two	rt.: abhaya mu. lt.: stem of lotus in dhyana mu.	youth	two	vajra	bodh. ornaments, va.: lotus throne	(Nirrtipada-krama-Bhattaraka)-Maitreya

one/two	two	rt.: lotus lt.: wish fulfilling jewel	mature	two		bodh. ornaments, va.: lotus throne	Pariskara-Vasita
one/two	two	rt.: stem of lotus lt.: cylindrical banner/flag	mature	two	lalita	bodh. ornaments, va.: lotus throne	Pariskara-Vasita
one/two	two	rt.: varada mu. lt.: stem of lotus in karana mu.	youth	two	vamalalita	bodh. ornaments, va.: lotus throne	Pita-Amoghapasa
one/two	two	embrace shakti in vajrahumkara mu.	mature	two	alidha, yab-yum	bodh. ornaments, va.: human figures	Pita-Chakra-Samvara
one*/two	two	rt.: axe, trident lt.:radish, bowl	corp.	two	ardha- paryanka	*elephant-head, bodh. ornaments, va.: mouse on lotus throne	Pita-Ganapati
one/two	two	rt.: vitarka mu. lt.: stem of lotus	youth	two	sattva	bodh. ornaments, va.: lotus throne on back of pig	Pita-Marici (fo-mu)
one/two	two	holding dharmachakra mu. with stem of lotus & book/manuscript	youth	two	vajra	bodh. ornaments, va.: lotus throne	Pitaprajnaparamita
one/two	two	rt.: varada mu. lt.: stem of lotus	youth	two	sopasraya	bodh. ornaments, va.: lotus throne	Pita-Tara
one/two	two	rt.: thunderbolt lt.: bell	youth	two	lalita	bodh. ornaments, va.: lotus throne	Pita-Vajrasattva
one/two	two	rt.: vitarka mu. lt.: Prajna Paramita book on lotus	youth	two	padma	bodh. ornaments, va.: lotus throne	Prajna-Paramita
one/two	two	rt.: sword lt.: book/manuscript	youth	two	vajra	bodh. ornaments, va.: lotus throne	Prajnacakra-Manjughosa (dan-po?)
one/two	two	rt.: lotus lt.: blue lotus	mature	two		bodh. ornaments, va.: lotus throne	Pranidhana-Vasita
one/two	two	rt.: karana mu. lt.: book/manuscript	mature	two	vajra	Buddha-like, monastic robe, rt. shoulder uncovered, va.: lotus throne	Purana-Kasyapa
one/two	two	rt.: varada mu. lt.: ear of rice	youth	two		bodh. ornaments, va.: lotus throne	Rab-bzad-ma

one/two	two	rt.: varada mu. lt.: ear of rice	youth	two		bodh. ornaments, va.: lotus throne	Rab-sbas-ma
one/two	two	rt.: abhaya mu. lt.: karana mu. with stem of lotus	youth	two	vajra	bodh. ornaments, va.: lotus throne	Rajalila-Manjusri
one/two	two	rt.: abhaya mu. on knee lt.: stem of lotus in vitarka mu.	youth	two	vamalalita	bodh. ornaments, va.: lotus throne	Rajalila-Manjusri (Bodhisattva)
one/two	two	rt.: varada mu. lt.: dhyana mu. with wish fulfilling jewel	mature	two	dhyana	Buddha-like, va.: pair of lions or horses	Ratnasambhava
one/two	two	rt.: bell lt.: wish fulfilling jewel	youth	two	dhyana, yab-yum	bodh. ornaments, va.: pair of lions or horses	Ratnasambhava
one/two	two	rt.: jewel lt.: dhyana mu.	youth	two	vajra	bodh. ornaments, va.: lotus throne	Ratnasambhava
one/two	two	rt.: varada mu. lt.: dhyana mu.	youth	two	vajra	bodh. ornaments, va.: lotus throne	Ratnasambhava
one/two	two	holding precious jewel	youth	two	vajra, vab-yum	bodh. ornaments, va.: horse throne	Ratnasambhava
one/two	two	rt.: bhumisparsa mu. lt.: dhyana mu.	mature	two	dhyana	Buddha ornamaments, monastic robe, va.: lotus throne	Sakyamuni Buddha
one/two	two	rt.: upraised with index finger pointing up lt.: at side with index finger pointing down	child	two	sama- bhanga	Buddha ornamaments, monastic robe, va.: lotus throne	Sakyamuni Buddha
one/two	two	dharmachakra mu.	mature	two	dhyana	Buddha ornamaments, monastic robe, va.: lotus throne	Sakyamuni Buddha
one/two	two	rt.: vitarka mu. lt.: varada mu.	mature	two	dhyana	Buddha ornamaments, swastika on chest, monastic robe, va.: lotus throne	Sakyamuni Buddha
one/two	two	uttarabodhi mu.	mature	two	dhyana	Buddha ornamaments, monastic robe, va.: coil of snakes with	Sakyamuni Buddha

						the serpents hood covering the head	
one/two	two	rt.: supports head lt.: rests on side	mature	two	parinirvana	laying on right side, Buddha ornamaments, monastic robe, va.: lotus throne	Sakyamuni Buddha
one/two	two	rt.: sword on lotus lt.: sword on lotus	youth	two	vajra	bodh. ornaments, va.: lotus throne	Samantabhadra
one/two	two	rt.: jewels lt.: on hip	mature	two	dhyana	bodh. ornaments, va.: lotus throne	Samantabhadra
one/two	two	rt.: crossed thunderbolts lt.: dhyana mu.	mature	two	sattva	bodh. ornaments, va.: lotus throne	Samantabhadra
one/two	two	rt.: varada mu. lt.: white lotus	youth	two	vajra	bodh. ornaments, va.: lotus throne	Sarasvati
one/two	two	rt.: varada mu. lt.: ear of rice	youth	two		bodh. ornaments, va.: lotus throne	Sarasvati
one/two	two	playing a lute	youth	two	vamalalita	bodh. ornaments. va.: lotus throne	Sarasvati (devi)**
one/two	two	srem of lotus with jewel in dharmachakra mu.	mature	two	sopasraya	bodh. ornaments, va.: lotus throne	Sarva-jina-pitamaha-Samanthabhadra
one/two	two	rt.: short staff/stick lt.: clenched at hip	mature	two	dhyana	bodh. ornaments, va.: lotus throne	Sarvasokatamonirghatamati
one/two	two	holds namaskara mu.	mature	two	dhyana	bodh. ornaments, va.: lotus throne	Sarvasokatamonirghatamati
one/two	two	rt.: thunderbolt lt.: throwing weapon	mature	two	dhyana	bodh. ornaments, va.: lotus throne	Sarvasokatamonirghatamati
one/two	two	rt.: varada mu. lt.: ear of rice	mature	two		bodh. ornaments, rich silk garments, va.: lotus throne	sByin-bzang-ma
one/two	two	rt.: varada mu. lt.: ear of rice	youth	two		bodh. ornaments, rich silk garments, va.: lotus throne	sByin-ma

one/two	two	dharmachakra mu. holding stem of lotus	youth	two	vajra	bodh. ornaments, va.: lion throne	Simhanada-Manjughosa**
one/two	two	dharmachakra mudra, stem of blue lotus	youth	two	lalita	bodh. ornaments, va.: lion or lion throne	Simhanada-Manjusri**
one/two	two	dharmachakra mu.	youth	two	vajra	bodh. ornaments, va.: lion	Simhavahana-Manjusri (Bodhisattva)t**
one/two	two	rt.: abhaya mu. lt.: dhyana mu.	mature	two	dhyana	Buddha-like, monastic robes, va.: lotus throne	Suparikirtitanamasri
one/two	two	dharmachakra mu.	mature	two	dhyana	Buddha-like, monastic robes, rt. shoulder uncovered, va.: lotus throne	Suvarnabhadravimalaratna-prabhasa
one/two	two	dharmachakra mu.	mature	two	dhyana	Buddha-like, monastic robes, rt. shoulder covered, va.: lotus throne	Suvarnabhadravimalaratna-prabhasavrata
one*/two	two	rt.: varada mu. lt.: dhyana mu.	mature	two	dhyana	*yellow orange Buddha-like, monastic robes, va.: lotus throne	Svaraghosaraja
one/two	two	rt.: human-skull drum lt.: sun disc	youth	two	astride	long loose robe, bodh. ornaments, va.: flying garuda with serpent in bealk	Srivajra
one/two	two	rt.: needle lt.: thread	youth	two	sama-bhanga	bodh. ornaments, va.: lotus throne	Sucisutradhara-Marici**
one/two	two	rt.: thunderbolt lt.: emerald	mature	two		bodh. ornaments, va.: lotus throne	Sudurjaya
one/two	two	rt.: thunderbolt lt.: jewel	mature	two	vamalalita	bodh. ornaments, bare breasted, va.: lotus throne	Sudurjaya (fo-mu)
one/two	two	rt.: crossed thunderbolts lt.: ears of corn	mature	two		bodh. ornaments, va.: lotus throne	Sumati
one/two	two	holds dharmachakra mu.	youth	two	vajra	bodh. ornaments,	Vadirad-Manjughosa

						va.: lotus throne	
one/two	two	holds dharmachakra mu.	youth	two	alidha	bodh. ornaments, va.: lotus throne	Vadisimha Manjughosa
one/two	two	playing a tambourine	youth	two	ardha- paryanka	bodh. ornaments, va.: lotus throne	Vadya
one/two	two	holds stems of flowers carrying three peacock feathers	youth	two	vamalalita	bodh. ornaments, va.: lotus throne	Vajradhatvisvari
one/two	two	rt.: varada mu. lt.: vase/vessel	youth	two		bodh. ornaments, va.: lotus throne	Vasudhara
one/two	two	playing lute	youth	two	sattva	bodh. ornaments, va.: lotus throne	Vina-Sarasvati
one/two	two	rt.: cylindrical banner/flag lt.: palm dawn on thigh	youth	two	vamalalita	bodh. ornaments, va.: lotus throne	Yasodhara(?)
one/two	two	rt.: varada mu. lt.: ear of rice	youth	two		bodh. ornaments, va.: lotus throne	Zla-shel-ma
one/two	four	prin. plays stringed instrument rt.: abhaya mu. lt.: serpent/snake	youth	two	dhyana	bodh, ornaments, va.: lotus throne	Arya-Ianguli
one/two	four	rt.: thunderbolt-topped staff/stick, lotus lt.: roasry, vase/vessel	youth	two	sama- bhanga	bodh. ornaments, va.: lotus throne	Anucara-Bhrkuti
one/two	four	rt.: abhaya mu., rosary lt.: abhaya mu., trident	youth	two	alidha	bodh. ornaments, va.: lotus throne	Anucara-Bhrkuti
one/two	four	prin. hold bow and arrow of flowers rt.: sword lt.: lotus	youth	two	pratyalidha	bodh. ornaments, va.: lotus throne	Arya-Manjughosa
one/two	four	rt.: varada mu. and garland of roses lt.: trident and vase/vessel	mature	two	vamalalita	Amitabha in crown, bodh. ornaments, va.: lotus throne	Bhrkuti
one/two	four	rt.: varada mu. and rosary lt.: trident and vase/vessel	mature	two	vamalalita	Amitabha in crown, bodh. ornaments, va.: lotus throne	Bhrkuti
one/two	four	rt.: vase/vessel and bow lt.: rosary and abhaya	mature	two	vamalalita	Amitabha in crown, bodh. ornaments,	Bhrkuti

						va.: lotus throne	
one/two	four	rt.: rosary and varada mu. lt.: short staff/stick(?) and vase/vessel	youth	two	vamalalita	bodh. ornaments, va.: lotus throne	<u>Bhrkuti (devi)</u>**
one/two	four	rt.: varada mu. and rosary lt.: short staff/stick and lotus	youth	two	sama- bhanga	bodh. ornaments, va.: lotus throne	<u>Bhrkuti-Tara</u>
one/two	four	rt.: peacock feather, vase/vessel lt.: jewel, varada mu.	mature	two		bodh. ornaments, va.: lotus throne	<u>Mahamayuri</u>
one/two	four	prin.: dharmachakra mu. rt.: abhaya mu. lt.: Prajna Paramita book on blue lotus	youth	two	vajra	bodh. ornaments, va.: lotus throne	<u>Prajna-Paramita</u>
one/two	four	rt.: sword, arrow lt.: bow, stem of lotus	youth	two	vajra	bodh. ornaments, va.: lotus throne	<u>Tiksna-Manjusri</u>**
one/two	four	rt.: sword, arrow lt.: stem of lotus with book/manuscript, bow	youth	two	vajra	bodh. ornaments, va.: lotus throne	<u>Tiksna-Manjusri (Bodhisattva)</u>**
one/two	four	rt.: Asoka bough, needle lt.: noose/snare, thunderbolt	youth	two		bodh. ornaments, va.: lotus throne	<u>Vadali</u>
one/two	four	prin.: bow of flowers and arrow rt.: sword lt.: lotus	youth	two	pratyalidha	bodh. ornaments, va.: lotus throne	<u>Vajrananga</u>
one/two	four	rt.: thunderbolt, needle lt.: noose/snare, Asoka bough	youth	two		bodh. ornaments, va.: lotus throne	<u>Varali</u>
one/two	six	rt.: thunderbolt, arrow, fist on thigh lt.: noose/snare, bow, (?)	youth	two	lalita	bodh, ornaments, va.: lotus throne	<u>Arya-Ianguli</u>
one/two	six	prin. hold bow and arrow of lotus buds rt.: sword, mirror lt.: lotus, asoka bough	youth	two	pratyalidha	bodh. ornaments, va.: lotus throne	<u>Arya-Manjughosa</u>
one/two	six	rt.: sword, varada mu., arrow lt.: book/manuscript, blue lotus, bow	youth	two	dhyana	bodh. ornaments, va.: lotus throne	<u>Manjusri</u>
one/two	six	rt.: branch, sword, (?) lt.: wheel, three flaming jewels, human skull-cup	youth	two	lalita	bodh. ornaments, va.: lotus throne	<u>Sadbhuja-Sarasvati (fo-mu)</u>
one/two	six	rt.: thunderbolt, ritual chopper,	youth	two	dhyana	bodh. ornaments,	<u>Samantabhadra</u>

		battle axe lt.: bell, skull-cup, head of Brahma				va.: lotus throne	
one/two	six	rt.: sword, crossed thunderbolts, wheel(?) lt.: bell, lotus, three jewels	mature	two	vajra	bodh. ornaments, va.: lotus throne	Samantabhadra
one/two	six	prin.: vajrahumkara mu. rt.: sword, vitarka mu. lt.: bow, lotus	youth	two	vajra, yab-yum	bodh. ornaments, va.: lotus throne	Vairocana-Manjuvajra
one/two	six	prin., bow of flowers and arrow of lotus buds rt.: sword, mirror lt.: lotus, Asoka bough with red flowers	youth	two	pratyalidha	bodh. ornaments, va.: lotus throne	Vajrananga
one/two	six	rt.: namaskara mu., varada mu., ears of corn lt.: book/manuscript, ears of corn, vase/vessel of jewels	youth	two		bodh. ornaments, va.: stands on a moon above a double lion	Vasudhara
one/three	two	rt.: encircles her yab's neck lt.: human skull-cupfilled with blood	mature	two	pratyalidha	bodh. ornaments, va.: lotus throne	Ratna-Krotishaurima
three/3-9	four	rt.: sword and arrow lt.: bow and book/manuscript	youth	two	vajra	bodh. ornaments va.: lotus throne	Bhramarasvara-Manjusri (Bodhisattva)**
three/six	two	dharmachakra mu. holding lotus stems with book/manuscripts	mature	two	vajra,	bodh. ornaments, va.: lotus throne	Guhya-Manjusri (Buddha)
three/six	two	dharmachakra mu. holding lotus stems with book/manuscripts and sword	mature	two	vajra,	bodh. ornaments, va.: lotus throne	Guhya-Manjusri (Buddha)
three/six	four	prin.: dharmachakra mu. rt.: abhaya mu. lt.: (?)	youth	two	sattva	bodh. ornaments, va.: lotus throne	Caturbhuja-Maitreya**
three/six	four	rt.: sword, arrow lt.: bow, book/manuscript	youth	two	vajra	bodh. ornaments, va.: lotus throne	Caturbhuja-Namasamgiti-Manjughosa**
three/six	four	prin.: dharmachakra mu. rt.: varada mu. lt.: twig of the nagakesara flower	youth	two	pralam-bapada	bodh. ornaments, va.: lotus throne	Maitreya
three/six	four	prin.: holds dharmachakra mu. rt.: karana mu. on knee lt.: wheel	youth	two	vamalalita	bodh. ornaments, va.: lotus throne	Trimukhacaturbhuja-Maitreya (Bodhisattva)**

three/six	six	rt.: wish fulfilling jewel, thunderbolt and wheel lt.: sword, bell and flower	mature	two	vajra	bodh. ornaments, va.: lotus throne	Akasagarbha
three/six	six	prin.: embrace shakti in vajrahumkara mu. rt.: sword, vitarka lt.: lotus, bow	mature	two	vamalalita, yab-yum	bodh. ornaments va.: lotus throne	Guhya-Manjuvajra
three/six	six	prin.: embrace shakti in vajrahumkara mu. rt.: sword, arrow lt.: lotus, bow	mature	two	vajra, yab-yum	bodh. ornaments va.: lotus throne	Guhya-Manjuvajra Buddha
three/six	six	prin.: hold vajrahumkara mu. embracing shakti rt.: vitarka, arrow lt.: bow, flower	youth	two	vamalalita, yab-yum	bodh. ornaments, va.: lotus throne	Guhya-Sadhana-Manjusri**
three/six	six	rt.: sword, thunderbolt, arrow lt.: noose/snare in tarjani mu., blue lotus, bow	youth	two	vamalalita	bodh. ornaments, va.: lotus throne	Ianguli
three/six	six	rt.: wheel, thunderbolt, lotus lt.: sword, flaming jewel, bell	mature	two	vajra	bodh. ornaments va.: lotus throne	Ksitigarbha
three/six	six	rt.: lotus, thunderbolt, flaming wheel(?) lt.: bell, sword, triple-jewel(?)	youth	two	vajra	bodh. ornaments, va.: lotus throne	Maitreya
three/six	six	prin.: embrace shaktu rt.: sword, arrow lt.: bow, blue lotus	youth	two	vajra, yab-yum	bodh. ornaments, va.: moon or lion	Manjuvajra
three/six	six	rt.: wheel, thunderbolt, jewel lt.: lotus, sword, empty hand	youht	two	vajra	bodh. ornaments, va.: lotus throne	Manjunatha**
three/six	six	rt.: prin.: embrace shakti with thunderbolt, bell in vajrahumkara mu.	youth	two	vajra, yab-yum	bodh. ornaments, va.: lotus throne	Manjusri-vajra**
three/six	six	rt.: flaming jewels, wheel, thunderbolt lt.: bell, sword, (?)	youth	two	vajra	bodh. ornaments, va.: lotus throne	Ratnasambhava
three/six	six	prin.: ritual chopper, human skull-cup rt.: (?), sword lt.: wheel, (?)	youth	two	sattva	bodh. ornaments, va.: lotus throne	Sadbhuja-Vajrasarasvati**

three/six	six	rt.: sword, arrow, abhaya mu. lt.: (?), bow, book/manuscript	youth	two	vajra	bodh. ornaments, va.: lotus throne	Trailokyavasyadhikara-Manjughosa**
three/six	six	prin.: embrace shakti rt.: yellow wheel, sword rt.: jewel, lotus	youth	two		bodh. ornaments, va.: lotus throne	Usnisa
three/6-9	four	prin. dharmachakra mu. rt.: varada mu. lt.: lotus stem	youth	two	vamalalita	bodh. ornaments, va.: lotus throne	Bhattaraka-Maitreya**
three/6-9	six	holding lotus, thunderbolt, sword, axe, noose/snare and tarjani mu.	mature	two			Bu-gzugs-bzang-ma
three/6-9	six	prin.: embraces shakti in vajrahumkara mu. rt.: lotus, arrow lt.: bow, sword	mature	two	vajra, yab-yum	bodh. ornaments, va.: lotus throne	Guhyasamaja-Manjuvara**
three/6-9	six	prin.: embraces shakti in vajrahumkara mu. rt.: lotus, arrow lt.: bow, sword	mature	two	vajra, yab-yum	bodh. ornaments, va.: lotus throne	Guhyasamaja-Manjuvara (Buddha)**
three/6-9	six	prin.: embrace shakti rt.: jewel, sword lt.: mongoose, lotus	corp.	two	lalita, yab-yum	bodh. ornaments, va.: lotus throne	Guhyasamaja-vinirgata-Pita-Jambhala
three*/6-9	six	rt.: lotus, thunderbolt, sword lt.: axe, noose/snare, tarjani mu.	mature	two		*wh., yw., rd., bodh. ornaments, va.: lotus throne	mDzes-pa'i-gzugs-can-ma
three*/6-9	eight	holding sword, lotus, circular banner/flag, crossed thunderbolts, peacock feathers, earring(?), varada mu., bowl	mature	two	ardha- paryanka	bodh. ornaments, va.: lotus throne	Mahasitavati
three/nine	six	rt.: thunderbolt, battle axe, arrow lt.: bow, cluster of leaves, noose/snare	youth	two	ardha- paryanka	bodh. ornaments, va.: lotus throne	Pita-Parnasabari
three/nine	eight	prin.: dharmachakra mu. rt.: goad/hook, arrow, thunderbolt lt.: bow, (?), noose/snare	youth	two	alidha	bodh. ornaments, va.: lotus throne	Astabhuja-Marici
three/nine	eight	prin.: needle and thread rt.: battle axe, noose/snare, bow	youth	two	alidha	bodh. ornaments, va.: chariot drawn	Astabhuja-Marici

		lt.: arrow, thunderbolt, leaves of asoka tree				by 7 pigs trampling on Prajna and Upaya	
three*/nine	ten	rt.: sword, thunderbolt, arrow, varada mu., parasol lt.: bow, banner/flag, jewel, battle axe, conch	mature	two	ardha-paryanka	*bl., tw., wh., bodh. ornaments, va.: lotus throne	<u>Mahapratisara</u>
four/eight	eight	rt.: thunderbolt, noose/snare, arrow, conch lt.: blue lotus, bow, goad/hook, tarjani mu.	youth	two	vajra	bodh. ornaments, va.: lotus throne	<u>Vajra-Tara</u>
four/eight	eight	rt.: thunderbolt, arrow, conch, varada mu. lt.: blue lotus, bow, goad/hook, noose/snare in tarjani mu.	youth	two	vajra	bodh. ornaments, va.: lotus throne	<u>Vajra-Tara</u>
four/12	eight	rt.: sword, wheel, trident, arrow lt.: battle axe, bow, noose/snare, thunderbolt	mature	two	lalita	*wh., yw., re., bodh. ornaments, va.: lotus throne	<u>Mahapratisara</u>
four/12	12	rt.: jewel, wheel, thunderbolt, arrow, sword, varada mu. lt.: thunderbolt, noose/snare, trident, bow, axe, conch	mature	two	vajra	bodh. ornaments, va.: lotus throne	<u>Mahapratisara</u>
five/ten	eight	prin.: dharmachakra mu. rt.: sword, arrow, thunderbolt	youth	two	vajra	bodh. ornaments, va.: lotus throne	<u>Astabhuja-Dharmadhatu-vagisvara -Manjughosa</u>**
five/ten	ten	prin.: hold discs at chest rt.: thunderbolt, arrow, karana mudra and short staff-stick (?) lt.: bow, flower, noose/snare and (?)	youth	two	sama-bhanga	bodh. ornaments, va.: chariot drawn by seven pigs	<u>Dasabhuja-Marici (fo-mu)</u> **

Yellow (Skt.: pita; Tib.: ser-po), Wrathful, Angry or Haughty Deities

Abbreviations:

as. = asana | bk. = black | bl. = blue | bodh. = bodhisattva
bn. = brown | corp. = corpulent | dhar. = dharmapala | gn. = green
lt. = left | mu. = mudra | pu. = purple | rd. = red
rt. = right | sc. = smokey | va. = vahana | wh. = white
yw. = yellow

(*) special variations or attributes noted within the entry.

(**) following deity's name indicates that the color is not noted in the source, kulesa's color is applied to the entry.

(eyes: 2-3, 6-9, etc.) in sources the deity's faces are noted, but the number of the eyes are not noted.

Head/Eyes	Hands	Objects Held	Body	Feet	Asana	Other Attributes	Deity Name
headless	two	rt.: knife that severs own head lt.: head	mature, nude	two		dhar. ornaments, va.: lotus throne	Vajrayogini
one*/two	two	holding treasure casque and gold lance with banner/flag	mature	two		*angry, gold shell armor, va.: elephant	bsTan-bsrung-mdzad-gnod-sbyin-mched-lnga
one*/two	two	rt.: flat bowl lt.: victory banner	mature	two	astride	*angry, silk garments, bejeweled, va.: red horse	Dam-pa-rin-chen-dpa'-rtsal
one*/two	two	holding treasure casque and turquoise lance with banner/flag	mature	two		*angry, copper shell armor, va.: dragon	bsTan-bsrung-mdzad-gnod-sbyin-mched-lnga
one*/two	two	rt.: noose/snare lt.: human skull-cup	mature	two	praty-alidha	*sow-head southern quarter	Yellow Sow-headed Noose-Holding Goddess
one*/two	two	rt.: citron lt.: mongoose	mature	two	raja-paryanka	*haughty, richly garbed, va.: lotus throne	dPa'-bo-chig-grub-pa-las-byung-ba'i-jambhala-lha-mang
one*/two	two	rt.: jewel lt.: mongoose	mature	two	vamalalita	*haughty, rich garments, va.: lotus throne	Ekantanayaka-Pita-Iambhala
one*/two	two	rt.: vase/vessel filled with gems	mature	two		*angry,	Gang-ba-bzang-po

		lt.: moongoose				richly armored, bodh. ornaments, va.: lotus throne	
one*/two	two	rt.: citron lt.: mongoose	mature	two	raja-paryanka	*angry richly armored, bodh. ornaments, va.: lotus throne	Gang-ba-bzang-po
one/two	two	rt.: varada mu. lt.: ear of rice	mature	two		silk garments, bodh. ornaments, va.: lotus throne	hPhags-ma
one*/two	two	large corpse on the shoulder and holding a skeleton in the hands	mature	two	alidha	*vulture-head, dhar. ornaments	Htamenma, "Yellowish-White Vulture-Headed One"
one*/two	two	holding thunderbolt	mature	two	alidha	*dog-head, dhar. ornaments	Ishvari, "Yellow Dog-Headed Rakshasi"
one*/two	two	holding razor	mature	two	alidha	*bat-head, dhar. ornaments	Ishvari, "Yellow Bat-Headed Delight-Goddess"
one*/two	two	holding noose/snare	mature	two	alidha	*goat-head, dhar. ornaments	Ishvari, "Yellow Goat-headed Mystic Goddess"
one*/two	two	rt.: lemon lt.: mongoose	corp.	two	vamalalita	*haughty, richly dresses, va.: lotus throne	Iambhala
one*/two	two	embrace shakti rt.: human skull-cup lt.: mongoose	corp.	two	yab-yum	*angry, richly dresses, va.: lotus throne	Iambhala
one*/two	two	rt.: lemon lt.: mongoose	corp.	two	alidha	*angry, bodh. ornaments, va.: Sankhamunda and Padmamunda	Iambhala
one*/two	two	rt.: jewel lt.: mongoose	corp.	two		*angry, richly dressed, va.: caprisoned horse	Iambhala
one*/two	two	rt.: citron lt.: mongoose	corp.	two	raja-paryanka, yab-yum	*angry, richly dressed, fancy leather boots	Iambhala
one*/two	two	rt.: citron ln varada mu.	corp.	two	alidha	multicolored garments,	Iambhala-ser-po-gtso-rkyang

		lt.: mongoose				bodh. ornaments, va.: gems	
one/two	two	rt.: stem of lotus in vitarka mu. on knee lt.: stem of lotus in vitarka mu. at chest	youth	two	vajra	bodh. ornaments, va.: lotus throne	Ianguli (fo-mu)**
one*/two	two	rt.: citron lt.: mongoose	mature	two	raja-paryanka	richly garbed, bejewled	Kilimili
one*/two	two	rt.: varada mu. lt.: bough of Asoka tree	mature	two	alidha	*angry, bodh. ornaments, va.: pig	Marici-Asokakanta
one/2-3	two	rt.: flaming jewel lt.: mongoose	mature	two	astride	richly garbed, va.: blue horse	gNod-sbyin-nor-bu-bzang-po
one*/2-3	two	rt.: sack of diseases lt.: torch	mature	two		*angry, blue silk garment	Hang-phan-ser-po-bya-ra-ba
one/two	two	rt.: divination arrow lt.: basin of jewels	mature	two		white silk garment, bejeweled, va.: tiger	Mi-g.yo-blo-bzang-ma
one*/two	two	rt.: cylindrical banner lt.: mongoose	corp.	two	lalita	*angry, richly armored, fancy boots, va.: lion	Pita-Iambhala
one*/two	two	rt.: citron lt.: mongoose	corp.	two	vamalalita	dhar. ornaments, va.: lotus throne	Pita-Iambhalavajra
one*/two	two	rt.: gem encrusted club lt.: treasure producing mongoose	mature	two		*yellow-green, angry, clothed in silks, sun and moon rests on shoulders, va.: treasure trunk	rNam-sras-ljang-ser-be-con-can
one*/two	two	rt.: citron lt.: treasure producing mongoose	mature	two	raja-paryanka	*angry, jeweled diadem, righly dressed, va.: lotus throne	rNam-thos-kyi-bu
one*/two	two	rt.: banner/flag lt.: treasure producing mongoose	mature	two		*angry, richly armored,	rNam-thos-sras

						va.: white lion	
one*/two	two	rt.: ladle of turquoise lt.: ladle of gold	mature	two**		*angry, hores-like, va.: lotus throne	Se-ba-rang-rta-rgyal-po'i-chibs
one*/two	four	rt.: varada mu. and rosary lt.: trident and vase/vessel	mature	two	alidha	*frowning bodh. ornament va.: lotus throne	Bhrkuti-Tara**
one*/two	four	prin.: casque rt.: club/cudgel lt.: mongoose	mature	two		*haughty, richly garbed, bejeweled, va.: lotus throne	Jinarsabha-Vaisravana
one*/two	four	prin.: shallow bowl, gem filled rt.: short staff/stick lt.: mongoose	mature	two		*angry, bodh. ornaments, va.: ;lotus throne	Jinarsabha-Vaisravana
one/two	six	rt.: thunderbolt, (?), arrow lt.: bow, (?), karana	youth	two	lalita	bodh. ornaments, va.: lotus throne	Janguli (fo-mu)**
one/three	two	rt. chapatedana mu. lt. : noose/snare	mature	two	alidha	dhar. ornaments, va.: Ganesa under foot on lotus throne	Aparajita
one/three	two	rt.: abhaya mu. lt.: noose/snare	mature	two	alidha	dhar. ornaments, va.: demons under foot on lotus throne	Aparajita
one/three	two	rt.: sword lt.: noose/snare	mature	two	astride	human skin on torso, tiger skin on loins, dhar. ornaments, va.: buffalo, syllable "rag"	bDud-mo-gshin-rje-lag-brgya-ma
one*/three	two	holding vajra-tipped noose/snare	mature, pendulous breasts, nude	two	ardha- paryanka	*angry, bodh. ornaments, va.: lotus throne	Bhrkuti
one*/three	two	rt.: held at waist lt.: jewel	mature, bird wings	two, bird- like	alidha	*bird head, ornaments, va.: serpent/snake on lotus throne	Bkah-gdams-lugs-Pita-Garuda
one/three	two	rt.: sword	mature	two		dhar. ornaments,	Candarosana

		lt.: serpent/snake over heart				protuding tongue, va.: lotus throne	
one/three	two	rt.: sword lt.: noose/snare in tarjani mu.	mature	two		dhar. ornaments, protuding tongue, va.: lotus throne	Candarosana
one/three	two	rt.: grass lt.: deer	mature, nude	two	alidha	dhar. ornaments, va.: corpse	Candesvari
one*/three	two	rt.: club with a skull finial lt.: tarjani mu. with noose/snare	mature	two	alidha	*head of a buffalo lapis horns with flaming points, dhar. ornaments, va.: white lion	Chos-rGyal-phyi-sgrub
one/three	two	rt.: club/cudgel with thunderbolt handle lt.: noose/snare	mature	two		bodh. ornaments,	dByug-pa-'jigs-byed
one/three	two	rt.: casque lt.: golden zor	mature	two		dhar. ornaments, peacock-feather cloak va.: hind	dPal-ldan-lha-mo-remadza
one/three	two	rt.: citron lt.: mongoose	mature	two	raja-paryanka	silk garments, bodh. ornaments, va.: lotus throne	hlam-po-'khyil-pa
one/three	two	rt.: ritual chopper lt.: human skull-cup	mature	two	ardha-paryanka	dhar. ornaments, va.: lotus throne	Kapalini
one/three	two	rt.: vajra-topped staff/stick lt.: noose/snare, embraces shakti	corp	two	alidha, yab-yum	dhar. ornaments, va.: prostrate human figures	Krodhaparajita**
one*/three	two	rt.: club/cudgel with skull finial lt.: tarjani with black noose/snare	mature	two	alidha	dhar. ornaments, va.: white lion	Las-kyi-gshin-rje
one/three	two	rt.: flaming jewel lt.: bowl of jewels	mature	two	astride	bejeweled, va.: horse	lHa-chen-gser-gyi-rgyal-po
one/three	two	rt.: miniature palace lt.: mongoose	mature	two		richly armored, va.: caprisoned horse	lNga-rten
one*/three	two	rt.: cylindrical banner/flag lt.: mongoose	corp.	two	lalita	*angry, armored, dhar. ornaments, va.: lion	Mahapita-Vaisravana

one*/three	two	rt.: cylindrical banner/flag with wish fulfilling jewel lt.: mongoose	corp.	two	astride	*angry, armored, fancy leather boots dhar. ornaments, va.: lion	Mahapita-Vaisravana
one/three	two	rt.: flaming jewel lt.: treasure producing mongoose	mature	two	astride	dhar. ornaments, va.: blue horse	Manibhadra-Yaksa
one/three	two	rt.: flaming jewel lt.: mongoose	mature	two	lalita	dhar. ornaments, va.: horse	Manibhadra-Yaksa
one*/three	two	rt.: citron lt.: treasure producing mongoose	mature	two	raja-paryanka	* angry, bodh. ornaments, va.: lotus throne	Manibhadra
one/three	two	rt.: varada mu. lt.: asoka branch	mature	two	vamalalita	dhar. ornaments, va.: chariot drawn by seven boars	Marici
one/three	two	rt.: basin of food lt.: mongoose	mature	two		*angry, haughty, bejewled, attrib.: syllable "*mam*" va.: tiger	Mi-g.yo-blo-bzang-ma
one/three	two	rt.: divination arrow lt.: flat bowl with food of a hundred tastes	mature	two		dhar. ornaments, va.: tigress	Mi-g.yo-glang-bzang-ma
one/three	two	right hands: ritual choppers left hands: serpents/snakes	corp.	*		*legs=snake coils, dhar. ornaments, va.: lotus throne	Nagarohi-Manjusri**
one/three	two	rt.: ear of corn lt.: bag made of a mongoose	mature	two		dhar. ornaments, va.: golden throne	Nor-lha-arya-jambhala
one/three	two	rt.: jewels lt.: ear of rice	mature	two		dhar. ornaments, va.: lotus throne	Nor-rgyun-ma-ba-glang-rdzi
one/three	two	rt.: citron lt.: treasure producing mongoose	mature	two	raja-paryanka	richly garbed, dhar. ornaments, va.: lotus throne	Nor-sbyin
one/three	two	holding noose/snare	mature	two	alidha, yab-yum	dhar. ornaments, with Yamantaka Gatekeeper of the South ,	Pasadhari

						va.: lotus throne	
one/three	two	rt.: treasure casque lt.: lance with banner/flag	mature	two		armor of gold, dhar. ornaments, va.: elephant	Phu-yi-gzhi-bdag-mdzod-lnga-spun-lnga
one/three	two	rt.: abhaya mu. lt.: harina mu.	corp.	two	alidha	dhar. ornaments, va.: prostrate human forms	Pita-Aparajita (fo-mu)
one/three	two	rt.: thunderbolt lt.: human skull-cup	mature, nude	two	ardha- paryanka	dhar. ornaments, va.: lotus throne	Pita-Vahari
one*/three	two	rt.: human skull-drum lt.: tantric staff/stick	mature, nude	two	alidha	*bull-head, dhar. ornaments, va.: bull	Pita Yamaraja
one/three	two	rt.: varada mu. lt.: dhyana mudra with wish fulfilling jewel	mature	two	ardha- paryanka	dhar. ornaments, va.: lotus throne	Ratna-Heruka
one*/three	two	rt.: cylindrical banner/flag lt.: mongoose	mature	two	lalita	*angry, long flowing garment with pants, va.: lion	Ratna-Pita-Jambhala
one/three	two	rt.: golden noose/snare lt.: porcupine	mature	two		dhar. ornaments, va.: fox-colored sea monster	rDo-rje-de-byin-chen-mo
one/three	two	rt.: golden vase/vessel lt.: golden basin with wish fulfilling jewel	mature	two	sattva	blue hair which falls to the left, dhar. ornaments, attribute: syllable "bhyo", va.: yellow mule	rGyas-pa'i-lha-mo
one/three	two	rt.: vase/vessel of nectar of life lt.: basin filled with jewels	mature	two		dhar. ornaments, va.: yellow horse	rGyas-pa'i-rgyal-chen
one*/three	two	rt.: ritual chopper lt.: human skull-cup	mature	two	ardha- paryanka	*bear-head, dhar. ornaments, va.: lotus throne	Rikshavaktra
one/three	two	rt.: precious vase/vessel lt.: iron goad/hook	mature	two		dhar. ornaments, va.: lotus throne	Rin-chen-mkha'-'gro-ma

one/three	two	rt.: ritual chopper lt.: human skull-cup	mature, nude	two	ardha-paryanka	dhar. ornaments, va.: lotus throne	Rin-chen-mkha'-'gro-ma
one*/three	two**	claws hold jewels	mature	two, claws		*bird-head, **wings dhar. ornaments, va.: lotus throne	Rin-po-che'i-khyung
one*/three	two	rt.: ritual chopper lt.: sack of diseases	mature, nude	two	ardha-paryanka	*lion-head, pendulous breasts, dhar. ornaments, va.: lotus throne	Rksavaktra
one/three	two	rt.: club/cudgel lt.: flat bowl with food	youth	two		dhar. ornaments, va.: wild dog	rMa-ri-rab-'byans-drag-mo
one/three	two	holds human skull-cup	mature	two		dhar. ornaments, va.: lotus throne	Sa-bdag-bu-mo-'bum-gyi-gtso-mo
one*/three	two	holds sceptre of crystal	mature	two		*mouse-head, dhar. ornaments, va.: lotus throne	Sa-bdag-rgan-rgon
one/three	two	rt.: precious vase/vessel lt.: trumpet	mature	two		full robe of golden silk, dhar. ornaments, va.: lotus throne	Sa-bdag-rgyal-po-'jig-rten-bdag
one/three	two	rt.: ritual chopper lt.: human skull-cup	mature	two	astride	dhar. ornaments, va.: deer	Sarad-devi
one/three	two	rt.: crossed thunderbolts lt.: casque of jewels	mature	two		dhar. ornaments, va.: lotus throne	Sarvabuddhadharmakosavati
one*/three	two	rt.: silver bow lt.: gold arrow	mature	two		*pale yellow, blue silk garment, dhar. ornaments, va.: lotus throne	sBal-te
one*/three	two	rt.: ritual chopper lt.: human skull-cup	mature, nude	two		*dark yw., no ornaments, va.: lotus throne	Sinnga-gling-ma
one*/three	two	rt.: divination arrow with yellow streamers lt.: magic mirror	mature	two		*orange, broad brimmed hat, dhar. ornaments, va.: lotus throne	Se-ba-bla-mkhyen

one/three	two	rt.: bow lt.: arrow of gold	mature	two		red turban, red spotted garment, dhar. ornaments, va.: red brown stag	<u>sKu-la-zhal-gyi-lha-btsan</u>
one*/two	two	rt.: citron lt.: treasure producing mongoose	mature	two		*angry, rich silk garments, bodh. prnaments, va.: lotus throne	<u>sPyod-pa'i-dbang-po</u>
one*/two	two	rt.: sword lt.: treasure producing mongoose	mature	two	astride	*angry, richly helmeted, richly armored, fancy leather boots, va.: caprisoned horse	<u>Yang-dag-shes</u>
one*/two	two	rt.: citron lt.: treasure producing mongoose	mature	two	raja- paryanka	*angry, dhar. ornaments, richly armored, fancy leather boots, va.: caprisoned horse	<u>Zhal-gyi-dbang-po</u>
one/three	two	holds poison arrow with a black notch	mature	two		dhar. ornaments, dress of human skin, attribute: syllable "la", va.: garuda-like bird	<u>Srivajra</u>
one/three	two	rt.: sickle lt.: skull-cup full of blood	mature, nude	two	astride	pendulous breasts, dhar. ornaments, peacock feather cloak, attribute: syllable "bhyo", va.: stag	<u>sTon-gyi-rgyal-mo</u>
one/three	two	rt.: heart lt.: human corpse	mature	two		dhar. ornaments, va.: lotus throne	<u>Tsandhali</u>
one/three	two	rt.: bow lt.: arrow	mature	two		dhar. ornaments, va.: lotus throne	<u>Tseurima</u>
one*/three	two	rt.: victory banner/flag lt.: mongoose	mature	two	aseat	angry, helmeted, richly dressed, dhar. ornaments, va.: white lion	<u>Vaisravana</u>

one/three	two	rt.: noose/snare lt.: tarjani mu.	mature	two		dhar. ornaments, va.: lotus throne	Vajrapasi
one/three	two	holds noose/snare	mature	two	alidha	dhar. ornaments, realm: Northern gate, va.: lotus throne	Vajrapasi
one/three	two	rt.: varada mu. lt.: ears of corn	mature	two		dhar. ornaments, va.: lotus throne	Vasudhara
one/three	two	rt.: varada mu. lt.: ear of rice	mature	two	raja- paryanka	dhar. ornaments, va.: lotus throne	Vasudhara
one/three	two	rt.: ritual chopper, embraces shakti lt.: human skull-cup, embraces shakti	mature	two	alidha, yab-yum	dhar. ornaments, va.: lotus throne	Vidya-Dhara
one/three	two	plays the lute	mature	two	pratyalidha	dhar. ornaments, va.: lotus throne	Vina
one*/three	two	rt.: human skull-drum lt.: divination arrow	corp.	two	alidha	*bull-head, dhar. ornaments, va.: bull	Yama
one/three	four	rt.: sword, noose/snare lt.: staff/stick, wheel	corp.	two	alidha	bodh. ornaments, va.: lotus throne	Dhvajagrakeyura (fo-mu)
one/three	four	rt.: mirror, serpent/snake lt.: trident, magic dagger	mature, pendulous breasts	two		dhar. ornaments, va.: hind	dPal-ldan-lha-mo-remati
one/three	four	rt.: jewel, human skull-cup lt.: flaming sword, trident	mature	two	alidha	dhar. ornaments, va.: lotus throne	mGon-po-ser-po
one/three	four	rt.: sword, goad/hook lt.: bell, noose/snare	mature	two		dhar. ornaments, va.: lotus throne	Vajraghandahari
one/three	six	rt.: sword, goad/hook and short staff/stick lt.: human skull-cup, noose/snare and severed human head	mature	two	alidha	vomits into skull-cup, dhar. ornaments, va.: prostrate human form	Bhrkuti-Tara**
one/three	10	rt.: swords lt.: noose/snares	mature	two	astride	dhar. ornaments, va.: buffalo, syllable "rag"	bDud-mo-gshin-rje-lag-brgya-ma
three*/6-9	six	prin.: embrace shakti rt.: citron, sword	corp	two		*angry, richly dressed,	Jambhala

		lt.: mongoose, lotus				fancy leather boots	
three/6-9	six	rt.: sword, thunderbolt, arrow lt.: tarjani mu. with noose/snare, blue lotus, bow	youth	two		bodh. ornaments, va.; lotus throne	Ianguli-Tara
three/nine	two	prin.: embrace shakti with ritual chopper, human skull-cup rt.: cylindrical victory banner, lotus lt.: snare/noose, mongoose	corp.	two	alidha	dhar. ornaments, va.: prostrate Ganesa forms	(Sadbhuja-Trimukha)-Mativardhana-(Dhanapala)-Pita-Mahakala
three*/nine	six	prin. embrace shakti rt.: sword, jewel lt.: wheel, lotus	mature	two	alidha	*wh., bk., rd., dhar. ornaments, va.: lotus throne	Aparajita
three*/nine	six	prin.: embrace shakti with ritual chopper, skull-cup rt.: victory banner/flag, blue lotus lt.: mongoose, snake	mature	two	alidha, yab-yum	*yellow-orange color, dhar. ornaments, va.: lotus throne	mGon-ser-nor-srung-blo-'phel-zhal-gsum-phyag-drug-pa
three*/nine	six	rt.: noose/snare, sword thunderbolt lt.: pestle, axe, tarjani mu.	mature	two	alidha	*rd., yw., wh., dhar. ornaments, va.: lotus throne	Pasadhari
three*/nine	six	rt.: wish fulfilling jewel, trident, short staff/stick lt.: bell, human skull-cup, trident-topped staff/stick	mature	two	pratyalidha, yab-yum	*wh., yw., rd., dhar. ornaments, va.: lotus throne	Ratna-Heruka
three*/nine	eight	rt.: thunderbolt, goad/hook, arrow, needle lt.: asoka branch, bow, thread, tarjani mu.	mature	two	vamalalita	*rd., yw., boar-head, bodh. ornaments, va.: supported by seven pigs	Marici
three/nine	eight	prin.: dharmachakra mu. with serpent/snake rt.: goad/hook, arrow, thunderbolt lt.: noose/snare, bow, karana mu.	mature	two	alidha	bodh. ornaments, va.: prostrate human bodies on lotus throne	Marici (with jade girdle)
three/nine	eight	prin.: needle, thread rt.: battle axe, noose/snare, bow lt.: arrow, thunderbolt, leaves of asoka tree	mature	two	alidha	dhar. ornaments, va.: chariot with seven pigs and tramples on Prajna and Upaya	Marici-Picuva
three/nine	eight	rt.: needle, battle axe, noose/snare lt.: thread, bow and arrow, thunderbolt, leaves of Asoka tree	mature	two	alidha	dhar. ornaments, va.: lotus throne	Samksipta-Marici

four*/12	four	rt.: rosary of human bones, human skull-cup filled with jewels lt.: ritual chopper, gem laden vase/vessel	corp.	two	alidha	*yw., wh., rd., gray, dhar. ornaments, va.: lotus throne	Dhana-vardhana-Pita-Caturmukha-(Sri-Mahakala)
four*/12	four	rt.: rosary, ritual chopper lt.: vase/vessel, human skull-cup	corp.	two	alidha	*yw., wh., rd., gray, dhar. ornaments, va.: lotus throne	Dhana-vardhana-Pita-Caturmukha-(Sri-Mahakala)
four*/12	four	rt.: sword, wheel lt.: noose/snare in tarjani mu., wooden pestle, trident against left shoulder	corp.	two	praty-alidha	*yw., rd., wh., gray dhar. ornaments, va.: lotus throne	Dhvajagrakeyura
four*/12	four	rt.: rosary, human skull-cup filled with jewels lt. : ritual chopper, gem filled vase/vessel	mature	two		dhar. ornaments, va.: lotus throne	dPal-mgon-zhal-bzhi-pa-ser-po-nor-'phel
four*/12	eight	rt.: sword, short staff/stick, wheel, arrow lt.: trident, noose/snare, bow, tarjani mu.	corp.	two	alidha	dhar. ornaments, va.: prostrate human form	Dhvajagrakeyura**
five/15	ten	prin.: rt. plam up at chest, lt. dhyana mu. rt.: thunderbolt, arrow, karana mudra and short staff-stick (?) lt.: bow, flower, noose/snare and (?)	mature	two	alidha	bodh. ornaments, va.: chariot drawn by seven pigs	Dasabhuja-Marici (fo-mu)**
five*/15	12	hold tantric symbols	mature	two	alidha	dhar. ornaments, va.: pig-drawn chariot	Vajradhatvisvari Marici
six*/18	12	rt.: sword, wooden pestle, arrow, wheel, thunderbolt, battle axe lt.: noose/snare, magic notched staff/stick topped with a skull-cup, Asoka bough, head of Brahma, bow, trident	mature	two	alidha	*rd., bl., gr., yw & wh., bl. sowv top head dhar. ornaments, va.: pig	Odiyana-Marici
six*/18	12	rt.: sword, wooden pestle, arrow, goad/hook, thunderbolt, battle axe lt.: noose/snare, skull-cup, Asoka bough, head of Brahma, bow, trident	mature	two	alidha	*rd., bl., gr., yw., wh., sow-like, dhar. ornaments, va.: lotus throne	Vajradhatvisvari Marici
eight*/24	16	rt.: magic notched staff/stick, lotus, arrow, thunderbolt, goad/hook, staff/stick, knife, abhaya mu. lt.: noose/snare in tarjani mu., skull-	mature	two	pratyalidha	*yw., bl., gr., bl., wh., rd., bl., smokey dhar. ornaments, va.: lotus throne	Prasanna-Tara

		cup, bow, magic notched stick, thunderbolt, noose/snare, head of Brahma, and vase/vesse of jewels				
nine/27	18	right hands: ritual choppers left hands: serpents/snakes	mature	*	*legs=snake coils, dhar. ornaments,	Nagaraksa-Manjusri**

Black (Skt.: krsna; Tib.: nag-po), Wrathful Deities

Abbreviations:

as. = asana	bk. = black	bl. = blue	bodh. = bodhisattva
bn. = brown	corp. = corpulent	dhar. = dharmapala	gn. = green
lt. = left	mu. = mudra	pu. = purple	rd. = red
rt. = right	sc. = smokey	va. = vahana	wh. = white
yw. = yellow			

(*) special variations or attributes noted within the entry.
(**) following deity's name indicates that the color is not noted in the source, kulesa's color is applied to the entry.
(eyes: 2-3, 6-9, etc.) in sources the deity's faces are noted, but the number of the eyes are not noted.

Head/Eyes	Hands	Objects Held	Body	Feet	Asana	Other Attributes	Deity Name
one*/two	two	rt.: razor lt.: intestines from deity's mouth	mature	two	alidha	*fox-head, dhar. ornaments	Htamenma, "Black Fox-Headed One"
one*/two	two	large corpse on the shoulder	mature	two	alidha	*crow-head, dhar. ornaments	Htamenma, "Black Crow-Headed One"
one*/two	two	holding human skull-cup filled with blood	mature	two	alidha	*tiger-head, dhar. ornaments	Ishvari, "Yellowish-Black Tiger-headed Rakshasi"
one*/two	two	holding command staff/stick	mature	two	alidha	*vulture-head, dhar. ornaments	Ishvari, "Greenish-Black Vulture-Headed Eater-Goddess"
one*/two	two	rt.: human corpse lt.: human skull-cup filled with blood	mature	two	alidha	*elephant-head, dhar. ornaments	Ishvari, "Greenish-Black Elephant-headed Big-Nosed Goddess"
one*/two	two	holding trident	mature	two	alidha	*leopard-head, dhar. ornaments	Ishvari, "Greenish-Black Leopard-headed great Goddess"
one*/two	two	holding noose/snare	mature	two	alidha	*sow-head, dhar. ornaments	Ishvari, "Black Sow-Headed Sow-Goddess"
one*/two	two	holding goad/hook	mature	two	alidha	*cuckoo-head, dhar. ornaments	Ishvari, "Black Cuckoo-Headed Mystic Goddess"
one*/two	two	holding human skull-cup	mature	two	alidha	*sow-head, dhar. ornaments	Ishvari, "Greenish-Black Serpent-Headed Mystic Goddess"
one*/two	two	rt.: human skull-cup	mature,	two	alidha	*angry,	(Kasmira-mahapandita-krama)-

		lt.: mongoose	nude			erect phallus, dhar. ornaments, prostrate human form on on lotus throne	Krsna-Jambhala
one/2-3	two	rt.: magic notched staff/stick lt.: noose/snare	mature	two		gold crown, robe of black silk	bDud-kyi-rgyal-po
one/2-3	two	axe	mature	two		hair tied into a tuft, black silk and blue garment	bDud-kyi-rgyal-po-ma-rungs-pa
one*/2-3	two	rt.: lance lt.: hurls a throwing lance	mature	two		*lion faced, turquoise hair, red and black silk garment with a train, six different bone ornaments	bDud-mgon
one*/2-3	two	rt.: battle lance with five points lt.: noose/snare	youth	two		dhar. ornaments, va.: blue mule	'Brog-chen-rdo-rje-bgegs-gtso
one*/2-3	two	rt.: red jeweled lance lt.: treasure producing mongoose	mature	two	astride	*angry, richly armored, high fancy boots, va.: caprisoned horse	'Brog-gnas
one*/2-3	two	rt.: sack of pestilence lt.: pair of dice	emaciat-ed, pend. breasts	two		*dark rd., ugly, dhar. ornaments	bSod-byed-nag-mo
one/2-3	two	rt.: lance with black banner/flag lt.: human skull-cup filled with blood and a noose/snare	mature	two		helmet, cuirass of iron, high black boots, va.: black horse with white heels	Byang-bdud-chen-po
one*/2-3	two	rt.: thunderbolt lt.: black noose/snare	mature, nude	two		*dog-head, hair to heels, bone ornaments	Dung-mig-ma
one*/2-3	two	serpent/snake	mature, winged	two		*head of a bird, wish fulfilling jewel in forehead, serpent in beak, va.: dying Naga	Garuda

one*/2-3	two*	*dog-like	dog-like, winged	two*		*dog head, *dog-like legs, snake-like tail with human head in coils, va.: tortoise	gNam-khyi-nag-po
one*/2-3	two	rt.: thunderbolt lt.: black noose/snare	mature, nude	two		*dog-head, hair to heels, ornaments of bones	gSer-mig-ma
one*/2-3	two	rt.: thunderbolt lt.: black noose/snare	mature, nude	two		*dog-head, bone ornaments	gYu-mig-ma
one*/2-3	two	rt.: thunderbolt lt.: black noose/snare	mature, nude	two		*dog-head bone ornaments,	Khar-mig-ma
one*/2-3	two	rt.: sword lt.: treasure producing mongoose	corp.	two		*angry, richly armored, fancy boots, va.: caprisoned horse	Kubera
one/three	two	rt.: ritual chopper lt.: human skull-cup, with tantric staff/ stick in crook of arm	corp.	two	partyalidha	dhar. ornaments, va.: human forms	Ajita-Mahakala**
one/three	two	rt.: club lt.: lance	mature	two	alidha	*black-purple, dhar. ornaments, va.: lotus throne	Arya-(Atisa)-krama-Mahadeva-srijvala-Mahakala
one/three	two	rt.: skull-topped staff/stick lt.: lance	corp	two	alidha	*black-purple, dhar. ornaments, va.: human form	Arya-(Atisa)-krama-Mahadeva-srijvala-Mahakala
one/ three	two	command staff/stick in crook of arms rt.: ritual chopper lt.: human skull-cup	corp	two	pralamba-pada	dhar. ornaments, va.: human forms, five dancing nude goddesses	Astatmaka-Panjara-Mahakala
one/ three	two	rt.: red lance with banner/flag lt.: reins of horse	mature	two	astride	dhar. ornaments, va.: red horse	bDud-btsan
one/three(?)	two	rt.: noose/snare lt.: sword	mature	two	astride	dhar. ornaments, va.: black horse with white heels	bDud-po-bye-ba-gung-ring
one*/three	two	rt.: lance lt.: throws lance	mature	two		*lion head long, loose robe,	bDud-mgon

						bone/ ornaments, syllable "du"	
one/three	two	rt.: magic staff/stick lt.: noose/snare	mature	two		black robe,	bDud-kyi-rgyal-po
one/three	two	rt.: conch-shell ritual chopper lt.: human skull-cup filled with blood	mature	two		dhar. ornaments, va.: wild bull syllable "traka"	bDud-mo-gshin-rje-mgo-dgu-ma
one/three	two	rt.: magic notched staff/stick lt.: axe	mature	two	astride	dhar. ornaments, va.: black horse	bDud-po-skos-rje-brang-dkar
one/three	two	rt.: ritual chopper lt.: human skull-cup	mature nude	two		bone and snake ornaments, shakti: to Mig-dmar	'Bebs-pa-mo
one/three	two	rt.: ritual chopper lt.: human skull-cup	mature nude	two		snakes and bone ornaments, shakti: to Tel-pa	Be-con-nag-mo
one/three	two	rt.: sword lt.: heart	corp	two	alidha	dhar. ornaments, lance in crook of lt. arm, va.: human forms on lotus throne	Beg-tse
one/three	two	rt.: sword lt.: human heart to mouth in tarjani mu.	corp.	two	partyalidha	dhar. ornaments, coat of mail over long robes, va.: prostrate horse and human form	Begtse-Mahakala
one/three	two	rt.: sword lt.: trident	corp.	two	alidha	dhar. ornaments, coat of mail over long robes, va.: human form	Begtse-Mahakala
one/three	two	rt.: red lance with banner/flag lt.: red noose/snare of the *btsan*	mature	two		dhar. ornaments, high leather boots, va.: red horse	bDud-btsan
one/three	two	rt.: conch shell chopper lt.: skull-cup filled with blood	mature	two		syllable "traka," white cloak, dhar. & jewel ornaments, va.: wild bull	bDud-mo-gshin-rje-mgo-dgu-ma

one/three	two	rt.: magic notched staff/stick lt.: axe	mature	two		dhar. ornaments, va.: black horse	bDud-po-skos-rje-brang-dkar
one/three	two	rt.: noose/snare lt.: rosary of human skulls	mature	two		dhar. ornaments, va.: black horse	bDud-rgyal-dpa'-bo-thod-phreng-can
one/three	two	rt.: ritual chopper lt.: human skull-cup	mature, nude	two		dhar. ornaments, shakti of Mig-dmar	'Bebs-pa-mo
one/three	two	rt.: ritual chopper lt.: human skull-cup filled with blood	mature, nude	two		dhar. ornaments, shakti of Tel-pa	Be-con-nag-mo
one/three	two	rt.: sword lt.: heart (?) and lance in crook of arm	corp.	two	alidha	cuirass & warrior weapons, va.: horse & prostrate human	Beg-tse**
one/three	two	rt.: sword lt.: lifts heart(?) to mouth in tarjani mu.	mature	two	party-alidha	coat of mail and covered in long flowing robe & fancy boots, va.: prostrate horse and human form	Begtse-Mahakala**
one/three	two	rt.: sword lt.: trident	mature	two	alidha	coat of mail and covered in long flowing robe & fancy boots, va.: human form	Begtse-Mahakala**
one/three	two	rt.: staff/stick lt.: alms bowl	corp.	two	alidha	dhar. ornaments, va.: human form	Bhagavad-Mahakala
one/three	two	rt.: ritual chopper lt.: human skull-cup with tantric staff/stick in crook of arm	mature	two	party-alidha	dhar. ornaments, long flowing robe, va.: prostrate human forms	Bhagavan-Mahakala**
one/three	two	rt.: skull-topped staff/stick lt.: human skull-cup and shakti	corp.	two	alidha, yab-yum	dhar. ornaments, va.: lotus throne	Bhayada(?)-Mahakala**
one/three	two	rt.: sword lt.: human skull-cup	mature, nude	two		copper teeth, dhar. ornaments, va.: nine headed wolf	bKa'-nyan-mthu-bo-che
one/three	two	holding btsan noose/snare	mature, nude	two		copper teeth, dhar. ornaments, va.: nine headed red tiger	bKa'-nyan-mthu-bo-che

one/three	two	holding bdud noose/snare	mature, nude	two		copper teeth, dhar. ornaments, va.: nine headed copper wild dog	bKa'-nyan-mthu-bo-che
one/three	two	rt.: bk. trident with four heads impaled lt.: dripping heart with two snakes	mature	two	alidha, yab-yum	dhar. ornaments, high boots, va.: lotus throne	Bran-bdud-(dasa-mara?)-Krsna-Yama
one/three	two	rt.: bk. trident lt.: heart	mature	two	alidha, yab-yum	dhar. ornaments, high boots, va.: horse	Bran-bdud-(dasa-mara?)-Krsna-Yama
one/three	two	rt.: human thigh-bone trumpet lt.: cylindrical banner/flag	corp.	two	sukha	dhar. ornaments, va.: human forms on lotus throne	Brahmana-Rupadhara-Mahakala**
one/three	two	rt.: human skull-drum lt.: human skull-cup	mature, nude	two	yab-yum	dhar. ornaments, embracing yab	Dam-tshig-gi-dbang-mo
one/three	two	rt.: short staff/stick lt.: an-i-in mu.	mature	two	alidha	dhar. ornaments, va.: lotus throne	Dandadhara-Bhairavavajra
one/three	two	rt.: magic notched staff/stick lt.: sack of diseases	mature	two		dhar. ornaments, va.: three-legged mule	dPal-ldan-lha-mo-'dod-khams-kyi-dbang-phyug-ma
one/three	two	holding goad/hook	mature	two		dhar. ornaments, va.: mule	dPal-ldan-lha-mo-remati
one/three	two	rt.:sandalwood club lt.: skull-cup filled with blood	mature	two		red turban, black garment, bejewled, va.: black horse with white heels	dPal-ldan-mgon-po-nag-po-chen-po
one/three	two	rt.: magic notched staff/stick lt.: mummified corpse, noose/snare	mature, pendulous breasts	two	astride	dhar. ornaments, va.: mule	Drag-po'i-lha-mo
one*/three	two	rt.: goad/hook lt.: human skull-cup	mature	two	vamalalita	*distorted with rage. one tooth, dhar. ornaments, va.: lotus throne	Ekajata
one*/three	two	rt.: (?) lt.: human skull-cup	corp.	two	alidha	*bull's head, dhar. ornaments,	Ekavira-Bhairavavajra

						va.: lotus throne	
one/three	two	rt.: ritual chopper lt.: human skull-cup	corp.	two		dhar. ornaments, va.: lotus throne	Ekavira-Kartaridhara-Mahakala
one/three	two	rt.: ritual chopper lt.: human skull-cup	corp.	two	alidha	dhar. ornaments, va.: human form	Ekavira-Kartaridhara-Mahakala
one/three	two	rt.: bell lt.: an-i-in mu.	mature	two	alidha	dhar. ornaments, va.: lotus throne	Ghantadhara-Bhairavavajra
one*/three	two	rt.: sword lt.: karana mu.	corp.	two	astride	dhar. ornaments, va.: horse	hBron-zhal-can
one/three	two	rt.: human skull-cup filled with blood lt.: mongoose	dwarfish, nude	two	alidha	rags, dhar. ornaments, va.: treasure owner	Jambhala-nag-po-Kha-che-pan-chen-lugs
one/three	two	rt.: ritual chopper lt.: human skull-cup	corp.	two	alidha	dhar. ornaments, va.: human corpse on sun disc	Jnana-krama-Navatmaka-Kartaridhara-Mahakala
one/three	two	rt.: ritual chopper lt.: human skull-cup	corp.	two	alidha	dhar. ornaments, va.: human corpse	Jnana-krama-Navatmaka-Kartaridhara-Mahakala
one/three	two	holds divination arrow	mature	two	astride	black turban, dhar. ornaments, va.: black horse	Jo-bo-mgon-chen
one/three	two	rt.: ritual chopper lt.: human skull-cup	mature	two	ardha-paryanka	dhar. ornaments, va.: prostrate human	Kakasya-Karma-Mahakala**
one/three	two	rt.: human skull-cup lt.: mongoose	mature, nude	two	alidha	dhar. ornaments, va.: Kubera	Kalajambhala
one/three	two	rt.: trident lt.: human skull-cup	mature	two		dhar. ornaments	Kangkaka
one/three	two	rt.: ritual chopper lt.: human skull-cup	corp.	two	praty-alidha	dhar. ornaments, va.: human form on lotus throne	Kartaridhara-Traksad-Mahakala**
one/three	two	rt.: ritual chopper lt.: human skull-cup	corp.	two	alidha,	dhar. ornaments, va.: lotus throne over two figures on horseback	Kartaridhara-Traksad-Mahakala**

one/three	two	rt.: sacrificial knife lt.: human skull-cup	dwarfish	two	alidha	dhar. ornaments, va.: corpse	Kasmira-mahapandita-(Sakyasri)-krama-Kartaridhara-Mahakala
one/three	two	rt.: ritual chopper lt.: human skull-cup	corp.	two	alidha	dhar. ornaments, va.: prostrate human form	Kasmira-mahapandita-(Sakyasri)-krama-Kartaridhara-Mahakala
one*/three	two	holds serpent/snake	corp., winged	two		*garuda-head, serpent/snake in beak, va.: prostrate figure with human body with snake coils	Krsna-Garuda
one/three	two	rt.: human skull-cup lt.: mongoose	corp.	two	alidha	dhar. ornaments, va.: prostrate human form	Krsna-Jambhala
one/three	two	rt.: human skull-cup lt.: mongoose	corp.	two	alidha	dhar. ornaments, va.: reclining crowned figure	Krsna-Jambhalavajra
one*/three	two	rt.: sword lt.:stem of lotus with book/manuscript in kartari mu.	youth	two	vajra	*calm, bodh. ornaments, va.: lotus throne	Krsna-Manjughosa
one/three	two	rt.: sword lt.: book/manuscript	corp.	two	praty-alidha	dhar. ornaments, va.: lotus throne	Krsna-Manjusri
one/three	two	rt.: sword lt.: human skull-cup	corp.	two	alidha	dhar. ornaments, va.: human forms	Krsna-Mararaja
one/three	two	rt.: battle axe lt.: tarjani mu.	corp.	two	alidha	dhar. ornaments, va.: bird	Krsna-Parnasabari
one/three	two	rt.: long knife lt.: noose/snare	corp.	two	alidha	dhar. ornaments, va.: lotus throne	Krsnaraksa
one/three	two	rt.: lance lt.: flower	corp.	two	astride	dhar. ornaments, va.: horse	Krsna-Rastradhipa (?)
one/three	two	rt.: lance lt.: human skull-cup	corp.	two	astride	dhar. ornaments, va.: horse	Krsna-Taksad
one/three	two	rt.: thunderbolt lt.: karana mu.	corp.	two	alidha	dhar. ornaments, va.: human form	Krsna-Vajravidarana (Buddha)
one/three	two	rt.: ritual chopper	corp.	two	alidha	dhar. ornaments,	Krsna-yaksa

		lt.: tarjani mu.				va.: lotus throne	
one/three	two	rt.: trident lt.: heart and black noose/snare	mature	two	astride	dhar. ornaments, va.: black horse	Las-kyi-mgon-po
one/three	two	rt.: trident lt.: heart and nopose/snare	mature	two		dhar. ornaments	Las-mgon
one/three	two	rt.: ritual chopper lt.: ritual skull-cup filled with blood	mature, nude	two		dhar. ornaments	lCags-kyu-ma
one*/three	two	rt.: thunderbolts lt.: black noose/snare	mature, nude	two		dhar. ornaments	lCags-mig-ma
one/three	two	rt.: sandal-wood club/cudgel lt.: iron bowl filled with elixir of life	mature	two		dhar. ornaments, high leather boots	Legs-ldan-nag-po
one/three	two	rt.: banner/flag lt.: heart with noose/snare	mature	two		dhar. ornaments	lHa-chen-dpal-'bar-ma-ning
one/three	two	rt.: sword lt.: human skull-cup	mature	two		dhar. ornaments, va.: lotus throne	Lha-mo
one/three	two	rt.: mirror lt.: noose/snare	mature	two		black silk garments, dhar. ornaments, va.: lotus throne on lake of flames	lHa-mo-nag-mo
one/three	two	rt.: trident lt.: human skull-cup	mature	two		black silk garment dhar. ornaments, va.: lotus throne	lHa-mo-nag-mo
one/three	two	rt.: ritual chopper lt.: human skull-cup	mature	two		blood drips from fangs, dhar. ornaments, va.: lotus throne	Ljan-lugs-Saptadas-atmaka- Tamra-kartaridhara-Mahakala
one/three	two	rt.: human thigh-bone trumpet lt.: human skull-cup filled with blood	mature	two		dhar. ornaments, va.: lotus throne	Mahakala-Brahmanarupa
one/three	two	rt.: trident lt.: human skull-cup	mature	two	vamalalita	dhar. ornaments, va.: lotus throne	Mahakala (deva)
one/three	two	holds command staff/stick	corp.	two	alidha	dhar. ornaments, va.: prostrate human form	Mahakala-gur
one/three	two	rt.: sword	corp.	two	sopasraya	dhar. ornaments,	Mahakali-Remati

		lt.: human skull-cup				va.: horse	
one/three	two	rt.: sword lt.: (?) with lance in crook of arm	corp.	two	alidha	dhar. ornaments, va.: prostrate human forms	Maharakta-Mahakala
one/three	two	rt.: ritual chopper, flaming sword lt.: human skull-cup, trident	corp	two		dhar. ornaments, va.: lotus throne	Mahasiddha-santigupta-krama-Caturbhuja-(Inana)-Mahakala
one*/three	two	rt.: lance lt.: human skull-cup	corp.	two		*lion-head, dhar. ornaments, va.: lotus throne	Mahakala-Simhamukha
one/three	two	rt.: sword lt.: human skull-cup	mature	two	astride	dhar. ornaments, va.: mule	Mahakali
one/three	two	rt.: human skull-drum lt.: human skull-cup	mature, nude	two	yab-yum	dhar. ornaments, va.: lotus throne	Mahakali-Dam-tshig-gi-dbang-mo
one/three	two	rt.: lance lt.: human heart	corp.	two	alidha	dhar. ornaments, va.: prostrate human form	Mahapandaka-Karma-Mahakala
one/three	two	rt.: sword lt.: sack of diseases	mature	two	astride	dhar. ornaments, va.: black mule	Ma-mo-rdo-rje-ba-lam
one/three	two	rt.: sword lt.: stem of blue lotus	mature	two	kneeling	dhar. ornaments, va.: lotus throne	Manjusri**
one/three	two	rt.: ritual chyopper lt.: human skull-cup	mature, nude	two		dhar. ornaments, va.: lotus throne	mChe-ba-mo
one*/three	two	rt.: thunderbolt lt.: noose/snare	mature, nude	two		*dog-head, hair to heels, va.: lotus throne	mChong-mig-ma
one/three	two	rt.: sandal wood club lt.: goad/hook	mature	two	alidha	dhar. ornaments, va.: male and female gshin-rje	mGon-po
one/three	two	rt.: sacrificial knife lt.: skull-cup	mature	two	alidha	dhar. ornaments, va.: corpses	mGon-po-bzhi-sbrags
one*/three	two	rt.: flaming club lt.: bloody ritual chopper	mature	two		*wild yak-head, richly garbed, dhar. ornaments, va.: lotus throne	mGon-po-traksad-'brong-zhal-can

one*/three	two	rt.: vandana mu. (?) lt.: sack of diseases	mature, nude	two		*scorpion-head, pendulous breasts, open genitals, snake ornaments, attrib.: syllable "ma" va.: camel	Nad-gtong-ma
one/three	two	ritual chopper, human skull-cup embrace shakti	corp.	two	sama-bhanga, yab-yum	dhar. ornaments, va.: prostrate human form	Nagarjuna-krama-Samatrka-Panjara-Mahakala**
one/three	two	rt.: ritual chopper lt.: skull-cup filled with blood, across bent arms is trident	mature	two		flaming thunderbolt wings, dragon-like feet, dhar. ornaments, va.: human forms	Nagarjuna-krama-Samatrka-Panjara-Mahakala
one/three	two	rt.: ritual chopper lt.: human skull-cup, tantric staff/stick in crook of arm	mature	two	partyalidha	dhar. ornaments, flowing robe, va.: prostrate human forms	Narayana-Mahakala
one/three	two	rt.: flaming sword lt.: saffron colored divination arrow	mature	two	astride	richly garbed, fancy boots, dhar. ornaments, va.: lapis colored horse	Nilasva-Krsna-Vaisravana
one/three	two	rt.: trident lt.: heart & noose/snare	corp.	two	astride	black iron bow & sandal wood club at side, dhar. ornaments, va.: black horse	Pandaka-Traksad-Mahakala
one/three	two	rt.: trident lt.: human heart	corp.	two	lalita	flowing robe, fancy boots, dhar. ornaments, va.: prostrate human and horse figures	Pandaka-Traksad-Mahakala
one/three	two	command staff/stick across arms rt.: ritual chopper lt.: human skull-cup	corp.	two	pralam-bapada, yab-yum	dhar. ornaments, va.: prostrate human form	Panjara-Mahakala**
one/three	two	command staff/stick across arms rt.: ritual chopper lt.: human skull-cup filled with blood	corp.	two	pralam-bapada, yab-yum	silk garments, dhar. ornaments, va.: obstacle creating demons	Panjara-Mahakala**

one/three	two	rt.: ritual chopper lt.: human skull-cup filled with blood	mature, nude	two		snake & bone ornaments, va.: lotus throne	Pho-nya-mo
one/three	two	rt.: magic dagger lt.: red noose/snare	mature, nude	two		dhar. ornaments, va.: lotus throne	Pho-nya-mo
one/three	two	rt.: thunderbolt lt.: magic dagger	mature	two	alidha	dhar. ornaments, va.: revived corpse	Purakali
one/three	two	rt.: ritual chopper lt.: human skull-cup	mature	two		dhar. ornaments, va.: lotus throne	Pu-tra-lcam-dral
one/three	two	rt.: ritual chopper lt.: snake noose/snare	mature	two		one eye in forehead, single tooth, dhar. ornaments, va.: red water bull	rDo-rje-brag-btsan-rDo-rje-dbang-drag-rtsal
one/three	two	rt.: lt.:	mature	two		garment of the skin of a wild man, dhar. ornaments, va.: three legged mule	rDo-rje-brag-btsan-rDo-rje-dbang-drag-rtsal
one*/three	two	rt.: sword lt.: lance	mature	two	astride	richly armored, va.: horse	Raudra-krsna-Vaisravana
one/three	two	rt.: jewel lt.: golden vase/vessel filled with jewels	mature	two		garment of black silk, va.: lotus throne	rDo-rje-bdud-'dul
one/three	two	rt.: hammer lt.: bellows	mature	two	astride	dhar. ornaments, va.: brown billy goat	rDo-rje-legs-pa
one/three	two	rt.: thunderbolt club lt.: black shrine	mature	two		bejeweled diadem, richly clothed, fancy leather boots, sun and moon rests on shoulders, va.: lotus throne	rNam-sras-drag-byed
one/three	two	rt.: magic notched stick lt.: sack of diseases	mature	two		dhar. ornaments, va.: black three legged mule	rDo-rje-remati
one/three	two	rt.: ritual chopper, sword lt.: human skull-cup, trident	corp.	two	lalita	dhar. ornaments, va.: prostrate human forms	rGva-lo-(tsa-ba)-htshal-lugs-Caturbhuja-(Jnana)-Mahakala**

one/three	two	rt.: black banner/flag lt.: noose/snare	mature	two		dhar. ornaments, black cloak, va.: horse	rLe-dpon-nag-po
one/three	two	rt.: ritual chopper lt.: human skull-cup	corp.	two	sama- bhanga	dhar. ornaments, va.: prostrate human form	rNog-lugs-Ekanta-Panjara-Mahakala**
one*/three	two	rt.: ritual dagger lt.: human head	mature	two		*frog-head, dress of blood, dhar. ornaments, va.: camel with six heads	sBal-mgo-khrag-mig
one/three	two	rt.: bow & arrow lt.: noose/snare of a snake	mature	two		dhar. ornaments, va.: lotus throne	sGo-bdud-chen-po
one/three	two	holds noose/snare	mature	two	astride	dhar. ornaments, human skin, va.: black horse	sGrol-byed-bdud-kyi-shan-pa
one/three	two	rt.: conch lt.: short staff/stick	corp.	two	lalita	dhar. ornaments, va.: human form	Shailadeva-Mahakala**
one*/three	two	rt.: sword lt.: human skull-cup	mature	two		*lion-head, dressed in black silk, dhar. ornaments, va.: lotus throne	Sha-za-nag-po
one/three	two	rt.: battle axe lt.: noose/snare	mature	two		cane head dress, cloak of snake and tiger skins, dhar. ornaments, va.: black horse with white heels	Shing-bya-can
one/three	two	rt.: bDud lance lt.: bDud noose/snare	corp.	two	astride	diadem of black silk, harness of iron, dhar. ornaments, va.: black bDud horse	sKos-rje-trang-dkar-dmag-gi-dpon
one/three	two	rt.: magic staff/stick lt.: axe	mature	two	astride	cloak of dark blue silk, dhar. ornaments, va.: black horse	sKos-rje-trang-dkar-dung-gi-dpon
one/three	two	rt.: human heart	mature	two	aseat	dressed human skins,	sKye-mthing-ma

		lt.: tarjani mu.				dhar. ornaments, va.: stag	
one/three	two	rt.: devours human heart lt.: goad/hook	mature	two	alidha	hair hangs to thigh, dhar. ornaments, attribute: syllable "ma", va.: corpse	sNying-bzan-ma
one/three	two	rt.: sword lt.: lance	mature	two		dhar. ornaments, va.: monkey	sPrel-nag-mig-gcig
one/three	two	rt.: human heart lt.: human skull-cup	mature	two		dhar. ornaments, va.: lotus throne	Srid-pa-chogs-byed-ma
one/three	two	rt.: human thigh-bone trumpet lt.: human skull-cup	corp	two	ardha-paryanka	dhar. ornaments, va.: prostrate human figure	Sri-Mahakala
one/three	two	crushing the sun and moon		mature	two	hair hangs to thigh, dhar. ornaments, attribute: syllable "ma", va.: black bird	Srog-bdud-ma
one/three	two	rt.: lance lt.: human skull-cup	corp.	two	astride	loose garment, dhar. ornaments, va.: horse	Taksad-Mahakala**
one/three	two	rt.: thunderbolt lt.: vase/vessel	mature	two	astride	dhar. ornaments, va.: black horse	Tha-'og-jo-bo-rgyal-mrshan
one/three	two	rt.: thunderbolt lt.: vase/vessel	mature	two	astride	dhar. ornaments, va.: white lion	Tha-'og-jo-bo-rgyal-mrshan
one/three	two	rt.: lance lt.: human skull-cup	mature	two	astride	black silk garments, dhar. ornaments, va.: horse	Tra-ksad
one/three	two	rt.: trident lt.: human skull-cup	mature	two		emaciated breasts, garments of ox skin and black silk, va.: lotus throne	Tsamundi
one/three	two	rt.: trident lt.: human skull-cup	mature	two		dhar. ornaments, va.: lotus throne	Tsamunti
one/three	two	rt.: trident lt.: ritual chopper	mature	two	aseat	orange hair, dhar. ornaments,	Tshe-bdud-nag-po-khrag-med

						va.: white lion	
one/three	two	rt.: ritual chopper & skull-cup-hilt knife lt.: human skull-cup filled with blood	mature, nude	two		dhar. ornaments, va.: lotus throne	Vajrasrinkhala
one/three	two	rt.: ritual chopper lt.: human skull-cup	mature	two	aseat	dhar. ornaments, va.: raven	Virakali
one/three	two	rt.: sandal-wood club lt.: vase/vessel filled with human blood	mature	two	aseat	dhar. ornaments, va.: tiger	Vyaghravahana-Mahakala
one/three	two	rt.: short staff/stick with skull finial lt.: noose/snare in karana mu.	corp.	two	astride	dhar. ornaments, va.: tiger	Vyaghravahana-Mahakala
one/three	two	rt.: sandal-wood staff/stick lt.: human skull-cup (?)	corp.	two	utkutika	dhar. ornaments, va.: tiger on lotus throne	Vyaghravahana-Mahakala
one/three	two	rt.: sword lt.: treasure producing mongoose	mature	two		dhar. ornaments, va.: lotus throne	Yaksi-Remati
one/three	two	rt.: sword lt.: treasure producing mongoose	corp.	two	sopasraya	dhar. ornaments, va.: horse	Yaksi-Remati
one/three	two	rt.: magic staff/stick lt.: freshly severed head	mature	two	alidha	dhar. ornaments, va.: lotus throne	Yum-bdud-mo-nag-mo-Khrag-'jag-ma
one*/three	two	rt.: thunderbolt lt.: black noose/snare	mature	two		*dog-head, dhar. ornaments, va.: lotus throne	Zangs-mig-ma
one/three	two	rt. ritual chopper lt.: human skull-cup	mature, nude	two		dhar. ornaments, va.: lotus throne	Zhags-pa-mo
one/three	four	prin. bhutadamara mu. rt.: thunderbolt lt.: tarjani mu.	mature	two	pratyalidha	dhar. ornaments, va.: trampling Aparajita	Bhutadamara
one*/three	four	rt.: ritual chopper and human skull-drum lt.: magic notched staff/stick and human skull-cup	mature	two	ardha-paryanka, yab-yum	*bluish-black dhar. ornaments, va.: human form	Buddha-Kapala
one/three	four	prin.: ritual chopper, human skull-cup rt.: sword lt.: parasol	corp.	two	alidha	dhar. ornaments, va.: human form	Caturbhuja-Mahakala
one/three	four	prin.: ritual chopper, human skull-cup	corp.	two	alidha	dhar. ornaments,	Caturbhuja-Mahakala

		rt.: sword lt.: trident				va.: human form	
one/three	four	rt.: sword, rosary of skulls lt.: trident, human skull-cup filled with blood	mature	two		dhar. ornaments,	Caturbhuja-Nagi-Remati
one/three	four	rt.: sword, rosary lt.: trident, human skull-cup	mature	two	sopasraya	dhar. ornaments, va.: horse	Caturbhuja-Nagi-Remati
one/three	four	rt.: jewel(?), sword lt.: human skull-cup, lance	corp.	two	alidha, yab-yum	dhar. ornaments, va.: human forms on lotus throne	Caturbhuja-Sri-Mahakala
one/three	four	rt.: ritual chopper, red skull-cup lt.: piercing weapon, trident with silk ribbons	skeletal-like	two		floral crown, dhar. ornaments	Dhumavati-(Sri)-Devi
one/three	four	rt.: human skull-cup, sword lt.: trident. staff/stick	mature, pendulous breasts	two	astride	dhar. ornaments, va.: horse	Dhumavati-(Sri)-Devi
one/three	four	rt.: flaming crystal sword, human skull-cup lt.: trident, sword-topped lsance	mature	two	astride	dhar. ornaments, va.: mule with eye in left flank	Dhumavati-(Sri)-Devi
one/three	four	rt.: sword, red banner/flag lt.: lance, trident	mature	two	astride	black silk head-dress, yellow trousers, bell around neck, va.: donkey with red spot on forehead	gSer-gyi-spu-gri-ma
one/three	four	prin.: ritual chopper, human skull-cup rt.: seord lt.: trident	corp.	two	lalita	dhar. ornaments, va.: prostrate human forms on lotus throne on triangle	Htshal-lugs-Caturbhuja-(Inana)-Mahakala**
one/three	four	prin.: vajrahumakra mu. rt.: human skull-drum lt.: magic notched staff/stick	youth	two	alidha	dhar. ornaments, va.: prostrate human forms on lotus throne	Kavaca-Krsna-Heruka**
one/three	four	rt.: sword, rosary of skulls lt.: human skull-cup, trident in crook of arm	mature	two	astride	dhar. ornaments, va.: ass of the raksasas	kLu-mo-remati-phyag-bzhi-ma
one/three	four	rt.: lance, axe lt.: bow and arrow, noose/snare	mature	two	astride	dhar. ornaments, va.: black horse	lHa-chen-khang-kas-drag-po

one/three	four	rt.: shield, sword lt.: jewel, ritual chopper	mature	two		dhar. ornaments, va.: chariot	lHa-min-dbang-po-thags-bzang
one/three	four	prin.: embrace shakti with human skull-cup and ritual chopper rt.: sword lt.: trident	corp.	two	lalita	dhar. ornaments, va.: form of Ganesa	Mahasiddha-santigupta-krama-Caturbhuja-(Jnana)-Mahakala
one/three	four	rt.: staff/stick, baton/mace lt.: staff/stick, human skull-cup	corp.	two	astride	*pigs head at rt. ear, dhar. ornaments, va.: horse	Mahakala-Taksad
one/three	four	rt.: sword, ritual chopper lt.: trident, human skull-cup	mature	two		dhar. ornaments, va.: lotus throne	Nagarjuna-krama-Caturbhuja-(mahadharmapala-Jnana)-Mahakala
one/three	four	rt.: sword, ritual chopper lt.: trident, human skull-cup	mature	two	lalita	dhar. ornaments, va.: prostrate human form	Nagarjuna-krama-Caturbhuja-(mahadharmapala-Jnana)-Mahakala
one/three	four	rt.: magic mirror, snake noose/snare lt.: trident, sacred knife of iron	mature	two		dhar. ornaments, va.: lotus throne	Prana-sadhana-Loha-kila-Svayambhu-rajni-Devi
one/three	four	rt.: corpse, sword with scorpion hilt lt.: mongoose, skull-cup filled with blood	mature	two	astride	dhar. ornaments, va.: red ass	Prana-sadhana-Loha-kila-Svayambhu-rajni-Devi
one/three	four	rt.: mirror, string(?) lt.: trident, magic dagger	corp.	two	sopasraya	dhar. ornaments, va.: lotus throne on horse	Prana-sadhana-Loha-kila-Svayambhu-rajni-Devi
one/three	four	rt.: battle axe, sword lt.: sack of diseases, noose/snare	dwarfish	two		dhar. ornaments, va.: lotus throne	rNon-po
one/three	four	rt.: rosary, ritual chopper lt.: human skull-cup, trident	corp	two	sama-bhanga	dhar. ornaments, va.: prostrate Ganesa	Sarva-vighna-vinayaka-Mahakala**
one/three	four	rt.: vajra-topped staff/stick, staff/stick lt.: cylindrical banner, (?)	corp.	two	lalita	dhar. ornaments, va.: lotus throne on the back of a lion	Simhasana-Ganapati-Mahakala**
one/three	four	rt.: trident, sword lt.: human skull-cup, cylindrical banner of victory	corp.	two	sukha	dhar. ornaments, va.: lion	Simhavahana-Taksad**
one/three	four	rt.: trident, sword	corp.	two	aseat	dhar. ornaments,	Trakshad Mahakala**

		lt.: cylindrical banner/flag, serpent/snake				va.: tiger	
one/ three	six	prin.: embrace shakti and hold ritual chopper and human skull-cup rt.: rosary, human skull-drum lt.: trident, noose/snare	corp	two	alidha	dhar. ornaments va.: Ganesa	Ayushpati Mahakala
one/ three	six	rt.:ritual chopper, karana, human skull-drum lt.: human skull-cup, trident, noose/snare	corp	two	alidha	dhar. ornaments, va.: human forms	Ayuspati Mahakala
one/three	six	rt.: rosary of human skulls, ritual chopper, human skull-drum lt.: trident, human skull-cup, noose/snare	corp	two	pratyalidha	dhar. ornaments, va.: elephant elephant-headed deity	Mahakala
one/three	six	rt.: ritual chopper, rosary of skulls, human skull-drum lt.: human skull-cup, trident , noose/snare	corp.	two	partyalidha	dhar. ornaments, va.: prostrate form of Ganesa	Natha-Mahakala**
one/three	six	rt.: ritual chopper, part of elephant-skin cape, human skull-drum lt.: human skull-cup, trident, noose/snare	corp.	two	alidha	dhar. ornaments, va.: prostrate human form on lotus throne	Ksiprakara-Sadbhuja-Inana-Mahakala
one/three	six	rt.: foot of elephant-cape with rosary, human skull-drum, ritual chopper lt.: trident, noose/snare, human skull-cup	corp.	two	alidha	dhar. ornaments, va.: prostrate Ganesa-like figure on lotus throne	Sadbhuja-Inana-Mahakala
one/three	six	prin.: ritual chopper, human skull-cup rt.: rosary of skulls, (?) lt.: trident, noose/snare	corp.	two	alidha	dhar. ornaments, va.: prostrate human form	Sadbhuja-Mahakala
one/three	six	rt.: ritual chopper, rosary of human heads, human skull-drum lt.: blood filled skull-cup, trident noose/snare with two thunderbolt tips	corp.	two	alidha	dhar. ornaments, va.: prostrate human form	Sadbhuja-Mahakala
one*/three	24	rt.: sword, thunderbolt, disk, jewels, goad/hook, arrow, lance, hammer, knife, bludgeon,tambourine, rosary lt.: bow, noose/snare, *tarjani mudra*, banner/flag, hammer, trident, cup,	mature	two	rajalila	*distorted with rage. one tooth, dhar. ornaments, va.: human form	Ekajata

		blue lotus, bell, ritual chopper, Brahma head, skull-cup					
three*/6-9	six	rt.: ritual chopper, human skull-cup, sword lt.: goad/hook, noose/snare, bow and arrow	mature	snake-like		*tiger-head, elephant-head, pig-head, dhar. ornaments,	Ha-sa-garbha
three/nine	two	rt.: ritual chopper lt.: human skull-cup	corp.	two	alidha	dhar. ornaments, va.: prostrate human figure on lotus throne	Kartaridhara-Mahakala**
three/nine	two	rt.: ritual chopper, trident lt.: bow & arrow, severed head of an enemy	mature	two	alidha	dhar. ornaments, va.: corpse	Ye-shes-mgon-po-phyag-bzhi-pa'i-'khor-lha-mo-tsandika
three/nine	four	prin.: embrace shakti rt.: human skull-cup with alarm staff/stick in crook of arm lt.: thunderbolt	mature	two	alidha	dhar. ornaments, va.: human figure	Mahakalavajra
three/nine	six	prin.: embrace shakti holding human skull-cup and ritual chopper rt.: sword, short staff/stick lt.: (?), flaming jewel	mature	two	alidha, yab-yum	dhar. ornaments, va.: lotus throne	Dandadhara-Bhairavavajra
three*/nine	six	rt.: axe, sword, thunderbolt lt.: tarjani mu., pestle, noose/snare	mature	two		*bk., wh., rd., dhar. ornaments, va.: king of the Vighnas	Khro-bo-bdud-rtsi-'khyil-ba
three/nine	six	prin.: ritual chopper, human skull-cup and embrace shakti rt.: thunderbolt, sword lt.: hold baton/mace, (?)	corp.	two	alidha, yab-yum	dhar. ornaments, va.: human form	Krsnari
three/nine	six	rt.: thunderbolt, sword, (?) lt.: human skull-cup, lotus, karana mu.	corp.	two	praty-alidha	dhar. ornaments, va.: sun disc on lotus on back of bull	Krsnari-Bhairavavajra
three/nine	six	rt.: thunderbolt, sword, ritual chopper lt.: human skull-cup, lotus, karana mu.	corp.	two	praty-alidha	dhar. ornaments, va.: sun disc on lotus on back of bull	Krsnarivajra (Buddha)
three/nine	six	prin.: embrace shakti with ritual chopper, human skull-cup rt.: thunderbolt, sword lt.: wheel, lotus	mature	two	alidha, yab-yum	dhar. ornaments, va.: prostrate human figures on lotus on back of kneeling bull	Krsnari-Yamantaka (=Bhairavavajra)

three/nine	six	prin.: embraces shakti with ritual chopper, human skull-cup rt.: staff/stick with thunderbolt finial, sword lt.: flaming jewel, lotus	corp,	two	partyalidha, yab-yum	dhar. ornaments, va.: lotus throne	<u>Yamantaka</u>
three*/nine	six	prin.: embrace shakti, ritual chopper, skull-cup rt.: jewel, sword lt.: wheel, lotus	mature	two	alidha	*cent. bull-head, dhar. ornaments, va.: human body on the back of a buffalo	<u>Yamantaka</u>
four/12	two	rt.: ritual chopper, sword lt.: human skull-cup, trident	corp.	two	lalita	dhar. ornaments, va.: prostrate human form	<u>rGva-lo-(tsa-ba)-hi-lugs-Caturbhuja-(Inana)-Mahakala</u>**
four/12	two	rt.: sword, ritual chopper lt.: sword, ritual chopper	corp.	two	alidha	dhar. ornaments, va.: lotus throne	<u>Seva-kala-sambaddha-Caturmukha-Sri-Mahakala</u>
four*/12	four	rt.: ritual chopper, skull-cup lt.: flaming sword, rosary of bones crook of arm; trident, a gold vase/vessel	mature	two		*wh., bk., wh., gray, dhar. ornaments, va.: lotus throne	<u>dPal-mgon-zhal-bzhi-pa-sgrub-dus-dang-'brel-ba</u>
four/12	four	rt.: ritual chopper, sword lt.: human skull-cup, lance	corp.	two	alidha	dhar. ornaments, va.: prostrate human form on lotus throne	<u>Guhya-nidhi-dhara-Sri-Mahakala</u>**
four/12	four	rt.: ritual chopper, skull-cup lt.: flaming sword, rosary of bones, trident & a gold vase/vessel filled with the elixir of life rests in one arm-crook	corp.	two	alidha	dhar. ornaments, va.: lotus throne	<u>Sadhana-kala-sambaddha-Caturmukha-Sri-Mahakala</u>
four/12	four	rt.: sword, ritual chopper lt.: rosary with trident, human skull-cup	corp.	two	alidha	dhar. ornaments, va.: lotus throne	<u>Sadhana-kala-sambaddha-Caturmukha-Sri-Mahakala</u>
four/12	four	rt.: sacrificial knife, skull-cup filled with blood and hearts of enemies lt.: flaming sword, a rosary of human skulls	corp.	two		dhar. ornaments, va.: lotus throne	<u>Seva-kala-sambaddha-Caturmukha-Sri-Mahakala</u>
four*/12	24	prin.: embrace shakti rt.: thunderbolt, sword, trident, knife, fire, arrow, thunderbolt, goad/hook, wheel, knife, rod, axe lt.: bell, plate, ritual wand, skull-cup, bow, noose/snare, jewel, lotus, mirror,	mature	two	alidha, yab-yum	*bl., rd., wt.,yw. dhar. ornaments va.: human forms	<u>Kalacakra</u>

		thunderbolt, chain, severed head of Brahma					
seven*/21	18	prin.: embrace shakti holding ritual chopper and human skull-cup other hands hold tantric symbols	corp.	18	alidha, yab-yum	*central head bull-like, dhar. ornaments, va.: human forms	Bhairava**
nine*/27	two	rt.: snake staff/stick lt.: lake of blood	mature	snake coils		*frog-heads, dhar. ornaments, va.: lotus throne	Yum-gcig-klu-mo-klog-khyug-ma
nine*/27	34	holds tantric symbols	mature, nude	16	alidha	*cent. bull-head, dhar. ornaments, wheel at breast, va.: animals and birds	Yamantaka
12/36	24	rt.: sword, thunderbolt, wheel, jewel, goad/hook, arrow, dart, hammer/mace, wooden pestle, ritual chopper, human skull-drum, rosary lt.: bow, noose/snare, tarjani mu., banner/flag, hammer/mace, trident, wine glass, lotus, bell, battle axe, Brahma's skull-cup	mature	two	pratyalidha	dhar. ornaments, va.: Indra, Brahma, Vishnu, Siva	Vidyujjvalakarali

Dark (Skt.: syama[11]), Purple, Brown (Skt.: babhru; Tib.: ja) or Smoke (grey) (Skt.: dhumavarna; Tib.: dud-kha) Colored Deities, Wrathful deities

Abbreviations:

as. = asana	bk. = black	bl. = blue	bodh. = bodhisattva
bn. = brown	corp. = corpulent	dhar. = dharmapala	gn. = green
lt. = left	mu. = mudra	pu. = purple	rd. = red
rt. = right	sc. = smokey	va. = vahana	wh. = white
yw. = yellow			

(*) special variations or attributes noted within the entry.
(**) following deity's name indicates that the color is not noted in the source, kulesa's color is applied to the entry.
(eyes: 2-3, 6-9, etc.) in sources the deity's faces are noted, but the number of the eyes are not noted.

Head/Eyes	Hands	Objects Held	Body	Feet	Asana	Other Attributes	Deity Name
one*/two	two	crossed on chest	mature	two	alidha	*dark brown, *lion-head, dhar. ornaments	Htamenma, "Dark-Brown Lion-Headed One"
one*/two	two	rt.: thunderbolt lt.: human skull-cup	mature	two	alidha	*yak-head, dhar. ornaments	Ishvari, "Dark-Brown Yak-headed Rakshasa Goddess"
one/2 -3	two	silk banner/flag	mature	two		purple, black cloak, dhar. ornaments	bDud-kye-dge-bsnyen
one*/2-3	two	rt.: ritual chopper lt.: "life roots" to mouth	dwarf, misshapen	two		*purple, goat head, dhar. ornaments,	bShan-pa
one*/2-3	two	rt.: precious vase/vessel lt.: crystal rosary	mature	two		*brown body color white turban, bejeweled, va.: dark blue horse	dPa'-bo-chen-po
one*/2-3	two	rt.: trident lt.: heart and noose/snare	mature	two		*dark brown color dhar. ornaments, va.: sun-lotus throne	Ekajati-Devi

[11] This form of *Garuda* is described as "multi-colored."

one*/2-3	two	serpent/snake	mature, winged	two		*head of a bird, multicolored, wish fulfilling jewel in forehead, serpent in beak, va.: dying Naga	Garuda[12]
one*/three	two	rt.: tiger head lt.: pair of dice	mature	two		*purple, *fierce, dhar. ornaments	bDe-bskyed-mkha'-'gro-ma
one/three	two	rt. : tiger head lt.: pair of dice	mature	two		purple dhar. ornaments,	bDe-bskyed-mkha'-'gro-ma
one/three	two	rt.: trident lt.: human skull-cup	mature	two		dhar. ornaments, va.:sun and moon discs on defeated enemies brown	bKa'-srung-chen-mo-rdo-rje-khro-gdong-ma
one/three	two	rt.: thunderbolt lt.: vase/vessel with elixir of life	mature	two		loose garment, bejeweled grey	bKa'-srung-lha-mo-rdo-rje-chen-mo
one/three	two	wheel in dharmachakra mu.	mature	two	ardha-paryanka, yab-yum	dhar. ornaments, va.: garuda	Buddha-Heruka
one*/three	two	rt.: encircles yab's neck lt.: human skull-cup	mature	two	pratyalidha, yab-yum	*light br. dhar. ornaments, va.: garuda	Buddha-Krotishaurima
one/three	two	rt.: banner/flag with head of sea dragon lt.: banner/flag with tiger-head finial	mature	two		dhar. ornaments, realm: East	Byi-nu-raja
one*/three	two	rt.: trident lt.: ritual chopper	corp.	two	astride	*lion head dhar. ornaments, flowing robes, fancy boots, horse on triangle	Camarimukha-Traksad-Makahala
one*/three	two	rt.: lance lt.: axe	mature	two	astride	*cherry-brown golden armor, va.: horse	dByi-rgyal-dmag-dpon
one*/three	two	rt.: tiger head lt.: pair of dice	mature	two		*purple, dhar. ornaments,	dPal-ldan-lha-mo-remati

[12] In the rNying-ma-pa sect style.

						va.: mule	
one/three	two	rt.: trident lt.: human heart	corp.	two		dhar. ornaments, high boots, va.: horse on lotus throne on prostrate human and horse forms	Dvags-pohi-lugs-Traksad-Makahala
one/three	two	rt.: black war banner/flag lt.: human heart to mouth, trident rests on lt. shoulder	corp.	two	lalita	dhar. ornaments, high boots, va.: black horse	Dvags-pohi-lugs-Traksad-Makahala
one*/three	two	rt.: sword with scorpion hilt lt.: human skull-cup	mature	two	vamalalita	*distorted with rage. one tooth, dhar. ornaments, va.: lotus throne	Ekajata
one*/three	two	rt.: bow lt.: arrow	corp.*	two		dark purple, face and body covered with eyes, dhar. ornaments	gZa'-bdud
one*/three	two	rt.: red lance with banner/flag lt.: red noose/snare	mature	two		* brown color, fancy leather boots, bejeweled, va.: red horse	kLu-btsan
one*/three	two	rt.: sandal wood club/cudgel with fire issuing from the head and water from the hilt lt.: iron bowl filled with the elixir of life	mature	two		*purple color, dhar. ornaments	Las-kyi-mgon-po
one*/three	two	rt.: ritual chopper lt.: human skull-cup	mature	two		*smokey-grey color dhar. ornaments	lHa-mo-drag-mo
one*/three	two	rt.: trident lt.: heart with noose/snare	mature	two	alidha	*dark brown, dhar. ornaments, va.: bodies of enemies on a sun and moon-lotus	lHa-mo-ekajati-sngags-srung
one*/three	two	rt.: flaming sword lt.: human skull-cup filled with blood and sack of diseases	mature	two	astride	*dark brown, dhar. ornaments, blood, grease, human fat spattered, va.: half mule, half Asiatic wild ass	Ma-gcig-rdo-rje-rab-brtan-ma

one/three	two	rt.: trident lt.: human skull-cup	mature	two		*ash gray, dhar. ornaments, va.: lotus throne	Mahavira
one*/three	two	rt.: magic notched stick lt.: goad/hook	mature	two	astride	*smoke-gray dhar. ornaments, va.: an ass	Na-ra-seng-ha
one*/three	two	rt.: skin of a human lt.: rosary of human heads	mature	two		*dark brown, yak-skin garment, va.: fire cloud	rDo-rje-khyung-lung-ma
one/three	two	rt.: sun disc lt.: moon disc	mature	two		*purple, dhar. ornaments, va.: lotus throne	Rahu
one*/three	two	rt.: vase/vessel lt.: mirror	mature	two		*dark brown, dhar. ornaments, va.: lotus throne	rGyal-yum-chen-mo-the-khyim
one*/three	two	rt.: goad/hook lt.: wish fulfilling jewel, banner/flag in crook of arm	mature	two		*red-purple leather helmet, cuirass of tourquoise, high boots, va.: lotus throne	sNgo-la-g.yu-rtse
one*/three	two	rt.: sword lt.: skull-cup, mongoose in the crook of arm	mature	two		*dark brown peacock parasol, dhar. ornaments, va.: lotus throne	Uddhata-vajra-paksa(?)-Remati
one*/three	two	rt.: sword lt.: human skull-cup	mature	two	sopasraya	*dark-brown dhar. ornaments, va.: horse	Uddhata-vajra-paksa(?)-Remati
one*/three	four	rt.: thunderbolt, sword lt.: human heart, noose/snare	mature	two		*ash gray, white silk garments, va.: white lion	Li-byin-ha-ra
one*/three	four	rt.: sword, trident lt.: banner/flag, a noose/snare	mature	two		*dark purple color, dhar. ornaments, va.: lion	Tshogs-bdag-mgon-po-seng-ge'i-gdan-can
one*/ three	six	prin.: embrace shakti and hold ritual chopper and human skull-cup rt.: rosary, human skull-drum	corp	two	alidha	*dark purple color, dhar. ornaments, va.: Ganesa	Ayuspati-Syama-Mahakala

		lt.: trident, noose/snare					
two*/six	four	rt.: censor with poisonous fumes, noose/snare, magic notched stick in crook of arm lt.: skull-cup-hilt knife, human skull-cup	mature	two		*dog-head and pig-head, dhar. ornaments, va.: lotus throne	gNos-lugs-(Mahadeva)-Traksad-Yama-yami-Mahakala
two*/six	four	rt.: trident, ritual chopper lt.: staff/stick, human skull-cup	corp.	two	alidha	*human head and dog-head, va.: horse on a lotus throne	gNos-lugs-(Mahadeva)-Traksad-Yama-yami-Mahakala
three/nine	six	prin.: embrace shakti holding wheel and bell in dharmachakra mu. rt.: sword and battle axe lt.: human skull-cup and plow-share	mature	four	ardha-paryanka, yab-yum	dhar. ornaments, va.: garuda	Buddha-Heruka
three*/nine	six	rt.: thunderbolt, corpse of a child, sword lt.: human skull-cup, mongoose, bell	mature	four		*rd., pu., wh., dhar. ornaments, va.: iron mule	dByings-kyi-ma-mo
four/12	six	rt.: ritual chopper, human skull-cup, club corp. lt.: battle axe, noose/snare, elephant hide cape		two		dhar. ornaments, va.: lotus throne	Canda-mukha-Caturmukha-(Sri-Mahakala)
four/12	six	rt.: ritual chopper, goad/hook, sword lt.: noose/snare, elephant hide cape, human skull-cup	corp.	two	alidha	dhar. ornaments, va.: lotus throne	Canda-mukha-Caturmukha-(Sri-Mahakala)
five/15	12	rt.: drum, ritual wand, goad/hook, noose/snare, thunderbolt, arrow lt.: tarjani mu., skull-cup, red lotus, jewel, wheel, bow	mature	two	pratyalidha	dhar. ornaments, va.: lotus throne	Mayajalakrama-Avalokitesvara**
five/15	12	rt.: sword, thunderbolt, goad/hook, noose/snare, trident, arrow lt.: shield, wheel, jewel, deer skin, human skull-cup, tarjani mu.	mature	two	pratyalidha	dhar. ornaments, va.: lotus throne	Mayajalakramakrodha-Lokesvara**
nine*/*	two	rt.: banner/flag lt.: snake noose/snare	corp	snake-coils		*raven head-capped, *eyes cover head and body, smok-gray color	gZa'-mchog-chen-po-rahula
nine*/18	two	rt.: goad/hook lt.: magic notched staff/stick	mature	two		*wolf heads, *brown color, blue silk garmnets	hPhar-ma-mgo-dgu

nine/27	four	prin.: bow, arrow rt.: victory banner/flag lt.: noose/snare	*	**		3=rd., 3=br., 3=wh., topped with raven-head, dark-brown colored, *covered with 1,000 eyes and face, **coils of snake, attribute: syllable "ra"	Khyab-'jug-chen-po

Natural Skin-coloredDeities:

Abbreviations:

as. = asana
bk. = black
bl. = blue
bodh. = bodhisattva
bn. = brown
corp. = corpulent
dhar. = dharmapala
gn. = green
lt. = left
mu. = mudra
pu. = purple
rd. = red
rt. = right
sc. = smokey
va. = vahana
wh. = white
yw. = yellow

(*) special variations or attributes noted within the entry.

(**) following deity's name indicates that the color is not noted in the source, kulesa's color is applied to the entry.

(eyes: 2-3, 6-9, etc.) in sources the deity's faces are noted, but the number of the eyes are not noted.

Head/Eyes	Hands	Objects Held	Body	Feet	Asana	Other Attributes	Deity Name
one/two	two	rt.: at ease lt.: human skull-cup	mature	two	sattva	guru ornaments, meditation cord, va.: antelope skin	Ajapalipada**
one/two	**two**	samadhi mu.	mature	two	vajra	guru ornaments, meditation cord, va.: antelope skin	Ajita**
one/two	two	rt.: fly whisk lt.: vitarka mu.	mature	two	rajalita	monastic robed, va.: guru cushion	Ananda**
one/two	two	rt. fly whisk lt.: incense burner	mature	two	pralamba-pada	monastic robed, va.: chinese-style chair	Angaja**
one/two	two	rt. alarm staff/stick lt.: alms bowl in dhyana mu.	mature	two	pralamba-pada	monastic robed, va.: lotus throne	Angaja**
one/two	two	rt.: jnana mu. lt.: an-i-in (middle class, middle life) mu.	mature	two	padma	monastic robed, va.: lotus throne	Asanga**
one/two	two	dharmachakra mu.	mature	two	vajra	pointed lama hood, monastic robe, shrine to rt., basket to lt.	Atisha**
one/two	two	holding mongoose	mature	two	vajra	monastic robed,	Bakula**

							va.: guru cushion	
one/two	two	holding mongoose	mature	two	vajra	monastic robed, va.: guru cushion	Bakula**
one/two	two	Tibetan temborin-in mu.	mature	two	sattva	monastic robe, pointed lama hood. va.: guru cushion,	Dharmakirti
one/two	two	Tibetan temborin-in mu.	mature	two	sattva	monastic robe, pointed lama hood. va.: guru cushion,	Dharmakirti
one/two	two	dhyana mu.	mature	two	sukha	monastic robe, both shoulders covered, va.: guru cushion	Dhitika
one/two	two	rt.: abhaya lt.: palm inward at chest	mature	two	sattva	monastic robe, both shoulders covered, pointed lama hood. va.: guru cushion	Dignaga
one/two	two	rt.: human skull-cup lt.: human skull-drum	mature	two	maharaja-lila	guru-like, round basket to the rt., va.: antelope skin	Dombipada
one/two	two	rt.: vitarka mu. lt.: alms bowl	mature	two	vajra	monastic robe, pointed lama hood. va.: guru cushion	dPal-ldan-Ye-shes
one/two	two	rt.: short sword lt.: trident	corp.	two	maha-rajalila	bejeweled, kingly, va.: raised throne	dPal-skyon
one/two	two	rt.: bhumisparsa mu. lt.: dhyana mu.	mature	two	lalita	monastic robe, va.: guru cushion	Gampopa
one/two	two	rt.: human skull-drum lt.: thunderbolt handled bell	mature	two	sattva	meditation cord, guru garments, va.: antelope skin	Ghantapada
one/two	two	rt.: thunderbolt lt.: bell	mature	two	sattva	meditation cord, guru garments, va.: antelope skin	Ghantapada
one/two	two	holding manuscript	mature	two	vajra	monastic robe,	Gopaka

						va.: guru cushion	
one/two	two	rt.: alarm staff/stick lt.: alms bowl	mature	two	vajra	monastic robe, right shoulder covered, va.: guru cushion	Gopaka
one/two	two	alms bowl in dhyana mu.	mature	two		monastic robe, right shoulder covered, va.: lotus throne	Gunadhya
one/two	two	rt.: abhaya mu. lt.: bhumisparsa mu.	mature	two	vajra	monastic robe, both shoulders covered, round basket to right, va.: lotus throne	Gunaprabha
one/two	two	rt.: abhaya mu. on knee lt.: abhaya mu. at chest	mature	two		monastic robe, both shoulders covered, va.: guru cushion	hBrom-ston-pa
one/two	two	rt.: vitarka mu. holding stem of lotus lt.: abhaya mu.	mature	two		monastic robe, both shoulders covered, va.: guru cushion	hBrom-ston-pa
one/two	two	rt.: rosary lt.: rests on knee	corp.	two	sattva	monastic robes, laughing, surrounded by dancing children, antelope skin	Hva-shang
one/two	two	rt.: rosary lt.: bag	corp.	two	sattva	monastic robes, laughing, surrounded by dancing children, antelope skin	Hva-shang
one/two	two	rt.: varada mu. lt.: abhaya mu.	mature	two		monastic robe, rt. shoulder uncovered, va.: guru cushion	Kala
one/two	two	holding golden earrings	mature	two	vajra	monastic robe, va.: guru cushion	Kalika
one/two	two	rt.: alarm staff/stick lt.: alms bowl	mature	two	vajra	monastic robe, rt. shoulder covered, va.: guru cushion	Kalika
one/two	two	rt.: alarm staff/stick	mature	two		monastic robe,	Kanaka

		lt.: alms bowl in dhyana mu.				right shoulder covered, va.: lotus throne	
one/two	two	dhyana mu.	mature	two	vajra	monastic robe, va.: guru cushion	Kanaka-Bharadvaja
one/two	two	string of jewels	mature	two		monastic robe, va.: guru cushion	Kanakavasta
one/two	two	rt.: alarm staff/stick lt.: alms bowl	mature	two		monastic robe, right shoulder covered, va.: lotus throne	Kanakavasta
one/two	two	rt.: alarm staff/stick lt.: alms bowl in dhyana mu.	mature	two	dhyana	Arhat-like, monastic-robed, rt. shoulder covered, va.: lotus throne	Kasyapa
one/two	two	rt.: alarm staff/stick lt.: alms bowl	mature	two		Arhat-like, monastic robed, va.: lotus throne	Kaundinya
one/two	two	rt.: vitarka mu. lt.: book/manuscript	mature	two	vajra	pointed lama-like hood, monastic robed, va.: guru cushion	Khri-chen-bLo-bzang-bsTan-pahi-Nyi-ma
one/two	two	rt.: thunderbolt in karana mu. lt.: bell in karana mu.	mature	two	vajra	pointed lama-like hood, monastic robed, va.: guru cushion	Khri-chen-Ngag-dBang-mChog-ldan
one/two	two	rt.: harina mu. lt.: human skull-cup	mature	two	sattva	guru-garbed, round basket to left, va.: antelope skin	Krsnacarin
one/two	two	rt.: human skull-cup lt.: harina mu.	mature	two	sattva	guru-garbed, meditation cord, round basket to right, va.: antelope skin	Lalitavajra
one/two	two	rt.: lotus stem in vitarka mu. with sword lt.: vase/vessel in dhyana mu. with lotus stem and manuscript	mature	two	vajra	pointed lama-like hood, monastic robed, va.: guru cushion	Lalitavajra-Rolpa Dorje
one/two	two	holds wrapped book/manuscript	mature	two	vajra	pointed lama-like hood, monastic robed, va.: guru cushion	Legs-pahi-shes-rab

one/two	two	rt.: human skull-cup	mature	two	sattva	guru-garbed, meditation cord, cape, va.: guru cushion	Luipada
one/two	two	dhyana mu.	mature	two		Arhat-like, monastic-robed, rt. shoulder covered, va.: guru cushion	Mahakasyapa
one/two	two	rt.: abhaya mu. lt.: dhyana mu. holding alms bowl	mature	'wo	vajra	Arhat-like, monastic-robed, rt. shoulder covered, va.: guru cushion	Mahapandita-Sumatijnana
one/two	two	rt.: bhumisparsa mu. lt.: jnana on ground	mature	two	vajra	guru garbed, round basket at left, va.: antelope skin	Maitripada
one/two	two	rt.: stem of lotus with flaming sword lt.: book/manuscript	corp.	two	maha- rajalila	fancy garbed, bejewled, va.: raised throne	Manjusrikirtti
one/two	two	rt.: skull-cup lt.: rests on knee	mature	two	vajra	guru-like, bearded, long loose hair, meditation cord, va.: antelope skin	Manjushrimitra
one/two	two	rt.: skull-cup lt.: book/manuscript	mature	two	vamalalita	Arhat-like, long loose hair, monastic-robed, va.: antelope skin	Mar-pa
one/two	two	rt.: book/manuscript lt.: abhaya mu.	mature	two	rajalila	Arhat-like, monastic robe, rt. shoulder covered, va.: guru cushion	Maudgalyayana
one/two	two	rt.: skull-cup lt.: cupped to ear	mature	two	sopasraya	Arhat-like, long loose hair, monastic-robed, va.: antelope skin and surrounded by stags & does	Milarapa
one/two	two	rt.:, behind thigh	mature	two	padma	snakes 'round halo,,	Nagarjuna

		lt.: bhumisparsa mu				monastic-robed, rt. shoulder covered, round basket at rt., va.: lotus throne	
one/two	two	rt.: vase/vessel with the nectar of life lt.: magic staff/stick	mature	two	sattva	Arhat-like, monastic-robed, rt. shoulder uncovered, va.: guru cushion	Nagasena
one/two	two	rt.: thunderbolt lt.: bell	mature	two	sattva	folded lama cap, monastic-robed, rt. shoulder covered, va.: guru cushion	Nam-mKhah-rGyal-mTshan
one/two	two	rt.: alarm staff/stick lt.: alms bowl in dhyana mu.	mature	two		Arhat-like, monastic-robed, rt. shoulder covered, va.: lotus throne	Nanda
one/two	two	rt.: lt.:	mature	two	sattva	long loose hair, small top-knot, monastic-robed, round basket at lt., va.: antelope skin	Naropa
one/two	two	rt.: ritual chopper lt.: human skull-cup	mature	two	maha- rajalila	Arhat-like, monastic-robed, rt. shoulder covered, va.: lotus throne	Ni-ma-grags
one/two	two	rt.: human skull-cup lt.: abhaya mu	mature	two		hooded, monastic-robed, round basket to right, va.: guru cushion	Padmasambhava
one/two	two	rt.: book/manuscript lt.: vitarka mu.	mature	two	vajra	pointed lama hood, monastic-robed, va.: guru cushion	Panditasiddhasvamin
one/two	two	rt.: abhaya mu lt.: (?) mu.	mature	two		lama-like hood, monastic-robed, rt. shoulder covered, va.: guru cushion	Panditasiddhasvamin
one/two	two	rt.: vitarka mu. lt.: book/manuscript	mature	two	vajra	Arhat-like, monastic-robed,	Panthaka

						rt. shoulder covered, va.: guru cushion	
one/two	two	rt.: alarm staff/stick lt.: alms bowl	mature	two		Arhat-like, monastic-robed, rt. shoulder covered, va.: lotus throne	Panthaka
one/two	two	rt.: human skull-drum lt.: bell	mature	two		bearded, long loose hair, meditation cord, round basket at left va.: antelope skin	Phadampa
one/two	two	rt.: book/manuscript lt.: alms bowl	mature	two	vajra	Arhat-like, monastic-robed, va.: guru cushion	Pindola-Bharadvaja
one/two	two	rt.: alarm staff/stick lt.: alms bowl	mature	two	dhyana	Arhat-like, monastic-robed, rt. shoulder covered, va.: lotus throne	Pindola-Bharadvaja
one/two	two	holding ornate crown	mature	two	vajra	Arhat-like, monastic-robed, va.: guru cushion	
one/two	two	rt.: vitarka mu. manuscript lt.: book/manuscript	mature	two	vajra	pointed lama hood, monastic-robed, va.: guru cushion	rGyal-tshab-rJe
one/two	two	rt.: vajra-topped axe lt.: severed human head	corp.	two	lalita	bodh. ornaments, va.: raised throne	rGya-mtsho-rnam-rgyal
one/two	two	rt.: vitarka mu. with lotus stem lt.: dhyana mu.	mature	two	vajra	pointed lama hood, monastic-robed, va.: guru cushion	rJe-dGe-hdun-grub
one/two	two	rt.: bhumisparsa mu. lt.: book/manuscript in dhyana mu.	mature	two	vajra	folded lama cap, monastic-robed, va.: guru cushion	rJe-drung-bLo-bzang-dpal-ldan
one/two	two	both hands rest behind the thighs	mature	two	vamalalita	Arhat-like, monastic-robed, rt. shoulder covered, round basket at right, va.: lotus throne	Sakyaprabha

one/two	two	rt.: book/manuscript lt.: dhyana mu.	mature	two	vamalalita	pointed hood, monastic-robed, rt. shoulder uncovered, round basket at right, va.: lotus throne	Sakyaprabha
one/two	two	holds an arrow	mature	two	sopasraya	loose hair, bearded, small top-knot, va.: lotus throne	Saraha
one/two	two	rt.: abhaya mu. lt.: rosary	mature	two	rajalila	Arhat-like, monastic-robed, va.: guru cushion	Sariputra
one/two	two	rt.: arrow and rests on a round basket lt.: holds (?) in vitarka mu.	mature	two	rajalila	Arhat-like, top knot, meditation cord, va.: antelope skin on guru cushion	Sabari (pada)
one/two	two	rt.: abhaya mu. lt.: rests on knee	mature	two	vajra	Arhat-like, monastic robe, rt. shoulder covered, va.: guru cushion	Sanakavasin
one/two	two	holds dharmachakra mu.	mature	two	vajra	Arhat-like, monastic robe, rt. shoulder covered, round basket behind right hip, va.: guru cushion	Santideva
one/two	two	rt.: vitarka mu. lt.: vitarka mu.	mature	two	lalita	pointed lama-hood, monastic-robed, va.: guru cushion	Sa-skya-Pandita-Kun-dgah-rGyal-mTshan
one/two	two	right hand rests over left, palms facing, similar to the buddhapatra mu.	mature	two		guru-like, monastic-robed, outer garment encircling body, va.: guru cushion	Shantarakshita
one/two	two	rt.: vitarka mu. lt.: rests on cushion in front of knee	mature	two	vira	pointed lama hood, monastic-robed, round basket on rt.,	Shantideva

						va.: guru cushion	
one/two	two	dharmachakra mu.	mature	two		pointed lama hood, monastic-robed, rt. shoulder covered, va.: guru cushion	Shes-rab-Seng-ge
one/two	two	rt.: thunderbolt on knee lt.: abhaya mu.	mature	two		lama-like hood, monastic-robed, rt. shoulder covered, va.: guru cushion	Siddhasangha
one/two	two	rt.: bow lt.: karana mu.	mature	two	sopasraya	bearded, long loose hair, small top-knot, monastic-robed, human-skin stole, peacock feather loin-cloth, va.: antelope skin	Shavaripada
one/two	two	rt.: magic dagger lt.: dhyana mu. holds skull-cup	mature	two	lalita	guru-like, loose hair, small top-knot, va.: antelope skin	Siddheshvara Humkara
one/two	two	rt.: flaming sword lt.: shield	mature	two	maharaja-lila	bodhisattva-like, va.: raised throne	Sin-tu-bzan-po
one/two	two	rt.: bhumisparsa mu. lt.: abhaya mu.	mature	two		Arhat-like, monastic-robed, rt. shoulder covered, va.: guru cushion	Sudarsana
one/two	two	holds dharmachakra mu	mature	two	vajra	Arhat-like, monastic-robed, rt. shoulder covered, vase/vessel with flower by right knee, va.: guru cushion	Svamimahapandita-Sumatidharmadhvaja
one/two	two	rt.: vitarka mu. holding stem of flower lt.: dhyana mu.	mature	two	vajra	lama-like hood, monastic-robed, rt. shoulder covered, va.: guru cushion	Svami-Vagisvarasumatisagara
one/two	two	rt.: bhumisparsa mu	mature	two	sattva	Arhat-like,	Tailikapada

		lt.: tarjani mu. in lap				monastic-robed, rt. shoulder covered, va.: guru cushion	
one/two	two	rt.: book/manuscript lt.: human skull-cup	mature	two		guru-like, bearded, antelope skin, round basket to rt., va.: lotus throne	Thod-sMyon-bSam-grub
one/two	two	rt.: human skull-drum lt.: human skull-cup	mature	two		guru-like, loose hair, meditation cord, round basket to rt., va.: antelope skin	Tilopa
one/two	two	rt.: vitarka mu. lt.: dhyana mudra with alms bowl	mature	two		Arhat-like, monastic-robed, rt. shoulder covered, va.: guru cushion	Upagupta
one/two	two	rt.: conch shell(?) lt.: rosary	corp.	two	sattva	smiling, monastic-robed, rt. shoulder covered, va.: guru cushion	Upasaka-Hva-san
one/two	two	rt.: fly whisk lt.: vase/vessel	mature	two	pralam- bapada	top-knot, monastic-robed, rt. shoulder covered, to right a small tiger, to left a book case, va.: raised rectangular throne	Upasaka-Dharmatala
one/two	two	rt.: tarjani mu. lt.: fly whisk	mature	two	vajra	Arhat-like, monastic-robed, rt. shoulder covered, va.: guru cushion	Vajriputra
one/two	two	rt.: an-i-in mu. lt.: fly whisk	mature	two		Arhat-like, monastic-robed, rt. shoulder covered, va.: lotus throne	Vajriputra
one/two	two	rt.: tarjani mu. lt.: fly whisk	mature	two	vajra	Arhat-like, monastic-robed, rt. shoulder covered,	Vanavasin

						va.: guru cushion	
one/two	two	rt.: karana mu. lt.: fly whisk	mature	two	sattva	Arhat-like, monastic-robed, rt. shoulder covered, va.: guru cushion	Vanavasin

Calm Deities: Color not Designated in Sources

Abbreviations:

as. = asana	bk. = black	bl. = blue	bodh. = bodhisattva
bn. = brown	corp. = corpulent	dhar. = dharmapala	gn. = green
lt. = left	mu. = mudra	pu. = purple	rd. = red
rt. = right	sc. = smokey	va. = vahana	wh. = white
yw. = yellow			

(*) special variations or attributes noted within the entry.
(**) following deity's name indicates that the color is not noted in the source, kulesa's color is applied to the entry.
(eyes: 2-3, 6-9, etc.) in sources the deity's faces are noted, but the number of the eyes are not noted.

Buddha-like Deities:

Head/Eyes	Hands	Objects Held	Body	Feet	Asana	Other Attributes	Deity Name
one/two	two	holding dharmacakra mu.	mature	two	vajra	Buddha-like, monastic robe, va.: lotus throne	Anantaujas Buddha
one/two	two	holding sun disc in dhyana mu.	mature	two	vajra	Buddha-like, monastic robe, va.: lotus throne	Anantaujas Buddha
one/two	two	dyhana mu.	mature	two	vajra	Buddha-like monastic robe, va.: lotus throne	Asokasri Buddha
one/two	two	rt.: trunk of small tree lt.: roots of small tree	mature	two	vajra	Buddha-like, monastic robe, va.: lotus throne	Asokasri Buddha
one/two	two	rt.: abhaya mu. lt.: vitarka mu.	mature	two	vajra	Buddha-like, monastic robe, rt. shoulder covered, va.: lotus throne	Bhadrasri
one/two	two	rt.: abhaya mu.	mature	two	vajra	Buddha-like,	Bhadrasri Buddha

		lt.: vitarka mu.				monastic robe, rt. shoulder covered, va.: lotus throne	
one/two	two	rt.: stem of lotus in karana mu. lt.: branch	mature	two	vajra	Buddha-like, monastic robe, rt. shoulder covered, va.: lotus throne	Bhadrasri Buddha
one/two	two	rt.: vitarka mu. lt.: alms bowl in dhyana mu.	mature	two	vajra	Buddha-like, monastic robe, rt. shoulder covered, va.: lotus throne	Bhaiasjyaguru-Vaiduryaprabharaja
one/two	two	kanjo-in mu	mature	two	vajra	Buddha-like, monastic robes va.: lotus throne	Bhinnaklesa(?) Buddha
one/two	two	stem of lotus in dharmachakra mu.	mature	two	vajra	Buddha-like, monastic robes, rt. shoulder uncovered, va.: lotus throne	Brahma Buddha
one/two	two	abhaya mu. at chest	mature	two	vajra	Buddha-like, monastic robes, rt. shoulder uncovered, va.: lotus throne	Brahmadatta
one/two	two	dharmachakra mu.	mature	two	vajra	Buddha-like, monastic robes, va.: lotus throne	Brahmadatta Buddha
one/two	two	rt.: sun disc lt.: stem of lotus in karana mu,	mature	two	vajra	Buddha-like, monastic robes, rt. shoulder covered, va.: lotus throne	Brahmadatta Buddha
one/two	two	rt.: abhaya mu. lt.: dhyana mu.	mature	two	vajra	Buddha-like, monastic robes, rt. shoulder uncovered, va.: lotus throne	Brahmajyotirvikriditabhijna
one/two	two	rt.: bhumisparsa mu. lt.: dhyana mu.	mature	two	vajra	Buddha-like, monastic robes, va.: lotus throne	Brahmajyotirvikriditabhijna Buddha
one/two	two	rt.: stem of lotus in karana mu.	mature	two	vajra	Buddha-like,	Brahmajyotis Buddha

		lt.: dhyana mu.				monastic robes, rt. shoulder uncovered, va.: lotus throne	
one/two	two	rt.: bhumisparsa mu. lt.: dhyana mu.	mature	two	vajra	Buddha-like, monastic robes, rt. shoulder covered, va.: lotus throne	Brahman
one/two	two	holding horyuji temborin-in mu.	mature	two	vajra	Buddha-like, monastic robes, rt. shoulder covered, va.: lotus throne	Brahman Buddha
one/two	two	bhumisparsa mu.	mature	two	vajra	Buddha-like, monastic robes, rt. shoulder covered, va.: lotus throne	Candanasri
one/two	two	bhumisparsa mu.	mature	two	vajra	Buddha-like, monastic robes, va.: lotus throne	Candanasri Buddha
one/two	two	dhyana mu. with small tree	mature	two	vajra	Buddha-like, monastic robes, rt. shoulder covered, va.: lotus throne	Candanasri Buddha
one/two	two	bhumisparsa mu.	mature	two	vajra	Buddha-like, monastic robes, rt. shoulder covered, va.: lotus throne	Candraketu Buddha
one/two	two	rt.: thunderbolt lt.: alms bowl in dhyana mu.	mature	two		Buddha-like, monastic robes, rt. shoulder uncovered, va.: lotus throne	Citta-nirmita-Rsi-vidyajnana
one/two	two	dhyana mu.	mature	two	vajra	Buddha-like, monastic robes, rt. shoulder uncovered, va.: lotus throne	Dhanasri Buddha
one/two	two	flaming jewel in dhyana mu.	mature	two	vajra	Buddha-like, monastic robes,	Dhanasri Buddha

						rt. shoulder uncovered, va.: lotus throne	
one/two	two	dharmachakra mu.	mature	two	vajra	Buddha-like, monastic robes, rt. shoulder uncovered, va.: lotus throne	<u>Dharmaghosatathagata Buddha</u>
one/two	two	rt.: abhaya mu. lt.: dhyana mu.	mature	two	vajra	Buddha-like, monastic robes, rt. shoulder uncovered, va.: lotus throne	<u>Dharmasagaragra(?)-mativikriditabhijnaraja</u>
one/two	two	djharmachakra mu.	mature	two	vajra	monastic robes, rt. shoulder covered, va.: lotus throne	<u>Dhyanabhyudgataraja Buddha</u>
one/two	two	rt.: karana mu. lt.: karana mu. holding tip of robe	mature	two	vajra	Buddha-like, rt. shoulder covered, va.: lotus throne	<u>(Ekantanayaka)-Trisamayavyuha-Muni</u>
one/two	two	rt.: alarm staff/stick lt.: dhyana mu.	mature	two	rajalila	Buddha-like, monastic robe, va.: guru cushion	<u>Gavampati</u>
one/two	two	rt.:karana mu. lt.: book/manuscript in lap	mature	two	vajra	Buddha-like, monastic robe, rt. shoulder covered, va.: lotus throne	<u>Gaya-Kasyapa</u>
one/two	two	rt.: flaming jewel lt.: alms bowl in dhyana mu.	mature	two	vajra	Buddha-like, monastic robe, rt. shoulder uncovered, va.: lotus throne	<u>Guna-nirmita-Rsi-vidyajnana</u>
one/two	two	dhyana mu. lt.: alms bowl in dhyana mu.	mature	two	vajra	Buddha-like, monastic robe, rt. shoulder uncovered, va.: lotus throne	<u>Gunaprabha Buddha</u>
one/two	two	rt.: abhaya mu. lt.: dhyana mu.	mature	two	vajra	Buddha-like, monastic robe, rt. shoulder uncovered, va.: lotus throne	<u>hKhon-dan(?)-rgyags-pa-rnam-gnon</u>
one/two	two	rt.: flaming jewel	mature	two	vajra	Buddha-like,	<u>Indraketuvijya Buddha</u>

		lt.: parasol				monastic robe, rt. shoulder uncovered, va.: lotus throne	
one/two	two	rt.: abhaya mu. lt.: dhyana mu.	mature	two	vajra	Buddha-like, monastic robe, va.: lotus throne	Kanakamuni
one/two	two	rt.: crossed thunderbolts lt.: alms bowl in dhyana mu.	mature	two	dhyana	Buddha-like, monastic robe, rt. shoulder uncovered, va.: lotus throne	Karma-nirmita-Rsi-vidyajnana
one/two	two	rt.: wheel lt.: alms bowl in dhyana mu.	mature	two	dhyana	Buddha-like, monastic robe, rt. shoulder uncovered, va.: lotus throne	Kaya-nirmita-Rsi-vidyajnana
one/two	two	rt.: abhaya mu. lt.: dhyana mu.	mature	two	vajra	Buddha-like, monastic robe, rt. shoulder covered, va.: lotus throne	Kusuma Buddha
one/two	two	dhyana mu.	mature	two	vajra	Buddha-like, monastic robe, rt. shoulder covered, va.: lotus throne	Kusuma Buddha
one/two	two	rt.: abhaya mu. lt.: dhyana mu.	mature	two	dhyana	Buddha-like, monastic robe, rt. shoulder covered, va.: lotus throne	Kusumasri
one/two	two	rt.: abhaya mu. lt.: dhyana mu.	mature	two	vajra	Buddha-like, monastic robe, rt. shoulder covered, va.: lotus throne	Kusumasri Buddha
one/two	two	rt.: stem of lotus in karana mu. lt.: branch of tree	mature	two	vajra	Buddha-like, monastic robe, rt. shoulder uncovered, va.: lotus throne	Kusumasri Buddha
one/two	two	rt.: varada mu. over right knee lt.: dhyana mu.	mature	two	vajra	Buddha-like, monastic robe, rt. shoulder uncovered, va.: lotus throne	Mahabahu (Buddha)

one/two	two	dhyana mu.	mature	two	vajra	Buddha-like, monastic robe, rt. shoulder uncovered, va.: lotus throne	Mahabala Buddha
one/two	two	rt.: varada mu. lt.: dhyana mu.	mature	two	vajra	Buddha-like, monastic robe, rt. shoulder uncovered, va.: lotus throne	Mahaprabha (Buddha)
one/two	two	holds alms bowl with myrobalam leaves in dhyana mu.	mature	two	vajra	Buddha-like, monastic robe, rt. shoulder covered, va.: lotus throne	Maha-van-nirmita
one/two	two	rt.: abhaya mu. lt.: dhyana mu.	mature	two	vajra	Buddha-like, monastic robe, va.: lotus throne	Manidharin Buddha
one/two	two	rt.: abhaya mu. lt.: tarjani mu.	mature	two	vajra	Buddha-like, monastic robe, rt. shoulder covered, va.: lotus throne	Merusikhara-Muni
one/two	two	rt.: karana lt.: book/manuscriptat chest level	mature	two	vajra	Buddha-like, without usnisa monastic robe, rt. shoulder covered, va.: lotus throne	Nadi-Kasyapa
one/two	two	rt.: asoka branch lt.: serpent/snake in dhyana mu.	mature	two	vajra	Buddha-like, monastic robe, rt. shoulder uncovered, va.: lotus throne	Nagesvara Buddha
one/two	two	holds uttarabodhi mu.	mature	two	vajra	Buddha-like, monastic robe, rt. shoulder uncovered, va.: lotus throne	Naksatraraja Buddha
one/two	two	rt.: abhaya mu. lt.: dhyana mu.	mature	two	vajra	Buddha-like, monastic robe, rt. shoulder uncovered, va.: lotus throne	Naksatrarajavikridita Buddha

one/two	two	holding a flame	mature	two	sama-bhanga	Buddha-like, monastic robe, rt. shoulder uncovered, va.: lotus throne	Narakaloka (Buddha)
one/two	two	alms bowl in dhyana mu.	mature	two	sama-bhanga	Buddha-like, monastic robe, rt. shoulder uncovered, va.: lotus throne	Naraloka
one/two	two	dharmachakra mu.	mature	two	vajra	Buddha-like, monastic robe, rt. shoulder uncovered, va.: lotus throne	Narayana
one/two	two	dharmachakra mu.	mature	two	vajra	Buddha-like, monastic robe, rt. shoulder uncovered, va.: lotus throne	Narayana Buddha
one/two	two	rt.: monastery model lt.: stem of lotus in karana mu.	mature	two	vajra	Buddha-like, monastic robe, rt. shoulder uncovered, va.: lotus throne	Narayana Buddha
one/two	two	vase/vessel with lotus in dhyana mu.	mature	two	vajra	Buddha-like, monastic robe, rt. shoulder uncovered, va.: lotus throne	Nirmanakaya-Amitayus
one/two	two	alms bowl in dhyana mu.	mature	two	vajra	Buddha-like, monastic robe, rt. shoulder uncovered, va.: lotus throne	Nirmanakaya-Amitayus
one/two	two	rt.: thunderbolt lt.: alms bowl	mature	two	vajra	Buddha-like, monastic robe, rt. shoulder covered, va.: lotus throne	Padmasambhava
one/two	two	holding kanjo-in	mature	two	vajra	Buddha-like, monastic robe, rt. shoulder covered, va.: lotus throne	Osadhi Buddha
one/two	two	rt.: bhumisparsa mu. lt.: dhyana mu.	mature	two	vajra	Buddha-like, monastic robe,	Padmajyotirvikriditabhijna

						rt. shoulder covered, va.: lotus throne	
one/two	two	rt.: stem of lotus in karana mu. lt.: sun disc in dhyana mu.	mature	two	vajra	Buddha-like, monastic robe, rt. shoulder uncovered, va.: lotus throne	Padmajyotis Buddha
one/two	two	rt.: myrobalam branch in vitarka mu. lt.: begging bowl with leaf (myrobalam?) in dhyana mu.	mature	two	vajra	Buddha-like, monastic robe, rt. shoulder covered, va.: lotus throne	Panca-visa-salyoccheda-Bhaisajyaguru
one/two	two	rt.: bhumisparsa mu. lt.: dhyana mu.	mature	two	vajra	Buddha-like, monastic robe, rt. shoulder covered, va.: lotus throne	Parvatadhararaja Buddha
one/two	two	abhaya mu. at chest	mature	two	vajra	Buddha-like, monastic robe, rt. shoulder uncovered, va.: lotus throne	Prabhasasri
one/two	two	dharmachakra mu.	mature	two	vajra	Buddha-like, monastic robe, rt. shoulder uncovered, va.: lotus throne	Prabhasasri Buddha
one/two	two	holding three dimensional mandala	mature	two	vajra	Buddha-like, monastic robe, rt. shoulder uncovered, va.: lotus throne	Prabhasasri Buddha
one/two	two	rt.: bhumisparsa mu. lt.: dhyana mu.	mature	two	vajra	Buddha-like, monastic robe, rt. shoulder covered, va.: lotus throne	Prabhuta Buddha
one/two	two	holding kanjo-in mu.	mature	two	vajra	Buddha-like, monastic robe, rt. shoulder covered, va.: lotus throne	Pradipa Buddha
one/two	two	rt.: bhumisparsa mu. lt.: dhyana mu.	mature	two	vajra	Buddha-like, monastic robe, rt. shoulder covered, va.: lotus throne	Pradyota Buddha

one/two	two	holding kanjo-in mu.	mature	two	vajra	Buddha-like, monastic robe, rt. shoulder covered, va.: lotus throne	Prathamacittopadasamsayac-chedika(?)
one/two	two	dhyana mu.	mature	two	vajra	Buddha-like, monastic robe, rt. shoulder covered, va.: lotus throne	Rasmisamudgatasrikutaraja
one/two	two	dharmachakra mu.	mature	two	vajra	Buddha-like, monastic robe, rt. shoulder covered, va.: lotus throne	Ratnacandra Buddha
one/two	two	rt.: flaming jewel at chest lt.: sun disc(?)	mature	two	vajra	Buddha-like, monastic robe, rt. shoulder uncovered, va.: lotus throne	Ratnacandra Buddha
one/two	two	uttarbodhi mu.	mature	two	vajra	Buddha-like, monastic robe, rt. shoulder covered, va.: lotus throne	Ratnacandra Buddha
one/two	two	rt.: varada mu. lt.: dhyana mu	mature	two	vajra	Buddha-like, monastic robe, rt. shoulder covered, va.: lotus throne	Ratnacandrapadmapratimandi-tapandita(?)tejah-svaraghosaraja (Buddha)
one/two	two	rt.: bhumisparsa mu. lt.: dhyana mu.	mature	two	vajra	Buddha-like, monastic robe, rt. shoulder covered, va.: lotus throne	Ratnacandraprabha Buddha
one/two	two	rt.: flaming jewel at chest lt.: sun disc	mature	two	vajra	Buddha-like, monastic robe, rt. shoulder uncovered, va.: lotus throne	Ratnacandraprabha Buddha
one/two	two	rt.: bhumisparsa mu. lt.: dhyana mu.	mature	two	vajra	Buddha-like, monastic robe, rt. shoulder covered, va.: lotus throne	Ratnacandraprabha Buddha
one/two	two	holding parasol	mature	two	vajra	Buddha-like,	Ratnacchattrodgata (Buddha)

						monastic robe, rt. shoulder covered, va.: lotus throne	
one/two	two	holds gold parasol	mature	two	vajra	Buddha-like, monastic robe, rt. shoulder uncovered, va.: lotus throne	Ratnacchattrodgataprabha Buddha
one/two	two	rt.: bhumisparsa mu lt.: dhyana mu.	mature	two	vajra	Buddha-like, monastic robe, rt. shoulder covered, va.: lotus throne	Ratnagni
one/two	two	rt.: bhumisparsa mu lt.: dhyana mu.	mature	two	vajra	Buddha-like, monastic robe, rt. shoulder covered, va.: lotus throne	Ratnagni Buddha
one/two	two	rt.: flaming jewel lt.: stem of lotus with vase/vessel in dhyana mu.	mature	two	vajra	Buddha-like, monastic robe, rt. shoulder uncovered, va.: lotus throne	Ratnagni Buddha
one/two	two	dhyana mu	mature	two	vajra	Buddha-like, monastic robe, rt. shoulder covered, va.: lotus throne	Ratnangadyuti Buddha
one/two	two	dhyana mu	mature	two	vajra	Buddha-like, monastic robe, rt. shoulder covered, va.: lotus throne	Ratnangavyuhadyuti (Buddha)
one/two	two	rt.: jewel lt.: stem of lotus in karana mu.	mature	two	vajra	Buddha-like, monastic robe, rt. shoulder uncovered, va.: lotus throne	Ratnapadma Buddha
one/two	two	rt.: abhaya mu. lt.: dhyana mu.	mature	two	vajra	Buddha-like, monastic robe, rt. shoulder uncovered, va.: lotus throne	Ratnapadmavikramin Buddha
one/two	two	rt.: thunderbolt on end lt.: alms bowl in dhyana mu.	mature	two	vajra	Buddha-like, monastic robe, rt. shoulder uncovered,	Ratnaprabhasambhava Buddha

						va.: lotus throne	
one/two	two	dhyana mu.	mature	two	vajra	Buddha-like, monastic robe, rt. shoulder uncovered, va.: lotus throne	Ratnarcis Buddha
one/two	two	rt.: varada mu. lt.: end of robe at chest	mature	two	vajra	Buddha-like, monastic robe, rt. shoulder uncovered, va.: lotus throne	Rudrarupa Buddha
one/two	two	holding monastery (palace) over head	mature	two	vajra	Buddha-like, monastic robe, rt. shoulder uncovered, va.: lotus throne	Sailendraraja (Buddha)
one/two	two	rt.: lotus(?) lt.: dhyana mu.	mature	two	vajra	Buddha-like, monastic robe, rt. shoulder uncovered, va.: lotus throne	Samantadarsin (Jina)
one/two	two	rt.: abhaya mu. lt.: dhyana mu.	mature	two	vajra	Buddha-like, monastic robe, rt. shoulder uncovered, va.: lotus throne	Samantavabhasavyuhasri Buddha
one/two	two	rt.: sun disc lt.: branch	mature	two	vajra	Buddha-like, monastic robe, rt. shoulder uncovered, va.: lotus throne	Samantavabhasavyuhasri Buddha
one/two	two	holds dhyana mu.	mature	two	vajra	Buddha-like, monastic robe, rt. shoulder uncovered, va.: lotus throne	Samyaksambuddha-asoka
one/two	two	holds parasol	mature	two	vajra	Buddha-like, monastic robe, rt. shoulder covered, va.: lotus throne	Sans-rgyas-bdud-dan-yid-gnis-kun-hjoms(?)
one/two	two	rt.: sword lt.: dhyana mu.	mature	two	vajra	Buddha-like, monastic robe, rt. shoulder covered, va.: lotus throne	Sans-rgyas-byan-sems-hdul-ba

one/two	two	rt.: karana mu. with thunderbolt lt.: dhyana mu. with skull-cup, magic staff/stick in crook of arm	mature	two	vajra	Buddha-like, monastic robe, rt. shoulder uncovered, va.: lotus throne	Saroruhavajra
one/two	two	rt.: bhumisparsa mu. lt.: dhyana mu.	mature	two	vajra	Buddha-like, monastic robe, rt. shoulder uncovered, va.: lotus throne	Sarthavaha Buddha
one/two	two	rt.: bhumisparsa lt.: dhyana	mature	two	vajra	Buddha-like, monastic robe, rt. shoulder covered, alms bowl at feet, va.: lotus throne	Sauddhodani
one/two	two	rt.: abhaya mu. lt.: dhyana mu.	mature	two	vajra	Buddha-like, monastic robe, va.: lotus throne	Shan-mieh-cheng-ao fo
one/two	two	holds parasol	mature	two	vajra	Buddha-like, monastic robe, va.: lotus throne	Shan-mieh-mo-chang fo
one/two	two	holds kanjo-in mu.	mature	two	vajra	Buddha-like, monastic robe, rt. shoulder covered, va.: lotus throne	Simha Buddha
one/two	two	rt.: trident lt.: stem of lotus with sword	mature	two	vajra	Buddha-like, monastic robe, rt. shoulder covered, va.: lion on lotus throne	Simhanada
one/two	two	rt.: bhumisparsa mu. lt.: dhyana mu.	mature	two	vajra	Buddha-like, monastic robe, va.: lotus throne	Simhanada
one/two	two	dhyana mu.	mature	two	vajra	Buddha-like, monastic robe, rt. shoulder covered, va.: lotus throne	Smrtisri
one/two	two	dhyana mu.	mature	two	vajra	Buddha-like, monastic robe, rt. shoulder covered, va.: lotus throne	Smrtisri Buddha

one/two	two	rt.: sword lt.: book/manuscript in dhyana mu.	mature	two	vajra	Buddha-like, monastic robe, rt. shoulder uncovered, va.: lotus throne	Smrtisri Buddha
one/two	two	rt.: trunk of small tree lt.: roots of tree in dhyana mu.	mature	two	vajra	Buddha-like, monastic robe, rt. shoulder uncovered, va.: lotus throne	Sridatta Buddha
one/two	two	rt.: sun disc at chest lt.: stem of lotus in karana mu.	mature	two	vajra	Buddha-like, monastic robe, rt. shoulder uncovered, va.: lotus throne	Srinanda Buddha
one/two	two	rt.: sword lt.: book/manuscript	mature	two	vajra	Buddha-like, monastic robe, rt. shoulder covered, va.: lotus throne	Sui-yin-p'a-sa(t'i) fo
one/two	two	dhyana mu. with Mt. Meru	mature	two	vajra	Buddha-like, monastic robe, va.: lotus throne	Sumeruparvataraja Buddha
one/two	two	rt.: abhaya mu. lt.: dhyana mu.	mature	two	vajra	Buddha-like, monastic robe, rt. shoulder covered, va.: lotus throne	Sunaman
one/two	two	rt.: varada mu. lt.: dhyana mu.	mature	two	vajra	Buddha-like, monastic robe, rt. shoulder covered, va.: lotus throne	Sunamatathagata Buddha
one/two	two	kanjo-in mu.	mature	two	vajra	Buddha-like, monastic robe, rt. shoulder covered, va.: lotus throne	Sunetra Buddha
one/two	two	holds crown	mature	two	vajra	Buddha-like, monastic robe, rt. shoulder uncovered, va.: lotus throne	Suparikirtitanamasri Buddha
one/two	two	rt.: abhaya mu. lt.: dhyana mu.	mature	two	vajra	Buddha-like, monastic robe,	Suparikirtitanamasriraja

						rt. shoulder covered, va.: lotus throne	
ıe/two	two	in dharmachakra mu.	mature	two	vajra	Buddha-like, monastic robe, rt. shoulder covered, va.: lotus throne	Suradatta
ne/two	two	rt.: bhumisparsa mu. lt.: dhyana mu.	mature	two	vajra	Buddha-like, monastic robe, va.: lotus throne	Suradatta Buddha
one/two	two	in dhyana mu.	mature	two	vajra	Buddha-like, monastic robe, rt. shoulder uncovered, va.: lotus throne	Surasmi Buddha
one/two	two	in kan-jo mu.	mature	two	vajra	Buddha-like, monastic robe, rt. shoulder covered, va.: lotus throne	Suryagarbha Buddha
one/two	two	in dharmachakra mu.	mature	two	vajra	Buddha-like, monastic robe, rt. shoulder covered, va.: lotus throne	Suvarnaratnaprabhatathagata Buddha
one/two	two	rt.: bhumisparsa mu. lt.: dhyana mu.	mature	two	vajra	Buddha-like, monastic robe, rt. shoulder uncovered, va.: lotus throne	Suvikrantagamin Buddha
one/two	two	rt.: sword lt.: dhyana mu.	mature	two	vajra	Buddha-like, monastic robe, rt. shoulder uncovered, va.: lotus throne	Suvikrantasri Buddha
one/two	two	rt.: bhumisparsa mu. lt.: bhumisparsa mu.	mature	two	vajra	Buddha-like, monastic robe, rt. shoulder uncovered, va.: lotus throne	Suvikrantasri Buddha
one/two	two	rt.: varada mu. lt.: dhyana mu.	mature	two	vajra	Buddha-like, monastic robe, rt. shoulder uncovered, va.: lotus throne	Trikal-abhijna-raja

one/two	two	rt.: vitarka mu. lt.: vitarka mu.	mature	two	vajra	Buddha-like, monastic robe, rt. shoulder uncovered, va.: lotus throne	Trisamayavyuha Muni
one/two	two	rt.: abhaya mu. lt.: abhaya mu.	mature	two	vajra	Buddha-like, monastic robe, rt. shoulder covered, va.: lotus throne	Trisamayavyuha Muni
one/two	two	rt.: karana mu. lt.: book/manuscript in lap	mature	two	vajra	Buddha-like, monastic robe, rt. shoulder covered, va.: lotus throne	Uruvilva-Kasyapa
one/two	two	rt.: abhaya mu. lt.: dhyana mu.	mature	two	vajra	Buddha-like, monastic robe, rt. shoulder uncovered, va.: lotus throne	Vaidya Buddha
one/two	two	holds dharmachakra mu.	mature	two	vajra	Buddha-like, monastic robe, rt. shoulder covered, va.: lotus throne	Vajrabhedya Buddha
one/two	two	dhyana mu. with thunfderbolt on end	mature	two	vajra	Buddha-like, monastic robe, rt. shoulder uncovered, va.: lotus throne	Vajragarbha Buddha
one/two	two	holds dharmachakra mu.	mature	two	vajra	Buddha-like, monastic robe, rt. shoulder covered, va.: lotus throne	Vajragarbhapramardin
one/two	two	rt.: bhumisparsa mu. lt.: dhyana mu.	mature	two	vajra	Buddha-like, monastic robe, rt. shoulder uncovered, va.: lotus throne	Vajraksobhya
one/two	two	rt.: bhumisparsa mu. lt.: dhyana mu.	mature	two	vajra	Buddha-like, monastic robe, rt. shoulder covered, va.: lotus throne	Vajrasana-Muni
one/two	two	holds dhyana mu.	mature	two	vajra	Buddha-like, monastic robe,	Varuna

						rt. shoulder uncovered, va.: lotus throne	
one/two	two	holds dhyana mu.	mature	two	vajra	Buddha-like, monastic robe, rt. shoulder uncovered, va.: lotus throne	Varuna Buddha
one/two	two	holds wheel in dharmachakra mu.	mature	two	vajra	Buddha-like, monastic robe, rt. shoulder uncovered, va.: lotus throne	Varuna Buddha
one/two	two	rt.: abhaya mu. lt.: abhaya mu.	mature	two	vajra	Buddha-like, monastic robe, rt. shoulder uncovered, va.: lotus throne	Varuna Buddha
one/two	two	holds dhyana mu.	mature	two	vajra	Buddha-like, monastic robe, rt. shoulder uncovered, va.: lotus throne	Varunadeva Buddha
one/two	two	holds dharmachakra mu.	mature	two	vajra	Buddha-like, monastic robe, rt. shoulder uncovered, va.: lotus throne	Varunadeva Buddha
one/two	two	rt.: sun disc lt.: flowering branch	mature	two	vajra	Buddha-like, monastic robe, rt. shoulder uncovered, va.: lotus throne	Vikrantagamisri
one/two	two	dhyana mu.	mature	two	vajra	Buddha-like, monastic robe, rt. shoulder uncovered, va.: lotus throne	Vimala
one/two	two	holds dhyana mu.	mature	two	vajra	Buddha-like, monastic robe, rt. shoulder covered, va.: lotus throne	Vimala Buddha
one/two	two	rt.: flaming jewel lt.: sun disc	mature	two	vajra	Buddha-like, monastic robe, rt. shoulder uncovered, va.: lotus throne	Vimala Buddha

one/two	two	rt.: vitarka mu. lt.: dhyana mu.	mature	two	vajra	Buddha-like, monastic robe, rt. shoulder covered, va.: lotus throne	Vipasyin
one/two	two	rt.: bhumisparsa mu. lt.: dhyana mu.	mature	two	vajra	Buddha-like, monastic robe, rt. shoulder covered, va.: lotus throne	Vipasyin (Buddha)
one/two	two	holds dharmachakra mu.	mature	two	vajra	Buddha-like, monastic robe, rt. shoulder covered, va.: lotus throne	Viranandin
one/two	two	holds dharmachakra mu.	mature	two	vajra	Buddha-like, monastic robe, rt. shoulder covered, va.: lotus throne	Viranandin Buddha
one/two	two	rt.: abhaya mu. lt.: karana mu.	mature	two	vajra	Buddha-like, monastic robe, rt. shoulder covered, va.: lotus throne	Virasena
one/two	two	rt.: abhaya mu lt.: dhyana mu.	mature	two	vajra	Buddha-like, monastic robe, rt. shoulder covered, va.: lotus throne	Virasena Buddha
one/two	two	rt.: sword lt.: book/manuscript	mature	two	dhyana	Buddha-like, monastic robe, rt. shoulder uncovered, va.: lotus throne	Virasena Buddha
one/two	two	rt.: abhaya mu. lt.: dhyana mu.	mature	two	vajra	Buddha-like, monastic robe, rt. shoulder covered, va.: lotus throne	Vishvabhu
one/two	two	rt.: bhumisparsa mu. lt.: dhyana mu.	mature	two	vajra	Buddha-like, monastic robe, rt. shoulder covered, va.: lotus throne	Yasahketu Buddha
one/two	two	holds cuirass up to his chest	mature	two	vajra	Buddha-like,	Yuddhajaya Buddha

						monastic robe, rt. shoulder uncovered, va.: lotus throne	
one/two	two	rt.: sword lt.: coat of mail	mature	two	vajra	Buddha-like, monastic robe, rt. shoulder uncovered, va.: lotus throne	Yuddhajaya Buddha

Buddhas of Confession

one/two	two	dhyana mu.	youth	two	vajra	Buddha-like, monastic robe, rt. shoulder uncovered, va.: lotus throne	Jina-Amitabha
one/two	two	rt.: abhaya mu. lt.: dhyana mu.	youth	two	vajra	Buddha-like, monastic robe, rt. shoulder uncovered, va.: lotus throne	Jina-Amoghadarsin
one/two	two	in vitarka mu.	youth	two	vajra	Buddha-like, monastic robe, rt. shoulder uncovered, va.: lotus throne	Jina-Anantaujas
one/two	two	dhyana mu.	youth	two	vajra	Buddha-like, monastic robe, rt. shoulder uncovered, va.: lotus throne	Jina-Ashokashri
one/two	two	rt.: abhaya mu. lt.: dhyana mu.	youth	two	vajra	Buddha-like, monastic robe, rt. shoulder uncovered, va.: lotus throne	Jina-Bhadrasri
one/two	two	dharmachakra mu.	youth	two	vajra	Buddha-like, monastic robe, rt. shoulder uncovered, va.: lotus throne	Jina-Brahmadatta
one/two	two	rt.: bhumisparsa mu. lt.: dhyana mu.	youth	two	vajra	Buddha-like, monastic robe, rt. shoulder uncovered, va.: lotus throne	Jina-Brahmajyotis

one/two	two	rt.: bhumisparsa mu. lt.: dhyana mu.	youth	two	vajra	Buddha-like, monastic robe, rt. shoulder uncovered, va.: lotus throne	Jina-Brahman
one/two	two	rt.: bhumisparsa mu. lt.: dhyana mu.	youth	two	vajra	Buddha-like, monastic robe, rt. shoulder uncovered, va.: lotus throne	Jina-Buddha-Sakyamuni
one/two	two	rt.: varada mu. lt.: dhyana	youth	two	vajra	Buddha-like, monastic robe, rt. shoulder uncovered, va.: lotus throne	Jina-Candanasri
one/two	two	dhyana mu.	youth	two	vajra	Buddha-like, monastic robe, rt. shoulder uncovered, va.: lotus throne	Jina-Dhanasri
one/two	two	rt.: circular banner/flag lt.: dhyana mu.	youth	two	vajra	Buddha-like, monastic robe, rt. shoulder uncovered, va.: lotus throne	Jina-Indraketudhvaja
one/two	two	rt.: abhaya mu. lt.: varada mu.	youth	two	vajra	Buddha-like, monastic robe, rt. shoulder uncovered, va.: lotus throne	Jina-Kusumashri
one/two	two	uttarabodhi mu.	youth	two	vajra	snakes in halo, Buddha-like, monastic robe, rt. shoulder uncovered, va.: lotus throne	Jina-Nagesvararaja
one/two	two	vitarka mu.	youth	two	vajra	Buddha-like, monastic robe, rt. shoulder uncovered, va.: lotus throne	Jina-Narayana
one/two	two	rt.: bhumisparsa mu. lt.: dhyana mu.	youth	two	vajra	Buddha-like, monastic robe, rt. shoulder uncovered, va.: lotus throne	Jina-Padmajyotis

one/two	two	rt.: abhaya mu. lt.: dhyana mu.	youth	two	vajra	Buddha-like, monastic robe, rt. shoulder uncovered, va.: lotus throne	Jina-Parikirtita-Namashri
one/two	two	vitarka mu.	youth	two	vajra	Buddha-like, monastic robe, rt. shoulder uncovered, va.: lotus throne	Jina-Prabhasashri
one/two	two	uttarabodhi mu.	youth	two	vajra	Buddha-like, monastic robe, rt. shoulder uncovered, va.: lotus throne	Jina-Ratnacandra
one/two	two	rt.: bhumisparsa mu. lt.: dhyana mu.	youth	two	vajra	Buddha-like, monastic robe, rt. shoulder uncovered, va.: lotus throne	Jina-Ratnacandraprabha
one/two	two	rt.: bhumisparsa mu. lt.: dhyana mu.	youth	two	vajra	Buddha-like, monastic robe, rt. shoulder uncovered, va.: lotus throne	Jina-Ratnagni
one/two	two	rt.: abhaya mu. lt.: dhyana mu.	youth	two	vajra	Buddha-like, monastic robe, rt. shoulder uncovered, va.: lotus throne	Jina-Ratnapadma
one/two	two	dhyana mu.	youth	two	vajra	Buddha-like, monastic robe, rt. shoulder uncovered, va.: lotus throne	Jina-Ratnarcis
one/two	two	rt.: varada mu. lt.: dhyana mu.	youth	two	vajra	Buddha-like, monastic robe, rt. shoulder uncovered, va.: lotus throne	Jina-Samantadarshin
one/two	two	abhaya mu.	youth	two	vajra	Buddha-like, monastic robe, rt. shoulder uncovered, va.: lotus throne	Jina-Samantavabhasa
one/two	two	dhyana mu. with Mt. Meru	youth	two	vajra	Buddha-like, monastic robe,	Jina-Shailendraraja

						rt. shoulder uncovered, va.: lotus throne	
one/two	two	dharmachakra (horyuji temborin-in) mu.	youth	two	vajra	Buddha-like, monastic robe, rt. shoulder uncovered, va.: lotus throne	<u>Jina-Shuradatta</u>
one/two	two	dhyana mu.	youth	two	vajra	Buddha-like, monastic robe, rt. shoulder uncovered, va.: lotus throne	<u>Jina-Smritishri</u>
one/two	two	rt.: sword lt.: dhyana mu.	youth	two	vajra	Buddha-like, monastic robe, rt. shoulder uncovered, va.: lotus throne	<u>Jina-Suvikranta</u>
one/two	two	vitarka mu.	youth	two	vajra	Buddha-like, monastic robe, rt. shoulder uncovered, va.: lotus throne	<u>Jina-Vajragarbha</u>
one/two	two	dhyana mu.	youth	two	vajra	Buddha-like, monastic robe, rt. shoulder uncovered, va.: lotus throne	<u>Jina-Varuna</u>
one/two	two	vitarka mu.	youth	two	vajra	Buddha-like, monastic robe, rt. shoulder uncovered, va.: lotus throne	<u>Jina-Varunadeva</u>
one/two	two	bhumisparsa mu.	youth	two	vajra	Buddha-like, monastic robe, rt. shoulder uncovered, va.: lotus throne	<u>Jina-Vikratna</u>
one/two	two	dhyana mu.	youth	two	vajra	Buddha-like, monastic robe, rt. shoulder uncovered, va.: lotus throne	<u>Jina-Vimala</u>
one/two	two	dharmachakra mu. holding stems of lotus rt. shoulder lotus with sword lt. shoulder lotus with book/manuscript	youth	two	vajra	Buddha-like, monastic robe, rt. shoulder uncovered, va.: lotus throne	<u>Jina-Vimaloshnisha</u>

one/two	two	dharmachakra mu.	youth	two	vajra	Buddha-like, monastic robe, rt. shoulder uncovered, va.: lotus throne	Jina-Viranandin
one/two	two	rt. abhaya mu. lt.: varada	youth	two	vajra	Buddha-like, monastic robe, rt. shoulder uncovered, va.: lotus throne	Jina-Virasena
one/two	two	holding a coat of mail	youth	two	vajra	Buddha-like, monastic robe, rt. shoulder uncovered, va.: lotus throne	Jina-Yuddhajaya
one/two	two	rt.: bhumisparsa mu. lt.: dhyana mu.	youth	two	vajra	Buddha-like, monastic robe, rt. shoulder uncovered, va.: lotus throne	Jyotisprabha (?) Buddha

Bodhisattva-like Deities:

one/two	two	rt.: lotus (*padma*) stem with blossom at shoulder lt.: dhyana mu.	mature	two	sattva	bodh. ornaments, va.: lotus throne	Abhyudgatosnisa(?) (Bodhisattva)
one/two	two	rt.: rosary lt.: vase/vessel filled with elixer of life	mature	two	alidha	bodh. ornaments, va.: goat	Agni
one/two	two	rt.: stem of lotus in vitarka mu. lt.: stem of lotus in kartari-hasta mu.	mature	two	vamalalita	bodh. ornaments, va.: lotus throne	Agni-bhaya-trana-Tara
one/two	two	rt.: short staff/stick lt.: thunderbolt	youth	two	vama-lalita	bodh. ornaments, va,: lotus throne	A-lieh-ka-ma hsi-mu
one/two	two	rt.: varada mu. lt.: stem of lotus with shrine in kartari-hasta mu.	youth	two	lalita	bodh. ornaments, va.: lotus throne	Amita-parakrama(?) (Tara)
one/two	two	rt.: sword lt.: karana mu.	mature	two	vama-lalita	bodh. ornaments, va.: lotus throne	Amoghavikramin (Bodhisattva)
one/two	two	holding crossed thunderbolts and (?)	mature	two	sattva	bodh. ornaments,	Amritakundalin

						va.: lotus throne	
one/two	two	holding conch shell	youth	two	vama-lalita	bodh. ornaments, va.: lotus throne	Anantasvaraghosa
one/two	two	rt.: rosary lt. vase/vessel	mature	two	sattva	bodh. ornaments, va.: lotus throne	Angirodeva
one/ two	two	holding goad/hook	mature	two	alidha	bodh. ornaments, va.: lotus throne	Ankusha
one/two	two	rt.: wheel lt.: human skull-cup	youth	two	ardhapar-yanka	bodh. ornaments, va.: lotus throne	Anucara-Buddha-daki
one/two	two	rt.: sword lt.: human skull-cup	youth	two	ardhapar-yanka	bodh. ornaments, va.: lotus throne	Anucara-Karma-daki
one/two	two	rt.: abhaya mu. lt.: vase/vessel	youth	two	sopasraya	bodh. ornaments, va.: lotus throne	Anucara-Nivarana-viskambhin
one/two	two	rt.: lotus lt.: human skull-cup	youth	two	ardhapar-yanka	bodh. ornaments, va.: lotus throne	Anucara-Padma-daki
one/two	two	rt.: flaming jewel lt.: human skull-cup	youth	two	ardhapar-yanka	bodh. ornaments, va.: lotus throne	Anucara-Ratna-daki
one/two	two	anjali mudra with book/manuscript across forearm	youth	two	sama-bhanga	bodh. ornaments, va.: lotus throne	Anucara-Sudhana-kumara
one/two	two	rt.: palm down over lt. lt.: lotus at waist	youth	two	sama-bhanga	bodh. ornaments, va.: lotus throne	Anucara-Tara
one*/two	two	holding vase/vessel with elixir of life to chest	lower snake-like			*snakes in hair bodh. ornaments, va.: lotus throne	Apalala-nagaraja
one*/two	two	rt.: karana mu. lt.: vase/vessel with elixir of life	lower snake-like			*snakes in hair bodh. ornaments, va.: lotus throne	Apalala-nagaraja
one/two	two	rt.: flame in varada mu. lt.: book/manuscript with lotus	youth	two	vajra	bodh. ornaments, va.: lotus throne	Arya-Cunda-Tara
one/two	two	rt.: stem of lotus in vitarka mu. lt.: stem of lotus in kartari-hasta mu.	youth	two	vama-lalita	bodh. ornaments, va.: lotus throne	Asta-bhaya-trana Tara
one/two	two	rt.: (?)	youth	two	sattva	bodh. ornaments,	Astami Tithi

		lt.: dhyana mu.				va.: lotus throne	
one/two	two	rt.: goad/hook lt.: vase/vessel	mature	two	pralamba-pada	bodh. ornaments, va.: lotus throne	Ayurvashi-Devi
one/two	**two**	**rt.:** peacock feathers in simha-karna mu. lt.: thunderbolt	youth	two	vamalalita	bodh. ornaments, va.: lotus throne	Bhadrakara
one/two	two	rt.: varada mu. lt.: stem of lotus in kartari-hasta mu.	youth	two	lalita	bodh. ornaments, va.: lotus throne	Bhairavi (Tara)
one/two	two	rt.: alms bowl lt.: myrobalam fruit	mature	two	rajalila	bodh. ornaments, va.: lotus throne	Bhaishajya Devi
one/two	two	rt.: sun disc lt.: human skull-cup	corp.	two	rajalila	wreath, bodh. ornaments, large vase/vessel at rt. knee, va.: lotus throne	Birbapa
one/two	two	rt.: varada mu. lt.: lotus in karana mu.	youth	two	vamalalita	bodh. ornaments lotus throne	Bkah-gdams-Tara
one/two	two	rt.: thunderbolt lt.: vase/vessel filled with peacock feathers	youth	two	vamalalita	bodh. ornaments, flowing cloak, va.: lion	bKra-sis-tshe-rin-ma
one/two	two	rt.: thunderbolt lt.: tarjani mu.	youth	two	vamalalita	bodh. ornaments va.: elephant	Brahma-Indra
one/two	two	rt.: lotus lt.: tarjani mu.	youth	two	vamalalita	bodh. ornaments, va.: lotus throne	Brahman-(deva)
one/two	**two**	**rt.: arrow** **lt.: bow and stem of lotus**	**corp.**	**two**	maha-rajalila	bodh. ornaments, fancy boots, va.: raised throne	bSes-gnen-bzan
one/two	two	rt.: stem of lotus lt.: wheel	youth	two	vamalalita	bodh. ornaments, va.: lotus throne	Buddhabodhi
one/two	two	rt.: flaming sword lt.: dhyana mu.	youth	two	sopasrayas	bodh. ornaments, va.: lotus throne	Buddhosnisa (Bodhisattva)
one/two	two	holding a wheel	mature	two	sattva	bodh. ornaments va.: lotus throne	Cakra

one/two	two	rt.: abhaya mu. lt. human skull-cup	youth	two	sopasraya	bodh. ornaments, va.: lotus throne	Camunda-(devi)
one/two	two	dhyana mu.	youth	two	vamalalita	bodh. ornaments, va.: lotus throne	Candraprabha
one/two	two	dhyana mu.	youth	two	vajra	bodh. ornaments, va.: lotus throne	Candraprabha (Bodhisattva)
one/two	two	rt.: stem of lotus with blossom at shoulder level lt.: stem of lotus with blossom at shoulder level	youth	two	vamalalita	bodh. ornaments, va.: lotus throne	Cittotpada(=adhimukti?)-Vasita
one/two	two	rt.: thunderbolt lt.: lotus	youth	two	vamalalita	bodh. ornaments, va.: lotus throne	Cittotpadacaryabhumi (fo-mu)
one/two	two	rt.: lotus in vitarka mu. lt.: lotus in kartari mu.	youth	two	vamalalita	bodh. ornaments, va.: lotus throne	Cora-bhaya-trana Tara
one/two	two	rt.: parasol lt.: abhaya mu.	youth	two	rajalila	bodh. ornaments, va.: lotus throne	Chattra
one/two	two	rt.: vase/vessel lt.: abhaya mu.	youth	two	sattva	bodh. ornaments, va.: lotus throne	Ch'i-miao p'u-sa
one/two	two	rt.: vitarka lt.: vitarka	youth	two	vamalalita	bodh. ornaments, va.: lotus throne	Chiu-t'o p'u-sa
one/two	two	rt.: fruit lt.: branch	youth	two	vajra	bodh. ornaments, va.: lotus throne	
one/two	two	rt.: karana mu. lt.: human skull-cup	youth	two	vamalalita	bodh. ornaments, va.: lotus throne	Chuang-yen-mu
one/two	two	serpent/snake	youth	two		bodh. ornaments, va.: sea dragon	Chu-lHa
one/two	two	rt.: abhaya mu. lt.: dhyana mu	mature	two	vajra	bodh. ornaments, va.: lotus throne	Chu-p'in-ting fo
one/two	two	rt.: flowering branch lt.: flower bud	youth	two	sattva	bodh. ornaments, va.: lotus throne	Citra(?) (devi)
one/two	two	rt.: stem of lotus in vitarka mu. lt.: stem of lotus in kartari mu.	youth	two	vamalalita	bodh. ornaments va.: lotus throne	Daka-bhaya-trana Tara

one/two	two	rt.: stem of lotus in vitarka mu. lt.: stem of lotus in kartari mu.	youth	two	vamalalita	bodh. ornaments, va.: lotus throne	Danda-bhaya-trana-Tara
one/two	two	rt.: sword lt.: cymbal	youth	two	sattva	bodh. ornaments, va.: lotus throne	Dasami Tithi
one/two	two	rt.: stems of lotus with flaming sword lt.: wheel	corp.	two	maha- rajalila	fancy boots, bodh. ornaments, va.: raised throne	dBan-phyug
one/two	two	rt.: flaming jewel lt.: vase/vessel	youth	two	vamalalita	bodh. ornaments, va.: lotus throne	dByug-gu-ma-bhagini-traya
one/two	two	rt.: vajra-topped goad/hook lt.: noose/snare	corp.	two	lalita	bodh. ornaments, va.: lotus throne	Devendra
one/two	two	rt.: jewel(?) lt.: stem of flower in vitarka mu.	youth	two	vajra	bodh. ornaments, va.: lotus throne	Dhanada
one/two	two	rt.: conch shell lt.: bell	youth	two	sattva	bodh. ornaments, va.: lotus throne	Dhanus (deva)
one/two	two	rt.: lotus(?) lt.: lotus(?) in karana mu.	youth	two	vajra	bodh. ornaments, va.: lotus throne	Dharmavajri
one/two	two	rt.: flower (lotus?) lt.: flower (lotus?)	youth	two	vamalalita	bodh. ornaments, va.: lotus throne	Dharmavajri (fo-mu)
one/two	two	rt.: stem of lotus in vitarka mu. lt.: jewel in dhyana mu.	mature	two	vajra	bodh. ornaments, va.: lotus throne	Dharmodgata
one/two	two	rt.: abhaya mu. lt.: cylindrical banner/flag	mature	two	lalita	bodh. ornaments, va.: lotus throne	Dhvaja
one/two	two	victory banner/flag	matue	two	virasena	bodh. ornaments, va.: lotus throne	Dhvajagra(?) (Buddha)
one/two	two	rt.: stem of lotus in varada mu. lt.: stem of lotus in karana mu.	youth	two	vamalalita	bodh. ornaments, va.: lotus throne	Divasanta-ratrikruddha-Tara
one/two	two	rt.: abhaya lt.: vase/vessel	youth	two	vajra	bodh. ornaments, va.: lotus throne	Duhkhadahana-Tara
one/two	two	holding triangle	youth	two	vamalalita	bodh. ornaments, va.: lotus throne	Duhkhadahana-Tara
one/two	two	rt.: lotus	youth	two	sattva	bodh. ornaments,	Dundubhisvara (Bodhisattva)

		lt.: harina mu.				va.: lotus throne	
one/two	two	rt.: in lap holding staff/stick(?) lt.: abhaya mu.	youth	two	sattva	bodh. ornaments, va.: lotus throne	Durdantadamaka
one/two	two	holds thunderbolt on point in dhyana mu.	mature	two	vajra	bodh. ornaments, va.: lotus throne	Durgati-Shodhanaraja
one/two	two	rt.: abhaya mu. lt.: stem of lotus in kartari mu.	youth	two	lalita	bodh. ornaments, va.: lotus throne with fire in lower left	Dves-agni-prasamani (Tara)
one/two	two	dhyana mu.	youth	two	sattva	bodh. ornaments, va.: lotus throne	Dvibhuja-Dharmadhatuvagisvara (Buddha)
one/two	two	rt.: sword lt.: wheel	youth	two	sattva	bodh. ornaments, va.: lotus throne	Dvibhuja-Pratisara
one/two	two	rt.: thunderbolt lt.: stem of lotus	mature	two	vamalalita	bodh. ornaments, va.: lotus throne	Dyuti(?) (Buddha)
one/two	two	rt.: thunderbolt lt.: bell	youth, bare breasts	two	vamalalita	bodh. ornaments, va.: lotus throne	Ekadasa (deva)
one/two	two	rt.: stem of lotus in vitarka mu. lt.: shrine in dhyana mu.	mature	two	vajra	bodh. ornaments, va.: lotus throne	Gangadevi
one/two	two	rt.: abhaya mu. lt.: stem of lotus in kartari mu.	youth	two	vamalalita	bodh. ornaments, va.: lotus throne	Garbha-suvarna-sutra-Sri
one/two	two	rt.: rosary lt.: vase/vessel	youth	two	sattva	bodh. ornaments va.: lotus throne	Gautamadeva
one/two	two	rt.: abhaya lt.: stem of lotus in kartari mu.	youth	two	lalita	bodh. ornaments, va.: lotus throne with chain	Ghora-matsarya-srnkhala-mocani-(Tara)
one/two	two	rt.: stem of lotus in varada mu. lt.: stem of lotus in karana mu.	youth	two	vamalalita	bodh. ornaments va.: lotus throne	gNan-lugs Sadanga Tara
one/two	two	rt.: fly-whisk lt.: rosary	corp.	two	lalita	bodh. ornaments, va.: horse	gNan-than-lha
one/two	two	rt.: wheel lt.: conch shell	corp	two	rajalila	bodh. ornaments, va.: lotus throne	gZi-brjid-can

one/two	two	rt.: arrow lt.: bow	youth	two	vamalalita	bodh. ornaments, va.: lotus throne	Hai-pi-mu
one/two	two	rt.: stem of lotus in vitarka mu. lt.: stem of lotus in kartari mu. at chest level	youth	two	vamalalita	bodh. ornaments, va.: lotus throne	Hasti-bhaya-trana Tara
one/two	two	rt.: human skull-drum lt.: flaming jewel	corp.	two	maha-rajalila	bodh. ornaments, fancy boots, va.: raised throne	hOd-snan-ni-ma
one/two	two	rt.: abhaya mu. lt.: vase/vessel	youth	two	sattva	bodh. ornaments, va.: lotus throne	Hsiang-fu-yu-kuei p'u-sa
one/two	two	rt.: abhaya mu. on knee lt.: abhaya mu.	youth	two	sattva	bodh. ornaments, va.: lotus throne	Hua-kuang-man-t'ien p'u-sa
one/two	two	rt.: abhaya mu. lt.: flower (lotus?)	youth	two	vajra	dhar. ornaments, va.: lotus throne	Humsvara-nadini-Tara
one/two	two	rt.: abhaya mu. on knee lt.: rests behind thigh	youth	two	sattva	bodh. ornaments, va.: lotus throne	Isvara (deva)
one/two	two	rt.: abhaya mu. lt.: stem of lotus in kartari	youth	two	lalita	bodh. ornaments, va.: lotus throne and snake in lower left	Irsya-sarpa-vis-apaharani-(Tara)
one/two	two	rt.: goad/hook lt.: noose/snare	youth	two	vajra	bodh. ornaments, va.: lotus throne	Iagadvasi(?)-Tara
one/two	two	rt.: stem of lotus in vitarka mu. lt.: stem of lotus in kartari mu.	youth	two	vamalalita	bodh. ornaments, va.: lotus throne	Iala-bhaya-trana-Tara
one/two	two	holds rosary in vitarka mu.	youth	two	vamalalita	bodh. ornaments, va.: lotus throne	Ialiniprabhakumara
one/two	two	rt.: rosary(?) lt.: trident	youth	two	vajra	bodh. ornaments, va.; lotus throne	Ianguli-Tara
one/two	two	rt.: wheel lt.: rests behind left thigh	youth	two	vajra	bodh. ornaments, va.: lotus throne	Iayosnisa (Buddha)
one/two	two	dharmachakra mu.	youth	two	vamalalita	bodh. ornaments, va.: lotus throne	Iih-kung t'ien
one/two	two	vajrahumkara mu.	youth	two	vajra	bodh. ornaments, va.: lotus throne	Iina-Vajradhara

one/two	two	rt.: bhumisparsa mu. lt.: dhyana mu	mature	two	vajra	bodh. ornaments, va.: lotus throne	Inanaguru
one/two	two	rt.: tapering stick/staff (?) lt.: karana mu.	youth	two	sattva	bodh. ornaments, va.: lotus throne	Inanakara (Bodhisattva)
one/two	two	rt.: wheel lt.: rests behind left thigh	youth	two	vajra	bodh. ornaments, va.: lotus throne	Ivalanalosnisa(?) (Buddha)
one/two	two	holding fly whisk	youth	two	sattva	bodh. ornaments, va.: lotus throne	Kaladhvaja(?)-(devi)
one/two	two	holding vase/vessel	youth	two	rajalila	bodh. ornaments, va.: lotus throne	Kalasha
one/two	two	dhyana mu.	mature	two	vajra	bodh. ornaments, va.: lotus throne	Kamalosnisa(?) (Buddha)
one/two	two	rt.: (?) lt.: staff/stick	youth	two	vamalalita	bodh. ornaments, va.: lotus throne	Kanya (deva)
one/two	two	rt.: rosary lt.: vase/vessel	youth	two	sattva	bodh. ornaments, va.: lotus throne	Karkata(?)deva Bodhisattva
one/two	two	in tarjani mu.	youth	two	vajra	bodh. ornaments, va.: lotus throne	Karmavajri
one/two	two	rt.: crossed thunderbolts lt.: karana mu.	youth	two	sattva	bodh. ornaments, va.: lotus throne	Karmavajri (fo-mu)
one/two	two	rt.: fly whisk lt.: lance	youth	two	vajra	bodh. ornaments, va.: peacock	Karttikeya(?) (deva)
one/two	two	holding sword-tipped lance	youth	two	sattva	bodh. ornaments, va.: lotus throne	Kaumari(?)-(devi)
one/two	two	rt.: baton/mace lt.: dhyana mu.	mature	two	sattva	bodh. ornaments, va.: lotus throne	Kesini (devi)
one/two	two	rt.: staff/stick lt.: abhaya mu.	mature	two	vamalalita	bodh. ornaments, vahana: bullock	Krsna-Dharmaraja
one/two	two	rt.: abhaya mu. lt.: stem of lotus in kartari mu.	youth	two	lalita	bodh. ornaments, va.: lotus throne with thief in lower right	Kudrsti-cora-upadrava-nivarani (Tara)

one/two	two	rt.: sword lt.: shield	youth	two	ardha-paryanka	bodh. ornaments, va.: lotus throne	Kumbha
one/two	two	rt.: sword lt.: (?)	youth	two	sattva	bodh. ornaments, va.: lotus throne	Kumbha(?) (deva)
one/two	two	rt.: karana mu. lt.: rosary	youth	two	vamalalita	bodh. ornaments, va.: lotus throne	Lan-mu-ta-lieh-ta-na-ma hsi-mu
one/two	two	rt.: flaming sword lt.: disc/wheel/shield (?)	corp.	two	raja-paryanka	bodh. ornaments, vahana: throne	lHahi-dban-ldan
one/two	two	rt.: arrow lt.: bow	corp.	two	raja-paryanka	bodh. ornaments, va.: lotus throne	lHahi-dban-phyug
one/two	two	rt.: bell lt.: rests on thigh	youth	two	vamalalita	bodh. ornaments, va.: lotus throne	Ling-chui t'ien
one/two	two	dhyana mu.	youth	two	sattva	bodh. ornaments, va.: lotus throne	Locanaprabha
one/two	two	rt.: abhaya mu. lt.: shallow bowl	youth	two	vamalalita	bodh. ornaments, va.: lotus throne	Lung-chung-sheng-mu
one/two	two	rt.: alms bowl with fruit lt.: (?)	youth	two	sattva	bodh. ornaments, va.: elephant on lotus throne	Lung-yu t'ien
one/two	two	rt.: human skull-drum lt.: bell	mature	two	ardha-paryanka	bodh. ornaments, va.: lotus throne	Ma-cig-Lban-sgron
one/two	two	rt.: thunderbolt lt.: abhaya	mature	two	sattva	bodh. ornaments, va.: lotus throne	Mahajina
one/two	two	rt.: flowering branch lt.: harina mu.	youth	two	vamalalita	bodh. ornaments, va.: lotus throne	Mahamati (Bodhisattva)
one/two	two	rt.: thunderbolt lt.: thunderbolt	youth	two	sattva	bodh. ornaments, va.: lotus throne	Mahodgatosnisa(?)
one/two	two	rt.: wheel lt.: rests behind left knee	youth	two	vajra	bodh. ornaments, va.: lotus throne	Mahosnisa (Buddha)
one/two	two	rt.: thunderbolt lt.: bell	youth	two	sattva	bodh. ornaments, va.: lotus throne	Makara (deva)
one/two	two	rt.: thunderbolt	mature	two	vamalalita	bodh. ornaments,	Ma-lieh-ka-ma hsi-mu

		lt.: branch				va.: lotus throne	
one/two	two	holds beaded necklace(?) rosary(?)	youth	two	sattva	bodh. ornaments, va.: lotus throne	Malya (fo-mu)
one/two	two	rt.: varada mu. lt.: katari mu. with endless knot	youth	two	lalita	bodh. ornaments, va.: lotus throne	Mangalarthakari(?) (Tara)
one/two	two	rt.: abhaya mu. lt.: katari mu. with stem of lotus	youth	two	lalita	bodh. ornaments, va.: lotus throne with lion	Mana-simha-bhaya-trana (Tara)
one/two	two	rt.: thunderbolt lt.: human skull-cup	youth	two	sattva	bodh. ornaments, va.: lion	Mangala-Dirghayushi
one/two	two	rt.: short staff/stick lt.: mongoose	youth	two	vamalalita	bodh. ornaments, va.: lotus throne	Manohara-Vasudhara
one/two	two	rt.: ritual chopper lt.: human skull-cup	youth	two	sattva	bodh. ornaments, va.: lotus throne	Mantranudharani (fo-mu)
one/two	two	rt.: rosary lt.: vase/vessel	youth	two	sattva	bodh. ornaments, va.: lotus throne	Markata(?) deva
one/two	two	namaskara mu.	youth	two	sattva	bodh. ornaments, va.: lotus throne	Mei-ming fo-mu
one/two	two	rt.: thunderbolt-topped axe lt.: flower	youth	two	ardha-paryanka	bodh. ornaments, va.: lotus throne	Mesa
one/two	two	rt.: wheel lt.: conch shell	corp	two	sopasraya	bodh. ornaments, va.: raised throne	Mihi-sen-ge
one/two	two	rt.: human skull-drum lt.: sun disc(?)	mature	two	ardha-paryanka	bodh. ornaments, va.: lotus throne	Mina
one/two	two	rt.: (?) lt.: human skull-drum	touth	two	sattva	bodh. ornaments, va.: lotus throne	Mina (deva)
one/two	two	baton/mace (?)	youth	two	vamalalita	bodh. ornaments, va.: lotus throne	Ming-tien tsun-mu
one/two	two	rt.: vase/vessel lt.: palm down on thigh	youth	two	vamalalita	bodh. ornaments, va.: lotus throne	Ming-yueh-mu
one/two	two	rt.: varada mu. lt.: stem of lotus in kartari mu.	youth	two	lalita	bodh. ornaments, va.: lotus throne	Mi-pham-rgyal-mo (Tara)

one/two	two	rt.: stem of lotus in vitarka mu. lt.: stem of lotus in kartari mudra at chest	mature	two		bodh. ornaments, va.: lotus throne	Naga-bhaya-trana Tara
one/two	two	rt.: drum sticks lt.: drum under left arm	mature	two	vamalalita	bodh. ornaments, va.: lotus throne	Nandisvara (deva)
one/two	two	rt.: human skull-drum lt.: trident	mature	two	vamalalita	bodh. ornaments, va.: lotus throne	Nandisvara (deva)
one/two	two	holding wheel	youth	two	sattva	bodh. ornaments, va.: lotus throne	Narayana (deva)
one/two	two	rt.: wheel lt.: abhaya mu.	youth	two	sattva	bodh. ornaments, va.: lotus throne	Narayani (devi)
one/two	two	rt.: magic throwing stick lt.: holds (?)	mature	two	sattva	bodh. ornaments, va.: lotus throne	Navami-Tithi
one/two	two	dharmachakra mu.	youth	two	vajra	bodh. ornaments, va.: lotus throne	Navasikhin(?) (Buddha)
one/two	two	rt.: abhaya mu. at chest level lt.: abhaya mu. at chest level	youth	two	sattva	bodh. ornaments, va.: lotus throne	Nien-yu p'u-sa
one/two	two	rt.: sword lt.: rests at waist	youth	two	sama-bhanga	bodh. ornaments, va.: lotus throne	Nivaranaviskambhin
one/two	two	rt.: varada mu. lt.: stem of lotus in kartari mudra with vase/vessel	mature	two		bodh. ornaments, va.: lotus throne	Nor-gter-ma (Tara)
one/two	two	rt.: thunderbolt lt.: bell	mature	two	vajra, yab-yum	bodh. ornaments, va.: lotus throne	Padmasambhava
one/two	two	rt.: human skull-drum lt.: human skull-cup with lotus	mature	two	sopasraya	bodh. ornaments, magic dagger in sash, va.: lotus throne	Padmasambhava
one/two	two	rt.: human skull-drum lt.: mirror	mature	two	sopasraya	bodh. ornaments, magic dagger in sash, va.: lotus throne	Padmasambhava
one/two	two	rt.: wheel lt.: bow and arrow	youth	two	vajra	bodh. ornaments, va.: lotus throne	Pacaka-Tara

one/two	two	rt.: lotus lt.: abhaya mu	mature	two	lalita	bodh. ornaments, va.: lotus throne	Padma
one/two	two	rt.: flaming jewels lt.: crescent moon(?)	youth	two	vamalalita	bodh. ornaments, va.: lotus throne	Padmacarya-Paramita
one/two	two	rt.: abhaya mu. lt.: lotus stem in kartari mu.	mature	two	vamalalita	bodh. ornaments, va.: lotus throne	Pancatmika-Tara
one/two	two	rt.: varada mu. lt.:stem of lotus in kartari mu. with thunderbolt	mature	two	lalita	bodh. ornaments, va.: lotus throne	Paramjaya(?) (Tara)
one/two	two	holding vase/vessel	youth	two	vajra	bodh. ornaments, va.: lotus throne	Paripurna-Tara
one/two	two	holding bowl of fruit	youth	two	ardha-paryanka	bodh. ornaments, va.: lotus throne	Phala
one/two	two	rt.: thunderbolt lt.: jewel	mature	two	vamalalita	bodh. ornaments, va.: lotus throne	Prabhakari (fo-mu)
one/two	two	rt.: vitarka mu. lt.: rests on knee	mature	two	rajalila	bodh. ornaments, va.: lotus throne	Prabhaketu
one/two	two	rt.: vase/vessel lt.: harina mu.	mature	two	vamalalita	bodh. ornaments, va.: lotus throne	Prabhamati (Bodhisattva)
one/two	two	rt.: sword lt.: Prajna Paramita book/manuscript	mature	two	vajra	bodh. ornaments, va.: lotus throne	Prajnacakra
one/two	two	rt.: crossed thunderbolt lt.: dhyana mu.	mature	two	sattva	bodh. ornaments, va.: lotus throne	Prajnakuta
one/two	two	rt.: vitarka mu. lt.: rests on knee	mature	two	sattva	bodh. ornaments, va.: lotus throne	Pranidhanamati
one/two	two	rt.: varada mu. lt.: stem of lotus in kartari mu. with begging bowl	youth	two	lalita	bodh. ornaments, va.: lotus throne	Prasanta(?) (Tara)
one/two	two	rt.: sword lt.: wheel	mature	two		bodh. ornaments, va.: lotus throne	Pratisara (fo-mu)
one/two	two	holding anjali mu	mature	two	alidha	bodh. ornaments, va.: lotus throne	Punarvasu

one/two	two	stems of lotus in dharmachakra mu.	mature	two	maha-rajalila	bodh. ornaments, va.: lotus throne	Pundarika
one/two	two	rt.: varada mu. lt.: stem of lotus in kartari mu. with jewel	mature	two	lalita	bodh. ornaments, va.: lotus throne	Punyavarada (Tara)
one/two	two	rt.: baton/mace with trident finial & banners lt.: vitarka mu.	mature	two	vamalalita	bodh. ornaments, va.: lotus throne	Punyesvari
one/two	two	rt.: monastery model lt.: mongoose	mature	two	astride	fancy boots, bodh. ornaments, va.: horse	Purnabhadra
one*/two	two	rt.: wheel lt.: mongoose	mature	two	lalita	*angry, richly atrmored, bodh. ornaments, va.: lotus throne	Purnabhadra
one/two	two	rt.: staff/stick lt.: karana mu.	youth	two	vajra	bodh. ornaments, va.: lotus throne	Raganisudana-Tara
one/two	two	rt.: trident lt.: fan (?)	youth	two	sopasraya	bodh. ornaments, va.: lotus throne	Raganisudana-Tara
one/two	two	rt.: abhaya mu. lt.: stem of lotus in kartari mu.	mature	two	lalita	bodh. ornaments, va.: lotus throne	Rag-augha-vegavarta-sosani (Tara)
one/two	two	rt.: varada mu. lt.: vase/vessel	youth	two	ardha-paryanka	bodh. ornaments, va.: lotus throne	Rasavajra
one*/two	two	rt.: jewel lt.: serpent/snake in karana mu.	youth	two	vajra	*five snakes in hair, bodh. ornaments, va.: lotus throne	Ratnacuda
one/two	two	rt.: flaming jewels lt.: abhaya mu.	youth	two	sattva	bodh. ornaments, va.: lotus throne	Ratnamukuta
one/two	two	rt.: varada mu. over right knee lt.: dhyana mu.	mature	two	vajra	bodh. ornaments, va.: lotus throne	Ratnashikhin
one/two	two	rt.: crossed thunderbolts lt.: rosary	youth	two	vamalalita	bodh. ornaments, va.: lotus throne	Ratnavajri
one/two	two	rt.: jewel at chest lt.: tarjani mu.	youth	two	vajra	bodh. ornaments, va.: lotus throne	Ratnavajri

one/two	two	rt.: flaming jewels lt.: karana mu.	youth	two	vamalalita	bodh. ornaments, va.: lotus throne	Ratnavajri (fo-mu)
one/two	two	rt.: conch shell lt.: palm down on thigh	youth	two	vamalalita	bodh. ornaments, va.: lotus throne	Ratnavijaya
one/two	two	rt.: staff/stick lt.: palm down on thigh	youth	two	vamalalita	bodh. ornaments, va.: lotus throne	Ratnesvari(?)
one/two	two	rt.: crossed thunderbolts lt.: wish fulfilling banner/flag	mature	two		bodh. ornaments, va.: lotus throne	Ratnolka
one/two	two	rt.: stem of lotus which rises to shoulder lt.: disc	mature	two	vamalalita	bodh. ornaments, va.: lotus throne	Rddhi-Vasita
one/two	two	rt.: stem of lotus with thunderbolt lt.: bell	corp.	two	maha- rajalila	bodh. ornaments, fancy boots, va.: raised throne	Rin-chen-phyag
one/two	two	rt.: short staff/stick lt.: chain	corp.	two	maha- rajalila	bodh. ornaments, fancy boots, va.: raised throne	rNam-par-gnon
one/two	two	rt.: goad/hook lt.: noose/snare	corp.	two	maha- rajalila	bodh. ornaments, fancy boots, va.: raised throne	rNam-rgyal
one/two	two	holds sun (?) disc over head	youth	two	ardha- paryanka	bodh. ornaments, va.: lotus throne	Rupavajra
one/two	two	rt.: vitarka mu. lt.: vase/vessel in dhyana mu.	mature	two	vajra	bodh. ornaments, va.: lotus throne	Sadaprarudita
one/two	two	rt.: thunderbolt lt.: abhaya mu.	mature	two	sattva	bodh. ornaments, va.: lotus throne	Sakra (deva)
one/two	two	dharmachakra mu.	mature	two	vajra	bodh. ornaments, va.: lotus throne	Sakyasimha (Buddha)
one/two	two	rt.: full bloomed lotus lt.: dhyana mu.	mature	two	vajra	bodh. ornaments, va.: lotus throne	Samkusumita
one/two	two	rt.: abhaya mu. lt.: stem of lotus in kartari mu.	mature	two	lalita	bodh. ornaments, va.: lotus throne, and dakini in lower right	Samsaya-pisaca-bhaya-trana-Tara

one/two	two	holds trident	mature	two	sattva	bodh. ornaments, va.: lotus throne	Sankari(?) (devi)
one/two	two	rt.: spiral top baton/mace lt.: rests on thigh, palm up (vandana mudra?)	mature	two	vamalalita	bodh. ornaments, va.: lotus throne	Sankhapadma
one/two	two	rt.: sword lt.: (?)	mature	two	lalita	bodh. ornaments, va.: lotus throne	Sankhapali (devi)
one/two	two	rt.: sword lt.: mongoose	corp.	two	sopasraya	bodh. ornaments, va.: horse	Sankhapali (devi)
one/two	two	rt.: thunderbolt lt.: bell, embracing shakti	mature	two	vajra, yab-yum	bodh. ornaments, va.: lotus throne	Santa-Sahaja-Guhyapati
one/two	two	rt.: varada mu. lt.: stem of lotus in kartari mu.	mature	two	vajra	bodh. ornaments, va.: lotus throne	Sarva-bhaya-trana-Tara
one/two	two	rt.: ritual chopper lt.: human skull-cup	mature	two	sopasraya	bodh. ornaments, va.: raised throne	Sa-skyon
one/two	two	rt.: (?) lt.: wish fulfilling jewel	mature	two	sopasraya	bodh. ornaments, va.: lotus throne	Sasthi-Tithi
one/two	two	rt.: conch-shell lt.: abhaya mu.	youth	two	sama-bhanga	bodh. ornaments, va.: lotus throne	Satakratu
one/two	two	holds conch-shell	youth	two	sopasraya	bodh. ornaments, va.: lotus throne	Satakratu
one/two	two	rt.: thunderbolt lt.: noose/snare	youth	two	vajra	bodh. ornaments, va.: lotus throne	Sattvavajri
one/two	two	rt.: thunderbolt lt.: karana mu	youth	two	vamalalita	bodh. ornaments, va.: lotus throne	Sattvavajri (fo-mu)
one/two	two	dhyana mu. with thunderbolt on lotus	youth	two	vajra	bodh. ornaments, va.: lotus throne	Shakya-Kulendra
one/two	two	rt.: abhaya mu. lt.: jewel	youth	two	vamalalita	bodh. ornaments, bare breasted, va.: lotus throne	Shan-sha-ou-lieh t'ien
one/two	two	rt.: vitarka mu. lt.: abhaya mu.	youth	two	rajalila	bodh. ornaments, va.: lotus throne	Shantendriya

one/two	two	rt.: large fruit of karma lt.: yak hair fly whisk	youth	two	pralamba- pada	bodh. ornaments, va.: lotus throne	Sharmana
one/two	two	rt.: abhaya mu. lt.: rests on cushion behind thigh	youth	two	sopasraya	bodh. ornaments, bare breasted, va.: lotus throne	Shih-i-wo-shih-ma-mu
one/two	two	rt.: sword tipped lance lt.: abhaya	youth	two	sattva	bodh. ornaments, va.: lotus throne	Shih-lei-yen t'ien
one/two	two	rt.: abhaya mu. on knee lt.: abhaya mu. at chest	youth	two	vamalalita	bodh. ornaments, va.: lotus throne	Shih-miao-chin-kang
one/two	two	holds endless knot	youth	two	sopasraya	bodh. ornaments, va.: lotus throne	Shrivatsa
one/two	two	rt.: vase/vessel lt.: abhaya mu.	youth	two	vajra	bodh. ornaments, va.: lotus throne	Siddhida-Tara
one/two	two	rt.: abhaya mu. lt.: vase/vessel	youth	two	sopasraya	bodh. ornaments, va.: lotus throne	Siddhi-sambhava-Tara
one/two	two	rt.: stem of lotus in vitarka mu. lt.: kartari mu. at chest level	youth	two	vamalalita	bodh. ornaments, va.: lotus throne	Simha-bhaya-trana Tara
one/two	two	rt.: cylindrical banner lt.: rests palm down on thigh	youth	two	sukha	bodh. ornaments, va.: lotus throne	Simhadhvaja
one/two	two	rt.: hammer/mace lt.: book/manuscript	mature	two	raja- paryanka	bodh. ornaments, va.: raised throne	sNa-tshogs-gzugs
one/two	two	rt.: vajra-topped goad/hook lt.: noose/snare	mature	two	maha- rajalila	bodh. ornaments, va.: raised throne	sNa-tshogs-gzugs
one/two	two	rt.: abhaya on knee lt.: dhyana mu.	mature	two	sattva	bodh. ornaments, va.: lotus throne	Sokanirghatanamati
one/two	two	holding flowing scarf over head	youth	two	ardha- paryanka	bodh. ornaments, va.: lotus throne	Sparsavajra
one/two	two	rt.: mirror (?) lt.: (?)	mature	two	sama- bhanga	bodh. ornaments, va.: lotus throne	Sramana (fo-mu)
one/two	two	rt.: abhaya mu. lt.: flaming jewel	mature	two	lalita	bodh. ornaments, loose garment, va.: lotus throne	Sresthiputri

one/two	two	rt.: thunderbolt lt.: (?)	corp.	two	alidha	bodh. ornaments, va.: lotus throne	Sri-Ucarya-Vajrapani**
one/two	two	rt.: thunderbolt lt.: chain	youth	two	vamalalita	bodh. ornaments, va.: lotus throne	Srnkhala(?)
one/two	two	rt.: abhaya mu. lt.: stem of lotus in kartari mu.	mature	two	sopasraya	bodh. ornaments, va.: lotus throne	Sruta-nama-Nivarana-viskambhin
one/two	two	rt.: sword lt.: book/manuscript	youth	two	vajra	bodh. ornaments, va.: lotus throne	Sthiracakra-Manjughosa
one/two	two	rt.: (?) lt.: flaming jewel	corp.	two	maha- rajalila	bodh. ornaments, va.: raised throne	sTobs-po-che
one/two	two	rt.: hem of garment lt.: bell	corp.	two	vamalalita	bodh. ornaments, va.: lotus throne	Sucandra
one/two	two	rt.: three peacock feathers lt.: harina mudra (?)	youth	two	vamalalita	bodh. ornaments, va.: lotus throne	Sudarsana (Bodhisattva)
one/two	two	rt.: namaskara mu. holding book/manuscript at chest	youth	two	vamalalita	bodh. ornaments, va.: lotus throne	Sudhanakumara
one/two	two	dhyana mu. with vase/vessel	mature	two	vajra	bodh. ornaments, va.: lotus throne	Sugata-Aparimitayur-jnana
one/two	two	holding wheel	youth	two	vajra	bodh. ornaments, va.: lotus throne	Sukhada-Tara
one/two	two	holding sun disc(?)	youth	two	sopasraya	bodh. ornaments, va.: lotus throne	Sukha-sadhana-Tara
one/two	two	rt.: lotus with thunderbolt on end in karana mu. lt.: harina mu.	youth	two	vamalalita	bodh. ornaments, va.: lotus throne	Sumerukuta (Bodhisattva)
one/two	two	rt.: jewel (?) lt.: karana mu. in lap	youth	two	vamalalita	bodh. ornaments, va.: lotus throne	Sumerusikharadhararaja (Bodhisattva)
one/two	two	holds namaskara mu	youth	two	sattva	bodh. ornaments, va.: lotus throne	Surya (deva)
one/two	two	rt.: fish lt.: fish	mature	two	sopasraya	bodh. ornaments, va.: lotus throne	Survana-Matsya
one/two	two	rt.: stem of lotus with book/manuscript	youth	two	vamalalita	bodh. ornaments,	Suryavairocana (Bodhisattva)

		lt.: harina mu.				va.: lotus throne	
one/two	two	rt.: varada mu. lt.: stem of lotus	mature	two	lalita	bodh. ornaments, va.: lotus throne	<u>Svapnadesaka-Tara</u>
one/two	two	rt.: fly whisk lt.: branch of tree	youth	two	pralam- bapada	bodh. ornaments, va.: lotus throne	<u>Sramana (devi)</u>
one/two	two	sun disc in modified dharmachakra mu.	youth	two	sopasraya	bodh. ornaments, bare breasted, va.: lotus throne	<u>Suryaprabha (deva)</u>
one/two	two	rt.: vase/vessel lt.: rests on thigh in dhyana mu.	youth	two	vamalalita	bodh. ornaments, va.: lotus throne	<u>Ta-chi-fen-mu</u>
one/two	two	rt.: stem of lotus lt.: stem of lotus	youth	two	vamalalita	bodh. ornaments, va.: lotus throne	<u>Tatthata(?)</u>
one/two	two	holding a bodhisattva crown	youth	two	sopasraya	bodh. ornaments, va.: lotus throne	<u>Tejorasyusnisa</u>
one*/two	two	rt.: sun disc lt.: held on hip	youth	two		*pink color, bodh. ornaments, realm: South-East , va.: human being	<u>Tejosnisa</u>
one/two	two	holding rosary	youth	two	vamalalita	bodh. ornaments, va.: lotus throne	<u>T'ien-jung-mu</u>
one/two	two	rt.: wheel lt.: rests behind left thigh	youth	two	vajra	bodh. ornaments, va.: lotus throne	<u>Tiksnosnisa (Buddha)</u>
one/two	two	holds dharmachakra mu.	youth	two	vamalalita	bodh. ornaments, va.: lotus throne	<u>To Tsun-mu</u>
one/two	two	rt.: disc lt.: abhaya mu. in lap	youth	two	vajra	bodh. ornaments, va.: lotus throne	<u>Tejausnisa(?) (Buddha)</u>
one/two	two	rt.: wheel lt.: rests behind left thigh	youth	two	vajra	bodh. ornaments, va.: lotus throne	<u>Tejausnisa(?) (Buddha)</u>
one/two	two	rt.: severed head by hair lt.: throwing staff/stick	mature	two	vamalalita	bare breasted, bodh. ornaments, va.: lotus throne	<u>Trayodasa (deva)</u>
one/two	two	holds shepherd-like staff	youth	two	sopasraya	bodh. ornaments, va.: lotus throne	<u>Tsui-neng-san-lu p'u-sa</u>

one/two	two	rt.: human skull-drum(?) lt.: rests behind thigh	youth	two	vamalalita	bodh. ornaments, va.: lotus throne	<u>Tula (deva)</u>
one/two	two	rt.: varada lt.: stem of lotus in kartari	youth	two	lalita	bodh. ornaments, va.: lotus throne	<u>Tura-vira (Tara)</u>
one/two	two	rt.: bhumisparsa mu lt.: dhyana mu.	youth	two	vajra	bodh. ornaments, va.: lotus throne	<u>Tu-sheng fo</u>
one/two	two	rt.: abhaya mu., stem of lotus lt.: karana mu., stem of lotus	youth	two	vamalalita	bodh. ornaments, va.: lotus throne	<u>Tzu-chu-lin Tara (fo-mu)</u>
one/two	two	rt.: varada mu. lt.: stem of lotus in kartari mu.	youth	two	lalita	bodh. ornaments, va.: lotus throne	<u>Ujjvaladyuti(?) (Tara)</u>
one/two	two	rt.: vitarka mu. above head lt.: vitarka mu. at shoulder	youth	two	vamalalita	bodh. ornaments, va.: lotus throne	<u>Uma</u>
one/two	two	rt.: flowering branch lt.: simha-karna mu.	youth	two	sattva	bodh. ornaments, va.: lotus throne	<u>Upakesini(?) (devi)</u>
one/two	two	holding vase/vessel with the nectar of life	youth	*		*coils of a snake, halo surrounded by seven serpents, bodh. ornaments, va.: sea waves	<u>Upananda-Nagaraja</u>
one/two	two	rt.: lotus lt.: creepers	youth	two		bodh. ornaments, va.: lotus throne	<u>Upapatti-Vasita</u>
one/two	two	rt.: stems of lotus lt.: stems of lotus	youth	two	vamalalita	bodh. ornaments, va.: lotus throne	<u>Upapatti-Vasita</u>
one/two	two	rt.: (?) lt.: thunderbolt	youth	two	vamalalita	bodh. ornaments, va.: lotus throne	<u>Upayakausalya-Paramita</u>
one/two	two	rt.: abhaya mu. lt.: dhyana mu.	youth	two	sopasraya	bodh. ornaments, va.: lotus throne	<u>Urna(?) (fo-mu)</u>
one/two	two	rt.: thunderbolt lt.: bell	youth	two	vajra	bodh. ornaments, va.: lotus throne	<u>Uttamasri (Buddha)</u>
one/two	two	rt.: lt.:	youth	two		bodh. ornaments, va.: lotus throne	
one/two	two	rt.: thunderbolt on end	youth	two	vajra	bodh. ornaments,	<u>Vajrabhasa</u>

		lt.: (?)				va.: lotus throne	
one/two	two	rt.: abhaya mu. lt.: abhaya mu.	youth	two	sattva	bodh. ornaments, va.: lotus throne	<u>Vajrabhasa</u>
one/two	two	rt.: wheel lt.: (?)	youth	two	vamalalita	bodh. ornaments, va.: lotus throne	<u>Vajracakra</u>
one/two	two	rt.: flaming jewels lt.: thunderbolt	youth	two	vamalalita	bodh. ornaments, va.: lotus throne	<u>Vajracarya-Paramita</u>
one/two	two	rt.: spindle lt.: abhaya mu.	youth	two	sopasraya	bodh. ornaments, va.: lotus throne	<u>Vajradanta</u>
one/two	two	rt.: karana mu. wioth thunderbolt lt.: dhyana mu.	youth	two	vajra	bodh. ornaments, va.: lotus throne	<u>Vajradhatu</u>
one/two	two	rt.: crossed thunderbolts at chest lt.: bellat thigh	youth	two	vajra	bodh. ornaments, va.: lotus throne	<u>Vajradvidarana</u>
one/two	two	holds bhutadamara mu.	youth	two	sopasraya	bodh. ornaments, va.: lotus throne	<u>Vajragra (fo-mu)</u>
one/two	two	rt.: abhaya mu. at mouth lt.: bhumisparsa mu.	youth	two	sattva	bodh. ornaments, va.: lotus throne	<u>Vajrahasa</u>
one/two	two	rt.: (?) over shoulder lt.: (?) over shoulder	youth	two	sattva	bodh. ornaments, va.: lotus throne	<u>Vajrahasa (Bodhisattva)</u>
one/two	two	dharmachakra mu. with wheel	youth	two	vajra	bodh. ornaments, va.: lotus throne	<u>Vajrahetu</u>
one/two	two	rt.: wheel lt.: abhaya mu. on knee	youth	two	sattva	bodh. ornaments, va.: lotus throne	<u>Vajrahetu</u>
one/two	two	rt.: thunderbolt lt.: **bell**	youth	two	vajra	bodh. ornaments, va.: lotus throne	<u>Vajrakarma</u>
one/two	two	rt.: banner/flag with wish fulfilling jewel lt.: crossed thunderbolts on lotus	youth	two		bodh. ornaments, va.: lotus throne	<u>Vajrakarmaparamita</u>
one/two	two	rt.: circular banner lt.: bhumisparsa mu.	youth	two	sattva	bodh. ornaments, va.: lotus throne	<u>Vajraketu</u>
one/two	two	rt.: circular banner lt.: karana mu.	youth	two	sattva	bodh. ornaments, va.: lotus throne	<u>Vajraketu (Bodhisattva)</u>

one/two	two	rt.: goad/hook lt.: vase/vessel	youth	two	astride	bodh. ornaments, long loose robe, va.: deer	Vajralocani
one/two	two	rt.: karana mu. on thigh lt.: karana mu. on thigh	youth	two	sattva	bodh. ornaments, va.: lotus throne	Vajramusti (Bodhisattva)
one/two	two	rt.: karana mu. in lap lt.: karana mu. in lap	youth	two	sattva	bodh. ornaments, va.: lotus throne	Vajramusti (Bodhisattva)
one/two	two	rt.: sword lt.: wheel	youth	two	pralam- bapada	bodh. ornaments, va.: lotus throne	Vajrapanjara-bhasita-Pratisara
one/two	two	rt.: varada mu. lt.: stem of lotus	youth	two	vajra	bodh. ornaments, va.: lotus throne	(Vajra) Panjarabhasita-Vajratara
one/two	two	holds shepherd-like crook	youth	two	sattva	bodh. ornaments, va.: lotus throne	Vajraraja (Bodhisattva)
one/two	two	rt.: axe lt.: axe	youth	two	sattva	bodh. ornaments, va.: lotus throne	Vajraraja (Bodhisattva)
one/two	two	elaborate piece of cloth or coat of mail	youth	two	vajra	bodh. ornaments, va.: lotus throne	Vajraraksa
one/two	two	holds kanjo-in mu.	youth	two	sattva	bodh. ornaments, va.: lotus throne	Vajraraksa
one/two	two	rt.: jewel in vismaya mu. lt.: bell(?)	youth	two	vajra	bodh. ornaments, va.: lotus throne	Vajraratna
one/two	two	rt.: baton/mace(?) lt.: karana mu.	youth	two	sattva	bodh. ornaments, va.: lotus throne	Vajraratna
one/two	two	under cloth at chest holding wheel	youth	two	vajra	bodh. ornaments, va.: lotus throne	Vajratejas
one/two	two	rt.: sun disc(?) lt.: rests on knee	youth	two	sattva	bodh. ornaments, va.: lotus throne	Vajratejas
one/two	two	rt.: sword lt.: book/manuscript(?)	youth	two	vajra	bodh. ornaments, va.: lotus throne	Vajratiksna
one/two	two	rt.: trident lt.: noose/snare	youth	two	astride	bodh. ornaments, va.: horse	Vajra-Vinayaka
one/two	two	rt.: skull-topped staff/stick	youth	two	ardha-	bodh. ornaments,	Vajrayaksi

		lt.: flowering branch			paryankha	va.: lotus throne	
one/two	two	rt.: bhumisparsa mu. lt.: (?)	youth	two	vajra	bodh. ornaments, va.: lotus throne	Vajrosnisa (Buddha)
one/two	two	rt.: rosary lt.: vase/vessel	youth	two	sopasraya	bodh. ornaments, va.: lotus throne	Vasisthadeva
one/two	two	holds cylindrical banner with foliage	youth	two	sattva	bodh. ornaments, va.: lotus throne	Vasumati(?) (devi)
one/two	two	holds fly whisk	youth	two	astride	bodh. ornaments, va.: white stag	Vayu
one/two	two	holds scarf	youth	two	astride	bodh. ornaments, va.: white stag	Vayu
one/two	two	holds fly whisk	youth	two	sattva	bodh. ornaments, va.: lotus throne	Vayu (deva)
one/two	two	rt.: abhaya mu. lt.: karana mu.	youth	two	vajra	bodh. ornaments, va.: four-wheeled chariot	Vemacitrin
one/two	two	rt.: varada mu. lt.: stem of lotus in kartari mu	youth	two	lalita	bodh. ornaments, va.: lotus throne	Vidya (Tara)
one/two	two	holding wheel	youth	two	sopasraya	bodh. ornaments, va.: lotus throne	Vijaya (male)
one/two	two	rt.: goad/hook lt.: palm down on thigh	youth	two	vamalalita	bodh. ornaments, va.: lotus throne	Vijaya (male)
one/two	two	holding namaskara mu.	youth	two	vamalalita	bodh. ornaments, va.: lotus throne	Vijaya (male)
one/two	two	rt.: abhaya mu. lt.: wheel	youth	two	vamalalita	bodh. ornaments, va.: lotus throne	Vijaya (Bodhisattva)
one/two	two	vitarka mu. in lap with bow	youth	two	vamalalita	bodh. ornaments, va.: lotus throne	Vijaya (devi)
one/two	two	rt.: wheel lt.: behind left thigh	youth	two	vajra	bodh. ornaments, va.: lotus throne	Vijayosnisa (Buddha)
one/two	two	rt.: wheel lt.: behind left thigh	youth	two	vajra	bodh. ornaments, va.: lotus throne	Vikrantosnisa (Buddha)

one/two	two	rt.: thunderbolt lt.: (?) disc	youth	two	vamalalita	bodh. ornaments, va.: lotus throne	Vimala (fo-mu)
one/two	two	rt.: vitarka mu. lt.: flower	youth	two	vajra	bodh. ornaments, va.: lotus throne	Vimalaprabhakumara
one/two	two	rt.: trident lt.: rosary	corp	two	maha- rajalila	bodh. ornaments, va.: raised throne	Visnugupta
one/two	two	rt.: abhaya lt.: vitarka mu. with stem of lotus	youth	two	vajra	bodh. ornaments, va.: lotus throne	Vishvamatr
one/two	two	rt.: serpent/snake lt.: over thigh in abhaya mu.	youth	two	vamalalita	bodh. ornaments, va.: lotus throne	Varuna (deva)
one/two	two	holds vase/vessel with nectar of life	youth	*		coils of a serpent/snake, bodh. ornaments, va.: sea waves	Varuna Nagaraja
one/two	two	rt.: sword lt.: cymbal(?)	youth	two	vamalalita	bodh. ornaments, va.: lotus throne	Vrscika (deva)
one/two	two	rt.: baton/mace(?) lt.: palm up on thigh	youth	two	vamalalita	bodh. ornaments, va.: lotus throne	Wei-yen-mu
one/two	two	rt.: shrine lt.: mongoose(?)	youth	two	astride	bodh. ornaments, va.: lotus throne	Yaksa-Purnabhadra
one/two	two	rt.: wheel lt.: conch shell	cirp.	two	maha- rajalila	bodh. ornaments, va.: raised throne	Zla-bahi-hod
one/two	two	rt.: short staff/stick lt.: chain	corp.	two	maha- rajalila	bodh. ornaments, va.: raised throne	Zla-bas-byin
one/two	four	rt.: noose/snare, wheel lt.: sword, karana mu.	youth	two	sattva	bodh. ornaments, va.: lotus throne	Aparajita-Tara
one/two	four	rt.: flowering branch and thunderbolt lt.: bell and human skull-cup	youth	two	ardha- paryanka	bodh. ornaments, va.: lotus throne	Bhumivajra
one/two	four	rt.: cylindrical banner/flag and rosary lt.: vase/vessel and lotus with sword	youth	two	vajra	bodh. ornaments, va.: swan	Brahman-(deva)
one/two	four	prin.: karana mu. at chest rt.: varada mu lt.: short staff/stick	youth	two	vajra	bodh. ornaments va.: lotus throne	Caturbhuja-cintamanirajni (fo-mu)

one/two	four	prin.: wish-fulfilling jewel rt.: flower lt.: flower	youth	two	vamalalita	bodh. ornaments, va.: lotus throne	Caturbhuja-Vayu (deva)
one/two	four	prin.: karana mu. (back of hands touching) rt.: abhaya mu. lt.: stem of lotus	youth	two	vajra	bodh. ornaments, va.: lotus throne	Cina-Tara (fo-mu)
one/two	four	rt.: noose/snare, abhaya mu. lt.: arrow(?), noose/snare	mature	two	virasena	bodh. ornaments, va.: lotus throne	Dhvajagra(?) (Buddha)
one/two	four	prin.: at chest in vitarka mu. rt.: abhaya mu. lt.: flower	youth	two	vajra	bodh. ornaments, va.: lotus throne	Jayada-(fo-mu)
one/two	four	rt.: ritual chopper, shield lt.: human skull-cup, cymbal	youth	two	vamalalita	bodh. ornaments, va.: lotus throne	Li-shih t'ien
one/two	four	prin.: anjali mu. rt.: flaming jewels lt.: lotus	youth	two	sopasraya	bodh. ornaments, va.: lotus throne	Manidharin
one/two	four	rt.: vitarka, ritual choppper lt.: human skull-cup, axe	youth	two	vajra	bodh. ornaments, va.: lotus throne	Mantranudharani (fo-mu)
one/two	four	rt.: (?), flaming jewel lt.: flower, vase/vessel	youth	two	sattva	bodh. ornaments, va.: lotus throne	Marasudana-Tara
one/two	four	rt.: sword, thunderbolt lt.: bell, human skull-cup	youth	two	ardha-paryankha	bodh. ornaments, va.: lotus throne	Ragavajra
one/two	four	rt.: serpent/snake, moon disc lt.: trident, magic dagger	mature	two		bodh. ornaments, va.: mule	Rang-byung-lHa-mo
one/two	four	rt.: (?), thunderbolt lt.: bell, (?)	mature	two	sopasraya	bodh. ornaments, va.: lotus throne	Sakra (deva)
one/two	four	prin.: hold goad/hook crossed over head rt.: varada mu. lt.: stem of lotus with book/manuscript	mature	two	sopasraya	bodh. ornaments, va.: bird (garuda?)	Samkusumita-Tara
one/two	four	prin.: anjali mu. over the head rt.: sword lt.: lotus stem in karitari mu.	mature	two	vamalalita	bodh. ornaments, va.: lotus throne	Sokavinodana-Tara

one/two	four	rt.: sword, thunderbolt lt.: noose/snare, tarjani mu.	youth	two	sopasraya	bodh. ornaments, va.: lotus throne	Trailokyavijaya-Tara
one/two	four	rt.: abhaya mu., rosary lt.: cylindrical banner, vase/vessel	youth	two	vajra	bodh. ornaments, va.: lotus throne	Usnisa-Tara
one/two	four	rt.: rosary, varada mu. lt.: staff/stick, vase/vessel	youth	two	paryanka	bodh. ornaments, va.: lotus throne	Usnisvijaya-Tara
one/two	four	rt.: thunderbolt, short lance lt.: noose/snare, human skull-cup	youth	two	ardha-paryankha	bodh. ornaments, va.: lotus throne	Vajrabimba
one/two	four	rt.: arrow, goad/hook lt.: bow, human skull-cup	youth	two	ardha-paryankha	bodh. ornaments, va.: lotus throne	Vajraraudri
one/two	four	rt.: skull-topped staff/stick, goad/hook lt.: trident topped magic staff/stick, human skull-cup	youth	two	ardha-paryankha	bodh. ornaments, va.: lotus throne	Vajrasaumya
one/two	four	rt.: lance, conch shell lt.: wheel, human skull-cup	youth	two	ardha-paryanka	bodh. ornaments, va.: lotus throne	Vagvajra
one/two	four	prin.: conch and wheel rt.: hammer/mace lt.: bow	youth	two		bodh. ornaments, va.: lotus throne	Vishnu
one/two	four	rt.: baton-like staff/stick, wheel lt.: flaming jewels, conch shell	youth	two	vajra	bodh. ornaments, va.: garuda	Vishnu-Upendra
one/two	four	rt.: thunderbolt, sword lt.: abhaya mu., noose/snare	youth	two	vajra	bodh. ornaments, va.: lotus throne	Vijaya-Tara
one/two	four	rt.: jewels(?), noose/snare lt.: wish fulfilling jewel, (?)	youth	two	sopasraya	bodh. ornaments, va.: lotus throne	Varuna (deva)
one/two	four	rt.: sword, (?) lt.: noose/snare, chain	youth	two	sopasraya	bodh. ornaments, va.: lotus throne	Yo-chu t'ien
one/two	six	rt.: thunderbolt, karana, simha-karna mu. lt.: flower, sword, karana mu.	mature	two	vama-lalita	bodh. ornaments, va.: lotus throne	Anangavajra (Bodhisattva)
one/two	six	rt.: rosary, triple jewels(?), abhaya mu.(?) lt.: vase/vessel, stem of lotus, baton/mace	youth	two	vajra	bodh. ornaments, va.: lotus throne	Mahasanti-Tara

one/two	six	rt.: rosary, varada mu., short staff/stick lt.: lotus, vase/vessel, shallow bowl	youth	two	vajra	bodh. ornaments, va.: lotus throne	Mahasanti-Tara
one/two	six	rt.: sword, axe, in abhaya mu. lt.: lotus, trident, noose/snare	mature	two	sattva	bodh. ornaments, va.: lotus throne	Pratyangira
one/two	six	rt.: sword, arrow, abhaya mu. lt.: vase/vesse, bow, karana mu.	mature	two	vajra	bodh. ornaments, va.: lotus throne	Sahasrapramardani (fo-mu)
one/two	six	rt.: rosary, goad/hook, abhaya mu. lt.: flower, (?), flower	mature	two	sattva	bodh. ornaments, va.: lotus throne	Sokavinodana-Tara
one/two	six	rt.: rosary, thunderbolt, abhaya mu. lt.: human skull-cup, noose/snare, vase/vessel	youth	two	bhadra	bodh. ornaments, va.: lotus throne	Utnauti(?)-Lokesvara
one/two	six	prin.: thunderbolt in uttarabodhi mu rt.: rosary, arrow lt.: wheel, bow	youth	two	vajra	bodh. ornaments, va.: lotus throne	Vajradhatu (Buddha)
one/two	eight	rt.: thunderbolt, trident, goad/hook, sword lt.: fruit(?), triden, short staff/stick, vase/vessel	youth	two	vajra	bodh. ornaments, va.: lotus throne	Mangalaloka-Tara
one/two	eight	rt.: staff/stick, goad/hook, thunderbolt, sword(?) lt.: triple jewels, noose/snare, baton/mace, vase/vessel	youth	two	vajra	bodh. ornaments, va.: lotus throne	Mangalotpadana-Tara
one/two	eight	prin.: over head in karana mu. rt. arrow, wheel, sword lt.: bow, conch shell, noose/snare	mature	two	vajra	bodh. ornaments, va.: lotus throne	Pravira(?)-Tara
one/two	eight	rt.: thunderbolt, arrow, wheel, sword lt.: thunderbolt, bow, jewel, noose/snare	mature	two	vamalalita	bodh. ornaments, va.: lotus throne	Pravira(?)-Tara (fo-mu)
one/two	ten	rt.: rosary, sword, arrow, goad/hook, varada mu. lt.: noose/snare, (?), bow, tarjani(?) mu., bell	youth	two	vajra	bodh. ornaments, va.: lotus throne	Kanakavarna-Tara
one/two	ten	rt.: karana mu., trident, thunderbolt, arrow, sword lt.: (?), bow, bell, lotus, noose/snare	youth	two	vajra	bodh. ornaments, va.: lotus throne	Kanakavarna-Tara
one/two	12	holding tantric symbols	youth	two	sama-	bodh. ornaments,	Srivadirat (Bodhisattva)

					bhanga	va.: lotus throne	
one/two	18	all hands hold lotus va.: lotus throne	youth	two	vajra	bodh. ornaments,	Astadasabhuja-Padmanartesvara
one/two	22	prin.: namaskara mu. with thunderbolt and bell other hands hold tantric symbols	youth	two	lalita	bodh. ornaments, va.: lotus throne	Caturvimsatibhuja-Ekajata (devi)
one/three	two	rt.: jewel lt.: vase/vessel	youth	two	vamalalita	bodh. ornaments, va.: lotus throne	Bahya-sadhana-Zhan-blon-rdo-rje-Marajit
one/three	two	rt.: varada mu. lt.: stem of lotus	youth	two	sama-bhanga	bodh. ornaments, va.: lotus throne	Bhattarika-Kapala-Tara
one/three	two	rt.: sword-like staff/stick lt.: shallow bowl filled with jewels	youth	two	astride	bodh. ornaments, va.: feline-like animal	Kirtirajavajra
one/three	two	rt.: magic divination arrow lt.: book/manuscript	youth	two	astride	long loose robe, bodh. ornaments, va.: lotus throne	sKyon-btsun-de-mo
one/three	four	prin.: embrace shakti in vajrahumkara mu. rt.: trident lt.: human skull-cup	youth	two	vamalalita, yab-yum	bodh. ornaments, va.: bull	Isana
three/six	four	prin.: vajrahumkara mu. rt.: arrow (?) lt.: bow	youth	two	vajra, yab-yum	bodh. ornaments, va.: lotus throne	Yogambara (Buddha)
three/six	six	prin.: dharmachakra mu. rt.: thunderbolt, arrow lt.: lotus, bow	youth	two	vajra	bodh. ornaments, va.: lotus throne	Grahamatrika
three/six	six	prin.: dharmachakra mu. rt.: lotus, three jewels lt.: noose/snare, staff/stick baton(?)	youth	two	vajra	bodh. ornaments, va.: lotus throne	Grahamatrika
three/six	six	rt.: sword, trident, (?) lt.: goad/hook, human skull-cup, mongoose	youth	two	vajra	bodh. ornaments, va.: lotus throne	Kruddha-kali-Tara
three/six	six	rt.: triple jewels, baton/mace, thunderbolt lt.: flat bowl of jewels, noose/snare, knife(?)	mature	two	alidha	bodh. ornaments, va.: prostrate human bodies	Sadbhuja-Jambhala

three/six	six	prin.: hold (?) at chest level rt.: thunderbolt, wheel lt.: three flaming jewels, sword	youth	two	vajra	bodh. ornaments, va.: lotus throne	Vajragandha (fo-mu)
three/six	six	prin.: sun disc rt.: thunderbolt, branch lt.: sword, three jewels(?)	mature	two	vajra	bodh. ornaments, va.: lotus throne	Vajrarupa (fo-mu)
three/six	eight	rt.: thunderbolt, arrow, conch shell, abhaya mu. lt.: lotus, bow, (?), noose/snare	youth	two	vajra	bodh. ornaments, va.: lotus throne	Astabhuja-Vajratara (fo-mu)
three/six	eight	rt.: flaming jewels, trident tipped baton/mace, arrow, thunderbolt lt.: karana mu., bow, noose/snare goad/hook	youth	two	vamalalita	bodh. ornaments, va.: lotus throne	Pratisara (fo-mu)
three/six	eight	rt.: Buddha image, goad/hook, abhaya mu., crossed thunderbolts lt.: abhaya mu., bow, vase/vessel, karana mu.	youth	two	vajra	bodh. ornaments, va.: lotus throne	Vijaya (fo-mu)
three/six	eight	prin.: crossed thunderbolts rt.: Buddha image, arrow, abhaya mu. lt.: abhaya mu., dhyana mu., bow	youth	two	vajra	bodh. ornaments, va.: lotus throne	Vijaya (fo-mu)
three/6-9	ten	holding tantric symbols	youth	two	vamalalita	bodh. ornaments, va.: lotus throne	Pancatmaka-Pratisara
three/nine	six	prin.: vajrahumkara mu. with thunderbolt, bell rt.: conch, sword lt.: skull-cup, bow	youth	two	sattva	bodh. ornaments, va.: lotus throne	Vajra-Catuhpitha
three/nine	six	prin.: vitarka mu. at chest rt.: thunderbolt, arrow lt.: lotus, bow	youth	two	vajra	bodh. ornaments, va.: lotus throne	Vidyarajni-Grahamatrka
three/nine	eight	prin.: crossed thunderbolts rt.: Buddha image, arrow, varada mu. lt.: abhaya mu., vase/vessel, bow	youth	two	vajra	bodh. ornaments, va.: lotus throne	Vijaya (fo-mu)
three/nine	12	prin.: embrace shakti others: tantric symbols	mature	two	alidha, yab-yum	bodh. ornaments, va.: lotus throne	Pancabuddha-Samvararaja (Buddha)
three/nine	20	prin.: embrace shakti	mature	two	alidha,	bodh. ornaments,	Chakradhararaja (Buddha)

		rt. & lt.: tantric symbols			yab-yum	va.: subdued deities	
four/eight	two	wheel	youth	two	sama-bhanga	bodh. ornaments, va.: lotus throne	Brahman
four/eight	two	holding conch shell	youth	two	kneeling	bodh. ornaments, va.: lotus throne	Devendra-Satakratu
four/eight	eight	rt.: word, wheel, baton/mace, arrow lt.: noose/snare, axe, bow, karana mu.	mature	two	vamalalita	bodh. ornaments, va.: lotus throne	Pratisara (fo-mu)
four/eight	eight	prin.: vajrahumkara mu. rt.: sword, short staff/stick, arrow lt.: bow, noose/snare, thunderbolt	youth	two	alidha	bodh. ornaments, va.: lotus throne	Trailokyaraja
four/eight	12	rt.: flaming jewel, thunderbolt, arrow, sword, varada mu., (?) lt.: (?), noose/snare (pasha, zhags-pa), trident, bow,, axe, conch	mature	two	vajra	bodh. ornaments, va.: lotus throne	Pratisara
five/ten	eight	prin.: dharmachakra mu. rt.: sword, arrow, thunderbolt lt.: bow, bell, dhyana mu.	youth	two	vajra	bodh. ornaments,	Astabhuja-Dharmadhatu-vagisvara-Manjughosa
seven/14	16	prin.: karana mu. at chest other hands hold tantric symbols	mature	two	alidha	bodh. ornaments, va.: lotus throne	Sarvarthasadhana-Tara (fo-mu)

Other Deities:

one/two	two	rt.: lance lt.: mongoose	mature	two	astride	rich military garb, va.: horse	Atavaka
one/two	two	rt.: sword lt.: mongoose	corp	two	astride	fancy helmet, princely cuirass, bejeweled, va.: horse	Bijakundalin
one*/two	two	rt.: red lance lt.: flat bowl	mature	two		mitered hat monastic robed, jeweled necklace	bDud-btsan-dpa'-bo-hum-ri
one*/two	two	rt.: alarm staff/stick (Jizo's Staff) lt.: flat bowl	mature	two		mitered hat monastic robed,	bDud-btsan-dpa'-bo-hum-ri

							jeweled necklace	
one/two	two	rt.: jewel lt.: mongoose and embraces shakti	mature	two	vamalalita, yab-yum	bodh. ornaments, va.: lotus throne	Ekavira-sadhana-vinirgata-Bahudeva-Jambhala
one/two	two	rt.: varada lt.: abhaya mu. at chest level	mature	two	rajalila	monastic robed, va.: guru cushion	Katyayana**
one/two	two	rt.: cylindrical banner/flag lt.: treasure producing mongoose	corp	two	alidha	armored torso, loose jacket with full pants, bodh. ornaments, va.: lotus throne	Maharaja-Vaisravana
one/two	two	vase/vessel	mature	*		*coils of a snake rather than legs, serpents around halo, bodh. ornaments, va.: sea waves	Nanda-Nagaraja
one/two	two	holds serpent/snake	mature	*		*coils of a snake rather than legs, serpents around halo, bodh. ornaments, va.: sea waves	Nanda-Nagaraja
one/two	two	rt.: sword lt.: abhaya mu.	youth	two	sattva	bejeweled, va.: lotus throne	Raksasa
one/two	two	rt.: human thigh-bone trumpet lt.: human skull-drum	mature	two	raja-paryanka	yogi robes, va.: tiger skin	rGyal-po-grub-dbang-chen-po
one/two	two	rt.: lance lt.: wheel	corp.	two	maha-rajalila	bodh. ornaments, va.: raised throne	Rudra-Cakrin
one/two	two	rt.: wavy-bladed knife lt.: mongoose	mature	two		richly helmeted, flowing garments, va.: horse	Samjneya
one/three	two	rt.: stem of lotus with bell lt.: stem of lotus with thunderbolt	mature, nude	two	vajra, yab-yum	no ornaments, va.: lotus throne	Sahaja-Go-bzlog
three*/six	six	rt.: lotus, flaming jewels and sword lt.: vase/vessel, axe and jewel	mature, nude	four	alidha	*rt. head: pig, cent. head: elephant. lt. head: human,	Ajna-vinivarta-Ganapati

va.: goddess on lotus throne

Wrathful, Angry or Haughty Deities: Color not Designated in Sources

Abbreviations:

as. = asana	bk. = black	bl. = blue	bodh. = bodhisattva
bn. = brown	corp. = corpulent	dhar. = dharmapala	gn. = green
lt. = left	mu. = mudra	pu. = purple	rd. = red
rt. = right	sc. = smokey	va. = vahana	wh. = white
yw. = yellow			

(*) special variations or attributes noted within the entry.
(**) following deity's name indicates that the color is not noted in the source, kulesa's color is applied to the entry.
(eyes: 2-3, 6-9, etc.) in sources the deity's faces are noted, but the number of the eyes are not noted.

Dharmapala:

Head/Eyes	Hands	Objects Held	Body	Feet	Asana	Other Attributes	Deity Name
one/one	two	holds iron ritual chopper	mature	two		single hair, dhar. ornaments, va.: iron mule	Srog-bdag-rgyal-chen
one*/two	two	rt.: axe lt.: mongoose	mature	two	lalita	*angry dhar. ornaments, va.: lotus throne	Badidar-a
one*/two	two	rt.: thigh-bone trumpet lt.: human skull-cup	mature	two	kneeling	*angry, long white beard, dhar. ornaments, va.: human form	Bram-zehi
one*/two	two	rt.: thigh-bone trumpet lt.: rosary	mature	two	kneeling	*angry long white beard, dhar. ornaments, va.: human form	Bram-zehi
one*/two	two	rt.: noose/snare lt.: mongoose	corp.	two	vamalalita	*angry bodh. ornaments, va.: human forms	Chen-ta-lo (mahayaksasenapati)
one*/two	two	rt.: cane-like staff/stick lt.: crystal rosary	mature	two		*slightly angry, lama-like dress,	Chu-rgyud-dge-bsnyen

						dhar. ornaments	
one*/two	two	rt.: human skull-drum lt.: bell	youth	two	ardha-paryanka	*calm face, dhar. ornaments, va.: lotus throne	Ekamatrka
one*/two	two	rt.: karana mu. lt.: wish-fulfilling jewel	youth	two	sattva	*angry, bodh. ornaments, va.: lotus throne	Lieh-k'o-ta-ch'ia t'ien
one*/two	two	rt.: ritual chopper lt.: human skull-cup with magic notched staff/stick in crook of arm	youth	two	alidha	*calm, dhar. ornaments, va.: prostrate human figures on lotus throne	Mahasukha-Dakini-mata
one*/two	two	rt.: jewel-topped staff/stick lt.: mongoose	mature	two	lalita	*angry, dhar. ornaments, va.: lotus throne	Sedkiku-yi barigci
one*/two	two	rt.: sword lt.: mongoose	corp.	two	vamalalita	*angry, dhar. ornaments, va.: lotus throne	So-ni-lo (mahayaksasenapati)
one/two	two	rt.: thunderbolt lt.: (?)	corp.	two	alidha	bodh. ornaments, va.: lotus throne	Sri-Ucarya-Vajrapani**
one*/two	two	rt.: wheel lt.: mongoose	corp	two	vamalalita	*angry, dhar. ornaments, va.: lotus throne	P'i-chieh-lo (mahayaksasenapati)
one*/two	two	rt.: trident lt.: mongoose	mature	two	lalita	*angry, dhar. ornaments, va.: lotus throne	Vatadhara (?)
one*/two	four	rt.: ritual chopper and sword lt.: human skull-cup and magic notched staff/stick	youth, nude	two	ardha-paryanka	*animal-form head dhar. ornaments, va.: disc on human forms	Bhattarika-Kapalini(?)
one*/2-3	two	wheel	mature	two	alidha	*lion head dhar. ornaments, va.: lotus throne	Chakradhara (?)
one*/2-3	two	rt.: sword lt.: mongoose	corp.	two	vamalalita	dhar. ornaments, va.: human forms	Chu-tu-lo (mahayaksasenapati)
one*/2-3	two	rt.: jewel-topped staff/stick	mature	two	lalita	*angry,	Cimeg-i barigci

		lt.: mongoose				dhar. ornaments, va.: lotus throne	
one/2-3	two	rt.: ritual chopper lt.: human skull-cup	youth	two	ardha-paryanka	bodh. ornaments va.: lotus throne	Karkata
one/three	two	rt.: sword, lt.: goad/hook	mature	two	ardhapary-akana	dhar. ornaments, va.: lotus throne	**Ajinai cogtu**
one/three	two	rt.: ritual chopper lt.: human skull-cup, with tantric staff/stick in crook of arm	corp.	two	partyalidha	dhar. ornaments, va.: human forms	Ajita-Mahakala
one/ three	two	rt.: ritual chopper lt.: human skull-cup	aged	two	astride	dhar. ornaments, pendulous breasts, va.: horse	Akasambara
one/three	two	rt.: thunderbolt lt.: bell	corp.	two	alidha	dhar. ornaments, va.: lotus throne	Amoghatrana(?)-Vajrapani
one/three	two	rt.: thunderbolt lt.: noose/snare	corp.	two	alidha	dhar. ornaments, va.: lotus throne	Alpacanda-Vajrapani
one/three	two	rt.: crossed thunderbolts	corp.	two	ardhapar-yanka	dhar. ornaments, va.: human form	Amritakundalin
one/three	two	rt.: knife lt.: fly whisk	corp.	two	alidha	dhar. ornaments, va.: lotus throne	Angaraka
one/three	two	rt.: ritual chopper lt.: human skull-cup	corp	two	alidha	dhar. ornaments, va.: human form	Antara-Sadhana Dharmaraja
one/ three	two	rt.: ritual chopper lt.: human skull-cup	corp	two	alidha	dhar. ornaments, va.: human form	Antara-sadhana Yamaraja
one/three	two	rt.: trident lt.: human skull-cup	corp.	two	lalita	dhar. ornaments, companion by lt. knee, va.: human forms	Antara-sadhana-Zhan-blon-rdo-rje-Marajit
one/three	two	rt.:human skull-drum lt.: magic notched stick	youth	two	ardhapar-yanka	dhar. ornaments, va.: lotus throne	Anucara-Karma-dakini
one/three	two	rt.: ritual chopper lt.: human skull-cup	mature, nude	two	ardhapar-yanka	dhar. ornaments, human form	Anucara-Nagi-karmakari
one/three	two	human skull-drum lt.: magic notched staff/stick	youth, nude	two	ardhapar-yanka	dhar. ornaments, va.: lotus throne	Anucara-Padma-dakini

one/three	two	rt.: human skull-drum lt.: magic notched staff/stick	youth	two	ardhapar- yanka	dhar. ornaments, va.: lotus throne	Anucara-Ratna-dakini
one/three	two	human skull-drum lt.: magic notched staff/stick	youth, nude	two	ardhapar- yanka	dhar. ornaments, va.: lotus throne	Anucara-Vajra-dakini
one/three	two	rt.: ritual chopper lt.: human skull-cup	mature, nude	two	ardhapar- yanka	dhar. ornaments, va.: human forms	Anucara-Vajra-karmakari
one*/three	two	rt.: ritual chopper lt.: human skull-cup	youth	two	vama- lalita	*form of pig dhar. ornaments, va.: lotus throne	Anucara-Varahi
one*/three	two	rt.: ritual chopper lt.: human skull-cup	youth, nude	two	ardhapar- yanka	*form of dog dhar. ornaments, va.: lotus throne	Anucara-Yaksa-karmakari
one*/three	two	rt.: ritual chopper lt.: human skull-cup	youth, nude	two	ardhapar- yanka	*form of dog dhar. ornaments, va.: lotus throne	Anucara-Yama-karmakari
one/ three	two	rt.: goad/hook lt.: noose/snare, staff/stick	youth	two	alidha	dhar. ornaments, va.: lotus throne	Apada-vimocani-Tara
one*/three	two	rt.: skull-topped staff/stick lt.: noose/snare	corp. nude	two	vamalalita	*bull-head, erect phallus, dhar. ornaments, va.: bull copulating with a female	Bahya-Sadhana-Yamaraja
one*/three	two	rt.: lance lt.: human skull-cup	mature	two	astride	*bull-head, loose garments, bow & quiver of arrows, dhar. ornaments, va.: horse	Bhumipala (?)
one*/three	two	rt.: ritual chopper lt.: human skull-cup	mature, nude	two	alidha	*head of boar, dhar. ornaments, va.: prostrate human forms , on lotus throne	Brahmana-sridhara-krama- Vajravahari
one/three	**two**	**rt.:** mace-like staff/stick lt.: wheel	corp.	two	alidha, yab-yum	dhar. ornaments, va.: prostrate human forms , on lotus throne	Bhagavad-Bhayanasana
one/three	two	rt.: short staff/stick	corp.	two	astride	dhar. ornaments,	bSe-khrab-can

		lt.: noose/snare around the neck of a human fig.				loose garments, fancy leather boots, va.: horse	
one/three	two	rt.: sword lt.: human skull-drum	mature	two	lalita	dhar. ornaments, long flowing garments, va.: lotus throne	Bugr-a-kala
one/three	two	crystal thunderbolt	mature, nude	two		dhar. ornaments, va.: blue horse with black back	Bya-khri-mig-gcig-ma
one/three	two	rt.: trident lt.: human skull-cup	mature, nude,	two	ardha-paryanka	dhar. ornaments, pendulous breasts, va.: lotus throne	Camundi
one/three	two	noose/snare	mature, nude	two	alidha	dhar. ornaments, va.: human forms	Cauri (fo-mu)
one/three	two	rt.: thunderbolt lt.: fly-whisk (?)	corp.	two	alidha	dhar. ornaments, va.: human forms	Ch'a-sang
one/three	two	rt.: ritual chopper lt.: human skull-cup	mature	two	vira	dhar. ornaments, va.: garuda-like bird	Chiang-lin yo-mu
one/three	two	vajrahumkara mu.	youth, nude	two	alidha	dhar. ornaments, va.: human forms	Chiao-wan-shou-yin (fo-mu)
one/three	two	rt.: serpent/snake lt.: vitarka mu.	mature, nude	two	alidha	dhar. ornaments, va.: human forms	Ch'ih-ch'ien (fo-mu)
one/three	two	large pestle(?)	mature, nude	two	alidha	dhar. ornaments, va.: human forms	Ch'ih-kuan (fo-mu)
one/three	two	rt.: human skull-cup lt.: ritual chopper	mature	two	virasena	dhar. ornaments, va.: garuda-like bird	Damstradhara-(yo-mu)
one/three	two	rt.: human skull-cup lt.: ritual chopper	mature	two	virasena	dhar. ornaments, va.: garuda-like bird	Dandadhara (yo-mu)
one/three	two	holding (?)	youth, nude	two	alidha	bejeweled, garland of human heads va.: human body on lotus throne	Dharmadhatu (fo-mu)
one/three	two	rt.: thunderbolt lt.: tarjani mu.	corp.	two	alidha	dhar. ornaments, va.: lotus throne	Divasanta-ratrikruddha-Tara

one/three	two	rt.: baton/mace lt.: human skull-cup	corp.	two	lalita	dhar. ornaments, va.: horse	Dvibhuja-srimati-Devi
one/three	two	holding length of chain	mature, nude, pendulous breasts	two	ardha- paryanka	dhar. ornaments, va.: lotus throne	Ekajati
one/three	two	rt.: wheel lt.: fly whisk	corp.	two	alidha	dhar. ornaments, va.: lotus throne	Fa-chiu-ku yo-chu
one/three	two	rt.: karana mu. lt.: abhaya mu.	mature, nude	two	alidha	dhar. ornaments, va.: prostrate human form	Gauri (fo-mu)
one/three	two	rt.: horn of antelope lt.: bell	mature	two		dhar. ornaments, va.: white horse	gTsod-rva-can
one/three	two	rt.: ritual chopper lt.: human skull-cup	mature, nude	two	ardha- paryanka	dhar. ornaments, va.: lotus throne	Guhya-Dakini
one*/three	two	rt.: (?) lt.: human skull-cup	corp., nude	two	ardha- paryanka	*bull-head, erect phallus, dhar. ornaments, va.: bull	Guhya-Sadhana-Yamaraja
one*/three	two	rt.: staff/stick topped with goad/hook lt.: karana mu.	mature, nude	two	ardha- paryanka	pendulous breast, dhar. ornaments, va.: lotus throne	Guhyesvari
one/three	two	rt.: vajra topped staff/stick lt.: noose/snare	mature	two	ardha- paryka	dhar. ornaments, va.: lotus throne	Gunakara
one/three	two	rt.: flaming sword lt.: noose/snare, lance in crook of arm	mature	two	astride	golden harness, dhar. ornaments, va.: red horse with white heels	Gyang-rje-btsan-po
one/three	two	rt.: sword lt.: bell	corp.	two	alidha	dhar. ornaments, va.: lotus throne	Hu-mo-chin-kang
one/three	two	holding stringed instrument	mature, nude	two	alidha	dhar. ornaments, va.: lotus throne	Jalinidhara(?) (fo-mu)
one/three	two	rt.: thunderbolt lt.: human skull-cup filled with blood	corp	two	alidha	dhar. ornaments, va.: prostrate human	Jvalanala(?) (Buddha)

						form	
one/three	two	rt.: ritual chopper(?) lt.: human skull-cup	corp.	two	rajalila	dhar. ornaments, va.: garuda-like bird	Kaladhvaja(?)-(yo-mu)
one/three	two	rt.: dice lt.: human skull-cup	mature	two	vamalalita	pendulous breasts, dhar. ornaments, va.: crane-like bird	Kalaratri
one/three	two	rt.: knife lt.: tarjani mu.	corp.	two	alidha	dhar. ornaments, va.: lotus throne	Kala-Yaksa
one/three	two	rt.: ritual chopper lt.: human skull-cup, magic notched staff/stick in crook of arm	youth	two	ardha-paryka	dhar. ornaments, va.: prostrate human forms on lotus throne	Kali Kruddha Varahi
one/three	two	rt.: staff/stick capped with thunderbolt lt.: human skull-cup	mature, nude	two	sattva	dhar. ornaments, va.: human skin on mule	Kamadhatvishvari Parvati
one/three	two	rt.: sword lt.: sack of diseases	corp.	two	vamalalita	dhar. ornaments, va.: horse	Kamesvari
one*/three	two	rt.: tantric staff/stick lt.: flat bowl of jewels with trident tipped magic notched staff/stick in crook of arm	corp.	two	ardha-paryanka	*lion-head, dhar. ornaments, va.: prostrate human form	Karma-simhasya
one/three	two	rt.: ritual chopper lt.: human skull-cup	mature	two	ardha-paryanka	dhar. ornaments, va.: lotus throne	Kauveri
one/three	two	rt.: sword lt.: an-i-in mu.	mature	two	alidha	dhar. ornaments, va.: lotus throne	Khadgadhara-Bhairavavajra
one/three	two	rt.: staff/stick lt.: mongoose	mature	two		long loose garments, dhar. ornaments, va.: lotus throne	Khadgapani
one/three	two	rt.: thunderbolt lt.: noose/snare and embraces shakti	corp.	two	alidha, yab-yum	dhar. ornaments, va.: lotus throne supported by human figures	Krodha-Guhyapati
one/three	two	rt.: thunderbolt lt.: rests on thigh, palm up holding (?)	corp.	two	vamalalita	dhar. ornaments, va.: lotus throne	Kumbhira yao-ch'a-ta-chiang
one/three	two	rt.: abhaya mu.	mature,	two	alidha	dhar. ornaments,	Kuncikadhara (fo-mu)

		lt.: (?)	nude			va.: prostrate human figure	
one/three	two	rt.: ritual chopper lt.: human skull-cup	mature, nude	two		dhar. ornaments, left leg is held in the crook of the left arm, va.: prostrate human figure	Kurmapadi-Vahari
one/three	two	rt.: lance lt.: noose/snare	mature	two	astride	dhar. ornaments, va.: horse	lHa-chen-zangs-rva
one/three	two	rt.: banner/flagof black silk lt.: black noose/snare	mature	two	astride	black cloak, va.: black horse	lHa-sa'i-bdud-btsan-mthu-bo-che
one/three	two	rt. lance lt.: bell	corp.	two	alidha	bodh. ornaments, va.: lotus throne	Ling-shen-t'iao-fu-chin-kang
one/three	two	rt.: ritual chopper lt.: human skull-cup with magic notched staff/stick in crook of arm	youth	two	ardha-paryka	bodh. ornaments, va.: prostrate human figure	Loka-dakini
one/three	two	rt.: sword lt.: karana mu.	mature	two	partyalidha	dhar. ornaments, va.: lotus throne	Mahakarmesvara
one/three	two	noose/snare in anjali mu., sword rests in crook of right arm	mature	two	lalita	dhar. ornaments, va.: lotus throne	Mahakrodha
one/three	two	rt.: flaming jewels lt.: goad/hook	corp.	two	partyalidha	horse-head in hair, dhar. ornaments, va.: lotus throne	Maharatnesvara
one/three	two	rt.: thunderbolt lt.: karana mu.	corp.	two	alidha	dhar. ornaments, va.: lotus throne	Mahasukha (Buddha)
one/three	two	rt.: thunderbolt lt.: bell	mature	two	alidha	dhar. ornaments, va.: lotus throne	Mahosthavajra
one/three	two	rt.: ritual chopper lt.: human skull-cup	mature, nude	two	*	*right leg bent, left leg kicked and held in crook of arm, dhar. ornaments, va.: lotus throne	Maitri-Dakini
one/three	two	holds necklace or jeweled cord	youth	two	alidha	dhar. ornaments,	Malya

						va.: lotus throne	
one/three	two	rt.: flaming jewels lt.: (?)	mature	two	alidha	dhar. ornaments, va.: lotus throne	Matsarya-Bhairavavajra
one/three	two	rt.: rosary lt.: lance	mature	two		dhar. ornaments, va.: blue horse	Me-thar
one/three	two	rt.: flaming hammer lt.: bellows	mature	two		dhar. ornaments, va.: goat	mGar-nag
one/three	two	rt.: ritual chopper lt.: human skull-cup	mature	two		dhar. ornaments, va.: lotus throne	mGon-bdud-bya-rog-gdong-can
one/three	two	rt.: white ya-tsha lt.: lance	mature	two		dhar. ornaments, va.: white horse	mGon-po-jag-lha
one/three	two	rt.: baton/mace lt.: rests on thigh, palm up holding (?)	mature	two	vamalalita	dhar. ornaments, va.: lotus throne	Mi-ch'i-lo yao-ch'a-ta-chiang
one/three	two	rt.: sword lt.: human skull-cup	mature	two	ardha- paryanka	dhar. ornaments, va.: lotus throne	Mithuna
one/three	two	rt.: holds golden razor lt.: moon disc	mature	two		red pointed braids, dhar. ornaments, va.: lotus throne	Nag-mo-gnod-sbyin
one/three	two	rt.: lance lt.: human skull-cup	mature	two	alidha	dhar. ornaments, va.: clouds	Navajatimdhara
one/three	two	rt.: victory banner/flag lt.: mongoose	corp.	two	lalita	dhar. ornaments, va.: lion	Navatmaka-Mahapita-Vaisravana
one/three	two	rt.: branch lt.: bell	corp.	two	alidha	dhar. ornaments, va.: lotus throne	Neng-huai-wu-yen-chin-kang
one/three	two	prin.: embrace shakti in bhutadamara mu. rt.: thunderbolt lt.: staff/stick	corp.	two	alidha, yab-yum	dhar. ornaments, va.: lotus throne	Neng-sheng-mo-chang-chin-kang
one/three	two	rt.: sword lt.: bowl	mature	two	astride	dhar. ornaments, human skin-cape, va.: horse trodding on prostrate human figure	Nilesvari

one/three	two	rt.: ritual chopper lt.: human skull-cup	corp.	two	vamalalita	dhar. ornaments, va.: crawling female form	<u>Nirrti-Raksasa</u>
one/three	two	rt.: sword in human skull-cup lt.: mongoose	mature	two		dhar. ornaments, va.: lotus throne	<u>Nor-'dzin-rgyal-mo-rab-brtan-ma</u>
one/three	two	rt.: magic notched staff/stick lt.: tarjani mu. shining ring above	mature	two	vira	dhar. ornaments, va.: antelope skin	<u>Padmasambhava</u>
one/three	two	rt.: thunderbolt lt.: magic dagger	mature	two	alidha	curled hair, bejeweled, loose garment, va.: tiger	<u>Padmasambhava</u>
one/three	two	rt.: thunderbolt lt.: tarjani mu.	mature	two	alidha	dhar. ornaments, va.: prostrate human forms	<u>Padmasambhava</u>
one/three	two	rt.: an-i-in mu lt.: lotus	corp.	two	alidha	dhar. ornaments, va.: lotus throne	<u>Padmadhara-Bhairavavajra</u>
one/three	two	holds lotus	mature, nude	two	alidha	dhar. ornaments, va.: human form	<u>Padmadhara (fo-mu)</u>
one*/three	two	rt.: vase/vessel rt.: vase/vessel, trident tipped magic notched staff/stick in crook of arm	corp.	two	ardha- paryanka	*lion-head, dhar. ornaments, va.: prostrate human figure	<u>Padma-simhasya</u>
one/three	two	rt.: ritual chopper lt.: human skull-cup	mature	two	rajalalia	dhar. ornaments, va.: serpent/snake	<u>Pasadhara (yo-mu)</u>
one/three	two	rt.: thunderbolt lt.: rests on thigh, palm up holding (?)	corp.	two	vamalalita	dhar. ornaments, va.: lotus throne	<u>Po-ch'ai-lo yao-ch'a-ta-chiang</u>
one/three	two	rt.: goad/hook lt.: mongoose	corp.	two	vamalalita	dhar. ornaments, va.: lotus throne	<u>Po-hu-lo (mahayaksasenapati)</u>
one/three	two	rt.: thunderbolt lt.: human skull-cup, magic staff/stick in crook of arm	mature, nude	two	ardha- paryka	dhar. ornaments, va.: prostrate human figure	<u>Prajnalokakrtya</u>
one/three	two	rt.: shrine lt.: serpent/snake	mature	two	alidha	dhar. ornaments, va.: prostrate human figures	<u>Prajnapani</u>

one*/two	two	rt.: cylindrical banner/flag lt.: mongoose	corp.	two	lalita	*angry, dhar. ornaments, va.: lotus throne	Prakama-sri-dada-Vaisravana
one*/three	two	bow and arrow of leaves and flowers	corp.	two	alidha	*bull-head, dhar. ornaments, va.: bull copulating with human	Pratyalidha-Bhairavavajra
one/three	two	holding vase/vessel	mature, nude	two	alidha	dhar. ornaments, va.: human form	Pukkasi (fo-mu)
one/three	two	rt.: (?) lt.: axe	mature, nude	two	alidha	dhar. ornaments, va.: human form	Pu-lun tsu-shih
one/three	two	rt.: sword lt.: lotus bud	corp.	two	alidha	dhar. ornaments, va.: lotus throne	Qar-a bagr-a
one/three	two	rt.: sun disc lt.: moon disc	corp.	two	alidha	dhar. ornaments, va.: chariot drawn by horse	Rahua-(deva)
one/three	two	rt.: ritual chopper lt.: human skull-cup	corp.	two	alidha	pig(?) in hair, dhar. ornaments, va.: human forms	Ratnadaka
one/three	two	rt.: jewel lt.: human skull-cup, magic staff/stick in crook of arm	mature, nude	two	ardha-paryanka	dhar. ornaments, va.: lotus throne	Ratna-Dakini
one/three	two	rt.: jewel lt.: vase/vessel	mature, nude	two	ardha-paryanka	dhar. ornaments, va.: lotus throne	Ratna-Dakini
one*/three	two	rt.: flaming jewels lt.: serpent/snake	mature	two**		*bird-head, bird wings, **bird-like with serpent, dhar. ornaments, va.: serpent/snake	Ratna-Garuda
one*/three	two	rt.: ritual chopper lt.: human skull-cup, trident tipped magic staff/stick in crook of arm	corp.	two	ardha-paryanka	*lion-head, dhar. ornaments, va.: prostrate human figure	Ratna-simhasya
one/three	two	rt.: sword lt.: noose/snare	corp.	two		dhar. ornaments, va.: elephant	rGyal-po-grub-dbang-chen-po

one/three	two	rt.: crystal rosary lt.: copper flageolet	mature	two		dhar. ornaments, va.: gray cow	rDo-rje-sna-yon-ma
one/three	two	rt.: thunderbolt-topped staff/stick lt.: human skull-cup	corp.	two		pendulous breasts, dhar. ornaments, va.: horse	Remati
one/three	two	holds noose/snare	mature	two	alidha	pendulous breasts, loose wrap as a body covering, dhar. ornaments, va.: lotus throne	Revati
one/three	two	rt.: cane staff/stick lt.: white banner/flag	corp.	two		red-spotted cloak, dhar. ornaments, va.: black horse	Rin-po-che'i-mtshar-sdug-can
one/three	two	rt.: white staff/stick lt.: white conch shell	mature	two	astride	red spotted garment, dhar. ornaments, va.: black horse	rle'i-rgyal-po
one/three	two	rt.: baton/mace lt.: bell	mature	two	alidha	dhar. ornaments, va.: lotus throne	Sankara(?)vajra
one/three	two	rt.: staff/stick lt.: abhaya mu.	mature, nude	two	alidha	dhar. ornaments, va.: prostrate human figure	Sabari (fo-mu)
one/three	two	rt.: (?) lt.: alarm staff/stick	mature, nude	two	alidha	dhar. ornaments, va.: prostrate human figure	Sabari (fo-mu)
one/three	two	rt.: varada mu. lt.: stem of lotus in kartari mu.	youth	two	lalita	dhar. ornaments, va.: lotus throne	Sabari (Tara)
one/three	two	holding a lute	mature	two	ardha-paryanka	dhar. ornaments, va.: lotus throne	Sabdavajra
one/three	two	holding Mount Sumeru	mature	two		wears only loin cloth, va.: lotus throne	Sa-'dzin-lag-pa-chen-po
one/three	two	embraces shakti in vajrahumkara mu.	mature	two	alidha, yab-yum	dhar. ornaments, va.: prostrate human figures	Sahaja-Kalachakra
one/three	two	rt.: grasps tongue lt.: grasps heart from prostrate human	mature, nude	two	kneeling	pendulous breasts, va.: prostrate human	Sakali

		form				form	
one/three	two	rt.: flaming jewels lt.: bell	corp.	two	alidha	dhar. ornaments, va.: lotus throne	Samantadharavajra(?)
one/three	two	rt.: ritual chopper lt.: skull-cup, magic staff/stick in crook of arm	youth	two	ardha-paryanka	dhar. ornaments, va.: prostrate human figure	Samayadakini
one/three	two	rt.: thunderbolt lt.: serpent/snake	mature	two	alidha	dhar. ornaments, va.: lotus throne	Samda-biruv-a
one/three	two	rt.: sword, wheel lt.: axe, noose/snare	corp.	two	alidha	dhar. ornaments, va.: lotus throne	Samgramatarini (fo-mu)
one/three	two	rt.: shepherd-like staff/stick lt.: tarjani mu.	corp.	two	alidha	dhar. ornaments, va.: lotus throne	Sankhambara
one/three	two	rt.: sickle lt.: human skull-cup	mature, nude	two	aseat	pendulous breasts, dhar. ornaments, va.: stag	Sarad-rajni
one*/three	two	rt.: noose/snare lt.: human skull-cup	mature	two	ardha-paryankha	*leoppard-head dhar. ornaments, va.: lotus throne	Sardulavaktra
one*/three	two	rt.: ritual chopper lt.: sack of diseases	mature, nude	two	ardha-paryankha	*tiger-head, pendulous breasts, dhar. ornaments, va.: lotus throne	Sardulavaktra
one/three	two	rt.: ritual chopper lt.: human skull-cup, magic staff/stick in crook of arm	youth	two	ardha-paryankha	dhar. ornaments, va.: prostrate human figure	Sarvadakini
one/three	two	rt.: ritual chopper lt.: human skull-cup, tantric staff/stick in crook of arm	mature	two	pralam-bapada	dhar. ornaments, va.: prostrate human forms	Sarva-sasanaraksa-pradhana-Vajrapanjara
one*/three	two	rt.: skull-topped staff/stick lt.: human skull-cup	corp.	two	lalita	*parasol over head, dhar. ornaments, va.: mule or horse	Sasanaraka-pradhana-Parvati
one/three	two	rt.: crossed thunderbolt lt.: bell	corp.	two	alidha	dhar. ornaments, va.: lotus throne	Satrumjayavajra
one/three	two	rt.: magic notched staff/stick	mature	two	astride	pendulous breasts,	sGrol-byed-dpal-ldan-remadzi

		lt.: magic ball of thread				va.: camel	
one/three	two	rt.: vajra-topped staff/stick lt.: reins of horse	mature	two	astride	loose-flowing hair, loose garments, va.: horse	sGrol-gin-Yam-sud
one*/three	two	rt.: wheel lt.: human skull-cup with trident-tipped magic staff/stick	corp.	two	ardha-paryanka	*lion-head, dhar. ornaments, va.: prostrate human figure	Simhasya
one/three	two	rt.: trident lt.: staff/stick	mature	two	vamalalita	garuda flies over head, dhar. ornaments, va.: horse	Simnus-un ejen
one/three	two	rt.: ritual chopper lt.: human skull-cup	mature	two	ardha-paryanka	sagging breasts, dhar. ornaments, va.: lotus throne	Siva-Dakini
one/three	two	rt.: club/cudgel upright in his palm	mature	two	alidha	helmeted, shining armor; richly booted, va.: clouds and waves	Skandha
one/three	two	rt.: sword lt.: banner/flag	mature	two		helmeted, richly armored, va.: lotus throne	sNang-sel-khrab-gyon
one/three	two	rt.: abhaya mu. lt.: chain with orbs hanging from each ends	mature, nude	two	alidha	bone. ornaments, va.: human body	Sphotadhara (fo-mu)
one/three	two	rt.: ritual chopper lt.: (?)	mature	two	lalita	dhar. ornaments, va.: garuda-like bird	Sphotadhara(?) yo-mu
one/three	two	rt.: knife lt.: reins of horse	corp.	two	astride	loose garments, fancy boots, va.: horse	sPyan-gi-mgo-can
one/three	two	rt.: sack of diseases lt.: shallow bowl with (?)	corp.	two	alidha	dhar. ornaments, va.: prostrate human form	sPyi-sgrub-ma
one*/three	two	rt.: ritual chopper lt.: human skull-cup	corp.	two	**	*animal-head, **right leg high-kicking, dhar. ornaments, va.: prostrate human	Srgala-mukha-Pisaca

form

one/three	two	rt.: sword lt.: human skull-cup	mature	two	ardha-paryankha	loose garment, dhar. ornaments, va.: prostrate human form	Srikantha
one/three	two	rt.: thunderbolt lt.: bell	corp.	two	partyalidha	dhar. ornaments, va.: lotus throne	Srivajrachakra
one/three	two	rt.: ritual chopper lt.: human skull-cup	mature	two	ardha-paryanka	sagging breasts, dhar. ornaments, va.: lotus throne	Srnkhala-Dakini
one/three	two	holds dagger/knife and is skinning the figure upon which he is standing	corop.	two	ardha-paryanka	dhar. ornaments, va.: partially skinned human figure	Srog-bdag-ko-san
one/three	two	rt.: abhaya mu. on knee lt.: held to cheek	youth	two	sopasraya	dhar. ornaments, va.: lotus throne	Su-chi-i-t'ien p'u-sa
one/three	two	holds sun disc	mature, nude	two	alidha	dhar. ornaments, va.: crouched human form	Suryadhara (fo-mu)
one/three	two	rt.: be-ribboned, vajra-topped hammer lt.: (?)	mature	two	astride	loose garment, va.: goat with twisted horns	Suvajra
one/three	two	rt.: skull topped staff/stick lt.: magic staff/stick	corp.	two	ardha-paryanka	pendulous breasts, dhar. ornaments, va.: lotus throne	Tegus cogtu cing eke
one/three	two	rt.: long knife lt.: human skull-cup	mature	two		dhar. ornaments, long flowing robe, va.: lotus throne	Tegus cogtu cing mudur-tu
one/three	two	holds sack of lightning and hail	mature,	two	alidha	hair hangs to the thigh, blue silk pants, dhar. ornaments, va.: sun disc and moon disc	Thog-'phen-ma
one/three	two	rt.: (?) lt.: bell	corp.	two	alidha	dhar. ornaments, va.: lotus throne	T'iao-fu-tu-wu-chin-kang

one/three	two	rt.: noose/snare lt.: (?)	corp.	two	alidha	dhar. ornaments, va.: lotus throne	Ti-la-pa
one/three	two	holds bhutadamara mu. with thunderbolt & bell	mature	two	alidha	dhar. ornaments, va.: lotus throne	Trailokyavijayavajra
one/three	two	rt.: sword lt.: human skull (?)	mature	two	lalita	dhar. ornaments, va.: horse	Tribhav-adhipati-Mahamata
one/three	two	rt.: staff / stick with wheel finial lt.: silver broom	mature	two		dhar. ornaments, va.: low carriage with four wheels	Tsang-kun-lcags-kyi-'khor-lo-can
one/three	two	rt.: sword lt.: cymbal(?)	mature	two	alidha	dhar. ornaments, va.: prostrate human form	Tse-la-pa-la-ka fo-mu
one/three	two	rt.: thunderbolt lt.: fire	corp.	two	ardha-paryanka	dhar. ornaments, va.: prostrate human figures	Ucarya
one/three	two	rt.: flaming jewels (?) lt.: harina mu. (?)	mature	two	alidha	dhar. ornaments, va.: human body	Ulkadhara (fo-mu)
one/three	two	rt.: sword lt.: wheel at chest	mature	two	alidha	dhar. ornaments, va.: human bodies	Ushnishajvala
one/three	two	rt.: sword lt.: human skull-cup	mature, nude	two	ardha-paryanka	dhar. ornaments, pendulous breasts, va.: lotus throne	Vagraja
one/three	two	rt.: ritual chopper lt.: human skull-cup, magic staff/stick in crook of left arm	mature	two	alidha	dhar. ornaments, va.: lotus throne	Vairocani
one/three	two	rt.: wheel lt.: human skull-cup	mature	two	alidha	dhar. ornaments, va.: lotus throne	Vajrabhumi
one/three	two	rt.: wish fulfilling jewel lt.: human skull-cup	mature	two	alidha	dhar. ornaments, va.: lotus throne	Vajranala
one/three	two	rt.: crossed thunderbolts lt.: human skull-cup	mature	two	alidha	dhar. ornaments, va.: lotus throne	Vajranila
one/three	two	rt.: goad/hook lt.: embraces shakti in vitarka mu.	corp.	two	alidha	dhar. ornaments, va.: lotus throne	Vajrankusa

one/three	two	rt.: thunderbolt lt.: bell and embraces shakti	corp.	two	partyalidha	dhar. ornaments, va.: prostrate human forms	?-Vajrapani
one/three	two	rt.: ritual chopper lt.: human skull-cup, magic staff/stick in crook of arm	mature	two	alidha	flowing hair, dhar. ornaments, va.: lotus throne	Vajrapranava
one*/three	two	rt.: sun disc lt.: moon disc with trident tipped magic staff/stick	mature	two	ardha-paryanka	*lion headed, dhar. ornaments, human skin-cape, va.: prostrate human figure	Vajra-simhasya
one/three	two	rt.: branch lt.: human skull-cup	mature	two	alidha	dhar. ornaments, va.: lotus throne	Vajrodaka
one/three	two	rt.: ritual chopper lt.: human skull-cup, magic staff/stick in crook of arm	mature, nude	two	ardha-paryanka	dhar. ornaments, va.: lotus throne	(Varahi) Indra-dakini
one/three	two	rt.: short staff/stick with skull finial lt.: human skull-cup	mature	two	astride	dhar. ornaments, va.: bullock	Varsa-devi
one/three	two	rt.: thunderbolt-topped goad/hook lt.: human skull-cup	mature, nude	two		pendulous breasts, dhar. ornaments, va.: lotus throne	Varsa-rajni
one/three	two	rt.: wavy-bladed knife lt.: human skull-cup	mature, nude	two	astride	pendulous breasts, dhar. ornaments, va.: mule	Vasanta-rajni
one/three	two	rt.: sword lt.: magic dagger	corp.	two	astride	pendulous breasts, dhar. ornaments, va.: human-like, tailed animal who is devouring a person	Vidyadevi
one/three	two	holding a garland	mature, nude	two	alidha	dhar. ornaments, va.: human form	Vidyuddhara (fo-mu)
one/three	two	rt.: thunderbolt lt.: karana mu.	corp.	two	alidha	dhar. ornaments, va.: lotus throne	Vimalakasa
one/three	two	holding lute	mature	two	alidha	dhar. ornaments, va.: prostrate human form	Vinadhara (fo-mu)

one/three	two	rt.: ritual chopper lt.: human skull-cup	mature	two	ardha-paryanka	dhar. ornaments, va.: prostrate human figure	Vishvadakini
one/three	two	rt.: abhaya mu. lt.: (?)	mature, nude	two	alidha	dhar. ornaments, va.: prostrate human figure	Vitana(?)dhara (fo-mu)
one*/three	two	rt.: hammer/mace lt.: banner/flag	corp.	two	astride	*bull-head, dhar. ornaments, va.: goat	Vrati-Karmara-Kala
one/three	two	holds noose/snare	corp.	two	alidha	dhar. ornaments, va.: lotus throne	Vrksambara
one/three	two	rt.: wheel lt.: conch shell	mature	two	ardha-paryanka	dhar. ornaments, va.: lotus throne	Vrsa
one*/three	two	rt.: ritual chopper lt.: sack of diseases	mature, nude	two	ardha-paryanka	*bull-head, pendulous breasts, dhar. ornaments, va.: lotus throne	Vrsabhavaktra
one/three	two	holds dharmachakra mu.	mature	two	sama-bhanga	helmeted, armored, va.: lotus throne	We-to
one/three	two	rt.: noose/snare in tarjani mu. lt.: sword	mature	two		black clothes, va.: black horse	Yab-gcig-bdud-rje-nag-po
one*/three	two	rt.: staff-stick with skull finial lt.: noose/snare	corp.	two	alidha	*bull-head, dhar. ornaments, va.: bull in intercourse with human form	Yama
one/three	two	holds sack of diseases	corp.	two	vamalalita	cuirass, loose garments, va.: lotus throne	Yama-daksad (?)
one/three	two	holds flaming tooth	mature, nude	two		dhar. ornaments, va.: lotus throne	Yama daksdi
one/three	two	rt.: tusk lt.: noose/snare	mature	two	sama-bhanga	dhar. ornaments, va.: lotus throne	Yamadanda (?)
one/three	two	holds club	mature,	two		dhar. ornaments,	Yama dandi

			nude			va.: lotus throne	
one/three	two	rt.: ritual chopper lt.: tarjani mu.	mature	two	astride	dhar. ornaments, va.: horse	Yamadandin
one/three	two	rt.: knife lt.: human skull-cup	mature	two	ardha-paryanka	pendulous breasts, dhar. ornaments, va.: human form	Yamajaya (?)
one/three	two	rt.: hair of human figure lt.: rests on figure's back	mature	two	alidha	hood-like head-dress, dhar. ornaments, va.: clouds	Yamangaraka
one/three	two	rt.: staff/stick topped with a skull lt.: human skull-cup	mature	two	alidha	dhar. ornaments, va.: corpse which rests on a bull	Yamari
one/three	two	rt.: goad/hook lt.: karana mu.	mature	two	alidha	dhar. ornaments, va.: lotus throne	Ya-wa-ti
one/three	two	rt.: skull-topped staff/stick lt.: held up with fingers spread apar	mature	two	alidha	dhar. ornaments, va.: clouds	Yayati
one/three	two	rt.: banner/flag of red silk lt.: btsan noose/snare	mature	two		red turban, red cloak with three folds, dhar. ornaments, va.: red horse	Yer-ba'i-rdzong-btsan-mthu-bo-che
one/three	two	rt.: three flaming jewels lt.: vase/vessel	corp.	two	alidha	dhar. ornaments, long loose garment, va.: prostrate human form	Zhan-blon
one/three	two	rt.: triple jewel lt.: jewel	corp.	two	sukha	dhar. ornaments, va.: prostrate human forms	Zhan-blon-rdo-rje-bdud-hdul
one/three	four	rt.: sword, arrow lt.: wheel, bow	youth	two	alidha	loose garments, dhar. ornaments, va.: lotus throne	Paripacaka-Tara
one/three	four	rt.: abhaya mu. and staff/stick lt.: flowering branch and lotus	corp.	two	alidha	dhar. ornaments, va.: lotus throne	Agni-bhayatrana (Avalokitesvara)
one/three	four	prin. embrace shakti in bhutadamara mu.	corp.	two	alidha	dhar. ornaments, va.: human form	Amritakundalinvajra

		rt.: thunderbolt lt.: wheel					
one/three	four	rt.: thunderbolt, goad/hook lt.: human skull-cup, noose/snare	nude	two	alidha	dhar. ornaments va.: human forms	<u>Arthasadhana-Varahi</u>
one/three	four	rt.: sword, ritual chopper lt.: human skull-cup, abhaya mu.	corp.	two	alidha	dhar. ornaments, va.: lotus throne	<u>Caturbhuja-cintamanicakra-Tara (fo-mu)</u>
one/three	four	rt.: (?), ritual chopper lt.: karana mu. (?)	corp.	two	alidha	dhar. ornaments, va.: human form under left foot	<u>Cinakrama-Tara</u>
one*/three	four	prin.: embrace shakti with thunderbolt, bell in vajrahumkara rt.: ritual chopper lt.: human skull-cup	mature	two	ardha-paryanka, yab-yum	*angry dhar. ornaments, va.: lotus throne	<u>Chakrasamvara</u>
one/three	four	rt.: ritual chopper, sword lt.: human skull-cup, magic notched staff/stick	youth, nude	two	ardha-paryanka	dhar. ornaments, va.: lotus throne	<u>Guhyajnana-(dakini)</u>
one/three	four	prin.: dharmachakra mu. with ritual chopper rt.: human skull-drum lt.: magic notched staff/stick	youth	two	alidha	dhar. ornaments, va.: prostrate human forms on lotus throne	<u>Kavaca-Candika</u>
one/three	four	prin.: dharmachakra mu. with ritual chopper rt.: human skull-drum lt.: magic notched staff/stick	youth, nude	two	alidha	dhar. ornaments, va.: prostrate human form on lotus throne	<u>Kavaca-Mohini</u>
one/three	four	prin.: vajrahumakra mu. right hand holds lotus rt.: human skull-drum lt.: magic notched staff/stick	youth	two	alidha	dhar. ornaments, va.: prostrate human forms on lotus throne	<u>Kavaca-Padmanartesvara</u>
one/three	four	prin.: vajrahumakra mu. right hand holds sword rt.: human skull-drum lt.: magic notched staff/stick	youth	two	alidha	dhar. ornaments, va.: prostrate human form on lotus throne	<u>Kavaca-Paramasava</u>
one/three	four	prin.: dharmachakra mu. with ritual chopper rt.: human skull-drum lt.: magic notched staff/stick	youth	two	alidha	dhar. ornaments, va.: prostrate human forms on lotus throne	<u>Kavaca-Sancalini</u>

one/three	four	prin.: dharmachakra mu. with ritual chopper rt.: human skull-drum lt.: magic notched staff/stick	youth	two	alidha	dhar. ornaments, va.: prostrate human forms on lotus throne	Kavaca-Santrasini
one/three	four	prin.: vajrahumakra mu. with jewel rt.: human skull-drum lt.: magic notched staff/stick	youth	two	alidha	dhar. ornaments, va.: prostrate human forms on lotus throne	Kavaca-Vajrasurya
one/three	four	prin.: dharmachakra mu. with human skull-cup rt.: human skull-drum lt.: magic notched staff/stick	youth, nude	two	alidha	dhar. ornaments, va.: prostrate human forms on lotus throne	Kavaca-Yamini
one/three	four	rt.: sword, thunderbolt lt.: wheel, noose/snare	corp.	two	alidha	dhar. ornaments, va.: lotus throne	Ma-ha-car-a
one/three	four	rt.: sword, thunderbolt lt.: wheel, noose/snare	corp.	two	alidha	dhar. ornaments, va.: lotus throne	Ma-ha-car-a
one/three	four	rt.: wheel, noose/snare(?) lt.: thunderbolt, wavy-blade knife	youth	two	alidha	dhar. ornaments, va.: lotus throne	Sarvarthasadhana-Varahi
one/three	four	rt.: noose/snare, bell lt.: sword, thunderbolt	corp.	two	alidha	dhar. ornaments, va.: buffalo	Sanmukha-Bhairavavajra Buddha
one/three	four	rt.: trident, ritual dagger lt.: moon disc, serpent/snake	mature	two	astride	pendulous breast, dhar. ornaments, va.: horse on prostrate human form	Svayambhu-rajni
one/three	four	prin.: embrace shakti in bhutadamara mu. rt.: thunderbolt lt.: (?)	corp.	two	alidha, yab-yum	dhar. ornaments, va.: human forms	Tejo(?)vajra
one/three	four	rt.: ritual chopper lt.: human skull-cup, magic staff/stick in crook of arm	mature	two		dhar. ornaments, left leg is held in the crook of the left leg, va.: prostrate human figures	Urdhavapadi-Varahi
one/three	four	prin.: embrace shakti with skull-cup, wheel-crested staff/stick rt.: thunderbolt lt.: notched staff/stick	mature	two	alidha, yab-yum	dhar. ornaments, va.: human figure with sword	Usnisachakravartin

one/three	four	rt.: sword, wheel lt.: lotus, tarjani mu.	mature, nude	two	alidha	dhar. ornaments, pendulous breasts, va.: lotus throne	Vadi-pramardini-Tara
one/three	four	rt.: staff/stick, sack of diseases lt.: human skull-cup, noose/snare	mature	two	ardha-paryanka	dhar. ornaments, pendulous breast, va.: lotus throne	Vaisravana (female)
one/three	four	rt.: goad/hook, throwing staff/stick lt.: bow, skull-cup	mature	two	alidha	dhar. ornaments, va.: prostrate human figure	Vajrabhrkuti (fo-mu)
one/three	four	rt.: flower, thunderbolt lt.: bell, skull-cup	mature	two	alidha	dhar. ornaments, va.: prostrate human form	Vajrabhumi (fo-mu)
one/three	four	rt.: thunderbolt, ritual chopper lt.: human skull-cup, skull-topped staff/stick	mature	two	ardha-paryanka	dhar. ornaments, va.: lotus throne	Vajra-Nairatma
one/three	four	rt.: thunderbolt, abhaya mu. lt.: noose/snare, human skull-cup	mature	two	alidha	dhar. ornaments, va.: lotus throne	Vajraputtali(?) (fo-mu)
one/three	four	rt.: (?) lt.: wheel, skull-cup	mature	two	alidha	dhar. ornaments, va.: prostrate human figure	Vajrasabda (fo-mu)
one/three	four	rt.: staff/stick, (?) lt.: magic staff/stick, skull-cup	mature	two	alidha	dhar. ornaments, va.: prostrate human form	Vajrasanti (fo-mu)
one/three	four	rt.: wheel, axe lt.: karana mu., throwing staff/stick	mature	two	sopasraya	dhar. ornaments, va.: lotus throne	Vishnu (deva)
one/three	four	rt.: fly whisk, (?) lt.: wheel, wheel	mature	two	vamalalita	dhar. ornaments, va.: garuda	Vishnu (deva)
one/three	four	prin.: embrace shakti	mature	two	alidha, yab-yum	dhar. ornaments, va.: human body	Vajravetala
one/three	four	rt.: short staff/stick, triple jewels lt.: (?), (?)	mature	two	vamalalita	dhar. ornaments, va.: lotus throne	Yaksa (deva)
one/three	six	rt.: trident, staff/stick, sword lt.: human skull-cup, goad/hook, noose/snare	corp.	two	vamalalita	dhar. ornaments, va.: prostrate human forms on lotus throne	Guhya-Sadhana-Zhan-blon-rdo-rje-Marajit

one/three	six	prin.: embrace shakti in bhutadamara mu. with thunderbolt & vajra rt.: staff/stick, noose/snare lt.: dagger, human skull-cup	corp.	two	alidha, yab-yum	dhar. ornaments, va.: lotus throne	Humkaravajra
one/three	six	prin.: bhutadamara mu. rt.: axe, goad/hook lt.: noose/snare, thunderbolt	mature	two	alidha	dhar. ornaments, va.: lotus throne	Kamarajavajra
one/three	six	prin. embrace shakti with thunderbolt(?), skull-cup rt.: sword, trident lt.: flaming jewels, (?)	corp.	two	alidha, yab-yum	dhar. ornaments, va.: lotus throne	Raga-Bhairavavajra
one/three	six	prin.: hold an-i-in mu. other hands hold tantric symbols	mature	two	alidha	dhar. ornaments, va.: lotus throne	Tu-yen-chin-kang
one/three	six	prin.: hands over head others hold tantric symbols	mature	two	alidha	dhar. ornaments, va.: lotus throne	Vajrosnisacakravartiraja
one*/three	12	prin.: embrace shakti with thunderbolt, bell in vajrahumkara rt.: human skull-drum, staff/stick with banner, battle axe, ritual chopper, elephant hide in tarjani mudra lt.: magic staff/stick, fredshly severed human head, noose/snare, human skull-cup, elephant hide in tarjani mudra	mature	two	ardha-paryanka, yab-yum	*angry dhar. ornaments, va.: lotus throne	Chakrasamvara
one/three	16	prin.: embrace shakti all hands hold skull-cup with sacred image	mature	two	alidha, yab-yum	dhar. ornaments, va.: lotus throne	Vishva(?)daka (Buddha)
three/nine	two	prin.: embrace shakti with ritual chopper and human skull-cup rt.: swords lt.: flaming jewel, flower	corp., nude	two	alidha, yab-yum	dhar. ornaments, va.: lotus throne	Padma-krodha
three/nine	two	prin.: embrace shakti in semui-in mu. rt.: thunderbolt, serpent/snake lt.: bell, serpent/snake	corp.	two	alidha, yab-yum	snake held in teeth, dhar. ornaments, va.: snake also held in hands and mouth	Trimukha-sadbhuja-Canda
three*/nine	four	prin.: hold bow and arrow rt.: thunderbolt lt.: lotus	corp	two	alidha	*horsehead over brows dhar. ornaments, va.: lotus throne	Atisha-Hayagriva

three/nine	four	rt.: sword, human skull-cup lt.: thunderbolt, trident	corp.	two	lalita	dhar. ornaments, va.: horse	Dhumavati (devi)
three/nine	four	prin.: embrace shakti with staff/stick, skull-cup rt.: thunderbolt lt.: magic staff/stick	mature	two	alidha, yab-yum	dhar. ornaments, va.: lotus throne	Vajrakala
three/nine	four	prin.: embrace shakti with human skull-cup, crossed thunderbolts rt.: thunderbolt lt.: magic staff/stick	mature	two	alidha, yab-yum	dhar. ornaments, va.: human body	Vajrakundalin
three/nine	four	prin.: embrace shakti with human skull-cup, sword rt.: thunderbolt lt.: magic staff/stick	mature	two	alidha	dhar. ornaments, va.: human body	Vajrasurya
three/nine	four	prin.: embrace shakti and hold sword, human skull-cup rt.: thunderbolt lt.: magic staff/stick	mature	two	alidha	dhar. ornaments, va.: human body	Vajrayaksa
three/nine	six	rt.: viratka mu., thunderbolt, bowels lt.: karana mu., abhaya mu., bowels	corp	two	alidha	dhar. ornaments, clenches bowels in teeth, va.: lotus throne	Amr(i)tabinduvajra
three/nine	six	prin. embrace shakti rt.: thunderbolt, jewel lt.: sword, lotus	mature	two	alidha, yab-yum	dhar. ornament, va.: lotus throne	Amritakundalin
three/nine	six	rt.: axe, sword, thunderbolt lt.: tarjani mu., club, two rings	mature	two	ardhapar-yanka	dhar. ornaments, va.: human form on lotus throne	Amritakundalin
three/nine	six	prin.: embrace shakti rt.: thunderbolt and sword lt.: flaming jewel and flower	mature	two	alidha, yab-yum	dhar. ornaments, va.: lotus throne	Buddha-krodha
three/nine	six	rt.: crossed thunderbolts, thunderbolt, vajra-topped staff/stick lt.: staff/stick, noose/snare, tarjani mudra	corp.	two	alidha	dhar. ornaments, va.: lotus throne	Dhumavarna-Krodha-Bhurkumkuta
three/nine	six	prin.: embrace shakti and holds skull-cup and ritual chopper	corp.	two	alidha, yab-yum	dhar. ornaments, va.: lotus throne	Gauri (fo-mu)

		rt.: sword, wheel lt.: thunderbolt, flaming jewels					
three/nine	six	prin.: embrace shakti rt.: axe, jewel lt.: sword, lotus	mature	two	alidha, yab-yum	dhar. ornaments, va.: lotus throne	<u>Kamaraja</u>
three/nine	six	prin.: embrace shakti with human skull-cup and ritual chopper rt.: sword , wheel lt.: karana mudra, (?)	mature	two	alidha, yab-yum	dhar. ornaments, va.: lotus throne	<u>Khadgadhara-Bhairavavajra</u>
three/nine	six	rt.: goad/hook,, thunderbolt, karana mudra lt.: baton/mace, noose/snare, karana mu.	corp.	two	alidha	dhar. ornaments, va.: lotus throne	<u>Khro-bo-sme-brcegs</u>
three/nine	six	prin.: bhutadamara mu. rt.: thunderbolt, sword lt.: noose/snare, lance	corp.	two	alidha	dhar. ornaments, va.: lotus throne	<u>Khro-bo-sMe-ba-brTegs-pa</u>
three/nine	six	prin.: embrace shakti in vajrahumkara mu. rt.: goad/hook, noose/snare lt.: human skull-cup, skull-topped staff/stick	mature, nude	two	alidha, yab-yum	dhar. ornaments, va.: prostrate human forms on lotus throne	<u>Krodha-humkara</u>
three/nine	six	prin.: bhutadamara mu. rt.: sword, thunderbolt lt.: lotus, noose/snare	corp.	two	alidha	dhar. ornaments, va.: lotus throne	<u>Krodha-Sme-brtsegs</u>
three/nine	six	prin.: embrace shakti with skull-cup and ritual chopper rt.: sword, (?) lt.: wheel, flaming jewel	corp.	two	alidha, yab-yum	dhar. ornaments, va.: lotus throne	<u>La-ka-la-ti (fo-mu)</u>
three/nine	six	prin.: embrace shakti rt.: sword, flaming jewels(?) lt.: wheel, (?)	cirp>	two	alidha, yab-yum	dhar. ornaments, va.: lotus throne	<u>Matsarya-Bhairavavajra</u>
three/nine	six	prin.: embrace shakti with ritual chopper and human skull-cup rt.: sword, lotus lt.: wheel, (?)	mature	two	alidha, yab-yum	dhar. ornaments, va.: lotus throne	<u>Padmadhara-Bhairavavajra</u>
three/nine	six	prin.: hold baton-like staff/stick & human skull-cup against chest rt.: axe, mongoose	corp.	two	alidha	dhar. ornaments, va.: prostrate human forms	<u>Prajnapani</u>

		lt.: noose/snare, mongoose				
three/nine	six	rt.: lotus, sword, thunderbolt lt.: bell, axe, noose/snare	corp.	two	alidha	dhar. ornaments, va.: lotus throne	Prajnantakavajra
three/nine	six	prin.: embrace shakti rt.: goad/hook, sword lt.: flaming jewel, flower	corp., nude	two	alidha, yab-yum	dhar. ornaments, va.: lotus throne	Ratna-krodha
three/nine	six	rt.: thunderbolt, goad/hook, (?) lt.: noose/snare, (?), (?)	corp.	four	alidha	dhar. ornaments, va.: bull	Sanmukha-Bhairavavajra
three/nine	six	rt.: thunderbolt, staff/stick with crossed thunderbolt finial, vjara topped goad/hook lt.: staff/stick with thunderbolt finial, noose/snare, tarjani mu.	mature	two	partyalidha	dhar. ornaments, va.: lotus throne	sMe-brtsegs (dud-kha)
three/nine	six	prin.: embraces shakti with ritual chopper, human skull-cup rt.: wheel, sword lt.: flaming jewel, lotus	corp.	two	partyalidha, yab-yum	dhar. ornaments, va.: lotus throne	Usnisachakravartin
three/nine	six	prin.: embrace shakti rt.: wheel, jewel lt.: sword, lotus	mature	two	alidha, yab-yum	dhar. ornaments, va.: lotus throne	Ushnishacakravartin
three/nine	six	prin.: embrace shakti rt.: trident, sword lt.: flaming jewel, flower	corp.	two	alidha, yab-yum	dhar. ornaments, va.: lotus throne	Vajra-krodha
three/nine	six	prin.: embrace shakti in dharmachakra mu. with ritual dagger rt.: thunderbolts lt.: karana mu.	corp.	two	alidha, yab-yum	dhar. ornaments, spread vajra-tipped wings, va.: lotus throne	Vajrakumara
three/nine	six	prin.: embrace shakti in vajrahumkara mu. rt.: wheel, sword lt.: goad/hook, noose/snare	mature	two	vamalalita	dhar. ornaments, va.: lotus throne	Vajramrta
three/nine	six	prin.: embrace shakti rt.: thunderbolt, jewel lt.: sword, lotus	mature	two	alidha	dhar. ornaments, va.: lotus throne	Vajrapatala
three/nine	six	prin.: bowl with three jewels rt.: thunderbolt, wheel	mature	two	alidha	dhar. ornaments, va.: lotus throne	Vajrarasa (fo-mu)

		lt.: sword, vitarka mu.					
three/nine	six	prin.: hold lute rt.: thunderbolt, (?) lt.: hold sword, (?)	mature	two	vajra	dhar. ornaments, va.: lotus throne	Vajrasabda (fo-mu)
three/nine	six	rt.: thunderbolt, chain, arrow lt.: human skull-cup, noose/snare, bow	mature	two	lalita	dhar. ornaments, va.: lotus throne	Vajrasrinkhala (fo-mu)
three/nine	six	rt.: thunderbolt, wheel, tarjani mu. lt.: bell, axe, noose/snare	mature	two	alidha	dhar. ornaments, va.: lotus throne	Yamantakavajra
three/nine	six	prin.: embrace shakti rt.: axe, jewel lt.: sword, lotus	mature	two	alidha	dhar. ornaments, va.: lotus throne	Yamari
three/nine	12	holding tantric symbols	corp.	two	alidha	dhar. ornaments, va.: chariot borne on the back of pigs	Dvadasabhuja-Marici (fo-mu)
three/nine	12	prin.: embrace shakti in vajrahumkara mu. and holding thunderbolt, bell chopper crossed thunderbolts topped short staff/stick, (?) lt.: peacock feather, noose/snare, peacock feathers magic staff/stick, (?)	corp.	two	alidha, yab-yum	dhar. ornaments, va.: bodies of subdued deities	Samvararaja (Buddha)
three/nine	16	prin.: embrace shakti others hold human skull-cup with animal forms inside	mature	two	alidha, yab-yum	dhar. ornaments, va.: prostrate human forms	Buddhadaka (Buddha)
three/nine	16	prin.: embrace shakti rt.: human skull-cups with animals(?) lt.: human skull-cups with Buddha images	corp.	two	alidha	dhar. ornaments, va.: human forms	Ratnadaka
three/nine	16	prin.: sword, noose/snare other hands hold tantric symbols	corp	two	alidha	dhar. ornaments, va.: prostrate human bodies	Sarvarthasadhana-Tara-(fo-mu)
three/nine	16	prin.: embrace shakti in vajrahumkara mu. and hold thunderbolt, bell other hands hold tantric symbols	mature	two	alidha, yab-yum	dhar. ornaments, va.: human forms	Sastradhara-Hevajra (Buddha)
four/12	two	rt.: lance with banner lt.: lance with banner	corp.	two	alidha	dhar. ornaments, va.: lotus throne	Ukeger-un ejen

four/12	six	rt.: sword, axe, ritual chopper lt.: human skull-cup, goad/hook, noose/snare	corp.	two	alidha	dhar. ornaments, va.: lotus throne	Kapalamalin
four/12	eight	rt.: thunderbolt, arrow, (?), sword lt.: noose/snare, bow, pestle(?), conch shell(?)	youth	two	alidha	dhar. ornaments, va.: human forms on lotus throne	Jvalanala-(=Vajrajvalanalarka[?])
four/12	eight	rt.: sword, human skull-drum, human skull-cup, thunderbolt lt.: magic notched stick, lotus, lotus bud, tarjani	corp.	two	alidha	pendulous breasts, dhar. ornaments, va.: lotus throne	Pithisvari-Uddiyana-Tara
five/15	six	rt.: staff/stick, sword, ritual chopper lt.: noose/snare, thunderbolt, karana mu.	corp.	six*		*1st pr. ardhaparyanka 2nd&3rd pr. alidha, va.: bull in intercourse with prostrate woman	Sanmukha
five*/15	eight	prin.: pestle, skull topped staff/stick rt.: sword, wheel, human skull-drum lt.: human skull-cup, bow & arrow, noose/snare	corp., nude	two	alidha	*cent. bull-head, erect phgallus, dhar. ornaments, va.: four prostrate human figures	Samksipta-Bhairava
five*/15	16	prin. embrace shakti, hold thunderbolt and human skull-cup other hands hold tantric symbols	corp.	two	alidha, yab-yum	*central head bull-like, dhar. ornaments, va.: Hindu deities on lotus throne	Bhairavavajra
six/18	26	prin.: vajrahumakra mu. other hands hold tantric symbols	corp.	two		dhar. ornaments, va.: prostrate human figures	Vajravega
eight/24	16	prin.: vajrahumkara mu. rt.: noose/snarw, sword, axe, goad/ hook, arrow, hammer/mace, wheel lt.: tarjani mu., vase/vessel, lance, magic notched staff/stick, bow, (?)	corp.	four	alidha	dhar. ornaments, va.: human forms	Amara-vajra-devi
eight/24	16	all hold human skull-cups prin.: embrace shakti	mature, nude	two	alidha, yab-yum	dhar. ornaments, va.: disc on a multitude of prostrate human figures	Vajradaka
nine*/27	two	rt.: sword lt.: severed human head in karana mu.	corp.	two	alidha	*horse head in hair dhar. ornaments,	Dasagriva

						va.: lotus throne	
nine*/27	eight	prin.: embrace shakti other hands hold tantric symbols	mature	two	alidha, yab-yum	*central head bull-like, dhar. ornaments, va.: prostrate human forms on lotus throne	<u>Bhairavavajra Buddha</u>
nine*/27	26	prin.: embrace shakti holding ritual chopper, human skull-cup rt. & lt.: tantric symbols	corp.	14	alidha, yab-yum	dhar. ornaments, va.: prostrate human forms on lotus throne	<u>Kalarindra(?)-Mahisanana</u>

<u>Bodhisattva-like:</u>

one*/two	two	rt.: vajra-topped axe lt.: mongoose	mature	two	lalita	*angry bodh. ornaments, va.: lotus throne	<u>Badidar-a</u>
one*/two	two	rt.: peacock feathers lt.: thunderbolt mu.: simha-karna	youth.	two	vama- lalita	*angry bodh. ornaments, va.: lotus throne	<u>Bhadrakara</u>
one*/two	two	rt.: thunderbolt lt.: bell	youth	two	ardha- paryanka	*angry, bodh. ornaments, va.: lotus throne	<u>Dhanu</u>
one*/two	two	rt.: staff/stick baton lt.: mongoose	corp.	two	vamalalita	*angry bodh. ornaments, va.: lotus throne	<u>Indra-(mahayaksasenapati)</u>
one*/two	two	rt.: flaming jewels lt.: rests on thigh	youth	two	vamalalita	*angry, bodh. ornaments, va.: lotus throne	<u>Kalagni (deva)</u>
one*/two	two	rt.: axe lt.: karana mu.	youth	two	ardha- paryanka	bodh. ornaments, va.: lotus throne	<u>Kanya</u>
one*/two	two	rt.: vitarka mu. lt.: wish fulfilling jewel	youth.	two	sattva	bodh. ornaments, va.: lotus throne	<u>Ketugraha (deva)</u>
one*/two	two	holding vase/vessel	mature, nude	two	sama- bhanga	*angry, bodh. ornaments, va.: lotus throne	<u>Krodha-Bhurkumkuti(?)</u>
one*/two	two	rt.: karana mu.	youth	two	sattva	*angry,	<u>Lieh-k'o-ta-ch'ia t'ien</u>

		lt.: wish-fulfilling jewel				bodh. ornaments, va.: lotus throne	
one*/two	two	rt.: trident lt.: rosary	youth	two	lalita	*angry, bodh. ornaments, va.: lotus throne	Paripurna-Tara
one*/two	two	rt.: abhaya mu. on knee lt.: at side of face	youth	two	sopasraya	*angry, bodh. ornaments, va.: lotus throne	Shan-ch'eng-ming-yang-t'ien p'u- sa
one*/two	two	rt.: wheel lt.: conch shell	youth	two	ardha-paryanka	*angry, dhar. ornaments, va.: lotus throne	Simha
one*/two	two	rt.: human skull-drum lt.: karana mu.	mature	two	ardha-paryanka	*angry, bodh. ornaments, va.: lotus throne	Tula
one*/two	ten	all hold thunderbolts	youth	two	sattva	*angry, bodh. ornaments, va.: lotus throne	Krodha-Candaravajra
one/2-3	two	rt.: battle axe lt.: severed human	youth	two	alidha	bodh. ornaments va.: ;lotus throne	Dvitiya-Bhadra
one*/2-3	two	rt.: arrow lt.: bow	youth	two	alidha	*angry, bodh. ornaments, va.: lotus throne	Dvitiya-Jaya
one*/2-3	two	rt.: human skull-drum lt.: jewel	youth	two	alidha	*angry, bodh. ornaments, va.: lotus throne	Dvitiya-Nanda
one*/2-3	two	rt.: short sword lt.: shield	youth	two	alidha	*angry, bodh. ornaments, va.: lotus throne	Dvitiya-Purna
one*/2-3	two	rt.: lance lt.: sun disc	youth	two	alidha	*angry, bodh. ornaments, va.: lotus throne	Dvitiya-Sunya
one*/2-3	two	rt.: baton/mace lt.: palm up on thigh	corp.	two	vamalalita	*angry, bodh. ornaments, va.: lotus throne	E-ni-lo yao-ch'a-ta-chiang
one/three	two	holding vase/vessel	youth	two	sama-	bodh. ornaments,	Fen-nu Wei-chi fo-mu

					bhanga	va.: lotus throne	
one*/three	two	playing lute	youth	two	ardha-paryanka	*angry, bodh. ornaments, va.: lotus throne	Gandharva yaksa (?)
one*/three	two	rt.: trident lt.: human skull-cup	youth	two	alidha	*angry, bodh. ornaments, va.: lotus throne	Mahagati
one*/three	two	rt.: goad/hook lt.: simha-karna mu. on thigh	youth	two	vamalalita	*angry, bodh. ornaments, va.: lotus throne	Maharajavara
one*/three	two	rt.: varada mu. lt.: stem of lotus in kartari mu, with thunderbolt	mature	two	lalita	*angry, bodh. ornaments, va.: lotus throne	Ripuchakra-vinasini (Tara)
one*/three	two	rt.: sword lt.: (?)	mature	two	vamalalita	*angry, bodh. ornaments, va.: lotus throne	Tamodghatamati(?) (Bodhisattva)
one*/three	two	rt.: trident lt.: tarjani mu.	mature	two	alidha	*angry, bodh. ornaments, va.: lotus throne	Trtiya-Bhadra
one*/three	two	rt.: ritual chopper-topped staff/stick lt.: severed human head	mature	two	alidha	*angry, bodh. ornaments, va.: lotus throne	Trtiya-Jaya
one*/three	two	rt.: thunderbolt-topped staff/stick lt.: branch with flower	youth	two	alidha	*angry, bodh. ornaments, va.: lotus throne	Trtiya-Sunya
three*/6-9	six	rt.: crossed thunderbolts, wheel, lotus lt.: bell, three jewels, sword	mature	two	vajra	*angry, bodh. ornaments, va.: lotus throne	Tara (fo-mu)
three/nine	four	prin.: embrace shakti holding thunderbolt and human skull-cup rt.: (?) lt.: magic notched staff/stick	corp.	two	alidha, yab-yum	bodh. ornaments va.: human form	Bhayadavajra
three/nine	six	rt.: thunderbolt, sword, wheel lt.: goad/hook, noose/snare, tarjani mu.	mature	two	alidha	bodh. ornaments, va.: lotus throne	Astakapi-Acala
three/nine	six	rt.: thunderbolt, sword, wheel	mature	two	alidha	bodh. ornaments,	Astakapi-Acala

		lt.: goad/hook, noose/snare, karana mu.				va.: lotus throne	
four*/12	eight	prin.: anjali mu. rt.: rosary, arrow, wheel lt.: cylindrical banner, bow, vase/vessel	youth	two	vamalalita	*angry, bodh. ornaments, va.: lotus throne	Astabhuja-Tara

Other:

one*/two	two	rt.: ritual chopper lt.: human skull-cup, magic notched staff/stick in crook of left arm	mature, nude	two	arhdha- paryanka	*angry, garland of freshly severed heads, bejeweled, va.: lotus throne	dPyal-lugs-Vajravahari
one*/two	two	rt.: sword lt.: tarjani mu.	mature	two	vamalalita	*angry, fancy boots, loose garment, va.: kneeling elephant	Gunaraja
one*/two	two	rt.: sword lt.: serpent/snake	mature, winged	two		*bird-head, bird-legged, bejeweled, va.: serpent	Karma-Garuda
one*/two	two	rt.: banner/flag lt.: human skull-cup	mature	two	astride	*angry, loose garment, va.: horse	Karmaraja
one*/two	two	rt.: short baton/mace lt.: mongoose	mature	two	vamalalita	*angry, bodh. ornaments, va.: lotus throne	P'o-i-lo (mahayaksasenapati)
one*/two	two	rt.: noose/snare in vitarka mu. lt.: mongoose	mature	two	lalita	*angry, long flowing garment, va.: lotus throne	Samjneya
one*/2-3	two	rt.: wheel lt.: serpent/snake	human, winged	two		*garuda head, bird-like legs clutching snake, dhar. ornaments, va.: serpent/snake	Buddha-Garuda
one*/2-3	two	rt.: sword lt.: noose/snare	mature	two	alidha	*angry, cuirass of mail,	Cittaraja

						va.: lotus throne	
one*/2-3	two	rt.: thunderbolt lt.: human skull-cup	corp.	two	astride	*haughty, long flowing robes, va.: lion	Damcan Vajradsadhu
one*/2-3	two	holds noose/snare of sun-rays	mature	two		*snake-head, loin-cloth of snakes, va.: white tiger	Hang-phan
one*/three	two	rt.: sword lt.: reins of horse	corp.	two	astride	*angry fancy garments va.: horse	bDud-gin
one/three	two	rt.: sword lt.: reins of horse	corp.	two	astride	loose garments, fancy boots, va.: horse	bDud-gin
one/three	two	rt.: sword lt.: heart (?) and lance in crook of arm	corp.	two	alidha	cuirass & warrior weapons, va.: horse & prostrate human form	Beg-tse
one/three	two	rt.: goad/hook lt.: human skull-cup	mature, nude	two	ardha- paryanka	pendulous breasts, dhar. ornaments, va.: lotus throne	Ghatini
one*/three	two	rt.: knife lt.: reins of horse	corp.	two	astride	*angry, loose, flowing hair, loose garments, va.: horse	Gin-chen-srog-bdag
one/three	two	rt.: dagger lt.: severed human head	corp.	two	sama- bhanga	bone ornaments, va.: lotus throne	Ham-san-mi-dmar
one/three	two	rt.: sun disc lt.: moon disc	mature	two	alidha	pendulous breasts, hood-like headress, bejeweled	Kalapasi
one/three	two	rt.: banner/flag with otter head lt.: black snake noose/snare	mature	two		snake in hair, garment of scorpions, va.: white spotted tortoise	kLu-bdud-rdo-rje-spyan-gcig-ma
one/three	two	holding vase/vessel	mature, nude	two	sama- bhanga	long flowing hair, va.: lotus throne	Krodha-Bhurkumkuti(?)
one/three	two	rt.: (?)	mature,	two	alidha	dhar. ornaments,	Naro (Nadi) dakini (fo-mu)

		lt.: magic notched staff/stick	nude			pendulous breasts va.: prostrate human forms	
one*/three	two	rt.: lance lt.: mongoose	corp.	two	lalita	*angry, red helmet, battle dress, va.: blue horse	Nilasva-Raktasula-Vaisravana
one*/three	two	rt.: short jewel topped staff/stick lt.: mongoose	mature	two	lalita	*angry, dhar. ornaments, va.: lotus throne	Peyadhara (?)
one*/three	two	rt.: vajra topped sword lt.: mongoose	mature	two	lalita	*angry, flowing garments, va.: lotus throne	Pidahara (?)
one*/three	two	holding serpent/snake	corp.	two		*bird-head, serpent in beak, winged, dhar. ornaments, va.: prostrate figure snake coils	Puspa-Garuda
one/three	two	rt.: ritual chopper lt.: human skull-cup	mature	two	ardha-paryanka	sagging breasts, dhar. ornaments, va.: lotus throne	Raksa-Dakini
one/three	two	rt.: fly whisk lt.: shrine	corp.	two	alidha	richly armored, va.: lotus throne	Raudra-Vaisravana
one/three	two	rt.: jewel topped staff/stick lt.: mongoose	mature	two	lalita	dhar. ornaments, va.: lotus throne	Saktidhara (?)
one*/three	two	holds serpent/snake	mature	two	alidha	*bird-like head, serpent/snake in beak, bird wings, va.: lotus throne	Tantra-krama-Sabala-Kalacakra-Garuda
one*/three	two	rt.: abhaya mu. lt.: tarjani mu.	mature	two, bird-like	alidha	*bird-like, spread bird wings, va.: prostrate human form	Upadesa-krama-Sabala-Garuda
one/three	two	rt.: thunderbolt lt.: serpent/snake	mature	two, bird-like		*bird-like, spread bird wings, legs clutch snake,	Vajra-Garuda

						va.: serpent/snake	
three*/six	18	prin.: book/manuscript other hands: tantric symbols	corp	two	alidha	*angry, richly armored dhar. ornaments, va.: dragon	Nartakavara-Vaisravana
three/nine	six	rt.: baton/mace (?), mongoose, three jewels lt.: noose/snare, (?), mongoose	youth	two	vamalalita	dhar. ornaments, va.: lotus throne	Sadbhuja-Iambhalavajra
three*/nine	six	rt.: axe, jewel, mongoose lt.: noose/snare, human skull-cup, mongoose	corp.	two	alidha	richly robed, va.: human forms	Iambhala-Zhal-gSum-Phyag-drug
nine/27	four*	prin.: bow, arrow rt.: sea-dragon-topped staff/stick lt.: noose/snare	corp.*	snake coils		*eye on each forearm, *face on stomach, dhar. ornaments	Grahottamaraja-Rahu
nine*/*	two	rt.: banner/flag lt.: bow and arrow	corp.	snake-coils		*raven head-capped, *eyes cover head and body, smok-gray color	gZa'-mchog-rgyal-po-rahula

Color Plates

Photo credits:

Plates I-XXIV,
Vassilios Spiros Sarioglou, M.F.A.
Thesaloniki, Greece.

Plate I.

Life of Sakyamuni Buddha
Karma Thupten, aka Karma Lama (Tibetan)
Distemper, fine silver, & 24k. gold on muslin, 44" h. x 31" w.
Kathmandu (Kantipur), Nepal
1989 (in the 18th Century Style)

This *thangkas*, like a medieval tapestry, abounds with vibrant images/scenes. Each refers to an incident in the life of *Sakyamuni Buddha*.

The central image, *Sakyamuni Buddha*, whose right hand is in the *bhumisparsa mudra* and left in the *dhyana mudra* holding a alms bowl (*patra, lhung-bzed*), sits in the *vajrasana* position and wears monastic robes of the northern tradition. He is surrounded by an aura, halo and flames, and sits upon a sun an moon disc supported by a lotus on a lion throne. *Saripatra*, one of *Sakyamuni's* principle disciples, stands to the right and *Maudgalyayana*, the other principle disciple, stands to the left of the *Buddha*.

In the aura surrounding The *Sakyamuni Buddha* are: heavenly figures, heavenly musicians, *Garuda*, a sky god and symbol of fruitfulness and the sun, *Naga* Princesses, *Makara* symbolizes the life giving power of the waters, unknown figures on rams, white lions, symbol of the lordly power of the spirit, royal caprisoned elephants. At the base of the lion throne are: *cintamani* jewels, the wheel of the law with fish, the endless knot, the sacred lotus, and the lions of the throne.

Above *Sakyamuni* , at the top of the *thangka* sits the *Adi-Buddha*, the Primordial Buddha (here represented by *Samantabhadra*) in *dhyana mudra* and *vajrasana*, in the *yab-yum* position with his consort. When *Samantabhadra* is shown as *Adi-Buddha* he is always portrayed nude and blue in color.

Between the representation of the *Adi-Buddha* and *Sakyamuni* are eight *Buddha* figures, all are gold in color. Seven surround a central figure whose garb is identical to the central *Sakyamuni Buddha*. This *Buddha* holds the *buddhasramana mudra* with red lotus in right hand and holds the *dhyana mudra* with alms bowl (*patra, lhung-bzed*) in the left. He sits in the *vajrasana* leg position. The garb of the surrounding seven differ slightly from the central figure and all sit in *vajrasana*. Their mudras include: *dharmachakra mudra, bhumisparsa mudra* with a *patra, dhyana mudra* and the right hand in the *abhaya mudra*. These figures could not be representations of the *Dhyani Buddhas* since their colors are not representative. They may possibly represent a number of the *Buddhas* of Confession.

The rest of the thangka relates to *Sakyamuni Buddha's* life. In the upper left hand corner is the representation of *Sakyamuni Buddha's* incarnation. Queen *Maya* dreams of a white elephant entering her womb, a form of immaculate conception. The dream and conception his portrayed here through the vehicle of a rainbow. **Below is** the interpretation of *Maya's* dream by a court sage who declares that the child will either be a *Chakravartin* (Universal Ruler) or a *Buddha*. Directly below this scene is the Birth of *Buddha*--Queen *Maya* journeys to Lumbini Park (Nepal), supports herself on a flowering *sala* tree, and *Sakyamuni Buddha* in the form of Prince *Siddhartha* is born miraculously through her right side. The babe takes seven steps (represented here by the seven lotus blossoms) to proclaim his spiritual eminence and cosmic nature. *Maya's* sister *Mahaprajapati* is in attendance, while above Hindu gods witness the birth from the vantage of the clouds. Following is the next major scene, Prince *Siddhartha* (*Sakyamuni Buddha*) basks in royal splendor, guarded by dragons overhead, while to the right a *garuda* and *makara* guard the palace. This is followed by one of the miracles that *Sakyamuni Buddha* performs concerns his jealous cousin *Devadatta* (shown to the right) who looses a mad elephant in the vicinity of *Sakyamuni Buddha*. He calms the mad elephant and the other elephants rejoice. **Finally, in the lower left hand corner** Prince *Siddhartha* rides forth on his favorite horse after taking leave of his sleeping wife *Yasodhara* and his sun *Rahul*.

In the upper right appears a scene that is associated with *Sakyamuni Buddha's* pre-birth. He appears in the *Tushita* heaven where he accepts the life of a *Buddha*, transmits the *Buddha*-lineage to *Amitabha Buddha* (the future *Buddha*, who now reigns in the *Tushita* heaven) and descends to earth.

Below is a representation of an emaciated figure of *Buddha*, before his Enlightenment and during his period of fleshly mortification. He is surrounded by figures playing musical instruments. This is followed by *Sakyamuni Buddha* in meditation and attended by two figures.

Following, Prince *Siddhartha* renounces his princely status and cuts his hair. This is The Great Renunciation. His hair is carried by a celestial being to the heavens.

Beneath this scene, is a representation of *Sakyamuni Buddha* during the period of his Enlightenment being tempted by *Mara* (the evil force) and his minions. As they hurl all forms of temptations at him, the aura of his spirit rebuffs them all and they fall harmlessly to the ground as lotus blossoms.

Across the bottom are scenes which apply to the *Buddha's* life after Enlightenment: *Sakyamuni Buddha's* first sermon, after his Enlightenment, in Deer Park, Sarnath, being given to the five disciples who had abandoned him; and, the death of *Sakyamuni Buddha*.

Plate I.

Plate II.

Sakyamuni Buddha **(detail) Life of Sakyamuni Buddha**

Karma Thupten, aka Karma Lama (Tibetan)
Distemper, fine silver, & 24k. gold, 44" h. x 31" w.
Kathmandu (Kantipur), Nepal
1989 (in the 18th Century Style)

Plate II.

Plate III.

Life of Sakyamuni Buddha
Karma Thupten, aka Karma Lama (Tibetan)
Distemper, fine silver, & 24k. gold, muslin, 44" h. x 38.5" w.
Kathmandu (Kantipur), Nepal
1993 (in the 15th Century Style)

The style of this *Life of Sakyamuni Buddha* is of the 15th Century style. Not only does it differ in style from Plate I, but also the cinamagraphic approach differs. The scenes proceed clockwise from the upper right panel. This panel depicts *Sakyamuni Buddha* in Tushita heaven where he transmits the *Buddha* lineage to *Maitreya,* the Buddha-to-Be.

The second panel indicates the conception of *Buddha*. *Maya's* dream of the white elephant (an Asian symbol of royalty) is set within a curtained pavilion.

Following, is a panel which depicts the birth of *Prince Siddhartha* (*Sakyamuni Buddha*). Maya stands with her right hand clutching the *sala* tree. In addition this panel portrays the lustration.

The next two panels depict Atisha's pronouncement that *Prince Siddhartha* is either a *Chakravartin* (Universal Ruler) or a *Buddha*. And, *Prince Siddhartha* is taken to the temple where he is honored by the gods.

The seventh panel indicates the First Concentration at the Plowing Festival. This is followed to the lower right and across the bottom (in a double register) by a series of panels indicating the trraining of *Prince Siddhartha* in the princely ways and representations of his royal leisure.

Second from the bottom on the left hand side is a panel which depicts the Great Renunciation. Here *Prince Siddhartha* cuts his princely locks as he renounces the ease of a royal household for that of an ascetic. Beside him a figure holds a *bodhisattva* crown.

A series of panels depicts *Sakyamuni Buddha's* life prior to his Enlightenment. These panels portray the ascetic life, mortification, the acceptance of honey and milk from Nandabala.

The Enlightenment is depicted by the large central panel. In this *Sakyamuni Buddha* is flanked by *Saripatra*, one of *Sakyamuni's* principle disciples, on the right and *Maudgalyayana*, the other principle disciple, on left. He sits in front of a blue throne back, is surrounded by a trefoil arch, and is supported by the traditional lion throne. Surrounding, are representations of *Mara's* temptations--fearful demons, amorous couples and maidens. On either side of his head are discs--sun (*surya, nyi-ma*) and moon (*chandra, zla-ba*)--and topping his ushnisa is a small golden shrine (*chaitya* or *stupa, mchod-rten*)

The panels of the top two registers--with the exception of the two already noted above--deal with *Sakyamuni Buddha's* pastoral life including the Sermon at Deer Park, the monkey's gift, the multiplication of images, the death of *Sakyamuni Buddha*--the Parinirvana, the cremation in Self-Created Fire, and the depositing of relics.

Across the top of the *thangka* are a series--twenty--of niches. The niche at the far left is inhabited by *Sakyamuni Buddha*. The rest are filled by various lama and *arhat*-like figures.

On either side of the right and left life-panel registers are a series of niches--eleven on the right and eleven on the left. The top eight niches on both sides are peopled by the sixteen *arhats* of the Indian tradition. The bottom three niches on either side are displayed three wrathful deities on the left and three calm deities on the right--the middle right being *Ganapati*.

Plate III.

Plate IV.
Sakyamuni Buddha **(detail)** **Life of Sakyamuni Buddha**
Karma Thupten, aka Karma Lama (Tibetan)
Distemper, fine silver, & 24k. gold, muslin, 44" h. x 38.5" w.
Kathmandu (Kantipur), Nepal
1993 (in the 15th Century Style)

Plate IV.

Plate V.

<u>The Bardo Mandala</u> or <u>Thub-pa-drug Mandala</u> or <u>The Chonyid Bardo Mandala</u> (Mandala of the Six Wrathful and Six Peaceful Buddhas or "The Transitional State of the Experiencing of Rreality")
Karma Thupten, aka Karma Lama (Tibetan)
Distemper, fine silver, & 24k. gold, 43 1/4" h. x 33" w.
Kathmandu (Kantipur), Nepal
1989 (in the 18th Century Style)

The *Thub-pa-drug Mandala* contains the 102 deities of the visual manifestation of the Tibetan *Book of the Dead*. All *Buddha* powers are illustrated in this *tantric mandala*. It alludes the overcoming of all after-death obstacles in the six worlds which leads to abhorrent re-births.

In the upper center of the *thangka*, directly above the large *mandala* are six figures. The upper central figure is a representation of the *Adi-Buddha*, the primordial *Buddha* in the form of *Kun-tu-bzang-po*, blue in color, nude and in the *yab-yum* position with his *shakti*. Directly below the *Adi-Buddha* is the representation of *rNam-par-snag-mdzad* in the *yab-yum* position with his *shakti*. He is white and holds in his right hand at his breast the thunderbolt and in his left hand the bell. *rNam-par-snag-mdzad* in a celestial appearance represents *Adi-Buddha*, here, however, here he occupies the zenith.

To the left of the *Adi-Buddha* is the first of the *Thub-pa-drug*, a white *Buddha* with vina or lute is known by the name of *brGya-byin* or *Pi-bang hChang-pa* (the "lute-Player"). This *Buddha* reigns over the World of the Gods and his syllable is "*Om*." To the right of the *Adi-Buddha* is the green *Thag-bZang-ris* who holds a flaming sword and reigns over the World of the Fighting Titans. His syllable is "*Ma*." To the left of *rNam-par-snag-mdzad* stands ththe yellow *Sha-skya Seng-ge* holding a alms bowl. *Sha-skya Seng-ge's* realm is the World of Men and his syllable is "*Ni*." To the right of *rNam-par-snag-mdzad* stands the blue *Senge-Rab-rten*, who holds in his hand the sacred manuscript. *Senge-Rab-rten's* realm is the World of Animals and his syllable is "*Pad*." The other two *Thub-pa-drug* are centered on the left and right sides of the *mandala*, between the *mandala* and the edge. On the left stands the red *Khar-hBar-ma* who reigns over the World of the Insatiable Monsters and holds a vessel of nectar. His syllable is "*Me*." Across the *mandala* on the right is the sixth *Thub-pa-drug*, *Me-lCe hChang-pa* who here holds a conch shell, symbolic of water, but may also be shown holding a flame. *Me-lCe hChang-pa* reigns over the World of Hells and his syllable is "*Hum*."

In the four corners of the *thangka* are four five-light-colored circles (*mandalas*) further representing the peaceful deities. In upper left hand corner *mandala* are five yellow deities dressed as *bodhisattvas*. The zenith is occupied by a yellow deity the *Dhyani Buddha Ratnasambhava* in the *yab-yum* position, accompanied by: *Dhyani Bodhisattva Aksogharba* (left) with *Dhupa* (below left) and *Dhyani Bodhisattva Samantabhadra* (right) with *Mala* (below right). In the upper right hand corner within the small *mandala* are five red deities garbed as *bodhisattvas*. The zenith is occupied by the red deity the *Dhyani Buddha Amitabha* in the *yab-yum* position, accompanied by: *Dhyani Bodhisattva Avalokitesvara* (left) with *Aloka* (below left) and *Dhyani Bodhisattva Manjusri* (right) with *Gita* (below right). In the lower right hand corner is another *mandala* which holds again five green deities. The deity at the zenith is the *Dhyani Buddha Amoghasiddhi* in the *yab-yum* position, accompanied by: *Dhyani Bodhisattva Vajrapani* (left) and *Naivedya* (below left) and *Dhyani Bodhisattva Sarvanivaranaviskambhin* (right) and *Gandha* (below right). Finally, in the lower left hand corner is a *mandala* which holds four white deities, while the one at the zenith is the blue *Dhyani Buddha Aksobhya* in the *yab-yum* position accompanied by: *Dhyani Bodhisattva Ksitigarbha* (left) and *Puspa* (below left) and *Dhyani Bodhisattva Maitreya* (right) and *Lasya* (below right).

There are four door keepers if the *mandala* who are represented in the *yab-yum* position with their *saktis*. On the left side of the *thangka*, directly above figure of *Khar-hBar-ma* stands a ferocious yellow deity in the garb of a *dharmapala*, the Door-Keeper *Yamantaka* with his *sakti Pasadhari* who guards the south. Below the figure of *Khar-hBar-ma* stands a fierce white deity, the Door-Keeper *Vijaya* with his *sakti Ankusa* (Tib.: *Chags-kyu-ma*) who guards the east. On the right side of the *thangka*, above the figure of *Me-lCe hChang-pa* stands a red ferocious deity in the garb of a *dharmapala* is the Door-Keeper *Hayagriva* with his sakti *Vajrasrinkhala* who guards the west. Finally, below the figure of *Me-lÇe hChang-pa* stands a fierce green deity, the Door-Keeper *Amritadhara* with his sakti *Kinkini-Dhari* (Tib.: *Dril-bu-ma*) who guards the north. Directly below the *mandala* in the bottom center are six other deities. Centered, top is the representation of the white *rDo-rje Sems-dpah* His representation here is as the nadir.

Below *rDo-rje Sems-dpah* are five deities. These are the *Vidyadharas* or Knowledge-Holding Deities. Centered is a blue deity named the Supreme Knowledeg-Holding Deity, Lotus Lord of the Dance. On either side of this figure are four deities all in similar poses. To the far left is the yellow deity named the Knowledge-Holder Having Power Over Duration of Life. To the left is the white deity named the Earth-Abiding Knowledge-Holder. To the right of *rDo-rje Sems-dpah* is the red deity named the Knowledge-Holder of the Great Symbol. To the far right is the green deity named the Self-Evolved Knowledge-Holder.

The *mandala* proper is made up of two outer four-colored flaming rings filled with forty eight wrathful deities: The outer ring consists of twenty-four animal headed *Yoginis* and four *Yoginis* of the Door. The inner circle consists of eight human headed *Kerimas*, eight *Htamenmas* and four Female Door Keepers.

In the sacred center amid vibrant, ever burning, celestial flames are the wrathful emanations of the *Thag-bZang-ris*. They are the ferocious *Herukabuddhas*, the wrathful emanations of the *Dhyani Buddhas* and that of the *Adi-Buddha* (*Samanthabadra*) with their *shaktis*..

Plate V.

Plate VI.

The Wrathful Deities **(detail) The Bardo Mandala or Thub-pa-drug Mandala or The Chonyid Bardo Mandala (Mandala of the Six Wrathful and Six Peaceful Buddhas or "The Transitional State of the Experiencing of Reality")**

Karma Thupten, aka Karma Lama (Tibetan)

Distemper, fine silver, & 24k. gold on muslin, 43 1/4" h. x 33" w.

Kathmandu (Kantipur), Nepal

1989 (in the 18th Century Style)

Plate VI.

Adi-Buddha, and is the primordial *Buddha* of all *mandalas*. He is surrounded at the cardinal points by four identical white deities whose right hand is in the *bhumisparsa mudra* and the left in the *vitarka mudra*. These four figures may represent *rDo-rje Sems-dpah* which then would call forth the five-fold *rDo-rje Sems-dpah*.

At the gates of the inner sanctuary are represented a red guardian (north), gold guardian (east), white guardian (south) and yellow guardian (west). On the inner points are red, gold, white and white guardians, respectively.

In the four inner corners are represented four white deities dressed as *bodhisattvas*, each are bracketed by two *mahasiddhas* or *gurus*. *Ushnishavijaya*, the deity in the upper left hand corner has eight arms. The principle arms hold a *visva-vajra* (right) and a demon snare (left). The other right hands hold an image of *Buddha*, an arrow and the *bhumisparsa mudra* while the left hands hold the *abhaya mudra*, a bow, and the *dhyana mudra*. The upper right and lower left deity figures are identical. They are white, the right hand in the *tarjani mudra* rests on the knee while the left is raised to the chest in the *tarjani mudra*. Flowers bloom at both shoulders. The iconography clearly identifies this deity as the *Kandiravani Tara*. The lower right figure is a mirror image of the other two.

Across the top of the *mandala* are twelve niches in which figures appear. From left to right appear *Sakyamuni Buddha*, *Vajrasattva* and ten *mahasiddhas* or *arhats* (Indian and Tibetan holy men). They are tentatively identified as: *Atisha*, *Khadub*, *Dharmakirti*, *Dignaga*, *Gedundub*, *Shantideva*, *Chandrakirti*, *Sakya Pandita*, *Bhsadra* and *Panthaka*. Likewise, across the bottom corresponding niches appear. From left to right appear: 1) a yellow deity dressed as a *bodhisattva* with three heads and four arms, the principle arms hold a *ghanta* (bell) and *vajra*, the deity's *vahana* (transport or throne) is a *garuda*, 2) a yellow deity dressed as a *bodhisattva* with one heads and two arms holding a *ghanta* (bell) and *vajra*, the deity's *vahana* is a white elephant, 3) a red-orange deity dressed as a *bodhisattva* with one head and four arms, the principle arms hold a *ghanta* (bell) and *vajra*, the deity's *vahana* is a blue-green goat, 4) a blue deity dressed as a *bodhisattva* with one head and two arms, holding a *goad* and *cintamani* jewel, the deity's *vahana*) is a tan bullock, 5) a green deity dressed as a *bodhisattva* with one head and two arm, the deity's *vahana* is a human figure on all fours, 6) a white deity dressed as a *bodhisattva* with one head and two arms holding a *ghanta* (bell) and *vajra*, the deity's *vahana* (is a red bullock, 7) a pale blue-green deity dressed as a *bodhisattva* with one head and two arms, the left holds a *cintamani* jewel, the deity's *vahana* is a white ram, 8) a yellow deity dressed as a *bodhisattva* with one head and two arms holding a *ghanta* (bell) and *vajra*, the deity's *vahana* is a brown horse, 9) a white deity dressed as a *bodhisattva* with one head and four arms, the deity's *vahana* is a tan bullock, 10) a yellow deity dressed as a *bodhisattva* with one head and two arms, the deity's vahana is a red boar, 11) the *dharmapala Jambhala*, the deity's *vahana* is a white lion, and 12) an *mahasiddha* or *arhat*.

Plate VII.

Shato Mandala with rDo-rje Sems-dpah or Mandala of the Supreme Buddha Vajrasattva
Karma Thupten, aka Karma Lama (Tibetan)
Distemper, fine silver, & 24k. gold on muslin, 47" h. x 43" w.
Kathmandu (Kantipur), Nepal
1989 (in the 18th Century Style)

The *Mandala of the Supreme Buddha Vajrasattva*, another *tantric mandala*, presents in its center *rDo-rje Sems-dpah* (Dorje Sempe)(Skt.: *Vajrasattva*) in the *yab-yum* position with his *Prajna*. He is white and holds at his breast in his right hand the *dorje* (Skt.: *vajra*) and in his left hand the *dril-bu* (Skt.: *ghanta*). *rDo-rje Sems-dpah* in a celestial appearance represents

Plate VII.

Plate VIII.

<u>rDo-rje</u> <u>Sems-dpah</u> <u>Mandala</u> (Skt.: *Vajra-sattva*) (Purification Mandala)

Karma Thupten, aka Karma Lama (Tibetan)
Distemper, fine silver, & 24k. gold on muslin, 30" h. x 24 1/2" w.
Kathmandu (Kantipur), Nepal
1989 (in the 18th Century Style)

The *bodhisattva rDo-rje Sems-dpah* (Skt.: *Vajrasattva*) is the embodiment of Purification, personifies the purity of the awareness of ultimate reality. He, the primordial *Buddha* of all mandalas, reflecting all *Buddha*-qualities. Sometimes, he is named as the sixth *Dhyani Buddha* and assumes the collective qualities of the *Dhyanis*. His white coloration coupled with the robes and ornaments of a *bodhisattva* become his prime iconographical manifestation. He, represented with one face and two arms, holds in his right hand over his heart a ceremonial thunderbolt (*vajra, rdo-rje*) symbolic of "Ultimate Reality" (*Sunya*), and with his left hand resting on his hip, clasps a ceremonial bell, symbolic of "Wisdom" (*Prajna*). At times *rDo-rje Sems-dpah* is represented by the form and aspect of *rDo-rje-hChang* (Dorje Chang) (Skt.: *Vajradhara*).

In this *mandala rDo-rje Sems-dpah* is shown in the center presented in the *yab-yum* (Chin.: *yin-yang*) position with his consort (*Saktí*). He holds in his right hand over his heart a ceremonial thunderbolt (Skt.: *vajra*; Tib.: *dorje*) symbolic of Ultimate Reality (*Sunya*), and with his left hand resting on his hip he clasps a ceremonial bell (Skt.: *ghanta*), symbolic of Wisdom (*Prajnâ*). His consort holds in her left hand a skull cap (Skt.: *kapala*), symbol of "Oneness Absolute," and in her right hand a ceremonial knife (Skt.: *katri*), symbolic of the destruction of Ignorance. *rDo-rje Sems-dpah* is surrounded on the four cardinal points by representations of himself without his consort. These representations are surrounded by the various sacred, protective gates and rings of a *mandala*.

Centered and above, one finds the representation of *rDo-rje-hChang* (*Vajradhara*). *rDo-rje-hChang* is the first *tantric* manifestation of *Sakyamuni Buddha* and also one of the anthropomorphic representation of *Adi-Buddha*, the primordial *Buddha*.

Below and to the left of *rDo-rje-hChang* is the representation of *Tilopa* (*Teo*) an Indian *tantric yoga* who influenced *Padma Karpo*. Opposite, to the right, rests *Naropa* (*Narlo*), a second important Indian *yoga* who influenced *Marpa*. Below *Tilopa*, on the left, is *Marpa*, the great translator of Buddhist and *tantric* texts and one of the founding figures of the *bKa'-brgyud-pa* Order. Opposite *Marpa*, on the right is the renowned *Milarepa*, a student of *Marpa*. Because he lived on nettle soup during much of his long meditations, *Milarepa* is shown with green skin. His renown comes from his poetry, his saintliness and, as *Marpa*, a founder of the *bKa'-brgyud-pa* Order. Below *Marpa*, on the left, is depicted *Gampopa* (*Tapo*)(1079-1153), a student of *Milarepa* and also considered as a founder of the *bKa'-brgyud-pa* Order. Opposite *Gampopa*, on the right, the first *Karmapa Lama* of the *bKa'-brgyud-pa* Order, *Dusum Khyenpa* is represented. Across the bottom, left to right are depicted *Gonpo Pena* (Protector of the *Sa-skya-pa* Order), *Guru Trakpo* (a wrathful manifestation of *Guru Rinpoche*) *Padmasambhava* (Tib., *Guru Rinpoche* or *Lopon Rinpoche*, the Indian Tantric master and founder of the *rNying-ma-pa* Order), *Shindoma* (consort of *Padmasambhava*), and *dPal-ldan-lha-mo* (the wrathful protectoress of the *dGe-lugs-pa* Order and guardian of Lhasa).

Even though this *mandala* includes the four major orders of Tibetan *Vajrayana* Buddhism, the iconographic emphasis appears to be weighted toward the *bKa'-brgyud-pa* Order. This is considered to be a very powerful *mandala* due to the fact that the third ring, the cemetery, is included. The inclusion of the third ring with the representation of the eight sacred cemeteries is normally this ring is reserved for *mandalas* dedicated to wrathful deities.

Plate VIII.

1989 (in the 18th Century Style)

sPyan-ras-gZigs (Skt.: *Avalokiteshvara*; Eng. phonetic trans.: *Chenrezig*), the beautiful youth, the *bodhisattva*, that embodies compassion, the desire that all things be free from suffering and dissatisfaction. The *Dhyani Buddha Amitabha* created him from a light which sprung from his right eye. He resided in that pure land called *Potala*. *sPyan-ras-gZigs* observed through clairvoyance that sentient beings were becoming enlightened which pleased him. Yet he realized that no matter how many sentient beings were becoming enlightened, there would always be more who were not enlightened. Three times he made this observation and this disheartened him. He considered these three different occasions and said, "How can I possibly help these sentient beings?" With this third questioning he lost his *bodhicittsa* motivation and the power of his despair exploded his head into countless pieces. His body was reassembled by *Buddha Amitabha* and *Vajrapani* into a very powerful form with eleven heads and a thousand arms, *sPyan-ras-gZigs Phyag-sTong sPyan-sTong*. *sPyan-ras-gZigs*, the patron saint of Tibet, is considered to be reincarnated in the Dalai Lamas. In China he is known as *Kuan-yin*.

The central positioning of *sPyan-ras-gZigs Phyag-sTong sPyan-sTong Mandala* typifies the compositional make-up of mandalas dedicated to this deity. The deity is shown here in the form give him by *Buddha Amitabha* and *Vajrapani*. On each of his one thousand hands an eye appears in the center of the palm which symbolizes the union of wisdom (the eye) and skillful means (the hand). In this form *sPyan-ras-gZigs Phyag-sTong sPyan-sTong* possesses a white body, stands on a moon disc and a lotus blossom. He has eight main hands, the first two of which clasps the wish fulfilling gem to his heart, the next five hold a lotus symbol of compassion, a bow and arrow representing method and wisdom, a vase containing the nectar of immortality, a crystal rosary, an eight-spoked wheel representing the teachings of Buddha, and the eighth hand is presented with the open palmed gesture (*mudrâ*) of generosity and mercy. He has three rows of three colored faces, representing the three manifestation bodies or the principal aspects of *Buddha* or of Buddhahood: red (*dharmakaya*), white (*sambhogakaya*), and green (*nirmanakaya*). Above these nine heads is the blue wrathful face of *Vajrapani* and the red face of *Buddha Amitabha*.

sPyan-ras-gZigs Phyag-sTong sPyan-sTong stands upon a lotus throne, surrounded by a nimbus, all floating upon a cosmic blue background.

In this *thagka sPyan-ras-gZigs Phyag-sTong sPyan-sTong* is surrounded by sixteen small rainbow circled, orb-projecting *mandalas*. The upper central mandala is *Sakyamuni Buddha*, the rest of the *mandalas* depict forms of *sPyan-ras-gZigs*, an other representation of *Sakyamuni BuddhaT*, Green *Tara*, and other peaceful and wrathful deities. Of note is the representation of *Vajrapani* behind a radiant rainbow in the bottom center of the *thangka*.

Plate IX.

sPyan-ras-gZigs Phyag-sTong sPyan-sTong Mandala (Chenrezig Chaktong Chentong Mandala) (The Thousand-Armed Avaloki-teshvara Mandala)
Karma Thupten, aka Karma Lama (Tibetan)
Distemper, fine silver, & 24k. gold on muslin, 40 1/2" h. x 27 1/4" w.
Kathmandu (Kantipur), Nepal

Plate IX.

Plate X.

<u>sPyan-ras-gZigs</u> <u>Phyag-bZhi-pa</u> (Chenrezig Chazhi-pa)(Four-Armed Avalokiteshvara)
Karma Thupten, aka Karma Lama (Tibetan)
Distemper, fine silver, & 24k. gold, muslin, 19" h. x 14 1/2" w.
Kathmandu (Kantipur), Nepal
1989 (in the 18th Century Style)

sPyan-ras-gZigs (Skt.: *Avalokiteshvara*; Eng. phonetic trans.: *Chenrezig*), the beautiful youth, the *bodhisattva*, that embodies compassion, the desire that all things be free from suffering and dissatisfaction. The *Dhyani Buddha Amitabha* created him from a light which sprung from his right eye. He resided in that pure land called *Potala*. *sPyan-ras-gZigs* observed through clairvoyance that sentient beings were becoming enlightened which pleased him. Yet he realized that no matter how many sentient beings were becoming enlightened, there would always be more who were not enlightened. He is the *bodhisattva* of Compassion.

sPyan-ras-gZigs Phyag-bZhi-pa is shown here sitting in the full lotus posture on a sun and moon disc supported by a lotus blossom. His body is white in color and he wears the five silk robes and the jeweled ornamentation of a *bodhisattva*. Generally, a *bodhisattva's* color is that of his/her *kulesa*. In *sPyan-ras-gZigs Phyag-bZhi-pa'* case, *Dhyani Buddha Amitabha*, whose color is red. The white *sPyan-ras-gZigs* is frequently the color found in Nepal, however, he may rightly be represented as red in color.

In his principle hands he clasps the wish fulfilling gem to his heart. In his other two hands he holds a crystal rosary and the blue flower of compassion. *sPyan-ras-gZigs* has many forms, but he can always be recognized by the gray-green deer skin draped over his left shoulder.

In this representation he is depicted against a landscape that both depicts that beautiful land, *Potala*, and indicates the strong influence of Chinese landscape painting in Tibetan art. This influence was present from the Kingdom of Tibet's earliest associations with the Empire of China. Of further note is the well-spring seen gushing forth from the mountain on the left, *sPyan-ras-gZigs Phyag-bZhi-pa* has strong associations with such well-springs, as does his *sakti* (consort) *sGrol-ma-ljang-gu* (Green *Tara*).

Plate X.

Plate XI.

<u>sGrol-ma</u> <u>lJan-gu</u> (Drolma Jang) (Skt.: *Syamatara*) (Green Tara)
Karma Thupten, aka Karma Lama (Tibetan)
Distemper, fine silver, & 24k. gold, muslin, 41 1/2" h. x 30 3/4" w.
Kathmandu (Kantipur), Nepal
1988 (in the 14th Century Style)

As the Green Savioress, *sGrol-ma lJan-gu* or the Green *Tara,* one of 21 *Tara,* is the patron goddess of Tibet. She possesses considerable importance in the Tibetan pantheon.

Târâ is known as the "Savioress," the "Deliveress" as she aids people in crossing the Ocean of Existence as well to soothe their tribulation filled lives. The Green *Târâ* presides over the evening hours. She embodies the motherly aspect of compassion and accompanies *sPyan-ras-gZig* (Skt.: *Avalokiteshvara*). Therefore, because of her compassionate nature she is the *shakti* of *sPyan-ras-gZig* also a god of considerable importance in Tibet.

sGrol-ma lJan-gu's body is green and she sits in royal posture on the moon disc (symbolic of her soothing human suffering during the night, her sphere of influence) and lotus flower, while her extended right leg rests on a lotus blossom. She holds the blue lotuses of compassion in her hands.

The throne upon which *sGrol-ma lJan-gu's* sits is surrounded by a multi-layered shrine within the details of which are found various animals, mythic beasts and beleaguered humans. These are found in the smallest detail. The shrine, reminiscent of the sacred Mt. Meru, is crowned by three stupas. The total is surrounded by a bhodi tree, sacred to *Sakyamuni Buddha*, in which can be seen various birds.

Plate XI.

Plate XII.

dPal-ldan lHa-mo (Paldan Lhamo) (Skt.: *Srí Deví*)
Karma Thupten, aka Karma Lama (Tibetan)
Distemper, fine silver, & 24k. gold, muslin, 23" h. x 18" w.
Kathmandu (Kantipur), Nepal
1989 (in the 18th Century Style)

She, in a *tantric* manifestation, the "Glorious One," protectoress of the *dGe-lugs-pa* sect and guardian of the capital, Lhasa, raises feelings of horror. As a *dharmapala* (protector of religion) *dPal-ldan lHa-mo* appears hideously wrathful. Her wrath is directed not towards the believer but towards the enemies of religion, the unbeliever.

This wrathful goddess, colored blue, has but one face, three eyes and two arms. She grasps a club-staff in her right hand, while in her left she holds a skull cap of a child born of an incestuous union, brimming with blood and fat. A freshly drawn tiger-skin girds her waist and a human skin drapes her shoulders. A poisonous snake and a lion's head hang from her earrings, while in her teeth *dPal-ldan lHa-mo* clutches a human corpse. Broken chains hang from her ankles and writhing snake belt girds her waist. The moon appears above a crown of five skulls in her hair which streams upwards. and the sun nestles in her navel.

Canopied by a peacock feather umbrella, *dPal-ldan lHa-mo* sits on a cannibal skin saddle, astride a mule, as she rides over a sea of menstrual blood and fat. Writhing, poisonous snakes serve as the reins for her mount which bears an eye on its rump. From the cannibal-skin saddle hangs a skull, a bag of poison potions and diseases, and divination dice. She is shown accompanied by the Lion-headed One and the Crocodile-headed One, who are *dPal-ldan lHa-mo's* frequent companions.

Plate XII.

Plate XIII.

Na-ro mKha'-spyod-ma (Skt.: *Sarvabuddha-dakini*)
Karma Thupten, aka Karma Lama (Tibetan)
Distemper, fine silver & 24 k gold, muslin, 21" h. x 16" w.
Kathmandu (Kantipur), Nepal
1989 (in the 18th Century Style)

A *dakini*, a female deity or magical, supernatural being who is able to fly through the air. Sometimes they are referred to a "Cloud Fairies." They are able to initiate novices into *tantra* and assist *yogin* in spiritual insights or grant them supernatural powers. A *dakini* may appear as a young girl in body with a lion, bird, dog or horse head.

In this *thangka Na-ro mKha'-spyod-ma*, patroness of the *Sa-skya-pa* Order and acolyte to *Vajravahari*, is shown with a human head, three eyes and a crown of five human skulls. In her right hand she holds a *karttrika* (ritual chopper) while in her left she raises to her lips a *kapala* (human skull-cup) filled with human blood and fat. A *khatvanga* (the magic stick of *Padmasambhava*) rests in the crook of her left arm. She appears nude but wears ornaments of carved human bones and human skulls. *Na-ro mKha'-spyod-ma* is red and stands in the *pratyalidhasana* (bow and arrow position) on the forms of the enemies of religion. A halo of flames surrounds her and a lotus supports her.

Directly below *Na-ro mKha'-spyod-ma* dances the *Citapati*, a pair of skeletons who are the enemies of thieves and often associated with *gShin-rje* (Skt.: *Yama*) the god of death. To the left and below rests a *kapala* with a tongue, nose, ears, eyes and brain representing the senses. To the right on a low table rests offerings normally brought to this deity. The total rests within a landscape of Chinese influence.

Plate XIII.

Plate XIV.

<u>Sha-kya</u> <u>Thub-pa</u> (Skt.: *Sakyamuni Buddha*)
Karma Thupten, aka Karma Lama (Tibetan)
Distemper, fine silver & 24 k gold on muslin, 21" h. x 16" w.
Kathmandu (Kantipur), Nepal
1993 (in the 18th Century Style)

In this *thangka*, a typical representation, *Sakyamuni Buddha* sits upon a lion throne in front of a lotus bordered aura. In front of the throne on a low table and flanking it are a number of offerings which are sacred to *Sakyamuni Buddha*. At the base of the thangka are two small deer which recall Deer Park where the Law was given.

Plate XIV.

Plate XV.

sPyan-ras-gZigs Phyag-bZhi-pa (Chenrezig Cha-zhipa)(Four-Armed Avalokiteshvara)
Tibeto-Nepali Artisan, Patan workshop
Copper alloy, cast & repoussé, 6" h. x 4" w. x 3 1/4" d.
Patan (Lalitapur), Nepal
20th Century

For a description of the iconography of *sPyan-ras-gZigs Phyag-bZhi-pa* see: *sPyan-ras-gZigs Phyag-bZhi-pa*, Plate X.

Plate XV.

Plate XVI.
<u>Buddha Image</u> (Sakyamuni Buddha [?] or Don-yod Grub-pa [?])
Tibeto-Nepali Artisan, Bhadgaon workshop
Polychromed wood and peacock feathers, 9" h. 4 3/4" w. x 3" d.
Bhadgaon (Bhaktapur), Nepal
c. 1988

Although most Tibetan craftsman cast their *Buddha* images in metal, there exist isolated instances of images produced in wood. However, the relative rarity of wood in Tibet makes a wooden Buddha image rather unusual. Most probably, this image was carved in Bhadgaon or Bhaktapur by a Nepali craftsman, who may be Buddhist. It is to be noted that this image is carved out of a single black of wood. Bhadgaon or Bhaktapur, in the Eastern Katmandu Valley, has been known for centuries as a center of fine wood carving.

The image with this combined *mudra* possesses several related interpretations. This image, seems to represents *Sakyamuni Buddha* since the color of the image is gold--the usual color of *Sakyamuni Buddha*. The right hand is in the *abhaya mudra* while the left hand rests, palm up, in the lap in the *dhyana mudra*. Although *Sakyamuni* may be shown in this *mudra*, it is more often a mudra used to represent the *Panca Buddha Don-yod Grub-pa* (*Dhyani Buddha Amoghasiddhi*), however, his color is green. Traditionally the *abhaya* is the *mudra* of protection or the blessing of fearlessness, while the *dhyana* represents meditation. In the *Theravada* tradition this *mudra* is interpreted as "calming the children" or "calming the angry children."

The aura (Tib.: *rgyab-yol*; Skt.: *prabha-mandala*), or Glory Arch backs the image. Frequently, in cast pieces, the arch is quite ornate with sacred animals and other iconographic images. Here, the arch is simplified and represents a flame motif on its outer border and forms an aura around the image. The peacock feathers, a sacred symbol of Enlightened Being, is frequently found in conjunction with the images.

Plate XVI.

Plate XVII.

Buddha Image (Sukhothai Style)
Thai Artisan
Cast bronze, 16" h. x 12 1/2" w. x 7" d.
Thailand
First half, 20th C.

The Thai *Theravada Buddha* images produced during the *Sukhothai* period are considered by many as the finest examples of the art of image making in Thailand. Indeed the *Sukhothai Buddha* images stand out among all images from the Orient for their grace and transcendental elegance.

The proportions of the figure are, in general, elongated. The arms and the legs as well as the trunk become fluid, as though there are no underlying bony structures. There is a strong parallel between the *Sukhothai Buddha* images and the representation of the human form (particularly the Virgin Mary) to be found in the Late Medieval and Eastern Orthodox traditions. Generally, in Thai *Sakyamuni Buddha* images as in the image here depicted, the *Buddha* is portrayed in the *bhumisparsa mudra* ("subduing Mara" or calling the Earth to Witness"). The *ushnisa* (the protuberance on the top of the head) of the *Sukhothai Buddha* images becomes extremely elongated and flame-like. The monastic robes are simple and undecorated. The end of the robe falls over the left shoulder and ends at the nipple-line.

Generally, *Sukhothai Buddhas* sits on a rather simple lotus throne as is the case with most of the images of Thailand. Later, when they are installed in a temple, the bases can become extremely elaborate. This image, a 20th Century production, presents the image of *Buddha* in the *Sukhothai* style, however, the throne upon which the fugure rests is more elaborate and mirrors the *Rattanakosin* Period.

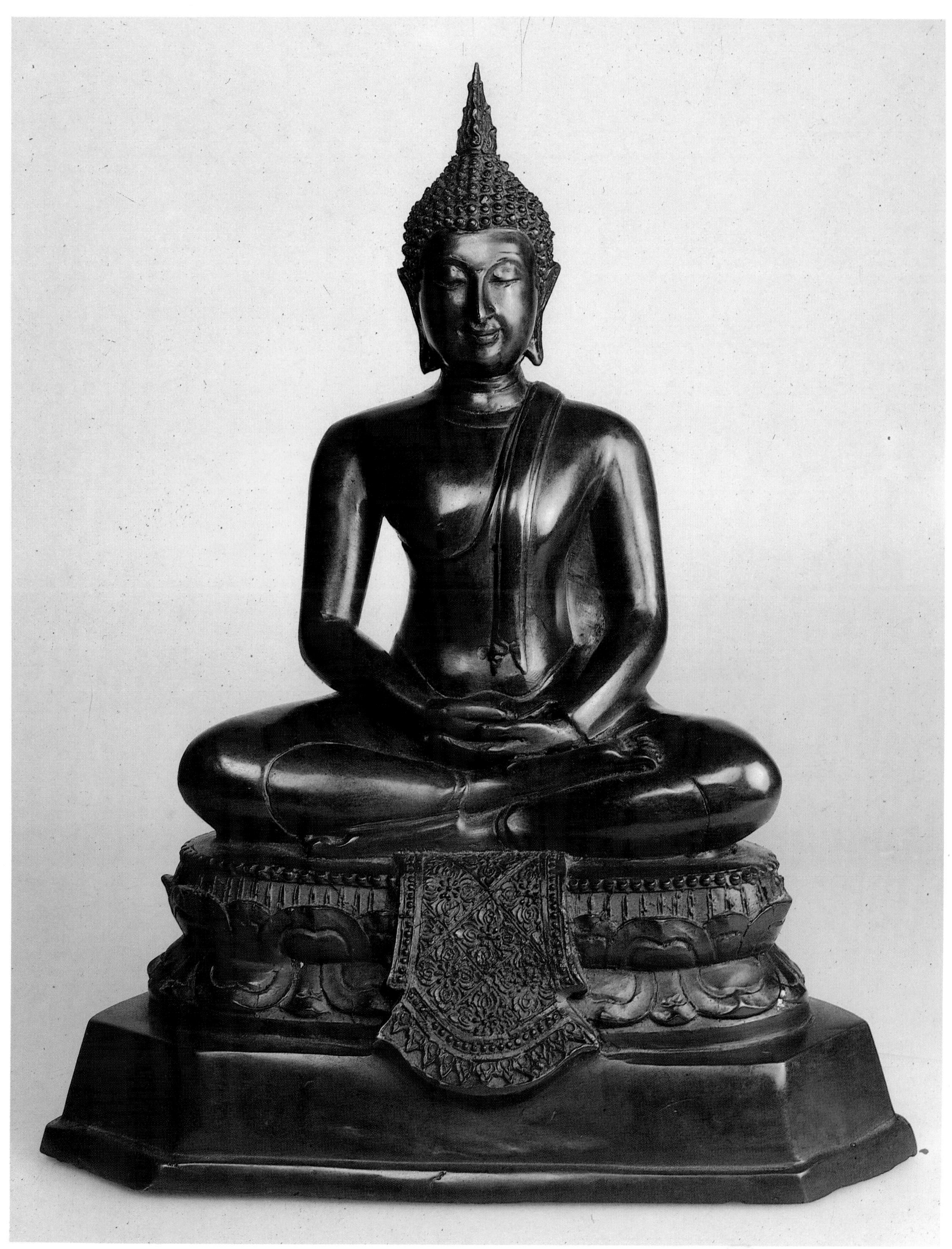

Plate XVII.

Plate XVIII.

Buddha Image **(Chieng Saen Style)**
Thai Artisan
Cast bras, 8 1/4" h. x 6" w. x 3 3/4" d.
Thailand
Late 18th C.

Chieng Saen images, unlike those of the *Sukhothai* style, bear a knob-like ushnisa which is likened to a lotus bud. The figures appear less supple than those of the *Sukhothai* style, and thereby somewhat more substantial, thick, and solid. The *Buddha* images' heads are rounder, the curls larger, the eyebrows arched in a half-moon shape, the eyes prominent and the chin well defined.

Generally, the image makers of the *Chieng Saen* style preferred seated *Buddhas*. The figures sit upright, back perpendicular to the ground. Unlike a majority of Thai images, these frequently assume the *vajrasena* foot position rather than the more regularly used *virasena* . As in this image the *Chieng Saen's* use of the bhumisparsa mudra (subduing *Mara*) predominates. The robe is open, covering the left shoulder and the flap falls to the nipple-line in mirrored serpentine folds.

This image sits on a lotus throne. As in most Thai *Buddha* images the "throne" is rather simple, not as elaborate as the Northern traditions.

Plate XVIII.

Plate XIX.

Buddha Image with Naga (Lop Buri Style)
Thai Artisan
Cast bronze, 8 3/4" h. x 2 3/4" w. x 2 1/2" d.
Thailand
Late 18th C

The *Lop Buri* period indicates the influence and to some extent the over-lordship of the Khmer empire in what is now Thailand. The strongest influence is to be seen in architecture. However, in larger sculptural works an important Khmer influence is to be noted.

The image of the *Buddha* is somewhat lighter than those of the preceding *Srivijaya* period of Thailand. Of importance is the appearance in many of the images of a diadem as well as a cone-like *ushnisa*.

This small image typifies the *Lop Buri* style. The right shoulder is bare and the robe flap falls to the waist. This figure sits in the *virâsena* position with his hands in the *dhyana mudra* (meditation hand position).

The preeminent feature of this image is the *Naga* (serpent). After his Enlightenment *Sakyamuni Buddha* spent many days in deep meditation. *Mara* (the evil one) sent torrential rains to disturb the *Buddha*. The *Naga*, King *Muchalinda*, rose up, spread his hood and protected *Sakyamuni Buddha* from the elements. This image became very popular during the *Lop Buri* period in Thailand. The image of *Sakyamuni Buddha* sits upon the coils of the *Naga* while the seven-headed hood protects him.

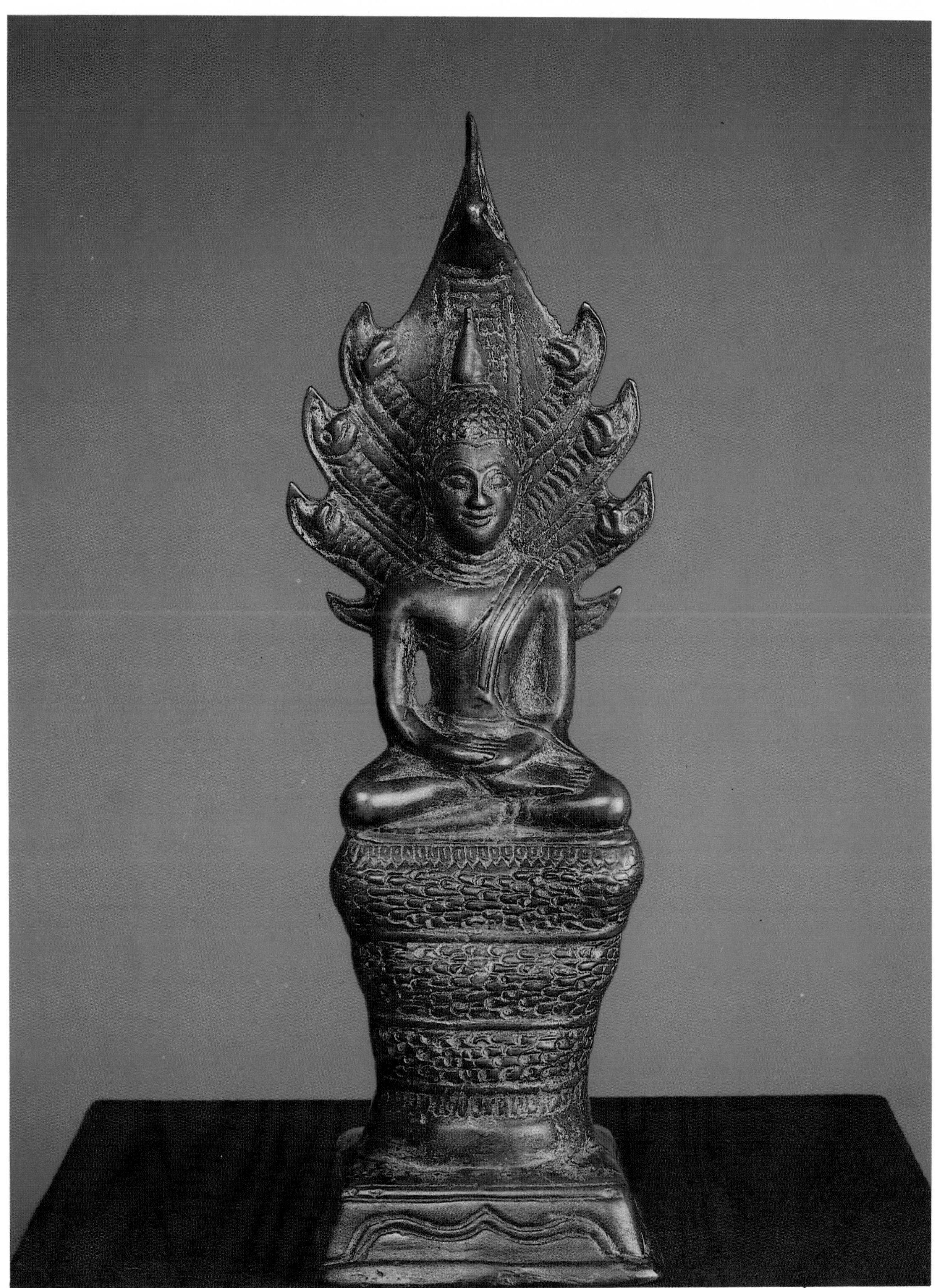

Plate XIX.

Amoghasiddhi) (the North [far left]); **Rin-chen-hByung-lDan** (Skt.: Ratnasambhava)(the South [2nd from left]); **Mi-bsKyod-pa** (Skt.: Aksobhya)(the Center); **rNam-par sNang-mDzad** (Skt.: Vairocana)(the East [2nd from right]); **hOd-dpag-med** (Skt.: Amitâbha)(the West [far right])
Tibetan Artisan, Patan workshop
Copper alloy, cast and repoussé, 4 3/4" h. x 3" w. x 2 1/4" d. (with attached aura, each)
Patan (Lalitapur), Nepal
1990

The *rGyal-ba-Rigs-lNga* (Skt.: *Panca Buddhas*) or the Five Mystic (*Dhyani*) Buddhas is a tradition that the *bKa'-brgyud-pa* and *dGe-lugs-pa* Orders espouse. The *Dhyani Buddhas* (*Buddhas* of Meditation) are a product solely of *Vajrayana* Buddhism. *Vajrayana* conceived of the world as being made up of five cosmic elements (Skt.: *skandhas*) which are embodied in the five *Dhyani Buddhas*. They spring from "the diamond-clear concentration of the *Adi-Buddha*" and from the *Dhyani Buddhas* come the *Dhyani Bodhisattvas*. When shown together, they are known as the *Panca Buddhas* (Skt.).

Dhyani Buddha Amoghasiddhi (Tib.: *Don-yod-Grub-pa*) -- the North. *Amoghasiddhi* personifies the element of *samskâra* (conformation). His coloration is green. He represents the rainy season. His cognition symbol is the the double thunderbolt and his *shakti* is *Tara.* His *Dhyani Bodhisattva* is *Visvapani.*

Dhyani Buddha Ratnasambhava (Tib.: *Rin-chen-hByung-lDan*) -- the South. The *Dhyani Buddha Ratnasambhava* represents the element *vedana* (sensation). He rules over the spring season and is colored yellow. He is the progenitor of the *ratna* (jewel) family. His cognition symbol is the jewel and his *shakti* is *Vajradhatisvari.* His *Dhyani Bodhisattva* is *Ratnapani.*

Dhyani Buddha Aksobhya (Tib.:*Mi-bsKyod-pa*) -- the Center. The element *vijnana* (consciousness) finds its manifestation in the *Dhyani Buddha Aksobhya. Aksobhya* who is portrayed in blue, represents the sense of hearing, the elements of Ether, Sound, and Winter. His cognition symbol is the thunderbolt and his *shakti* is *Mamaki*. His *Dhyani Bodhisattva* is *Vajrapani.*

Dhyani Buddha Vairocana (Tib.: *rNam-par sNang-mDzad*) -- the East. *Rupa* (form), the cosmic element manifests itself in the *Dhyani Buddha Vairocana.* He is white in color, and symbolizes Fall. He is the embodiment of Ideal Knowledge. *Vairocana* is ranked first among the *Dhyani Buddhas,* and, as such, is often placed in the sanctuary of a stupa. His cognition symbol is the discus and his *shakti* is *Locana*. His *Dhyani Bodhisattva* is *Samantabhadra*.

Dhyani Buddha Amitabha (Tib.: *hOd-dpag-med*) -- the West. The cosmic element *samjna* (name) finds its embodiment in *Buddha Amitabha,* the oldest of the *Buddhas* in Meditation. His color is red, and he symbolizes the vital fluid. He represents the summer season, and presides over the *Sukhâvati* heaven in silent meditation. His cognition symbol is the lotus and his *shakti* is *Pandara*. His *Dhyani Bodhisattva* is *Avalokiteshvara* (*Padmapani*).

Plate XX.

rGyal-ba-Rigs-lNga (Skt.: *Panca Buddhas*) (The Five Dhyani Buddhas); Don-yod-Grub-pa (Skt.:

Plate XX.

Plate XXI.

sMan-gyi bLa Bai-dur-ya hOd-kyi rGyal-po (Skt.: *Baishajyaguru Vaiduryaprabharaja*)(Medicine Buddha)

Tibeto-Nepali Artisan, Patan workshop
Copper alloy, cast and repoussé, 6" h. x 4" w. x 3 1/4" d.
Patan (Lalitapur), Nepal
1990

sMan-gyi bLa Bai-dur-ya hOd-kyi rGyal-po, but one of a number of Medicine *Buddhas*, demonstrates the power of healing. Of course, *Sakyamuni Buddha* reigns as the supreme healer.

The *Buddha* of Healing, *sMan-gyi bLa Bai-dur-ya hOd-kyi rGyal-po* (*Sanggye Menlha* as the shortened name-form) is depicted in the typical posture. He sits in the lotus position (*vajrasana*) on a lotus throne and wears the monastic robes of the Northern tradition. In this representation the borders of the robes are intricately engraved in a florid pattern. Normally, the exposed areas of his body are painted blue. In his left hand *sMan-gyi bLa Bai-dur-ya hOd-kyi rGyal-po* holds the iron alms bowl (*patra*) of the Buddhist monk out of which protrudes the *aura*, a medicinal plant. In his right hand, in the *vitarka mudra*, he holds the stem of an *aura* plant as well. *sMan-gyi bLa Bai-dur-ya hOd-kyi rGyal-po's* right hand is in the *varada mudra* (gift bestowing position).

In this *Buddha* image as in many others, the image is chased after casting, thereby bringing out wanted detail as well as the requisite surface decorations. Compare these Tibetan images with the Thai images which do not chase the images after casting.

Plate XXI.

Plate XXII.

Dsam-bha-la (Skt.: *Jambhala*)
Tibetan Artisan
Copper alloy, cast and repoussé, 4 3/4" h. x 6" w. x 3 1/4" d.
Tibet
early 19th Century

Dsam-bha-la is a *yi-dam* (tutelary deity), a *lokapala* (Guardian of the Quarters), and an important *dharmapala* ("Guardians of Religion" or "The Eight Terrible Ones"), who some feel emanates from the *Dhyani Buddha Ratnasambhava* while others from the *Dhyani Buddha Aksobhya*. This deity manifests the transmigration of the Hindu deity *Kubera* into the Tibetan pantheon of gods. He is the God of Wealth.

As a *dharmapala*, *Dsam-bha-la* ranks with the others as a deity of the eighth rank. He is the only one of the eight *dharmapala* who generally appears benign.

Dsam-bha-la costume denotes his standing--suitably rich and ornamented as if he were a king. His ornaments resemble more those of a *bodhisattva* than a *dharmapala*. On his head rest a five-leafed crown, and he wears earrings, a tight necklace, armlet, bracelet, anklet, a wide sash and fancy leather boots. In paintings his clothing glistens with rich brocaded colors.

His right hand holds a *bijapura* (citron) while his left clasps a treasure producing *nakula* (mongoose). *Dsam-bha-la's* rather robust appearance (pot belly) also belies his "God of Wealth" status. He sits in the *vama-lalitasana* on a raised throne which has three crossed thunderbolts (*visva-vajra*) on the entablature of the throne.

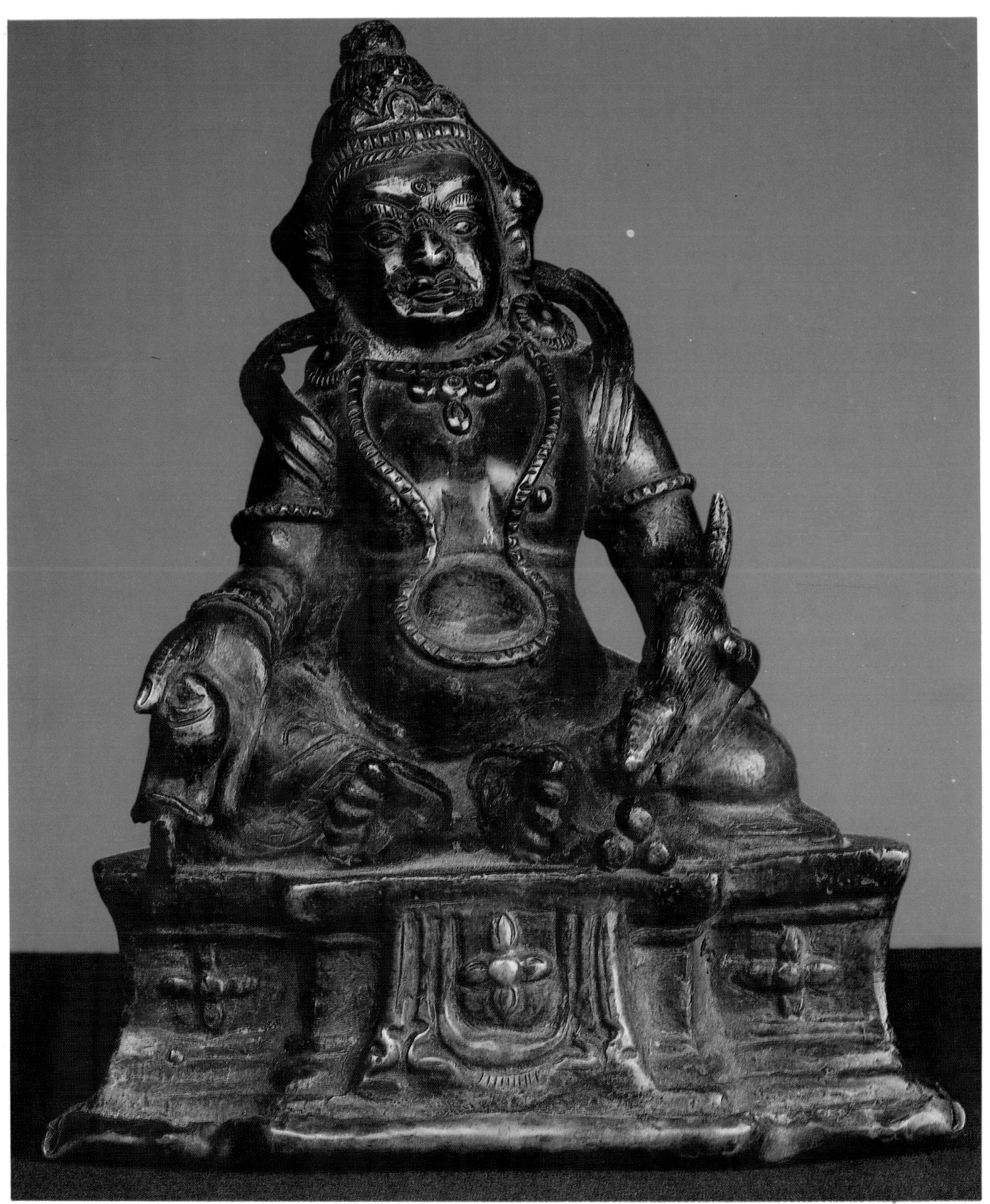

Plate XXII.

Plate XXIII.

Dung-dkar (Skt.: *Shanka*)
Tibetan Artisan
Silver, copper, conch and turquoise, formed and repoussé,
4 3/4" h. x 3" w. x 2 1/4"
20th C.

The *dung-dkar* is not only one of the eight sacred symbols of Buddhism, the sacred conch shell also has ceremonial use. This *dung-dkar* has a mouthpiece at the head of the shell, a long conical extension with a ball finial at its base, and a decorative banner shaped extension.

On the banner are eight repousée medallions of the eight sacred symbols: the precious parasol, the cylindrical banner of victory, the vase of spiritual treasure, the incomparable lotus, the golden fish, the white conch shell, the golden doctrinal wheel and the infinite knot of life. Also around the base of the mouthpiece are four medallions depicting the infinite knot of life, the vase of spiritual treasure, the white conch shell and the golden fish. These eight symbols bracket a writhing, fierce, fire-breathing dragon which clutches small conch shells in its four clawed feet. The whole surface is finely chased and repouséed in floral and geometric motifs

This *dung-dkar* is an instrument blown during certain religious ceremonies and as an iconographic device is frequently associated with calm or peaceful deities.

Plate XXIII.

Plate XXIV.

<u>Ga'u</u> (Skt.: *Gahu*)(Traveling Shrine)
Unknown Sino/Tibetan Artisan
Silver, gilded brass, copper, leather and fabric
Tibet
early 19th Century

Silver fronted *ga'us* were very often found in temple shrines and were displayed on the home's altar of virtually every Tibetan. Frequently, any number of charms and/or amulets would be found inside and a picture or small statuette of a deity would appear in the window. The two small metal bands or loops on either side of the *ga'u* are to support a leather shoulder strap by which this box could be easily transported from place to place, or on long journeys.

This shrine shaped *ga'u* exhibits a pierced-chased and repousséd silver, double-shouldered ogive arched, face-plate. Upon this face-plate, on either side of the opening, are attached gilded brass embossed representations of the Eight Auspicious Signs of *Buddha*--the precious parasol, the cylindrical banner of victory, the vase of spiritual treasure, the incomparable lotus, the golden fish, the white conch shell, the golden doctrinal wheel and the infinite knot of life. Also around the base of the mouthpiece are four medallions depicting the infinite knot of life, the vase of spiritual treasure, the white conch shell and the golden fish.

Above the opening rests an embossed representation of the Three Jewels (Tib.: *dkon-mchog-gsum*), symbol of the Holy Triad (the Buddha, the Law and the Fellowship), while below appears a monster mask (Tib.: *gzi-gdong*). The latter, is considered an auspicious emblem that wards off evil. Around the opening is a gilded brass border with two dragons (Tib.: *klu*; Skt.: *naga*) which serve as guardians.

The side walls are of copper, as is the detachable back plate. This *ga'u* is shown with its cloth and leather protective covering. The small spherical brass buttons are typical of Tibetan closures for these type of articles as well as clothing.

Plate XXIV.

Glossaries

Asana
Mudra
Attributes

Asana Glossary

Deities may be presented in a number of different leg poses. Whether standing, sitting or lying, these various poses are often referred to as *asanas*. In some cases *asana* referrers to the seat upon which the deity sit or stands. "The *Asanas* have likewise a spiritual significance. The *Vajraparyanka* attitude signifies meditation, the *Ardhaparyanka* and *Lalitasana* signify serenity, the *Alidha* heroism, the *Pratyalidha* destruction and loathsomeness, and the dancing attitude in *Ardhaparyanka* signifies wrath and horror." (BB)

The following refer only to the position of the legs, whether sitting or standing.

Adamantine -- A sitting position known as "The meditation posture" in which the legs are crossed with the soles of the both feet turned upward and resting on the opposite thighs. It is one of the two most common leg positions. This position is also known as: *Dhyanasana*, *Padmasana* , *Vajraparyankasana* or *Vajrasana*. (RG, EDS, BB)

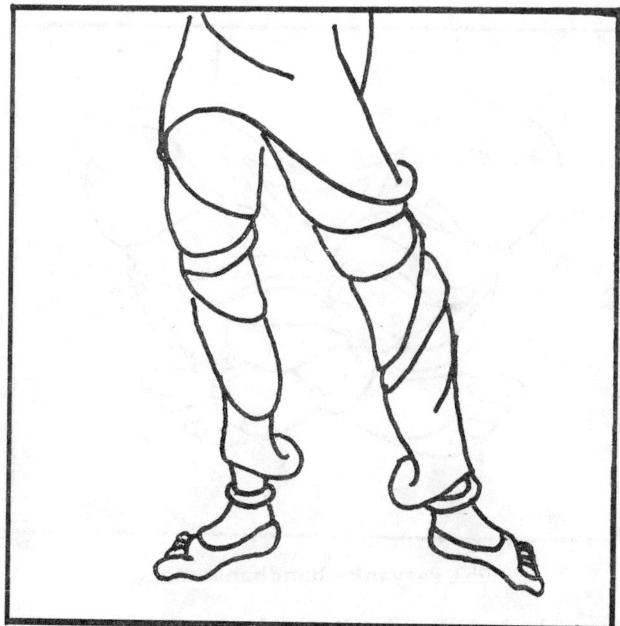

247. **Alidhasana**

Alidha or **Alidhasana** -- A standing pose with the left leg slightly bent and slightly in front of the right leg. The right leg is straight and the weight of the body is on this leg, the opposite of *pratyalidha*. Know as "drawing the bow." (RG, BB)

Ardhaparyanka or **Ardhaparyankasana (I)** -- A seated at ease pose in which the right knee is folded and raised and the left leg is crossed under and heel against the buttocks. The arm is frequently resting on the raised knee. Also known as *Maharajalilasana*. (RG, BB)

248. **Ardhaparyankasana (II)**

Ardhaparyanka or **Ardhaparyankasana (II)** -- A dancing attitude, a pose in which one foot is lifted, knee bent, heel close to thigh and the other leg is slightly bent. A position similar to that taken by *dakinis*. (AKG)

Bhadra or **Bhadrasana (I)** -- A seated posture similar to *kurmasana* in that the feet are drawn back towards the groin, however, the toes are held in the hands. (RG)

Bhadra or **Bhadrasana (II)** -- A seated pose in which both feet are pendent. (BB)

Dhyana or **Dhyanasana** -- A sitting position known as "The meditation posture" in which the legs are crossed with the soles of the both feet turned upward and resting on the opposite thighs. It is one of the two most common leg positions. This position is also known as: *Adamantine*, *Padmasana* , *Vajraparyankasana* or *Vajrasana*. (RG, EDS, BB)

European Pose -- A seated pose in which both feet are pendent, soles of the feet flat on the ground. An asana frequently used in the portrayals of *Maitreya*. Same as the *Western* pose or *Pralambapadasana*. (ML, RG, EDS)

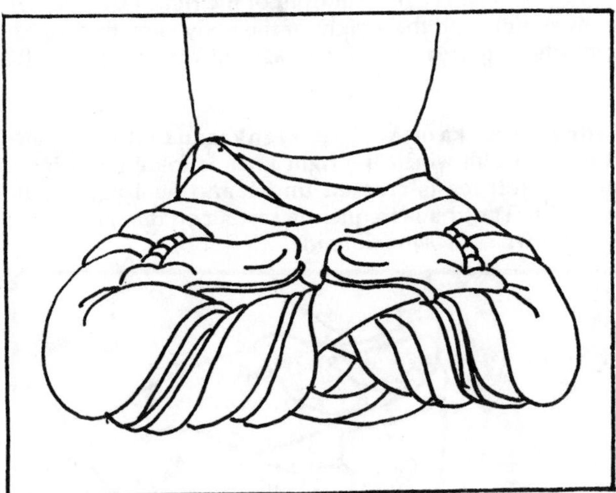

249. **Dhyanasana**

Kurma or **Kurmasana** -- A sitting pose in which the legs are crossed with the feet tucked under the buttocks. (RG)

Lalita or **Lalitasana** -- A sitting pose in which the divinity is on a pedestal with the left leg pendant, often resting on a lotus, and the right leg folded under, It is the opposite of *Vama-lalitasana*. This position is also known as: *Savya-lalitasana* or *Sukhasana*. (RG, AKG)

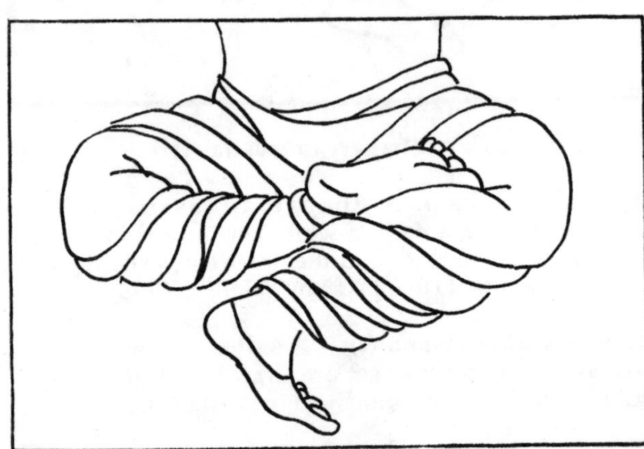

250. **Lalitasana**

Maharajalila or **Maharajalilasana** -- A seated at ease, a pose in which the right knee is folded and raised and the left leg is crossed under and heel against the buttocks. The arm is frequently resting on the raised knee. Also known as *Ardhaparyanka* or *Rajalilasana*. (RG)

Natya or Natyasana -- A variation of the *Ardhaparyankasana*. (BB)

Padma or **Padmasana (I)** -- A sitting position known as "The meditation posture" in which the legs are crossed with the soles of the both feet turned upward and resting on the opposite thighs. One of the two most common leg positions. This position is also known as: *Adamantine, Dhyanasana, Vajraparyankasana* or *Vajrasana*. (RG, EDS, BB)

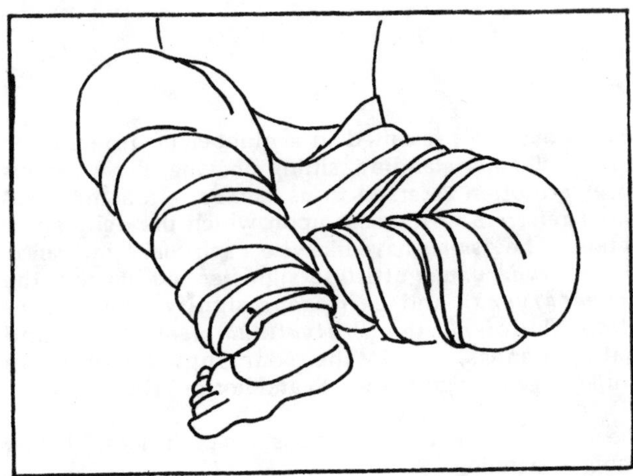

251. **Maharajalilasana**

Padma or **Padmasana (II)** -- A seated cross-legged pose, similar to *Kurmasana* except the feet are not drawn back towards the buttocks, but are left comfortably just behind the opposite knee. (RG)

Paryanka or **Paryankasana** -- A sitting position known as "The meditation posture" in which the legs are crossed with both feet invisible. (RG, BB)

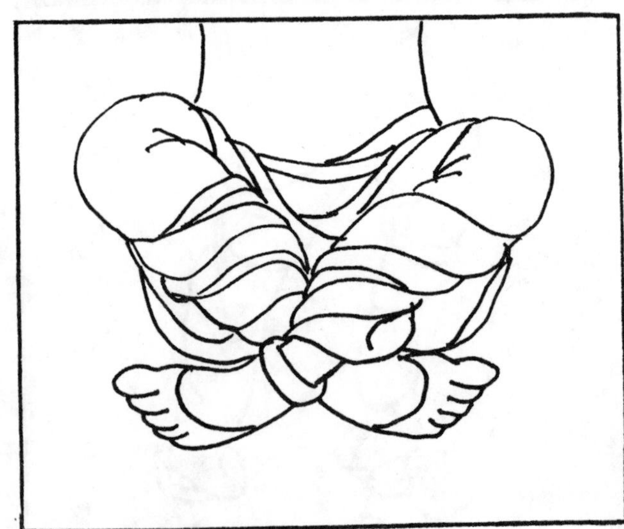

252. **Paryanka-bandhanasana**

Paryanka-bandhana or **Paryanka-bandhanasana** -- A sitting position that is similar to the *Paryankasana*, except the knees are raised to a mid-position. (EDS)

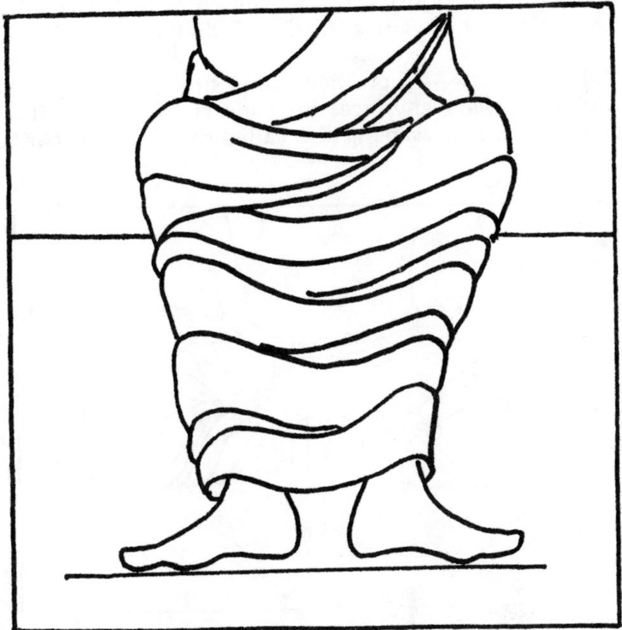

253. Pralambapadasana

Pralambapada or **Pralambapadasana** -- A seated pose in which both feet are pendent, soles of the feet flat on the ground. An asana frequently used in the portrayals of *Maitreya*. Same as the *Western* pose or *European Attitude*. (ML, RG, EDS)

254. **Pratyalidhasana**

Pratyalidha or **Pratyalidhasana** -- A standing pose with the right leg slightly bent and slightly in front of the left leg. The left leg is straight and the weight of the body is on this leg, the opposite of *Alidhasana*. (RG, BB)

Rajalila or **Rajalilasana** -- A seated pose known as "royal ease." Right knee is raised, left in usual folded position with left foot behind right heel. Right hand resting on right knee. (AG, AKG)

Raja-paryankasana -- A sitting pose in which the divinity is on a pedestal with the left leg pendant, the right leg folded with ankle resting on left knee. The left hand rests of the right ankle. (EDS)

255. **Samabhangasana**

Samabhanga or **Samabhangasana** -- A standing pose in which the feet are not spaced far apart and weight is frequently distributed evenly on both feet. There are instances in which the weight may be slightly transferred either on one leg or the other, but not in a hip-shot position or exaggerated weight transference. (BB)

Sattvasana -- A seated pose in which the legs are crossed, loosely and the soles are slightly visible. (AKG)

Savya-lalita or **Savya-lalitasana** -- A sitting pose in which the divinity is on a pedestal with the left leg pendant. This position is also known as: *Lalitasana* or *Sukhasana*. (RG)

Simha or **Simhasana** -- A seated pose similar to *kurmasana* except the palms of the hands are kept on the thigh with the fingers stretched and the eyes focus on the tip of the nose. (RG)

Sopasraya or **Sopasrayasana** -- A seated pose in which the legs are loosely locked (crossed) and the soles of the feet rest in front. (RG)

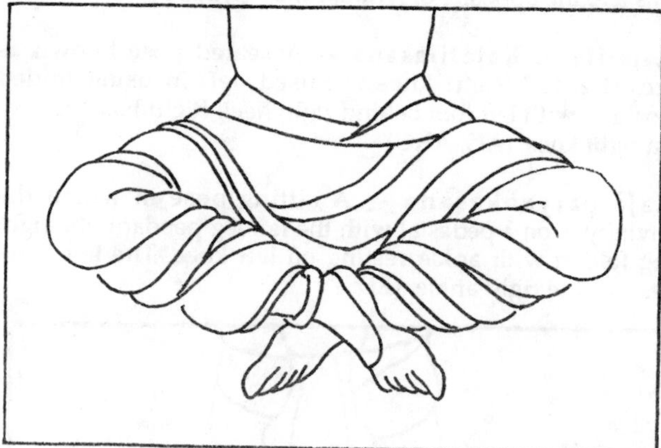

256. **Sattvasana**

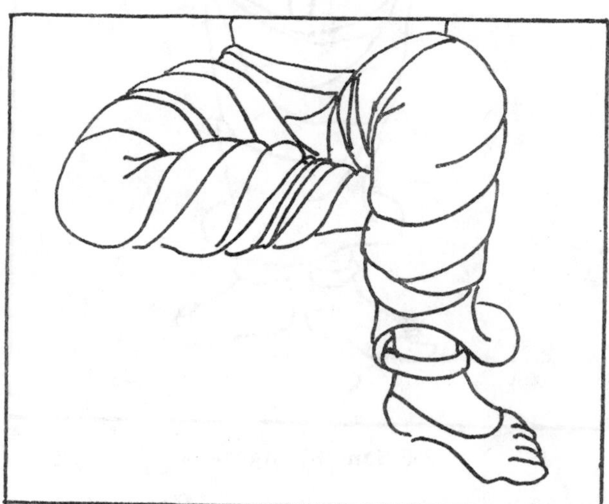

257. **Sukhasana**

Sukha or **Sukhasana** -- Seated in any comfortable position or a sitting pose in which the divinity is on a pedestal with the left leg pendant. This position is also known as: *Savya-lalitasana* or *Sukhasana.* (RG)

Utkutika or **Utkutikasana** -- A sitting position in which the soles of the feet are pressed together and drawn in towards the groin. (RG)

Swastika or **Swastikasana** -- Described as a cross-legged sitting position in which the toes touch opposite knees. (RG) It is not noted whether the toes are resting on top as in *vajrasana,* or beneath as a form of *paryanka-bandhasana.*

Vajra or **Vajrasana** -- A sitting position known as "The meditation posture" in which the legs are crossed with the soles of the both feet turned upward and resting on the opposite thighs. It is one of the two most common leg positions. This position is also known as: *Adamantine, Padmasana* or *Dhyanasana.* (RG, EDS, BB)

Vajra Attitude -- A position, either sitting or standing in which the deity embraces his consort or *sakti* in ritual intercourse. This asana is also called the *Yab-yum.* (AKG, AG)

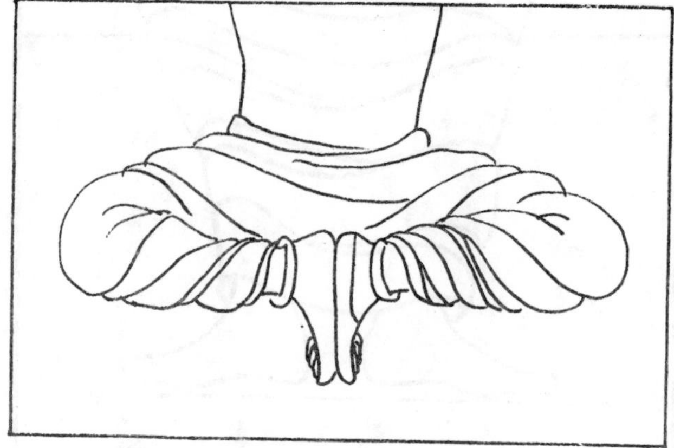

258. **Utkutikasana**

Vajraparyanka or **Vajraparyankasana** -- A sitting position known as in which the legs are crossed with the soles of the both feet turned upward and resting on the opposite thighs. It is one of the two most common leg positions. Listed as the same as *Dhyanasana.* (AKG)

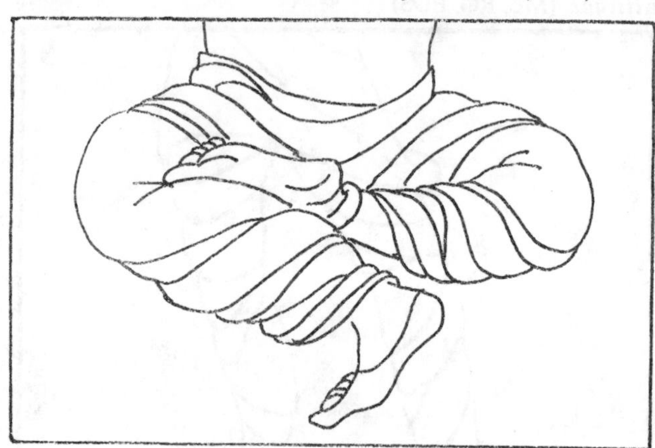

259. **Vama-lalitasana**

Vama-lalita or **Vama-lalitasana** -- A sitting pose in which the divinity is on a pedestal with the left leg pendant, often resting on a lotus, and the right leg folded under, It is the opposite of *Lalitasana.* (RG)

Vira or **Virasana** -- (Thai.: **Virasena**) A sitting pose known as the "Hero's pose" in which the left leg is resting on top of the right leg, toes touching the opposite knees. One of the two most common leg positions in Thai Buddha images. (RG)

Virasena -- The Thai form of Virasana.

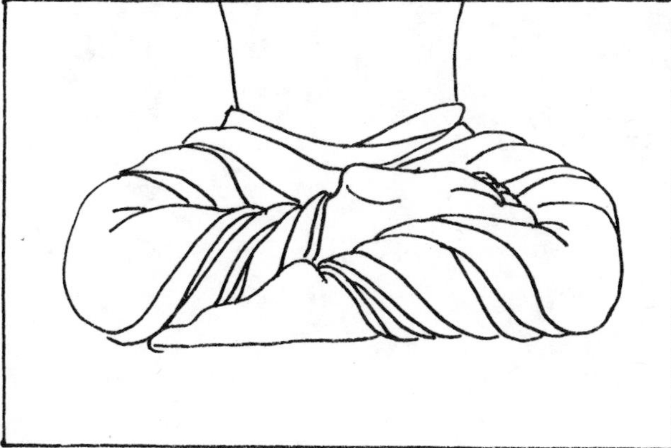

260. **Virasana**

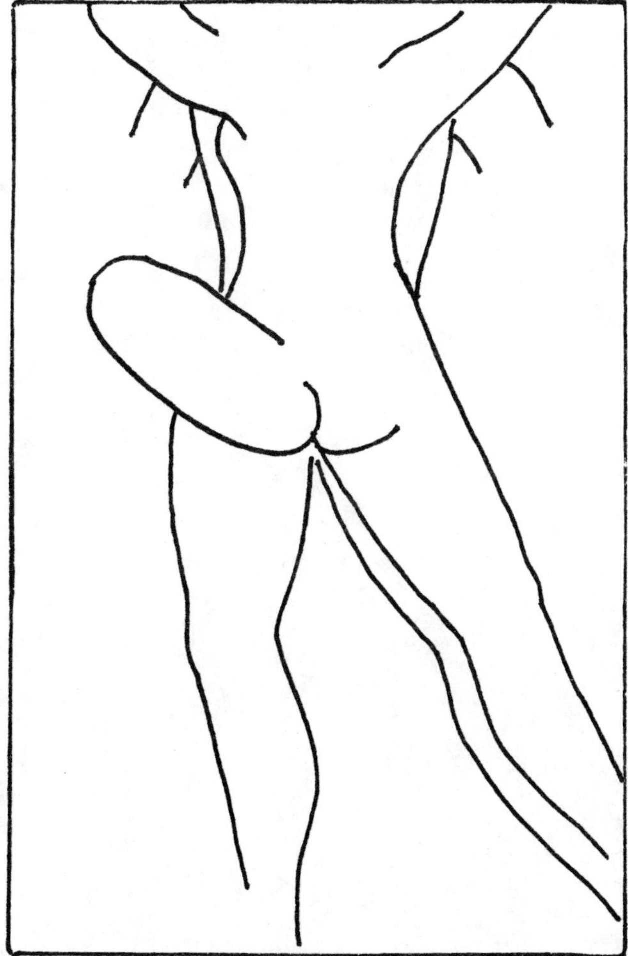

261. **Yab-yum (Alidhasana) II**

Western Pose -- A seated pose in which both feet are pendent, soles of the feet flat on the ground. An *asana* frequently used in the portrayals of *Maitreya*. Same as the *European Attitude* or *Pralambapadasana*. (ML, RG, EDS)

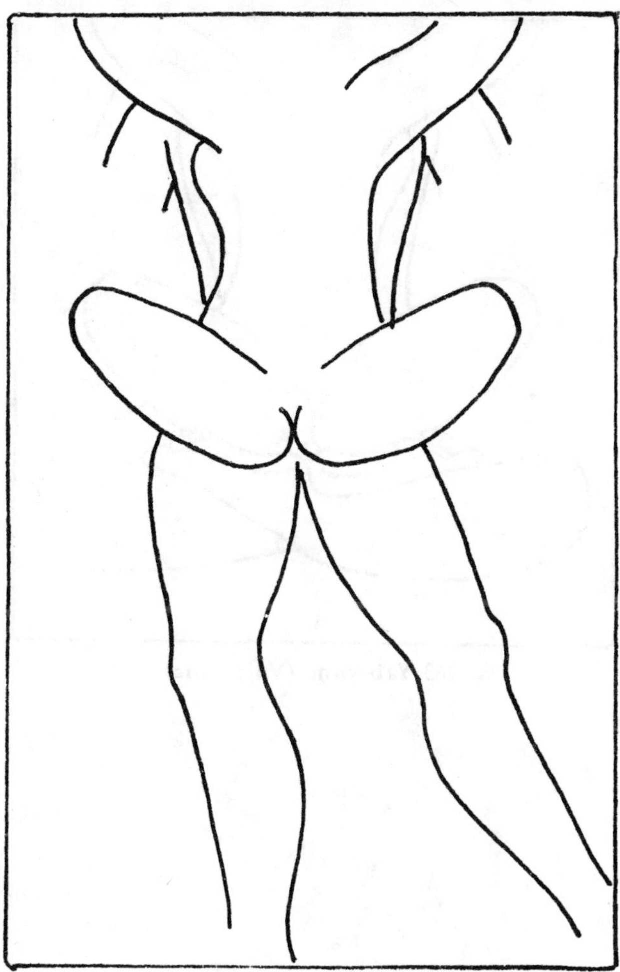

262. **Yab-yum (Alidhasana) III**

Yab-yum -- A position, either sitting or standing in which the deity embraces his consort or *sakti* in ritual intercourse. This *asana* is also called the *Vajra Attitude*. There are three major variations: I. Yab-yum (*vajrasana* or *virasana*) a seated union in which the yum's legs are wrapped around her yab's waist and frequently her arms encircle his neck; II. Yab-yum (*alidhasana*) a standing union (*alidhasana*) in which one of the yum's legs are wrapped around her yab's waist, the other is standing and frequently her arms encircle his neck; III. Yab-yum (*alidhasana*) a pose in which the yab is standing (*alidhasana*) in union and the yum's legs are wrapped around her yab's waist and frequently her arms encircle his neck. (AKG, AG)

Yoga or **Yogasana** -- A sitting position known as "The meditation posture" in which the legs are crossed with the soles of the both feet turned upward and resting on the opposite thighs. It is one of the two most common leg positions. This position is also known as: *Adamantine*, *Padmasana* or *Dhyanasana*. (RG, EDS, BB)

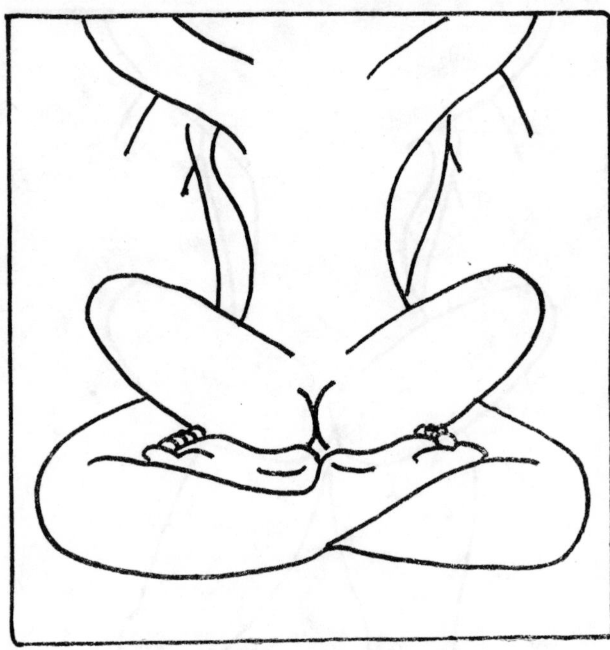

263. **Yab-yum (Vajrasana)**

Mudra or Hasta Glossary

Buddhas and *Bodhisattvas* and frequently other deities are shown with their hands forming a number of different ritualized and stylized poses--*mudras* or *hastas*. They may be holding different objects as well within these poses. Each singly and in combination have very specific meanings.

Abhaya mudra -- (Skt.: or *abhayamdada*)(Chin.: *Shih-wu-wei-yin*; Jap,: *semui-in*) The protection *mudra* or the blessing of fearlessness *mudra*. Generally, this position is shown with the palm(s) facing outward and the fingers extended upwards. It may also be shown with the arms in pendant and the palms facing downward with the fingers extended outward. A mudra frequently associated with *Sakyamuni Buddha* and *Dipankara*. (RG, AKG)

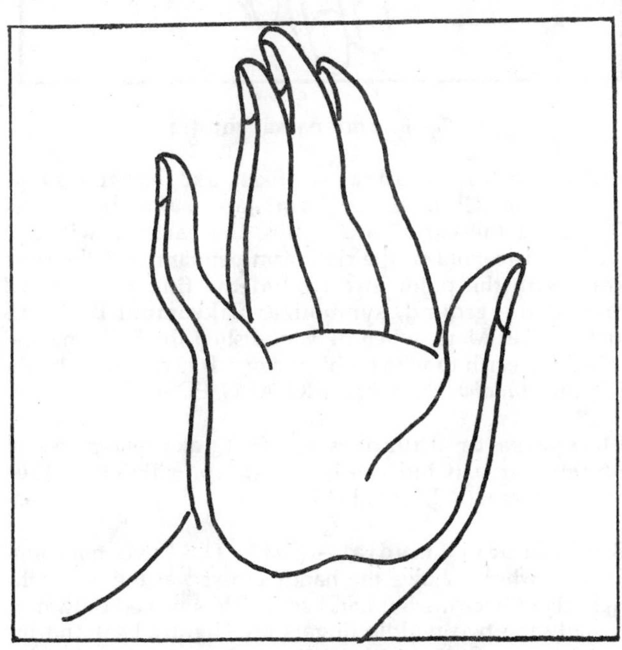

264. **Abhaya mudra (I)**

Abhayamdada mudra -- (Skt.: or *abhaya*)(Chin.: *Shih-wu-wei-yin*; Jap,: *semui-in*) See *abhaya*. (RG, AKG, EDS)

Abhiseka(na) mudra -- (Skt,)(Chin.: *kuan-ting-yin*; Jap.: *kanjo-in*) See *kanjo-in*. (EDS)

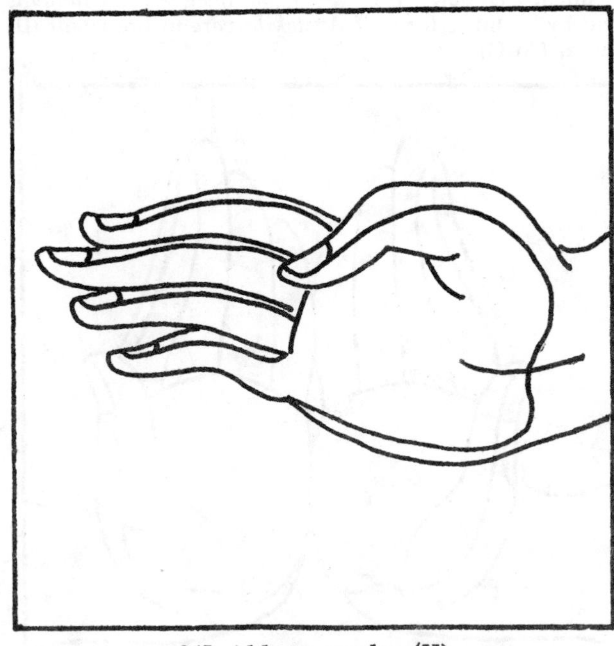

265. **Abhaya mudra (II)**

An-i-in -- (Jap.)(Chin.: *an-wei-yin*; Skt.: *vitarka* or *vyakhyana*) The act of preaching *mudra*, in addition, it represents argumentation or disputation. A variation on the *vitarka mudra* in which either the index, middle or ring finger touches the tip of the thumb. (EDS)

An-i-shoshu-in -- (Jap.)(Chin.: *an-wei she-ch'u-yin*) The calming *mudra*. A *mudra* in which the left hand is in the *vitarka mudra* and the right, level with the waist, palm is turned up with a slight rotation toward the center line, the thumb is separated from the fingers. (EDS)

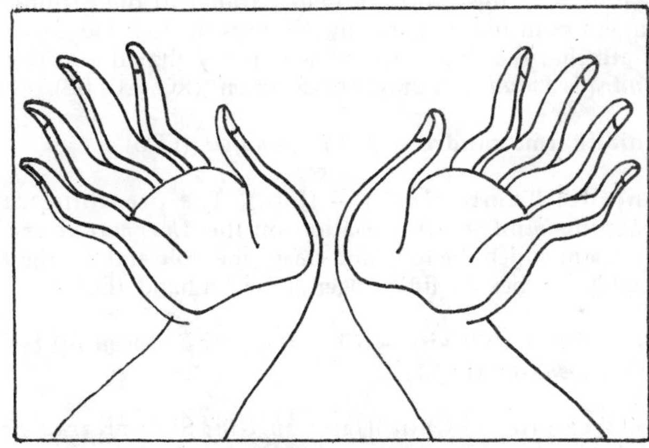

266. **Anjali mudra (I)**

Anjali mudra (I) -- (Skt.: or *vajra-anjalikarma*)(Chin.: *chin-kang ho-chang*; Jap.: *kongo-gassho*) Both hands are held above the head, the heels of the palm are touching, the fingers and thumbs spread outward and upward.

Frequently an object is held--e.g., an image of *Amitabha* is held by a tantric form of *Avalokitesvara* in the anjali (II) nudra. (AKG)

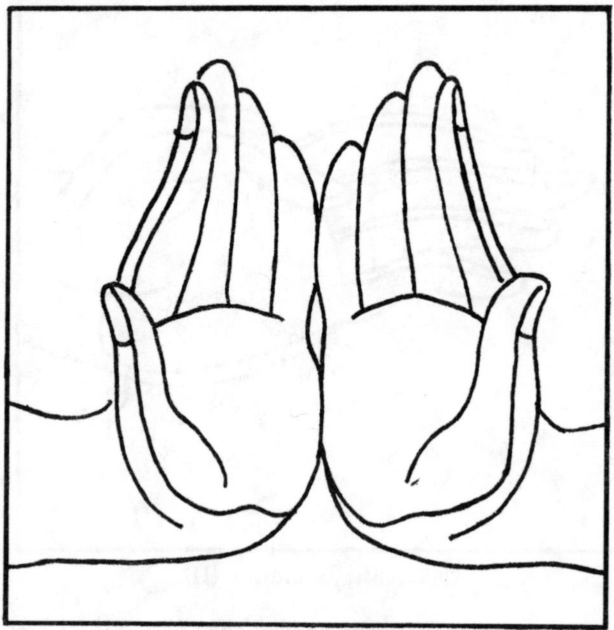

267. **Anjali mudra (II)**

Anjali mudra (II) -- (Skt.: or *vajra-anjalikarma*)(Chin.: *chin-kang ho-chang*; Jap.: *kongo-gassho*) The salutation or greeting *mudra*. There appears to be disagreement between the meaning of this *mudra* (*anjali*) and the *namaskara mudra*. Foucher, Getty and Gordon describe it as follows: to form this pose the hands are brought together (little fingers and the outside of the palms touching) forming a hollow. The hands, thus formed, rest against the chest and are held parallel to the ground, fingers pointing out and the thumbs on top. However, Bhattacharyya and Gopinatha Rao say that the *anjali mudra* is a *mudra* of prayer or devotion. (RG, AG, BB)

Anjalikarma mudra -- (Skt.) See *anjali*. (EDS)

Anjanta Temborin-in -- (Jap.) The preaching or teaching *mudra*. A variation on the *dharmachakra mudra* in which the left hand clasps the stole and the right slightly touches the little finger of the left hand. (EDS)

An-wei she-ch'u-yin -- (Chin.)(Jap.: *An-i-shoshu-in*) See *An-i-shoshu-in*. (EDS)

An-wei-yin -- (Chin.)(Jap.: *an-i-in*; Skt.: *vitarka* or *vyakhyana*) See *vitarka* or *an-i-in mudra*. (EDS)

Anzan-in -- (Jap.) A touching the ground *mudra* (*bhumisparsa*) variant in which the right hand touches the ground, palm down and the left hand is in *dhyana mudra*. (EDS)

Basara-un-kingo-in -- (Jap.)(Chin.: *chuan-yueh-lo-hung chin-kang-yin*; Skt.: *vajrahumkara*) Known as the "diamond mudra." A variation on the *vajrahumkara mudra* in which the fists are clenched and crossed at the wrists. (EDS, RG, AKG)

Bhasparsa mudra -- (Skt.: aka *bhumisparsa* or *bhusparsa*)(Chin.: *ch'u-ti-yin*; Jap.: *sokuchi-in*) See *bhumisparsa*. (RG, AKG,EDS)

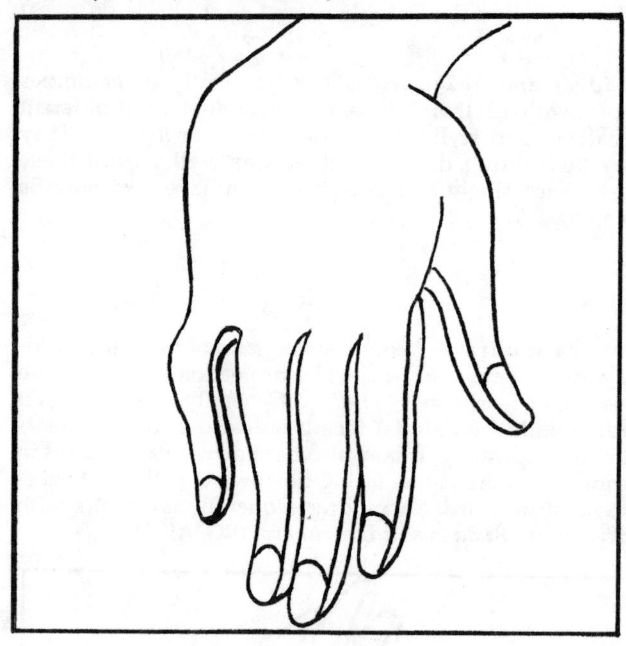

268. **Bhumisparsa mudra**

Bhumisparsa mudra -- (Skt.: aka *bhasparsa* or *bhusparsa*)(Chin.: *ch'u-ti-yin*; Jap.: *sokuchi-in*) The "touching the earth" or "calling the earth to witness" *mudra*. This *mudra*, the right arm pendant over the right knee with the palm inward and the fingers extended toward the ground, symbolizes Sakyamuni Buddha's victory over Mara, when he vanquished the Evil One and called the earth to witness his victory. It is also used by the *Dhyani Buddha Aksobhya*. (RG, AKG, EDS)

Bhusparsa or Bhuspars -- (Skt.: aka *bhasparsa* or *Bhumisparsa*)(Chin.: *ch'u-ti-yin*; Jap.: *sokuchi-in*)See *bhumisparsa*. (RG, AKG,EDS)

Bhutadamara mudra -- (Skt.) The "awe-inspiring" *mudra* which shows the hands crossed at the wrist, the right hand over the left hand and, palms turned outwards. Usually the two middle fingers are slightly bent and the hands may both hold additional symbols. This is frequently seen in the representations of the *Dhyani Bodhisattva Vajrapani* and *Bhutadamaravajrapani*. Sometimes called the *Trailokyavijaya mudra*. (RG, AKG)

Bodhasri mudra -- (Skt.: *jnana* or *vajra*)(Chin.: *chih-ch'uan-yin*; Jap.: *chi ken-in*) See *jnana*. (EDS, RG, AKG)

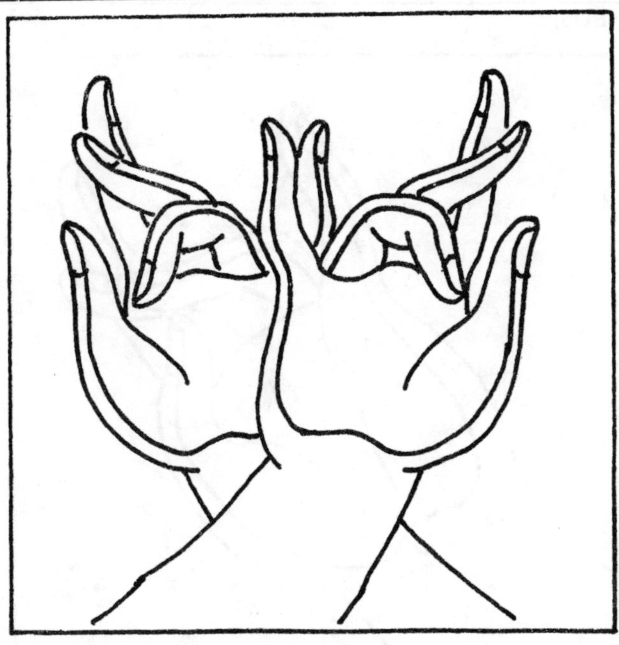

269. **Bhutadamara mudra**

Buddhapatra mudra -- (Skt.)(Chin.: *fo-puo-yin*; Jap.: *buppatsu-in*) See *buppatsu-in*. (EDS)

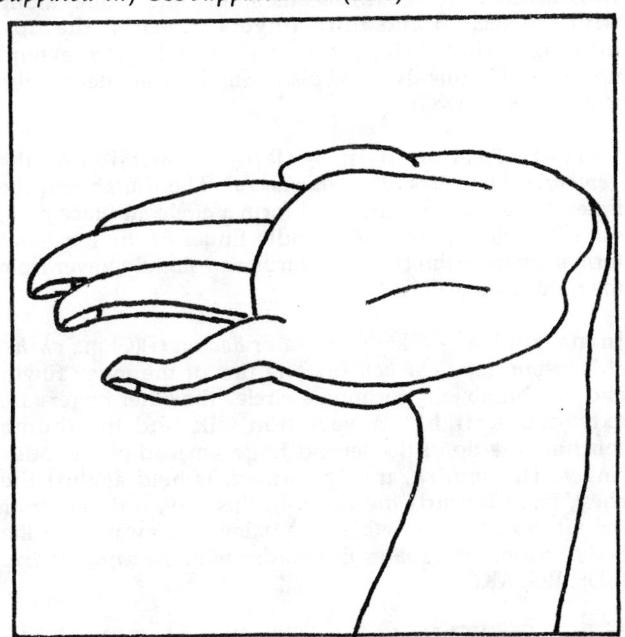

270. **Buddhasramana mudra**

Buddhasramana mudra -- (Skt.) The salutation or greeting *mudra*, another variation. In this *mudra* the right hand is lifted in line with the shoulder, the wrist bends backwards and the fingers and the palm face upwards. The fingers point outward, away from the body. Frequently Vasudhara and *Usnisvijaya* are depicted with this *mudra*. (RG, AKG)

Buppatsu-in -- (Jap.)(Chin.: *fo-puo-yin*; Skt.: *buddhapatra*) Known as "the alms bowl mudra." A mudra in which the two hands are separated, one over the other, fingers and thumbs together, and with palms facing each other. (EDS)

Chapatedana mudra -- (Skt.) A menacing, a slapping attitude in which the fingers are extended upwards, palm facing outward (forward). (BB)

Chih-ch'uan-yin -- (Chin.)(Jap.: *chi ken-in*; Skt.: *jnana* or *vajra* or *bodhasri*) See *jnana*. (EDS, RG, AKG)

Chi Ken-in -- (Jap.)(Skt.: *jnana* or *vajra* or *bodhasri*; Chin.: *chih-ch'uan-yin*:) Known as the *mudra* of the "knowledge fist." The left hand is in the tarjani mudra, the right hand grasps the extended index finger in its fist. (EDS, RG, AKG)

Chin-kang ho-chang -- (Jap.: *kongo-gassho*; Skt.: *anjali mudra* or *vajra-anjalikarma*) See *anjali mudra*. (RG, AKG, EDS)

Chuan-fa-lun-yin -- (Chin.)(Jap.: *temborin-in*: Skt.: *dharmachakra*) See *dharmachakra*. (RG, AKG, EDS)

Chuan-yueh-lo-hung chin-kang-yin -- (Chin.)(Jap.: *basara-un-kongo-in*; Skt.: *vajrahumkara*) See *vajrahumkara*. (RG, AKG,EDS)

Ch'u-ti-yin -- (Chin.)(Jap.: *sokuchi-in*; Skt.: *bhasparsa* or *bhumisparsa*) See *bhumisparsa*. (RG, AKG, EDS)

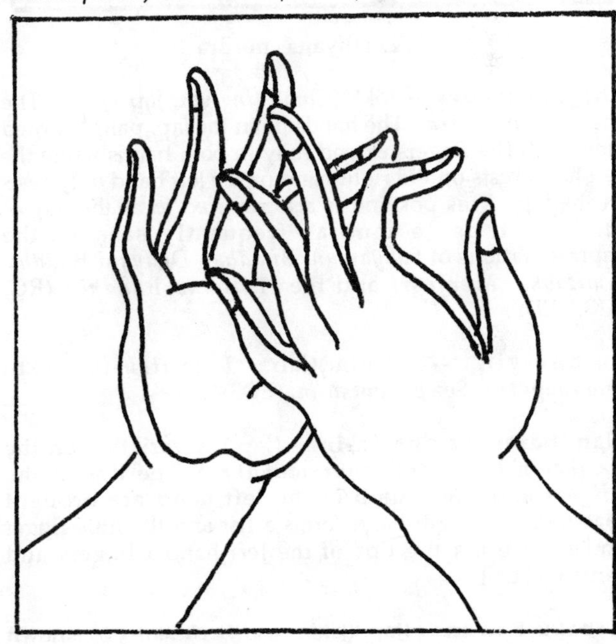

271. **Dharmachakra mudra**

Dharmachakra mudra -- (Skt.)(Chin.: *chuan-fa-lun-yin*; Jap.: *temborin-in*) The preaching or teaching *mudra*. It is often referred to as "Turning the Wheel of the Law" *mudra*. In each hand the thumb and the index fingers touch, the right hand palm faces outward and the left palm faces inward, covering the right hand. Usually, the hands are held in front of the chest. *Sakyamuni Buddha* and the *Dhyani Buddha Vairocana* as well as *Dhyani Bodhisattva Maitreya* are frequently shown in this *mudra*. (RG, AKG, EDS)

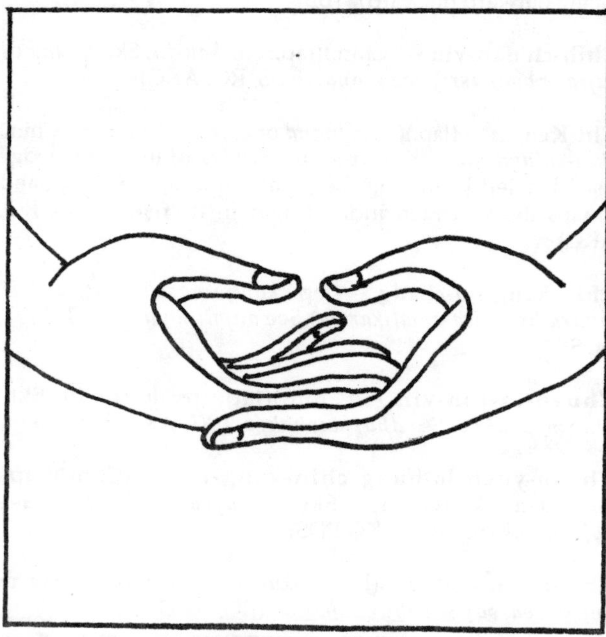

272. **Dhyana mudra**

Dhyana mudra -- (Skt.)(Chin.: *ting-yin*; Jap.: *jo-in*) The meditation *mudra*. The hands lie in the lap, palms turned upward. The fingers extend fully in both hands while the left hand rests on the right hand or the left hand only rests in the lap. This position is also referred to as the *yoga-mudra*. It is a mudra frequently seen in the representations of *Sakyamuni Buddha, Dhayani Buddha Amitabha, Manjusri* and the *Medicine Buddhas*.(RG, AKG, EDS)

Fo-puo-yin -- (Chin.)(Jap.: *buppatsu-in*; Skt.: *buddhapatra*) See *buppatsu-in*. (EDS)

Gandharan Temborin-in -- (Jap.) A variation on the *Temborin-in mudra* (*dharmachakra*). The tips of the fingers and the thumb of the left hand are brought together. The right hand forms a fist and the little-finger end rests upon the tips of the left hand's fingers and thumb. (EDS)

Gebaku Ken-in -- (Jap.)(Chin.: *wai-fu ch'uan-yin*) Known as the "outer bound fist." The two hands are joined, palms together, the fingers interlace and rest outside the palms. (EDS)

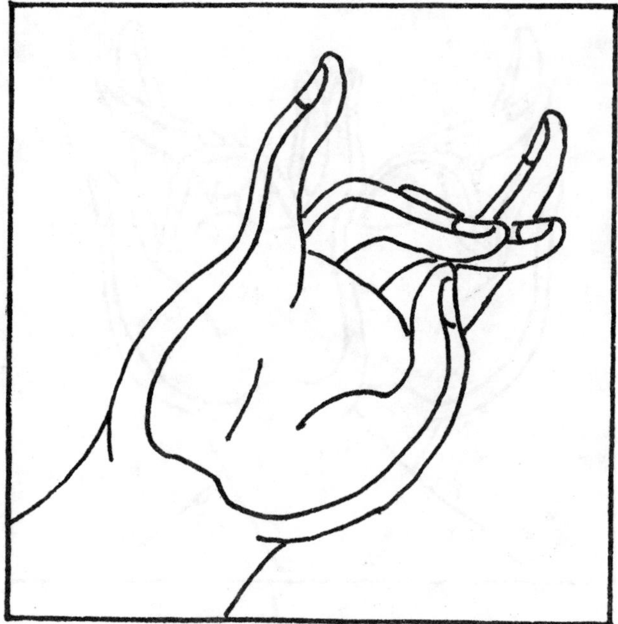

273. **Harina mudra**

Harina mudra -- (Skt.) In this *mudra* the thumb along with the second and third fingers touch at the tips, forming a ring. The little and index fingers extend upwards. Frequently, symbols or emblems are held in this manner. (RG, AKG)

Horyuji Temborin-in -- (Jap.) A variation of the *Temborin-in mudra* (*dharmachakra*). The thumb and the index finger of the right hand form a circle and face palm out. The thumb and the middle finger of the left hand form a circle , palm facing inwards and slightly lower from the right hand. (EDS)

Jnana mudra -- (Skt.: or *vajra* or *bodhasri*)(Chin.: *chih-ch'uan-yin*: Jap.: *chi ken-in*) The tips of the index finger and the thumb join, forming a circle, the other fingers are extended straight. A variation will find the thumb touching the tip of the second finger instead of the index finger. This *mudra*, thusly formed, is held against the chest, palm towards the chest. In this way, it differs from the *vitarka mudra* in which the palms face away from the body. Saunders equates this *mudra* with the *vajra mudra*. (EDS, RG, AKG)

Jo-in -- (Jap.)(Chin.: *ting-yin*: Skt.: *dhyana*) Known as the "*mudra* of concentration" (*dhyana*). There are a number of variants: first in which the hands are rotated palms at right angles on the axis;

-- **2** -- in which the tips of the thumbs touch and are slightly elevated;

-- **3** -- similar to two except the thumb and index fingers on both hands form a circle, the rest of the left hand fingers overlap the right;

-- **4** -- similar to three except the thumb and the middle finger form a circle; and
-- **5** -- similar to three except the thumb and the ring finger (third) join and form a circle. (EDS)

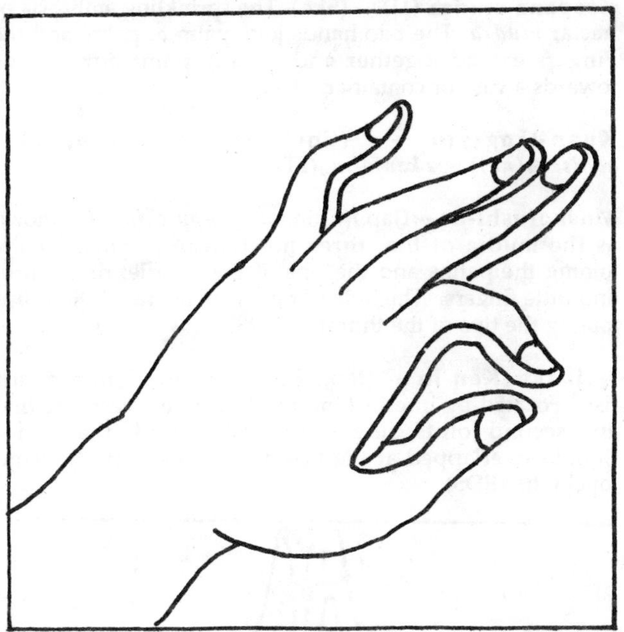

274. **Jnana mudra**

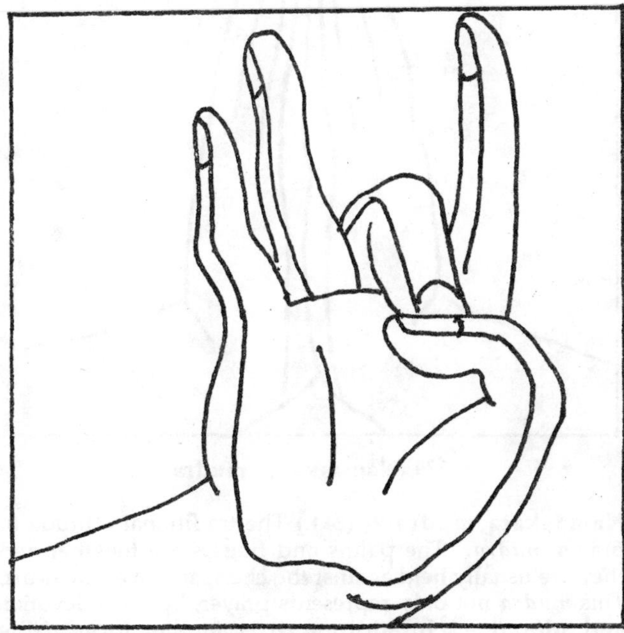

275. **Karana mudra**

Kanjo-in -- (Jap.)(Chin.: *kuan-ting-yin*; Skt.: *abhiseka(na)*) Known as the *mudra* of the "ceremony of unction." Formed by interlocking all fingers on the inside of the fists except the index finger and the thumb. The index fingers touch at the tips as do the thumbs and point upwards. (EDS)

Karana mudra -- (Skt.) The fascination *mudra*, indicates the hand stretched out, either horizontally or vertically, palm turned forward. The thumb presses down the middle two fingers, while the index and little fingers extend straight upwards. *Ekajata* and *Yama* are frequently shown in this mudra. (RG, AKG)

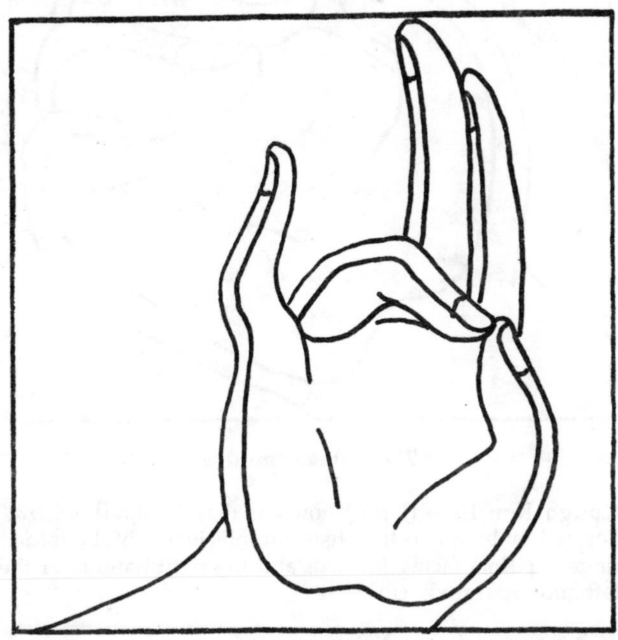

276. **Katari mudra**

Kartari mudra -- (Skt.) This *mudra* is held with the hands at shoulder level. The thumb and the third finger (ring finger) touch at the tips forming a circle. The index and second finger extend straight resembling rabbits ears or the horns of a deer. Frequently, symbols appear between these two fingers. (RG, AKG)

Kataka mudra -- (Skt.) A loose fist-like *mudra* in which the fingers bend together until the index finger and the thumb meet, forming an open tube. This position is frequently used in icons in which fresh flowers or other venerated objects are inserted. (RG, AKG)

Kichijo-in -- (Jap.) Known as the *mudra* of "good fortune." Formed by joining the tip of the thumb with that of the ring (third) finger, the other fingers extending upwards. (EDS)

Kimyo-gassho -- (Jap.) Known as the "diamond hand clasp." Similar to *anjali mudra*. (EDS)

Kongo-gassho -- (Jap.)(Chin.: *chin-kang ho-chang*; Skt.: *anjali* or *vajra-anjalikarma*) Known as the "diamond hand clasp." Similar to *anjali mudra* except the tips of the fingers and thumbs overlap and interlock. (RG, AKG,

EDS)

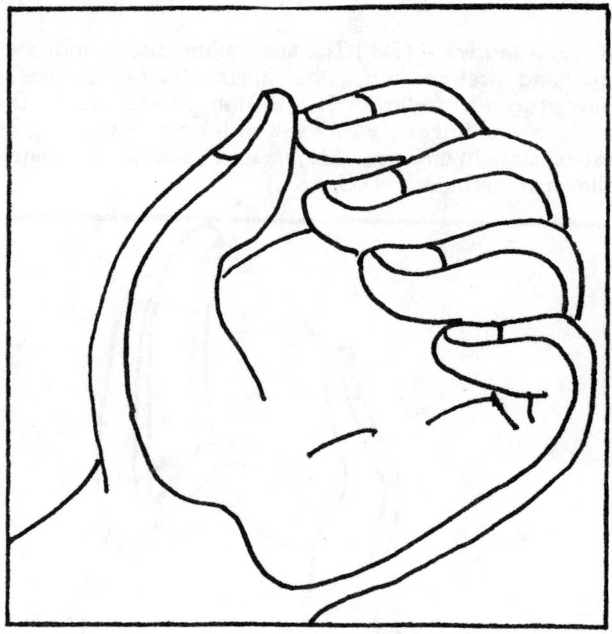

277. **Kataka mudra**

Kongo Ken-in -- (Jap.) Known as the "diamond *mudra*." Formed by both hands in fists, thumbs inside of the folded fingers, palms facing inwards and the right hand over the left and separated. (EDS)

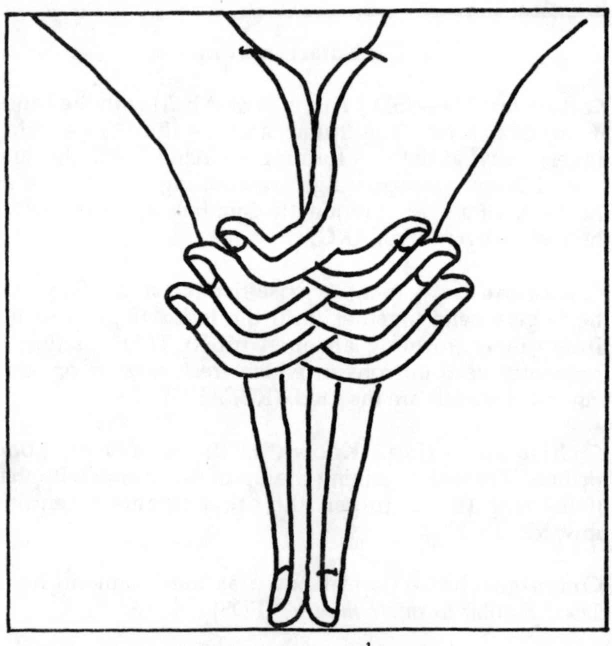

278. **Ksepana mudra (I)**

Ksepana mudra (I) -- (Skt.) The sprinkling ambrosia or nectar *mudra*. The two hands join, palm to palm, and the index fingers extend together and usually point downwards towards a vase or container. The other fingers and the thumbs are intertwined. (RG, AKG)

Ksepana mudra (II) -- (Skt.) The sprinkling ambrosia or nectar *mudra*. The two hands join, palm to palm, and the Fingers extend together and usually point downwards towards a vase or container. (BB)

Kuan-ting-yin -- (Chin.)(Jap.: *kanjo-in*; Skt.: *abhiseka(na)*) See *kanjo-in*. (EDS)

Mushofushi-in -- (Jap.)(Chin.: *wu-so-pu-chih-yin*) Known as the mudra of the "three mysteries." Formed by the joining the palms and the tips of the middle, ring (third) and little fingers. The index fingers are bent with their tips joining the tips of the thumbs. (EDS)

Naibaku Ken-in -- (Jap.) Known as the "outer bonds fist." Formed by interlocking the fingers between the first and second joints, fingers inward towards the palms, thumbs overlapped at the tips and the heels of the hand touching. (EDS)

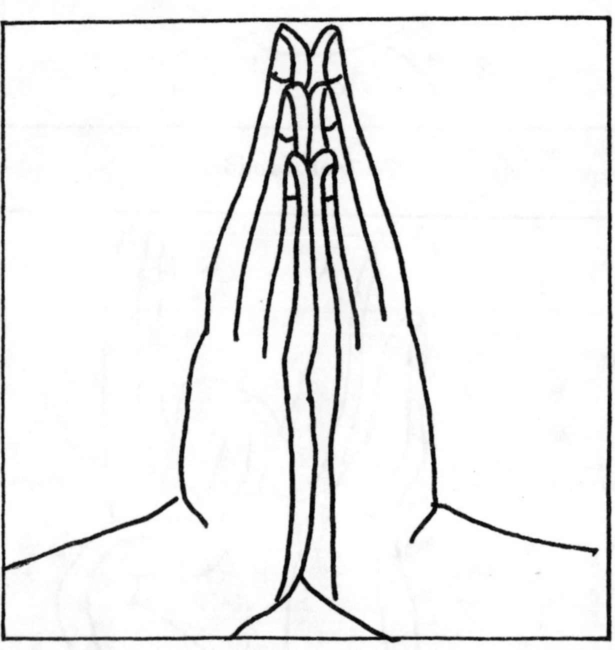

279. **Namaskara mudra**

Namaskara mudra -- (Skt.) The traditional attitude of prayer *mudra*. The palms and fingers are together and they are usually held against the chest, and over the heart. This *mudra* not only represents prayer, but also devotion and adoration. In addition, it is another form of the traditional form of greeting. In the case of some deities and object is held between the hands--*Avalokitesvara* holds a jewel. (RG, AKG)

Niwa-in -- (Jap.) A variant of the An-i-in (*vitarka*) *mudra*. The thumb is bent and the first knuckle is covered by the tips of the index and second fingers. The third finger is bent. The left hand crosses in front of the right hand at the wrists and the little fingers inter-lock. (EDS)

Ongyo-in -- (Jap.)(Chin.: *yin-hsing-yin*) Known as the *mudra* of "hiding forms." The left hand is formed into a fist, palm down, and the right hand, palm down and fingers extended rests slightly above the left. (EDS)

Renge-no-in -- (Jap.) The japanese equivalent of the Sanskrit for *uttarabhodi mudra.* (AG)

Sankaisaisho-in -- (Jap.) Known as the "Basara-un diamond" *mudra.* Both hands form a fist, thumb inside the fingers. The fists are crossed at the wrists, right in front of left. (EDS)

Sarvajrajendra -- (Skt.) The same as *anjali mudra.* (BB)

Segan-in -- (Jap.)(Skt.: *varada*) Known as the giving *mudra,* and similar to the *abhaya mudra,* fingers extended, pointing down and the palms out. (EDS)

Segan-semui-in -- (Jap.) Both hands have fingers extended, palm out, the right hand points upward and the left points downward. (EDS)

Semui-in -- (Jap.)(Chin.: *shih-wu-wei-yin;* Skt.: *abhaya* or *abhayamdada*) Known as the *mudra* which "grants the absence of fear." The fingers of the right hand are extended, palm out and the fingers point upwards, the left rests in the lap in *dhyana mudra.* (EDS)

Simha-karna mudra -- (Skt.) See *kataka mudra.* (RG, AKG)

Shih-yuan-yin -- (Chin.)(Jap.: *segan-in*) See *Varada mudra.* (EDS)

Shih-wu-wei-yin -- (Chin.)(Skt.: *abhaya* or *abhayamdada*) See *Semui-in.* (EDS)

Smadhi mudra -- (Skt.) See *dhyana mudra.*(RG, AKG)

Samputanjali -- (Skt.) The same as *anjali mudra.* (BB)

Sokuchi-in -- (Jap.)(Chin.: *ch'u-ti-yin;* Skt.: *bhasparsa* or *bhumisparsa*) Known as the mudra which touches the ground (*bhumisparsa*). A variant has the right hand pointing with the index finger at the ground. (EDS, RG, AKG)

Suci -- (Skt.) A mudra generally used in a dancing attitude. "All fingers are stretched with the tips joining at the end, so as to resemble a needle (*suci*)." (BB)

Tarjani mudra -- (Skt.) The menacing or making one aware of an error *mudra.* In this position the index finger extends upwards while the thumb tightly clasps the other three fingers in the palm of the hand. It is to be noted that the finger points upwards, never at someone. To point at someone is a gross breach of etiquette in the cultures of the Orient. A *mudra* frequently shown by *Marici* and other wrathful deities. (RG, AKG)

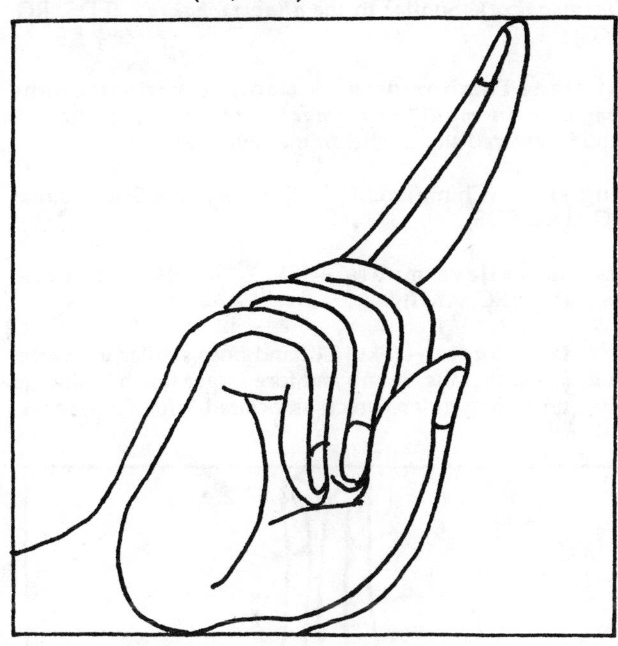

280. **Tarjani mudra**

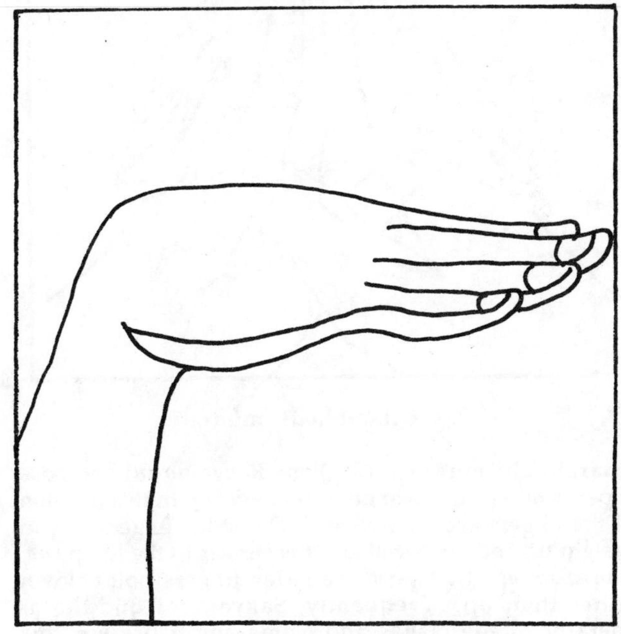

281. **Tarpana mudra**

Tarpana mudra -- (Skt.) The performance of homage (to the departed) *mudra.* The arms are bent at the elbow with the hands raised even with the shoulders. The fingers are slightly bent with the fingertips extending towards the shoulders. The palms of the hands face downwards. A *mudra* frequently shown by *Namasangiti*. (RG, AKG)

Temborin-in -- (Jap.)(Chin.: *chuan-fa-lun-yin*; Skt.: *dharmacakra*) Similar to the *ḍharmachakra*. (EDS, RG, AKG)

Tibetan Temborin-in -- (Jap.) A variant of the *Temborin-in mudra* (*dharmachakra*) in which the left hand is lowered slightly below the right. (EDS)

Ting-yin -- (Chin.)(Jap.; *jo-in*: Skt.: *dhyana*) See *dhyana*. (RG, AKG,EDS)

Trailokyavijaya mudra -- (Skt.) See *Bhutadamara mudra*. (RG, AKG)

Tripataka mudra -- (Skt.) A hand pose similar to *jnana mudra* in which the thumb and fore-finger touch while the other three fingers are erect, associated with *Paramasva*. (BB)

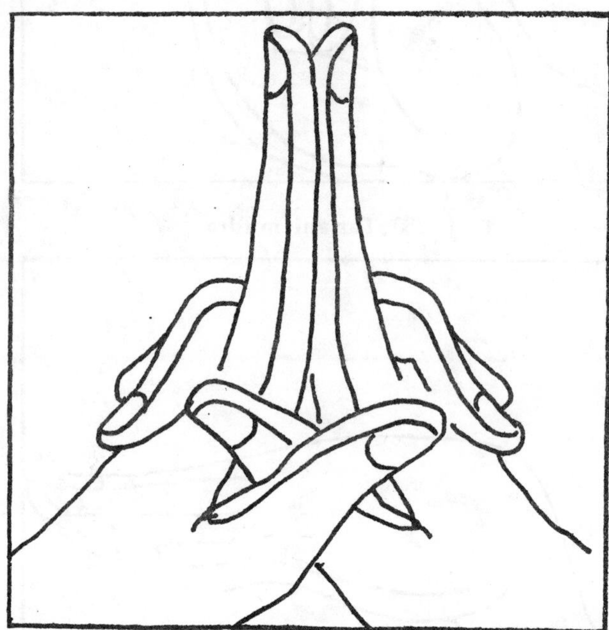

282. **Uttarabhodi mudra**

Uttarabodhi mudra -- (Skt.)(Jap: *Renge-no-in*) The pose of perfection or the best perfection *mudra*. In this position all the fingers are intertwined. The index fingers extend straight up and are together. It is similar to the *Ksepana mudra* except that pose the index fingers point down rather than up. Frequently, Sakyamuni Buddha as liberator of the Nagas and Namasangiti present this *mudra*. (RG, AKG)

Vajra mudra -- (Skt.: or *jnana* or *bodhasri*)(Chin.: *chih-ch'uan-yin*: Jap.: *chi ken-in*) *mudra*. The *mudra* of the knowledge fist, in which the right hand makes a fist, thumb enclosed, index finger extended upward, palm out; the left hand forms a fist, palm inward and encloses the extended index finger. (EDS)

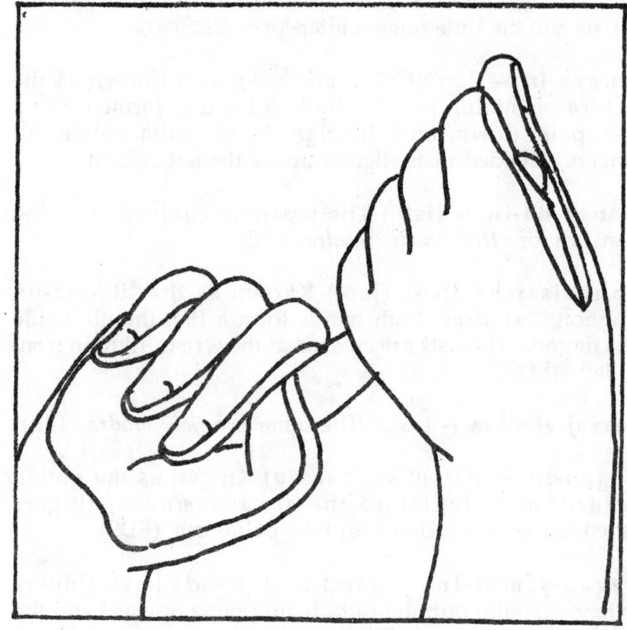

283. **Vajra mudra**

Vajra-anjalikarma mudra -- (Skt.: or *anjali*)-- (Chin.: *chin-kang ho-chang*; Jap.: *kongo-gassho*) (EDS, RG, AKG)

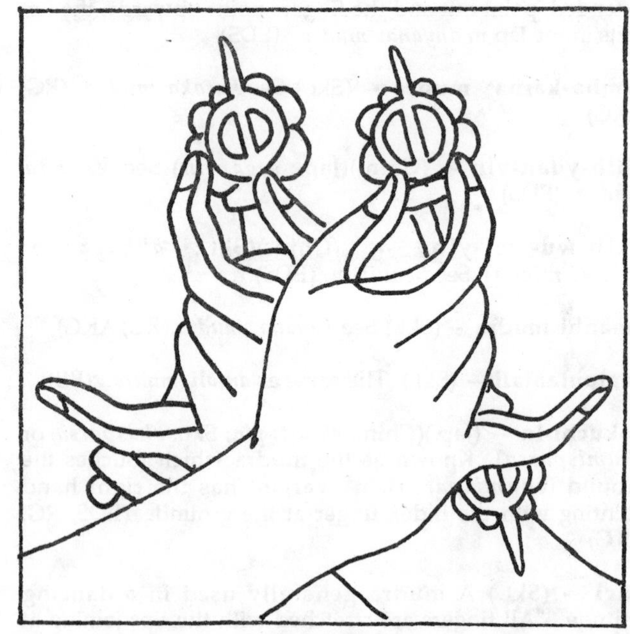

284. **Vajrahumkara mudra**

Vajrahumkara mudra -- (Skt.)(Chin.: *chuan-yueh-lo-hung chin-kang-yin*; Jap.: *basara-un-kongo-in*) The Buddha with supreme and eternal elements *mudra*, is the *mudra* in which the right hands clasp a *thunderbolt* (Tib.:

vajra, rdo-rje) and the left hand holds a bell (*ghanta, dril-bu*). The right hand crosses over the left at the wrist, palms facing inwards towards the chest and usually over the heart. *Vajradhara, Samvara, Trailokyavijaya* and the *Dhyani Buddhas* in the *yab-yum asana* present this *mudra*. (RG, AKG, EDS)

Vandana mudra -- (Skt.) A mudra in which the hand is held (usually) above the waist, fingers extended, palm up. Frequently objects are held in the palm of the hand. A mudra that is associated with Amoghapasa Lokesvara. (PB)

Vara mudra --(Skt.) See *varada mudra*. (RG, AKG)

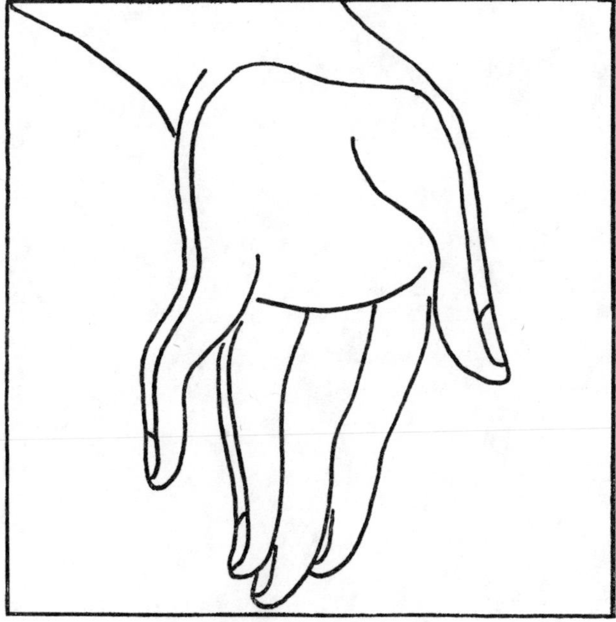

285. **Varada mudra**

Varada mudra --(Skt.)(Chin,: *shih-yuan-yin*; Jap.: *segan-in*) The gift bestowing or charity giving *mudra*, that in which the arms are stretched full length down the side with the hands held pendant with the fingers extended and the palm turned outwards. *Sakyamuni Buddha*, the white and green *Taras* as well as the *Medicine Buddhas* frequently hold this mudra.. (RG, AKG)

Vismaya mudra -- (Skt.) A *mudra* of astonishment or wonder in which the hands are brought up level with the shoulder, elbow bent, palm up. (RG, AKG)

Vitarka mudra -- (Skt.: or *vyakhyana*) (Chin.: *an-wei-yin*; Jap.: *an-i-in*) The act of preaching *mudra*, in addition, it represents argumentation or disputation. It is the position in which the fingers are extended upward, except the index finger which bends and touches the tip of the thumb. The palms turn outward. This mudra is frequently held by *Sakyamuni Buddha, Maitreya, Ksitigarbha* and *Akasagarbha*. (RG, AKG, EDS)

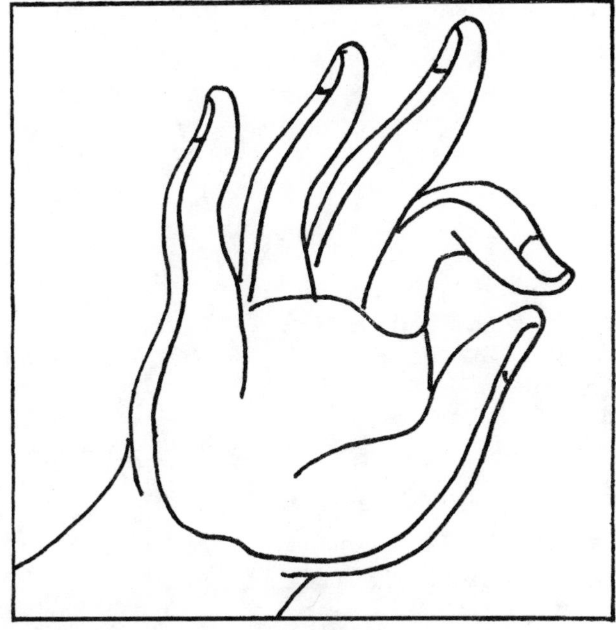

286. **Vitarka mudra**

Vyakhyana mudra -- (Skt.: or *vitarka*)(Chin.: *an-wei-yin*; Jap.: *an-i-in*) See *vitarka*. However B. Bhattacharyya equates it with the *dharmachakra mudra*. (RG, AKG, EDS)

Wai-fu ch'uan-yin -- (Chin.)(Jap.: *gebaku ken-in*) See *gebaku ken-in*. (EDS)

Wu-so-pu-chih-yin -- (Chin.)(Jap.: *mushofushi-in*) See *mushofushi-in*. (EDS)

Yin-hsing-yin -- (Chin.)(Jap.: *ongyo-in*) See *ongyo-in*. (EDS)

Attributes/Inconography and Vahanas

Deities frequently hold symbolic objects in their hands, such as weapons--e.g., axe, goad, sword, trident, etc.--plant forms--e.g., citron, lotus, ashoka branch, etc.--or other ordinary objects--e.g., vase, bowl, book, etc. These various objects often have important symbolic significance. Some objects are generally carried by wrathful deities or manifestations, whereas others are generally only carried by peaceful deities or emanations.

The term *vahanas* refers to the the support or the mount upon which a deity rests, stands or rides. *vahanas* may be animals--e.g., wild asses, horses or garudas, etc.--or human forms--e.g., alien gods, demons, living humans or corpses, etc.--or other natural forms--e.g., lotus, sun disc, moon disc or animal skins, etc. Most Buddha figures sit upon a lotus. *Maitreya* is often found sitting upon a throne. Some *mahasiddhas* sit upon animal skins. *Yamantaka* is usually found on the back of a bull, and *Vajrabhairava* stands upon human forms.

The symbols/vahanas listed below are the Sanskrit and/or Tibetan transliteral equivalents. They do not include the Chinese, Japanese or Mongolian transliteral equivalent. Where their iconographic meaning has been listed in the various sources, it will be listed following the primary term.

Airy horse -- (*rlung-rta*) or wind horse, a symbol of luck, also a *vahana*, vehicle, ridden frequently by calm or peaceful deities, particularly those of the Tibetan pantheons.

Aksamala -- (Skt.) see *rosary*.

Ambrosia -- see *elixir of life*.

Amrita -- (Skt.) see *elixir of life*.

Amrta -- (Skt.) see *elixir of life*.

Animals -- (unidentifiable) vahanas or vehicles ridden by deities, particularly those of the Tibetan pantheons.

Animal skin -- a vahana, vehicle, ridden frequently by Arhats, particularly those of the Tibetan pantheons.

Ankusa -- (Skt.) see *goad/hook*.

Ankusha -- (Skt.) see *goad/hook*.

Antelope skin -- see *skin, antelope*.

Arrow -- (*shara* or *bana, mdah*) it is frequently known as the "arrow of confession," to chase away forgetfulness and neglect and is a male element in counterpoint to the spindle. It is an instrument of *Kama*, used by *Marici* to inflict pain on *Mara*, as bow and arrow it symbolizes "Method and Wisdom."

Arrow, divination -- (*mdah-dar*) bound with five colored streamers and often used against demons.

A-ru-ra -- (Tib.) see *tree, myrobalan*.

Asiatic wild ass -- (*khyang*) see *ass, wild Asiatic*.

Asoka -- (Skt.) see *tree, Asoka*.

Asoka Flower -- see *flower, Asoka*.

Asrkkapala -- (Skt.) see *cup, human skull-, filled with blood*.

Ass, wild Asiatic -- (*khyang*) a *vahana*, vehicle, ridden by protective deities (*chos-skyong*), particularly those of the Tibetan pantheons. Frequently ridden by wrathful deities of the *chos-skyong* and *dam-can* classes.

Atapatra -- (Skt.) see *parasol*.

Aura -- see *halo*.

Axe -- (*parashu, dgra-sta*) an instrument of battle, as well as a symbol of building, a symbol of *tantric* manifestation used to subdue or destroy the enemies of religion (Buddhism) or on monks who have broken their vows. Frequently carried by wrathful deities of the *chos-skyong* and *dam-can* classes.

Ba-dan -- (Tib.) see *banner, cylindrical*.

Bag -- see *sack*.

Ball of thread -- see *thread, ball*.

Bana (Skt.) -- see *arrow*.

Band, white silk -- iconographic importance or meaning not noted in sources.

Banner/ flag, cylindrical of victory -- (*pataka, ba-dan* or *mtshan*) it is one of the "Eight Auspicious Symbols" which is erected on Mt. Meru or a symbol of victory over the enemies of religion.

Banner/ flag, flat -- (*dhvaja , rgyal-mtshan*) symbolic of victory.

Basket, round -- (*za-ma-thog*) symbolizes spiritual nourishment and often associated with *arhats* and *gurus*.

Basket of leaves -- iconographic importance or meaning not noted in sources.

Baton -- see *staff/stick, baton*.

Bdud-ta-kha -- (Tib.) English transliteral equivalent not noted in sources.

Bdud-kyi-khram-shing -- (Tib.) see *staff/stick, command*.

Bdud-rtsi -- (Tib.) see *elixir of life*.

Bear -- a vahana, vehicle, ridden by protective deities (*chos-skyong*), particularly those of the Tibetan pantheons.

Beer, Tibetan -- (*chang*) iconographic importance or meaning not noted in sources.

Bell -- (*ghanta, dril-bu*) it is a symbol frequently shown with the thunderbolt (*vajra*), used to summon deities, often associated with *Vajrasattva*, also symbolizes impermanence, symbol of the primeval female.

Bell, low, broad -- (*gshang*) used in ceremonies for fierce deities and to subdue or destroy the enemies of religion (Buddhism) or on monks who have broken their vows. Frequently carried by wrathful deities of the *chos-*

skyong and *dam-can* classes.

Bell, vajra-topped -- (*vajraghanta, rdo-rje-dril-bu*) see *bell*.

Bellows -- iconographic importance or meaning not noted in sources.

Beng -- (Skt.) see *mace*.

Bija -- (Skt.) see *seed*.

Bijapura -- (Skt.) see *citron*.

Bilvafala -- (Skt.) see *wood-apple*.

Bindu -- (Skt.) see *semen*.

Bird -- (unidentifiable) a *vahana*, vehicle, ridden by deities, particularly those of the Tibetan pantheons.

Bird , garuda-like -- (*khyung*) represents the mind which can instantaneously soar skyward and pervades all creatures, also a vahana, vehicle, ridden by deities, particularly those of the Tibetan pantheons.

Bla-khri-bzhugs -- (Tib.) see *cushion, guru*.

Blood sack -- see *sack, blood*.

Boar -- a *vahana*, vehicle, ridden by protective deities (*chos-skyong*), particularly those of the Tibetan pantheons and often associated with *Marici*.

Book/manuscript -- (*pustaka, sher-phyin*) usually symbolic of the *Prajnaparamita* (writings of Transcendental Wisdom) given to the *Nagas* by the *Buddha*.

Book/manuscript, Prajnaparamita -- (*pustaka, glegs-bam*) see *book/manuscript*.

Bottle, perfume.

Bow -- (*chapa* or *dhanus, gzhu-dang*) frequently known as the "bow of mercy," used by *Marici* to inflict pain on *Mara*, as bow and arrow it symbolizes Method and Wisdom.

Bowels -- usually carried by fierce deities and represents the demise of the enemies of religion (Buddhism). They may be held in the deity's mouth or twisted in his/her hands.

Bowl, alms -- (*patra, lhung-bzed*) a symbol associated with *Sakyamuni Buddha*, a begging bowl carried by wandering Buddhist monks, may also be carried by *Amitabha, Avalokitesvara* and *Manla* (Medicine Buddha).

Bowl, flat -- (*gshong*) used in ceremonies involving wrathful deities. Also, a symbol, when filled with jewels, or food that is associated with wealth bestowing deities or their companions. See also *nor-gshong*.

Bowl, silver alms -- (*par -bu*) see *bowl/alms*.

Box of spiritual treasures -- (*gter-bum*).

Brahmakapala -- (Skt.) see *head of Brahma*.

Brahmamukha -- (Skt.) see *faces of Brahma, four*.

Brahmasirah -- (Skt.) see *head of Brahma*.

Branch, Asoka -- a branch from the Tree of Consolation, *Sakyamuni Buddha* being born between the *asoka* tree and the *bodhi* tree .

Branch, Arura -- a medicinal plant that is frequently associated with the Medicine Buddhas.

Branch, burning juniper -- iconographic importance or meaning not noted in sources.

Branch, Myrobalan -- a medicinal plant that is frequently associated with the Medicine Buddhas.

Branch, Willow -- with which the nectar of life (*amrita*) is sprinkled, often used by the feminine *Kuan-yin*.

Branch of the wish-granting tree -- see *tree, wish granting*.

Brang-rgyas -- (Tib.) English transliteral equivalent not noted in sources.

Broom, silver -- iconographic importance or meaning not noted in sources.

Bse-bya bird -- a *vahana*, vehicle, ridden by protective deities (*chos-skyong*), particularly those of the Tibetan pantheons.

Bseg-shing -- (Tib.) see *staff/stick, heavy wooden*.

Bse-phur -- (Tib.) see *dagger, demon*.

Btsan-mdung -- (Tib.) see *lance, btsan*.

Btsan-sha -- (Tib.) see *meat, btsan*.

Buddha image -- either *Sakyamuni* or one of the *Dhyani Buddhas* (*kulesas*) found either in the head-dresses or hands of deities.

Buffalo, water -- a *vahana*, vehicle, ridden by protective deities (*chos-skyong*), particularly those of the Tibetan pantheons.

Bull -- a *vahana*, vehicle, ridden by protective deities (*chos-skyong*), particularly those of the Tibetan pantheons.

Bum-pa -- (Tib.) see *vase/vessel*.

Cage -- iconographic importance or meaning not noted in sources.

Caitya -- (Skt.) see *shrine*.

Cakra (Skt.) see *wheel*.

Camara -- (Skt.) see *whisk , fly-*.

Camel -- a *vahana*, vehicle, ridden frequently by calm or peaceful deities, particularly those of the Tibetan pantheons.

Candra -- (Skt.) see *disc, moon*.

Capa -- (Skt.) see *bow*.

Casaka -- (Skt.) same as *kapala*.

Casque, treasure -- (*sgrom-bu*) often associated with deities of wealth.

Censor -- iconographic importance or meaning not noted in sources.

Chain, iron -- (*phota* or *sphota* or *srinkhala, lcags-sgrog*) used to subdue or bind or destroy the enemies of religion (Buddhism). Frequently carried by wrathful deities of the *chos-skyong* and *dam-can* classes.

Chaitya -- (Skt.) see *shrine*.

Chakra -- (Skt.) see *wheel*.

Chalice -- iconographic importance or meaning not noted in sources.

Chamara -- (Skt.) see *whisk , fly-*.

Chandra -- (Skt.) see *disc, moon*.

Chang -- (Tib.) see *beer, Tibetan*.

Chapa -- (Skt.) see *bow*.

Chariot with seven horses -- a *vahana*, vehicle, ridden by protective deities (*chos-skyong*), particularly those of the Tibetan pantheons.

Chasaka -- (Skt.) same as *kapala*.

Chauri -- (Skt.) see *chowrie*.

Chopper, ritual -- (*karttrika , grig-gug*) symbolic of *Buddhasaktis, dakinis* and some *dharmapala*, a symbol of *tantric* manifestation, it is used to cut the "life roots" of religious enemies.

Chorten -- (Tib.) see *shrine*.

Chowrie -- (Skt.) B. Bhattasharyya define "*chowrie*" as *chamara*. [1]

Chintamani -- (Skt.) see *jewel, wish fulfilling*.

Chu-gri -- (Tib.) see *knife, wavy-bladed*.

Chu'i-rkyal-pa -- (Tib.) see *sack of blood*.

Churi -- (Skt.) see *knife*.

Chu-srin -- (Tib.) see *Sea elephant or dragon*.

Chu-yi-zhags-pa -- (Tib.) see *noose/snare, water*.

Cintamani -- (Skt.) see *jewel, wish fulfilling*.

Citron -- (*bijapura, jambhara, skyu-ru-ra*) represents the seed of the universe and is frequently held by deities of wealth, particularly in conjunction with a mongoose.

Club/cudgel -- (*parigha, dbyug-to*) a weapon of battle, a symbol of tantric manifestation. Used to subdue or destroy the enemies of religion (Buddhism) or on monks who have broken their vows. Frequently carried by wrathful deities of the *chos-skyong* and *dam-can* classes.

Club/cudgel, jeweled -- see *club/cudgel*.

Club/cudgel, human corpse -- (*zhing-dbyag* or *khram-ban*) see *club/cudgel*.

Club/cudgel, sandal-wood -- see *club/cudgel*.

Club/cudgel with skull finial -- (*thod-dbyug*) see *club/cudgel*.

Coat of mail -- (*khrab*) iconographic importance or meaning not noted in sources. Held frequently by calm Buddha-like deities.

Conch shell -- as an offering bowl or a horn spiraling to the right. It is one of the Eight Auspicious Symbols used to frighten away demons and a *vahana*, vehicle, ridden frequently by calm or peaceful deities, particularly those of the Tibetan pantheons.

Coral stick -- see *stick/staff, coral*.

Cord, meditation -- (*sgom-thag*) a cord which crosses the left shoulder and the right crossed leg, used during meditation exercises, usually shown on *gurus* and *arhats*.

Corn, ear -- iconographic importance or meaning not noted in sources.

Corpse -- (*prea* or *mrtaka* or *sava*) a *vahana*, vehicle, ridden by protective deities (*chos-skyong*), particularly those of the Tibetan pantheons.

Cow -- a *vahana*, vehicle, ridden by protective deities (*chos-skyong*), particularly those of the Tibetan pantheons--e.g., *rDo-rje-sna-yon-ma*.

Crown, Bodhisattva -- described as a five-leafed crown and is usually shown on calm deities.

Crown, Dharmapala -- described as a five-skulled crown and is usually shown on protective deities (*chos-skyong*).

Cross, sacred thread -- (*ma-mo-mdos*) part of an important ceremony and provides an abode for a deity.

Cudgel -- see *club/cudgel*.

Cup -- iconographic importance or meaning not noted in sources.

Cup, human skull- -- (*kapala, thod-pa*) it is a symbol that is frequently carried by *dharmapalas* filled with the blood of the enemies of religion, a *tantric* manifestation.

Cup, human skull-, filled with blood -- (*asrkkapala*) see *cup, human skull-*.

Cup, human skull-, filled with flesh -- (*mamsakapala*) see *cup, human skull-*.

Cushion, guru -- (*bla-khri-bzhugs*) a *vahana*, vehicle, ridden frequently by *gurus* or *mahagurus*, particularly those of the Tibetan pantheons.

Cymbals -- (*si-nen* or *rol-mo*) used to call the hungry demons to accept the ritual offerings.

Dagger, demon -- (*bse-phur*) used to subdue or destroy the enemies of religion (Buddhism) or on monks who have broken their vows. Frequently carried by wrathful deities of the *chos-skyong* and *dam-can* classes.

Dagger, magic -- (*kila* , *phur-bu*) a triple edged dagger, a symbol of tantric manifestation, stops demons from inflicting evil.

Dam-shing -- (Tib.) see *stick , magic throwing*.

Damaru -- (Skt.) see *drum, human skull*.

Danda -- (Skt.) see *staff/stick, short*.

Darpana -- (Skt.) see *mirror*.

Dart -- (*sakti*) iconographic importance or meaning not noted in sources, but similar to *arrow*.

Dbyug-pa -- (Tib.) see *staff/stick with skull finial*.

Dbyug-to -- (Tib.) see *club/cudgel*.

Deer, doe or **Deer, stag** -- a *vahana*, vehicle, ridden frequently by calm or peaceful deities, particularly those of the Tibetan pantheons.

Deer skin -- see *skin, deer*.

Demon -- a *vahana*, vehicle, ridden by protective deities (*chos-skyong*), particularly those of the Tibetan pantheons.

Dgra-sta -- (Tib.) see *axe*.

Dgra-zor -- (Tib.) see *sickle*.

Dhanus -- (Skt.) see bow.

Dhupa -- (Skt.) see incense.

Dhvaja -- (Skt.) see *banner/flag, flat*.

Diamond throne -- a *vahana*, vehicle, ridden frequently by calm or peaceful deities, particularly those of the Tibetan pantheons.

Dice -- (*sho-rde'u*) iconographic importance or meaning not noted in sources, but carried by fierce deities--e.g., *dPal-ldan-lha-mo*.

Dipa -- (Skt.) see *lamp*.

Disc, moon -- (*chandra, zla-ba*) a symbol of "Relative Truth," with the sun disc it symbolizes the revelation to the "Twin Unity."

Disc, sun -- (*surya, nyi-ma*) a symbol of "Absolute Truth," with the moon disc it symbolizes the revelation to the "Twin Unity."

Dmar-gtor (Tib.) see *lance, throwing*.

Donkey -- a *vahana*, vehicle, ridden by protective

---

[1] B. Bhattasharyya define "*chowrie*" as: "*Camara*. -- chowrie or the fly-whisk consisting of the tail of a yak" (p. 191). Yet he uses the term "*chowrie* jewel" when describing the iconography of *Maitreya Bodhisattva* (p. 11). Further, when describing the various forms of Avalokitesvara, he assigns the "chowrie" as a symbol (pp. 186, 187 and 188), however, when viewing the respective images (Pls. LXII - No. 79, LXIII - No. 82, LXIV - Nos. 85 & 87, LXVII - No. 100, and LXVIII - No. 102) the images in no way resemble a fly-whisk (*camara*), rather, they are staff-like with a prominent finial (jewel?).

deities (*chos-skyong*), particularly those of the Tibetan pantheons.

Dpag-bsam-shing (Tib.) see *tree, wish-granting*.

Dragon – a *vahana*, vehicle, ridden by protective deities (*chos-skyong*), particularly those of the Tibetan pantheons.

Dragon, cloud (*mega, hbrug*) Symbolizes the thundering voices which proclaim the teachings of Buddha

Dril-bu (Tib.) see *bell*.

Drum -- (*rnga*) used during religious ceremonies to call deities and to frighten away demons.

Drum, fish head -- (*mo-yu*) see *drum*.

Drum, human skull (*damaru, thod-rnga*) It is symbolic of Tantric manifestation

Drum, small -- (*rnga'u-chung*) see *drum*.

Dug-thun -- (Tib.) English transliteral equivalent not noted in sources.

Dung-dkar -- (Tib.) see *shell , conch*.

Eagle(s) -- a vahana, vehicle, ridden frequently by calm or peaceful deities, particularly those of the Tibetan pantheons.

Earrings, golden -- iconographic importance or meaning not noted in sources.

Elephant(s) -- a *vahana*, vehicle, ridden frequently by calm or peaceful deities, particularly those of the Tibetan pantheons.

Elephant-headed person -- a representation of the Hindu deity *Ganesa* and a *vahana*, vehicle, ridden by protective deities (*chos-skyong*), particularly those of the Tibetan pantheons.

Elephant skin -- see *skin, elephant*.

Elixir of life -- (*amrita, bdud-rtsi*) a liquid, sometimes referred to as ambrosia which imparts not only all wisdom but entré to Enlightenment. The liquid which is frequently held in a *kalasha* (one of the Eight Auspicious Symbols).

Emerald -- iconographic importance or meaning not noted in sources.

Ewer -- see *vase/vessel, spouted*.

Faces of Brahma, four -- (*Brahmamukha*) iconographic importance or meaning not noted in sources.

Falcon -- a *vahana*, vehicle, ridden by deities of the Tibetan pantheons and a symbol whose iconographic importance or meaning is not noted in sources.

Fan -- iconographic importance or meaning not noted in sources.

Feathers, peacock (*mayurapiccha*) a symbol associated with *Mahamayuri, Mamaki, Sri-Devi*.

Fire -- a weapon of war and purification.

Fish -- the golden fish, one of the "Eight Auspicious Symbols."

Flag -- see *banner, flag*.

Flageolet -- a musical instrument frequently carried by wrathful deities of the *chos-skyong* and *dam-can* classes--e.g., *rDo-rje-sna-yon-ma*.

Flat pan -- see *pan, flat*.

Fly whisk -- see *whisk, fly*.

Flower(s) -- (unidentified) iconographic importance or meaning not noted in sources.

Flower, Asoka -- a red flower with ragged edges symbolic of Marici (yellow) and *Kurukulla* and from the "Tree of Consolation," it is sacred in India and related to chastity.

Flower, Kunda -- iconographic importance or meaning not noted in sources.

Flower, Priyangu -- iconographic importance or meaning not noted in sources.

Frog -- iconographic importance or meaning not noted in sources, but frequently held by wrathful deities.

Fruit, myrobalan -- iconographic importance or meaning not noted in sources, however, often associcated with the Medicine Buddhas.

Gada -- (Skt.) see *staff/stick* or *staff/stick, tantric*.

Garment (go-zu) -- iconographic importance or meaning not noted in sources.

Garuda -- a mythic-bird *vahana*, vehicle, ridden frequently by calm or peaceful deities, particularly those of the Tibetan pantheons.

Garuda-like bird -- (*khyung*) -- a *vahana*, vehicle, ridden frequently by deities, particularly those of the Tibetan pantheons.

Gdugs -- (Tib.) see *parasol*.

Genii -- a *vahana*, vehicle, ridden by protective deities (*chos-skyong*), particularly those of the Tibetan pantheons.

Ghanta -- (Skt.) see *bell*.

Glegs-bam -- (Tib.) see *book/manuscript Prajnaparamitra*.

Goad/hook -- (*ankusha, lcags-kyu*) is symbolic of *tantric* manifestations, often carried by protective deities "to bring into their power the three worlds" or "to tear out the hearts of infidels."

Goad/hook, vajra-topped -- (*vajrankusa*) is symbolic of *tantric* manifestations, often carried by protective deities "to bring into their power the three worlds" or "to tear out the hearts of infidels."

Goat -- a *vahana*, vehicle, ridden frequently by calm or peaceful deities, particularly those of the Tibetan pantheons.

Gong -- (*'khar-rnga*) used in ceremonies for fierce deities and to subdue or destroy the enemies of religion (Buddhism) or on monks who have broken their vows. Frequently carried by wrathful deities of the *chos-skyong* and *dam-can* classes.

Go-zu -- (Tib.) see *garment [go-zu]*.

Gri -- (Tib.) see *knife*.

Grig-gug -- (Tib.) see *chopper*.

Gru-gu -- (Tib.) see *thread, ball*.

Gshang -- (Tib.) see *bell, low, broad*.

Gshong -- (Tib.) see *bowl, flat*.

Gter-bum -- (Tib.) see *box of spiritual treasures*.

Gyung-drung -- (Tib.) see *swastika*.

Gzhu-dang -- (Tib.) see *bow,*.

Gzi-gdong -- (Tib.) see *mask, monster*.

Halo or Aura -- (*hOd-hkhor*) symbolizes the "Circle of Light" which results from Enlightenment.

Hammer/mace -- (*mudgara* or *tho-ba*) an instrument of battle, a symbol of *tantric* manifestation used in ceremonies for fierce deities and to subdue or destroy the enemies of religion (Buddhism) or on monks who have broken their vows. Frequently carried by wrathful deities of the *chos-skyong* and *dam-can* classes.

Hbrug -- (Tib.) see *dragon, cloud.*

Head, severed -- a symbol held by wrathful deities and represents a head of an enemy of religion.

Head of Brahma -- (*Brahmakapala* or *Brahmasirah.*

Heart -- a symbol held by wrathful deities and represents the heart of an enemy of religion.

Heavy wooden staff see *staff/stick, heavy wooden.*

Hen -- iconographic importance or meaning not noted in sources.

Hgan-di -- (Tib.) see *staff/stick* or *staff/stick tantric.*

Hindu deities -- a *vahana*, vehicle, ridden by protective deities (*chos-skyong*), particularly those of the Tibetan pantheons, also often associated with *Avalokitesvara.*

Hkhar-gsil -- (Tib.) see *staff/stick, alarm* or *staff/stick, begging.*

Hkhor-lo -- (Tib.) see *wheel.*

Hod-hkhor -- (Tib.) see *halo or aura.*

Hook -- see *goad/hook.*

Horn, antelope -- iconographic importance or meaning not noted in sources.

Horse -- a *vahana*, vehicle, ridden frequently by both calm or wrathful deities, particularly those of the Tibetan pantheons.

hPrul-gyis -- (Tib.) see *staff/stick, short.*

Human corpse club -- see *club/cudgel, human corpse.*

Human, man -- a *vahana*, vehicle, ridden by protective deities (*chos-skyong*), particularly those of the Tibetan pantheons.

Human skin -- see *skin, human.*

Human skull-cup -- see *cup, human skull-.*

Human skull-drum -- see *drum, human skull.*

Human thigh-bone trumpet -- see *trumpet, human thigh-bone.*

Human, woman -- a *vahana*, vehicle, ridden by protective deities (*chos-skyong*), particularly those of the Tibetan pantheons.

Ichneumon -- see *mongoose.*

Incense -- (*dhupa*) used in religious ceremonies to purify and to call the gods.

Incense burner -- see *censor.*

Intestines -- of the enemies of religion and often shown being chewed in the mouths of wrathful deities or twisted in their hands.

Jackal -- a *vahana*, vehicle, ridden by protective deities (*chos-skyong*), particularly those of the Tibetan pantheons.

Jambhara -- (Skt.) see *citron.*

Jar -- see *kalasha.*

Jewel(s) -- (*ratna, mani, nor-bu*) symbolizes the preciousness of the teachings of Buddha, the perfection of the Law.

Jewels, flaming -- (*nor-bu-me-har*) see *jewels.*

Jewels, three (*triratna*) symbolic of the *Buddha, Dharma* and *Sangha*, see also *jewels.*

Jewel, wish fulfilling (*chintamani, yid-bzhin-nor-bu*) the gem that fulfills all wants, the sixth sense, the vehicle of the divine essence.

Jizo's Staff -- see *staff/stick, alarm.*

Ju-tig -- (Tib.) see *thread, sacred.*

Kalasha -- (Skt.) see *vase.*

Kamandalu -- (Skt.) see *Vase/vessel, spouted.*

Kapala -- (Skt.) see *human skull-cup.*

Karppar -- (Skt.) same as *kapala.*

Kartri -- (Skt.) see *karttrika.*

Karttari -- (Skt.) see *karttrika.*

Karttrika -- (Skt.) see *chopper.*

Kattara -- (Skt.) English transliteral equivalent not noted in sources.

Keys -- iconographic importance or meaning not noted in sources.

Khadga -- (Skt.) see *sword.*

Khakkhara -- (Skt.) see *staff/stick, alarm* or *staff/stick, begging.*

Khar-gil -- (Tib.) see *staff/stick, alarm* or *staff/stick, begging.*

'Khar-rng -- (Tib.) see *gong.*

Kha-ti -- (Tib.) English transliteral equivalent not noted in sources.

Kha-tram -- (Tib.) English transliteral equivalent not noted in sources.

Kha-tvam-ga -- (Tib.) see *staff/stick, magic.*

Khatvanga -- (Skt.) see *staff/stick, magic.*

Khetaka -- (Skt.) see *shield.*

Kharab -- (Skt.) see *coat of mail.*

Khrag-mtsho -- (Tib.) see *lake of blood.*

Khram-bam -- (Tib.) see *club, mummified corpse.*

Khram-shing -- (Tib.) see *staff/stick, magic notched.*

Khri-snyan-sa-le -- (Tib.) see *skin, antelope.*

Khyang -- (Tib.) see *ass, wild Asiatic.*

Khyung -- (Tib.) see *garuda-like bird.*

Kila -- (Skt.) see *dagger, magic.*

Klu -- (Tib.) see *serpent/snake.*

Klu-shing -- (Tib.) see *staff/stick, snake.*

Knife -- (*churi, gri*) used to subdue or destroy the enemies of religion (Buddhism) or on monks who have broken their vows. Frequently carried by wrathful deities of the *chos-skyong* and *dam-can* classes.

Knife, skull-cup-hilt -- see *knife.*

Knife, wavy-bladed -- (*chu-gri*) see *knife.*

Knot, endless -- the "infinitely interwoven knot of life" and one of the "Eight Auspicious Symbols."

Kundika -- (Skt.) see *vase/vessel, spouted.*

Kuthara -- (Skt.) English transliteral equivalent not noted in sources.

Kyi-mdung -- (Tib.) see *lance, piercing weapon.*

Ladle -- iconographic importance or meaning not noted in sources.

Lake of blood -- (*khrag-mtsho*) a symbol generally associated with fierce deities either being held in the hand or being ridden across--e.g., *dPal-ldan-lha-mo.*

Lamp -- (*dipa*) associated with religious ceremonies, a light of spiritual awareness, a symbol which calls deities and frightens away demons.

Lance -- (*mdung*) used to subdue or destroy the enemies of religion (Buddhism). Frequently carried by wrathful deities of the *chos-skyong* and *dam-can* classes.

Lance, btsan -- (*btsan-mdung*) see *lance*.

Lance, piercing weapon -- (*shagti, kyi-mdung* or *mdung*) used to subdue or destroy the enemies of religion (Buddhism). Frequently carried by wrathful deities of the *chos-skyong* and *dam-can* classes.

Lance, sword tipped -- (*shagti, shag-gri*) used to subdue or destroy the enemies of religion (Buddhism). Frequently carried by wrathful deities of the *chos-skyong* and *dam-can* classes.

Lance, throwing -- (*dmar-gtor*) used to subdue or destroy the enemies of religion (Buddhism). Frequently carried by wrathful deities of the *chos-skyong* and *dam-can* classes.

Lcags-kyu -- (Tib.) see *goad/hook*.

Lcags-sgrog -- (Tib.) see *chain, iron*.

Leash of disease -- (*nad-zhags*) used to destroy the enemies of religion (Buddhism). Frequently carried by wrathful deities of the *chos-skyong* and *dam-can* classes.

Lemon -- (*jambhara*) see also *citron*. It is a symbol frequently associated with *Jambhala*. and other deities of wealth

Lhung-bzed -- (Tib.) see *bowl, alms*.

Lion -- (*simha, seng*) symbolizes bravery and the eager spirit of the believer, also a *vahana*, vehicle, ridden frequently by calm or peaceful as well as wrathful deities, particularly those of the Tibetan pantheons.

Lioness -- a *vahana*, vehicle, ridden by protective deities (*chos-skyong*), particularly those of the Tibetan pantheons.

Lion throne -- a *vahana*, vehicle, ridden frequently by calm or peaceful deities, particularly those of the Tibetan pantheons.

Lion, winged -- a *vahana*, vehicle, ridden frequently by wrathful deities, particularly those of the Tibetan pantheons.

Lotus -- (*padma*) a symbol of self creation or self existence, the feminine principle, of every *Buddha* and *bodhisattva*. It is one of the "Eight Auspicious Symbols," also a *vahana*, vehicle, ridden frequently by calm or peaceful deities, particularly those of the Tibetan pantheons.

Lotus, blue -- (*utpala* or *nilotpala*) The night flower, symbolic of the green *Tara*.

Lotus, double -- (*visvapadma*) see lotus, iconographic importance or meaning not noted in sources.

Lotus, pink -- see lotus, iconographic importance or meaning not noted in sources.

Lotus, red -- see lotus, iconographic importance or meaning not noted in sources.

Lotus throne -- a *vahana*, vehicle, ridden frequently by calm or peaceful deities, particularly those of all Buddhist pantheons.

Lute -- (*vina, pi-wang*) iconographic importance or meaning not noted in sources.

Mace -- see *staff/stick, tantric*; or *staff/stick, baton*.

Makara -- (Skt.) see *"sea elephant"* or *dragon*.

Mala -- (Skt.) see *rosary*.

Ma-mo-mdos -- (Tib.) see *cross, sacred thread*.

Mamsakapala -- see *cup, human skull-, filled with flesh*.

Mandala -- (Skt.) a sacred circle containing mystic diagrams, deities, and *tantric* symbols, divided geometrically, generally two dimensional, but may be three dimensional as well.

Mani -- (Skt.) see *jewel*.

Manuscript -- see *book/manuscript*.

Mask, monster -- (*gzi-gdong*) see *makara*.

Mayura -- (Skt.) see *peacock*.

Mayurapiccha -- (Skt.) see *feathers , peacock*.

Mchod-rten -- (Tib.) see *shrine*.

Mdah -- (Tib.) see *arrow*.

Mdah-dar -- (Tib.) see *arrow, divination*.

Mdung -- (Tib.) see *lance, piercing weapon*.

Meat, btsan -- (*mtsan-sha*) carried exclusively by wrathful deities, the flesh of demons.

Meditation cord -- see *cord, meditation*.

Mega -- (Skt.) see *dragon, cloud*.

Me-long -- (Tib.) see *mirror*.

Mirror -- (*darpana, me-long* or *'phrul-gyi-me-long*) symbolizes the image of the void, indicates the transitory nature of material things.

Mkhar-gsil -- (Tib.) see *staff/stick, alarm*.

Mongoose -- (*nakula* or *ichneumon, nehu-li*) A symbol usually associated with *Jambhala*, a deity of wealth, a receptacle of and an animal which vomits out gems.

Moon -- a *vahana*, vehicle, ridden frequently by calm or peaceful deities, particularly those of the Tibetan pantheons.

Moon disc -- see *disc, moon*.

Mo-yu -- (Jap.) see *drum, fish-head*.

Mrtaka -- (Skt.) see *corpse, human*.

Mtshan -- (Tib.) see *banner/flag*.

Mtshan-cha'i-'khor-lo -- (Tib.) see *wheel, sharp-weaponed*.

Mudgara -- (Skt.) see *hammer/mace*.

Mule -- a *vahana*, vehicle, ridden by protective deities (*chos-skyong*), particularly those of the Tibetan pantheons.

Musala -- (Skt.) see *pestle*.

Myrobalan -- (Skt.) see *tree, myrobalan*.

Nad-rkyal -- (Tib.) see *sack of diseases*.

Nad-zhags -- (Tib.) see *leash of disease*.

Naga -- a snake deity and a *vahana*, vehicle, ridden by protective deities (*chos-skyong*), particularly those of the Tibetan pantheons. see *serpent/snake*.

Nakula (Skt.) see *mongoose*.

Necklace -- iconographic importance or meaning not noted in sources.

Nectar of life -- see *elixir of life*.

Needle -- (*suci*) used to sew shut the eyes and mouths of non-believers and enemies of religion.

Nehu-li -- (Tib.) see *mongoose*,.

Ne'u-le'i-rkyal-pa -- (Tib.) see *sack*,

ichneumon skin.

Nilotpala -- (Skt.) same as *utpala.*

Noose/snare -- (*pasha, zhags-pa*) a weapon used to bind the host of Mara and used to subdue or destroy the enemies of religion (Buddhism) or on monks who have broken their vows. Frequently carried by wrathful deities of the *chos-skyong* and *dam-can* classes.

Noose/snare, snake -- (*sbrul-zhags*) see noose/snare.

Noose/snare of sun-rays -- (*nyi-zcr-zhags-pa*) see noose/snare.

Noose/snare, vajra-tipped -- (*vajrapasha, rdo-rje-zhags-pa*) see noose/snare.

Noose/snare, water -- (*chu-yi-zhags-pa*) see noose/snare.

Nor-bu -- (Tib.) see *jewel.*

Nor-bu-me-har -- (Tib.) see *jewel, flaming.*

Nor-gshong -- (Tib.) see *pan, flat.*

Nyi-ma -- (Tib.) see *disc, sun.*

Nyi-zer-zhags-pa -- (Tib.) see *noose/snare of sun-rays.*

Otter head -- (*sram-gyi*) iconographic importance or meaning not noted in sources.

Padma -- (Skt.) see *lotus.*

Padma throne -- see *lotus throne.*

Pan, flat -- (*nor-gshong*) a symbol, frequently filled with jewels, or food and associated with wealth bestowing deities or their companions.

Parasol -- (*atapatra, gdugs*) a particular symbol of the goddess *Sitatapatra* as well as *Usnisasita* and *Pancaraksa.* It is one of the "Eight Auspicious Symbols," a symbol of protection.

Parashu -- (Skt.) see *axe.*

Par-bu -- (Tib.) see *bowl, silver alms.*

Parigha -- (Skt.) see *club/cudgel.*

Pasha -- (Skt.) see *noose/snare.*

Pataka -- (Skt.) see *banner, cylindrical.*

Patra -- (Skt.) see *bowl, alms.*

Peacock -- (*mayura, rma-bya*) a *vahana,* vehicle, ridden frequently by calm or peaceful deities, particularly those of the Tibetan pantheons, generally associated with *Amitabha.*

Peacock feathers -- see *feathers, peacock.*

Peacock throne -- a vahana, vehicle, ridden frequently by calm or peaceful deities, particularly those of the Tibetan pantheons, generally associated with *Amitabha.*

Pearl -- see *jewel.*

Pearl, flaming -- see *jewel, flaming.*

Pestle -- (*musala*) a device appropriate to both Buddhism and Hinduism, iconographic importance or meaning not noted in sources.

'Phang -- (Tib.) see *spindle.*

Phatka -- (Skt.) see *tusk.*

Phota -- (Skt.) see *chain.*

Phreng-ba -- (Tib.) see *rosary.*

'Phrul-gyi-me-long -- (Tib.) see *mirror.*

Phur-bu -- (Tib.) see *magic dagger.*

Phyed-rnga -- (Tib.) see *tambourine.*

Piercing weapon -- see *lance.*

Pig -- a vahana, vehicle, ridden by protective deities (*chos-skyong*), particularly those of the Tibetan pantheons and often associated with *Marici.*

Pi-wang -- (Tib.) see *lute.*

Plow-share -- a device which is held by the wrathful central *Heruka* deities of the *Bardo Mandala.*

Pomegranate -- iconographic importance or meaning not noted in sources.

Porcupine -- iconographic importance or meaning not noted in sources.

Prajna Paramita book -- see *book/manuscript, Prajna Paramita.*

Preta -- (Skt.) see *corpse, human.*

Priyangu flower -- see *flower, Priyangu.*

Purse -- iconographic importance or meaning not noted in sources.

Pustaka -- (Skt.) see *book/manuscript.*

Radish -- an iconographic device usually associated with *Ganesa.*

Ral-gri -- (Tib.) see *sword.*

Rat -- a *vahana,* vehicle, ridden frequently by calm or peaceful deities--e.g., *Ganesa*--particularly those of the Tibetan pantheons.

Ratna -- (Skt.) see *jewel.*

Razor -- (*spu-gri*) used to subdue or destroy the enemies of religion (Buddhism) or on monks who have broken their vows. Frequently carried by wrathful deities of the *chos-skyong* and *dam-can* classes.

Rdo-rje -- (Tib.) see *thunderbolt.*

Rdo-rje-dril-bu -- (Tib.) see *bell, vajra-topped.*

Rdo-rje-hprul-gyis -- (Tib.) see *staff/stick, short vajra-topped.*

Rdo-rje-rgya-gram -- (Tib.) see *thunderbolts, crossed.*

Rdo-rje-zhags-pa -- (Tib.) see *noose/snare, vajra-tipped.*

Rdo-zor -- (Tib.) see *sling.*

Rgyal-mtshan -- (Tib.) see *banner,/flag, flat.*

Rice, ear -- iconographic importance or meaning not noted in sources.

Ritual wand -- see *wand, ritual.*

Rkang-gling -- (Tib.) see *trumpet , human thigh-bone.*

Rkyal-pa -- (Tib.) see *sack.*

rLung-rta -- (Tib.) see *Airy horse.*

Rma-bya -- (Tib.) see *peacock.*

Rnga -- (Tib.) see *drum.*

Rnga'u-chung -- (Tib.) see *drum, small.*

Rnga-yab -- (Tib.) see *whisk , fly-.*

Rol-mo -- (Tib.) see *cymbals.*

Rooster -- a *vahana,* vehicle, ridden frequently by wrathful or angry deities, particularly those of the Tibetan pantheons.

Rosary -- (*mala* or *akasamala, phreng-ba*) a circle of beads often made from dried fruit, carved bones, human skulls or beads, a device used during prayer, a religious offering associated with *Aksayamati-Bodhisattva,* and a special symbol of *Avalokitesvara, Prajnaparamita, Cunda, Bhrkuti,* and certain wrathful deities (rosary of skulls).

Rtse-gsum -- (Tib.) see *trident.*

Sabre -- (*shang-lang*) similar to *sword* but used

less often, a symbol-weapon to subdue or destroy the enemies of religion (Buddhism) or on monks who have broken their vows. Frequently carried by wrathful deities of the *chos-skyong* and *dam-can* classes.

Sack -- (*rkyal-pa*) iconographic importance or meaning not noted in sources.

Sack, ichneumon skin (*ne'u-le'i-rkyal-pa*) see *sack*.

Sack of blood -- (*chu'i-rkyal-pa*) used by wrathful deities, see *sack*.

Sack of diseases (*nad-rkyal*) used by wrathful deities, see *sack*.

Sakti -- (Skt.) see *dart*.

Sava -- (Skt.) see *corpse, human*.

Sbrul-zhags -- (Tib.) see *noose/snare, snake*.

Sceptre -- see *staff/stick*.

Scepter, white crystal -- (*shel-gyi-'gying-dkal*) iconographic importance or meaning not noted in sources.

Scroll -- see *book/manuscript*.

Sea elephant or sea dragon -- (*makara, chu-srin*) see *sea monster*.

Sea Monster -- (*makara*) a *vahana*, vehicle, ridden by protective deities (*chos-skyong*), particularly those of the Tibetan pantheons, often shown around *Sakyamuni Buddha* as a protective device..

Seed -- (*biju*) iconographic importance or meaning not noted in sources.

Semen -- (*bindu, thig-le*) iconographic importance or meaning not noted in sources.

Seng -- see *lion*.

Serpent/snake -- (*naga, klu*) a device related to *Naga*, a water symbol, enemy of *Garuda* the air symbol.

Serpent, black -- iconographic importance or meaning not noted in sources.

sGom-thag -- (Tib.) see *cord, meditation*.

Sgrom-bu -- (Tib.) see *casque*.

Shag-gri -- (Tib.) see *lance, sword tipped*.

Shagti -- (Skt.) see *lance, piercing weapon*.

Shakujo -- (Jap.) see *staff/stick, alarm*.

Shang-lang -- (Tib.) see *sabre*.

Shankha -- (Skt.) see *shell , conch*.

Shara -- (Skt.) see *arrow*.

Shel-gyi-'gying-dkal -- (Tib.) see *scepter, white crystal*.

Shell, conch -- (*shankha, dung-dkar*) one of the "Eight Auspicious Symbols," symbolic of diffusing the Law, of the teachings of Buddha.

Sher-phyin -- (Tib.) see *book/manuscript*.

Shield (*khetaka*) It is a symbol of *Dharma* and its ability to protect the devout.

Sho-rde'u -- (Tib.) see *dice*.

Shrine -- (*chaitya, stupa, mchod-rten*) represents the Buddhist universe, a Buddhist sanctuaty, it is within a stupa that the relics of Buddha were buried.

Sickle -- (*dgra-zor*) a weapon used to subdue or destroy the enemies of religion (Buddhism) or on monks who have broken their vows. Frequently carried by wrathful deities of the *chos-skyong* and *dam-can* classes.

Simha -- (Skt.) see *lion*.

Si-nen -- (Tib.) see *cymbals*.

Silver alms bowl -- see *bowl, silver alms*.

Skin, antelope -- (*khri-snyan-sa-le*) a *vahana* upon which *gurus* and *mahagurus* frequently sit.

Skin, deer -- iconographic importance or meaning not noted in sources.

Skin, elephant -- frequently worn by *dharmapalas* as a cloak.

Skin, human -- frequently worn by *dharmapalas* as a cloak.

Skull -- a symbol usually carried by wrathful deities, symbolizing the enemies of religion.

Skull-cup -- (Tib.) see *cup , human skull-*.

Skyu-ru-ra -- (Tib.) see *citron*.

Sling -- (*rdo-zor*) iconographic importance or meaning not noted in sources.

Snake -- a *vahana*, vehicle, ridden by protective deities (*chos-skyong*), particularly those of the Tibetan pantheons. See also *serpent/snake*.

Sphota -- (Skt.) see *chain*.

Spindle -- (*'phang*) a female element often associated with wrathful deities and is in counterpoint to the arrow (male element).

Spu-gri -- (Tib.) see *razor*.

Sow -- a *vahana*, vehicle, ridden by protective deities (*chos-skyong*), particularly those of the Tibetan pantheons and often associated with *Marici*.

Sram-gyi -- (Tib.) see *otter head*.

Srid-pa'i-ldem-shing -- (Tib.) see *staff/stick, three forked* .

Srinkhala -- (Skt.) see *chain, iron*.

Srnkhala -- (Skt.) see *chain, iron*.

Staff/stick, alarm -- (*Jizo's staff, shakujo, khakkhara, hkhar-gsil* or *mkhar-gsil*) a sounding staff with four rings representing the "Four Truths," carried by mendicants.

Staff/stick, baton -- (*gada, hgan-di*) or mace, a tantric symbol of *Mahakala*. When shown, it often rests across the crook of both arms.

Staff/stick, begging -- (*khakkhara, hkhar-gsil*) see *staff/stick, alarm*.

Staff/stick, command -- (*bdud-kyi-khram-shing*) iconographic importance or meaning not noted in sources.

Staff/stick, heavy wooden -- (*bseg-shing*) iconographic importance or meaning not noted in sources.

Staff/stick, Jizo's -- see *staff, alarm*.

Staff/stick, magic -- (*khatvanga, kha-tvam-ga*) said to have been first used by *Padmasambhava*, a ritual wand topped with either a *vajra*, skull, severed human head, trident or any combination of the fore mentioned, also associated with the *dakinis*.

Staff/stick, magic notched -- (*khram-shing*) used in ceremonies for wrathful deities and to subdue or destroy the enemies of religion.

Staff/stick, magic throwing -- (*dam-shing*) a ceremonial weapon used in rites for wrathful deities and to subdue or destroy the enemies of religion (Buddhism) or on monks who have broken their vows. Frequently carried by wrathful deities of the *chos-skyong* and *dam-can* classes.

Staff/stick, Padmasambhava's magic -- see *staff/stick, magic*.

Staff/stick, short, magic -- (*hprul-gyis-gandi*) usually held cradled across the fore-arms and carried by *Hayagriva*.

Staff/stick, skull finial -- (*danda, thod-dbyug-pa*) a short *tantric* staff usually topped with a skull finial.

Staff/stick, snake -- (*klu-shing*) iconographic importance or meaning not noted in sources.

Staff/stick, Tantric -- (*gada, hgan-di* or *beng*) amace often associated with *Mahakala*, it represents light and *tantric* manifestation.

Staff/stick, three forked -- (*srid-pa'i-ldem-shing*) iconographic importance or meaning not noted in sources.

Staff/stick, vajra-topped -- (*vajra-danda, rdo-rje-hprul-gyis*) iconographic importance or meaning not noted in sources.

Stag -- (Tib.) see *tiger*.

Sta-mo of iron -- English transliteral equivalent not noted in sources and a iconographic importance or meaning not noted in sources.

Stick -- see *staff/stick*.

String/thread -- see *thread, ball*.

Stupa -- (Skt.) see *shrine*.

Suci -- (Skt.) see *needle*.

Sula -- English transliteral equivalent not noted in sources

Sun -- a *vahana*, vehicle, ridden frequently by calm or peaceful deities, particularly those of the Tibetan pantheons.

Sun disc -- see *disc, sun*.

Surya -- (Skt.) see *disc, sun*.

Suryya -- (Skt.) same as *surya*.

Sutra -- (Skt.) see *thread, sacred*.

Swan -- a *vahana*, vehicle, ridden frequently by calm or peaceful deities, particularly those of the Tibetan pantheons.

Swastika -- (gyung-drung) symbolizes the esoteric doctrine of the Buddha.

Sweetmeat -- iconographic importance or meaning not noted in sources.

Sword -- (*khadga, ral-gri*) a symbol of enlightenment, often associated with *Manjusri* and his emanations, also used by protective deities against enemies of Buddhist creed.

Sword, flaming -- (*ye-shes-ral-gri*) the sword of wisdom.

Tabor or flat drum -- see *drum*.

Tambourine -- (*phyed-rnga*) a single membrane, shallow drum with a handle used in ceremonies for wrathful deities.

Thig-le -- (Tib.) see *semen*.

Tho-ba -- (Tib.) see *hammer*.

Thod-dbyug-pa (Tib.) see *club/cudgel with skull finial*.

Thod-gdengs -- (Tib.) see *toupet*.

Thod-pa -- see *cup, human skull-*.

Thod-rnga -- (Tib.) see *drum, human skull*.

Thread, ball -- (*gru-gu*) related to *sutra* and sacred thread cross, frequently held by protective deities.

Thread, sacred -- (*sutra, ju-tig*) used to sew shut the eyes and mouths of non-believers and the enemies of religion.

Thunderbolt -- (*vajra, rdo-rje*) a symbol used to destroy the enemies of religion, the form (five prongs) represents the *Pançabuddhas*, as "diamond scepter" it represents indestructibility, or wisdom which destroys passion, a masculine symbol (*linga*).

Thunderbolt, crossed -- (*vishva-vajra, rdo-rje-rgya-gram*).

Thun-zor -- (Tib.) English transliteral equivalent not noted in sources.

Tiger -- (*stag*) a *vahana*, vehicle, ridden by protective deities (*chos-skyong*), particularly those of the Tibetan pantheons.

Torch -- iconographic importance or meaning not noted in sources.

Tortoise -- a *vahana*, vehicle, ridden by protective deities (*chos-skyong*), particularly those of the Tibetan pantheons.

Toupet -- (*thod-gdengs*) various hair forms of deities (frequently wrathful deities or those associated with wrathful deities).

Tree, Asoka -- the "Tree of Consolation," *Sakyamuni Buddha* being born between the *asoka* tree and the *bodhi* tree.

Tree, Myrobalan -- (*a-ru-ra*) a medicinal plant, frequently associated with the Medicine Buddhas.

Tree, wish granting -- (*dpag-bsam-shing*) iconographic importance or meaning not noted in sources.

Triangle (*trikona*) Symbolic of the *Buddha*, *Dharma* and *Sangha*, a feminine symbol (*yoni*).

Trident -- (*trishula, rtse-gsum*) a symbol which has diverse connotations. It may represent creation, protection and descruction, or the *Buddha, Dharma* and *Sangha*, or the tree of life, or lightening, or one of the symbols of Buddha-hood.

Trikona -- (Skt.) see *triangle*.

Triratna -- (Skt.) see *jewel, three*.

Trishula -- (Skt.) see *trident*.

Trumpet, human thigh-bone -- (*rkang-gling*) a *tantric* device used to dispel demons and the enemies of religion, frequently carried by fierce deities.

Tse-bum -- (Tib.) see *vase/vessel of life*.

Tshe-bum -- (Tib.) see *vase/vessel of life*.

Tusk -- (*phatka*) a symbol of dominance, also often shown in conjunction with jewels as an indication of valuable gifts.

Utpala -- (Skt.) see *lotus, blue*.

Urn -- see *vase/vessel*.

Vajra -- (Skt.) see *thunderbolt*.

Vajrankusa -- (Skt.) see *goad/hook, vajra-topped*.

Vajradanda -- (Skt.) see *staff/stick, short vajra-topped*.

Vajraghanta -- (Skt.) see *bell, vajra-topped*.

Vajrapasha -- (Skt.) see *noose/snare, vajra-tipped*.

Vase/vessel -- (*kalasha , bum-pa* or *tse-bum*) thought to hold the nectar of life, the primordial water from which the universe was formed. It is one of the "Eight Auspicious Symbols."

Vase/vessel of life -- (*tshe-bum*) see *vase/vessel*.

Vase/vessel, spouted -- (*kamandalu* or *kundika*) see *vase/vessel*.

Vessel -- see *vase/vessel*.

Vessel, treasure -- see *casque, treasure*.

Vija -- (Skt.) see *bija*.

Vijapuraka -- (Skt.) same as *bijapura*.

Vina -- (Skt.) see *lute*.

Vishvapadma -- (Skt.) see *lotus, double*.

Vishva-vajra -- (Skt.) see *thunderbolts, crossed*.

Visvapadma -- (Skt.) see *lotus, double*.

Wand , ritual -- see *staff/stick,command*.

Water buffalo -- see *buffalo, water*.

Wheel -- (*chakra, hkhor-lo*) symbolic of the rotation of the world, of absolute completeness, the "Eightfold Path of Self Conquest" and the "Wheel of the Law." It is one of the "Eight Auspicious Symbols."

Wheel, sharp-weaponed -- (*mtshan-cha'i-'khor-lo*) associated with the deity *Khro-bo-ging-ka-ra*.

Whip -- iconographic importance or meaning not noted in sources.

Whisk , fly- -- (*chamara* or *chauri , rnga-yab*) A *tantric* symbol, it repels any obstacle to enlightenment, obedience to the Law, also a symbol of authority.

Willow -- a female symbol often associated with *Kuan-shis-yin p'u-sa*.

Wind wheel -- iconographic importance or meaning not noted in sources.

Wind wheel, flaming -- iconographic importance or meaning not noted in sources.

Wish fulfilling jewel -- see *jewel, wish fulfilling*.

Wish granting tree -- see *tree, wish granting*.

Wolf -- a *vahana*, vehicle, ridden by protective deities (*chos-skyong*), particularly those of the Tibetan pantheons.

Wolf, nine-headed -- a *vahana*, vehicle, ridden by protective deities (*chos-skyong*), particularly those of the Tibetan pantheons.

Wood-apple -- (*bilvafala*) iconographic importance or meaning not noted in sources.

Wreath, Rose -- iconographic importance or meaning not noted in sources.

Yak -- a *vahana*, vehicle, ridden by protective deities (*chos-skyong*), particularly those of the Tibetan pantheons.

Ya-tsha -- (Tib.) English transliteral equivalent not noted in sources.

Ye-shes-ral-gri -- (Tib.) see *sword, flaming*.

Yid-bzhin-nor-bu -- (Tib.) see *jewel, wish fulfilling*.

Za-ma-thog -- (Tib.) see *basket, round*.

Zhags-pa -- (Tib.) see *noose/snare*.

Zhing-dbyag -- (Tib.) see *club/cudgel, human corpse*.

Zla-ba -- (Tib.) see *disc, moon*.

Zor -- (Tib.) English transliteral equivalent not noted in sources.

Appendix I

Classes Group and Hierarchies

Classes, Groups and Hierarchies

In Mahayana Buddhism and particularly in the Vajrayana tradition, the deities are found in various classes, groups and hierarchies. Within the various sects the ranks can differ considerably, particularly within the lesser ranks. Adi-Buddha occupies the apex of the order within the various Northern pantheons, followed by the Dhyani Buddhas, Dhyani Bodhisattvas, Manushi Buddhas, Buddhas and Mahabodhisattvas. The following list does not purport to list the deities in ranked order. The first twelve are the most frequently known and are in a rough ranked-order. Beyond, the classes and groups are merely listed alphabetically.

Schematically the divinities form the following:

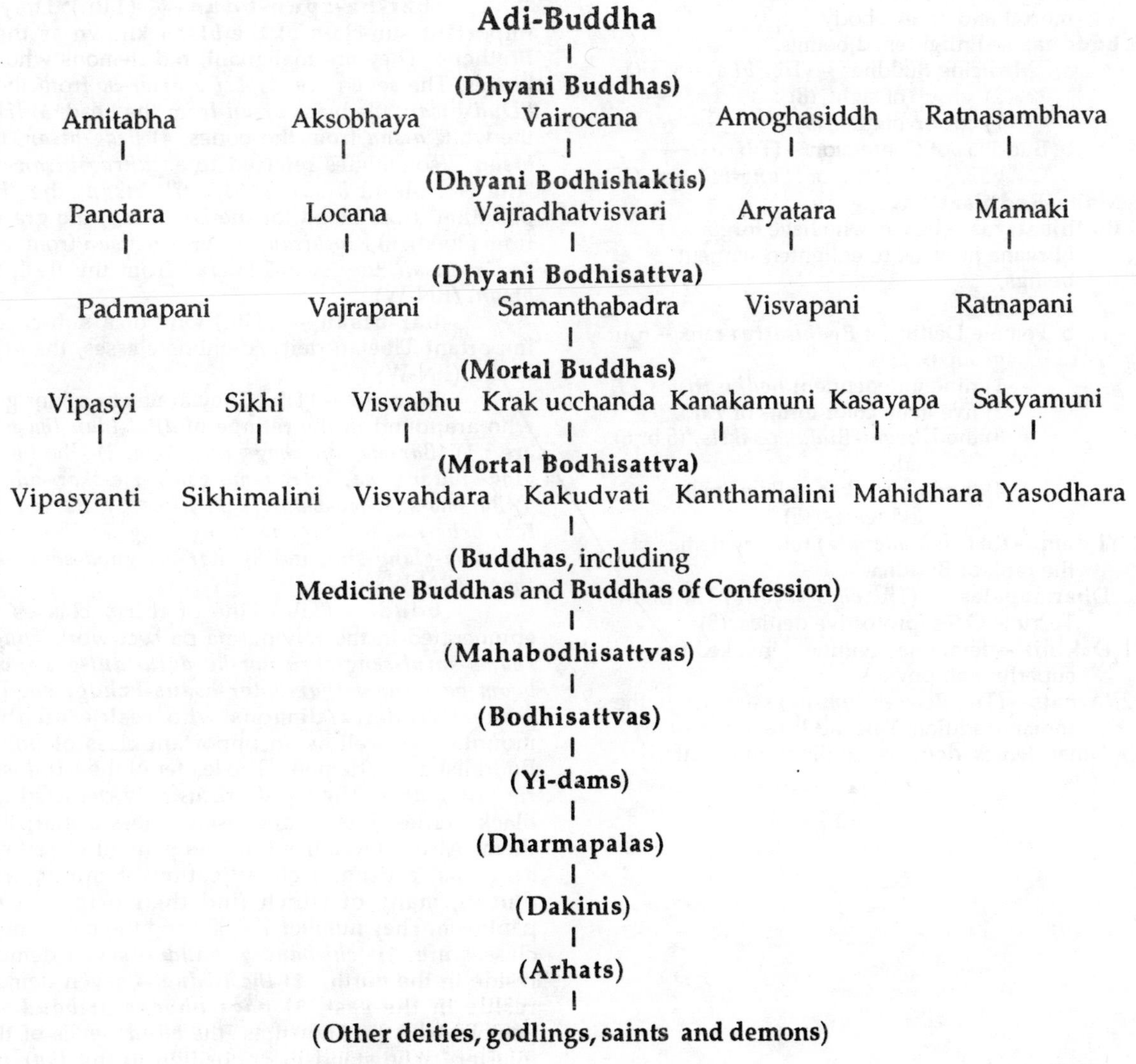

Hierarchy of Deities

1. **Adi-Buddha** -- primordial Buddha, Self-Creative, Self-Existent.
2. **Dhyani-Buddhas** -- Buddhas of Meditation, Celestial Buddhas, created by the Adi-Buddha and live in Nirvana. (5 or 6)[2]
3. **Dhyani-Buddhasaktis** -- Consorts of the Dhyani-Buddhas. (5 or 6)
4. **Dhyani-Bodhisattvas** -- live in heaven in Sambhogakaya or Body of Supreme Happiness,
   a. five are reflexes of the *Dhyani-Buddhas;* (5) or
   b. eight (including the five above). (8)
5. **Manushi-Buddhas** -- Buddhas who live or have lived on earth in Nirmanakaya, mortal and ascetic body.
6. **Buddhas** -- Enlightened beings,
   a. Medicine Buddhas -- (Tib.: *bLas-sMan*),
      2) group of eight, (8)
      1) group of nine, (9)
   b. Buddhas of Confession -- (Tib.: *bDe-gShegs-So-lNga* or *lTung-bShags*). (35)
7. **Maha-Bodhisattvas**
8. **Bodhisattvas** -- beings who have forgone Nirvana in order to enlighten sentient beings,
   a. Male,
   b. Female Deities of *Bodhisattva* rank -- four groups:
      1) nine independent *Bodhisattvas*, (9)
      2) five main color forms of *Tara*,
      3) the *Dhyani-Buddha-saktis*, (5 or 6) and
      4) the *Pancaraksa* or Five Spell Goddesses. (5)
9. **Yi-dam** -- (Skt.: *Ishtadevata*) tutelary deities of the rank of Buddha.
10. **Dharmapalas** -- (Tib.: *chos-skyong*) The Eight Terrible Ones, protective deities. (8)
11. **Dakinis** -- feminine divinities , invoked for superhuman powers.
12. **Arhats** -- (Tib.: *dGra-bCom-pa*) saints, 16 in the Indian tradition, Tibet adds two more. (18)
13. Other deities, demons, godlings and saints.

[2] Numbers in parenthesis are the accorded numbers of deities within the various classes or groups.

Classes, Groups, Hierarchies and Titles

The following are not listed in rank order, but are merely listed in alphabetical order.

arhats -- (Skt.) Buddhists "saints" of the Indian tradition who were responsible for the spread of Buddhism in Tibet. There are traditionally sixteen to whom are frequently added two more. (BO)

asuras -- (Skt.) A group of deities who seem to parallel the Tibetan *lha-ma-yin*. See *lha-ma-yin*. (RN-W)

'bar-ba-nyis-brgya-lnga-bcu -- (Tib.) They represent a group of 250 *dgra-lha*-like demons. (RN-W)

'bar-ba-spun-bdun -- (Tib.) They are an important sub-class of the *btsan* known as the "Seven Brothers." They are malignant, red demons who ride red horses. The seven are: **1)** *Tsi'u-dmar-po* from the egg, **2)** *bDud-btsan*, the black *btsan* from the head, **3)** *lHa-btsan*, the white *btsan* from the bones, **4)** *Brag-btsan*, the "rock *btsan*;" (sometimes referred to as *Khrag-btsan-dmar-po*, "the red blood *btsan*"), **5)** *Grib-btsan*, the "*btsan* of pollution" from blood (or the *Dri-btsan*, the green *btsan* from blood), **6)** *Klu-btsan, the* brown *btsan* from urine, and **7)** *Gri-btsan*, the "sword *btsan*" from the flesh See also *btsan*. (RN-W)

bar-btsan -- (Tib.) One of a sub-class of the important Tibetan deity/demons classes, the *btsan*. See *btsan*. (RN-W)

'bar-ma -- (Tib.) They are eight minor goddesses who are found in the retinue of *dPal-ldan-lha-mo*. They are : 1) *'Bar-ma-nyi-zhags-thogs-ma*, 2) *'Bar-ma-khyer-glog-'phreng-ma*, 3) *'Bar-ma-gshin-rje-skar-mda'-gdong*, 4)*'Bar-ma-srin-mo-mdung-'phen-ma*, 5) *'Bar-ma-klu-mo-lce-'bebs-ma*, 6) *'Bar-ma-rlung-bdag*, 7) *'Bar-ma-gnod-sbyin-ba-glang-sna*, and 8) *'Bar-ma-gnod-sbyin-khyung-thogs*. (RN-W)

bdud -- (Tib.) One of thirty classes that are enumerated in the rNying-ma pa sect work *Thugs-rje'i-rnams-sprul-seng-chen-nor-bu-dgra-'dul-gyis-nor-bdud-bcom-pa'i-rnam-thar-mdor-bsdus-bzhugs-so*. They are protective deity/demons who reside on the black mountain as well as an important class of Bon or pre-Buddhist deity/demons. The leader of the *bdud* is *rKong-rje-brang-dkar*. The *bdud* are usually depicted as fierce, black deities. Fits of unconsciousness are attributed to them. Also, they fall under the general classification of *dregs-pa*, a general classification of minor protective deities, many of which find their origin in the Bon pantheon. They number 100,000 and the major, noted sub-classes are: **1)** *'chi-bdag-gi-baud* -- seven demons who reside in the north, **2)** *lha'i-bdud* -- seven demons who reside in the east, **3)** *nags-phyogs-gi-bdud* -- seven demons who are known as "the *bdud* devils of the black quarter," who stand in opposition to the *dkar-phyogs-skyong-ba'i-srung-ma*, **4)** *nyon-mongs-pa'i-bdud* -- seven demons who reside in the south, yellow in color, ride yellow horses, hold sword and snare and cause illness to counteract harmful effects of the enemies of religion, **5)** *phung-po'i-bdud* -- seven demons who reside in the west, red in color, ride red horses, hold lance and snares, and cause illness to counteract harmful effects of the enemies of religion, **6)** *sa-bdud* -- known as "earth bdud" reside in the east and are a Bon deity, **7)** *rlung-bdud* -- known as the "wind bdud" reside in the north and are a Bon deity, **8)** *me-bdud* -- known as the "fire bdud" reside in the west and are a Bon deity, **9)** *chu-bdud* -- known as "water bdud" reside in the south and are a Bon deity, **10)** *lha-bdud* -- known as "sky bdud" reside in the sky and are a Bon deity, **11)** *ya-bdud* -- known as the "upper *bdud*," and **12)** *ma-bdud* -- known as the "lower *bdud*." (RN-W)

bdud-blon -- (Tib.) They represent a sub-class of deities known as the *blon-po* (or"ministers"), noted in rNying-ma-pa sect writings. See *blon-po*. (RN-W)

bdud-btsan -- (Tib.) They represent a minor class of deity/demons formed from the union of the *bdud* and the *btsan*. This class of deities is noted in rNying-ma-pa sect writings. Their leader is *'Byams-pa-khrag-mgo*. Also, they fall under the general classification of *dregs-pa*, a general classification of minor protective deities, many of which find their origin in the Bon pantheon. See also *btsan*. (RN-W)

bdud-gza' -- (Tib.) They are a group of deity/demons who are the product of a union between a *bdud* and a *gza'*. They are to be found in the retinue of *Pe-har*. (RN-W)

bdud-kyi-dge-bsnyen -- (Skt.: *upasaka*) They are a sub-class of the mountain deities *dge-bsnyen* (a term that is sometimes applied to *dharmapala* of a lower rank). See *dge-bsnyen*. (RN-W)

bdud-mo -- (Tib.) They are an important class of pre-Buddhits goddesses. The leader of the *bdud-mo* is the goddess *Nag-mo-khtrag-'jag* or *bDud-mo-ri-ti-nag-mo*. Usually depicted as fierce, black deity/demons. Fits of unconsciousness are attributed to them. One of a class of thirty that are enumerated in the rNying-ma pa sect work *Thugs-rje'i-rnams-sprul-seng-chen-nor-bu-dgra-'dul-gyis-nor-bdud-bcom-pa'i-rnam-thar-mdor-bsdus-bzhugs-so*. Also, they fall under the general classification of *dregs-pa*, a general classification of minor protective deities, many of which find their origin in the Bon pantheon. (RN-W)

bdud-sri-nag-po -- (Tib.) A sub-class of the *sri*, a group of demons who originated from thirteen eggs. See *sri*. (RN-W)

bgegs -- (Skt.: *vighna*) One of thirty classes that are enumerated in the rNying-ma pa sect work *Thugs-rje'i-rnams-sprul-seng-chen-nor-bu-dgra-'dul-gyis-nor-bdud-bcom-pa'i-rnam-thar-mdor-bsdus-bzhugs-so*. Also, they fall under the general classification of *dregs-pa*, a general classification of minor protective deities, many of which find their origin in the Bon pantheon. They reside in the Northeast and are obstacle creating demons who obstruct religious practices. Their master is the deity *Byi-na-ya-ga*. The are related to the *vighnas* or *bighnas* of India. (RN-W)

bgegs-sri -- A sub-class of the *sri*, a class of demons who originated from thirteen eggs. See *sri*. (RN-W)

bhiksu -- (Skt.)(Tib.: *dge-slong*) They are "fully-ordained priest," one-hundred are described in the retinue of the *Putra-ming-sring-gsum*. (RN-W)

bhutas -- (Skt.)(Tib.: *byung-po*) A group of deities who seem to parallel Tibetan *byung-po*. (RN-W)

bighnas -- (Skt.: aka *vighnas*) A Sanskrit terms which parallels the Tibetan bgegs. See *bgegs*. (RN-W)

bka'-nyan-ma-mo-bzhi -- (Tib.: aka *'khor-ma-mo-bzhi*) Another name for *'khor-ma-mo-bzhi*. See *'khor-ma-mo-bzhi*. (RN-W)

bka'-sdod-srung-ma-zhang-blon-dam-can-sde-dgu -- A title given to a group of nine minor deities who serve as servants of the Medicine Buddha. (RN-W)

bka'-srung-klu-btsan-'bar-ba-spun-bdun -- (Tib.) The title of a group of demons who are mentioned in rNying-ma-pa works and closely related to the *'bar-ba-spun-bdun*. (RN-W)

blon-po -- (Tib.) They represent a class of deities known as "ministers" noted in rNying-ma-pa sect writings. Also, they fall under the general classification of *dregs-pa*, a general classification of minor protective deities, many of which find their origin in the Bon pantheon. The five noted sub-classes are: **1)** *chos-blon* -- "religious" minister, **2)** *bdud-blon* -- "devilish" minister, **3)** *blon-po-so-gnyis* -- A group of thirty-two *dgra-lha*-like deities, **4)** *nang-blon*, and **5)** *phyi-blon*. (RN-W)

blon-po'i-phung-sri -- (Tib.) A tertiary class of the *phung-sri*. (RN-W)

blon-po-so-gnyis -- (Tib.) They represent a sub-class of deities known as the *blon-po* (or"ministers"), noted in rNying-ma-pa sect writings. See *blon-po*. (RN-W)

bon-nyid-dbyings-kyi-ma-mo -- (Tib.) They represent a sub-class of deity/demons known as the *ma-mo*, ancient Tibetan minor goddesses. See *ma-mo*. (RN-W)

bon-skyong -- (Tib.) They are guardian deity/demons of the Bon, and are similar to *dharmapala* and are related to the *nag-phyogs-gi-bdud*. A major sub-group is the *dbal* who originated from eggs. They are: 1) *gze-ma-dgu* -- (9) "the nine who quickly run," who have animal heads and are protectors of the Bon, 2) *mi-bzad-dbal-gyi-gyad-ma-dgu* -- (9) animal heads who are protectors of the Bon, 3) *byin-te-dgu* or *dbal-gyi-sgo-nga-tha-ma-dgu* -- (9) protectors of the Bon; associated with the khri'i-'a-mo, 4) *lhag-ma-bzhi* or *lhag-bsdud-ma* -- (4) reside in the four cardinal points, 5) *gyad-dmag-dpon-bzhi* -- four male and four animal *dbal*, which comprise two additional groups the a) *dbal-gyi-gyad-chen* -- (4) "giant of the I," and the b) animal I -- (4). (RN-W)

bon-skyong-srung-ma-sde-brgyad -- They represent eight diety-groups coming from the Bon faith. This class is made up of the *bon-skyong* and the *bon-srung* and is collective known as the *nag-phyogs-gi-bdud*. (RN-W)

bon-srung -- They are guardian deity/demons of the Bon and related to the *bon-srung*. See *bon-skyong*. (RN-W)

brag-btsan -- They represent a group of minor "guardians of the Buddhist doctrine," who are related to the to *chos-skyong*. See also *btsan*. (RN-W)

brag-gnyan -- (Tib.) They represent a sub-class of yellow, fierce deity/demons known as the *gnyan*, and noted in rNying-ma-pa sect writings. See *gnyan*. (RN-W)

brag-srin -- (Tib.) They represent a sub-class of rock dwelling deity/demons known as the *srin-mo*, and noted in rNying-ma-pa sect writings. See *srin-mo*. (RN-W)

bran-g.yog-mched-bzhi -- (Tib.: aka *srog-'phrog*) Another name for *srog-'phrog*. See *srog-'phrog*. (RN-W)

bra-nye -- (Tib.) They represent a sub-class of deity/demons known as the *rgyu-skar* (Skt.: *naksatra*) who reside in the realm "in between." See *rgyu-skar*. (RN-W)

brgya-byin -- (Tib.)("the hundred giver") They represent a group of deities who are frequently associated with *Pe-har*. (RN-W)

'brog-gnas-mched-lnga -- (Tib.) They represent a group of five *dgra-lha*-like deity/demons. (RN-W)

brog-mo -- (Tib.) They are a group of goddesses who reside in pastures and are made up of: 1) *brog-mo* -- a group of four, 2) *brog-mo* of the North -- a group of eight, and 3) *brog-mo* sisters -- a group of nine. (RN-W)

brtan-ma-bcu-gnyis -- (Tib.: aka *bstan-ma-bcu-gnyis*) They represent a group of twelve goddess, also known as *bstan-ma-bcu-gnyis*, whose mistress is *He-la-'bar-ma*, they are also in the retinue of *rDo-rje-g.yu-sgron-ma*. (RN-W)

bse -- (Tib.) A group of demons also *bsve* and *se*. A sub-group is the *se-ju-spun-bzhi* -- the four *se-ju* brothers. (RN-W)

bse-bdud -- (Tib.) They are the product from the union between the *bse* and *bdud*. See *bse* and *bdud*. (RN-W)

bse-btsan -- (Tib.) They are the product from the union between the *bse* and *btsan*. See *bse* and *btsan*. (RN-W)

bshan-pa-nyer-gcig -- (Tib.) They are known as "The twenty-one butchers" who take the life-breath of enemies of religion. They are found in the retinue of *lCam-sring*. (RN-W)

bstan-ma-bcu-gnyis -- (Tib.: aka *brtan-ma-bcu-gnyis*) They are twelve *bstan-ma* goddesses who are frequently in the train of *dPal-ldan-lha-mo*. (RN-W)

bstan-srung-ma -- (Tib.) They are "guardians of the Buddhist doctrine" and are related to the to *chos-skyong*. (RN-W)

btsan -- (Tib.) They are one of the most important Tibetan demon classes. They are usually described a ferocious red horsemen, astride red horses and carrying a red lance and snare. They are demons who reside in the rocks, and red rocky mountains. They are a minor protective deity. Their leader is *Srog-zan-dmar-po* or *Brag-btsan-srog-can* or rTsi'u-dmar-po (considered to be the chief leader). One of a class of thirty that are enumerated in the rNying-ma pa sect work *Thugs-rje'i-rnams-sprul-seng-chen-nor-bu-dgra-'dul-gyis-nor-bdud-bcom-pa'i-rnam-thar-mdor-bsdus-bzhugs-so*. Also, a *dregs-pa*, a general consideration of minor protective deity/demons, many of which find their origin in the Bon pantheon. The sub-groups are: 1) *'bar-ba-spun-bdun* -- commanders of the wild *btsan* demons, known as the seven brothers (*Dam-can-mched-bdun* or *Drag-btsan-mched-bdun* or *bTsan-rgod-'bar-ba* or *bTsan-rgod-zangs-ri-spun*). They are born from "blood eggs" and their names are: a) *Tsi'u-dmar-po*, b) *bDud-btsan* -- the black head-*btsan*, c) *lHa-btsan* -- the white bone-*btsan*, d) *Brag-btsan* -- the rock-*btsan*, e) *Khrag-btsan-dmar-po* -- the red blood-*btsan*, f) *gGib-btsan* -- the *btsan* of pollution, g) *Dri-btsan* -- the green *btsan* , h) *kLu-btsan* -- the brown *btsan* from urine, and i) *gRi-btsan* -- the sword *btsan*; the other *btsan* include: 2) *btsan-gyi-bud-med-dmar-mo* -- a female deity class, 3) *btsan-rgod-'bar-ba-spun-bdun*, 4) *btsan-chen* -- the great *btsan*, 5) *btsan-phran* -- the minor *btsan*, 6) *phyi-btsan* -- the outer *btsan*, 7) *nang-btsan* -- the inner *btsan*, 8) *bar-btsan* -- the middle *btsan*, 9) *chu'i-btsan* -- the water *btsan*, 10) *sa'i-btsan* -- the earth *btsan*, 11) *gnam-btsan* -- the sky *btsan*, 12) *g.ya'-btsan* -- the slate-mountain *btsan*, 13) *gangs-btsan* -- the glacier *btsan*, 14) *skyes-bu-btsan*, 15) *kha-btsan*, 16) *mdo-btsan*, 17) *sra-btsan*, 18) *dri-za'i-btsan* -- the btsan who resides in the East, 19) *gshin-rje'i-btsan* -- the btsan who resides in the South, 20) *klu'i-btsan* -- the btsan who resides in the West, and 21) *gnod-sbyin-btsan* -- the btsan who resides in the North. (RN-W)

btsan-chen -- (Tib.) They represent an important sub-class of deity/demons known as the *btsan*, ancient Tibetan demons. See *btsan*. (RN-W)

btsan-gyi-bud-med-dmar-mo -- (Tib.) They represent an important sub-class of deity/demons known as the *btsan*, ancient Tibetan demons. See *btsan*. (RN-W)

btsan-phran -- (Tib.) They represent an important sub-class of deity/demons known as the *btsan*, ancient Tibetan demons. See *btsan*. (RN-W)

btsan-rgod -- (Tib.) They are minor "guardians of the Buddhist doctrine" and are related to the *chos-skyong*. (RN-W)

btsan-rgyal -- (Tib.) They are minor "guardians of the Buddhist doctrine" and are related to the *chos-skyong*. (RN-W)

btsan-ma-bcu-gnyis -- They are a group of twelve goddess, also known as the *brtan-ma-bcu-gnyis*. (RN-W)

btsan-skyong-sde-dgu -- Thet represnet a group of nine *dgra-lha*-like minor deity/demons. (RN-W)

btsan-sri-dmar-po -- (Tib.) A sub-class of the *sri*, a group of deity/demons who originated from thirteen eggs. See *sri*. (RN-W)

bsve -- (Tib.) A group of minor deities. See *bse*. (RN-W)

btsa'-byed-mig-dmar -- They are a group of nine *dgra-lha*-like deities. (RN-W)

btsan-'gong -- They are a minor group of deity/demons who are the product from the union between the *btsan* and *'gong-po*. (RN-W)

btsan-gyi-dge-bsnyen -- (Tib.) They are a group of minor mountain deity/demons. See *dge-bsnyen*. (RN-W)

bstan-srung-ma -- (Tib.) They are a sub-group of guardian deity/demons known as *srung-ma* and are related to the *chos-skyong*. See *srung-ma*. (RN-W)

btsun -- (Tib.) Another name for *mtshun*. See *mtshun*. (RN-W)

byad-sri -- (Tib.) A sub-class of the *sri*, a group

of demons who are bringers of woes. See *sri*. (RN-W)

byes-sri -- (Tib.) A sub-class of the *sri*, a group of demons who originated from thirteen eggs. See *sri*. (RN-W)

byin-te-dgu -- (Tib.) A sub-group of the *bon-skyon*, a guardian deity. See the *dbal* of the *bon-skyong*. (RN-W)

byung-po -- (Skt.: *bhutas*) They represent a group of deity/demons who reside in the Northeast. They seem to parallel Indian *bhutas* and are obstacle producing demons. (RN-W)

cang-seng-spun-dgu -- They are a a minor class of deity/demons of the sub-group *dgra-lha-bcu-gsum*. See the *dgra-lha-bcu-gsum* of the *dgra-lha*. (RN-W)

chab-gnyan -- (Tib.) They represent a sub-class of yellow, fierce deity/demons known as the *gnyan*, and noted in rNying-ma-pa sect writings. See *gnyan*. (RN-W

che-sri -- (Tib.) A sub-class of the *sri*, a group of demons who are bringers of woes. See *sri*. (RN-W)

'chi-bdag -- (Tib.) A group of minor "enemy" deity/demons (*dgra-lha*) who protect the faithful. Of this group there is a sub-group known as the: *'chi-bdag-bcu-gnyis* -- A group of twelve *dgra-lha*-like deities. (RN-W)

'chi-bdag-bcu-gnyis -- A sub-group of minor "enemy" deity/demons (*dgra-lha*) who protect the faithful See *'chi-bdag*. (RN-W)

'chi-bdag-gi-bdud -- (Tib.) They represent a sub-class of protective deity/demons known as the *bdud*. They are seven demons who reside in the north, black in color, ride black horses, hold magic stick and snare and cause illness to counteract harmful effects of enemies of religion. See *bdud*. (RN-W)

'chi-med-nye-pa'i-dbang-po -- They are mountain deity/demons and the name given to the four companions of the mountain deity *bKra-bzang-zhing-skyong*. (RN-W)

'chi-sri -- (Tib.) A sub-class of the *sri*, a group of demons who are bringers of woes. See *sri*. (RN-W)

chos-blon -- (Tib.) They represent a sub-class of deity/demons known as the *blon-po* (or"ministers"), noted in rNying-ma-pa sect writings. See *blon-po*. (RN-W)

chos-rgyal -- (Tib.) The Tibetan transliteral equivalent of the Sanskrit for *dharmaraja*. (RN-W)

chos-skyong -- (Skt.: *dharmapala*) They are high ranking protective deities which corresponds to the *nang* and the *gsang-ba'i-chos-skyong*. (RN-W)

chu-bdud -- (Tib.) They represent a sub-class of protective deity/demons known as the *bdud*. See *bdud*. (RN-W)

chu-'dre-spun-dgu -- They represent a group of nine *dgra-lha*-like who reside in water. (RN-W)

chu-gnyan -- (Tib.) They represent a sub-class of yellow, fierce deity/demons known as the *gnyan*, and noted in rNying-ma-pa sect writings. See *gnyan*. (RN-W)

chu'i-btsan -- (Tib.) They represent an important sub-class of deity/demons known as the *btsan*, ancient Tibetan demons. See *btsan*. (RN-W)

chu-mig-chos-'bar -- (Tib.) They are Bon, beggar priests. (RN-W)

chung-sri -- (Tib.) A sub-class of the *sri*, a group of demons who originated from thirteen eggs. See *sri*. (RN-W)

chu-sri -- (Tib.) A sub-class of the *sri*, a group of demons who are bringers of woes. See *sri*. (RN-W)

dakas -- (Tib.) They are fierce angelic male deity/demons, counterparts to the *dakinis*. (RN-W)

dakini -- (Tib.) They are a class of fierce, angelic, female deity/demons noted in rNying-ma-pa sect writings. Their mistress is *Nag-mo-mgyogs-byed*. Also, a *dregs-pa*, a general consideration of minor protective deity/demons, many of which find their origin in the Bon pantheon. (RN-W)

dam-can -- (Tib.) They are "those bound by an oath"; colloquial term of *Chos-skyong*; often applied to non-Buddhist deity/demons converted or subdued and who become protectors of Buddhism. (RN-W)

dam-can-mo-rgyud -- (Tib.) A minor class of Tibetan demons. Of this group are the sub-classes known as the: 1) *mo-rgyud* -- female, and 2) *pho-rgyud* -- male. (RN-W)

dam-sri -- (Tib.) A sub-class of the *sri*, a group of demons who originated from thirteen eggs. See *sri*. (RN-W)

dar-ma'i-sri -- (Tib.) A sub-class of the *sri*, a group of demons who are bringers of woes. See *sri*. (RN-W)

dbal -- (Tib.) They represent a sub-class of deity/demons known as the *bon-skyong*, guardian deities of the Bon. See *bon-skyong*. (RN-W)

dbal-gyi-gyad-chen -- (Tib.) A sub-group of the *bon-skyon*, a guardian deity. See the *dbal* of the *bon-skyong*. (RN-W)

dbal-gyi-sgo-nga-tha-ma-dgu -- (Tib.) A sub-group of the *bon-skyon*, a guardian deity. See the *dbal* of the *bon-skyong*. (RN-W)

dbang-chen -- (Tib.) A group of minor Tibetan deity/demons. (RN-W)

dbang-ldan -- (Tib.) A group of minor Tibetan deity/demons. (RN-W)

dben-gnas-gncyn-gyi-srung-ma -- (Tib.) A infrequently used term for a group of guardian deities. (RN-W)

dbyug-gu-ma-spun-gsum -- (Tib.) They are three sister deities who are closely related to *Jambhala*. (RN-W)

deva -- (Skt.)(Chin.: *t'ien*; Tib.: *lha*) The name given to the term "god" (male). (WEC, RN-W)

devi -- (Skt.)(Chin.: *t'ien-mu*) The name given to the term "goddess." (RN-W)

dge-bsnyen -- (Skt.: *upasaka*) They are mountain deity and a term that is sometimes applied to *dharmapala* of a lower rank. They cause illness, and they number three hundred and sixty. They are comprised of four subgroups who are: 1) *bdud-kyi-dge-bsnyen* (120), 2) *btsan-gyi-dge-bsnyen* (120,) 3) *lha'i-dge-bsnyen* -- (120) white, and 4) *dge-bsnyen-nyi-shu-rtsa-gcig* -- known as the "twenty-one *dge-bsnyen*" and they are named after their abode. (RN-W)

dge-bsnyen-nyi-shu-rtsa-gcig -- (Tib.) They are a group of minor mountain deity/demons. See *dge-bsnyen*. (RN-W)

dge-slong -- (Tib.)(Skt.: *bhiksu*) The Tibetan transliteral equivalent of the Sanskrit for *bhiksu*. (RN-W)

dgos-sri -- (Tib.) A sub-class of the *sri*, a group of demons who are bringers of woes. See *sri*. (RN-W)

dgra-bcom-pa -- (Tib.) The Tibetan transliteral equivalent of the Sanskrit for Arhats. See *arhats*. (RN-W)

dgra-lha -- They represent a large group of "enemy gods" who sits on the right shoulder. They are deity/demons who protect worshipers from enemies. They are frequently personal deities and are attributed to helping worshipers in the increase of their property. The chief of the *dgra-lha* is *sKyu-brla-gsang-ba* (or *sKu-bla-gsang-ba* or *rDo-legs-dkar-po*). One of a class of thirty that are enumerated in the rNying-ma pa sect work *Thugs-rje'i-rnams-sprul-seng-chen-nor-bu-dgra-'dul-gyis-nor-bdud-bcom-pa'i-rnam-thar-mdor-bsdus-bzhugs-so*. Also, a *dregs-pa*, a general consideration of minor protective deities, many of which find their origin in the Bon pantheon. There are thirteen sub-groups called: 1) *dgra-lha-bcu-gsum* -- the thirteen *dgra-lha*; with a sub-group named *cang-seng-spun-dgu* -- (9) nine deities derived from *Lam-lha* one of the thirteen *dgra-lha*; distributors of wealth, 2) *dgra-lha-bdun* -- the seven *dgra-lha*; 3) *dgra-lha-mched-dgu* -- the nine *dgra-lha* brothers, 4) *dgra-lha-nyi-rtsa-gcig* -- the twenty-one *dgra-lha*, 5) *dgra-lha-sde-lnga* -- the five orders of *dgra-lha*, 6). *dmu-rabs-brgyud-dgra-lha* -- *dmu* lineage *dgra-lha*, 7) *gtsug-rabs-brgyud-dgra-lha* -- the first generation lineage *dgra-lha*, 8) *mi-rabs-brgyud-dgra-lha* -- lineage of mankind *dgra-lha*, 9) *mi-thub-dgra-lha-spun-gsum* -- three *dgra-lha* brothers, 10) *pha-mes-brgyud-dgra-lha* -- ancestral lineage *dgra-lha*, 11) *phyi-rabs-brgyud-dgra-lha* -- lineage of later generations *dgra-lha*, and 12) *rlung-rta-dar-ba'i-dgra-lha* -- four animals of the "wind horse" flag. (RN-W)

dgra-lha-bcu-gsum -- (Tib.) They represent a sub-class of deity/demons known as the *dgra-lha*, ancient Tibetan minor deities. See *dgra-lha*. (RN-W)

dgra-lha-bdun -- (Tib.) They represent a sub-class of deity/demons known as the *dgra-lha*, ancient Tibetan minor deities. See *dgra-lha*. (RN-W)

dgra-lha-mched-dgu -- (Tib.) They represent a sub-class of deities known as the *dgra-lha*, ancient Tibetan minor deities. See *dgra-lha*. (RN-W)

dgra-lha-nyi-rtsa-gcig -- (Tib.) They represent a sub-class of deity/demons known as the *dgra-lha*, ancient Tibetan minor deities. See *dgra-lha*. (RN-W)

dgra-lha-sde-lnga -- (Tib.) They represent a sub-class of deity/demons known as the *dgra-lha*, ancient Tibetan minor deities. See *dgra-lha*. (RN-W)

dgra-sri-dar-ma -- (Tib.) A sub-class of the *sri*, a group of demons who originated from thirteen eggs. See *sri*. (RN-W)

dharmaraja -- (Skt.)(Tib.: *chos-rgyal*) Known as the "King of Religion.". (RN-W)

dikpala -- (Skt.) Deities which are similar to *lokapala*. (RN-W)

dkar-phyogs-skyong-ba'i-srung-ma -- (Tib.) The collective name used for *'jig-rten-las-'das-pa'i-srung-ma* and *'jig-rten-pa'i-srung-ma*, who are "gaurdians protecting the white quarter" when they stand in opposition to the *nag-phyogs-gi-bdud*. (RN-W)

dma'-them-pa-dgu -- (Tib.) They represent a group of nine *dgra-lha*-like deity/demons. (RN-W)

dmu -- (Tib.) They are a purple-brown class of early Tibetan deity/demons noted in rNying-ma-pa sect writings. Their leader is *Ga-pa-li-dor*. Also, a *dregs-pa*, a general consideration of minor protective deities, many of which find their origin in the Bon pantheon. The sub-classes are: 1) *dmu-chen* -- the Great *dmu*, one of two main groups of *dmu*, and 2) *dmu-phran* -- the Minor *dmu*, one of two main groups of *dmu*. (RN-W)

dmu-bdud -- (Tib.) It is a class of deity/demons who originated from the union of the *dmu* and the *bdud*. Their leader is *dMu-bdud-nag-po-bk(h)rag-med*. One of a class of thirty that are enumerated in the rNying-ma pa sect work *Thugs-rje'i-rnams-sprul-seng-chen-nor-bu-dgra-'dul-gyis-nor-bdud-bcom-pa'i-rnam-thar-mdor-bsdus-bzhugs-so*. Also, a *dregs-pa*, a general consideration of minor protective deities, many of which find their origin in the Bon pantheon. (RN-W)

dmu-chen -- (Tib.)("the great *dmu*") They represent a sub-class of deity/demons known as the *dmu*, ancient Tibetan minor deities. See *dmu*. (RN-W)

dmu-phran -- (Tib.)("the minor *dmu*") They represent a sub-class of deity/demons known as the *dmu*, ancient Tibetan minor deities. See *dmu*. (RN-W)

dmu-bdud -- (Tib.) A class of important early Tibetan deity/demons who resulted from the union between the *bdud* and *dmu*; Their chief is *Ga-pa-li-dor* or *dMu-bdud-nag-po-bk(h)rag-med*. They possess two main sub-classes: 1) *dmu-chen* -- "the great *dmu*" and 2) *dmu-phran* -- "the minor *dmu*." (RN-W)

dmu-rabs-brgyud-dgra-lha -- (Tib.) An infrequently used term for a group of guardian deities. They represent a sub-class of deity/demons known as the *dgra-lha*, ancient Tibetan minor deities. See *dgra-lha*. (RN-W)

'dod-rigs-sman-ba-bco-brgyad -- (Tib.) They are a group of eighteen *dgra-lha*-like deity/demons. (RN-W)

'dod-pa'i-sde-brgyad -- (Tib.) They represent a group of deity/demons who are amongst the *dregs-pa*, a general consideration of minor protective deities, many of which find their origin in the Bon pantheon. This group has eight sub-classes: 1) *dkar-po-lha-i-sde* -- who are white, 2) *dmar-po-btsan-gyi-sde* -- who are red, 3) *nag-po-bdud-kyi-sde* -- who are black, 4) *lhra-bo-gza'yi-sde* -- who are varicolored, 5) *smug-po-dmu-yi-sde* -- who are brown, 6) *sha-za-srin-po'i-sde*, 7) *dkor-bdag-rgyal-po'i-sde*, and 8) *nda-bdag-ma-mo'i-sde*. (RN-W)

dpa'-bo -- (Tib.) They are the "heroic type" protective deities of the *chos-skyong/dharmapala* types. (RN-W)

drag-byed-sprul-pa'i-ma-mo -- (Tib.) They represent a sub-class of deity/demons known as the *ma-mo*, ancient Tibetan minor goddesses. See *ma-mo*. (RN-W)

drag-gshed-brgyad -- (Tib.) A group of protective deities made up of *dPal-ldan-lha-mo*, *mGon-po*, *rNam-thos-sras*, *gShin-rje*, *lcam-sring*, *Tshangs-pa-dkar-po*, *rTa-mgrin*, and *sShin-rje*. (RN-W)

drang-srong -- (Tib.) They represent group of

deity/demons who reside in the upper sphere or the Southeast. (RN-W)

dregs-pa -- They are known as the "haughty ones," colloquial term for the *'jig-rten-pa'i-srung-ma*. A generalized group of minor protective deity/demons, both male and female, of a lower rank. In isolated instances it is a term applied to higher ranking *dharmapalas*. Most of the *dregs-pa* were aboriginal Tibetan deities associated with the Bon pantheon. There are five noted sub-classes: 1) *dregs-pa'i-sde-dpon-bco-brgyad* -- (18) rulers of the *dregs-pa*, 2) *dregs-pa'i-sde-dpon-sum-bcu* -- (30) rulers of the *dregs-pa*, 3) *dregs-pa'i-gtso-bo-bdun-cu-rtsa-gnyis* -- (72) rulers of the *dregs-pa*, 4) *dregs-pa-sde-brgyad* -- a group of *dregs-pa* frequently invoked in magic ceremonies, comprising six sub-classes: a) *phyi-yi-sde-brgyad*, b) *nag-gi-sde-brgyad*, c) *gsang-ba'i-sde-brgyad*, d) *mchog-gi-sde-brgyad*, e) *sprul-pa-sde-brgyad*, and f) *snang-srid-sde-brgyad*; and 5) *dregs-pa-pho-bdun*. (RN-W)

dregs-pa-bzhi -- (Tib.: aka *las-mdzad*) Another name for *las-mdzad*. See *las-mdzad*. (RN-W)

dregs-pa'i-gtso-bo-bdun-cu-rtsa-gnyis -- (Tib.) They represent a sub-class of deity/demons known as the *dregs-pa*, ancient Tibetan minor deities. See *dregs-pa*. (RN-W)

dregs-pa'i-mtsho-sman -- (Tib.) They rêpresent a sub-class of deity/demons known as the *sman*, ancient Tibetan minor goddesses. See *sman*. (RN-W)

dregs-pa'i-sde-dpon-bco-brgyad -- (Tib.) They represent a sub-class of deity/demons known as the dregs-pa, ancient Tibetan minor deities. See *dregs-pa*. (RN-W)

dregs-pa'i-sde-dpon-sum-bcu -- (Tib.) They represent a sub-class of deity/demons known as the dregs-pa, ancient Tibetan minor deities. See *dregs-pa*. (RN-W)

dregs-pa-pho-bdun -- (Tib.) They represent a sub-class of seven black male deity/demons known as the *dregs-pa*, ancient Tibetan minor deities. See *dregs-pa*. (RN-W)

dregs-pa-sde-brgyad -- (Tib.) They represent a sub-class of deity/demons known as the dregs-pa, ancient Tibetan minor deities. See *dregs-pa*. (RN-W)

dri-btsan -- (Tib.) They represent an important sub-class of deity/demons known as the *btsan*, ancient Tibetan demons. See *btsan*. (RN-W)

dri-za -- (Skt.: *gandharvas*) They are a class of early Tibetan deity/demons who reside in the East and are noted in rNying-ma-pa sect writings. Also, a *dregs-pa*, a general consideration of minor protective deities, many of which find their origin in the Bon pantheon. (RN-W)

dri-za'i-btsan -- (Tib.) They represent an important sub-class of deity/demons known as the *btsan*, ancient Tibetan demons. See *btsan*. (RN-W)

dri-za'i-rgyal-po -- (Tib.)(Skt.: *gandharvas*) The Tibetan transliteral equivalent of the Sanskrit for *gandharvas*. (RN-W)

dus-bzhi-lha-mo (Tib.: aka *dus-kyi-bdag-mo* or *dus-kyi-rgyal-mo*)("queens of the four seasons") A group of deities related to *dPal-ldan-lha-mo*. They are: *dPyid-kyi-rgyal-mo*, *dByar-gyi-rgyal-mo*, *sTon-gyi-rgyal-mo* and *dGun-gyi-rgyal-mo*. (RN-W)

dus-dug-sprul-pa'i-ma-mo -- (Tib.) They represent a sub-class of deity/demons known as the *ma-mo*, ancient Tibetan minor goddesses. See *ma-mo*. (RN-W)

dus-kyi-bdag-mo (Tib.: aka *dus-bzhi-lha-mo* or *dus-kyi-rgyal-mo*)("queens of the four seasons") Another name for *dus-bzhi-lha-mo*. See *dus-bzhi-lha-mo*. (RN-W)

dus-kyi-rgyal-mo (Tib.: aka *dus-bzhi-lha-mo* or *dus-kyi-bdag-mo*)("queens of the four seasons") Another name for *dus-bzhi-lha-mo*. See *dus-bzhi-lha-mo*. (RN-W)

dus-sri -- (Tib.) They represent a sub-class of deity/demons known as the *sri*, ancient Tibetan minor deities who bring woes. See *sri*. (RN-W)

gandharvas -- (Skt.)(Tib.: *dri-za'i-rgyal-po*) They are a group of deity/demons which are both to be found in Indian and Tibetan pantheons. A term applied to Zur-phud-lnga-pa, who is considered as an emanation of Pe-har. (RN-W)

gangs-btsan -- (Tib.) They represent a sub-class of yellow, fierce deity/demons known as the *gnyan*, and noted in rNying-ma-pa sect writings. See *gnyan*. (RN-W)

garuda -- (Skt.) They represent a group of bird-like deity/demons (sky). See *khyung*. (RN-W)

gdon -- They are demons (424) who injure children and create obstacles, 1) *gdon-phal-pa-bzhi* -- (4) common *gdon*, 2) *gdon-chen-bco-lnga* -- (15) great *gdon*, 3) *gdon-chen-bco-brgyad* -- (18) great *gdon*, d. *gnas-gdon*, 4) *las-gdon*, and 5) *lus-gdon*. (RN-W)

gdon-chen-bco-lnga -- (Tib.) They represent a sub-class of deity/demons known as the *gdon*, ancient Tibetan minor deities. See *gdon*. (RN-W)

gdon-chen-bco-brgyad -- (Tib.) They represent a sub-class of deity/demons known as the *gdon*, ancient Tibetan minor deities. See *gdon*. (RN-W)

gdong-can-gnyis -- (Tib.: aka *'jigs-rung*) Another name for *'jigs-rung*. See *'jigs-rung*. (RN-W)

gdon-phal-pa-bzhi -- (Tib.) They represent a sub-class of deity/demons known as the *gdon*, ancient Tibetan minor deities. See *gdon*. (RN-W)

gsang-ba'i-sde-brgyad -- (Tib.) They represent a sub-class of deity/demons known as the dregs-pa, ancient Tibetan minor deities. See *dregs-pa*. (RN-W)

gsangs-bde-hjigs-gsum -- (Tib.) The Tibetan transliteral equivalent of the Sanskrit for *Ishtadevata*. See *Ishtadevata*. (RN-W)

gi-khod-sum-brgya-drug-bcu -- They are a group of 360 *dgra-lha*-like deity/demons. (RN-W)

gin -- (Tib.) An alternate spelling for *ging*. See *ging*. (RN-W)

ging -- (Tib.) They are minor deity/demons. Originally a term applied to a group of Bon deities. The leader of the ging is *Srog-bdag-srongs-pa*. Also known as *'gying* and *gying*. Frequently a term applied to deities of the rNying-ma-pa sect and bKa'-rgyud-pa sects denoting hero (*dpa'-bo*), messenger (*pho-nya*) or officer (*las-mkhan*). One of a class of thirty that are enumerated in the rNying-ma pa sect work *Thugs-rje'i-rnams-sprul-seng-chen-nor-bu- dgra-'dul-gyis-nor-bdud-bcom-pa'i-rnam-thar-mdor-bsdus-bzhugs-so*. Also, a *dregs-pa*, a general consideration of minor protective deities, many of which find their origin in the Bon pantheon. Fifteen sub-classes are noted, they are:1) *las-kyi-rigs-kyi-ging* -- (4) blue; two male, two female, 2) *lha'i-ging-chen* -- (4) the four great *ging,* 3) *padma-rigs-kyi-ging* -- (4) red; two male, two female, 4) *rdo-rje-rigs-kyi-ging* -- (4) white; two male, two female, 5) *rin-chen-rigs-kyi-ging* -- (4) yellow; two male, two female, 6) *snags-bdag-ging-chen-bco-brgyad* -- (18) nine males, nine females, 7) *ging-chen* -- great *ging,* 8) *ging-phran* -- minor *ging,* 9) *ging-pho* -- male *ging,* 10) *ging-mo* -- female *ging,* 11) *ging-'dzin* -- (42) a group of forty two, 12) *sgrol-ging* -- aka *gsang-ba'i-sgrol-ging,* 13) *gsang-ba'i-sgrol-ging* -- aka *sgrol-ging,* 14) *pho-dgu* -- the male *ging,* whose sub-class is the nine *sngags-bdag-ging-chen-bco-brgyad,* and 15) *mo-dgu* -- the female *ging.* (RN-W)

ging-chen -- (Tib.) They represent a sub-class of deity/demons known as the *ging,* ancient Tibetan minor deities. See *ging.* (RN-W)

ging-'dzin -- (Tib.) They represent a sub-class of deity/demons known as the *ging,* ancient Tibetan minor deities. See *ging.* (RN-W)

ging-mo -- (Tib.) They represent a sub-class of deity/demons known as the *ging,* ancient Tibetan minor deities. See *ging.* (RN-W)

ging-phran -- (Tib.) They represent a sub-class of deity/demons known as the *ging,* ancient Tibetan minor deities. See *ging.* (RN-W)

ging-pho -- (Tib.) They represent a sub-class of deity/demons known as the *ging,* ancient Tibetan minor deities. See *ging.* (RN-W)

ganga-gnyan -- (Tib.) They represent a sub-class of yellow, fierce deity/demons known as the *gnyan,* and noted in rNying-ma-pa sect writings. See *gnyan.* (RN-W)

gnam-btsan -- (Tib.) They represent an important sub-class of deity/demons known as the *btsan,* ancient Tibetan demons. See *btsan.* (RN-W)

gnam-gnyan -- (Tib.) They represent a sub-class of yellow, fierce deity/demons known as the , and noted in rNying-ma-pa sect writings. See *gnyan.* (RN-W)

gnam-sman -- (Tib.) They are an important class of monor deity/demons and a sisterhood of deities. The leader of the *gnam-sman* is the goddess *Thog-gi-bu-yug.* They are of pre-Buddhist origin and some feel that they are a sub-division of the *sman-mo* class. One of a class of thirty that are enumerated in the rNying-ma pa sect work *Thugs-rje'i-rnams-sprul-seng-chen-nor-bu-dgra-'dul-gyis-nor-bdud-bcom-pa'i-rnam-thar-mdor-bsdus-bzhugs-so.* Also, a *dregs-pa,* a general consideration of minor protective deities, many of which find their origin in the Bon pantheon. They are frequently consorts of the *lha* and are related to medicine deities. There are three noted sub-classes: a. *sman-ma* -- a sisterhood of lake dwelling deities, b. *sman-mo* -- a sisterhood of deities who dwell in the sky, and c. *sman-btsun* -- an alternate name of *sman-mo,* or a distinct class of *sman-mo.* See *sman.* (RN-W)

gnam-sri -- (Tib.) They represent a sub-class of deity/demons known as the *sri,* ancient Tibetan minor deities who bring woes. See *sri.* (RN-W)

gnas-gdon -- (Tib.) They represent a sub-class of deity/demons known as the *gdon,* ancient Tibetan minor deities. See *gdon.* (RN-W)

gnas-srung -- (Tib.) They are guardians of holy pilgrimage places. They are also a sub-group of guardian deity/demons known as *srung-ma* and are related to the *chos-skyong.* See *srung-ma.* (RN-W)

gnod-sbyin -- (Tib.)(Skt.: *yaksa*) They are protective male deity/demons who reside in the North. The leader of the *gnod-sbyin* is the deity *Yaksa-me-dbal.* They were subduedby *Padmasambhava* and lost their identity by being equated by the *yaksas* and *yaksis* of India. One of a class of thirty that are enumerated in the rNying-ma pa sect work *Thugs-rje'i-rnams-sprul-seng-chen-nor-bu-dgra-'dul-gyis-nor-bdud-bcom-pa'i-rnam-thar-mdor-bsdus-bzhugs-so.* Also, a *dregs-pa,* a general consideration of minor protective deities, many of which find their origin in the Bon pantheon. (RN-W)

gnod-sbyin-btsan -- (Tib.) They represent an important sub-class of deity/demons known as the *btsan,* ancient Tibetan demons. See *btsan.* (RN-W)

gnod-spyin-chen-po -- (Tib.)Skt.: *maha-yaksa*)("the great *yaksa*") A group of *yaksa* or *gnod-sbyin* who are set apart (maha) from the others of the class. See also *gnod-sbyin* and *yaksa.* (RN-W)

gnod-sbyin-mo -- (Tib.)(Skt.: *yaksis*) They are protective female deity/demons who reside in the North. The leader of the *gnod-sbyin* is the goddess *Ma-mo-nag-mo Mon-mo-nag.* They were subdued by *Padmasambhava* and lost their identity by being equated by the *yaksas* and *yaksis* of India. One of a class of thirty that are enumerated in the rNying-ma pa sect work *Thugs-rje'i-rnams-sprul-seng-chen-nor-bu-dgra-'dul-gyis-nor-bdud-bcom-pa'i-rnam-thar-mdor-bsdus-bzhugs-so.* Also, a *dregs-pa,* a general consideration of protective deities, many of which find their origin in the Bon pantheon. (RN-W)

gnod-sri -- (Tib.) They represent a sub-class of deity/demons known as the *sri,* ancient Tibetan minor deities who bring woes. See *sri.* (RN-W)

gnyan -- (Tib.) They represent an important and well known class of yellow, fierce deity/demons who reside between earth and sky, or green meadows and virforests. They are evil demons and cause lameness. Also, a class of deities noted in rNying-ma-pa sect writings. Further, a *dregs-pa,* a general consideration of minor protective deities, many of which find their origin in the Bon pantheon, They number 400,000 and possess twenty-six sub-groups, which are: 1) *brag-gnyan* -- rock *gnyan,* 2) *chab-gnyan* -- river *gnyan,* 3) *chu-gnyan* -- West *gnyan,* 4) *chu-gnyan* -- river *gnyan,* 5) *gangs-gnyan* -- (21) glacier *gnyan,* 6) *gnam-gnyan* -- sky *gnyan,* 7) *gnyan-chen-sde-bzhi* -- the four orders of the great *gnyan,* 8) *g.ya'-gnyan* -- slate *gnyan,* 9) gza'-gnyan -- planets *gnyan,* 10) gzha'-gnyan -- rainbow *gnyan,* 11) *me-gnyan* -- fire *gnyan,* 12) *me-gnyan* -- South *gnyan,* 13) *mtsho-gnyan* -- lake *gnyan,* 14) *nags-gnyan* -- forest *gnyan,* 15) *nyi-gnyan* -- sun *gnyan,* 16) *rdo-gnyan* -- stone *gnyan,* 17) *rdza-gnyan* -- mud *gnyan,* 18) *rlung-gnyan* -- North *gnyan,* 19) *rlung-gnyan* -- wind *gnyan,* 20) *rytsi-gnyan* -- tree *gnyan,* 21) *sa-gnyan* -- earth *gnyan,* 22) *shing-gnyan* -- East *gnyan,* 23) *shing-gnyan* -- tree *gnyan,* 24) *skar-gnyan* -- stars *gnyan,* 25) *spprin-gnyan* -- cloud *gnyan,* and 26) *zla-gnyan* -- moon

They represent a
...ons known as the
...a sect writings. See
...ib.) They are a class of
...ma-pa sect writings. Also,
...eration of minor protective
...nd their origin in the Bon
...des the following sub-classes: 1)
...rog-lha -- They are depicted the
...u-lha -- They are guardians of the
They are guardians of the human
...W)
...dgu -- (Tib.) They represent a
...deity/demons. (RN-W)
...hey represent a sub-class of
...sri, ancient Tibetan minor
...RN-W)
...represent a sub-class of
...n as the *'gong-po*, and
...s. they are described as
...of turquoise." They
...*ng-po*. (RN-W)
...deity/demons who
...to the *rgyal-po*.
...*po* and they are
..." They appear
...thirty that are
...*Thugs-rje'i-*
...*is-nor-bdud-*
...*s-so*. Also, a
...r protective
...in the Bon
...hree major
...le up of: 1)
...rothers, 2)
...thers, and
...s; and the
...sub-class
...*-po*, and
...*po*. (RN-
...esent a
...as the
...s. See
...e five
...rtant
...ient
...tant
...ent
...nd
...a
...e

An alternate
-spun-bdun.
g for *'bar-*
regions
lesses
do-
")
huma...
body
gro...

a
ons
ce The
th rank.
etimes th
. (RN-W)
-ma -- (Tib.:
for *'jig-rten-pa'*
N-W)
ib.: aka *'jig-rten-*
a-'das-pa'i-srung-
dregs-pa; and are
eres inhabited by
tly use mediums
me claim that Pe-
as-'das-pa'i-srung-
phyi-nang-gsang-
-can-gnyis) A group
and include: *Chu-*
(RN-W)
dgu -- (Tib.) They
deity/demons known
mons. See *klu-bdud*.
resent a sub-class of
cient Tibetan minor
W)
deities associated with
odol ("Liberation by
known as the Chonyid
periencing of Reality").
. (WE-W)
present the sub-class of
ancient Tibetan minor
-W)
represent an important
n as the *btsan*, ancient
W)
drug-bcu -- (Tib.) They
-like deity/demons. (RN-
(Tib.: aka *bka'-nyan-ma-*
ted to *dPal-ldan-lha-mo*

gcod-kyi-gying-brgyad) They are minor demons who are known as the "eight butchers who wield swords." (RN-W)

grub-thob -- (Tib.)(Skt.: *Mahasiddha*) They are the "Eighty-Four great Sorcerers," saints and miracle workers. (RN-W)

grul-bum -- (Tib.)(Skt.: *kumbhandhas*) They are supernatural beings who accompany *dharmapalas*. (RN-W)

gsang-ba'i-chos-skyong -- (Tib.) They are protective deities who are identical to the *'jig-rten-las-'das-pa'i-srung-ma* when considered under the collective name *phyi-nang-gsang-ba'i-chos-skyong*. (RN-W)

gsang-ba'i-sgrol-ging -- (Tib.) They represent a sub-class of deity/demons known as the *ging*, ancient Tibetan minor deities. See *ging*. (RN-W)

gsang-yum -- (Tib.)(Skt.: *guhya-shakti*) A term applied to "secret consorts." (RN-W)

gshin-rje -- (Tib.) They are demons who reside in the South. The leader of the *gshin-rje* is *Yama-Raja*. They are male demons of death believed to be pre-Buddhist deity/demons and later associated with the Hindu *Yama*. One of a class of thirty that are enumerated in the rNying-ma pa sect work *Thugs-rje'i-rnams-sprul-seng-chen-nor-bu-dgra-'dul-gyis-nor-bdud-bcom-pa'i-rnam-thar-mdor-bsdus-bzhugs-so*. Also, a *dregs-pa*, a general consideration of protective deities, many of which find their origin in the Bon pantheon. (RN-W)

gshin-rje'i-btsan -- (Tib.) They represent an important sub-class of deity/demons known as the ***btsan***, ancient Tibetan demons. See *btsan*. (RN-W)

gsjin-rje-mo -- (Tib.) They are female demonesses of death believed to be pre-Buddhist deity/demons and later associated with the Hindu *Yama*. The leader of the gshin-rje is *Srog-bdag-mo* or *Yum-mchog-sgrol-byed-nag-mo*. One of a class of thirty that are enumerated in the rNying-ma pa sect work *Thugs-rje'i-rnams-sprul-seng-chen-nor-bu-dgra-'dul-gyis-nor-bdud-bcom-pa'i-rnam-thar-mdor-bsdus-bzhugs-so*. Also, a *dregs-pa*, a general consideration of minor protective deities, many of which find their origin in the Bon pantheon. (RN-W)

gter-bdag -- (Tib.) These minor deity/demons are proprietors of treasures. (RN-W)

gter-gyi-srung-ma-sde-bzhi -- (Tib.) They are "the four orders of treasure gods." (RN-W)

gtod -- (Tib.) They are evil demons who cause muteness. (RN-W)

gtsug-rabs-brgyud-dgra-lha -- (Tib.) An infrequently used term for a group of guardian deities. They represent a sub-class of deity/demons known as the *dgra-lha*, ancient Tibetan minor deities. See *dgra-lha*. (RN-W)

guhya-shakti -- (Skt.)(Tib.: *gsang-yum*) A term applied to "secret consorts." (RN-W)

gur-lha-bcu-gnyis -- (Tib.) A class of deity/demons who are in the company of *Gur-gyi-mgon-po-lha-brgyad*. They are: *Putra-nag-po, Bhadra-nag-po, Srin-mo-ral-gcig-ma, Klong-rdol-bla-ma, Ekajati, dPal-ldan-lha-mo-'dod'khams-dbang-phyug-ma, Nag-po-gnod-sbyin* and *NAg-mo-gnod-sbyin*. (RN-W)

gyad-dmag-dpon-bzhi -- (Tib.) They represent

a sub-class of deity/demons known as the *bon-skyong*, guardian deities of the Bon. (RN-W)

g.ya'-btsan -- (Tib.) They represent an important sub-class of deity/demons known as the *btsan*, ancient Tibetan demons. See *btsan*. (RN-W)

g.ya'-gnyan -- (Tib.) They represent a sub-class of yellow, fierce deity/demons known as the *gnyan*, and noted in rNying-ma-pa sect writings. See *gnyan*. (RN-W)

gying -- (Tib.) They are protective deity/demons, and generally fierce in countenance. Two sub-classes are noted: 1) *srog-hgcod-kyi-gying-brgyad* -- "the eight life cutting *gying*"; fiercely *gshin-rje*-like in form, and 2) *sgrol-'gying-chen-bzhi*. (RN-W)

g.yu-sgron-mched-lnga -- (Tib.) They are goddesses known as the"five turquoise lamp sisters." (RN-W)

gza' -- (Tib.) They represent varicolored deity/demons who reside in the upper sphere or in between. Their leader is the deity *gZa'-bdud-rahula*. One of a class of thirty that are enumerated in the rNying-ma pa sect work *Thugs-rje'i-rnams-sprul-seng-chen-nor-bu-dgra-'dul-gyis-nor-bdud-bcom-pa'i-rnam-thar-mdor-bsdus-bzhugs-so*. Also, a *dregs-pa*, a general consideration of minor protective deities, many of which find their origin in the Bon pantheon, with a sub-group known as: *gza'-bdud* -- known as the eyes, heart and liver emanation. (RN-W)

gza'-bdud -- (Tib.) They represent a sub-class of deity/demons known as the *gza'*, ancient Tibetan minor deities who bring woes. See *gza'*. (RN-W)

gza'-chen-brgyad -- (Tib.) They represent a sub-class of deity/demons known as the *mgon-po*, ancient Tibetan minor deities who bring woes. See *mgon-po*. (RN-W)

gza'-gnyan -- (Tib.) They represent a sub-class of yellow, fierce deity/demons known as the *gnyan*, and noted in rNying-ma-pa sect writings. See *gnyan*. (RN-W)

gzed -- (Tib.) They are minor evil demons who cause muteness. (RN-W)

gze-ma-dgu -- (Tib.) They represent a sub-class of deity/demons known as the *bon-skyong*, guardian deities of the Bon. (RN-W)

gzha'-gnyan -- (Tib.) They represent a sub-class of yellow, fierce deity/demons known as the *gnyan*, and noted in rNying-ma-pa sect writings. See *gnyan*. (RN-W)

gzhi-bdag -- (Tib.)("foundation-owners") They represent a class of deity/demons noted in rNying-ma-pa sect writings who reside on mountains, or passes, or narrow ledges, or boats and bridges, or roads. Also, a *dregs-pa*, a general consideration of minor protective deities, many of which find their origin in the Bon pantheon, 1) *shing-chen-bzhi'i-gzhi-bdag* -- (4) the *gzhi-bdag* of the four great woods, 2) *gzhi-bdag* -- who dwell in passes, 3) *gzhi-bdag* -- who dwell on narrow ledges, 4) *gzhi-bdag* -- who dwell on boats and bridges, 5) *gzhi-bdag* -- who dwell on roads, and are related to the *lam-lha*, and 6) *sgang-drug-gzhi-bdag-bcu-gnyis* -- "twelve *gzhi-bdag* ruling the six ridges." (RN-W)

gzhon-sri -- (Tib.) They represent a sub-class of deity/demons known as the **sri**, ancient Tibetan minor deities who bring woes. See *sri*. (RN-W)

hbar-ba-spun-bdun -- (Tib.) spelling for *'bar-ba-spun-bdun*. See *'bar-b* (RN-W)

hbar-ma -- (Tib.) An alternate spell *ma*. See *'bar-ma*. (RN-W)

htamenmas -- (Skt.) They reside i of the brain. They are animal- or bird-head and are associated with the second state Thodol ("Liberation by hearing on the After known as the Chonyid Bardo ("Transition Experiencing of Reality"). (WE-W)

hu-shis-che -- The Chinese equivalent ofthe Sanskrit for *lokapala*. (WE

ishtadevata -- (Skt.) They repr deities which correspond to the Tibeta *gDSangs-bde-hjigs-gsum*. They are tutela rank of Buddha. (RN-W, BO)

'jig-rten-las-'das-pa'i-srung-m are powerful, high-ranking deity/der passed beyond the six spheres of existe protective deities of eighth, ninth and ten *'jig-rten-pa'i-srung-ma, they are* som called *phyi-nang-gsang-ba'i-chos-skyong*

'jig-rten-ma-'das-pa'i-srung *'jig-rten-pa'i-srung-ma*) Another name *srung-ma*. See *'jig-rten-pa'i-srung-ma*. (R

'jig-rten-pa'i-srung-ma -- (T *ma-'das-pa'i-srung-ma*) See *'jig-rten-m* *ma*. They are also sometimes known as deity/demons who exist within sph animated beings. They are freque through which they communicate. So *har* is their chief. With the *'jig-rten-* *ma, they are* sometimes they are calle *ba'i-chos-skyong*. (RN-W)

'jigs-rung -- (Tib.: aka *gdong* of deities related to *dPal-ldan-lha-m* *srin-gdong* and *Seng-ge'i-gdong-can*.

jo-bo-klu-bdud-mched- represent an important sub-class of as the *klu-bdud*, ancient Tibetan d (RN-W)

keg-sri -- (Tib.) They rep deity/demons known as the *sri*, a deities who bring woes. See *sri*. (RN

kerimas -- (Skt.) They are the second state of the Bardo-T hearing on the After Death Plane") Bardo ("Transitional State of the E They are also Cemetery goddesse

lceb-sri -- (Tib.) They re deity/demons known as the *sri*, deities who bring woes. See *sri*. (R

kha-btsan -- (Tib.) The sub-class of deity/demons know Tibetan demons. See *btsan*. (RN-

khas-drag-sum-brgya- represent a group of 360 *dgra-lha* W)

'khor-ma-mo-bzhi -- *mo-bzhi*) A group of deities rel

and which includes: *Srog-bdud-ma, sNying-bzan-ma, Thog-'phren-ma* and *Nad-gton-ma*. (RN-W)

khrag-btsan-dmar-po -- (Tib.) They represent an important sub-class of deity/demons known as the *btsan*, ancient Tibetan demons. See *btsan*. (RN-W)

'khrung-lha -- (Tib.) They represent an indeterminate group of "birth deities." One is born within the aura of the deity's influence. Frequently the *'khrung-lha* is a local *gzhi-bdag, sa-bdag, btsan* or other deity/demon. (RN-W)

klu -- (Tib.) (Skt.: *naga*) They are a class of generally blue, serpent deities who reside below the water or springs in the black sphere, or in the meadows and whose realm is the West. They are a class of deities noted in rNying-ma-pa sect writings. Their leader is *Ya-ba-mgo-dgu*. Also, a *dregs-pa*, a general consideration of minor protective deities, many of which find their origin in the Bon pantheon. They number 100,000. There are eight noted sub-groups of the *klu*, they are: 1) *klu-bram-ze'i-rigs* -- red, mouse-headed *klu*, 2) *klu-byol-song-gi-rigs*, 3) *klu-dkar-rigs*, 4) *klu-dmangs-rigs* -- blue, ox-headed *klu*, 5) *klu-gdol-pa'i-rigs* -- blue, lizard-headed *klu*, 6) *klu-rgyal-rigs* -- white, horse-headed *klu*, 7) *klu-rje-rigs* -- yellow, goose-headed *klu*, and8) *klu-sman* -- product of a union between the *klu* and the *sman*. (RN-W)

klu-bdud -- (Tib.) They are deity/demons who reside in streams and confluences of rivers. They are the product of the untion of the *klu* and the *bdud*. Their leader is the deity *kLu-bdud-nag-po-mgo-dgu* or *Nag-po-mgo-dgu*. One of a class of thirty that are enumerated in the rNying-ma pa sect work *Thugs-rje'i-rnams-sprul-seng-chen-nor-bu-dgra-'dul-gyis-nor-bdud-bcom-pa'i-rnam-thar-mdor-bsdus-bzhugs-so*. Also, a *dregs-pa*, a general consideration of minor protective deities, many of which find their origin in the Bon pantheon. There are two noted sub-groups: 1) eight *klu-bdud* sisters, and 2) *jo-bo-klu-bdud-mched-dgu* -- nine *klu-bdud* brothers which cause bilious diseases. (RN-W)

klu-bram-ze'i-rigs -- (Tib.) They represent a sub-class of deity/demons known as the *klu*, ancient Tibetan minor deities. See *klu*. (RN-W)

klu-brog-mo -- (Tib.) They are a group of minor deity/demons who are the product from the union between the *klu* and the *brog-mo*. There are two noted sub-groups of the *klu-brog-mo*, they are: 1) eight queens -- human bodies with animal heads, 2) four queens -- human bodies with yak heads. (RN-W)

klu-btsan -- (Tib.) They are a group of minor deity/demons who are the product from the union of the *klu* and *btsan*. They number 100,000. (RN-W)

klu-bum --(Tib.) They are related to the *klu* and are an ancient Tibetan minor deity/demons. (RN-W)

klu-byol-song-gi-rigs -- (Tib.) They represent a sub-class of deity/demons known as the *klu*, ancient Tibetan minor deities. See *klu*. (RN-W)

klu-chen-brgyad -- S(Tib.) They represent a sub-class of deity/demons known as the *mgon-po*, ancient Tibetan minor deities who bring woes. See *mgon-po*. (RN-W)

klu-dkar-rigs -- (Tib.) They represent a sub-class of deity/demons known as the *klu*, ancient Tibetan minor deities. See *klu*. (RN-W)

klu-dmangs-rigs -- (Tib.) They represent a sub-class of deity/demons known as the *klu*, ancient Tibetan minor deities. See *klu*. (RN-W)

klu-gdol-pa'i-rigs -- (Tib.) They represent a sub-class of deity/demons known as the *klu*, ancient Tibetan minor deities. See *klu*. (RN-W)

klu'i-btsan -- (Tib.) They represent an important sub-class of deity/demons known as the *btsan*, ancient Tibetan demons. See *btsan*. (RN-W)

klu-mo -- (Tib.)(Skt.: *nagis*) The are pre-Buddhist female deity/demons known as water spirits. The mistress is the goddess *Yum-klu-mo-yaksa-nag-mo* or *Yaksa-nag-mo*. One of a class of thirty that are enumerated in the rNying-ma pa sect work *Thugs-rje'i-rnams-sprul-seng-chen-nor-bu-dgra-'dul-gyis-nor-bdud-bcom-pa'i-rnam-thar-mdor-bsdus-bzhugs-so*. Also, a *dregs-pa*, a general consideration of minor protective deities, many of which find their origin in the Bon pantheon. (RN-W)

klu-rgyal-rigs -- (Tib.) They represent a sub-class of deity/demons known as the *klu*, ancient Tibetan minor deities. See *klu*. (RN-W)

klu-rje-rigs -- (Tib.) They represent a sub-class of deity/demons known as the *klu*, ancient Tibetan minor deities. See *klu*. (RN-W)

klu-sman -- (Tib.) They represent a sub-class of deity/demons known as the *klu*, as well as the sub-class of deities known as the *sman*, both ancient Tibetan minor deities. See *sman* and *klu*. (RN-W)

klu-sri-sngon-po -- (Tib.) A sub-class of the *sri*, a group of demons who originated from thirteen eggs. See *sri*. (RN-W)

klu-srin -- (Tib.) They are a group of minor deity/demons who are the product of the union between the *klu* and the *srin-mo*. (RN-W)

khrag-'tung-lnga-bcu-rtsa-brgyad -- (Tib.) They are a minor deity/demon class who are known as the "fifty-eight blood drinkers" which are invoked by the rNying-ma-pa sect sect during a dgra-lha incantation. (RN-W)

khri'i-'a-mo -- (Tib.) They are associated with the *byin-te-dgu* (who represent a sub-class of deity/demons known as the *bon-skyong*, guardian deities of the Bon). (RN-W)

'khrung-lha -- (Tib.) They minor deities, related to the *lha* and are birth gods. (RN-W)

khyung -- (Tib.) They are bird-like deities whose realm is the sky. They are frequently shown in opposition to the *klu* (*nagas*). (RN-W)

kumbhandhas -- (Skt.) They are similar to the Tibetan *grul-bum* who are supernatural beings who accompany *the dharmapalas*. (RN-W)

lam-lha -- (Tib.) They are road demons and are related to the road *gzhi-bdag*. (RN-W)

lang-ka-bzhi -- They are fierce deity/demons who are related to the *srin-po* and *srin-mo*. They are ruled by the *lang-ka'i-bdag-po-drug-cu*. There are four noted sub-classes: a. *las-kyi-rigs-kyi-lang-ka* -- dark green, b. *padma-rigs-kyi-lang-ka* -- red, c. *rdo-rje-rigs-kyi-lang-ka* -- four white, d. *rin-chen-rigs-kyi-lang-ka* -- yellow. (RN-W)

lang-ka'i-bdag-po-drug-cu -- They are sixty,

fierce deity/demons who rule the *lang-ka-bzhi*. (RN-W)

las-byed-mtsho-sman -- (Tib.) They represent a sub-class of deity/demons known as the *sman*, ancient Tibetan minor goddesses. See *sman*. (RN-W)

las-gdon -- (Tib.) They represent a sub-class of deity/demons known as the *gdon*, ancient Tibetan minor deities. See *gdon*. (RN-W)

las-kyi-pho-nya -- (Tib.) They represent a sub-class of deity/demons known as the *pho-nya*, ancient messenger deities. See *pho-nya*. (RN-W)

las-kyi-rigs-kyi-ging -- (Tib.) They represent a sub-class of deity/demons known as the *ging*, ancient Tibetan minor deities. See *ging*. (RN-W)

las-kyi-rigs-kyi-lang-ka -- (Tib.) They represent a sub-class of deity/demons known as the *lang-ka-bzhi*, ancient Tibetan minor deities. See *lang-ka-bzhi*. (RN-W)

las-mdzad -- (Tib.: aka *dregs-pa-bzhi*) A group of deities related to dPal-ldan-lha-mo and includes: *Khyab-'jug-chen-po, bTsan-rgod, bDud-mgon*, and *Li-byin-ha-ra*. (RN-W)

las-mkhan -- (Tib.) They are a class of deity/demons who are known as "officers" and are related to the *ging*. (RN-W)

lce-spyang-ma-brgyad -- (Tib.) They are demon/deities whose origin may have been in India. See *lha-mo*. (RN-W)

ldan-pa-spun-dgu -- (Tib.) They are a group of nine *dgra-lha*-like deities. (RN-W)

lha -- (Tib.)(Skt.: *deva*) They are white Gods who reside on the white mountain and the upper spheres. They are ruled by *Mahadeva* (*lHa-chen-nam-dbang-phyug-mahadeva*) and are thought to be regarded as purely Tibetan deities who bring harm and to cause madness. They lost their original identity after being equated with the *devas* of India. One of a class of thirty that are enumerated in the rNying-ma pa sect work *Thugs-rje'i-rnams-sprul-seng-chen-nor-bu-dgra-'dul-gyis-nor-bdud-bcom-pa'i-rnam-thar-mdor-bsdus-bzhugs-so*. Also, a *dregs-pa*, a general consideration of minor protective deities, many of which find their origin in the Bon pantheon. As a class, they number 100,000. A sub-class is the: *mdud-lha-sum-brgya-drug-bcu* -- *lha* of the knots, a group of 360 *dgra-lha*-like *lha*. (RN-W)

lha-bdud -- (Tib.) They represent a sub-class of protective deity/demons known as the *bdud*. See *bdud*. (RN-W)

lha-btsan -- (Tib.) They represent an important sub-class of deity/demons known as the *btsan*, ancient Tibetan demons. See *btsan*. (RN-W)

lha-chen-brgyad -- (Tib.) They represent a sub-class of deity/demons known as the *mgon-po*, ancient Tibetan minor deities. See *mgon-po*. (RN-W)

lhag-bsdud-ma -- (Tib.) They represent a sub-class of deity/demons known as the *bon-skyong*, guardian deities of the Bon. (RN-W)

lhag-ma-bzhi -- (Tib.) They represent a sub-class of deity/demons known as the *bon-skyong*, guardian deities of the Bon. (RN-W)

lha'i-bdud -- (Tib.) They represent a sub-class of protective deity/demons known as the *bdud*. They are seven demons who reside in the east, white in color, ride white horses, holds flower and snare, they cause illness to counteract harmful effects of the enemies of religion. See *bdud*. (RN-W)

lha'i-dge-bsnyen -- (Tib.) They are a group of minor mountain deity/demons. See *dge-bsnyen*. (RN-W)

lha'i-ging-chen -- (Tib.) They represent a sub-class of deity/demons known as the *ging*, ancient Tibetan minor deities. See *ging*. (RN-W)

lha-ma-yin -- (Tib.) (Skt.: *asuras*) They represent a class of deities noted in rNying-ma-pa sect writings. Their leader is *Thang-bzang-ring-skyes*. Also, a *dregs-pa*, a general consideration of minor protective deities, many of which find their origin in the Bon pantheon. (RN-W)

lha-mo -- (Tib.) They are goddesses whose leader is *Uma-devi*. They may have been originally Tibetan deities rather than a group adapted from India. One of a class of thirty that are enumerated in the rNying-ma pa sect work *Thugs-rje'i-rnams-sprul-seng-chen-nor-bu-dgra-'dul-gyis-nor-bdud-bcom-pa'i-rnam-thar-mdor-bsdus-bzhugs-so*. Also, a *dregs-pa*, a general consideration of minor protective deities, many of which find their origin in the Bon pantheon There are two noted sub-groups: a. *ma-mo-mched-dgu* -- sisterhood of nine, b. *lce-spyang-ma-brgyad* -- eight animal headed. (RN-W)

lha-mtshams -- (Tib.) They represent a sub-class of deity/demons known as the *rgyu-skar* (Skt.: *naksatra*) who reside in the realm "in between." See *rgyu-skar*. (RN-W)

lha-sri -- (Tib.) They represent a sub-class of deity/demons known as the *sri*, ancient Tibetan minor deities who bring woes. See *sri*. (RN-W)

li-byin-thong-gar -- (Tib.) They are a group of thirteen deity/demons who are found in the retinue of *Pe-har*, and appear to be dancers. (RN-W)

lokapala -- (Skt)(Chin.: *hu-shis-che*) They are a group of deities who are similar to the Tibetan *phyogs-skyong*. They are "Guardians of the Four Cardinal Points." (RN-W)

lo-sri -- (Tib.) They represent a sub-class of deity/demons known as the *sri*, ancient Tibetan minor deities who bring woes. See *sri*. (RN-W)

lus-gdon -- (Tib.) They represent a sub-class of deity/demons known as the *gdon*, ancient Tibetan minor deities. See *gdon*. (RN-W)

lus-lha -- (Tib.) They represent a sub-class of minor deity/demons known as the *'go-ba'i-lha-lnga*, and noted in rNying-ma-pa sect writings. See *'go-ba'i-lha-lnga*. (RN-W)

ma-bdud -- (Tib.) They represent a sub-class of protective deity/demons known as the *bdud*. See *bdud*. (RN-W)

ma-gza'-dam-gsum -- (Tib.) A group of three deities comprising: *Ma-mo-ekajati, Rahu* and *Dam-can-rdo-rje-legs-ma*. (RN-W)

mahasiddha -- (Skt.)(Tib.: *grub-thob*) See *grub-thob*. (RN-W, BO)

maha-yaksa -- (Skt.)(Tib.: *gnod-spyin-chen-po*)(the great *yaksa*) See *gnod-spyin-chen-po*. (RN-W)

ma-mo -- (Tib.)(Skt.: *matrka*) These goddesses are ancient Tibetan deities and are similar to the *matrka* (Skt.). The leader of theis class is *Srid-pa'i-rgyal-mo* (*dPal-*

ldan-lha-mo). They are very unpleasnat, fierce looking deities, usually black, with emaciated and pendulous breasts. They are bringers of the illness called *dal-yams*. They were subdued by Padmasambhava. One of a class of thirty that are enumerated in the rNying-ma pa sect work *Thugs-rje'i-rnams-sprul-seng-chen-nor-bu-dgra-'dul-gyis-nor-bdud-bcom-pa'i-rnam-thar-mdor-bsdus-bzhugs-so*. Also, a *dregs-pa*, a general consideration of monor protective deities, many of which find their origin in the Bon pantheon. There are six noted sub-groups: 1) *bon-nyid-dbyings-kyi-ma-mo,* 2) *drag-byed-sprul-pa'i-ma-mo,* 3) *dus-dug-sprul-pa'i-ma-mo,* 4) *mkha'-klong-dbyings-kyi-ma-mo,* 5) *rang-bzhin-mkha'-nyid-ma-mo,* and 6) *rdzu-'phrul-klong-gi-ma-mo.* (RN-W)

ma-mo-mched-dgu -- (Tib.) They are demon/deities whose origin may have been in India. See *lha-mo*. (RN-W)

ma-mtshun -- (Tib.) They represent a sub-class of deity/demons known as the *mtshun*, ancient Tibetan minor deities. They are also known as *tshun, btsun* or *mes-btsun*. See *mtshun*. (RN-W)

ma-nges-dgu-shor -- (Tib.) They represent a sub-class of deity/demons known as the *sri*, ancient Tibetan minor deities who bring woes. See *sri*. (RN-W)

ma-sangs -- Theey are a group of pre-Buddhist deities, many of whom reside in mountains. The leader of the ma-sangs deities is *sPyi-bdud-dgu-rum-rtse* or *sPyid-bdud-rgyal-po-gu-ru-ma*. One of a class of thirty that are enumerated in the rNying-ma pa sect work *Thugs-rje'i-rnams-sprul-seng-chen-nor-bu-dgra-'dul-gyis-nor-bdud-bcom-pa'i-rnam-thar-mdor-bsdus-bzhugs-so*. Also, a *dregs-pa,* a general consideration of minor protective deities, many of which find their origin in the Bon pantheon. There are two noted sub-groups: 1) a group of nine brothers, and 2) a group of seven brothers. (RN-W)

matrka -- (Skt.)(Tib.: *ma-mo*) They represent a sub-class of deity/demons known as the *ma-mo*, ancient Tibetan minor goddesses. See *ma-mo*. (RN-W)

mchod-pa'i-lha-mo -- (Tib.) They are a group of five goddesses who serve higher ranking divinities with items of sensual pleasure. They are found in the retinue of *Pe-har*. (RN-W)

mchog-gi-sde-brgyad -- (Tib.) They represent a sub-class of deity/demons known as the *dregs-pa,* ancient Tibetan minor deities. They are also to be found in the personal train of *Pe-har*. See *dregs-pa*. (RN-W)

mdo-btsan -- (Tib.) They represent an important sub-class of deity/demons known as the *btsan*, ancient Tibetan demons. See *btsan*. (RN-W)

mdud-lha-sum-brgya-drug-bcu -- (Tib.) They represent an important sub-class of deity/demons known as the *lha*, ancient Tibetan demons. See *lha*. (RN-W)

me-bdud -- (Tib.) They represent a sub-class of protective deity/demons known as the *bdud*. See *bdud*. (RN-W)

me-bzhi -- (Tib.) They represent a sub-class of deity/demons known as the *rgyu-skar* (Skt.: *naksatra*) who reside in the realm "in between." See *rgyu-skar*. (RN-W)

med-sri -- (Tib.) They represent a sub-class of deity/demons known as the *sri*, ancient Tibetan minor deities who bring woes. See *sri*. (RN-W)

me-gnyan -- (Tib.) They represent a sub-class of yellow, fierce deity/demons known as the *gnyan*, and noted in rNying-ma-pa sect writings. See *gnyan*. (RN-W)

mes-btsun -- (Tib.) They represent a sub-class of deity/demons known as the *mtshun*, ancient Tibetan minor deities. They are also known as *tshun, btsun* or *mes-btsun*. See *mtshun*. (RN-W)

me-sri -- (Tib.) They represent a sub-class of deity/demons known as the *sri*, ancient Tibetan minor deities who bring woes. See *sri*. (RN-W)

mgon-po -- (Tib.) They represent a class of various minor forms of Mahakala. The leader of the *mgon-po* is the deity *Mahakala* (Skt.). They lost their identity, having been assumed into the Buddhist tradition and practice. They are related to the *bdud-mgon*. One of a class of thirty that are enumerated in the rNying-ma pa sect work *Thugs-rje'i-rnams-sprul-seng-chen-nor-bu-dgra-'dul-gyis-nor-bdud-bcom-pa'i-rnam-thar-mdor-bsdus-bzhugs-so*. Also, a *dregs-pa*, a general consideration of minor protective deities, many of which find their origin in the Bon pantheon. There are six noted sub-groups: 1) *lha-chen-brgyad* -- a group of eight, 2) *klu-chen-brgyad* -- a group of eight, 3) *gza'-chen-brgyad* -- a group of eight, 4) *rgya-skar-nyi-shu-rtsa-brgyad* -- a group of twenty eight, 5) *phyogs-skyong-bcu* -- a group of ten, and 6) *rje-yi-mgur-lha-bcu-gsum* -- a group of thirteen. (RN-W)

mgur-lha-bcu-gsum -- (Tib.) They are a group of protective, Tibetan mountain deities. (RN-W)

mi-bzad-dbal-gyi-gyad-ma-dgu -- (Tib.) They represent a sub-class of deity/demons known as the *bon-skyong*, guardian deities of the Bon. (RN-W)

mi-la-spun-dgu -- (Tib.) They represent a group of nine *dgra-lha*-like deities. (RN-W)

mi-rabs-brgyud-dgra-lha -- (Tib.) They represent a sub-class of deity/demons known as the *dgra-lha*, ancient Tibetan minor deities. See *dgra-lha*. (RN-W)

mi-thub-dgra-lha-spun-gsum -- (Tib.) They represent a sub-class of deity/demons known as the *dgra-lha*, ancient Tibetan minor deities. See *dgra-lha*. (RN-W)

mkha'-'gro -- (Tib.)(Skt. dakini) They are a class of goddesses who are related to the *dakini* of India. The mistress of the *mkha'-'gro* is the goddess *Nag-mo-mgyogs-byed*. One of a class of thirty that are enumerated in the rNying-ma pa sect work *Thugs-rje'i-rnams-sprul-seng-chen-nor-bu-dgra-'dul-gyis-nor-bdud-bcom-pa'i-rnam-thar-mdor-bsdus-bzhugs-so*. Also, a *dregs-pa*, a general consideration of minor protective deities, many of which find their origin in the Bon pantheon. (RN-W)

mkha'-klong-dbyings-kyi-ma-mo -- (Tib.) They represent a sub-class of deity/demons known as the *ma-mo*, ancient Tibetan minor goddesses. See *ma-mo*. (RN-W)

mkha'-lding -- (Tib.) A group of monor Tibetan demon/dieties. (RN-W)

mkhar-gyi-rtse-lha-gnyan-po -- (Tib.) A group of monor Tibetan demon/dieties. They are thirteen evil peak-gods of castles. (RN-W)

mo-dgu -- (Tib.) They represent a sub-class of deity/demons known as the *ging*, ancient Tibetan minor deities. See *ging*. (RN-W)

mo-lha -- (Tib.) They represent a sub-class of minor deity/demons known as the *'go-ba'i-lha-lnga*, and noted in rNying-ma-pa sect writings. See *'go-ba'i-lha-lnga*. (RN-W)

mon-mo-shva-na-nag-mo-drug -- (Tib.) They are a group of six black "messenger" deity/demons who are *Mon pho-nya* and are in the retinue of *lHa-chen-mgon-polcam-dral-traksad-gnyis-lugs*. (RN-W)

mo-rgyud -- (Tib.) They represent a sub-class of deity/demons known as the *dam-can-mo-rgyud*, ancient Tibetan minor deities. See *dam-can-mo-rgyud*. (RN-W)

mo-sri -- (Tib.) They represent a sub-class of deity/demons known as the *sri*, ancient Tibetan minor deities who bring woes. See *sri*. (RN-W)

mtshams -- (Tib.: aka *'tshams*) An alternate spelling for *'tshams*. (RN-W)

mtshams-(gyi)-srung-(ma) -- (Tib.)("border guardians") They are a sub-group of guardian deity/demons known as *srung-ma* and are related to the *chos-skyong*. See *srung-ma*. (RN-W)

mtsho-sman -- (Tib.) They represent a sub-class of deity/demons known as the *sman*, ancient Tibetan minor goddesses. See *sman*. (RN-W)

mtsho-gnyan -- (Tib.) They represent a sub-class of yellow, fierce deity/demons known as the *gnyan*, and noted in rNying-ma-pa sect writings. See *gnyan*. (RN-W)

mtshon-srin -- (Tib.) They represent a sub-class of rock dwelling deity/demons known as the *srin-mo*, and noted in rNying-ma-pa sect writings. See *srin-mo*. (RN-W)

mtsho-sman -- (Tib.) They are Tibetan deity/demons who reside in large lakes. (RN-W)

mtshun -- They are also known as *tshun*, *btsun* or *mes-btsun*, they are ancestral spirits and are regarded by some as evil. There are two noted sub-classes: 1) *pha-mtshun* -- male, which possesses two sub-groups: a) *pha-mtshun-yab-lha-spun-drug* -- "brotherhood of the six father gods," and b) *pha-mtshun-dgra-lha-spun-dgu* -- "brotherhood of the nine *dgra-lha*," 1) *ma-mtshun* -- female. (RN-W)

mu-stegs-pa -- (Skt.: *tirthika*) Their leader is the *(dpon) Gu-lang-raksa* or *Kala-nag-po*. Not a member of aboriginal Tibetan deities, but appear derived from the Indian *tirthika*. One of a class of thirty that are enumerated in the rNying-ma pa sect work *Thugs-rje'i-rnams-sprul-seng-chen-nor-bu-dgra-'dul-gyis-nor-bdud-bcom-pa'i-rnam-thar-mdor-bsdus-bzhugs-so*. Also, a *dregs-pa*, a general consideration of minor protective deities, many of which find their origin in the Bon pantheon. (RN-W)

nad-kyi-bu-mo-spun-lnga -- (Tib.) They are minor deity/demons who are goddesses of epidemics. (RN-W)

nad-sri -- (Tib.) They represent a sub-class of deity/demons known as the *sri*, ancient Tibetan minor deities who bring woes. See *sri*. (RN-W)

naga -- (Skt.)(Tib.: *klu*) The equivalent of the Tibetan *kLu* and are serpent deities which in Tibet take on greater importance than the Indian variety. See *klu*. (RN-W)

nagis -- (Skt.)(Tib.: *klu-mo*) A group of *naga*-related deities which are found in the retinue of *dPal-ldan-lha-mo*. (RN-W)

nags-gnyan -- (Tib.) They represent a sub-class of yellow, fierce deity/demons known as the *gnyan*, and noted in rNying-ma-pa sect writings. See *gnyan*. (RN-W)

nag-gi-sde-brgyad -- (Tib.) They represent a sub-class of deity/demons known as the *dregs-pa*, ancient Tibetan minor deities. See *dregs-pa*. (RN-W)

nags-phyogs-gi-bdud -- (Tib.)("the *bdud* devils of the black quarter") They are evil demons who are still being converted to protectors. They also represent a sub-class of protective deity/demons known as the *bdud*. They are also related to the *bon-skyong* and the *bon-srung*. They are seven demons who stand in opposition to the *dkar-phyogs-skyong-ba'i-srung-ma*. See *bdud*. (RN-W)

naksatra -- (Skt.) They are Indian minor deities which are similar to the 4Tibetan *rgyu-skar*. See *rgyu-skar*. (RN-W)

nang -- (Tib.) They are a group of deities who correspond to the *chos-skyong* and the *gsang-ba'i-chos-skyong*. See *chos-skyong* and *gsang-ba'i-chos-skyong*. (RN-W)

nang-blon -- (Tib.)("minister of internal affairs") They represent a sub-class of deities known as the *blon-po* (or"ministers"), noted in rNying-ma-pa sect writings. See *blon-po*. (RN-W)

nang-btsan -- (Tib.) They represent an important sub-class of deity/demons known as the *btsan*, ancient Tibetan demons. See *btsan*. (RN-W)

nor-lha -- (Tib.) They are gods of wealth. and are related to *Jambhala*, *Kubera* and *Vaisravana*. (RN-W)

nye-sri -- (Tib.) They represent a sub-class of deity/demons known as the *sri*, ancient Tibetan minor deities who bring woes. See *sri*. (RN-W)

nyi-gnyan -- (Tib.) They represent a sub-class of yellow, fierce deity/demons known as the *gnyan*, and noted in rNying-ma-pa sect writings. See *gnyan*. (RN-W)

nyon-mongs-pa'i-bdud -- (Tib.) They represent a sub-class of protective deity/demons known as the *bdud*. See *bdud*. (RN-W)

'od-ldan-mtsho-sman -- (Tib.) They represent a sub-class of deity/demons known as the *sman*, ancient Tibetan minor goddesses. See *sman*. (RN-W)

padma-rigs-kyi-ging -- (Tib.) They represent a sub-class of deity/demons known as the *ging*, ancient Tibetan minor deities. See *ging*. (RN-W)

padma-rigs-kyi-lang-ka -- (Tib.) They represent a sub-class of deity/demons known as the *lang-ka-bzhi*, ancient Tibetan minor deities. See *lang-ka-bzhi*. (RN-W)

padma-rigs-kyi-pho-nya -- (Tib.) They represent a sub-class of deity/demons known as the *pho-nya*, ancient messenger deities. See *pho-nya*. (RN-W)

pancatathagatha -- (Skt.) The five tathagatha Buddhas: *Aksobhya*, *Vairocana*, *Ratnasambhava*, *Amitabha* and *Amoghasiddhi*. (RN-W)

pha-mes-brgyud-dgra-lha -- (Tib.) They represent a sub-class of deity/demons known as the *dgra-lha*, ancient Tibetan minor deities. See *dgra-lha*. (RN-W)

pha-mtshun -- (Tib.) They represent a sub-class of deity/demons known as the *mtshun*, ancient Tibetan minor deities. They are also known as *tshun*, *btsun* or *mes-btsun*. See *mtshun*. (RN-W)

pha-mes-(brgyud)-kyi-srung-ma -- (Tib.) ("ancestral protective deities") They are a sub-group of guardian deity/demons known as *srung-ma* and are related to the *chos-skyong*. See *srung-ma*. (RN-W)

pha-mtshun-dgra-lha-spun-dgu -- (Tib.) They represent a sub-class of deity/demons known as the *mtshun*, ancient Tibetan minor deities. They are also known as *tshun*, *btsun* or *mes-btsun*. See *mtshun*. (RN-W)

pha-mtshun-yab-lha-spun-drug -- (Tib.) They represent a sub-class of deity/demons known as the *mtshun*, ancient Tibetan minor deities. They are also known as *tshun*, *btsun* or *mes-btsun*. See *mtshun*. (RN-W)

pho-dgu -- (Tib.) They represent a sub-class of deity/demons known as the *ging*, ancient Tibetan minor deities. See *ging*. (RN-W)

pho-lha -- (Tib.) They are personal protective deity second to *dgra-lha*. See *'go-ba'i-lha-lnga*. (RN-W)

pho-nya -- (Tib.) They are a class of deity/demons who are generally known as messenger deities. They number 360, and there are four noted sub-groups: 1) *las-kyi-pho-nya* -- green; carries a bell, 2) *padma-rigs-kyi-pho-nya* -- red; carries a lotus, 3) *rdo-rje-rigs-kyi-pho-nya* -- white, carries a hook, and 4) *rin-chen-rigs-kyi-pho-nya* -- yellow, carries a snare. (RN-W)

pho-nya'i-mtsho-sman -- (Tib.) They represent a sub-class of deity/demons known as the *sman*, ancient Tibetan minor goddesses. See *sman*. (RN-W)

pho-rgyud -- (Tib.) They represent a sub-class of deity/demons known as the *dam-can-mo-rgyud*, ancient Tibetan minor goddesses. See *dam-can-mo-rgyud*. (RN-W)

pho-sri -- (Tib.) They represent a sub-class of deity/demons known as the *sri*, ancient Tibetan minor deities who bring woes. See *sri*. (RN-W)

'phrin-las-bzhi'i-lha-mo -- (Tib.) A group of deities related to *dPal-ldan-lha-mo* which include: *Zhi-ba'i-lha-mo*, *rGyas-pa'i-lha-mo*, *dBang-gi-lha-mo* and *Drag-pa'i-lha-mo*. (RN-W)

phung-po'i-bdud -- (Tib.) They represent a sub-class of protective deity/demons known as the *bdud*. See *bdud*. (RN-W)

phyi-ba'i-chos-skyong -- (Tib.) They are deities who are identical to the *'jig-rten-pa'i-srung-ma* when considered under the collective name *phyi-nang-gsang-ba'i-chos-skyong*. (RN-W)

phyi-blon -- (Tib.)("minister of external affairs")They represent a sub-class of deities known as the *blon-po* (or"ministers"), noted in rNying-ma-pa sect writings. See *blon-po*. (RN-W)

phyi-btsan -- (Tib.) They represent an important sub-class of deity/demons known as the *btsan*, ancient Tibetan demons. See *btsan*. (RN-W)

phyi-nang-gsang-ba'i-chos-skyong -- (Tib.) The collective name often used for *'jig-rten-las-'das-pa'i-srung-ma* and *'jig-rten-pa'i-srung-ma*. (RN-W)

phyi-rabs-brgyud-dgra-lha -- (Tib.) An infrequently used term for a group of guardian deities. They also represent a sub-class of deity/demons known as the *dgra-lha*, ancient Tibetan minor deities. See *dgra-lha*. (RN-W)

phyi-yi-sde-brgyadd -- (Tib.) They represent a sub-class of deity/demons known as the *dregs-pa*, ancient Tibetan minor deities. See *dregs-pa*. (RN-W)

phyogs-skyong -- (Tib.)(Skt.: *lokapala*) The Tibetan transliteral equivalent of the Sanskrit for lokapala, the "Guardians of the Four Cardinal Points." (RN-W, BO)

phyogs-skyong-bcu -- (Tib.) They represent a sub-class of deity/demons known as the *mgon-po*, ancient Tibetan minor deities. See *mgon-po*. (RN-W)

phyugs-lha-spun-bdun -- (Tib.) They are a minor group of deity/demons known as cattle deities. (RN-W)

phyva -- (Tib.) They are little known class of demon/deities noted in Nebesky-Wojkowitz. (RN-W)

phyva-sman -- (Tib.) They are a group of deity/demons who are the result of the union between a *phyva* and a *sman*. (RN-W)

pisacas -- (Skt.) A group of minor deities. (RN-W)

Pleiads -- (Eng.) They represent a sub-class of deity/demons known as the *rgyu-skar* (Skt.: *naksatra*) who reside in the realm "in between." See *rgyu-skar*. (RN-W)

putra -- (Tib.) A class of deity/demons. (RN-W)

putra-ming-sring-gsum -- (Tib.) A sub-class of deity/demons mad up of two dark-blue brothers and their sister. They are: *Putra-nag-po*, *Bhadra-nag-po* and *Srin-mo-ral-gcig-ma*. (RN-W)

raksasas -- (Skt.) They represent a group of giant deity/demons with human bodies, with supernatural powers, and which are similar to the *srin-po*. See *srin-po*. (RN-W)

raksasis -- (Skt.) They represent a group of giant deity/demons with human bodies, with supernatural powers, and which are similar to the *srin-mo*. See *srin-mo*. (RN-W)

rang-bzhin-mkha'-nyid-ma-mo -- (Tib.) They represent a sub-class of deity/demons known as the *ma-mo*, ancient Tibetan minor goddesses. See *ma-mo*. (RN-W)

rdo-gnyan -- (Tib.) They represent a sub-class of yellow, fierce deity/demons known as the *gnyan*, and noted in rNying-ma-pa sect writings. See *gnyan*. (RN-W)

rdo-rje-rigs-kyi-ging -- (Tib.) They represent a sub-class of deity/demons known as the *ging*, ancient Tibetan minor deities. See *ging*. (RN-W)

rdo-rje-rigs-kyi-lang-ka -- (Tib.) They represent a sub-class of deity/demons known as the *lang-ka-bzhi*, ancient Tibetan minor deities. See *lang-ka-bzhi*. (RN-W)

rdo-rje-rigs-kyi-pho-nya -- (Tib.) They represent a sub-class of deity/demons known as the *pho-nya*, ancient messenger deities. See *pho-nya*. (RN-W)

rdza-gnyan -- (Tib.) They represent a sub-class of yellow, fierce deity/demons known as the *gnyan*, and noted in rNying-ma-pa sect writings. See *gnyan*. (RN-W)

rdzi'u-sum-brgya-drug-bcu -- (Tib.) They are a group of 360 *dgra-lha*-like deity/demons known as "the herdsmen." (RN-W)

rdzu-'phrul-klong-gi-ma-mo -- (Tib.) They represent a sub-class of deity/demons known as the *ma-mo*, ancient Tibetan minor goddesses. See *ma-mo*. (RN-W)

remati-mched-bzhi -- (Tib.) A group of four deities in the retinue of dpal-ldan-lha-mo. They are: *Remati, Rema-dza, Rema-dzu* and *Remati-ti*. (RN-W)

remati-mched-gsum -- (Tib.) A group of three deities in the retinue of *dPal-ldan-lha-mo*. They are: *dPal-ldan-lha-mo-remati, dPal-ldan-rema-rdza, dPal-ldan-rema-dzu*. (RN-W)

rgan-sri -- (Tib.) A sub-class of the *sri*, a group of demons who originated from thirteen eggs. See *sri*. (RN-W)

rgyal-chen -- (Tib.)("the great *rgyal*") A sub-class of the *rgyal-po*, a group of minor protective deity/demons. See *rgyal-po*. (RN-W)

rgyal-'gong -- (Tib.) They are true Tibetan deities who reside in castles or temples and monasteries. They were created from a union of the *rgyal-po* and the *'gong-po*. (RN-W)

rgyal-mo-gsim-ma -- (Tib.) They are a group of sixteen deity/demons who are in the personal train of *Pehar*. (RN-W)

rgyal-phran -- (Tib.)("the minor *rgyal*") A sub-class of the *rgyal-po*, a group of minor protective deity/demons. See *rgyal-po*. (RN-W)

rgyal-po -- (Tib.) They are deity/demons who bring illness and cause insanity. Their leader is the demon *Maharaja* (*Pe-har* or *rGyal-po-`chen-po* or *Khyung-chen-klu-'brug*). One of a class of thirty deities that are enumerated in the rNying-ma pa sect work *Thugs-rje'i-rnams-sprul-seng-chen-nor-bu-dgra-'dul-gyis-nor-bdud-bcom-pa'i-rnam-thar-mdor-bsdus-bzhugs-so*. Also, a *dregs-pa*, a general consideration of minor protective deities, many of which find their origin in the Bon pantheon. There are five sub-groups noted: 1) *rgyal-po-gnod-sbyin-mched-gsum* -- three *dgra-lha*-like deities, 2) *rgyal-po-'od-can-mched-gsum* -- three *dgra-lha*-like deities, 3) *rgyal-po-sku-lnga*, 4) *rgyal-chen* and 5) *rgyal-phran*. (RN-W)

rgyal-po-gnod-sbyin-mched-gsum -- (Tib.) They represent a sub-class of deity/demons known as the *rgyal-po*, ancient messenger deities. See *rgyal-po*. (RN-W)

rgyal-po-'od-can-mched-gsum -- (Tib.) They represent a sub-class of deity/demons known as the *rgyal-po*, ancient messenger deities. See *rgyal-po*. (RN-W)

rgyal-po-sku-lnga -- (Tib.) They represent a sub-class of deity/demons known as the *rgyal-po*, ancient messenger deities. They number five and some say that *Pe-har* is the head of this group. See *rgyal-po*. (RN-W)

rgyal-sri -- (Tib.) They represent a sub-class of deity/demons known as the *sri*, ancient Tibetan minor deities who bring woes. See *sri*. (RN-W)

rgyal-srid-dkar-po -- (Tib.) A sub-class of the *sri*, a group of demons who originated from thirteen eggs. See *sri*. (RN-W)

rgya-skar-nyi-shu-rtsa-brgyad -- (Tib.) They represent a sub-class of deity/demons known as the *mgon-po*, ancient Tibetan minor deities. See *mgon-po*. (RN-W)

rgyu-skar -- (Tib.)(Skt.: *naksatra*) They are a minor class of deity/demons who reside in the sphere "in between." They are the personification of lunar mansions, who number twenty-eight and consist of four noted sub-groups: 1) *bra-nye* -- seven deities of the first lunar mansion, 2) *lha-mttshams* -- seven deities of the sixteenth lunar mansions, 3) *me-bzhi* -- seven deities of the twelfth lunar mansions, 4) *Pleiads* -- the seven stars of the east. (RN-W)

rig-'dzin -- (Tib.) They represent a group of deity/demons who reside in the Northwest and are not indigenous to Tibet. (RN-W)

rigs-'dzin-brgyud-kyi-srung-ma -- (Tib.) A general term for all "guardian" deities of the Buddhist creed. They are also a sub-group of guardian deity/demons known as *srung-ma* and are related to the *chos-skyong*. See *srung-ma*. (RN-W)

rigs-gsum-mgon-po -- (Tib.) They are a triad of minor mountain deities. (RN-W)

rin-chen-rigs-kyi-ging -- (Tib.) They represent a sub-class of deity/demons known as the *ging*, ancient Tibetan minor deities. See *ging*. (RN-W)

rin-chen-rigs-kyi-lang-ka -- (Tib.) They represent a sub-class of deity/demons known as the *lang-ka-bzhi*, ancient Tibetan minor deities. See *lang-ka-bzhi*. (RN-W)

rin-chen-rigs-kyi-pho-nya -- (Tib.) They represent a sub-class of deity/demons known as the *pho-nya*, ancient messenger deities. See *pho-nya*. (RN-W)

rje-yi-mgur-lha-bcu-gsum -- (Tib.) They represent a sub-class of deity/demons known as the *mgon-po*, ancient Tibetan minor deities. See *mgon-po*. (RN-W)

rlung-bdud -- (Tib.) They represent a sub-class of protective deity/demons known as the *bdud*. See *bdud*. (RN-W)

rlung-gnyan -- (Tib.) They represent a sub-class of yellow, fierce deity/demons known as the *gnyan*, and noted in rNying-ma-pa sect writings. See *gnyan*. (RN-W)

rlung-rta-dar-ba'i-dgra-lha -- (Tib.) They represent a sub-class of deity/demons known as the *dgra-lha*, ancient Tibetan minor deities. See *dgra-lha*. (RN-W)

rma-rigs -- (Tib.) A shortened form of the deity/demon class known as the *rma-rigs-sum-brgya-drug-cu*. See *rma-rigs-sum-brgya-drug-cu*. (RN-W)

rma-rigs-sum-brgya-drug-cu -- (Tib.) They are known as brothers of *mZangs-pa'i-sras-mo-spun-dgu* and whose consorts are the *rma-sman*. They number 360. (RN-W)

rma-sman -- (Tib.) They represent a sub-class of deity/demons known as the *sman*, ancient Tibetan minor goddesses. See *sman*. (RN-W)

rmugs-pa-spun-dgu -- (Tib.) They are a group of nine *dgra-lha*-like deities. (RN-W)

rta-bdag-brgyad -- (Tib.) They are a group of deity/demons who are known as the "eight masters of the horse." Frequently they are associated with *rNam-thos-sras*. (RN-W)

rta-rgod-mched-brgyad -- (Tib.) They are a group of eight *dgra-lha*-like deities. (RN-W)

rta-sri -- (Tib.) They represent a sub-class of deity/demons known as the *sri*, ancient Tibetan minor deities who bring woes. See *sri*. (RN-W)

rtse-lha -- (Tib.) They are a class of deity/demons who reside in gates. (RN-W)

rtse-sman -- (Tib.) They represent a sub-class of deity/demons known as the *sman*, ancient Tibetan minor goddesses. See *sman*. (RN-W)

rudras -- (Skt.) A group of deity/demons whose origin, apparently, was India, but related to the *snags-bdag* through the deity *Rudra-thar-pa-nag-po*. Their leader is the deity *rDo-rje-bdud-'dul*. One of a class of thirty that are enumerated in the rNying-ma pa sect work *Thugs-rje'i-rnams-sprul-seng-chen-nor-bu-dgra-'dul-gyis-nor-bdud-bcom-pa'i-rnam-thar-mdor-bsdus-bzhugs-so*. Also, a *dregs-pa*, a general consideration of minor protective deities, many of which find their origin in the Bon pantheon. (RN-W)

rytsi-gnyan -- (Tib.) They represent a sub-class of yellow, fierce deity/demons known as the *gnyan*, and noted in rNying-ma-pa sect writings. See *gnyan*. (RN-W)

sa-bdag -- They are a group of green deities who reside below (water) in the black sphere, astrological and world-quarters (earth). They are malevolent deities causing crippling illnesses. They are noted in rNying-ma-pa sect and Bon writings. Also known as a *dregs-pa*, a general consideration of minor protective deities, many of which find their origin in the Bon pantheon. They number 100,000, among which are noted four sub groups: 1) *sa-bdag-bdud-'dul-chen-mo* -- eight deities of the eastern quarter, 2) *sa-bdag-btsan-'dul-chen-mo* -- eight deities of the northern quarter, 3) *sa-bdag-gza'-'dul-chen-mo* -- eight deities of the southern quarter, and 4) *sa-bdag-klu-'dul-chen-mo* -- eight deities of the western quarter. (RN-W)

sa-bdag-bdud-'dul-chen-mo -- (Tib.) They represent a sub-class of deity/demons known as the *sa-bdag*, ancient Tibetan deities. See *sa-bdag*. (RN-W)

sa-bdag-btsan-'dul-chen-mo -- (Tib.) They represent a sub-class of deity/demons known as the *sa-bdag*, ancient Tibetan deities. See *sa-bdag*. (RN-W)

sa-bdag-gza'-'dul-chen-mo -- (Tib.) They represent a sub-class of deity/demons known as the *sa-bdag*, ancient Tibetan deities. See *sa-bdag*. (RN-W)

sa-bdag-klu-'dul-chen-mo -- (Tib.) They represent a sub-class of deity/demons known as the *sa-bdag*, ancient Tibetan deities. See *sa-bdag*. (RN-W)

sa-bdud -- (Tib.) They represent a sub-class of protective deity/demons known as the *bdud*. See *bdud*. (RN-W)

sa-gnyan -- (Tib.) They represent a sub-class of yellow, fierce deity/demons known as the *gnyan*, and noted in rNying-ma-pa sect writings. See *gnyan*. (RN-W)

sa'i-btsan -- (Tib.) They represent an important sub-class of deity/demons known as the *btsan*, ancient Tibetan demons. See *btsan*. (RN-W)

sa-sri -- (Tib.) They represent a sub-class of deity/demons known as the *sri*, ancient Tibetan minor deities who bring woes. See *sri*. (RN-W)

sa-srin -- (Tib.) They represent a sub-class of rock dwelling deity/demons known as the *srin-mo*, and noted in rNying-ma-pa sect writings. See *srin-mo*. (RN-W)

se -- (Tib.: aka *bse*) An alternative spelling for *bse*. See *bse*. (RN-W)

se-ju-spun-bzhi -- (Tib.) They represent a sub-class of deity/demons known as the *bse*, ancient Tibetan demons. See *bse*. (RN-W)

ser-bdag-bco-brgyad -- (Tib.) They a group of deity/demons who are known as "the eighteen masters of hail." (RN-W)

sgang-drug-gzhi-bdag-bcu-gnyis -- (Tib.) They represent a sub-class of deity/demons known as the *gzhi-bdag*, ancient Tibetan minor deities. See *gzhi-bdag*. (RN-W)

sgrol-ging -- (Tib.) They represent a sub-class of deity/demons known as the *ging*, ancient Tibetan minor deities. See *ging*. (RN-W)

sgrol-'gying-chen-bzhi -- (Tib.) They represent a sub-class of the protective deity/demons known as the *gying*, ancient Tibetan minor deities. See *gying*. (RN-W)

sgo-lha -- (Tib.) They are a group of deity/demons who reside in gates. (RN-W)

sgrog-gcod-kyi-gying-brgyad -- (Tib.) They represent a sub-class of the protective deity/demons known as the *gying*, ancient Tibetan minor deities. See *gying*. (RN-W)

sgo-sri -- (Tib.) They represent a sub-class of deity/demons known as the *sri*, ancient Tibetan minor deities who bring woes. See *sri*. (RN-W)

shan-pa -- (Tib.) They represent deity/demons who are known as "butchers," so called of many *dharmapala*. There is one noted sub-group, the *shan-pa-nag-po* -- black butcher. (RN-W)

shan-pa-nag-po -- (Tib.) They represent a sub-class of deity/demons known as the *shan-pa*, ancient Tibetan minor deities. See *shan-pa*. (RN-W)

sha-zan -- (Tib.) They represent a sub-class of deity/demons known as the *lang-ka-bzhi*, ancient Tibetan minor deities. See *lang-ka-bzhi*. (RN-W)

shing-chen-bzhi'i-gzhi-bdag -- (Tib.) They represent a sub-class of deity/demons known as the *gzhi-bdag*, ancient Tibetan minor deities. See *gzhi-bdag*. (RN-W)

shing-gnyan -- (Tib.) They represent a sub-class of yellow, fierce deity/demons known as the *gnyan*, and noted in rNying-ma-pa sect writings. See *gnyan*. (RN-W)

skar-gnyan -- (Tib.) They represent a sub-class of yellow, fierce deity/demons known as the *gnyan*, and noted in rNying-ma-pa sect writings. See *gnyan*. (RN-W)

sku-gsung-thugs-yon-tan-'phrin-las-kyi-mgon-po-sde-lnga -- (Tib.) They are a group of generally fierce, protective deities which represent various emanations of the body. (RN-W)

sku'i-rgyal-po -- (Tib.) They are five ministers associated with *Pe-har*. They may be part of the *blon-po* class.(RN-W)

sku-lha -- (Tib.) They represent a sub-class of minor deity/demons known as the *'go-ba'i-lha-lnga*, and noted in rNying-ma-pa sect writings. See *'go-ba'i-lha-lnga*. (RN-W)

sku-lnga -- (Tib.) They are a group of five ministers associated with *Pe-har*. They may be part of the *blon-po* class. (RN-W)

skyes-bu-btsan -- (Tib.) They represent an important sub-class of deity/demons known as the *btsan*, ancient Tibetan demons. See *btsan*. (RN-W)

skyes-bu-chen-po'i-srung-ma -- (Tib.) ("guardians of the great saints") They are a group of higher ranking protectors of religious law. They are also a sub-group of guardian deity/demons known as *srung-ma* and are related to the *chos-skyong*. See *srung-ma*. (RN-W)

skyobs-pa'i-spun-dgu -- (Tib.) They represent a group of nine *dgra-lha*-like deity/demons. (RN-W)

slob-dpon-brgyud-kyi-srung-ma -- (Tib.) They are deity-protectors of religious preceptors. They also are a sub-group of guardian deity/demons known as *srung-ma* and are related to the *chos-skyong*. See *srung-ma*. (RN-W)

sman -- (Tib.) They are an important class of deities.One of a class of thirty that are enumerated in the rNying-ma pa sect work *Thugs-rje'i-rnams-sprul-seng-chen-nor-bu-dgra-'dul-gyis-nor-bdud-bcom-pa'i-rnam-thar-mdor-bsdus-bzhugs-so*. Also, a *dregs-pa*, a general consideration of minor protective deities, many of which find their origin in the Bon pantheon. *sMan* deities are frequently consorts of the *lha* and are related to medicine (*sMan*) deities, 1) *sman-ma* -- a sister-hood of lake dwelling deities, 2) *sman-mo* -- goddesses who dwell in the sky. The "mistress" of the *aman-mo* is the goddess *Srid-pa-chags-byed-ma*, 3) *sman-btsun* -- an alternate name of *sman-mo* or a sub-class of *sman-mo*, 4) *gnam-sman* -- a sisterhood of deities who dwell in the. The leader of the *gnam-sman* is the goddess *Thog-gi-bu-yug*. They are of pre-Buddhist origin and some feel that they are a sub-division of the *sman-mo* class, 5) *mtsho-sman* -- *sman* who dwell in the lakes, the queens are *mTsho-sman-rgyal-mo-mkhro'i-gtso* and *mTsho-sman-ru-phyug-rgyal-mo*, consisting of four sub-groups: a) *'od-ldan-mtsho-sman* -- a sub-group of the *mtsho-sman*, b) *dregs-pa'i-mtsho-sman* -- a sub-group of the *mtsho-sman*, c) *pho-nya'i-mtsho-sman* -- a sub-group of the *mtsho-sman*, as well as, d) *las-byed-mtsho-sman* -- a sub-group of the *mtsho-sman*; 6) *rtse-sman* -- an earth dwelling *sman*, 7) *sman-phran* -- The "mistress" of the *sman-phran* is the goddess *sMan-phran-'bum-gyi-gtso-mo*, 8) *klu-sman* -- *sman* who are the product of the union with a *klu*. The "mistress" of the *klu-sman* is the goddess *mDzes-ma'i-'od-phro-ma*, 9) *phyva-sman* -- similar to the *klu-sman*. They are products of a union between the little known class of *phyva* deities and the *sman*, and 10) *rma-sman* -- consorts of the *rma-rigs* who number 100,000. (RN-W)

sman-btsun -- (Tib.) They represent a sub-class of deity/demons known as the *sman*, ancient Tibetan minor goddesses. See *sman*. (RN-W)

sman-ma -- (Tib.) They represent a sub-class of deity/demons known as the *sman*, ancient Tibetan minor goddesses. See *sman*. (RN-W)

sman-mo -- (Tib.) They represent a sub-class of deity/demons known as the *sman*, ancient Tibetan minor goddesses. See *sman*. (RN-W)

sman-phran -- (Tib.) They represent a sub-class of deity/demons known as the *sman*, ancient Tibetan minor goddesses. See *sman*. (RN-W)

sme-ba -- (Tib.) They are a group of deity/demons who are associated with the *spar-sme-tshe-lha-sum-brgya-drug-bcu*. (RN-W)

snags-bdag-ging-chen-bco-brgyad -- (Tib.) They represent a sub-class of deity/demons known as the *ging*, ancient Tibetan minor deities. See *ging*. (RN-W)

snang-srid-sde-brgyad -- (Tib.) They represent a sub-class of deity/demons known as the *dregs-pa*, ancient Tibetan minor deities. See *dregs-pa*. (RN-W)

sngags-bdag -- (Tib.) They are a group of eighteen deities noted by Nebesky-Wojkowitz. (RN-W)

sngags-bdag-bco-brgyad -- (Tib.) They are a group of deities related to the *sngags-srung*. They are known as the "guardian of the Mantras." (RN-W)

sngags-bdag-dregs-chen-bco-brgyad -- (Tib.) They are a group of deities related to the *sngags-srung*. They are known as the "guardian of the Mantras." (RN-W)
273

sngags-bdag-ging-chen-bco-brgyad -- (Tib.) They represent a sub-class of deity/demons known as the *ging*, ancient Tibetan minor deities. See *ging*. (RN-W)

sngags-srung -- (Tib.) They are a class of deity/demons known as "Guardian of Mantras." The leader of the *sngags-srung* is the goddess *Ekajati* or *Ma-mo-sngags-kyi-srung-ma*. They are purely Buddhist in source. They are related to the *sngags-bdag-bco-brgyad* ("the eighteen masters of the Mantras"). One of a class of thirty that are enumerated in the rNying-ma pa sect work *Thugs-rje'i-rnams-sprul-seng-chen-nor-bu-dgra-'dul-gyis-nor-bdud-bcom-pa'i-rnam-thar-mdor-bsdus-bzhugs-so*. Also, a *dregs-pa*, a general consideration of minor protective deities, many of which find their origin in the Bon pantheon. There are noted two sub-groups: 1) *sngags-bdag-bco-brgyad* -- "the eighteen masters of the mantra" and 2) *sngags-bdag-dregs-chen-bco-brgyad* -- guardian of mantras. (RN-W)

spar-kha -- (Tib.) They are a class of deity/demons who are associated with the *spar-sme-tshe-lha-sum-brgya-drug-bcu*. (RN-W)

spar-sme-tshe-lha-sum-brgya-drug-bcu -- (Tib.) They are a group of 360 *dgra-lha*-like deities who are associated with the *sme-ba* and *spar-kha*. (RN-W)

sprin-gnyan -- (Tib.) They represent a sub-class of yellow, fierce deity/demons known as the *gnyan*, and noted in rNying-ma-pa sect writings. See *gnyan*. (RN-W)

sprul-pa-sde-brgyad -- (Tib.) They represent a sub-class of deity/demons known as the *dregs-pa*, ancient Tibetan minor deities. See *dregs-pa*. (RN-W)

spyang-zhon-lha-mo-mched-gsum -- (Tib.) They are a class of three deity/demonesses who ride on wolves and are *dgra-lha*-like in character. (RN-W)

spyan-rnon-sum-brgya-drug-bcu -- (Tib.) They represent a group of 360 *dgra-lha*-like deities who are known as "the three hundred sixty sharp eyed ones." (RN-W)

sra-btsan -- (Tib.) They represent an important sub-class of deity/demons known as the *btsan*, ancient Tibetan demons. See *btsan*. (RN-W)

sri -- (Tib.) They are a class of deity/demons who orginated from 13 eggs. There are noted thirteen sub-groups: 1) *bdud-sri-nag-po* -- black; reside in the mountains of the *bdud*; human bodies with kyung head, 2) *btsan-sri-dmar-po* -- reside in the mountains of the *btsan*, human bodies with owl head; human bodies and pig head, 3) *byes-sri* -- reside on the peaks of nine mountains; human bodies with horse head, 4) *chung-sri* -- reside under beds; human bodies with weasel head, 5) *dam-sri* -- nine black deities who reside in meditation locales and where three valleys meet, 6) *dgra-sri-dar-ma* -- reside on enemy borders; human bodies with yak head, 7) *gri-sri-ngan-pa* -- reside in weapon points; human bodies with stag head, 8) *klu-sri-sngon-po* -- blue; reside in the ocean; human bodies with snake head, 9) *mo-sri* -- reside in the ocean; human bodies with camel head, 10) *pho-sri* -- reside in mountain peaks; human bodies with wolf head, 11) *rgan-sri* -- reside in the bodies of relatives; human bodies with fox head, 12) *rgyal-srid-dkar-po* -- white; reside in temples; human bodies with pig head, and 13) *god-sri* -- reside in caves; human bodies with goats head. (RN-W)

sri -- (Tib.) They are a class of deity/demons who, unlike those born of eggs, but are bringers of woes. There are thirty-four noted sub-groups: 1) *bgegs-sri* -- obstacle *sri*, 2) *byad-sri* -- wicked *sri*, 3) *che-sri* -- *sri* who attack adults, 4) *'chi-sri* -- death *sri*, 5) *chu-sri* -- water *sri*, 6) *dar-ma'i-sri* -- *sri* of manhood, 7) *dgos-sri* -- desire *sri*, 8) *dus-sri* -- sixty time *sri*, 9) *god-sri* -- *sri* of being, 10) *gnam-sri* -- sky *sri*, 11) *gnod-sri* -- injury *sri*, 12) *gzhon-sri* -- youth *sri*, 13) *keg-sri* -- harm *sri*, 14) *lceb-sri* -- suicide *sri*, 15) *lha-sri* -- *sri* of hatred, 16) *lo-sri* -- year *sri*, 17) *ma-nges-dgu-shor* -- heretic women, 18) *me-sri* -- fire *sri*, 19) *med-sri* -- *sri* of not being, 20) *mo-sri* -- ugly, nude, wrinkled skin, 21) *mo-sri* -- black; reside in the ocean; human bodies with bitch head, 22) *nad-sri* -- illness *sri*, 23) *nye-sri* -- human bodies with scorpion head, 24) *pho-sri* -- iron gray; big bellied, 25) *rgyal-sri* -- white; human bodies with lion head, 26) *rta-sri* -- horse *sri*, 27) *sa-sri* -- earth *sri*, 28) *sgo-sri* -- gate *sri*, 29) *ya-ma-dam-sri* -- men who broke their oaths, 30) *yar-pa'i-sri* -- adolescence *sri*, 31) *yo-ma-dam-sri* -- male *sri*, 32) *zhag-sri* -- thirty day *sri*, 33) *za-ma'i-sri* -- food *sri*, and 34) *zla-sri* -- twelve month *sri*. (RN-W)

srid-pa-chags-pa'i-lha-dgu -- (Tib.) They are a group of eight protective mountain deities who reign in relation to mountains from which they derive their name. (RN-W)

srid-pa'i-'dre-dgu -- (Tib.) They are a group of nine *dgra-lha*-like demon/deities. (RN-W)

srid-pa'i-lha-dgu -- (Tib.) They are a group of nine *dgra-lha*-like demon/deities. (RN-W)

sring-lcam-bzhi-bcu-zhe-lnga -- (Tib.) They are a group of forty-five *dgra-lha*-like demon/deities. (RN-W)

sring-mo -- (Tib.) They represent a sub-class of rock dwelling deity/demons known as the *srin-mo*, and noted in rNying-ma-pa sect writings. See *srin-mo*. (RN-W)

sring-mo-bzhi -- (Tib.)("four sisters") They represent a sub-class of rock dwelling deity/demons known as the *srin-mo*, and noted in rNying-ma-pa sect writings. Also a group of four deities who accompany *dPal-ldan-lha-mo*. They are: *lHa-i-sring-mo-byis-pa'i-dur-byed-ma*, *gShin-rje'i-sring-mo-mtshan-byed*, *kLu'i-sring-mo-rnam-byed* and *gNod-sbyin-sring-mo-rlung-byin*. (RN-W)

sring-mo-dmar-mo-bzhi -- (Tib.) A class of deity/demons known as the "four red sisters" who are found in the retinue of *Pe-har*. (RN-W)

srin-mo -- (Tib.)(Skt.: *raksasis*) They are pre-Buddhist goddesses who reside in the earth and rocks. The mistress of the *srin-mo* is the goddesss *Bal-mgo-khrag-mig*. They were subdued by *Padmasambhava* and lost their identity by being equated by the *raksasas* and *raksasis* of India. One of a class of thirty that are enumerated in the rNying-ma pa sect work *Thugs-rje'i-rnams-sprul-seng-chen-nor-bu-dgra-'dul-gyis-nor-bdud-bcom-pa'i-rnam-thar-mdor-bsdus-bzhugs-so*. Also, a *dregs-pa*, a general consideration of protective deities, many of which find their origin in the Bon pantheon. This class has four noted sub-groups: 1) *brag-srin* -- dwell in the earth and rocks, 2) *sa-srin* -- dwell in the earth and rocks, 3) *mtshon-srin* -- weapons *srin*, and 4) *sring-mo-bzhi* -- four goddesses who are in the retinue of *dPal-ldan-lha-mo*. (RN-W)

srin-po -- They reside in the Southwest. They are Pre-Buddhist deities who reside in the earth and rocks. The leader of the *srin-po* is *Raksa-glog-'phreng*. They were subdued by *Padmasambhava* and lost their identity by being equated by the *raksasas* and *raksasis* of India. One of a class of thirty that are enumerated in the rNying-ma pa sect work *Thugs-rje'i-rnams-sprul-seng-chen-nor-bu-dgra-'dul-gyis-nor-bdud-bcom-pa'i-rnam-thar-mdor-bsdus-bzhugs-so*. Also, a *dregs-pa*, a general consideration of protective deities, many of which find their origin in the Bon pantheon. (RN-W)

srog-bdag -- (Tib.: aka *srog-gi-bdag-po*)("master of life") The shorten form of the class, *srog-gi-bdag-po*. See *srog-gi-bdag-po*. (RN-W)

srog-gcod-kyi-gying-brgyad -- (Tib.: aka *srog-hgcod-kyi-gying-brgyad* or *gri-thogs-bshan-pa-brgyad*) An alternative spelling for *srog-hgcod-kyi-gying-brgyad*. See *srog-hgcod-kyi-gying-brgyad*. (RN-W)

srog-gi-bdag-po -- (Tib.: aka *srog-bdag*)("master of life") They represent a group of deity/demons who accompany *Pe-har*. The related sub-classes are: 1) *srog-gi-bdag-po-chen-po*, 2) *srog-gi-bdag-gi-dmag-dpon-gsum*.(RN-W)

srog-gi-bdag-po-chen-po -- (Tib.) They represent a sub-group of deity/demons *srog-gi-bdag-po* who accompany *Pe-har*. (RN-W)

srog-gi-bdag-gi-dmag-dpon-gsum -- (Tib.) They represent a sub-group of deity/demons *srog-gi-bdag-po* who accompany *Pe-har*. (RN-W)

srog-hgcod-kyi-gying-brgyad -- (Tib.: aka *srog-gcod-kyi-gying-brgyad*)("the eight life-cutting *gying*") They represent a sub-class of deity/demons known as the *gying*, ancient Tibetan minor deities. See *gying*. (RN-W)

srog-lha -- (Tib.) They represent a sub-class of minor deity/demons known as the *'go-ba'i-lha-lnga*, and noted in rNying-ma-pa sect writings. See *'go-ba'i-lha-lnga*. (RN-W)

srog-'phrog -- (Tib.: *bran-g.yog-mched-bzhi*) A group of deities related to dpal-ldan-lha-mo. They include: *dDud-mo-remati*, *Nad-kyi-bdag-mo*, *sKye-mthing-ma* and *Khri-sman-sa-le-ma*. (RN-W)

srung-ma -- (Tib.) They represent a group of

deities known as "guardians" which refers to *chos-skyong;* see also *'jig-rten-las-'das-pa'i-srung-ma* who are powerful, high-ranking deities, 1) *bstan-srung-ma* -- "guardians of the Buddhist doctrine" and refers to *chos-skyong,* 2) *dkar-phyogs-skyong-ba'i-srung-ma* -- "guardians protecting the white quarter," the collective name for the *'jig-rten-las-'das-pa'i-srung-ma* and the *'jig-rten-pa'i-srung-ma;* in opposition to the *bdud* class *nags-phyogs-gi-bdud,* 3) *gnas-srung* -- "border guardians," 4) *'jig-rten-las-'das-pa'i-srung-ma* -- "gods and goddesses who have passed beyond the six spheres of existence," one of two main groups of powerful, high ranking deities (deities of the eighth and ninth rank), 5) *'jig-rten-pa'i-srung-ma* -- reside in animated spheres, they are fierce, take active part in religious life and are sometimes called *dregs-pa* ("haughty ones"), 6) *mtshams-(gyi)-srung-(ma)* -- "border guardians," 7) *pha-mes-(brgyud)-kyi-srung-ma* -- "ancestral protective deities," 8) *rigs-'dzin-brgyud-kyi-srung-ma* -- guardian deities of Buddhist creed, 9) *skyes-bu-chen-po'i-srung-ma* -- "guardians of the great saints," high ranking protectors of religious law, and 10) *slob-dpon-brgyud-kyi-srung-ma* -- protectors of religious preceptors. (RN-W)

stag-po -- (Tib.) They are a group of deity/demons who are in the personal train of Pe-har and are described as "giants." (RN-W)

the-brang -- (Tib.: aka *the'u-rang*) A variant spelling of *the'u-rang*. See *the'u-rang.* (RN-W)

the'u-brang -- (Tib.: aka *the'u-rang*) A variant spelling of *the'u-rang*. See *the'u-rang.* (RN-W)

the'u-rang -- (Tib.: aka *the'u-brang, the-brang*) They are a class of deities who reside in the sphere in between or rocky caves. Their chief is *(sKyes-bu) gNam-the'u-dkar-po.* They are demons of an evil nature, cause quarrels and disunity as well as influence weather and bring hail-storms. They originated from the fat of a cosmic turtle. One of a class of thirty that are enumerated in the rNying-ma pa sect work *Thugs-rje'i-rnams-sprul-seng-chen-nor-bu-dgra-'dul-gyis-nor-bdud-bcom-pa'i-rnam-thar-mdor-bsdus-bzhugs-so.* Also, a *dregs-pa,* a general consideration of minor protective deities, many of which find their origin in the Bon pantheon. There are two noted sub-groups: 1) a group of three hundred and sixty, and 2) *the'u-rang-sgo-srung* -- eleven Gate Guards. (RN-W) **101,**

the'u-rang-sgo-srung -- (Tib.: aka *the'u-rang*) A variant spelling of *the'u-rang*. See *the'u-rang.* (RN-W)

thugs-dkar-sum-brgya-drug-bcu -- (Tib.) They are a group of 360 *dgra-lha*-like deity/demons. (RN-W)

thugs-kyi-rgyal-chen -- (Tib.: aka thugs-kyi-rgyal-po) The title sometimes given to the five chief deities of the *sku'i-rgyal-po.* (RN-W)

thugs-kyi-rgyal-po -- (Tib.: aka thugs-kyi-rgyal-chen) The title sometimes given to the five chief deities of the *sku'i-rgyal-po.* (RN-W)

t'ien -- (Chin.) The Chinese transliteral equivalent of the Sanskrit for deva. See *deva.* (RN-W)

t'ien-mu -- (Chin.) The Chinese transliteral equivalent of the Sanskrit for devi. See *devi.* (RN-W)

tirthika -- (Skt.) They are the Indian equivalent of *mu-stegs-pa.* (RN-W)

'tshams -- (Tib.: aka *mtshams*) They represent a class of deities noted in rNying-ma-pa sect writings. Their leader is *Ya-ba-mgo-dgu.* Also, a *dregs-pa,* a general consideration of minor protective deities, many of which find their origin in the Bon pantheon. (RN-W)

tshe-ring-mched-lnga -- (Tib.) They represent a class of five deity/demons who are known as the "Five Long Lived Sisters" who are in the train of *dPal-ldan-lha-mo.* (RN-W)

tshongs-dpon -- (Tib.) They represent a class of five deity/demons who are known as traders deities. (RN-W)

tshun -- (Tib.) They represent a sub-class of deity/demons known as the *mtshun,* ancient Tibetan minor deities. They are also known as *tshun, btsun* or *mes-btsun.* See *mtshun.* (RN-W)

upasaka -- (Skt) They are a group of minor mountain deity/demons. See *dge-bsnyen.* See *dge-bsnyen.* (RN-W)

vighna -- (Skt.: aka *bighna*) They are obstacle creating demons. See *bgegs.* (RN-W)

wer ma -- (Tib.) They represent a group of deities who are known as"the angry, ferocious and fearless ones." They are road deities and there are two noted sub-groups: 1) group of 180, and 2) group of 360. (RN-W)

ya-bdud -- (Tib.) They represent a sub-class of protective deity/demons known as the *bdud.* See *bdud.* (RN-W)

yaksas -- (Skt.)(Tib.: *gnod-sbyin*) They are a relatively important class of misshapen, dwarf-like, savage, male, forest dwelling deities. They feed on human flesh. See also *gnod-sbyin.* (RN-W)

yaksis -- (Skt.)(Tib.: *gnod-sbyin-mo*) They are a relatively important class of misshapen, dwarf-like, savage, female, forest dwelling deities. They feed on human flesh. See *gnod-spyin-mo.* (RN-W)

ya-ma-dam-sri -- (Tib.) They represent a sub-class of deity/demons known as the *sri,* ancient Tibetan minor deities who bring woes. See *sri.* (RN-W)

yar-pa'i-sri -- (Tib.) They represent a sub-class of deity/demons known as the *sri,* ancient Tibetan minor deities who bring woes. See *sri.* (RN-W)

yi-dam -- (Tib.) Personal protectors or tutelary deities chosen by individuals for personal guidance and protection. (BO)

yo-ma-dam-sri -- (Tib.) They represent a sub-class of deity/demons known as the *sri,* ancient Tibetan minor deities who bring woes. See *sri.* (RN-W)

yul-lha -- (Tib.)("country gods") They reside on the meadow mountain, they are considered as "country gods." Their leader is the deity *lHa-rabs-shams-po.* One of a class of thirty that are enumerated in the rNying-ma pa sect work *Thugs-rje'i-rnams-sprul-seng-chen-nor-bu-dgra-'dul-gyis-nor-bdud-bcom-pa'i-rnam-thar-mdor-bsdus-bzhugs-so.* Also, a *dregs-pa,* a general consideration of minor protective deities, many of which find their origin in the Bon pantheon (RN-W)

za-ma'i-sri -- (Tib.) They represent a sub-class of deity/demons known as the *sri,* ancient Tibetan minor deities who bring woes. See *sri.* (RN-W)

zhag-sri -- (Tib.) They represent a sub-class of deity/demons known as the *sri,* ancient Tibetan minor deities who bring woes. See *sri*. (RN-W)

zla-gnyan -- (Tib.) They represent a sub-class of yellow, fierce deity/demons known as the *gnyan*, and noted in rNying-ma-pa sect writings. See *gnyan*. (RN-W)

zla-sri -- (Tib.) They represent a sub-class of deity/demons known as the *sri*, ancient Tibetan minor deities who bring woes. See *sri*. (RN-W)

Appendix II

Vajrayana Orders/Schools

Vajrayana Orders[3] /Schools

bKa'-gdams-pa -- (Phon. Eng.: *Kadampa*) An order founded by Atisha and reformed by Tsong-kha-pa and associated with the Reting Monastery. It was a forerunner and absorbed into the *dGe-lugs-pas*. (AKG)

bKa'-brgyud-pa -- (Phon. Eng.: *Kagyupa*) One of the four prominent orders ("Four Great Waves of Buddhism") in Tibet, which along with the *Sas-kya-pa* order is one of the "middle orders." Frequently known as the "Red Hats." An order founded in the eleventh century by *Mar-pa*, one of the apostles was *Milarepa* followed by *Gampopa*. (GT, AKG, ML)

Bodong -- See: *Bo-dong-pa*. (ML)

Bo-dong-pa -- (Phon. Eng.: *Bodongpa*) A sub-order of the Samding Monastery. Founded by Bo-dong Pan-chen Phyogs-las-rnam-rgyal

Bu-lugs-pa -- (Phon. Eng.: *Bulukpa*) A sub-order of the Zhalu Monastery. An order founded by Bu-ston Rin-chen-grub-pa, also csalled *Zha-lu-pa*. (ML, GT)

Bupa -- See: *Bu-lugs-pa*. (ML)

Cho -- See: *gCod*.

dGe-lugs-pa -- (Phon. Eng.: *Gelukpa*) One of the four prominent orders ("Four Great Waves of Buddhism") in Tibet, the latest order. Founded in the fifteenth century by *Tsongkhapa* as a reformed *bKa'-gdams-pa* order, also known as the "Yellow Hats." Closely associted with the order is the Ganden Monsatery, founded by *Tsongkhapa*, it is the home of of the "official head" of the order known as the Ganden Tripa (not the Dalai Lama). (AKG, ML)

Dzokchenpa -- See: *rDzogs-chen-pa*.

gCod -- (Phon. Eng.: *Cho*)A school of meditation which evolved from the teachings of *Pha-dam-pa Sangs-rgyas* (GT)

Gelukpa -- See: *dGe-lugs-pa*.

Kadampa -- See: *bKa'-gdams-pa*.

Kagyupa -- See: *bKa'-brgyud-pa*.

Karmapa -- See: *Kar-ma-pa*.

Kar-ma-pa -- (Phon. Eng.: *Karmapa*) A sub-order of the *bKa'-brgyud-pa* order. Known as the "Black hats." (GT)

Kar-ma bKa'-brgyud-pa -- (Phon. Eng.: *Karma Kagyupa*) See: *Kar-ma-pa*. (ML)

Nyingmapa -- See: *rNying-ma-pa*.

Padampa -- See: *Pha-dam-pa*.

Pha-dam-pa -- (Phon. Eng.: *Padampa*) A tantric school founded by Pha-dam-pa. (BO)

Phag-mo-gru-pa -- (Phon. Eng.: *Phakmo-trupa*) A sub-order of the *bKa'-brgyud-pa* order. (GT)

Phakmotrupa -- See: *Phag-mo-gru-pa*.

rDzogs-chen-pa -- (Phon. Eng.: *Dzokchenpa*) A tantric tradition which is allied with the rNying-ma-pa tradition. (GT, RN-W)

rNying-ma-pa -- (Phon. Eng.: *Nyingmapa*) One of the four prominent orders ("Four Great Waves of Buddhism") in Tibet. The most ancient order, founded by *Padmasambhava* in the eighth century. It is associated with the red hats and owes some of its importance to the Fifth Dalai Lama who also considered himself a *rNying-ma-pa*. (AKG, RT)

Sakyapa -- See: *Sa-skya-pa*.

Sa-skya-pa -- (Phon. Eng.: *Sakyapa*) One of the four prominent orders ("Four Great Waves of Buddhism") in Tibet, which along with the *bKa'-brgyud-pa* order is one of the "middle orders." An order founded by Kunga Nyingpo and Sakya Pandita in the eleventh century. The Sakya Monastery is the center of the order. (BO)

Shalupa -- See: *Zha-lu-pa*.

Shichepa -- See: *Zhi-byed-pa*.

Zha-lu-pa -- (Phon. Eng.: *Shalupa*) A Buddhist school. (GT)

Zhi-byed-pa -- (Phon. Eng.: *Shichepa*)A school which evolved from the teachings of *Pha-dam-pa Sangs-rgyas*. See also *Bu-lugs-pa*. (BO, GT)

---

[3] The term "order(s)" is used here, rather than the more popular term "sect." Since, as Robert Thurman states "'sect' is a term derived from the history of Protesytantism, and implies . . . major doctrinal or institutional divergence from an established religion. . . ." The orders of Buddhism in Tibet all upheld the tenants of the Triple Jewels (Buddha, Dharma, Community) and the Triple Vehicles.

Appendix III

Tibetan Alphabets

Tibetan Alphabet

The Tibetan aplhabet(s) as shown below are those utilized by Clark and Nebesky-Wojkowitz, and those that appear within this compilation. For a complete alaphabet refer to Sarat Chandra Das' *A Tibetan-English Dictionary.*

Ka -- **(WEC, RN-W)**
bKa
bsKa
dKa
rKa
sKa

Kha -- **(WEC, RN-W)**
hKha
mKha

Ga -- **(WEC, RN-W)**
brGa
dGa
hGa
mGa
nGa
rGa
sGa
snGa

Nga -- **(WEC, RN-W)**
lNga
mNga
rNga
sNga

Ca -- **(WEC, RN-W)**
bCa
gCa
lCa

Cha -- **(WEC, RN-W)**
gCha
hCha
mCha

Ja -- **(WEC, RN-W)**
hJa
lJa
rJa

Nya -- **(WEC)**
Ni(y)a **(RN-W)**
bsNya
bsNi(y)a
gNya
gNi(y)a
rNya
rNi(y)a
sNya
sNi(y)a

Ta -- **(WEC, RN-W)**
brTa
bsTa
gTa
lTa
rTa
sTa

Tha -- **(WEC, RN-W)**
mTha

Da -- **(WEC, RN-W)**
bDa
bsDa
gDa
hDa
mDa
rDa
sDa

Na -- **(WEC, RN-W)**
gNa
mNa
rNa
sNa

Pa -- **(WEC, RN-W)**
dPa
lPa
sPa

Pha -- **(WEC, RN-W)**
hPha

Ba -- **(WEC, RN-W)**
dBa
hBa
sBa

Ma -- **(WEC, RN-W)**
dMa
rMa
sMa

Tsa -- **(RN-W)**
C(h)a-- **(WEC)**
bTsa
bC(h)a
gTsa
gC(h)a
hTsa
hC(h)a
mTsa
mC(h)a

rTsa
rC(h)a

Tsha -- (RN-W)
mTsha

Dza -- (RN-W)
hDza
mDza
rDza

Za -- (WEC, RN-W)
bZa
gZa

Zha -- (RN-W)
bZha
gZha

hO -- (WEC)
'O -- (RN-W)

Ya -- (WEC, RN-W)
gYa

Ra -- (WEC, RN-W)

La -- (WEC, RN-W)

Sha -- (RN-W)
S(h)a -- (WEC)
bSha
bSa
gSha
gSa

Ha -- (WEC, RN-W)
lHa

U -- (WEC, RN-W)

A -- (WEC, RN-W)

Deity List

Deity List

Below is the list of deities that appear within this compilation--i.e., the deity entries, pages 1-636. Not all of the below appear within the Deity Identification Charts.

- A -

Abhasarasmi (?)
Abhasavara(?)-Tathagata Buddha
Abhayamdada
Abheda
Abhijna-krama-Rakta-Jambhala
Abhijnaraja
Abhimukha
Abhimukha Bodhisattva
Abhimukhi
Abhimukhi (fo-mu)
Abhyudgataraja Buddha
Abhyudgatosnisa(?) (Bodhisattva)
Abida
Abiday-a
Abinca
A-bse-rgyal-ba
Acala
Acala-Amitayus
Acala (fo-mu)
Acalaketu-Lokesvara
Acala-Vajrapani
Acarya-Vajrapani
Acata(?)-Lokesvara
Achala
A-ch'u
Acokottamasri
Adhimukticharya
Adhimuktivasita
Adi-Buddha
Adi-Dharma
Adi-kalayana Deities
Adi-Prajna
Aditya
Advaya
Aghora-Mahakala
Agni
Agni-bhayatrana-(Avalokitesvara)
Agni-bhayatrana-Tara
Agni (deva)
Agra(?)matirajatathagata Buddha
Agulas-un erketu qagan
Aizen
Ajapalipada
Ajaya
Ajinai cogtu
Ajita
Ajita Mahakala
Ajna-vinivarta-Ganapati
A-jo-dge-bsnyen-chen-po
Akarsani(?) (devi)
Akasa debel-tu
Akasa-Dhatu-Ishvari
Akasaganja
Akasagarbha
Akasagarbha-Lokesvara
Akasambara
Akasanetra (Bodhisattva)
Aksayamati
Aksayamati-Lokesvara
Aksobhya
Aksobhyavajra
Aksyajnankaranda
A-lag-gser-rtse-stag-ri
A-lieh-ka-ma hsi-mu
Aloka
Aloke
Alpacanda-Vajrapani
Amara-vajra-devi
A-me-ya
Amida
Amida Nyorai
Amindev-a
Amin-u ejen
Amitabha
Amitabha (Bodhisattva)
Amitabha-Lokesvara
Amitabha-Manjusri
Amita-parakrama(?)-(Tara)
Amitaprabha
Amitayuh
Amitayus
Amitayus (Buddha)
Amitayus Jina
A-mi-to
A-mi-to fo
Am-kri-mi-dmar
Am-nye-rma-chen
Amoga-pasa
Amoghadarsin (Bodhisattva)
Amoghadarsin Buddha

Amoghankusa-Avalokitesvara
Amoghapasa
Amoghapasa-isvara-(= Lokesvara)-Avalokitesvara (Bodhisattva)
Amoghapasa-Lokesvara (BB 185)
Amoghapujamani-Avalokitesvara
Amoghasiddhi
Amoghatrana(?)-Vajrapani
Amoghavikramin (Bodhisattva)
Amr(i)tabinduvajra
Amritadhara
Amritakundalin
Amritakundalinvajra
Amrta-kundali
Amrtakundali
Amrtaprabha-Lokesvara
Amtan-u vcir eke
A-nan
Ananda
Anandadi-Lokesvara
Anangavajra (Bodhisattva)
Anantajaya
Anantamukhi
Anantasvaraghosa
Anantaujas
Anantaujas Buddha
Angaja
Angaraka
Ang-chi-li-t'ien p'u-sa
Ang-chi-ta tsun-che
Anggiri
Anghan burhan
Anghora-Mahakala
Angirodeva
Aniruddha
Ankusadhara (yo-mu)
Ankusha
Ankusi (fo-mu)
Anoku Kwan-non
Antara-Sadhana-Dharmaraja
Antarasadhana-Manjughosa
Antara-sadhana-Yamaraja
Antara-sadhana-Zhan-blon-rdo-rje-Marajit
Anucara-Avalokitesvara
Anucara-Bhrkuti
Anucara-Buddha-daki
Anucara-Ekajata
Anucara-Karma-daki
Anucara-Karma-dakini
Anucara-Maitreya
Anucara-Manjusri
Anucara-Nagi-karmakari
Anucara-Nivarana-viskambhin
Anucara-Padma-daki
Anucara-Padma-dakini
Anucara-Rakta-Amoghapasa
Anucara-Rakta-Hayagriva
Anucara-Ratna-daki
Anucara-Ratna-dakini
Anucara-Sudhana-Kumara
Anucara-Tara
Anucara-Vajra-dakini
Anucara-Vajra-karmakari
Anucara-Varahi
Anucara-Yaksa-karmakari
Anucara-Yama-karmakari
Anucarin (?) Buddha
Apada-vimocani-Tara
Apalala-Nagaraja
Aparajita
Aparajita-Tara
Aparajita-yaksa
Apayajaha
A-pi-ta tsun-che
A-pi-t'e tsun-che
A-po-kun-sdud
Arapacana
Arapacana-Manjughosa
Arban nigen nigur-tu Qomsim bodhi-satuva
Archismati
Ardhacaturth-aksara-Avalokitesvara
Arhat
Ariabalo
Arnadavan
Arslan kolgetu
Arslan terigutu
Arthadarsin Buddha
Artha-Pratisamvita
Artha-Pratisamvit
Arthasadhana-Varahi
Arya-Atisa
Arya-(Atisa)-krama-Caturbhuja-Sita-Ganapati
Arya-(Atisa)-krama-Caturdakini-parivara-Hayagriva
Arya-(Atisa)-krama-Garudapaksavat-Hayagriva
Arya-(Atisa)-krama-Mahadeva-srijvala-Mahakala
Arya-(Atisa)-krama-Pancatmaka-Sita-Jambhala
Arya-(Atisa)-krama-Sadaksara-

Avalokitesvara
Arya-(Atisa)-krama-Sahaja-Ekavira-Hayagriva
Arya-(Atisa)-krama-Simha-vahana-Traksad-Makahala
Arya (Atisa)-krama-Sita-Tara
Arya-Avalokitesvara
Arya-Cunda-Tara
Aryadeva
Aryadev-a
Arya-Janguli
Arya-Manjughosa
Arya-Marici
Arya-(Mula)-Syama-Tara
Arya-Namasangiti
Arya-Pala
Arya-Sarasvati
Arya-Sitatapatra
Arya-Tara
Aryavajravarahi
Aryavalokitesvara
Aryavalokitesvara-(Arya-Pala)
Asanga
Asary-a
A-shih-to tsun-che
Ashokashri
Ashokottamashri
A-shos
Ashtamangala-Devi
Ashuku
A-shuo-shih
A-shva
Asoka Buddha
Asokakanta
Asokakanta-Marici
Asokasri
Asokasri Buddha
Asokatathagata Buddha
Asokottamashri
Asta
Asta-bhaya-trana-Avalokitesvara
Asta-bhaya-trana-Tara
Astabhuja-Dharmadhatuvagisvara-Manjughosa
Astabhuja-Kurukulla
Astabhuja-Marici
Astabhujapita-Marici
Astabhuja-Tara
Astabhuja-Vajratara (fo-mu)
Astadasabhuja-Padmanartesvara
Astakapi-Acala
Astamahabhaya-Tara
Astami Tithi
Astatmaka-Panjara-Mahakala
Asuraloka
Asvajit
Asvapatis
Atavaka
Atisha
A-ti-sha Tsu-shih
Atisha-Hayagriva
A-tzu-ta tsun-che
Avaivartikacakrasambhavasri[?]
Avaivartikasrichakra Buddha
Avalokita
Avalokita-Lokesvara
Avalokitesvara
A-wa-glang-mgo
A-wa-niu-t'ou yo-chu
A-wo-dge-mjo
Ayuhsadhana-Sita-Samvara
Ayuqu metu ma-ha-kala
Ayurdhara-Sita-Vaisravana
Ayur-vardhana-Sita-Caturmukha-(Sri-Mahakala)
Ayur-vardhana-Sita-Vaisravana
Ayurvashi-Devi
Ayur-Vasita
Ayushpati-Mahakala
Ayusi
Ayuspati-Mahakala
Ayuspati-Syama-Mahakala

- B -

Babhru-nila-Hayagriva
Ba-dan-ser-po-can
Badidar-a
Badm-a
Badm-a singq-a muka
Badr-a
Bagali-budr-a
Bagatur-un ayimag
Bahubhuja-Cunda (devi)
Bahya-Sadhana-Dharmaraja
Bahya-Sadhana-Yamaraja
Bahya-Sadhana-Zhan-blon-rdo-rje-Marajit
Baishajyaguru-Vaiduryaprabharaja
Bajar bidarana
Bajar-binayaga

Bajar-biriv-a
Bajar-dakini
Bajar eke locani
Bajar garudi
Bajar-gunragm-a
Bajarpani
Bajar-ruda
Bajar-satuva
Bajar singq-a muka
Bajar varahi
Bajar yamubala
Bakkula
Bakula
Ba-ku-la
'Ba-la-ba
Balaparamita
Bal-yul-gangs
Bal-yul-gser-phug
Bam-srin-dred-kyi-gdong-can
Banabas
Bandaga
Bang-lha
Bang-rim-gsum-gyi-ma-mo
Ba-ra-dhva-za-bsod-snoms-len
Ba-ra-dhva-za-gser-can
'Bar-ba-spun-bdun
Bar-gyi-khyab-'jug-rahu'i-rtsis
Ba-ri-lugs-Amitayus
Ba-ri-lugs-Pacatmaka-Amoghapasa
Bari-lugs-Sita-Tara
Bar-lha-sogs-ra
'Bar-ma
'Bar-ma-dbang-ldan-bdud-'dul-ma
'Bar-ma-glog-'phreng-ma
'Bar-ma-gnod-sbyin-ba-glang-sna
'Bar-ma-gnod-sbyin-khyung-hogs
'Bar-ma-gshin-rje-skar-mda'-gdong
'Bar-ma-khyer-glog-'phreng-ma
'Bar-ma-klu-mo-lce-'bebs-ma
'Bar-ma-nyi-zhags-thogs-ma
'Bar-ma-rlung-bdag
'Bar-ma-rlung-stag-gru-'dzin-ma
'Bar-ma-srin-mo-mdung-'phen-ma
Bar-snang-brgya-byin-khra-bo
Bar-snang-gi-'gong-po
Bars terigutu
Bars terigutu eke
Bar-thel-khra-bo
Bar-the(l)-khra-ba
Bar-thil-khra-bo
Bar-yul-gangs
Basa buruga
Ba-to Kwan-non
Bayasqulang cog-tu
Bayildugan-i masids darugci
Bal-yul-gangs
bCom-ldan-reg-chig
bCon-kha-pa
bCon-kha-pa-chen-po
bCud-ldan-zas-kyi-bdag
bCu-gcig-zhal
bCu-gcig-zhal-hjigs-pa-brgyad-skyobs
bDag-med
bDe-ba-sbyin-pahi-sGrol-ma
bDe-bskyed-mkha'-gro-ma
bDe-chen-grags-pa
bDe-chen-mKhah-la-spyod-pahi-yum
bDe-'gro-gsang-yum
bDe-gryas-byed-ma
bDe-gsegs-Tshe-dan-ye-ses-dpag-med-mgon
bDe-gShegs-So-lNga
bDe-mchog
bDe-mchog-dkar-po
bDe-mchog-dkar-po-tshe-sgrub
bDe-mchog-khro-bo-rig-tshig
bDe-mchog-lhan-skyes
bDe-mchogs-mkhah-lden
bDe-mchog-phyag-gnis
bDe-mchog-rdo-rje-mkhah-ldin
bDe-mchog-rdor-sems
bDe-mchog-rdor-sems-dpah
bDe-rgyas-byed-ma
bDe-sgrub-ma
bDud
bDud-btsan
bDud-btsan-dpa'-bo-hum-ri
bDud-gin
bDud-gza'-mig-dkar
bDud-gza'-smin-dkar-mo
bDud-kun-gtso-remadzu
bDud-kye-dge-bsnyen
bDud-kyi-dmag-dpon
bDud-kyi-rgyal-po
bDud-kyi-rgyal-po-A-po-kun-sdud
bDud-kyi-rgyal-po-bSe'i-skyes-by-shogs(?)-can-sdud
bDud-kyi-rgyal-po-bTsan-mgo-dmar-po
bDud-kyi-rgyal-po-Kha-stongs-me-'bar
bDud-kyi-rgyal-po-ma-rungs-pa
bDud-kyi-rgyal-po-Mi-nag-spres-mgo-can
bDud-kyi-rgyal-po-sPyi-phyir-phur-byed
bDud-kyi-rgyal-po-srog-gi-bdag

bDud-kyi-rgyal-po-sTag-mgo-can
bDud-kyi-rgyal-po-'Ug-mgo-can
bDud-ma-hal-khyi-ting-ting-ma
bDud-ma-rungs-pa-mon-bu-bhata
bDud-mchog-ma-nu-yaksa
bDud-mdung-khyim
bDud-mgon
bDud-mgon-bsam-pa-don-grub-pa
bDud-mgon-bya-rog-gdong-can
bDud-mgon-seng-gdong
bDud-mo-bkra-bzang-ma
bDud-mo-'bum-gyi-gtso-mo
bDud-mo-gshin-rje-lag-brgya-ma
bDud-mo-gshin-rje-mgo-dgu
bDud-mo-gshin-rje-mgo-dgu-ma
bDud-mo-gsod-byed-ma
bDud-mo-kha-'bar-ma
bDud-mo-me-yi-kha-rlangs
bDud-mo-nag-mo-khrag-'thung
bDud-mo-phung-khrol-ma
bDud-mo-ral-bsigs-pa
bDud-mo-remati
bDud-mo-re-ma-ti
bDud-mo-ri-ti-nag-mo
bDud-mo-rno-myur
bDud-mo-ro-langs-ma
bDud-mo-seng-gdong-ma
bDud-nag-rkang-gcig
bDud-pho-re-ti-'gong-yag
bDud-po-bye-ba-gung-ring
bDud-po-kha-mtshun-yaksa
bDud-po-ma-ru-rtse
bDud-po-rog-ti
bDud-po-sha-zan
bDud-po-skos-rje-brang-dkar
bDud-po-ze-ra-rva-skyes
bDud-rci-hkhyil-pa
bDud-rgyal-dpa'-bo-'phreng-can
bDud-rgyal-dpa'-bo-thod-phreng-can
bDud-ri-ti-'gong-nyag
bDud-rje-stong-bdud
bDud-rtsi-hkhyil-ba
bDud-rtsi-hkhyil-va
bDud-rtsi-'khyil-ba
bDud-rtsi-lus-can-ma
bDud-rtsi-spyan-ma
bDug-spos-kyi-khyung
bDug-spos-ma
bDun-po-raksa'i-mgo-g.yag
'Bebs-pa-mo
Be-con-nag-mo
Be-dkar
Beg-ce
Begce ma-ha-kala
Beg-tse
Beg-tse-can
Beg-tse-lcam-dral
Begtse-Mahakala
Beg-tse-mGon-po
Beng ma-ha-kala
Benten
Benzaiten
Be-rag-khyung-btsun
Be-ri-yi-mtsho-nag
Be'u-'byin-chu-yi-zhags-pa-can
'Be-yi-chab-bzhi-rdzong-'phrang
bGegs-'dul-ma
bGegs-rgyal-bina-yaka
Bhadra
Bhadrakara
Bhadra-nag-po
Bhadrapala
Bhadrasri
Bhadrasri Buddha
Bhadrasvaresvara(?)raja-Manjughosa
Bhagavad-Bhayanasana
Bhagavad-Mahakala
Bhagavan-Aksobhya
Bhagavan-Aksobhya-Vajrasattva
Bhagavan-Amitabha
Bhagavan-Amoghasiddhi
Bhagavan-Mahakala
Bhagavan-Ratnasambhava
Bhagavan-Vairocana
Bhagavan-Vajrasattva
Bhagavat-Mahakala
Bhagavat-Mahakala-bhratr-traya
Bhaiasjyaguru-Vaiduryaprabharaja
Bhairava
Bhairavavajra
Bhairavavajra Buddha
Bhairavi-(Tara)
Bhaisajyaguru
Bhaisajyagurutathagata Buddha
Bhaishajya-Devi
bHa-ra-dHva-dza-bSod-sNyoms-len
bHa-ra-dHva-dza-gSer-can
Bharali
Bhattaraka-Maitreya
Bhattarika-Kapala-Tara
Bhattarika-Kapalini(?)
Bhayada(?)-Mahakala

Bhayadavajra
Bhaya-nasana-Krodha-Samvara
Bhima
Bhimadarsana
Bhinnaklesa(?) Buddha
Bhodi-nar-i nomugadqagci vcir-a-bani
Bhramarasvara-Manjusri (Bodhisattva)
Bhrkuti
Bhrkuti (devi)
Bhrkuti (fo-mu)
Bhrkuti-Tara
Bhrngi
Bhumi
Bhumi-bajar eke
Bhumi-bala
Bhumipala (?)
Bhumivajra
Bhutadamara
Bhutadamara-Anuttara-Vajrapani
Bhutadamara-Vajrapani
Bhutadamara-Vajrapani (Buddha)
Bibasi
Bidali eke
Bidy-a-devi
Bigci ma-ha-kala
Biger
Bighna
Bigna-daka
Bigna-taka
Bi-har
Bi-har-dmar-po-dgra-lha-skyes-gcig
Bi-har-rgyal-po
Bijakundalin
Biji kundali
Bikstipatra
Bikuchi
Bilig baramid
Bilig-un cinadu kijaghar-a kuruksen
Bimacidiri
Binzuru sama
Birakca debel-tu eke
Birbapa
Birisa
Birubagsi
Birudaki
Bishamon
Bisman
Bisman tegri
Bisman tngri
Bi ugei eke
Biysirama

Bkah-gdams-Avalokitesvara
Bkah-gdams-lha-bzhihi-nan-gi-sgrol-ma
Bkah-gdams-lha-bzhihi-nan-gi-spyan-ras-gzigs
Bkah-gdams-lugs-Nila-(Candarosana)-Acala
Bkah-gdams-lugs-Pita-Garuda
Bkah-gdams-Tara
bKa'i-bya-ra-ba
bKa'-nyan-btsan-rgod-gter-gyi-bdag
bKa'-nyan-mthu-bo-che
bKa'-rgyud-pa'i-grub-dbang-chen-po
bKa'-rgyud-pa'i-mgon-po-ber-nag-can
bKa'-rgyud-pa'i-rgyal-po-grub-dbang-chen-po
bKa'-sdod-ma
bKa'-srung-brag-lha-mgon-po
bKa'-srung-chen-mo-rdo-rje-khro-gdong-ma
bKa'-srung-lha-mo-rdo-rje-chen-mo
bKra-bzang-ma
bKra-bzang-zhing-skyong
bKra-shis-dpa'-gyi-rtsal
bKra-shis-gzi-'od-'bar
bKra-shis-lha-brag-dkar-po
bKra-shis-lHa-mo-brGyad
bKra-shis-mgon-chen
bKra-shis-'od-'bar
bKra-shis-tshe-ring-ma
bKra-shis-tshe-yi-lha-mo-lnga
bKras-sis-che-rin-ma
bKra-sis-don-byed
bKra-sis-skye-bahi-sGrol-ma
bKra-sis-snan-bahi-sgrol-ma
bKra-sis-tshe-rin-ma
bLa-med-phyag-rdor-hbyun-po-hdul-byed
bLo-bzang-Chos-rgyan
bLo-bzang-Don-grub
bLo-bzang-Grags-pa
bLo-bzang-rGya-mTsho
bLo-bzang-sKal-bzang
bLo-bzang-Ye-shes
bLo-bzan-ma
bLo-ldan-mchog-sred
Boa-shi-Ssan-ddo
Bodhisattva
Bod-skyong-brtan-ma'i-gtso-mo-g.Yu-yi-sgron
Bon bamo
Bon-'jang-brag-(dang)-stag-lung-ri
Bon-kun-tu-bzang-po
Bon-ri-mgo-dgu
Bo-satsu
Brag-btsan
Brag-btsan-chen-po-A-shva

Brag-btsan-dmar-po
Brag-btsan-dmar-po-stong-gi-rje
Brag-btsan-srog-zan
Brag-btsan-srog-zan-dmar-po
Brag-btsan-stong-sde-rje
Brag-dkar-Brag-nag
Brag-dkar-bya-rgod
Brag-dkar-rygal-po
Brag-dmar-btsan
Brag-dmar-gnam-skas-lcags-phur-can
Brag-dmar-ri-mo-ldang-lha-brag
Brag-lha-btsan-po-gdug-pa-'dul
Brag-lHa-mGon-po
Brag-nag-btsan-rgod
Brag-'phen-'od-bzang-lag-dgu
Brahma
Brahma Buddha
Brahmadanda-Lokesvara
Brahmadatta
Brahmadatta Buddha
Brahma (deva)
Brahma-Indra
Brahmajyotirvikriditabhijna
Brahmajyotirvikriditabhijna Buddha
Brahmajyotis Buddha
Brahman
Brahmana-Rupa-Mahakala
Brahmana-Rupadhara-Mahakal
Brahmana-sridhara-krama-Vajravahari
Brahman Buddha
Brahman (deva)
Bram-ze-Dpal-hdzin-lugs-kyi-rdo-rje
Bram-zehi
Bran-bdud-(dasa-mara?)-Krsna-Yama
Bran-bdud-gshin-rje-nag-po
Bran-bdud-gsin-rje-nag-po
Bran-kha-dpal
Bre-nag-sde-lnga
brGya-byin
brGya-byin-dkar-po
brGya-byin-sras-mo-gnam-mtsho
Brhaspati
Bril-phrom-rdo-rje-g.yu-drung
Brin-gyi-bkra-shis-tshe-ring
'Brog-bza'-lha-lcam-ma
'Brog-chen-rdo-rje-bgegs-gtso
'Brog-gnas
'Brog-gnas-kyi-sde-dpon-chen-po-gnyan-rje-sNgo-la-g.yu-rtse
'Brog-gnas-lha-yi-dge-bsnyen
'Brog-gnas-rma-rgyal-spom-che
'Brog-gnyan-'phya-ba
'Brog-srin-chu-srin-gyi-gdong-can
Brong-rdza-gangs
brTan-ma-bcu-gnyis
brTan-ma-dril-dkar
'Brug-gang?-seng-gsum
'Brug-rgyal-ma
bSe-bdud-ngu-ru-keng
bSe-bdud-ngu-ru-ki
bSe'i-khrab-can
bSe'i-skyes-by-shogs(?)-can-sdud
bSe-khrab
bSe-khrab-can
bSe-mi-'brong-ri-smug-pa
bSe-rag-rgyal-po-gzhon-nu-dpal
bSes-gnen-bzan
bSe-te-re
bShan-pa
bShan-pa-glang-mgo-can
bShan-pa-mi-zan
bSil-bahi-chal
bSil-bahi-tshal-chen-mo
bsKal-pa-bzang-po
bSod-byed-nag-mo
bSod-nams-mchog-ster-ma
bSre(r)-rag-rgyal-po-gzhon-nu-dpal
bsTan-bsrung-mdzad-gnod-sbyin-mched-lnga
bsTan-ma-bcu-gnis
bsTan-ma-bcu-gnyis
(bsTan-srun-chen-po-ye-ses)-mgon-po-phyag-bzhi-pa-klu-sgrub-lugs
bsTan-srung-chen-po-ye-shes-mgon-po-phyag-bzhi-pa-Klu-sgrub-lugs
bsTan-srung-grib-rDo-rje-shog-rgod-rtsal
bsTan-srung-kun-gyi-sde-dpon-rdo-rje-gur
bsTan-srun-gtso-mo-dmag-zor-lha
bsTan-srun-kun-gtso-rDo-rje-gur
bsTan-srung-rdzong-btsan-pa
bsTan-srung-rgyal-chen-shel-khrab
bSve-skyes-bu-ra-'jigs-pa
bTsan-bsod-nams-'od-'bar
bTsan-chen-jag-pa-me-len
bTsan-dmar-chen-po
bTsan-'gong-dmar-po
bTsan-'gong-mi-ring-dmar-po
bTsan-gyi-dge-bsnyen
bTsan-gyi-dmag-dpon
bTsan-la-ra-mo-sman-gcig-ma
bTsan-la-rol-pa'i-sman-gcig-ma
bTsan-mchog-gri-btsan-'thu-bo
bTsan-mda'-ra-ba

bsTan-mgo-dmar-po
bTsan-mgon-bya-rog-gdong-can
bTsan-po-khrab-kyi-dgra-lha
bTsan-po-phung-kha-nag-po
bTsan-po-yam-shud-srog-len
bTsan-rgod
bTsan-rgod-'bar-ba
bTsan-rgod-Bya-'ug-pa
bTsan-rgod-dmag-dpon-'bar-ba
bTsan-rgod-lCags-skud-dmar-po
bTsan-rgod-legs-pa-don-grub
bTsan-rgod-pa-don-grub
bTsan-rgod-Phun-tshogs-bkra-shis
bTsan-rgod-rdo-rje
bTsan-rgod-rDo-rje-'bar-ba
bTsan-rgod-Thog-lha-me-'bar
bTsan-rgod-zangs-ri-spun-bdun
bTsan-rgyal-lCags-skud-dmar-po
bTsan-rgyal-yam-shud-dmar-po
bTsan-shar-dregs-pa
bTsan-sha-za-khrag-'thung
bTsan-zangs-ri-'khyil-pa
bTsan-zho-khyung-gi-grib-btsan
bTsun-chung-me-tog-pa
bTsun-mo-dpe-'phreng-ma
bTsun-mo-mang-dge-dmar-mo
bTsun-mo-uma-devi
bTsun-mo-zangs-kyi-phreng-ba-can
Buddha
Buddhabodhi
Buddhabodhiprabhavasita
Buddhadaka (Buddha)
Buddha-Dakini
Buddha-Garuda
Buddha garudi
Buddha-Heruka
Buddha-Kapala
Buddha-Kila
Buddha-krodha
Buddha-Krotishaurima
Bud-dha-Kro-ti-shva-ri-ma
Buddha-Locana
Buddha-Locana (fo-mu)
Buddhapalita
Buddha-ruda
Buddhashakti
Buddhosnisa (Bodhisattva)
Budha
Budha (deva)
Bugr-a-kala
Bu-gzugs-bzang-ma

Bujig-ci eke
Bumi-bajar-eke
Buridugsen
Burin gerel-tu
Burin-i oggugci
Burnavasu
Burqan
Bu-ston-lugs-dpal-mgon-beng-dmar
Butcho
Butsu
Bu-xian
Bya-khra-sngon-mi
Bya-khri-mig-gcig-ma
Bya-khri-mig-gcig-po
Byakusangai
Byaku-i Kwan-non
Bya-ma-bye-ri
Byams-pa
'Byams-pa-khrag-mgo
Byams-pa-phyag-bzhi-pa
Byams-pa-phyag-gnis-pa
Byan-chub-rdo-rje-sems-dpah
Byan-chub-sems-dpah-Sa-yi-snin
Byang-bdud-chen-po
Byang-'brog-'khor-'dul-ma
Byang-chub-sems-dpa'
Byang-gi-gangs-dkar
Byang-gi-gnam-mtsho-phyug-mo
Byang-gi-gnyan-chen-thang-lha
Byang-gi-ma-ting-ting-mo-btsan
Byang-gi-sman-btsun-de-mo-btsun
Byang-gi-ting-ting-ting-mo-shag
Byang-phyug-ma-mo
Byang-stod-dmar-gyi-mtsho-bdag
Byan-Las-kyi-mkhah-hgro-ma
Bya-nyal-go-ra-gnam-gyi-ri
Bya-rgod-kyi-gdong-pa-can
Bya-rgod-sprung-ri
Bya-rgod-spungs-po'i-ri-bo'i-sa-bdag
Bya-rgod-thang-nag
Bya-rog-gdong-pa
Bya-ru
Bya-'ug-brag-btsan
Bya-'ug-pa
Bye-ba-gung-ring
Bye-ba-rkang-ring
Byi-lam-sngon-mo
Byi-na-ya-ga
Byin-chung-phyug-po
Byi-nu-raja
Byis-pa-'khar-dbyug-thog-pa

'Byung-ba-chags-pa'i-dgra-lha
bZang-po
bZan-po
bZe-yi-ma-mo-mched-gsum
bZhad-ma
bZhag-ra-lha-rtse

- C -

Cagan acala
Cagan cakr-a-sambar-a
Cagan car-a
Cagan dar-a eke
Cagan erlig qagan
Cagan ganapati
Cagan jambhala
Cagan ma-ha-kala
Cagan manjusri
Cagan naran saran
Cagan sikurtei
Cagan usun tngri
Cagan varaki
Caghan sigurtei
Caghlasi ugei gereltu
Caghlasi ugei nasutu
Cagh-un kurde
Cag-un salmaci
Cakra
Cakr-a-sambar-a
Camarimukha-Traksad-Makahala
Camunda (devi)
Camundi
Camundri
Candali
Candali-Dakini
Candali (fo-mu)
Canda-mukha-Caturmukha-(Sri-Mahakala)
Candanasri
Candanasri Buddha
Can-dan-dpal
Candarosana
Canda-Vajrapani-(chun)
Candesvari
Candika-Devi
Candra
Candra (deva)
Candrakanti(?)-Gauri-Tara
Candrakanti(?)-Tara
Candrakanti(?)-Tara (fo-mu)
Candraketu Buddha
Candrakirti
Candraprabha
Candraprabha (Bodhisattva)
Candraprabha-Lokesvara
Candravairocana (Bodhisattva)
Canggi guscunm-a
Cangkya Rolpa Dorje
Cara bala
Caraka
Carali eke
Carcika
Carcika (fo-mu)
Caryatantra-Amitayus
Casang
Caturayudha-Atiguhya-Vaisravana
Caturbhuja
Caturbhuja-Acala
Caturbhuja-Acalavajra
Caturbhuja-Amitayus
Caturbhuja-Avalokitesvara
Caturbhuja-Avalokitesvara (Bodhisattva)
Caturbhuja-cintamanicakra-Tara (fo-mu)
Caturbhuja-cintamanirajni (fo-mu)
Caturbhuja-Cunda (devi)
Caturbhuja-Cunda (fo-mu)
Caturbhuja-Heruka
Caturbhuja-(jnana)-Mahakalanucara-Candika-Devi
Caturbhuja-Mahakala
Caturbhuja-Maitreya
Caturbhuja-Nagi-Remati
Caturbhuja-Namasamgiti-Manjughosa
Caturbhuja-Prajnaparamita (fo-mu)
Caturbhuja-rakta-Avalokitesvara (Bodhisattva)
Caturbhuja-rakta-Ganapati
Caturbhuja-rakta-Lokesvara
(Caturbhuja)-Sita-Amitayus
Caturbhuja-Sita-Sarasvati
Caturbhuja-Sri-Mahakala
Caturbhuja-Vayu (deva)
Caturmaharajas
Caturmukha-Karmayoga-Mahakala
Caturmukhastabhuja-Hayagrivavajra
Caturvimsatibhuja-Ekajata (devi)
Catuspada-Acala
Cauri (fo-mu)
Ceceg-un cogtu
Cenggel-un eke

Cerig-un okin tngri
Ces-rab-seng-ge
Ceti(?) (yo-mu)
Cha'a-chi-ni fo-mu
Chad-pahi-hjigs-skyobs
Chags-'khor-nyon-mongs-bdud
Chags-kyu-ma
Chags-pa-hjoms-pahi-sGrol-ma
Chakdor
Chakna Natsho Dorje
Chakna Rinchen
Chakradhara (?)
Chakradhararaja (Buddha)
Chakrapani
Chakrasamvara
Chakravartin
Champa
Cham Sing
Chamunda
Chamunda (devi)
Chana Dorje
Chandraprabha
Ch'ang-lu fo-mu
Ch'ang sheng-fo
Chan-hsiang Mi-lo fo
Chans-pa
Chans-pahi-hod-zer-rnam-par-rol-bas-mnon-par-mkhyen-pa
Chans-pas-byin
Chan-t'an-kung-te fo
Ch'an-ting-hsien-sheng-wang fo
Ch'an-ting Po-lo-mi-mu
Ch'ao-ting fo
Ch'a-sang
Chatrosnisa
Chattra
Chaturbhuja-Sitatara
Che-bdag-mgon-po
Che-dpag-med
Che-dpag-med-phyag-bzhi-pa
Che-mchog-yon-tan-lha-tshogs
Ch'eng-chiu fo
Ch'eng-chiu-i-ch'ieh Chiu-tu fo-mu
Ch'eng-hu Shou-ch'ih-chin-kang
Ch'eng-so Kuan-shih-yin
Chenrezik
Chenrezik Chak-tong Chen-tong
Chenrezik Chak-zhi-pa
Chen-shih-ming-tsun-ssu-pei Wen-shu
Chen-shih-ming Wen-shu p'u-sa
Chen-ta-lo (mahayaksasenapati)
Chen-ta-lo yao-ch'a-ta-chiang
Chen-tan Chiu-tu fo-mu
Che-zhes-gtsug-'chang-'od-'bar-ma
Che-zhes-gtsug-gi-'od-'chang-ma
Chia-chu-yen
Chia-li-chia tsun-che
Chia-lo-ts'a-pu tsu-shih
Chiang (?Feng)-yin Wen-shu p'u-sa
Chiang-lin yo-mu
Chia-no-chia-fa-ts'o tsun-che
Chia-no-chia-po-li-to-she tsun-che
Chiao-wan-shou-yin (fo-mu)
Chia-she
Chia-yeh
Chia-yeh fo
'Chi-bdag-'joms-pa
'Chi-bdag-las-btsan-bdud
Chichi gyalmo
Chi-chih p'u-sa
Ch'i-chu-wu-ch'u p'u-sa
Chieh-chen-shih-chu-mu
Chieh-chi fo
Chieh-fa-shih-mu
Chieh-i-shih-mu
Chieh-po-chia tsun-che
Chieh-shih-pan-ts'ai-mu
Chieh-t'o-tou-chan fo-mu
Chieh-yin-fo
Chieh-yin-san-t'u p'u-sa
Ch'ien-ts'ui-sui fo-mu
Chi-Guo
Ch'ih-ch'ien (fo-mu)
Ch'ih-chien Wei-lo-wa-chin-kang
Chih-ch'iu t'ien-mu hu-fa
Ch'ih-cho fo-mu
Ch'ih-cho yo-mu
Ch'ih-chu fo
Ch'ih-chui Wei-lo-wa-chin-kang
Ch'ih-chung Wei-lo-wa-chin-kang
Chih-ch'un t'ien-mu hu-fa
Ch'ih-hsiang fo-mu
Ch'ih-hsiang-mu
Ch'ih-hsiang-shui-mu
Chih-hsia t'ien-mu hu-fa
Chih-hsing-chin-kang fo-mu
Chih-hsing fo-mu
Ch'ih-hsu-mi-feng-wang p'u-sa
Ch'ih-hua fo-mu
Ch'ih-hua-mu
Chih-hui-k'ung-hsiang fo-mu
Chih-hui Po-lo-mi-mu

Chih-hui-ting p'u-sa
Ch'ih-jih fo-mu
Ch'ih-ka-pu-la Hsi-chin-kang
Ch'ih-kou fo-mu
Ch'ih-kou yo-mu
Ch'ih-kuan (fo-mu)
Ch'ih-kuo t'ien-wang
Ch'ih-lien-hua fo-mu
Ch'ih-lien-hua Wei-lo-wa-chin-kang
Ch'ih-liu-hsing fo-mu
Ch'ih-lun-wang fo
Ch'ih-man fo-mu
Ch'ih-man-mu
Ch'ih-men fo-mu
Ch'ih-men-so fo-mu
Ch'i-hou Avalokitesvara (Bodhisattva)
Ch'i-hou-Isvara(= Lokesvara)-Avalokitesvara (Bodhisattva)
Ch'i-hou Kuan-shih-yin
Ch'i-hou Kuan-shih-yin p'u-sa
Ch'i-hou-tzu-tsai Kuan-shih-yin
Ch'i-hou tzu-tsai Kuan-shih-yin p'u-sa
Ch'ih-p'a Miao-yin fo-mu
Ch'ih-pang Wei-lo-wa-chin-kang
Ch'ih-pang yo-mu
Ch'ih-pang Yung-pao hu-fa
Ch'ih-ping-ch'i Hsi-chin-kang fo
Ch'ih-p'i-p'a fo-mu
Ch'ih-shan-wang fo
Ch'ih-sheng fo-mu
Ch'ih-sheng yo-mu
Ch'ih-shuang-teng fo-mu
Chi-hsiang-ch'ang-shou t'ien-mu hu-fa
Ch'i-hsiang P'u-hsien p'u-sa
Chi-hsiang-yuan-man Chiu-tu fo-mu
Ch'ih-teng fo-mu
Ch'ih-teng mu
Ch'ih-tien fo-mu
Chih-tung t'ien-mu hu-fa
Ch'i-hu Yung-pao hu-fa
Ch'ih-wang fo-mu
Ch'ih Wei-lo-wa-chin-kang
Ch'ih-wei Po-lo-mi-mu
Ch'ih-yao-shih fo-mu
Ch'ih-ya yo-mu
Ch'ih-yuan-ku fo-mu
Chi-kuang
Chi-kuang-chi-hsiang-wang fo
Chi-kuang fo-mu
Ch'i-kuo
Chi-lieh-ti-ka t'ien
Chi-li-na
Chi-li-ssu-na-pa tsu-shih
Ch'i-lung-pai Pu-lu-chin-kang
'Chi-med-nye-pa'i-dbang-po
Ch'i-miao p'u-sa
Chin-cho-chin-kang
Ching-chin-chun fo
Ch'ing-ching fo
Ch'ing-ching-kuang-yu-hsi-shen-t'ung fo
Ch'ing-ching-shih fo
Ching-chin-hsi fo
Ching-chin Po-lo-mi-mu
Ch'ing Chiu-tu fo-mu
Ch'ing-hsiang-tzu-tsai Kuan-shih-yin
Ch'ing-hsiang tzu-tsai Kuan-shih-yin p'u-sa
Ch'ing-i Shou-ch'ih-chin-kang
Ching-kang-ling-mu
Ching-ming Wen-shu
Ch'ing-mu tsu-shih
Chi'ng Pu-tung-chin-kang
Chin-kang-ch'a-ka-mu
Chin-kang-chieh-hsing
Chin-kang-chieh-hsing fo
Chin-kang-chieh P'i-lu fo
Chin-kang-chien fo-mu
Chin-kang-chih-hsing p'u-sa
Chin-kang-ch'ih p'u-sa
Chin-kang-cho
Chin-kang-cho fo-mu
Chin-kang-cho-mu
Chin-kang-ch'uang-kai p'u-sa
Chin-kang-ch'uang p'u-sa
Chin-kang-ch'uan p'u-sa
Chin-kang-ch'uan-yin p'u-sa
Chin-kang-fa fo
Chin-kang-fa fo-mu
Chin-kang-fa p'u-sa
Chin-kang-feng-mu
Chin-kang-fen-nu fo-mu
Chin-kang-hai-mu
Chin-kang-hsiang fo-mu
Chin-kang-hsiao p'u-sa
Chin-kang-hsien p'u-sa
Chin-kang-hsi-hsiao p'u-sa
Chin-kang-hsi-mu p'u-sa
Chin-kang-hsing fo
Chin-kang-hsing Po-lo-mi-mu
Chin-kang-hsing-wang Chi-kuang fo-mu
Chin-kang-huo-mu
Chin-kang-jih
Chin-kang-jou-shan fo-mu

Chin-kang-kan-ta-li
Chin-kang-kan-ta-li fo-mu
Chin-kang-kan-t'o-lo fo-mu
Chin-kang-kou
Chin-kang-kou-mu
Chin-kang-kung-shih Chiu-tu fo-mu
Chin-kang-ling-mu
Chin-kang-lun p'u-sa
Chin-kang-miao-fa Kuan-shih-yin
Chin-kang-miao-fa p'u-sa
Chin-kang-min-chieh p'u-sa
Chin-kang-pao fo-mu
Chin-kang-pao-hu p'u-sa
Chin-kang-pao p'u-sa
Chin-kang-pi-ta-la
Chin-kang-pu-huai fo
Chin-kang-pu-huai Kuan-shih-yin
Chin-kang p'u-sa
Chin-kang-pu-tung fo
Chin-kang-se fo-mu
Chin-kang-se-hsiang fo-mu
Chin-kang-shan-hsien p'u-sa
Chin-kang-sheng fo-mu
Chin-kang-sheng-mu
Chin-kang-shih
Chin-kang-shui-mu
Chin-kang-shuo-fa p'u-sa
Chin-kang-so fo-mu
Chin-kang-t'an
Chin-kang-ta-pao-mu
Chin-kang-ta-pao p'u-sa
Chin-kang-ta-ti p'u-sa
Chin-kang-te-wei p'u-sa
Chin-kang-ti fo-mu
Chin-kang-ti-mu
Chin-kang-ting
Chin-kang-ting-chuan-lun-wang
Chin-kang-ting fo
Chin-kang-tsang p'u-sa
Chin-kang-wang p'u-sa
Chin-kang-wei fo-mu
Chin-kang-wei-kuang p'u-sa
Chin-kang-wen-shu pi-mi fo
Chin-kang-yao-ch'a
Chin-kang-yao-ch'a p'u-sa
Chin-kang-yeh-ch'a p'u-sa
Chin-kang-yeh fo-mu
Chin-kang-yeh p'u-sa
Chin-kang-yin p'u-sa
Chin-kang-yin-yuan p'u-sa
Chin-kang-yu fo-mu
Chin-kang-yung-shih
Chin-kang-yung-shih fo
Chin-kang-yung-shih fo-mu
Chin-kang-yung-shih p'u-sa
Chin-kang-yung-shih Shang-lo-wang fo
Chin-kang-yu p'u-sa
Chin-kang-yü p'u-sa
Chinnamunda-(Vajravarahi)
Chin-se-pao-kuang-ju-lai fo
Chin-se-pao-kuang-miao-hsing-ch'eng-chiu-ju-lai
Ch'i-shih Wen-shu p'u-sa
Ch'i-shih Yung-pao hu-fa
Chi-tu-hsing t'ien
Chiu-ting fo
Chiu-t'o p'u-sa
Ch'iu-ts'ai fo-mu
Chiu-tu fo-mu
Chiu-tu-mu
Chi Wei-lo-wa-chin-kang
Ch'iy-kuo
Chochyong
Chode gyatshoi jang
Chogs-bdag-dmar-chen
Chogyel
Chok-kyong
Chonyid Kuntuzangpo
Chos-bdag-bkra-shis-dpal
Chos-bdag-brag-btsan-Zangs-phur-can-pa
Chos-bdag-byang-bdud-pa
Chos-bsgrags-rgya-mtsho
Chos-dbyins-gsun-dban
Chos-dbyin-gsun-gi-dban-phyug
Chos Grags
Chos-gter-gyi-srung-ma
Chos-hphags
Chos-kyi-rdo-rje-ma
Chos-kyi-rgyal-po
Chos-kyi-rgyal-po-gnod-sbyin-Yang-dag-shes
Chos-legs-rnam-rgyal
Chos-nyid-Kun-tu-bzang-po
Chos-rGyal
Chos-rGyal-gSang-sGrub
Chos-rgyal-gsan-sgrub
Chos-rgyal-las-kyi-gshin-rje-mthing-ga
Chos-rgyal-las-kyi-gshin-rje-mthin-ga
Chos-rgyal-li-byin-ha-ra-legs
Chos-rGyal-Nang-sGrub
Chos-rGyal-phyi-sgrub
Chos-rGyal-phyi-sgrub-ma-he'i-gdong-can
Chos-rgya-mcho-mchog-gi-blos-rnam-par-rol-

bar-mnon-par-mkhyen-pahi-rgyal-po
Chos-sgrags-rgya-mchohi-dbyans
Chos-sgrags-rgya-mtshohi-dbyans
Chos-skyon
Chos-skyong
Chos-skyong-ba'i-rgyal-po
Chos-skyong-chen-mo
Chos-skyong-chen-po
Chos-skyong-dregs-pa-lcam-sring
Chos-skyong-gnod-sbyin-dmar-po
Chos-skyong-gza'-bdud-chen-po-rahula
Chos-skyong-mahakala
Chou-t'an-kung-te fo
Chou-tsa-chuang-yen-kung-te fo
Chuang-pi-pa tsu-shih
Ch'uang-ting fo
Ch'uang-ting-pei-yen
Ch'uang-ting-pei-yen fo-mu
Ch'uang-ting-po-yen fo-mu
Chuang-yen-mu
Ch'uan-heng-san-chieh Kuan-shih-yin
Ch'uan-heng-san-chieh Kuan-shih-yin p'u-sa
Chuan-lun-ting
Chuan-pi-ni fo-mu
Chu-ch'a-pan-t'o tsun-che
Ch'u-chu-chang p'u-sa
Chu-chu t'ien
Ch'u-chu-wu-nan Chiu-tu fo-mu
Ch'u-chu-wu-tu Chiu-tu fo-mu
Ch'u-fan-nao fo
Chuhi-hjigs-skyobs
Chu-hsiang fo-mu
Ch'u-kai-chang t'ien-mu
Chu-klun-hod-srun
Chu-lHa
Chu-lha-dkar-po
Chu-lhahi-ha
Chu-liu-sun fo
Ch'u-mieh-kuei-wang-chin-kang
Ch'u-mo-chin-kang
Chu-na-she-mou-ni fo
Chung
Chung-tieh-kuang-huan Kuan-shih-yin
Chun-ti
Chu-p'in-ch'a-ka fo
Chu-p'in t'ien-mu
Chu-p'in-ting fo
Chu-rgyud-dge-bsnyen
Chu-rgyud-rgyal-po
Chu-shou Yung-pao hu-fa
Chusinmo
Chu-srin-gdong-can
Chu-srin-mo
Chu-srin-pa'i-rgyal-po-lcags
Ch'u-tu fo-mu
Chu-tu-lo (mahayaksasenapati)
Chu-tu-lo yao-ch'a-ta-chiang
Ch'u-tz'u-chueh-i fo
Ch'u-wu-ch'u Chiu-tu fo-mu
Cida-raja
Cig-car-dmar-po
Ci-hdod-char-hbebs-mGon-dkar-mtshan
Cimeg-i barigci
Cinakrama-Tara
Ci-namira
Cina-Tara (fo-mu)
Cintamani-Avalokitesvara
Cintamani-chakra
Cintamanichakra-Avalokitesvara
Cintamanichakra-sita-Tara
Cintamani-Lokesvara
Cintamani-Rakta-Mahakala
Cintamani-Sita-Mahakala
Citipati
Citra(?) (devi)
Cittadhatu-Lokesvara
Citṭa-Hevajra
Citta-nirmita-Rsi-vidyajnana
Cittaraja
Citta-Vasita
Cittavisramana-Avalokitesvara
Cittotpada(=adhimukti?)-Vasita
Cittotpadacaryabhumi (fo-mu)
Cod-dpan-mgrin-bzang-ma
Cod-pan-mgrin-bzang-ma
Cog-i oggugci
Cog-la-mtshal-rtse
Cog-la-tshal-rtse
Cogtu candan
Cogtu ma-ha-kala
Cogtu okin tngri
Cogtu qogulai-tu
Confession Buddhas
Cora-bhayatrana-(Avalokitesvara)
Cora-bhayatrana-Tara
Cudapanthaka
Cunda
Cundra
Cunti
Cur-a-bandaga

- D -

Dabara inggadi
Dag-lha-sgam-bu
Dagun-u eke
Dagun-u vcir eke
Dai-ko-ku
Dai-nichi Nyorai
Dai-sei-shi
Daka-bhaya-trana-Tara
Dakamukha-Guhyasadhana-Traksad-Makahala
Dakini
Dakini-bhayatrana-(Avalokitesvara)
Dakini (fo-mu)
Dakiraja
Dalai-Lama
Dalai-Lama-Kalpabhadrasamudra
Dalha
Damasrim-a
Dam-can
Dam-can-chos-rgyal
Dam-can-mched-bdun
Dam-can-mgar-ba-Nag-pohi-mtshan
Dam-can-rDo-rje-Legs-pa
Dam-can-remati
Dam-can-shel-ging-dkar-po
Damcan-Vajradsadhu
Dam-can-zhing-skyong-nag-po
Dam-chen-Chos-kyi-rgyal-pohi-zhabs
'Dam-gyi-'ben-rgyal-sbyang-ri
Dam-pa-rin-chen-dpa'-rtsal
Dam-pa-Sangs-rgyas
Dam-sangs
'Dam-srang-rgyal-po
Damstradhara (yo-mu)
Dam-tshig-gi-dbang-mo
Dam-tshig-gi-ma-mo
Dam-tshig-mkhah-hgro
Dana-Paramita
Dan-'bag-zhang-go
Dance Deities
Danda-bhayatrana-(Avalokitesvara)
Danda-bhayatrana-Tara
Dandadhara-Bhairavavajra
Danda(dhara)-Mahakala
Dandadhara (yo-mu)
Danda-Mahakala
Dan-po-sems-skyed-the-chom-gcod-mzad
Dara-eke
Dar-'dzin-skyes-ri-mthon-po
Dasabhuja-Marici (fo-mu)
Dasabhujasita Marici
Dasa-bhumi-pati-Maitreya
Dasagriva
Dasa-girv-a
Dasa-Kundali
Dasami Tithi
Da-shi-zhi
Dayang gyalpo
dBal-chan-ram-pa
dBal-gyi-mgar-ba
dBang-'dus-gryal-chen
dBang-gi-gshin-rje
dBang-gi-lha-mo
dBang-mdzod-nor-gyi-bdag
dBang-mo
dBang-phyug
dBang-phyug-chen-po
dBang-phyug-khrag-'thung-ma
dBang-phyug-mahadeva
dBang-phyug-remati
dBang-phyug-ye-shes-mgon
dBang-po-brgya-byin
dBang-po-Zhi
dBang-rgya-byin
dBang-sdud-lcags-kyus-'dren-ma
dBan-mchog-ster-bahi-sgrol-ma
dBan-phyug
dBan-pohi-tog-gi-rgyal-mchan-gyi-rgyal-po
dBa'-ri-dbi-hu-brag-nag-po
dBugs-len-bdud-kyi-bshan-pa
dBu-lnga-sman-phran-gtso
dBus-kyi-'brug-lha-ga-pa
dByangs-can-ma
dByans-can-ma-dkar-mo
dByans-can-ma-dkar-mo-phyag-bzhi-pa
dByans-can-ma-dmar-po
dByar-gyi-lha-mo
dByar-gyi-rgyal-mo
dByig-gNyen
dByings-khyug-nor-'dzin-ma
dByings-kyi-ma-mo
dByi-rgyal-dmag-dpon
dByug-gu-ma-bhagini-traya
dByug-gu-ma-spun-gsum
dByug-pa-'jigs-byed
dByug-sNgon-can
dByug-snon-can
Demchok
Deva

Devadevata-Lokesvara
Devaloka (Buddha)
Devaputra
Devaraja
Devendra
Devendra-Satakratu
Devi
dGah-bo
dGa'-ldan-'brog-ri'i-dge-bsnyen
dGe-bsnen-Dharma
dGe-bsnen-dharma-ta-la
dGe-bsnyen-'bo-rong
dGe-bsNyen-Dharma
dGe-bsNyen-Dhar-ma-tah-la
dGe-bsnyen-mkha'-ri-lcam-dral
dGe-bsnyen-nyi-shu-rtsa-gcig
dGe-bsnyen-rdo-rje-dbang-drag
dGe-bsnyen-rdo-rje-legs-pa
dGe-bsnyen-ston-ka-rgyal-mtshan
dGe-hdun-grub-pa
dGe-lha
dGe-ri-lcam-dral
dGon-gsar-bla-ma'i-dkon-mchog
dGra-bgegs-'dul-mdzad-ma
dGra-bgegs-'dul-mdzad-pa
dGra-dpun-hjoms-mdzad-ma
dGra-lha
dGra-lha-chen-po
dGra-lha-dpe-har
dGra-lha-gdong-btsan
dGra-lha'i-rgyal-po-gnas-chung
dGra-lha'i-rgyal-po-lcam-dral
dGra-lha-ja-mun
dGra-lha-khyim-la-ske-thung
dGra-lha-ma-lha-bu-rdzi
dGra-lha-mgon-po-dmar-po
dGra-lha-rdor-legs-dkar-po
dGra-lha-rgyal-chen-rnam-thos-sras
dGra-lha-sku-la-gsang
dGra-lha-skyes-gcig
dGra-lha-skyes-gcig-bu
dGra-lha-sku-la-gsang
dGra-lha-spun-gsum
dGra-lha-sTong-btsan-pa
dGra-lha-thab-lha-gyu-mo
dGra-nag-gsin-rje-gsed
dGra-nags
dGra-sman-gshog-dkar
dGun-gyi-lha-mo
dGun-gyi-rgyal-mo
dGyes-pa'i-rdo-rje

Dhana
Dhanada
Dhanada-Tara
Dhanada-Tara (fo-mu)
Dhanasri
Dhanasri Buddha
Dhana-vardhana-Pita-Caturmukha-(Sri-Mahakala)
Dhanu
Dhanus (deva)
Dharani-vinirgata-Marici
Dharani-vinirgata-Vasudhara-Devi
Dharinis
Dharma
Dharmacakra-Lokesvara
Dharmadhara
Dharmadhatu (fo-mu)
Dharmadhatu-Lokesvara
Dharma-Dhatu-Samantabhadra
Dharmadhatu-Vagisvara
Dharmadhatuvagisvara (Buddha)
Dharmaghosatathagata Buddha
Dharmakirti
Dharm-a-kirti
Dharma-kirti-sagara
Dharmakirtisagaraghosa
Dharmamegha
Dharmamegha (fo-mu)
Dharmapala
Dharma Pratisamvita
Dharmaraja
Dharmasagaragra(?)mativikriditabhijnaraja
Dharmasanka-samadhi Manjusri
Dharmavajra
Dharmavajri
Dharmavajri (fo-mu)
Dharma-Vasita
Dharmodgata
Dhatarattha
Dhi-dhi-ka
Dhitika
Dhritarastra
Dhrtarastra
Dhumavarna-Krodha-Bhurkumkuta
Dhumavati (devi)
Dhumavati-(Sri)-Devi
Dhupa
Dhupa (fo-mu)
Dhupatara
Dhupema
Dhvaja

Dhvajagra(?) (Buddha)
Dhvajagrakeyura
Dhvajagrakeyura (fo-mu)
Dhvajosnisa
Dhyanabhyudgataraja Buddha
Dhyanaparamita
Dhyani Bodhisattvas
Dhyani Buddhas
Dhyani Buddhashakti
Dichapma
Digambara
Digambara-Devi
Dignaga
Dilba
Dinnaga
Din sangma
Dipa
Dipa (fo-mu)
Dipa Namsel
Dipani
Dipankar-a
Dipankara Buddha
Dipatara
Dipayugmadhara (fo-mu)
Dipika
Diridisdiri
Divasanta-ratrikruddha-Tara
Di-zang
dKah-ma(?)-Dandadhara-Mahakala
dKar-mo'i-nyi-zla'i-thod-'phreng
dKar-mo-ni-zla-lcam-dral
dKar-mo-nyi-zla-lcam-dral
dKar-mo-zla-mdans-kyi-sgrol-ma
dKar-po-spyan-gcig
dKar-po-spyan-('u?)
dKar-sgang-rin-chen-phug-pa
dKor-bdag-chen-po
dKor-bdag-rgyal-chen-bi-ha-ra
dKor-bdag-rgyal-po
dMag-bskul-gnyan-rje-gong-sngon
dMag-dpon-dgra-'ḍul
dMag-gi-lbang-ging
dMag-zor-gyi-rgyal-mo-remati
dMag-zor-ma
dMigs-pa
dMrig-pa-g.yag-mgo
dMu-bdud-bkrag-med-nag-po
dMu-bdud-dkar-po
dMu-bdud-dmu-rgyal-dga'-bo
dMu-bdud-nag-po-bk(h)rag-med
dMu-'bri-rje
dMu-lcam-mgrin-sngon
dMu-rabs-brgyud-kyi-dgra-lha
dMu-rje-brtson-thogs-rje
dMu-rje-btsan-po
dMu-rje-btsan-po-'khor-lo-bsgyur
dMu-rje-gos-sngon
dMu-rje-gsang-ba'i-mi-kun
dMu-rje-ko-long-tho-long
dMu-rje-lang-dang-bskol-po-rje
dMu-rje-lha-gnyan
dMu-rje-nag-po-kha-med
dMu-shad-rje-rgyal-gtong-po-rje
dMu-theng-snang-dang-gtso-bo-brgyad
dNgul-chu'i-gzhi-bdag-lCags-skud-pa
dNgul-mig-ma
dNos-grub-scol-bahi-sGrol-ma
'Dod-dgu-chags-pa'i-dgra-lha
Doljang
Dolkar
Dolma Jangu
Dolma Karpo
Dombini (fo-mu)
Do-mbi-pa
Dombipada
Domdong Chen
Dom-gdon-can
Dom-gdong-ma
Dom- mgo-glang-gi-snying
Dom- mgo-glang-snying
Dom-nag-'phrang-rtse-gser-gsham-che
Domton
Don-grub
Don-grub-dban-chen
Don-grub-pa
Don-hgrub
Don-thams-cad-sgrub-pahi-sGrol-ma
Don-yod-grub-pa
Donyo Dhupa
Don-yod-zhags-pa
Don-zhags-lha-lna-Ba-ri-lugs
Don-zhags-[lha-lna]-kha-che-pan-chen-lugs
Don-zhags-ser-po
Door Goddesses
Door-Keepers
Dorben gar-tu maqakala
Dorben gar-tu qomsim bodhi-satuva
Dorje Bod Khamchyong
Dorje Chang
Dorje Chenchima
Dorje Dagmo Gyal
Dorje Ge Chitso

Dorje Jikche
Dorje Khado
Dorje Kundag
Dorje Kundagma
Dorje Kunsang
Dorje Lumo
Dorje-lutru
Dorje Man Chiba
Dorje Naljorma
Dorje Pagmo
Dorje Phagmo
Dorje Phakmo
Dorje Polgyi-yum
Dorje Sempa
Dorje Yama Chyong
Dorje Yamasil
Dorje Yingchi Wang Chugma
Dorje Zulema
Dorleg
Do Sangma
Dotugadu erlig qagan
dPa'-bo-chen-po
dPa'-bo-chig-grub-pa-las-byung-ba'i-jambhala-lha-mang
dPa'-bo-dur-khrod-bdag-po-yab-yum
dPa'-bo-khro-'bar
dPa'-brtan-bzlog-med
dPa'-brtan-dmag-dpon-(chen-po)
dPag-dpon-mdung-rtse
dPag-med-gnon-ma
dPah-bo-chig-sgrub-las-byun-bahi-dzambha-la-lha-man
dPah-bohi-sde
dPal-byin
dPal-bzan
dPal-dgyes
dPal-dus-kyi-hkhor-lo
dPal-gsan-ba-bdus-pa
dPal-gSang-ba-hDus-pa
dPal-gyi-Be-hu
dPal-gyi-gra-bu-lung
dPal-gyi-'jag-ma-lung
dPal-gyi-lha-mo
dPal-hjam-pahi-rdo-rje
dPal-'Khor-lo-bde-mchog
dPal-'Khor-lo-sdom-pa
dPal-Kye-rdo-rje
dPal-ldan-dMag-zor-gyi-rgyal-mo-remati
dPal-ldan-dmag-zor-remati
dPal-ldan-dmag-zor-rgyal-mo
dPal-ldan-gSan-ba-hdus-pa-che
dPal-ldan-ha-ri
dPal-ldan-jo-mo-yang-gha-bza'
dPal-ldan-lha-mo
dPal-ldan-lha-mo-dMag-zor-ma
dPal-ldan-lha-mo-'dod-khams-dbang-phyug-ma
dPal-ldan-lha-mo-'dod-khams-kyi-dbang-phyug-ma
dPal-ldan-lha-mo-'dod-pa-khams-gyi-dbang-phyug-ma
dPal-ldan-lha-mo-(dud-gsol-ma)
dPal-ldan-lha-mo-dud-gsol-mar-grags-pa-'dod-khams-dbang-phyug-ma
(dPal-ldan)-lha-mo-dud-sol-ma-(rgrags-pa-hdod-khams-dban-phyug-ma)
dPal-ldan-lha-mo-phyag-gnis-ma
dPal-ldan-lha-mo-rdo-rje-nam-gru-ma
dPal-ldan-lha-mo-remadza
dPal-ldan-lha-mo-remati
dPal-ldan-mgon-po
dPal-ldan-mgon-po-nag-po-chen-po
dPal-ldan-mgon-po-phyag-bzhi-pa
dPal-ldan-mkha'-'gro-mched-lnga
dPal-ldan-rema-dzu
dPa-ldan-rema-rdza
dPal-ldan-remati
dPal-ldan-Ye-shes
dPal-legs-ldan-nag-po-chen-po
(dPal-mgon)-zhal-bzhi-dkar-po-tshe-bhpel
(dPal-mgon)-zhal-bzhi-dmar-po-dban-sdud
dPal-mgon-zhal-bzhi-pa-bsnen-dus-dan-hbrel-ba
dPal-mgon-zhal-bzhi-pa-bsnyen-dus-dang-'brel-ba
dPal-mgon-zhal-bzhi-pa-dkar-po-tshe-'phel
dPal-mgon-zhal-bzhi-pa-dmar-po-dbang-sdud
(dPal-mgon)-zhal-bzhi-pa-gdon-gnan-can
dPal-mgon-zhal-bzhi-pa-gdon-gnyan-can
dPal-mgon-zhal-bzhi-pa-ser-po-nor-'phel
dPal-mgon-zhal-bzhi-pa-sgrub-dus-dang-'brel-ba
dPal-mgon-zhal-bzhi-pa-sgrub-dus-dan-hbrel-ba
dPal-mgon-zhal-bzhi-pa-sngon-po-nyams-sgrol
(dPal-mgon)-zhal-bzhi-pa-snon-po-nams-sgrol
(dPal-mgon)-zhal-bzhi-ser-po-nor-bhpel
dPal-mo-snin-gi-gser-thig-can
dPal-rdo-rje-hkhor-lo
dPal-rdo-rje-'jigs-byed
dPal-rdo-rje-nag-po-bstan-bsrung-yongs-rdzogs
dPal-rtsa-ri

dPal-sbyin
dPal-skyon
dPal-ye-shes-mgon-pa-mahakala-dpa'-bo-chen-po
dPa'-rtsal-che-ba'i-dgra-lha
dPa'-snying-che-ba'i-dgra-lha
dPe-dkar
dPe-dkar-gsung-gi-rgyal-po
dPe-dkar-sku'i-rgyal-po
dPe-dkar-thugs-kyi-rgyal-po
dPe-dkar-yon-tan-rgyal-po
dPe-ha-ra
dPe-kar
dPung-g.yas-dgra-lhar-sprul-pa-dang
dPung-g.yon-ma-mor-sprul-pa-dang
dPyal-lugs-rdo-rje-phag-mo
dPyal-lugs-Vajravahari
dPyid-kyi-lha-mo
dPyid-kyi-rgyal-mo
Drag-btsan-mched-bdun
Drag-chen-srid-pa'i-rgyal-mo
Drag-gi-gshin-rje
Drag-po-hkhor-lo-can
Drag-po'i-lha-mo
Drag-po'i-rgyal-chen
Drag-rtsal-thog-'bebs
Drag-shad-mGon-po
Drang-ba'i-mi-bo-che
Drang-srong
Drang-srong-bkra-shis
Drang-srong-blo-ldan
Drang-srong-chen-po-gza'-bdud-rahula
Drang-srong-dal-'gro
Drang-srong-dkar-po
Drang-srong-drag-po-gtsug-rgyan
Drang-srong-gza'-bdud-sgra-can-'dzin
Drang-srong-'od-stong-ldan
Drang-srong-zla-ba
Dran-pahi-dpal
Dra'u'i-tshan-mtsho-dkar-po
Drdha-Prthivi (devi)
Dred-gdong-ma
Dregs-pa-bdud-kyi-rgyal-po-Chags-'khor-nyon-mongs-bdud
Dregs-pa-bdud-kyi-rgyal-po-'Chi-bdag-las-btsan-bdud
Dregs-pa-bdud-kyi-rgyal-po-Ma-rig-'khrul-ba'i-bdud
Dregs-pa-bdud-kyi-rgyal-po-Phung-po-lus-len-bdud
Dregs-pa-bdud-kyi-rgyal-po-Ruma(?)-gzug-rnyen(?)-bdud
Dregs-pa'i-lha-gnyan-mthu-bo-che
Dregs-pa'i-mnga'-bdag-gNyan-rje-gung-sngon
Dri-btsan
Dri-chab-kyi-khyung
Dri-chab-ma
Dri-chha-ma
Dri-gtsang-zhags-pa
Dril-bu'i-khyung
Dril-bu-ma
Dril-bu-pa
Dri-ma-med-pa
Dri-rdo-rje-ma
Dri-za'i-'dul-ba'i-khyung
Dri-za-zur-phud-lnga-pa
Droljang
Drolkar
Drolma
Drolma Jangu
Drolma Karpo
Drung-yig-chen-mo
Dsa-ba-ri
Dsam-bha-la
Dsam-bha-la-ser-po
Du-ba-'jug-ring
Du-ba-mjug-ring
Dubi eke
Dudging
Dud-nag-sel-bahi-sGrol-ma
Dug-lnahi-zhug-rnu-kun-hjoms-Sman-gyi-bla
Dug-sel-ma
Duhkhadahana-Tara
Dui vcir eke
Dukar Chemma
Dukor
Dundubhisvara (Bodhisattva)
Dung-dkar-gYas-hKhyil
Dung-dkar-ri-rgyal-gser-gyi-ri
Dung-gha-bza'
Dung-gi-rdo-rje
Dung-mig-ma
Dung-skyong-dkar-po
'Dun-raja-ha
Dupoma
Dupthop chen
Duradqui cogtu
Durangama
Durangama (fo-mu)
Durdantadamaka
Durdharsha
Durgati-Shodhanaraja

Durgottarini-Tara
Durgottarini-Tara (fo-mu)
Durjaya
Dur-khrod-bdag-po
Dur-khrod-bdag-po-lcam-dral
Dur-khrod-ma-mo-gsum
Dur-khrod-mgon-po-yab-yum
Durlo Depo
Dus-dgrahi-dban-po-Ma-hehi-zhal
Dus-'dzin-se-bya
Dus-gsum-mnon-mkhyen-rgyal-po
Dus guscunma
Dus-hkhor-khyun-khra-rgyud-lugs
Dus-hkhor-lhan-skyes
Dus-'k'or
Dus-kyi-hkhor-lo
Dus-kyi-hkor-lohi-mtsan
Dus-kyi-zhags-pa
Dus-kyi-zhags-pa-ma
Dus-kyi-zhags-pa-mo
Dus-ldan
Dus-lha
Dus-mtshan-ma
Dus-yum-lha-mo
Duti(?) (yo-mu)
Dvadasa (deva)
Dvadasabhuja-Marici (fo-mu)
Dvags-pohi-lugs-Traksad-Makahala
Dvang-phyug-ma
Dvang-po-rgya-byin
Dvaradhara (fo-mu)
Dvarapala
Dvaratalakadhara (fo-mu)
Dves-agni-prasamani (Tara)
Dvibhuja-Dharmadhatuvagisvara (Buddha)
Dvibhuja-Ekajata (fo-mu)
Dvibhuja-Heruka
Dvibhuja-Maitreya
Dvibhuja-Marici
Dvibhuja-Padmanartesvara-Avalokitesvara
Dvibhuja-Parnasabari
Dvibhuja-Prajnaparamita
Dvibhuja-Pratisara
Dvibhuja-Samvara
Dvibhuja-srimati-Devi
Dvibhuja-Usnisa-vijaya
Dvibhuja-Vajra-Nairatma
Dvibhuja-Vajrasarasvati
Dvitiya-Bhadra
Dvitiya-Jaya
Dvitiya-Nanda
Dvitiya-Purna
Dvitiya-Sunya
Dyuti(?) (Buddha)
Dza-ba-ri
Dzam-bHa-la-dkar-po
Dzam-bHa-la-Nag-po
Dzambh-la-dkar-po-lha-lna-jo-bohi-lugs
Dzambh-la-dmar-po-(srog-sgrub)-sa-lugs
Dzambh-la-ljan-khu-hdus-hkhor-lugs
Dzambh-la-nag-po-(kha-che-pan-chen-lugs)
Dzambha-la-ser-po
Dzam-bha-la-ser-po
Dzambha-la-ser-po-gtso-rkyan
Dzam-bHa-lha-Nag-po
Dzam-bHa-la-Zhal-gSum-Phyag-drug
Dzam-po-'khyil-pa
Dza-sa-dmar-po
Dzi-na-mi-tra

- E -

Ebul-un okin tngri
Ed-un cogtu
Egeci deguu
Eight Fears Avalokitesvara
Eight Fears Tara
Eight Mothers
Ekabhaisajyavajra
Ekadara-skyes-cig-po
Ekadasa (deva)
Ekadasamukha
Ekadasamukha-Astabhayatrana-(Arya-Avalokitesvara)
Ekadasamukha-Avalokitesvara
Ekadasamukha-Avalokitesvara (Bodhisattva)
Ekadasamukha-Mahakarunika
Ekajata
Ekajata (devi)
Ekajata-Tara
Ekajati
Ekajati-Devi
Ekajati-ral-gcig-ma
Ekamatri-Shri-Devi
Ekamatrka
Ekantanayaka-Pita-Jambhala
(Ekantanayaka)-Trisamayavyuha-Muni
Ekavira-Bhairava
Ekavira-Bhairavavajra
Ekavira-Kartaridhara-Mahakala

Ekavira-sadhana-vinirgata-Bahudeva-Jambhala
Elements deities
Emgeg-i tasulagci
Emma-o
Emma-ten
Em-un qatun
E-ni-lo yao-ch'a-ta-chiang
En-ko Kwan-non
E-nyams-ra-mdo'i-spe-na
Erdem-un gerel-tu
Erdeni gerel gargacgi
Erdeni-in oron
Erdeni lingqu-a-tu
Erdeni saran
Erdeni saran gerel-tu
Erdeni-tu sira jambhala
Erh-pei Chi-kuang fo-mu
Erh-pei Chin-kang-miao-yin fo-mu
Erh-pei Fa-chieh-miao-yin fo
Erh-pei I-chi fo-mu
Erh-pei Lien-hua-miao-wu-tzu-tsai Kuan-shih-yin
Erh-pei Mi-lo
Erh-pei Pan-jo fo-mu
Erh-pei Sui-ch'iu fo-mu
Erh-pei T'ien-mu hu-fa
Erh-pei Yeh-i fo-mu
Erh-shih-ssu-pei I-chi fo-mu
Erikeci eke
Er-jiang
Erke barigci
Erketu oki ilagugsan
Erlig-jin jarghaqci
Erlik qan
Esrua
Esru-a

- F -

Fa-chieh-miao-yin-tzu-tsai fo
Fa-chiu-ku yo-chu
Fa-hai-sheng-hui-yu-hsi-shen-t'ung-ju-lai
Fa-hai-shen-yin-ju-lai
Fa-hsing-miao-yin-tzu-tsai fo
Fa-hsin-hsing-ti fo-mu
Fa-kuang
Fa-kuang fo-mu
Fa-na-p'o-ssu tsun-che
Fang-pien Po-lo-mi-mu
Fan-wang
Fan-wang t'ien
Fa-she-lo-fo-to tsun-che
Fa-sheng tsu-shih
Fa-ti
Fa-ti hu-fa
Fa-yin-ju-lai fo
Fa-yun
Fa-yun fo-mu
Fen-chu hu-fa
Feng-t'ien
Fen-nu-miao-yueh-chin-kang
Fen-nu-mu
Fen-nu Shou-ch'ih-chin-kang
Fen-nu Wei-chi fo-mu
Five Great Kings
Five Long Life Sisters
Five Senses Goddesses
Fo
Fo-hai Kuan-shih-yin
Fo-hai Kuan-shih-yin fo
Fo-mu Shou-ch'ih-chin-kang fo
Fo-ting
Fo-ting p'u-sa
Fo-t'o-ka-pa-la
Fo-t'o-ka-pa-la chin-kang
Fo-t'o-ka-pu-la fo
Fo-t'o-p'u-t'i-mu
Four Seasons Goddesses
Fo-yen
Fo-yen fo-mu
Fudo
Fudo-Myo-o
Fu-gen
Fuku jo-ju
Fuku-kenjaku
Fu-do Myo-o
Fu-mo Shou-ch'ih-chin-kang
Fu-mo Shou-ch'ih-chin-kang fo
Fu-tzu-tsai-mu

- G -

Ga-ba-dgu-brtsegs
Gabala erike-tu
Gabala-tu ki vcir
Ga-byang

Ga-byang-spun-gsum
Gadadhara-Syama-pita-Vaisravana
Gadagadu erlig qagan
Gaganaganja-Lokesvara
Gagananjanja
Gaganaraja
Gag-ca em-tu vcir eke
Gajar-un jiruken
Gajar-un okin tngri
Gal erdeni-tu
Gal tngri
Galudani
Gampopa
Ganapati
Ganapati (deva)
Ganapatihrdaya
Ganavagasa
Gan-ba-bzan-po
Gandha
Gandhahasti
Gandhahastin (Bodhisattva)
Gandharva-yaksa (?)
Gandhatara
Gandhavajra
Gandhema
Ganesa
Gangadevi
Gan-gahi-lha-mo
Gang-ba-bzang-po
Gang-ba-bzang-po-gcig-char-dmar
Gangs-btsan-pa
Gangs-chen-mched-lnga
Gangs-chen-mdzod-lnga
Gangs-dkar-rgyal-po
Gangs-dkar-ri-bo-(rnam-gsum)
Gangs-dkar-sha-med
Gangs-dkar-sha-med-ma
Gangs-gnyan-nyi-shu-rtsa-gcig
Gangs-kyi-yum-chen-g.yu-bun-ma)
Gangs-kyi-yum-chen-ma
Gangs-ri-ltar-dkar-btsan-rgod-dmag-dpon-che
Gangs-yum-kun-bzang
Ganiy-a
Ga-pa-li-dor
Gaqai terigutu eke
Garbha(?)-Hevajra
Garbha-suvarna-sutra-Sri
Garg-a-bani
Gargar-a
Gar-gyi-glog-ltar-'du-ma
Garma
Gar-mdzad-ma
Garuda
Garudapaksavat-Kilapada-Panjara-Mahakala
Garuda-Samvara
Garuda-Samvararaja (Buddha)
Garudayuta-Vajrapani
Gasalang ugei
Gasalang ugei degedu
Gauri (fo-mu)
Gauri-Tara
Gautama Buddha
Gautamadeva
Gavampati
Gaya gasib
Ga-ya-hod-srun
Gaya-Kasyapa
Gay-a-raja
gCer-bu-lag-rdum
gCug-dgu
gCug-tor-can
gCur-tor-sGrol-ma
gDong-dmar-ma
gDon-po-drug-pa
gDugs-dkar-can-ma
gDul-dKah-sNgon-po
Gedundub
Geg Moma
Gegs-mthar-byed
Ger bukun-i-ayugulugci
Gerel-sakiqci
Gerel-un cogtu
Ghajar-un jiruken
Ghandhatara
Ghantadhara-Bhairavavajra
Ghantapada
Ghantapani
Ghasiba
Ghasmari
Ghasmari (fo-mu)
Ghatini
Ghirdhima
Ghoracandi
Ghora-matsarya-srnkhala-mocani-(Tara)
Gin-chen-srog-bdag
Gingcen ganabadi
Ging-chen-dkar-po-srog-gi-bdag
Ging-chen-sna-khrid
Ging-ka-ra
Ging-mo-rdo-rje-mkha'-'gro-ma
Gita
Gita (fo-mu)

Gi'u-then-po-sa-yi-lha
Glang-chen-'gyings-ri
Glang-chen-po
Glang-dar-ma
Glang-gi-raja
Glan-mgo-can
Glan-pohi-hjigs-skyobs
Gleng-gzhi-'grub-pa'i-dgra-lha
Glu-ma
gNam-bkyos-sa-yi-tshangs-pa-ching-gis-chos-kyi-rgyal-po'i-rigs-kyi-bsrung-ma
gNam-dkar-po
gNam-gyi-brgya-byin-dkar-po
gNam-gyi-bya-khyung-heng-phan
gNam-gyi-dkar-po
gNam-gyi-'gong-po
gNam-gyi-gza'-chen-lha-rgod
gNam-gyi-yo-cha-dkar-po-chen-po
gNam-khyi-nag-po
gNam-lha-byang-chub
gNam-lha-byang-sman-mthing-gi-go-zu-can
gNam-lha-dkar-po
gNam-lha-dkar-po-(byang-chub)
gNam-lha-zhe-sdang-khen-pa-rgan-po
gNam-mtsho
gNam-phyi-bdud-rgyal-nam-mkha'i-mdzod-dzin-ma
gNam-phyi-mched-gsum
gNam-rde'u-dkar-po
gNam-ru-ru-rtse-thod-dkar-can
gNam-sde-dkar-po
gNam-sman-thog-gi-bu-yug
gNam-the-dkar-po
gNam-thel-dkar-po
gNam-the'u-dkar-po
gNam-thib-dkar-po
gNan-lugs Sadanga Tara
gNan-lugs-sgrol-dkar
gNan-lugs Sita Tara
gNan-sgrol-yan-lag-drug-pa
gNan-than-lha
gNas-kha-ba-dkar-po
gNod-mdzes-rgyal-po
gNod-sbyin-a-pa-ra-dzi-ta
gNod-sbyin-aparajita
gNod-sbyin-bshan-pa
gNod-sbyin-bya-rog-gdong-can
gNod-sbyin-chen-po-zangs-kyi-beg-tse-can
gNod-sbyin-dban-ldan
gNod-sbyin-dgra-lha-chen-po-pu-tra
gNod-sbyin-dmar-nag
gNod-sbyin-'dul-ba'i-khyung
gNod-sbyin-gan-ba-bzan-po
gNod-sbyin-gang-ba-bzang-po
gNod-sbyin-gangs
gNod-sbyin-gangs-bzang
gNod-sbyin-ma-ru-rtse
gNod-sbyin-mgon-po-mon-bu-pu-tra
gNod-sbyin-mo-hphrog-ma
gNod-sbyin-mo-sngon-mo
gNod-sbyin-nag-po
gNod-sbyin-nor-bu-bzang-po
gNod-sbyin-nor-bu-bzan-po
gNod-sbyin-nor-gyi-rgyal-po
gNod-sbyin-remati
gNod-sbyin-re-ma-ti
gNod-sbyin-rgyal-thang
gNod-sbyin-sgrol-gying-bshan-pa
gNod-sbyin-shan-pa-gri-thogs
gNod-sbyin-sring-mo-rlung-byin
gNod-sbyin-srin-mo'i-gdong-pa
gNod-sbyin-yaksa-me-dbal
gNod-sbyin-yaksa-sha-me-dbal
gNod-sbyin-zangs-kyi-ral-pa-can
gNod-sbyin-zhang-blon-rdo-rje-bdud-'dul
gNos-lugs-(Mahadeva)-Traksad-Yama-yami-Makahala
gNyan
gNyan-chen-g.yu-rtse
gNyan-chen-thang-lha
gNyan-gyi-remati
gNyan-ljang-rdo-rge-blo-gros
gNyan-ma-ma-le-gu
gNyan-po-brag-srin-kumara
gNyan-po-ri-Gangs-ri-rtse
gNyan-po-sku-lha-gyer-'dzom
gNyan-rgyal-mtsho-nag-rba-ri-gnyan
gNyan-rje-gong-sngon
gNyan-rje-gung-sngon
gNyan-spar-ba-dung-mgo-g.yu'i-thor-tshugs-can
gNyan-stag-dmar-po
Gobaga
'Go-ba'i-dgra-lha-spun-gsum
Go-bzlog-lhan-skyes
Go-chahi-bskyed-byed-ma
Go-chahi-dpah-bo-drug
Go-chahi-gsin-rje-ma
Go-chahi-he-ru-ka-nag-po
Go-chahi-padma-gar-dban
Go-chahi-rdo-rje-ni-ma
Go-chahi-rdo-rje-phag-mo

Go-chahi-rdo-rje-sems-dpah
Go-chahi-rmons-byed-ma
Go-chahi-rnam-snan
Go-chahi-rta-mchog
Go-chahi-skrag-byed-ma
Go-chahi-tsandi-ka
Go-'dre-min-ga
Gokarmo
Gom-kar
Gompo Chakdruk
Gong-De-Tian
Gong-po-bse-rag-spun-dgu
'Gong-po-khu-le-lag-dgu
'Gong-po-yam-shud-dmar-po
Gopaka
Gopala-Vasudhara
Go-san-ze
Gos-dkar-mo
Gos-ster-ma-dkar-mo
Gotama
Grahamatrika
Grahottamaraja-Rahu
Grib-btsan
Gri-btsan
Gri-gug-mgon-po
Gri-phug-spyang-ri-rtse-rgyal
Grismadevi
Grogs-byed-mgo-dkar-mgo-sngon
Grogs-lha
Gro-shod-bod-kyi-dmag-rje
Gro-shod-bod-kyi-sgang-dmag-rje
Grub-snyan-lag-pa-can
Grub-thob-chen
Grva-pa-mnon-ses-lugs-kyi-dzambha-la-dmar-po
Grva-pa-mngon-shes-lugs-kyi-jambhala-dmar-po
gSal-ja-gangs
gSan-bahi-bdag-po-khro-bo
gSan-bahi-bdag-po-rDo-rje-hdzin
gSan-bahi-mdzod-hdzin-dPal-mgon
gSan-bahi-mkhah-hgro
gSan-ba-rab-khros-rDo-rje-hdzin
gSan-bdag-lhan-skyes-zhi-ba
gSan-bdus
gSang-ba-hdus-pa
gSang-ba'i-las-mgon
gSang-ba'i-mkha'-'gro-ma
gSang-'dus-las-byung-ba'i-jam-ser
gSang-hdus-hJam-rDor
gSan-hdus-hjam-pahi-rdo-rje
gSan-hdus-hjigs-rten-dban-phyug
gSan-hdus-las-byun-bahi-dZambha-la-ser-po
(gSan-hdus-las-byun-bahi)-khro-bo-bgegs-mthar-byed
gSan-hdus-lhan-skyes
gSan-hdus-mi-bskyod-pa
gSan-hdus-mi-bskyod-rdo-rje
gSan-sgrub-Zhan-blon-rdo-rje-bdud-hdul
gSan-snags-rjes-bzin
gSans-snags-chen-mo
gSer-behu
gSer-bzan-dri-ma-med-pahi-dpal
gSer-bzan-dri-med
gSer-bzan-dri-med-rin-chen-snan
gSer-bzan-dri-med-rin-chen-snan-brtul-zhugs-pa
gSer-chen-mkh'-lding-klu-mo
gSer-gyi-hKhor-lo
gSer-gyi-Nya
gSer-gyi-ri-bdun-sa-bdag
gSer-gyi-spu-gri-ma
gSer-mdog-can-gyi-sgrol-ma
gSer-mig-ma
gSer-thub
gShan-pa-ma-ru-rtse
gShan-pa-mi-zan
gShan-pa-sku-mdog-can
gShen-Lha-od-dkar
gShin-gyi-pho-rog
gShin-rje
gShin-rje-brag-thabs
gShin-rje-chos-kyi-rgyal-po
gShin-rje-dam-sri-ma-nag-mo
gShin-rje-dkar-po
gShin-rje-dmar-po
gShin-rje-'dul'ba'i-khyung
gShin-rje-dus-mtshan-ma
gShin-rje-gsed
gShin-rje-gsed-dmar
gShin-rje-gsed-dmar-po
gShin-rje-gShed
gShin-rje-gShed-dGra-nag
gShin-rje-gShed-dMar-po
gShin-rje-gshed-pa-dmar-po
gShin-rje-gshed-po
gShin-rjehi-pho-na-mo
gShin-rje'i-rgyal
gShin-rje'i-pho-nya
gShin-rje'i-pho-nya-mo
gShin-rje'i-rgyal
gShin-rje'i-sring-mo-mtshan-byed

gShin-rje-ma-rungs-pa-mon-bu-putra
gShin-rje-ma-ru-rtse
gShin-rje-mig-dmar
gShin-rje-mthar-byed
gShin-rje-mtshan-mo
gShin-rje-nan-grub
gShin-rje-phebs-ma
gShin-rje-ser-po
gShin-rje-snon-po
gShin-rje-sreg-ma
gShin-rje'-sring-mo-mtshan-byed
gShin-rje-stag-mgo-can
gShin-rje-tshe-bdag-nag-po
gShin-rje-yama-raja
gShin-stag-'thab
gSod-byed-nag-mo-ral-can
gSod-ma
gSung-gi-mgon-po-beng-dmar-po
gSun-gi-rgyal-po
gSung-mchog
gSung-sprul-'bri-byed
gSun-kyai-rdor
gSun-sprul-chen-po
gTad-dkar-'gro-bzang-ma
gTad-dkar-hgro-bzan-ma
gTad-lha
gTal-dkar-'gro-bzang-ma
gTer-bdag-chen-po-gshog-rgod-rtsal
gTer-bdag-dge-ri-lcam-dral
gTer-bsrung-rGyal-ba-thod-dkar
gTer-chen-pahi-Bum-pa
gTer-gyi-bsrung-ma
gTer-srung-dregs-pa-lnga
gTi-mug-glan-pohi-hjigs-sgrol-lha-mo
gTing-skyes-blon-po-mtshan-lnga
gTor-bdag-chen-po-ban-chen-po
gTsang-gi-jo-mo-nags-rgyal
gTsangs-gi-khu-le-lag-dgu
gTsang-gi-lha-rgod-mdud-rtse
gTsang-kha'i-g.yu-mtsho-sngon-mo
gTsod-rva-can
gTso-mo-remati
gTsug-na-rin-chen
gTsug-rabs-brgyud-kyi-dgra-lha
gTsug-tor-can
gTsug-tor-gdugs-dkar
gTsug-tor-hKhor-bsGyur
gTsug-tor-hkhor-los-sgyur-ba
gTsug-tor-rnam-par-rgyal-bahi-sgrol-ma
gTsug-tor-rnam-par-rgyal-ma
gTsug-tor-rnam-par-rgyal-mahi-zhabs
gTsug-tor-rnam-rgyal
gTsug-tor-rnam-rgyal-phyag-gnis-ma
gTum-mo
gTum-po-zhal-gsum-phyag-drug-pa
Guang-Mu
Guan-Yin
Guhya-Aksobhyavajra Buddha
Guhya-Dakini
Guhya-isvara(=Lokesvara)-Avalokitesvara
Guhyajnana-(dakini)
Guhyaka-kruddha-Vajradhara
Guhya-Manjusri (Buddha)
Guhya-Manjuvajra
Guhya-Manjuvajra Buddha
Guhya-nidhi-dhara-Sri-Mahakala
Guhya-pati
Guhyapati-Vajradhara
Guhyasadhana-Avalokitesvara
Guhya-Sadhana-Dharmaraja
Guhya-Sadhana-Hayagriva
Guhyasadhana-Kurukulla
Guhyasadhana-Manjughosa
Guhya-Sadhana-Manjusri
Guhya-Sadhana-Yamaraja
Guhya-sadhana-Zhan-blon-rdo-rje-Marajit
Guhya-samaja
Guhyasamaja-Aksobhya
Guhyasamaja-Aksobhyavajra (Buddha)
Guhyasamaja-Lokesvara (Buddha)
Guhyasamaja-Manjuvara
Guhyasamaja-Manjuvara (Buddha)
(Guhyasamaja-uddhrta)-Krodha-Vighnantaka
Guhyasamaja-vinirgata-Pita-Jambhala
Guhya-Vajraksobhya Buddha
Guhyesvari
Gu-lang-raksa
Gumba
Guna-Amitayus
Gunadhya
Gunakara
Gun-a-kar-a
Guna-nirmita-Rsi-vidyajnana
Gunaprabha
Gunaprabha Buddha
Gunaraja
Guna-raja
Gungs-btsan-pa
Gung-sman-ma
Gung-sman-rgyal-mo
Gungyi gyalmo
Gurgyi gompo

Gur-gyi-mgon-po-lha-brgyad
Gur-las-gzuns-pahi-rdo-rje-sGrol-ma
Gur ma-ha-kala
Gur-mgon-lcam-dral
Gur-mgon-lha-brgyad
Gur-mgon-phur-zhabs-khyung-gshog-can
Gur-mgon-phur-zhabs-(khyun-sog)-can
Gur-rkyang-rngog-lugs
Gur-rkyan-rnog-lugs
Gurugulli okin tngri
Gur-yum-can-Klu-sgrub-lugs
Gutagar bayasqulang
Gutagar ilagugci
Gutagar qogusun
Gutagar sayin
Gutagar tegusugsen
Gyaltshab
Gyalwa sengge ngaro
Gyang-rje-btsan-po
g.Ya'-spang-brgya-byin
g.Ya'-spang-mtshams-kyi-skyes-gcig-po
g.Ya'-spang-skyes-gcig
Gyelwa-rig-nga
Gyepe Dorje
Gyer-rgod-dgra-lha'i-rgyal-po
Gyer-rgod-lha-btsan
Gyi-ling-'phar-ma
Gying-chen-sna-'khrid
Gying-mgon-bya-rog-gdong-can
Gyo-ran Kwan-non
g.Yu-bya-gshog-gcig
g.Yu-dril-rdo-rje-gzugs-legs
g.Yu'i-dril-snyan-si-li-ma
g.Yu'i-sman-gcig-ma
gYul-las-sin-tu-rnam-par-rgyal-ba
g.Yu-lung-gangs
gYu-mig-ma
g.Yu-mtsho-klu-sman-hor-brag
gYung-drung-phyug-mo
gYung-mo
g.Yu-phreng-ma
g.Yu-phreng-rgyal-mo
g.Yu-phu-brag-dkar-'ja'-tshom-ri
g.Yu-phu'i-rtse-lha-mthu-bo-che
g.Yu-ri-sngon-po
g.Yu-sgron-dkar-mo
g.Yu-sgron-mched-lnga
gZa'-bdud
gZa'-bdud-gha-ra-nag-po
gZa'-bdud-nyid-du-sprul-pa-dang
gZa'-bdud-rahula
gZa'-chen-brgyad
gZa-chen-rahu
gZah-mchog-rgyal-po-Ra-hu-la
gZahn-gyis-mi-thub-ma
gZah-yum
gZah-yum-rig-pahi-rgyal-mo
gZa'-mchog-chen-po-rahula
gZa'-mchog-rgyal-po-rahula
gZa'-rgod-dug-gi-spu-gri
gZa'-thams-cad-kyi-yum
gZa'-the-ljang-khu
gZe-yi-ma-mo-'phen-bzang
gZha-brag-lha-rtse
gZhan-gyis-Mi-thub-ma
gZhan-las-rgyal
gZhi-bdag-dpal-ldan
gZhi-bdag-ga-byang
gZhi-bdag-khang-ka'i-rgyal-po
gZhon-nu-ma
gZi-brjid-can
gZi-brjid-mthah-yas
gZig-gdong-ma
gZig-gi-mjug-ma-can
gZig-shubs-thig-le'inang-gnas-pa'i
gZugs-can-snying-po-ho-thog-tha'i-si-chen-hum-tha'i-ji
gZugs-med-rlung-ltar-'du-ma
gZugs-rdo-rje-ma
gZungs-las-byung-ba'i-lha-mo-nor-rgyun-ma
gZuns-las-byun-bahi-hOd-zer-can-ma
gZuns-las-byun-bahi-lha-mo-nor-rgyun-ma

- H -

Ha
Hai-pi-mu
Halahala-Lokesvara
Hal-khyi'i-kha-khrid
Hal-kyi-nag-po-rgyal-po'i-khyi
Ham-san-mi-dmar
Ha-ngi-phan
Hang-ne
Hang-phan
Hang-phan-ser-po-bya-ra-ba
Han-lin fo-mu
Hannya
Hanuman
Hanumat
Harihara-Lokesvara

Harihariharivahanobdhava
Harihariharivahanobdhava-Lokesvara
Hariharivahana-Lokesvara
Ha-ri-rdo-rje-ya-ma
Hariti
Hariti (deva)
Hariti-Yaksini
Harivahana-Lokesvara
Ha-sa-garbha
Ha-sham-mi-dmar
Ha-shang-mi-dmar
Hasti-bhayatrana-(Avalokitesvara)
Hasti-bhayatrana-Tara
Hastivahana-Samantabhadra
Hasya
Hayagriva
Hayagriva-Lokesvara
Hayagrivavajra
Haye Kwan-non
hBar-bahi-hod-can-ma
hBar-ba-spun-bdun
hBar-ma
hBar-ma-dbang-ldan-bdud-'dul-ma
hBar-ma-gnod-sbyin-ba-glang-sna
hBar-ma-gnod-sbyin-khyung-thogs
hBar-ma-gshin-rje-skar-mda'-gdong
hBar-ma-khyer-glog-'phreng-ma
hBar-ma-klu-mo-lce-'bebs-ma
hBar-ma-nyi-zhags-thogs-ma
hBar-ma-rlung-bdag
hBar-ma-rlung-stag-gru-'dzin-ma
hBar-ma-srin-mo-mdung-'phen-ma
hBe-yi-chab-bzhi-rdzong-'phrang
hBras-bu-ma
hBrog-gnas
hBrom-ston-pa
hBron-zhal-can
hByams-pa-khrag-mgo
hByung-ba-chags-pa'i-dgra-lha
hByung-po-hDul-byed
hChi-bdag-las-btsan-bdud
hChi-med-nye-pa'i-dbang-po
hChi-med-rdo-rje-lha-mo
hDod-chags-chu-bohi-rba-klon-skems-mdzad-ma
hDod-dgu-chags-pa'i-dgra-lha
hDod-Khams-dBang-phyug-dMag-zor-ma
hDod-khams-dban-phyug-ma
hDod-pa-ma
hDod-rguhi-dpal-ster-rNam-thos-sras
hDod-rGyal
hDod-rgyal-dmar-po
hDud-rTsi-hKhyil-pa
Hei Fa-ti
Hei Pu-lu-chin-kang
Hei Ta-p'eng
Hei-ti-chin-kang fo
Hei-ti Wei-lo-wa-chin-kang
Hei Ts'ui-sui-chin-kang fo
Hei wu-mien shih-erh-pei Kuan-shih-yin p'u-sa
He-la-'bar-ma
He-li Di
Hemanta-devi
Hemanta-Rajni
He-nga-bod-kyi-rje-btsan
Heramba
Heruka
Herukabuddhas
Heruki
Hevajra
Hevajrakrama-Kurukulla
hGam-dpal-dvyangs
hGo-ba'i-dgra-lha-spun-gsum
hGong-po-khu-le-lag-dgu
hGong-po-yam-shud-dmar-po
hGro-ba-bzan-po
hGro-ba-hdul-ba
hGro-ba-hgugs-pahi-sGrol-ma
hGro-bZang-ma
hGro-bzan-lugs-Nilambaradhara-Vajrapani
hGro-bzan-ma
Hindu Deities
Hiyoi
hJam-dbyan-chos-dbyin-gsun-gi-dban-phyug-brgyad-pa
hJam-dbyangs
hJam-dbyan-gsan-sgrub
hJam-dBynags-dKar-po
hJam-dByangs-dMar-ser
hJam-dByangs-sMra-Seng
hJam-dbyan-nag-gi-rgyal-po
hJam-dbyans-a-ra-pa-tsa-na
hJam-dbyans-brtan-pahi-hkhor-lo
hJam-dbyans-chos-dbyin-gsun-gi-dban-phyug-brgyad-pa
hJam-dbyans-dkar-po
hJam-dbyan-sengehi-sgra
hJam-dbyans-nag-po
hJam-dbyans-nan-sgrub
hJam-dbyans-ses-rab-hkhor-lo-dan-po
hJam-dbyans-sgra-bzan-dban-phyug-rgyal-po

hJam-dbyans-smra-bahi-senge
hJam-dpal
hJam-dpal-bshes-gnyen
hJam-dpal-dbyangs
hJam-dpal-dkar-po
hJam-dpal-grags-pa
hJam-dpal-naga-raksa
hJam-dpal-rnon-po
hJam-dpal-sku-yi-lha-tshogs
hJam-dpal-tshe-bdag
hJam-pal-gZhon-nu-Gyur-pa
hJam-pal-gzhon-nur-gyur-ba
hJam-po-hkhyil-ba
hJam-po-'khyil-pa
hJams-dbyans-a-ra-pa-tsa-na-dmar-ser-sa-lugs
hJams-dbyans-brtan-pahi-hkhor-lo
hJams-dbyans-dkar-po-kha-che-pan-chen-lugs
hJams-dbyans-gan-blo-mahi-bstod-sgrub-mar-grags-pa
hJams-dkar-ses-rab-hkhor-lo
hJams-dpal-rgyal-po-rol-ba
hJang-ri-smug-po
hJig-gsum-lhag-par-dban-du-byed-pahi-hjam-dbyans
hJig-rten-dban-phyug-dmar-po-phyag-bzhi-pa
hJig-rten-dban-phyug-halhala
hJig-rten-dban-phyug-ha-ri-ha-ri-la-zhon-pa
hJig-rten-dban-phyug-mgrin-snon-can
hJig-rten-dban-phyug-yi-ge-bdun-pa
hJig-rten-gsum-las-rnam-par-rgyal-bahi-sgrol-ma
hJig-rten-gsum-rgyal
hJig-rten-gyi-ma-mo
hJig-rten-gyi-mgon-po
hJig-rten-mkhah-hgro
hJigs-byed
hJigs-byed-bsdus-pa
hJigs-byed-dpah-gcig
hJigs-byed-ma
hJigs-byed-rdo-rje
hJigs-pa-brgyad-skyobs-Sgrol-ma
hJigs-pa'i-zer-mo-mig-gcig-ma
hJigs-pa-kun-skyob-sgrol-ma
hJigs-par-byed-pa'i-bdud-pho
hJigs-rten-dban-phyug-dmar-po-phyag-bzhi-pa
hJur-hgegs-sel-bahi-tshogs-bdag
hKhon-dan(?)-rgyags-pa-rnam-gnon
hKhor-ba-hjigs
hKhor-Buddha-da-ki
hKhor-Byams-pa
hKhor-Don-zhags-dmar-po
hKhor-gnod-sbyin-las-byed-ma
hKhor-gsin-rje-las-byed-ma
hKhor-Hjam-dpal
hKhor-Karma-da-ki
hKhor-Khro-gner-can-ma
hKhor-klu-mo-las-byed-ma
hKhor-las-kyi-mkhah-hgro-ma
hKhor-lo-bDe-mchog
hKhor-lo-Chen-po
hKhor-lo'i-khyung
hKhor-lo-sDom-pa
hKhor-lo-sdom-pa-dkar-po
hKhor-lo-sdom-pa-ser-po
hKhor-nag-can
hKhor-Nor-bzan-gzhon-nu
hKhor-Padma-da-ki
hKhor-padma-mkhah-hgro
hKhor-phag-mo
hKhor-Ral-gcig-ma
hKhor-Ratna-da-ki
hKhor-rdo-rje-las-byed-ma
hKhor-rdo-rje-mkhah-hgro
hKhor-rin-chen-mkhah-hgro
hKhor-rta-mgrin-dmar-po
hKhor-Sgrib-sel
hKhor-sgrol-ma
hKhor-Spyan-ras-gzigs
hKhyil-pa
Ho-brag-rma-gsum-rdza-khra
hOd-bsrun
hOd-bsrun-chen-po
hOd-dpag-med
hOd-dpal
hOd-de-gung-rgyal
hO-de-gung-rgyal
hOd-kyi-Tog
hOd-snan-ni-ma
hOd-srun
hOd-zer-can-bdud-rcuhi-ma
hOd-zer-can-ma
hOd-zer-can-ma-khab-skud-can-Bhattacharyya
hOd-zer-can-ma-rta-ljan-can
hOd-zer-can-phyag-bcu-ma
hOd-zer-can-phyag-brgyad-ma
hOd-zer-can-phyag-gnis-ma
hOd-zer-can-rdo-rje-dbyins-kyi-bdan-phyug-ma
hOd-zer-dpag-me
hOd-zer(?)-kun-hphags-dpal-brcegs-rgyal-po
Hong

Hor-chen-shog-yon-tan-sbu-yin-thu'i-dgon-gyi-gzhi-bdag-bTsan-rgod-dgra-'dul
Hosho
Hotei
Hou-hsing t'ien
hPhags-ma
hPhags-ma-dug-sel-ma
hPhags-ma-gDugs-dkar
hPhags-ma-gdugs-dkar-(po-can)
hPhags-ma-(rtsa-bahi)-sgrol-ljan
hPhags-ma-tsunda-ta-ra
hPhags-pa-Don-yod-zhags-pa
hPhags-pa-hjam-dpal
hPhags-pa-lHa
hPhags-pa-spyan-ras-gzigs
hPhags-skyes-po
hPhar-ma-mgo-dgu
hPhren-ba-ma
hPhreng-ba-ma
hPhrin-las
hPhrin-las-bdag-mo-ma-rung-pa
hPhrin-las-kyi-mgon-po-traksad
hPhrin-las-mGon-po-ma-nin-che
hPhrin-las-rgyal-po
hPhrin-las-sprul-pa-dran-sron-rig-pahi-ye-ses
hPhrog-'chang-ma
Hsiang-fu-yu-kuei p'u-sa
Hsiang-hsiang p'u-sa
Hsiao Shou-ch'ih-chin-kang
Hsiao-Vajrapani
Hsiao-yu-chih p'u-sa
Hsi-chin-kang
Hsien-ch'ien
Hsien-ch'ien fo-mu
Hsien-ch'ien p'u-sa
Hsien-hsing Shou-ch'ih-chin-kang
Hsien-sheng-wang fo
Hsien-te fo
Hsien wu-yu fo
Hsien wu-yu p'u-sa
Hsi-hsin-chin-kang
Hsi-lo-ho tsu-shih
Hsi-ta t'ien
Hsiung-wei Yung-po hu-fa
Hsiu-yao fo
Hsu-k'ung-hung-yin Chiu-tu fo-mu
Hsu-k'ung-mu p'u-sa
Hsu-k'ung-tsang
Hsu-k'ung-tsang p'u-sa
Hsu-k'ung-wang p'u-sa
Hsu-mi-chi p'u-sa
Hsu-mi-shan-wang fo
Htamenma
Htshal-lugs-Caturbhuja-(Jnana)-Mahakala
Htshal-lugs-kyi-[ye-ses]-mgon-po-phyag-bzhi-pa
Hua-kuang-man-t'ien p'u-sa
Huang Chi-kuang fo-mu
Huang Pu-lu-chin-kang
Huang Wu-neng-sheng fo-mu
Huan-hsi
Huan-hsi fo-mu
Hua Ta-p'eng
Hua-ti (r. shih) fo
Hu-Fa
Hui-lun Wen-shu
Hui-shih Po-lo-mi-mu
Hu-kuo hu-fa
Humkaravajra
Hu-mo-chin-kang
Hum-sgra-sgrog-pahi-sgrol-ma
Humsvara-nadini-Tara
Hung-chi Ts'ai-pao hu-fa
Hung-kuang-hsien-yao-p'u-t'i
Hung-kuang-hsien-yao-p'u-t'i fo
Hung-kuang P'i-lu fo
Hung-kuang Shih-chia-shih-tzu fo
Hung-kuang Vairocana (Buddha)
Hung-kuang Wei-lo-wa-chin-kang
Hung-kuang Wen-shu-chin-kang
Hung Miao-yin fo-mu
Hung-mu-hsing
Hung Pu-lo-wang-chin-kang
Hung ssu-pei Kuan-shih-yin p'u-sa
Hung Wei-lo-wa-chin-kang
Hung Wei-lo-wa-chin-kang fo
Hung-wei-sheng-chin-kang
Hung-yen Ti-ch'uang-wang fo
Huo t'ien
Huo-yen-kuang fo
Huo-yen-kuang-ting fo
Hva-san-dge-bsnen
Hva-shang

- I -

I-ch'ieh-ch'eng-chiu Chin-kang-hai-mu
I-ch'ieh-ch'eng-chiu Chiu-tu fo-mu
Indra
Indraketudhvajraraja

Indraketudhvajraraja Buddha
Indraketuvijya Buddha
Indra-(mahayaksasenapati)
Inigegci eke
Irsya-Bhairavavajra
Irsya-sarpa-vis-apaharani (Tara)
Isana
Istadevata
Isvara
Isvara (deva)
Isvara(=Lokesvara)-Avalokitesvara (Bodhisattva)
Itegel mahakala
I-ti hu-fa
I-yao-ta-ch'uan fu-mo hu-fa
I-yung Wei-lo-wa-chin-kang

- J -

Jagaddama-Vajrapani
Jagadvasi(?)-Tara
Jaghan dara eke
Jala-bhayatrana-(Avalokitesvara)
Jala-bhayatrana-Tara
Jalinidhara(?) (fo-mu)
Jalinikumara
Jaliniprabha
Jaliniprabhakumara
Jaliniprabha-Lokesvara
Jamadanda-Lokesvara
Jamaripada-krama-Vasudhara
Jambhala
Jambhala-dkar-po-lha-lnga-jo-bo'i-lugs
Jambhala-dmar-po-srog-sgrubs-sa-lugs
Jambhala-ljang-gu-dus-'khor-lugs
Jambhala-nag-po-Kha-che-pan-chen-lugs
Jambhala-ser-po-gtso-rkyang
Jambhala-Zhal-gSum-Phyag-drug
'Jam-dbyangs
'Jam-dpal-dbyangs
'Jam-dpal-sku-yi-lha-tshogs
'Jam-dpal-tshe-bdag
Jampa
Jampe Tshepdak
Jampeyang
'Jam-po-'khyil-pa
Jampol
Jangchub-sempa
Janggi gucan
'Jang-ri-smug-po
Janguli
Janguli (fo-mu)
Janguli-Tara
Jan-teng fo
Jatamukuta-Lokesvara
Jaya
Jaya (devi)
Jayada (fo-mu)
Jaya-Tara
Jayosnisa (Buddha)
Jedung Lozang Pelden
Jen-ju Po-lo-mi-mu
Jian-Lao
Jibqulang-un egesig dagatu
'Jig-rten-gyi-ma-mo
'Jig-rten-gyi-mgon-po
'Jigs-byed-rdo-rje
'Jigs-pa'i-zer-mo-mig-gcig-ma
'Jigs-par-byed-pa'i-bdud-pho
Jigten Sumgyal
Jih-kuang-pien-chao p'u-sa
Jih-kuang t'ien
Jih-kung t'ien
Jih t'ien
Jih-tsang fo
Jikoku
Jina-Amitabha
Jina-Amoghadarsin
Jina-Anantaujas
Jina-Ashokashri
Jina-Bhadrasri
Jina-Brahmadatta
Jina-Brahmajyotis
Jina-Brahman
Jina-Buddha-Sakyamuni
Jina-Candanasri
Jina-Dhanasri
Jina-Indraketudhvaja
Jina-Kusumashri
Jinamitra
Jina-Nageshvararaja
Jina-Narayana
Jina-Padmajyotis
Jina-Parikirtita-Namashri
Jina-Prabhasashri
Jina-Ratnacandra
Jina-Ratnacandraprabha
Jina-Ratnagni
Jina-Ratnapadma
Jina-Ratnarcis

Jinarsabha-Vaisravana
Jinasagara-Avalokitesvara
Jinasagara-Avalokitesvara (Buddha)
Jina-Samantadarshin
Jina-Samantavabhasa
Jina-Shailendraraja
Jina-Shuradatta
Jina-Smritishri
Jina-Suvikranta
Jina-Vajradhara
Jina-Vajragarbha
Jina-Varuna
Jina-Varunadeva
Jina-Vikratna
Jina-Vimala
Jina-Vimaloshnisha
Jina-Viranandin
Jina-Virasena
Jina-Yuddhajaya
Jing-gir-rgyal-po
Jirgugan gar-tu hayangriva
Jir-rten-skyon
Jiten chyong
Jizo
Jnana-Amitayus
Jnanadakini
Jnanadhatu-Lokesvara
Jnanaguru
Jnandakini
Jnanakara (Bodhisattva)
Jnanaketu
Jnana-krama-Navatmaka-Kartaridhara-Makahala
Jnanakrama-Simhavahana-Syama-Vaisravana
Jnana-Paramita
Jnana-sattva-Manjughosa
Jnana-Vasita
Jnanesvari
Jo-a-ti-sa
Jo-bo-'bo-lha
Jo-bo-chen-po
Jo-bo-g.ya'-spang
Jo-bo-g.yul-rgyal
Jo-bo-gze-rgyal
Jo-bo-klu-bdud-mched-dgu
Jo-bo-lha-bcas
Jo-bo-lugs-kyi-rTam-mGrin
Jo-bo-mchim-lha
Jo-bo-mgon-chen
Jo-bo-nges-sum
Jo-gai-sho
Jo-g.yag-btsan-gyi-rgyal-po
Jo-lugs-sgrol-dkar
Jo-mo-gangs
Jo-mo-gangs-dkar
Jo-mo-lha-ri
Jo-mo-nag-ri
Jo-vo-thugs-rje-chen-po
Jowothuji chenpo
Jug-un jagan
Ju-hsing-mu
Ju-huo-ch'ih-ch'eng Chiu-tu fo-mu
Ju-ichi-men Kwan-non
Ju-i Kuan-shih-yin
Ju-i-lun Kuan-yin
Ju-i-pao-lun pai Chiu-tu fo-mu
Ju-i-ta-pai Yung-pao hu-fa
Julaci eke
Jula joqiaqci
Jun-tei Kwan-non
Jun-u okin tngri
Jvalanala (=Vajrajvalanalarka[?])
Jvalanala(?) (Buddha)
Jvalanalosnisa(?) (Buddha)
Jyotisprabha (?) Buddha

- K -

Ka-chen-mched-brgyad-kod-ru-thur
K'ai-chu-pu tsu-shih
K'ai-hua Kuan-shih-yin
Kakasya-Karma-Mahakala
Kakasya-Karmanatha
Kakudvati
Kala
Kalacakra
Kalacakra-krama-Syama-Jambhala
Kalachakra
Kaladevi
Kaladhvaja(?) (devi)
Kaladhvaja(?) (yo-mu)
Kaladuti
Kalagni (deva)
Kalajambhala
Kalaketu(?) (devi)
Kalaketu(?) (yo-mu)
Kala-nag-po
Ka-la-pa-sa
Kalapasi
Kala-qasti

Kalaratri
Kalarindra(?)-Mahisanana
Kalasha
Kala-Yaksa
Kalayaksa-nag-po
Kalaya-vati
Ka-lha
Ka-lieh-ka-ta-t'ien p'u-sa
Kalika
Ka-li-ka tsun-che
Kali Kruddha Varahi
Kali Kruddha Varahi Nine-deities
Kalpokta-Kurukulla
Ka-lu-ti Shang-lo-wang fo
Kama
Kamadhatvishvari-Parvati
Kamadhatv-isvari
Kamalacandra-Lokesvara
Kamalosnisa(?) (Buddha)
Kamandalu-Lokesvara
Kamaraja
Kamarajavajra
Kamesvari
Kamini
Kami-suvari
Kam-po-gangs-ra-spram-mtsho-rtse
Kanaka
Kanaka-Bharadvaja
Kanakamuni
Ka-na-ka-pa-la-wei-tsa tsun-che
Kanakaprajnaparamita
Kanakaraja
Kanakavarna-Tara
Kanakavasta
Ka-na-ka-wa-ssu tsun-che
Ka-na-ya t'ien
Kan-ch'a-pa
Kan-cha-pa tsu-shih
Kangkaka
Kang-ka-nag-gi-klu-btsan
Kang-ka-thod-nag-bdud-btsan
Kang-kuang p'u-sa
Kan-lu-chin-kang
Kan-lu-t'an-chin-kang
Kan-lu-ti-chin-kang
Kanthamalini
Kanya
Kanya (deva)
Kao-li fo-mu
Kao-ta-ma-t'ien p'u-sa
Kapaladhara-Hevajra
Kapala-Hevajra
Kapalamalin
Kapalini
Ka-pan-pa-ti
Kapata
Karandvyuha-Lokesvara
Ka-ra-ra-tri
Karini
Karitei-mo
Karkata
Karkata(?)deva (Bodhisattva)
Karma-Amitayus
Karmadaka
Karma-Dakini
Karm-a-dakini
Karma-Garuda
Karm-a garudi
Karma-Heruka
Karmakila
Karma-Krotishaurima
Karma-nirmita-Rsi-vidyajnana
Karmaraja
Karm-a-raja
Karma-shugs-ldan
Karma-simhasya
Karm-a singq-a muka
Karmavajra
Karmavajri
Karmavajri (fo-mu)
Karma-Vasita
Karna-Tara
Kartaridhara-Mahakala
Kartaridhara-Traksad-Makahala
Karttikeya
Karttikeya(?) (deva)
Karunesvara-Avalokitesvara
Kasho-butsu
Kasmira-mahapandita-krama-Amoghapasa
Kasmira-mahapandita-krama-Hayagriva
(Kasmira-mahapandita-krama)-Krsna-Jambhala
Kasmira-mahapandita-krama-Sita-Manjughosa
Kasmira-mahapandita-krama-Sita-Tara
Kasmira-mahapandita-krama-Syama-Tara
Kasmira-mahapandita-(Sakyasri)-krama-Kartaridhara-Makahala
Ka-ssu-ma-li fo-mu
Kasyapa
Kasyapadeva
Katyayana

Kaumari(?) (devi)
Kaundinya
Kauveri
Kavaca-Candika
Kavaca-Krsna-Heruka
Kavaca-Mohini
Kavaca-Padmanartesvara
Kavaca-Paramasava
Kavaca-Sancalini
Kavaca-Santrasini
Kavaca-Vairocana
Kavaca-Vajrasattva
Kavaca-Vajrasurya
Kavaca-Vajravarahi
Kavaca-viras
Kavaca-Yamini
Kaya-Hevajra
Kaya-nirmita-Rsi-vidyajnana
Kayaraja
Kei barigci
Kei tngri
Kele-yin ukin tegri
Keng-rus-dkar-mo
Kermina
Kesini
Kesini (devi)
Ketu
Ketugraha (deva)
Kevajra
Keyuri
Kha-ba-dkar-po
Kha-ba-gang-bzang
Kha-ba-klo-'dril
Kha-che-dmar-po
Kha-chu'i-gzhi-bdag-mNgon-dga'
Khadgadhara-Bhairavavajra
Khadgapani
Khadiravani-Tara
Khadoma
Khadub
Kha-'dzin-shag-'debs-dgra-lha
Kha-la-me-'bar
Khal-kha'i-yul-gyi-chos-bdag
Khams-gsum-dban-hdus-spyan-ras-gzigs
Khams-gsum-dbugs-sdud-ma
Khams-gsum-g.yas-'debs-ma
Khams-gSum-rNam-rGyal
Khams-gsum-snying-gsod-ma
Khandaroha
Khanding
Kha-rag-khyung-btsun
Kha-rag-khyung-btsun-ma
Kha-reg-khyung-btsun-ma
Khar-hBar-ma
'Khar-mig-ma
Khasarpana
Khasarpana-Avalokitesvara
Khasarpana-Avalokitesvara (Bodhisattva)
Khasarpana-Lokesvara
Kha-sarpa-ni
Kha-shag-smug-ri
Kha-sha-snyu-ri
Kha-stongs-me-'bar
Kha-zas-(dang)-sprod-pa'i-dgra-lha
Khol-po-kundhali
Khol-po-kundha-li
'Khor-lo-bDe-mchog
Khorlo Demchok
'Khor-lo'i-khyung
'Khor-nag-can
Khor Waji
Khrag-btsan-dmar-po
Khrag-hthun
Khra-thogs-Canda-Vajrapani
Khri-chen-bLo-bzang-bsTan-pahi-Nyi-ma
Khri-chen-Ngag-dBang-mChog-ldan
Khri-ldan-dbang-po-'bar-ba-rgyal
Khri-shog-rgyal-mo'i-mtsho
Khri-shor-rgyal-mo-mched-dgu
Khri-sman-sa-le-ma
Khri-srong-lde'u-btsan
Khri-stag
Khri-stag-ral-mi-bo-che
Khro-bo-bdud-rtsi-hkhyil-ba
Khro-bo-bdud-rtsi-'khyil-ba
Khro-bo-chen-po
Khro-bo-dbyug-sngon-can
Khro-bo-ging-ka-ra
Khro-bo-gzhan-gyis-mi-thub
Khro-bo-hDud-rTsi-hKhyil-pa
Khro-bo-hDod-rgyal
(Khro-bohi-rgyal-po-hphags-pa)-Mi-gyo-snon-po-pus-btsugs-ma
Khro-bo-hum-mdzad
Khro-bo-me-brcegs
Khro-bo-Mi-gYo-ba
Khro-bo-padma
Khro-bo-rdo-rje
Khro-bordo-rje-sa-hog
Khro-bo-rin-chen
Khro-bo-sans-rgyas
Khro-bo-sMe-ba-brTegs-pa

Khro-bo-sme-brcegs
Khro-bo-sme-brtsegs
Khro-bo-sme-brtsegs-dud-kha
Khro-bo-sme-brtsegs-ljan-khu
Khro-bo-stobs-po-che
Khro-chen-vajra-ging-ka-ra
Khrodha
Khrodha-Amritakundalin
Khro gner can ma
Khro-gner-gyo-bahi-sgrol-ma
Khro-mo-sme-brcegs
Khro-mo-sMe-brTsegs
Khug-chos-g.yar-mo-bsil
Khu-le-lag-dgu
Khva-ta'i-gdong-pa-can
Khyab-hjugs-sbas
Khyab-'jug
Khyab-'jug-chen-po
Khyab-'jug-chen-po-rahula
Khyab-'jug-gnam-mtsho'i-bdag-po
Khyab-'jug-sgra-gcan-'dzin
Khyab-mjug-chen-po
Khyi'i-gdong-pa-can
'Khyil-pa
Khyim-nang-lha
Khyi-mo-dmar-mo-gzi-mig-ma
Khyi-mo-dmar-mo-mthing-mig-ma
Khyi-mo-dmar-mo-mtshal-mig-ma
Khyi-mo-dmar-nag-khrag-mig-ma
Khyi-mo-gser-mig-ma
Khyun
Khyung
Khyung-btsun-rdo-rje
Khyung-chen-klu-'brug
Khyung-dung
Khyung-'dus
Khyung-gi-gdong-pa-can
Khyung-gSer-mig-hKhyil-ba
Khyung-Khra
Khyung-lding-nag-po
Khyung-Nag
Khyung-nag-me'i-spu-gri-can
Khyung-nag (me-yi-spu-gri)
Khyung-rtse
Khyung-rtse-mthon-po
Khyung-sngon-'byung-po-'dur-ed-can
Khyung-tho-dung-ri
Khyung-tho-ri
Khyun-khra-man-nag-lugs
Khyun-ser-bkah-gdams-lugs
Kiang-san-kie
Kiao-ta-mo
Kichijo-ten
Kijagalal ugei jibqulang-tu
Kilimili
Kilinglegsen aguril-tu eke
Kilinglegsen duri-tu jou
Kilingtu eke
Killing-tu okin tngri
Kin-kang
Kinkini-Dhari
Kinnara
Kirti-raja-bajar eke
Kirtirajavajra
Kishi-mo-jin
Kkir ugei
kLu
kLu-bdan
kLu-bdud-bu-mo-dod-'dzin-ma
kLu-bdud-bu-mo-khrag-mig-ma
kLu-bdud-bu-mo-kyo-stor-ma
kLu-bdud-bu-mo-padma-'phreng
kLu-bdud-bu-mo-shel-mig-ma
kLu-bdud-bu-mo-stobs-mo-che
kLu-bdud-chen-mo-rgyas-'debs-ma
kLu-bdud-chen-mo-tshe-'dzin-ma
kLu-bdud-dom-nag-sdig-pa'i-mgo-bo-can
kLu-bdud-'gram-nag-ral-pa-can
kLu-bdud-gser-gyi-'phrog-zhu-can
kLu-bdud-gtsang-pa-sbrul-mgo-can
kLu-bdud-g.yag-mgo-can
kLu-bdud-khri-stong-ral-pa
kLu-bdud-khyags-pa-dkar-po
kLu-bdud-nagaraja
kLu-bdud-nag-po
kLu-bdud-nag-po-mgo-dgu
kLu-bdud-nag-po-sog-pa-med
kLu-bdud-nyu-le-nyab-kyi-lag-ring
kLu-bdud-rdo-rje-spyan-gcig-ma
kLu-bdud-sbrul-sna-khan-brag
kLu-bdud-sgo-ra-nag-po
kLu-bdud-stag-dgu-nam-mkha'-lding
kLu-bdud-tsang-pa'i-mgo-dgu
kLu-bdud-zhags-pa-dgur-bcings
kLu-bram-ze'i-rigs
kLu-btsan
kLu-byol-song-gi-rigs
kLu-chen-brgyad
kLu-chen-rgyal-po
kLu-dban
kLu-dban-gi-rgyal-po
kLu-dkar-rigs

kLu-dkar-rtse-mo
kLu-dmangs-rigs
kLu-'dul-ba'i-khyung
kLu-gcig-thod-dkar
kLu-gdol-pa'i-rigs
kLu-grub
kLu-gza'-nag-mo
kLuhi-hjigs-skyobs
kLuhi-sde
kLu'i-dbang-po
kLu'i-dge-bsnyen
kLu'i-rgyal-po-g.yag-gi-gzug-can
kLu'i-sring-mo-rnam-byed
kLu-mchog-klu-rgyal-dung-skyong
kLu-mo-ma-mo-spyan-gcig-ma
kLu-mo-nor-'dzin-ma
kLu-mo-remati-phyag-bzhi-ma
kLu-mo-re-ma-ti-(phyag-bzhi-ma)
kLu-mo-yaksa-nag-po
kLu-rGyal
kLu-rGyal-dGah-bo
kLu-rgyal-lba-ru
kLu-rGyal-Nye-dGah
kLu-rgyal-rigs
kLu-rGyal-sog-ma-med
kLu-rGyal-Varuna
kLu-rje-rigs
kLu-sgrub
kLu-sman-gtso-mo
kLu-sras-bu-lu
kLu-yi-bu-mo-mgo-dgu-ma
kLu-yi-sDe
Kodulku-yi barigci
Koke debel-tu dakini
Koke erlig qagan
Koke hayangriv-a
Koke raks-a
Kokuzo
Komoku
Kong-btsun-de-mo
Kong-btsun-de-mo-bod-khams-skyong
Kong-lha-kong-btsun-rgya-la
Kongo
Kongosatta
Kong-po'i-kong-btsun-de-mo
Kong-rje-brang-dkar
Kong-rje-dkar-po
Kong-srin-ba-glang-gi-gdong-can
Ko-pai fo-mu
Ko-pai-mu
Koyasu Kwan-non

Krakucchanda
Kre-shod-zhe-da-mched-brgyad
Krishnacari
Krishnayamari
Krodha-Acala
Krodha-Amritakundalin
Krodha-Aparajita
Krodha-Bhurkumkuti(?)
Krodha-Candaravajra
Krodhadevatas
Krodha-Guhyapati
Krodha-Hayagriva
Krodha-humkara
Krodha-Kamaraja
Krodha-Mahabala
Krodha-Niladanda
Krodha-Padmantaka
Krodhaparajita
Krodhaparajita (devi)
Krodhaparajitavajra
Krodha-Prajnantaka
(Krodharaja-arya)-Avani-nihita-janu-Nila-Acala
Krodha-Sme-brtsegs
Krodha-Sumbharaja
Krodha-Takkiraja
Krodha-Usnisachakravartin
Krodha-Vajrapani
Krodha-Vajrapatala
Krodha-Vighnantaka
Krodha-Yamantaka
Krodha-Yamari
Kro-dhi-mi-dmar
Krognyer-can-ma
Kro-ti-mi-dmar
Kro-ti-shva-ri-ma
Krsnacarin
Krsna-Dharmaraja
Krsna-Garuda
Krsna-Jambhala
Krsna-Jambhalavajra
Krsna-Manjughosa
Krsna-Manjusri
Krsna-Mararaja
Krsnapada
Krsna-Parnasabari
Krsnaraksa
Krsna-Rastradhipa (?)
Krsnari
Krsnari-Bhairavavajra
Krsnarivajra Buddha

Krsnari-Yamantaka (=Bhairavavajra)
Krsna-Taksad
Krsna-Vajravidarana (Buddha)
Krsna-yaksa
Krsnayamari
Krtanjali-Lokesvara
Kruddha-atiguhya-Hayagriva
Kruddha-kali-Tara
Ksanti-Paramita
Ksati-taraka-Nila-Caturmukha-(Sri-Mahakala)
Ksetrapala
Kshe-tra-Pah-la
Ksiprakara-Sadbhuja-Jnana-Mahakala
Ksitigarbha
Ksitigarbha-Lokesvara
Kuang-hui fo
Kuang-mu
Kuang-mu t'ien-wang
Kuang-pei Chun-t'i fo-mu
Kuang-te fo
Kuang-yen fo
Kuang-yin-ju-lai fo
Kuan-i fo
Kuan-shih-yin
Kuan-shih-yin p'u-sa
Kuan-ting-tsun-sheng Chiu-tu fo-mu
Kuan-tzu-tsai
Kuan-tzu-tsai pi-mi-fo
Kuan-tzu-tsai p'u-sa
Kuan-yin
Kuan-yin Ch'ien-shou
Kuan-yin Ch'ien-yen
Kuan-yin Pa-nam
Kuan-yin san-shih-erh-hsiang
Kuan-yin Sung-tzu
Kubera
Kuber-a
Kubera-svarottama(?)-Vaisravana
Kubir-a
Kudrsti-cora-upadrava-nivarani
Kuei-mu t'ien
Kuei-tzu-mu
Kui Gyalpo
Kui-tzu-mu-shen
Kujaku Myo-o
Kujici eke
Ku-la-ha-ri
Ku-la-mkha'-ri-ze-sngon-pa
Kule
Kulesa
Kulika Kings of Sambhala
Kulisesvari
Ku-lu-ku-lo fo-mu
Kumarabhuta-Manjusri
Kumbha
Kumbha(?) (deva)
Kumbhanda
Kumbhira yao-ch'a-ta-chiang
Kun-bzang-ma
Kunci
Kuncikadhara (fo-mu)
Kun-dgah-po
Kundhali
Kun-'dus-rgyal-po
K'ung-hsing fo-mu
Kung-p'i-lu yao-ch'a-ta-chiang
Kung-shih Yung-pao hu-fa
Kungsum de-mu eke
Kung-te-hua fo
Kung-te-yu-wang p'u-sa
Kun-gyi-'jigs-byed
Kun-nas-snan-ba-bkod-pahi-dpal
Kun-rig-rnams-par-snan-mzad
Kun-rigs
Kun-syo ming-wang
Kun-tu-bzang-po
Kun-tu-bzan-po-glan-chen-po
Kun-tu-ri-ka
Kuntu Sangpo
Kuo-pa-ka tsun-che
Kurmapadi-Vahari
Kurtekui vcir eke
Ku-ru-ku-le
Kurukulla
Kurukulla (fo-mu)
Kurukulla-Tara
Kurukulle
Ku-ru-kulle-gsan-sgrub
Kusel-un eke
Kusuma Buddha
Kusumashri
Kusumasri
Kusumasri Buddha
Kutagara-Vajrapani
Kwang-mu
Kwan-non
Kwan-ze-on
Kwomoku
Kyai-rdo-rje
Kyai-rdor-lhan-skyes
Kye-ba-rdo-rje

Kye Dorje
Kyehi-rdo-rje
Kye-rdo-rje
Kye-te-re
Kyin-thing-dangs-kyi-ra-mo-sman
Kyi vcir
Kyor-lung-chos-skyong

- L -

Labai debeltu eke
Lag-g.yas-gshin-rjer-sprul-pa-dang
Lag-g.yon-klu-btsan-sprul-pa-dang
Lag-nor-(dang)-sprod-pa'i-dgra-lha
Lag-pa
La-hu-la tsun-che
La-ka-la-ti (fo-mu)
Laksmi-krama-Ekadasamukha-Avalokitesvara
La-li-ta
Lalita Tripurasundari
La-li-ta tsu-shih
Lalitavajra
Lalitavajra-Rolpa-Dorje
Lama
Lam-bsTan
Lam-phran
Lam-phran-bsTan
Lan Chiu-tu fo-mu
Lang-ka-mgrin-bcu
Lan-mu-ta-lieh-ta-na-ma hsi-mu
Lan-pang-chin-kang
Lan Shou-ch'ih-chin-kang
La-phyi-gangs
Lasema
Las-gshin-dmar-po-khrag-mdog
Las-gshin-dmar-po-ma-ru-rtse-bzhis-skor-ba
Las-gshin-dpa' gcig
Las-gshin-lha-bcu-gsum
Las-gsin-dmar-po-ma-ru-rtse-bzhis-bskor-ba
Las-kyi-dban-chen
Las-kyi-gshin-rje
Las-kyi-khyun
Las-kyi-khyung
Las-kyi-Kro-ti-shva-ri-ma
Las-kyi-ma-mo
Las-kyi-mgon-po
Las-kyi-mgon-po-zangs-gri-can
Las-kyi-mkha'-'gro-ma
Las-kyi-mkhah-hgro-ma
Las-kyi-rdo-rje-ma
Las-mdzad-gtum-mo
Las-mgon
Las-mgon-bya-rog-gdon-can
Las-mgon-bya-rog-gdong-can
Las-mkhan-'brong-zhal-nag-po
Las-mkhan-chen-po-srog-bdag-ma-rungs-pa-gying-chen-dregs-pa'i-rgyal-po
Las-mkhan-dmar-po
Lasya
La-sya
Lasya (fo-mu)
Layigan
lCags-kyu'i-khyung
lCags-kyu-ma
lCags-mig-ma
lCags-sgrog-ma
lCags-skud-dmar-po
lCags-sgrog-gi-khyung
lCam-mo-shel-bza'
lCam-sring
lCang-ra-smug-po
Lechi Khado
Legs-ldan-nag-po
Legs-ldan-nag-po-srid-med-kyi-bu
Legs-mthon
Legs-nyes-stangs-'dzin
Legs-pahi-shes-rab
Legs-sbyor-gser-thang-yug-ge-ma
Le-gu-lag-ring
lGhags-sgrog-ma
Lha
lHa-bdud-lcags-khung-pa
lHa-brag-klu-btsan
lHa-btsan
lHa-btsan-mgon-lha-dkar-po
lHa-btsan-pa
lHa-btsan-rgyal-pa
lHa-btsun-bu-le
lHa-btsun-ku-le
lHa-bu-gangs-dkar[ma]
lHa-bzang-a-mo-lcam
lHa-chen-dbang-phyug-che
lHa-chen-brgyad
lHa-chen-dpal-'bar-ma-ning
lHa-chen-gnam-the-dkar-po
lHa-chen-gser-gyi-rgyal-po
lHa-chen-khang-kas
lHa-chen-khang-kas-drag-po
lHa-chen-ma
lHa-chen-mahadeva

(lHa-chen)-mgon-po-[lcam-dral]-traksad-gnos-lugs
lHa-chen-mgon-po-lcam-dral-traksad-gnyis-lugs
lHa-chen-nam-dbang-phyug-mahadeva
lHa-chen-zangs-rva
lHa-gnyan-chen-po-sNgo-la-g.yu-rtse
lHa-gnyan-sngo-la-g.yu-rtse
lHag-pa
lHahi-dban-ldan
lHahi-dban-phyug
lHa'i-bud-med
lHa'i-dbang-po-brgya-byin
lHa'i-dge-bsnyen
lHa'i-sring-mo-byis-pa'i-dur-byed-ma
lHa'i-srung-ma
lHa-mchog-jo-bo-chags-gling
lHa-mchog-khang-kas-chen-po
lHa-min-dbang-po-thags-bzang
Lhamo
lHa-mo
lHa-mo-candi-ka
lHa-mo-cunda-phyag-bzhi-ma
lHa-mo-cunda-phyag-man
lHa-mo-dal-byad
lHa-mo-dpal-chen-mo
lHa-mo-drag-mo
lHa-mo-Dud-sol-ma
lHa-mo-dung-gha-bza'
lHa-mo-dung-skyong-ma
lHa-mo-dun-skyon-ma
lHa-mo-e-ka-dza-ti
lHa-mo-ekajati
lHa-mo-ekajati-ral-gcig-ma
lHa-mo-ekajati-sngags-srung
lHa-mo-gos-dkar-mo
lHa-mo-hrol-ma-spyan-gcig-ma
lHa-mo-khro-gner-can-ma
lHa-mo-ma-ma-ki
lHa-mo-ma(m)-gha-bza'
lHa-mo-mgyogs-byed-nag-mo
lHa-mo-nag-mo
lHa-mo-nam-mkha'-gos-can
lHa-mo-nam-mkhahi-gos-can
lHa-mo-ral-gcig-ma
lHa-mo-ral-gcig-ma-phyag-ni-su-rca-bzhi-ma
lHa-mo-remati-gsang-sgrub
lHa-mo-ro-lans-ma
lHa-mo-shel-bza'-sman-gcig-ma
lHa-mo-spu-gri-ma
lHa-mo-sra-ma-na
lHa-mo-srog-sgrub-lcags-phur-ma-ran-byun-rgyal-ma
lHa-mo-srog-sgrub-lcags-phur-ma-rang-'byung-rgyal-mo
lHa-mo-ti-nu
lHa-mo-Tsandi-ka
lHa-mo-tsunda-dKar-mo
lHa-rabs-shams-po
lHa-rgod-thog-pa
lHa-rigs
lHa-ri-gyang-te
lHa-ri-sku-lha-ngo-mo-ri
lHa-ri-spo-mthon
lHa-sa'i-bdud-btsan-mthu-bo-che
lHa-sa'i-bka'-srung-ma-gcig-dpal-ldan-lha-mo
lHa-sman-bkra-sis-tshe-rin-ma
lHa-sman-sras-mo
lHa-sman-tshe-ring-mched-lnga
lHa-srung-phying-pa-dkar-po
lHa'u-g.yang-dkar
lHa-yi-dban
lHa-yi-bdan-po-brgya-byin-mtshan
lHa-yi-dge-bsnyen-drag-rtsal
lHa-yi-gtso-bo
lHo-nub-mgon-po-gri-gug-dmar-po
lHo-nub-mgon-po-gri-gug-dpah-po
lHo-Rin-chen-mkhah-hgro-ma
lHo-rong-gangs
lHo-yi-rong-lha-rgyal-mtshan
Li-byin-ha-ra
Li-byin-ha-ra-dkar-po
Lieh-k'o-ta-ch'ia t'ien
Lieh-sheng-chin-kang
Lieh-yen-chin-kang
Lien-hsu-ta-p'eng Shou-ch'ih-chin-kang
Lien-hua-ch'a-ka fo-mu
Lien-hua-hsing Po-lo-mi-mu
Lien-hua-kuang-yu-hsi-shen-t'ung fo
Lien-hua-miao-wu-tzu-tsai Kuan-shih-yin p'u-sa
Lien-hua-miao-wu-tzu-tsai Ma-t'ou-chin-kang
Lien-hua-ting fo
Light Goddesses
Ling-an-chin-kang
Ling-an t'ien-mu
Ling-chui t'ien
Lingqu-a gerel-tu
Ling-shen-t'iao-fu-chin-kang
Lin Wei-lo-wa-chin-kang
Li Po-lo-mi-mu
Li-shih t'ien

Liu-mien Wei-lo-wa-chin-kang
Liu-mien Wei-lo-wa-chin-kang fo
Liu-pei Chin-kang-miao-yin fo-mu
Liu-pei Miao-yin fo-mu
Liu-pei pai-i Chiu-tu fo-mu
Liu-pei Pu-lu-chin-kang
Liu-pei Yeh-i fo-mu
Liu-pei Yung-pao hu-fa
lJang-ra-smug-po
lJang-sden-chen-po
Ljan-lugs-Saptadas-atmaka-Tamra-kartaridhara-Makahala
lNa-rtsen
lNga-rten
Lob Sangma
Locana
Locanaprabha
Lo-ch'a
Lohakhadga Hayagriva
Lohanadi(?)-Vajrapani
Lo-hi-ta-yi-dge-bsnyen
Lo-hou-la tsun-che
Lo-hou-lo
Loka-dakini
Lokanatha
Lokanatha-raktaryy-Avalokitesvara
Lokapalas
Lokesvara
Lo-ku-lo tsun-che
Lo-ma-gyon-ma
Lo-ma-gyon-ma-phyag-bzhi-ma
Lo-ma-gyon-ma-phyag-drug-ma
Long Lived Sisters
Lo-tzu-tsai t'ien
Lozang Chogyan
Lozang Dondup
Lozang Gyathso
Lozang Kalzang
Lozang Yeshe
lTa-ba-mig-rno'i-dgra-lha
lTa-nan-rkun-pohi-ner-htshe-las-bzlog-ma
lTen-rgyas-hod-srun
lTun-bsags-kyi-sans-rgyas-so-lna
lTung-bShags
Lu
Lu Chiu-tu fo-mu
Lugs-gnis-gcig-tu-sgril-bahi-[ye-ses]-mgon-po-phyag-bzhi-pa
Lugs-gnyis-gcig-tu-bsgril-ba'i-ye-shes-mgon-po-phyag-bzhi-pa
Lu-hi-pa
Luhipada
Lu-hsi-pa tsu-shih
Luipada
Luma
Lung-chung-sheng-mu
Lung-shu tsu-shih
Lung-tsun-wang fo
Lung-yu t'ien
Lus-lha
Lus-nan-po
Lus-ngan
Luus-un erketu qagan
Luvang

- M -

Ma-chags-stong-gi-dgra-lha
Ma-cig-Lban-sgron
Madar terigutu
Ma-gcig-'dod-khams-dbang-phyug-rab-brtan-ma
Ma-gcig-dPal-ldan-lha-mo
Ma-gcig-dPal-ldan-lha-mo-remati
Ma-gcig-Lab-sgron
Ma-gcig-lha-mo
Ma-gcig-rdo-rje-khyung-lung-ma
Ma-gcig-rdo-rje-rab-brtan-ma
Ma-gcig-srid-pa'i-lha-mo-gdong-dmar-ma
Ma-gha-bza'
Ma-g.yo-ka-ba
Maha-abhayakari-Lokesvara
Maha-abhayaphalada-Lokesvara
Mahabahu
Ma-ha-bajar-suri
Mahabala
Ma-ha-bala
Mahabala Buddha
Mahabalavajra
Mahabhumika-Avalokitesvara (Bodhisattva)
Mahabhumika(?)-rakta-Avalokitesvara
Mahabodhisattva
Mahacandarosana
Mahacandrabimba-Lokesvara
Ma-ha-car-a
Mahachakra-Vajrapani
Mahachakra-Vajrapani Buddha
Mahacina-Tara
Mahadeva
Mahadeva-dkar-po

Mahagadi
Mahagati
Maha-Isvari
Mahajaya
Mahajina
Mahakala
Mahakala-Brahmanarupa
Mahakala (deva)
Mahakala-gur
Mahakala-mGon-dkar
Mahakala-mGon-po
Mahakala-Simhamukha
Mahakala-Taksad
Mahakalavajra
Mahakali
Mahakali-Dam-tshig-gi-dbang-mo
Mahakali-Remati
Ma-ha-karma-suri
Mahakarmesvara
Mahakasyapa
Mahakrita
Mahakrodha
Mahalaksmi-Devi
Ma-ha-lieh-tsu-wa-lieh-ma hsi-mu
Mahamanjubhuta-Lokesvara
Mahamanjudatta-Lokesvara
Ma-ha-mantra-nudhari
Mahamantranusarini
Mahamati
Mahamati (Bodhisattva)
Mahamaya
Ma-ha-ma-ya-la-na-mo
Mahamayavajra (Buddha)
Mahamayuri
Mahamayuri (fo-mu)
Ma-ha-mayuri
Mahamudra
Mahapadmesvara
Mahapancaraja
Mahapandaka-Karma-Mahakala
Mahapandita-Sumatijnana
Mahapatala-Lokesvara
Mahapita-Vaisravana
Mahaprabha (Buddha)
Mahapratisara
Ma-ha-pratisari
Mahapratyangira
Mahapratyangira (fo-mu)
Maharaja
Maharajalila-Manjusri
Maharaja-Vaisravana
Maharajavara
Maharakta-Ganapati
Maharakta-Mahakala
Maharatnakirti-Lokesvara
Maharatnakula-Lokesvara
Ma-ha-ratnasuri
Maharatnesvara
Mahasahasrabhuja-Lokesvara
Mahasahasrapramardani
Mahasahasrasuryya-Lokesvara
Mahasankhanath-Lokesvara
Mahasanti-Tara
Ma-ha-saqasra-paramardani
Mahasarasvati
Mahasiddharthesvara
Mahasiddhas
Mahasiddha-santigupta-krama-Caturbhuja-(Jnana)-Mahakala
Maha-sitavani
Mahasitavati
Mahasri-Tara
Mahasthamaprapta-Lokesvara
Mahasthamaprata
Mahasukha (Buddha)
Mahasukha-Dakini-mata
Mahasurvana-Vaisravana
Mahasuryyabimba-Lokesvara
Mahatari-Tara
Mahavajradhara
Mahavajradhatu-Lokesvara
Mahavajradhrk-Lokesvara
Mahavajranatha-Lokesvara
Mahavajrapani-Lokesvara
Mahavajrasattva-Lokesvara
Mahavajresvara
Mahavala
Maha-van-nirmita
Mahavidya
Mahavira
Mahavisvasuddha-Lokesvara
Mahavrati-Dharmaraja
Mahayaksasenapati
Mahayasa
Mahesvara
Mahesvara (deva)
Ma-hgags-pa
Mahidhara
Mahlaima
Mahodadhi
Mahodgatosnisa(?)
Mahosnisa (Buddha)

Mahosthavajra
Maijdari
Maitreya
Maitreya (pot-bellied)
Maitri-Dakini
Mai-tri-mkhah-spyod
Maitripada
Maja chenmo
Ma-ka-lieh t'ien
Makara (deva)
Makaravaktra
Mala
Ma-le-gu
Ma-lha
Ma-lieh-ka-ma hsi-mu
Ma-lieh-ka-ta-t'ien p'u-sa
Malya
Malya (fo-mu)
Ma-ma-chi fo-mu
Mamaki
Mamaki-Devi
Mamaki (fo-mu)
Ma-mchog-lce-spyang-mdung-'dzin
Ma-mo
Ma-mo-dom-gyi-mgo-can
Ma-mo-dred-kyi-mgo-can
Ma-mo-dur-bya'i-mgo-can
Ma-mo-dza-mun-ti
Ma-mo-ekajati
Ma-mo-gnod-sbyin-mdzes-ldan-ma
Ma-mo-gzig-gi-mgo-can
Ma-mo-'jig-pa'i-glog-'byin
Ma-mo-kang-ka'i-mgo-can
Ma-mo-nag-mo
Ma-mo-rdo-rje-ba-lam
Ma-mo-seng-ge-yi-mgo-can
Ma-mo-sgam-pa-ma
Ma-mo-sngags-kyi-srung-ma
Ma-mo-spyang-mo'i-mgo-can
Ma-mo-srid-pa'i-rgyal-mo-mgon-po-mahakala
Ma-mo-srin-po'i-khram-'debs
Ma-mo-stag-gi-mgo-can
Mana-simha-bhaya-trana (Tara)
Mandarava
Ma-ne-ne
Ma-ne-ne-gnam-sman-dkar-mo
Mangala
Mangala-Dirghayus
Mangala-Dirghayushi
Mangalaloka-Tara
Mangalarthakari(?) (Tara)
Mangalotpadana-Tara
Mang-nya-'u-ber
Mangyila bedurye ochi gyalpo
Mani-badr-a
Manibhadra
Manibhadra-Yaksa
Manidhara
Manidharin
Manidharin Buddha
Manipadma-Lokesvara
Manipali
Manjughosa
Manjukumara
Manjunatha
Manjunatha-Lokesvara
Manjushrimitra
Manjusri
Manjusri-Bhattaraka
Manjusri-Jananasattva
Manjusrikirtti
Manjusri-Manjughosa
Manjusri-vajra
Manjusri vcir
Manjuvajra
Manjuvajra-Guhyasamaja
Manla
Manohara-Vasudhara
Mantranudharani (fo-mu)
Mantrapala-Ekajati
Manushi Bodhisattvas
Manushi Buddhas
Manushi Buddhasshaktis
Ma-pham-pa
Mara
Mara-snying-za-ma
Marasudana-Tara
Marici
Marici-Asokakanta
Marici (fo-mu)
Marici-Picuva
Ma-rig-'khrul-ba'i-bdud
Marini
Marishi-ten
Markata(?) deva
Marmedze
Mar-mehi-ma
Mar-me'i-khyung
Mar-me-mdsad
Mar-pa
Ma-sang-g.ya'-spangs-skyes
Ma-sangs-g.ya'-spang-rdza-rgyal

Ma-sangs-kyung-'dus
Ma-sangs-spun-dgu
Ma-sangs-spyi-rje
Masi geigulun joqiaqci
Masi teyin boged darumtatu
Masi ugugada dagurisqagci
Matar terigutu eke
Ma-ting (t'ou?)-chin-kang
Ma-t'ou-chin-kang
Matsarya-Bhairavavajra
Matsyendra
Maudgalyayana
Maya
Mayajalakramaryavalokitesvara
Mayajalakrama-Avalokitesvara
Mayajalakramakrodha-Lokesvara
Mayajalakrama-Kurukulla
Ma-zhing-khyung-rtse
mChan-brjod-kyi-hjam-dbyans-phyag-bzhi-pa
mChan-dpal-sin-tu-yons-bsgrags
mChan-legs-yons-grags-dpal-gyi-rgyal-po
mChe-ba-mo
mChims-phu-btsan-rgod-chu-bo-ri
mChog-gi-rGyal-mTshan
mChong-mig-ma
mChu-so-bdud-du-sprul-pa-dang
mC'og-gi-dan-pohi-sans-rgyas
mDa'-la-brsan-mo-gdug-pa-'dul
mDzes-byed-padma-can
mDze-ma'i-'od-'phro-ma
mDzes-pa'i-gzugs-can-ma
Medicine Buddhas
Med-pa-yod-ces-dgra-lha
Me-duna
Mehi-hjigs-skyobs
Mei-ming fo-mu
Me-lce-'bar-ba
Me-lCe-hChang-pa
Me-lHa
Me-ltar-hbar-ba
Mengge cogcalagsan
Merusikhara-Muni
Mesa
Me-thar
Me-tog-Cher-rgyas
Me-tog-dpal
Me-tog-gi-khyung
Me-tog-ma
Me-tog-spungs-sems
Metoma
mGar-ba'i-mtshan-can
mGar-ba-nag-po
mGar-nag
mGo-bo-srin-por-spruyl-pa-dang
mGon-bdud-bya-rog-gdong-can
(mGon-bkah-bzhi)-mgon-dmar-dban-gi-rgyal-po
(mGon-bkah-gnis-pa)-mgon-dkar-yid-bzhin-nor-bu
(mGon-bkah-gsum-pa)-mgon-ser-(nor-bsrun)-blo-hpel-(zhal-gsum-phyag-drug-pa)
mGon-chen-bkra-shis-che
mGon-chung
mGon-dkar-yid-bzhin-nor-bu
mGon-dmar-dbang-gi-rgyal-po
mGon-dmar-rkan-glin-can
mGon-dmar-rkang-gling-can
mGon-ljang-tshe-bdag
mGon-ljan-tshe-bdag
mGon-mchog-nag-po-lte-dkar
mGon-po
mGon-po-am-gho-ra
mGon-po-bar-chad-kun-sel
mGon-po-bdun-cu-don-lnga
mGon-po-ben
mGon-po-ben-dkah-ma
mGon-po-Beng
mGon-po-beng-dka'-ma
mGon-po-beng-gter-ma
mGon-po-ben-gter-ma
mGon-po-ber-nag-zangs-gri-can
mGon-po-ber-nag-zans-gri-can
mGon-po-Bram-zehi-gZugs-can
mGon-po-'brong-ri
mGon-po-bya-rog-gdong-can
mGon-po-bzhi-sbrags
mGon-po-dkar-po
mGon-po-dmar-po
mGon-po-gcer-bu-zangs-gri-can
mGon-po-gcer-bu-zans-gri-can
mGon-po-gri-gug-dpa'-gcig
mGon-po-gri-gug-dpah-gcig
mGon-po-gri-gug-kha-che-pan-chen-lugs
mGon-po-gri-gug-(lha-dgu-ma)-dzna-na-lugs
mGon-po-gri-gug-lha-dgu-manyaja-na'i-lugs
mGon-po-gur
mGon-po-gzag-ldan
mGon-po-jag-lha
mGon-po-legs-ldan
mGon-po-legs-ldan-mched-gsum
mGon-po-legs-ldan-mche-gsum
mGon-po-lha-chen-dpal-'bar-jo-bo'i-lugs

mGon-po-lha-chen-dpal-hbar-jo-bohi-lugs
mGon-po-ljang-khu
mGon-po-mahakala
mGon-po-mgron-lha
mGon-po-Phyag-bZhi-pa
mGon-po-phyag-drug
mGon-po-phyag-drug-pa
mGon-po-phyin-kha
mGon-po-ser-po
mGon-po-srog-lha-dkar-po
mGon-po-sTag-zhon
mGon-po-taksad-[?]
mGon-po-(')thab-rkyen-sna-nag
mGon-po-traksad-'brong-zhal-can
mGon-po-traksad-dvags-pohi-lugs
mGon-po-traksad-dvags-po'i-lugs
mGon-po-traksad-gri-gug-sbrag-sgrub-ma
mGon-po-traksad-gri-gug-sbrags-sgrub-ma
mGon-po-traksad-gsang-sgrub-shva-na'i-zhal-can
mGon-po-traksad-gsan-sgrub-sva-nahi-zhal-can
mGon-po-traksad-hbron-zhal-can
mGon-po-traksad-ma-ning-ma
mGon-po-traksad-ma-nin-ma
mGon-po-traksad-rkang-thang-ma
mGon-po-traksad-rkan-than-ma
mGon-po-traksad-seng-zhon-jo-bo'i-lugs
mGon-po-traksad-sen-zhon-jo-bohi-lugs
mGon-po-yid-bzhin-nor-bu
mGon-po-zangs-gri-can-lha-bcu-bdun-ma-gyi-ljang-lugs
mGon-po-zans-gri-can-(lha-bcu-bdun)-gyi-ljang-lugs
mGon-po-zas-lha-dmar-po
mGon-ser-nor-srung-blo-'phel
mGon-ser-nor-srung-blo-'phel-zhal-gsum-phyag-drug-pa
mGo-yul-jo-mo-lha-ri
mGrin-bzan-ma
mGron-phu'i-dil-(dang)-thog-gi-ri
mGur-lha-bcu-gsum
mGyogs-pa-rta-yi-dgra-lha
Mi-'am-ci-ljon-rta-mgo
Miao-fa-chin-kang fo-mu
Miao-fa t'ien-mu
Miao-hua fo
Miao-i fo
Miao-kuang fo
Miao-mu fo
Miao-pao-t'ung-tzu
Miao-wu fo-mu
Miao-wu-mu
Miao-wu Ts'ai-pao hu-fa
Miao-yin mu
Miao-yin t'ien-mu
Miao-yin-tzu-tsai Wen-shu
Miao-yu-tsun-ti Wen-shu
Mi-bdud-'byams-pa-khrag-mgo
Mi-bskyod-pa
Mi-'byams-pa-khrag-mgo
Mi-bzad-ser-snahi-lcags-sgrog-hgrol-mdzad-ma
Mi-ch'i-lo yao-ch'a-ta-chiang
Mi-chi Pu-tung-chin-kang fo
Mi-chi Wen-shu-chin-kang fo
Mi-chou-sui-ch'ih fo-mu
Mi-dmar-bshan-pa
Mi-dmar-gshar-pa
Mi-dmar-khra-ma
Mi-dmar-khra-ma-srog-bdag
Migba
Mig-dang-snying-dang-mchin-pa-gsum
Mig-dmar
Mig-gcig-ma-mche-ba-can
Mig-med-khyung-bshon-'brug-lag
Mig-mi-bzang
Mi-gsod-se-shar
Mi-gyo-ba
Mi-gyo-ba-dkar-po
Mi-gyo-ba-dmar-po
Mi-gyo-ba-(khro-bo-gtum-po)-snon-po-bkah-gdams-lugs
Mi-gyo-ba-phyag-bzhi-pa
Mi-gyo-ba-snon-po
Mi-gyo-ba-sprehu-brgyad-pa
Mi-gyo-ba-zhabs-bzhi-pa
Mi-g.yo-blo-bzang-ma
Mi-g.yo-blo-bzan-ma
Mi-gyo-glan-bzan-ma
Mi-g.yo-glang-bzang-ma
Mi-gyo-pa
Mihi-sen-ge
Mi-hkhrugs-pa
Mi-k'o-pa
Mikyoba
Milarapa
Mi-la-ras-pa
Mi-la tsu
Mi-lo Fo
Mi-lo p'u-sa
Mi-mgon-dkar-po
Mi-mjed-zhin-bdag-Tshans-pa-che
Mina

Mina (deva)
Mi-nag-spres-mgo-can
Mi-na t'ien
Min-chieh-ting
Min-chieh-ting fo
Min-chieh Wen-shu
Min-chieh Wen-shu p'u-sa
Ming-chao fo
Ming-chou-hung-sheng Chui-tu fo-mu
Minggan gar-tu qomsim bodhi-satuva
Ming-hsiang fo
Ming-hsiang tsu-shih
Ming-hui p'u-sa
Ming-teng fo
Ming-tien tsun-mu
Ming-yen fo
Ming-yueh-mu
Mi-pham-mgon-po
Mi-pham-rgyal-mo (Tara)
Mi-phyed-pa
Mi-rabs-brgyud-kyi-dgra-lha
Mi-rgod-hjigs-skyobs
Mi-roku
Miroku butsu
Misshaku
Mi-te Wen-shu-shih-li fo
Mi-thub-dgra-lha-spun-gsum
Mithuna
Miti o gtargui-yin yabudal-tu
Mitra-krama-Sita-Amitayus
Mi'ugdung-drug-dgra-lha
Miyowa
Mjug-ma-rmu-ru-sprul-pa-dang
Mjug-ring
mKha'-dbyings-lha-mo
mKha'-'gro-dpal-ldan-nag-mo-mgyogs-byed-ma
mKha'-gro'i-gtso-mo-ce-spyang-ma
mKha'-'gro'i-gtso-mo-kun-bdag-srog-gcod-ma
mKha'-'gro-ma
mKhah-hGro
mKhah-hGro-Dom-gyi-gDong-can
mKhah-hgro-gos-snon-can
mKhah-hgrohi-hjigs-skyobs
(mKhah-hgro-ma)-gsan-ba-ye-ses
mKhah-hgro-ma-stag-don-can
mKhah-hGro-Seng-gehi-gDong-can
mKhah-hGro-sTag-gDong-can
mKha'-lding
mKha'-lding-gser-mig-'khyil-ba
mKha'-lding-rgyal-po
mKhar-bzang-rgyal-po
mKhas-grub-rje
mNag-gzhung-ma
mNgon-dga'-lha-khang-gi-chos-bdag-tshangs-pa-drag-po-bse-khrab-can
mNgon-Phyogs-dMar po
mNon-mkhyen-rgyal-po
Mo-brtsun-gung-rgyal
Modur taghanvacirtu
Mog-po-ri-(dang)-drag-shul-can
Moha-Bhairavavajra
Moha-hasti-bhaya-trani-devi (Tara)
Mojaghanjavala-Lokesvara
Mo-lha
Mon-bu-mthing-nag
Mon-bu-pu-tra
Monggol ganjur-un
Mo-ni-lo-(mahayaksasenapati)
Mo-ni-lo yao-ch'a-ta-chiang
Mon-ju
Mon-mo-gser-gyi-spu-gri-ma
Mon-mo-nag
Mon-mo-shva-na-nag-mo-drug
Mon-pa-gri-debs
Mon-pa-nag-po
Morin qogholai-tu
Mother Deities
Mou-ni fo
Mrityuvancana-Tara
mThah-yas-gnen
mThah-yas-rnam-rgyal
mThar-skyes-mgon-po
mThing-gi-zhal-bzang-ma
mThing-gi-zhal-bzang-ma-mthe-bo-pra-dang-me-long-pra
mThin-gi-zhal-bzan-ma
mThing-ya-ma-skyong
mTho-lding-gi-rgyal-chen
mThon-ba-don-yod
mThon-po-bkra-shis-rtse
mThu-chen-dgra-'dul
mThu-chen-ma-mo-(bcu-gnyis)
mThu-dpung-spos-ri-zlum-po
mTshan-dpal-sin-tu-yons-bsgrags
mTshan-legs
mTshan-legs-yons-bsgrags-dpal-gyi-rgyal
mTshan-legs-yons-grags-dpal
mTshan-thos-Sgrib-pa-rnam-par-sel
mTsho-skye-rdo-rje
mTsho-sman-g.yu-thang-cho-longs-(ma)
mTsho-sman-gzi-ldan-ral-gcig-ma
mTsho-sman-mthing-gi-lha-mo

mTsho-sman-nyi-ma'i-byan-gcig-ma
mTsho-sman-rgyal-mo-mkhro'i-gtso
mTsho-sman-ru-phyug-rgyal-mo
Mu-chien-lien
Mudgaradhara-Bhairavavajra
Muktiskandha Buddha
Mukunda
Mukundadhara (fo-mu)
Muni Buddha
Munindra
Muraja
Musical Instrument Deities
Mu-stegs-dgu-lag-nag-po
Mu-stegs-gu-lang-nag-pa
Mu-stegs-ha-shang-nag-po
Mu-stegs-kala-nag-po
Mya-nan-med-mchog-dpal
Mya-nan-med-pahi-dpal
Mya-nan-sel-bahi-sGrol-ma
Myang-bran-rgyal-chen
Myang-ngan-med-mchog-dpal
Myur-ma-dpah-mo
Myur-mdzad-ye-ses-phyag-drug-mgon
Myur-mdzad-Ye-ses-mgon-po-phyag-drug-pa
Myur-mdzad-ye-shes-kyi-mgon-po-phyag-drug-pa
Myur-shing-mgyogs-pa'i-dgra-lha
Myur-zhin-dpahi-sGrol-ma

____

- N -

Na-chia-hsi tsun-che
Nadapada
Nad-gtong-ma
Nadi-Dakini
Nadi gasib
Nadi-Kasyapa
Nad-kyi-bdag-mo
Naga
Naga-bhayatrana-(Avalokitesvara)
Naga-bhayatrana-Tara
Nagajati eke
Naganjuna baksi
Nagaraja
Naga-raja-bajar eke
Nagarajavajra
Nagaraksa-Manjusri
Nagarjuna
Nagarjun-a
Nagarjuna-krama-Caturbhuja-(mahadharmapala-Jnana)-Mahakala
Nagarjuna-krama-Samatrka-Panjara-Mahakala
Nagarohi-Manjusri
Nagasa-manjusri
Nagasena
Nagasen-a
Nagesvara Buddha
Nagesvaravajra Buddha
Nag-gi-lha-mo
Nag-mo
Nag-mo-chen mo
Nag-mo-gnod-sbyin
Nag-mo-khrag-'jag
Nag-mo-mgyogs-byed
Nag-po
Nag-po-bkhrag-med
Nag-po-gnod-sbyin
Nag-po-mdung-rtse-do-la-ri
Nag-po-mgo-dgu
Nag-po-sPyod-pa
Nag-shod-Nyang-spyang
Nags-na-gNas
Nags-rin-lugs-kyi-sgrol-dkar
Nairatma
Nairatma (fo-mu)
Naivedya
Na-ka-sai-na tsun-che
Naksatraraja Buddha
Naksatrarajavikridita Buddha
Na-lo-ch'a-chi-ni fo-mu
Na-lo-pa tsu-shih
Na-lo-yen fo
Na-lo-yen t'ien
Na-lo-yen t'ien-mu
Namasangiti
Namasangiti-Avalokitesvara
Namasangiti-Manjusri (Bodhisattva)
Nam-gru
Nam-gru-chen-mo
'Nam-gru-ma
Namgyelma
Namkha Gyaltsan
Namkhe nyingpo
Nam-mkhah-bka'-srung-dbang-gi-ma-mo-bdun
Nam-mkh-ah-dvyings-kyi-dvang-phyung-ma
Nam-mkhahi-gos-can-ma
Nam-mKhah-rGyal-mTshan
Nam-mkhah-rgyal-po
Nam-mkhahi-snin-po

Nam-mk'hai-snying-po
Nam-mkha'-sbar-'dzin
Namnang
Nam-pahi-srog-gsan-Baik-tse-che
Nampar Nangdze
Namru
Namtose
Namur-un okin tngri
Nanda
Nanda-Nagaraja
Nandi
Nandikesvara
Nandi luus-un qagan
Nandisvara (deva)
Nang-Lha
Nangsalma
Nang-sgrub-srin-gi-gdong-can
Nan-sgrub-Zhan-blon-rdo-rje-bdud-hdul
Nan-sheng fo-mu
Nan-son-las-sgrol-bahi-sGrol-ma
Narakaloka (Buddha)
Naraloka
Na-ra-seng-ha
Narayana
Narayana Buddha
Narayana (deva)
Narayana-Mahakala
Narayani (devi)
Na-rgyal-sen-gehi-hjigs-skyon
Naro-Khachoma
Na-ro-mkhah-spyod-ma
Naro-(Nadi)-dakini (fo-mu)
Naro ogtargui-yin yabudal-tu
Naropa
Na-ro-pa
Nartakavara-Rakta-Vaisravana
Nartakavara-Vaisravana
Natha-Mahakala
Natsho dorje khado
Nava-Bhutadamara-Vajrapani
Navajatimdhara
Navami-Tithi
Navasikhin(?) (Buddha)
Navatmaka-Mahapita-Vaisravana
Ne-btsan-gter-bdag-rag-mo-ri
Nei-ch'eng-ching-ming Wen-shu
Neng-chu t'ien-mu
Neng-huai-wu-yen-chin-kang
Neng-hung-chu-chang-chin-kang
Neng-hung-chu-ti t'ien-mu hu-fa
Neng-mieh-chu-k'u Chiu-tu fo-mu
Neng-sheng-chi-hsiang Chiu-tu fo-mu
Neng-sheng-mo-chang-chin-kang
Neng-sheng-san-chieh
Neng-sheng-san-chieh Chiu-tu fo-mu
Neng-sheng-san-chieh-chin-kang
Neng-sheng-san-chieh fo
Neng-sheng-san-chieh p'u-sa
Neng-ts'ui-wu-ti Chiu-tu fo-mu
Neng-ts'ui-yuan-mo Chiu-tu fo-mu
Neng-tung-san-chieh Chiu-tu fo-mu
Ner-sbas
Ne-ser-jo-bo-chen-po
Ne-ser-lha-yi-dge-bsnyen-chen-po
(Ne-sras-brgyad-kyi-nan-chen)-hPhags-pa-hjam-dpal
(Ne-sras-brgyad-kyi-nan-chen)-phyag-na-rdo-rje-ljan-khu
(Ne-sras-brgyad-kyi-nan-chen)-spyan-ras-gzig
Ne('u)-le-thod-dkar
Ngag-dbang-bstan-'dzin-rnam-rgyal-'jigs-med
Ngal-bsos-po
Ngan-song-sByongs-rGyal
Ngom-rgyal-mtsho-bkra
Ngonchyen gyalpo
Nidhema
Nidhi-Dandadhara-Mahakala
Nidubarujekci
Nieh-p'an-chi-mieh Chiu-tu fo-mu
Nien-yu p'u-sa
Niguca dakini
Niguca eke
Niguca erlig qagan
Niguca quriyanggui
Nikama-varsi-Sita-Mahakala
Nila-Acala
Nila-Acalavajra
Niladanda
Niladandavajra
Niladanda-Vajrapani
Niladanta
Nila-Dharmaraja-Karma-Yama
Nila-Hayagriva
Nilakantha-isvara (= Lokesvara)-Avalokitesvara (Bodhisattva)
Nilakantha-Lokesvara
Nilakantharyavalokitesvara
Nilambara-Dakini
Nilambaradhara
Nilambaradhara-Vajrapani
Nilandanta-vcir-bani
Nilandar-a

Nila-Parnasabari
Nila-Simhavaktra
Nila-suvari
Nilasva-Krsna-Vaisravana
Nilasva-Raktasula-Vaisravana
Nila-Tara (fo-mu)
Nila-Vahari
Nila-Vajrapani
Nila-Vajravidarana
Nila-Yamaraja
Nilesvari
Ni-ltar-snan-byed
Ni-ma-grags
Ni-ma-hod-zer-(can)
Nine Planet Deities
Ni-o
Nirbhayavigatatamoraja(?)
Nirmanakaya-Amitayus
(Nirrtipada-krama-Bhattaraka)-Maitreya
Nirrti-Raksasa
Nirukti-Pratisamvita
Nispanna-Tara
Nityanatha-Lokesvara
Niu-shou Yung-pao hu-fa
Niu-(r. hung)wei-sheng-chin-kang
Nivaranaviskambhin
Nivida eke
Ni-wo
Noghoghan dara eke
Nogugan dar-a eke
Noguge bayasqulang
Noguge ilagugci
Noguge qogusun
Noguge sayin
Noguge tegusugsen
Nomuqan eke
Nor-bdag-chen-po-kubera
Nor-bdag-stag-sgro-'dzin-pa
Nor-bu-bzang-po
Nor-bu-hdzin-pa
Nor-dpal
Nor-'dzin-rgyal-mo-rab-brtan-ma
Nor-gter-ma (Tara)
Norlha
Nor-lha
Nor-lha-arya-jambhala
Nor-rgyun-ma
Nor-rgyun-ma-ba-glang-rdzi
Nor-rgyun-ma-ba-lan-rdzi
Nor-rgyun-ma-dmar-mo
Nor-rgyun-ma-dza-ma-rihi-lugs
Nor-sbyin
Nor-sbyin-ma
Nor-skyong-ma
Nor-ster-ma-sngon-mo
Nrtya
Nrtya (fo-mu)
Nub-padma-mkhah-hgro-ma
Nyang-bran-rgyal-chen
Nya-ngenme-chhopal
Nyan-pa-rna-ba'i-dgra-lha
Nye-gnas-lcang-dkar
Nyi-ma
Nyi-ma-gzhon-nu
Nyi-ma'i-mig
Nyi-sang-pad
Nyo-i-rin
Nyo-i-rin Kwan-non

- O -

Obesuben bolugsan qatun
Ocirdara
'Od-bzang-po
'Od-de-gung-rgyal
'Od-de-'od-po-che
Oddiyana-Kurukulla
Od-dpag-med
'O-de-gung-rgyal
'O-di-gu-rgyal
Odiyana-Marici
'Od-kyi-rgyal-po-li-byan-ha-ra
'Od-lha-'bar-ba
'Od-zer-dpag-me
O-ka-ta-sha t'ien
Okin tngri
O-mi-to-fo
Ongge vcir eke
On gge-yin vcir eke
Opagme
Oqtarghui-in jiruken
'Or-du-su'i-yul-lha-jing-gir
Orgyan-sgrol-ma-gnas-kyi-dban-phyug-ma
Orui-dagan erdeni-tu
Osadhi Buddha
Ostaraki
Osung
Otege terigutu
Otoci
Ozer chemma

- P -

Pacaka-Tara
Padatika-Traksad-Makahala
Pad-dkar-ses-rab-gsal-byed
Padma
Padma-Amitayus
Pad-ma-bZang-po
Padmacarya-Paramita
Padmadaka
Padma-Dakini
Padm-a-dakini
Padma-Dakini (fo-mu)
Padma-dban-chen
Padmadhara-Bhairavavajra
Padmadhara (fo-mu)
Padma-dkar
Padma-gar-dban-phyag-bco-brgyad-pa
Padma-Garuda
Padm-a garudi
Padma-gsung-gi-lha-tshogs
Pad-ma-gtsug-phud-ma
Padma-hbyun
Padma-Heruka
Padmahi-hod-zer
Padmahi-hor-zer-rnam-par-rol-bas-mnon-par-mkhyen-pa
Padma'i-khyung
Pad-ma-'jigs-byed
Padmajyotirvikriditabhijna
Padmajyotirvikriditabhijna Buddha
Padmajyotis Buddha
Padma khado
Padma-khyun
Padmakila
Padma-krodha
Padma Krotishaurima
Pad-ma-Kro-ti-shva-ri-ma
Pad-ma-mkha'-'gro-ma
Padma-mkhah-hgro-ma
Padma-mthar-byed
Padmanartesvara
Padmanartesvara-Avalokitesvara (Bodhisattva)
Padmanartesvara-Hayagriva
Padmantaka
Padmapani
Padmapani-Avalokitesvara
Padmapani-Lokesvara
Padma-rgyal-po
Padma-ruda
Padmasambhava
Padma-sambha-va
Pad-ma-shugs-ldan
Padma-simhasya
Padma-taka
Padma-Tara
Padmavikasana-Avalolitesvara
Padmosnisa
Pad-phreng-ma
Pa-hou Pu-tung-chin-kang
Pai Chui-tu-fo
Pai Chu-p'in fo-mu
Pai-hao fo-mu
Pai-i fo-mu
Pai Lung-mu
Pai Lung-wang
Pai Ma-t'ou-chin-kang fo
Pai-ming-hui Chin-kang-hai-mu
Pai po-ta-li fo-mu
Pai Pu-tung-chin kang
Pai-san-kai
Pai-san-kai fo-mu
Pai-san-kai p'u-sa
Pai-san-ting fo
Pai Shang-lo-wang
Pai Shang-lo-wang fo
Pai Shou-ch'ih-chin-kang
Pai Wen-shu p'u-sa
Pa-ku-la tsun-che
Palduchi khorlo
Pa-lieh-sha-tsa-cha t'ien
Palsangwa dupa
P'a-lu-che-na
Pa-na-pa-ssu tsun-che
Pancabuddha-Samvararaja (Buddha)
Pancamukhadvadasabhuja-krsna-Avalokitesvara (Bodhisattva)
Pancaraksa
Pancatmaka-Amoghapasa
Pancatmaka-Pratisara
Pancatmika-Tara
Panca-visa-salyoccheda-Bhaisajyaguru
Pancharakshas
Pan-chen-blo-bzan-ye-ses
Pan-ch'en lo-pu-tsang ch'ui-chi chia-lo-ts'an
Pan-ch'en lo-pu-tsang yeh-shih
Pancika
Pandaka-Traksad-Makahala

Pandara
Pandaravasini
Pandaravasini-Devi
Pandaravasini (fo-mu)
Panditasiddhasvamin
Panjarabhasita-Vajratara
Panjara-Mahakala
Pan-jo-ch'u-mieh-chin-kang
Pan-jo fo-mu
Pan-ta-ka tsun-che
Panthaka
Pan-t'o-chia tsun-che
Pao-hua-yu-pu fo
Pao-huo fo
Pao-kuang fo
Pao-kuan p'u-sa
Pao-lien-hua-shan-chu-hsu-mi-shan-wang fo
Pao-pei ch'a-ka
Pao-san-sheng fo
Pao-san-sheng-kuang fo
Pao-sheng fo
Pao-shen-kuang-hui fo
Pao-ting fo
Pao-tsui-sheng-mu
Pao-tzu-tsai-mu
Pao-yueh-chih-yen-kuang-yin-tzu-tsai-wang-ju-lai
Pao-yueh fo
Pao-yueh-kuang fo
Pa-pei Chi-kuang fo-mu
Pa-pei Chin-kang-chiu-tu fo-mu
Pa-pei Fa-hsing-miao-yu-tzu-tsai Wen-shu
Paramasva
Paramitas
Paramjaya(?)-(Tara)
Parinispanna-Tara
Paripacaka-Tara
Paripurna-Tara
Pariskara-Vasita
Parnasabari
Parnasabari-Tara
Parnasavari
Parvatadhararaja Buddha
Pasadhara (yo-mu)
Pasadhari
Pa-sangs
Pasi (fo-mu)
Patadharini
Pa-ta-la tsun-che
Pa-ta-lieh-ka-lieh-ma hsi-mu
Pa-tsa-li-pu-ta-la tsun-che
Pe-dkar
Pe-dkar-chen-po
Pedma Jungne
Pe-har
Pe-ha-ra
Pe-har-nag-can (?)
Pe-har-rgyal-po
Pei-lien-hua-mu
Peldan Lhamo
Peldan Yeshe
Pel Dorje Jikje
Pel Khorlo Demchok
Pel Kyedorje
Pen-sheng Shang-lo-wang fo
Petali
Peyadhara (?)
Phadampa
Pha-dam-pa
Phag-dkar-ses-rab-gsal-byed
Phag-dkar-ses-rab-gsal-byed-(Yig-rnin-lugs)
Phag-gi-gdong-pa-can
Phag-mo
Phag-mo-dkar-mo
Phag-mo-dmar-mo
Phag-mo-don-grub
Phag-mo-don-thams-cad-sgrub-pa
Phag-mo-gnam-zhabs-ma
Phag-mo-khros-nag
Phag-mo-Kurma-pa-di
Phag-mo-ser-mo
Phag-mo-snon-mo
(Phag-mo-zhal-gnis-ma) indra-mkhah-spyod
'Phags-ma
'Phags-ma-remati
'Phags-skyes-po
Phag-ston-spyan-ston-Spyan-ras-gzigs
Phala
Pha-lha
Pha-mes-brgyud-kyi-dgra-lha
Phan-byed-ma
'Phar-ma-mgo-dgu
Phechopo
Philosophic Deities
Phi-rabs-brgyud-kyi-dgra-lha
Pho-brang-smug-ri-phan-men-brgyad
Pho-gyong-bza'
Pho-klu-bdud-thod-dkar
Pho-la
Pho-lha-gnam-theb-dkar-po
Pho-lha-Gyer-rgod-lha-btsan
Phons-pa-sel-bahi-sgrol-ma

Pho-nya
Pho-nya-mo
Pho-nya-rgya-lcam-ma
Phrag-dog-sprul-gyi-dug-rnams-yons-sel-ma
'Phrin-las
'Phrin-las-bdag-mo-ma-rung-pa
'Phrin-las-kyi-mgon-po-traksad
'Phrin-las-rgyal-po
'Phrog-'chang-ma
Phu-la-ha-ri
Phung-po-lus-len-bdud
Phung-po-rin-chen-zam-bu-lung
Phun-tshogs-bkra-shis
Phur-bu
Phur-bu-rag-pa
Phur-'debs-ma
Phur-pa-'phrin-las-lha-tshogs
Phu-yi-gzhi-bdag-mdzod-lnga-spun-lnga
Phyag-brgyad-sgrol-ma
Phyag-dor
Phyag-mdzod-chen-po
Phyag-na-rdo-rje
Phyag-na-rdo-rje-gtum-chen
Phyag-na-rdo-rje-zhi-ba
Phyag-na-rin-chen
Phyag-na-sna-tshogs-rdo-rje
Phyag-rDor-Drag-po-gSum-sGril
Phyag-rDor-Gos-sNgon
Phyag-rdor-gos-snon-can
Phyag-rdor-gos-snon-can-hGro-bzan-lugs
Phyag-rdor-gtum-chen-bsrun-bahi-mkhar-ras-chun-lugs
Phyag-rdor-gtum-chun
Phyag-rdor-gtum-chun-dmar-po
Phyag-rDor-gTum-chung
Phyag-rdor-gtum-po-khra-thogs
Phyag-rdor-hbyun-hdul-byed-gsar-ma
Phyag-rdor-hbyun-po-hdul-byed
Phyag-rdor-hkhor-chen
Phyag-rdor-khan-brtsegs
Phyag-rdor-mdo-lugs
Phyag-rdor-sa-lugs
Phyag-rdor-u-ca-rya
Phyag-rdor-u-tsa-rya
Phyihi-gsin-rje-rgyal-po
Phying-dkar-ba
Phying-dkar-pa
Phyi-rabs-brgyud-kyi-dgra-lha
Phyir-bZlog-Chen-mo
Phyir-bZlog-ma
Phyir-bzlog-ma-chen-mo
Phyir-mi-ldog-pahi-hkhor-lo-hbyun-bahi-dpal
Phyi-shar-ba-dan-khra-bo
Phyis-kyi-mgon-po
Phyog-gLang
Phyogs-skyong-bcu
Phyva-bsans
Phyva-sangs
Pi-bang-hChang-pa
P'i-chieh-lo-(mahayaksasenapati)
P'i-chieh-lo yao-ch'a-ta-chiang
Pidahara (?)
Pien-ju t'ien
Pi-lieh-wa-pa
Pi-ling-'phar-ma
P'i-lu fo
Pi-mi-ch'eng-chiu Wen-shu
Pi-mi-ch'eng-chiu Wen-shu p'u-sa
Pi-mi Chin-kang-pu-tung fo
Pi-mih-ma-t'eu-kin-kang
Pi-mi Ma-t'ou-chin-kang
Pi-mi tzu-tsai Kuan-shih-yin
Pi-mi Wen-shu
Pi-mi Wen-shu-chin-kang
Pi-mi Wen-shu-shih-li fo
Pi-mu-ko-li-ti t'ien
Pindapatra-Lokesvara
Pindola-Bharadvaja
P'in-mei
P'in-mei fo-mu
P'in-mei-wei-hsiang Chiu-tu fo-mu
Pin-ta-la-pa-la-to-tsa tsun-che
Pin-tu-lo-po-lo-to tsun-che
Pi-p'o-shih fo
Pi-sha-men
P'i-she-fou fo
Pita-Amoghapasa
Pita-Aparajita (fo-mu)
Pita-Chakra-Samvara
Pita-Ganapati
Pita-Jambhala
Pita-Jambhalavajra
Pita-Marici (fo-mu)
Pita-Parnasabari
Pitaprajnaparamita
Pita-Tara
Pita-Vahari
Pita-Vajrasattva
Pita-Yamaraja
Pithisvari-Uddiyana-Tara
Pi-tsu Chi-kuang fo-mu

Pi-wan-dbyans-can-ma
Po-ch'ai-lo yao-ch'a-ta-chiang
Po-hu-lo-(mahayaksasenapati)
Po-hu-lo yao-ch'a-ta-chiang
P'o-i-lo (mahayaksasenapati)
P'o-i-lo yao-ch'a-ta-chiang
P'o-lo-men Yung-pao hu-fa
Potapada-Lokesvara
Po-t'o-lo tsun-che
Prabhakari
Prabhakari (fo-mu)
Prabhaketu
Prabhamati (Bodhisattva)
Prabhasasri
Prabhasasri Buddha
Prabhuta Buddha
Pradipa Buddha
Pradip-Tara
Pradyota Buddha
Prajapati
Prajna
Prajnacakra
Prajnacakra-Manjughosa (dan-po?)
Prajnachakra-Sita-Manjughosa
Prajna-Citrasena
Prajna-daka
Prajnakuta
Prajnaloka
Prajnalokakrtya
Prajnalokakrtya-sita-Vajravarahi
Prajna-Nairatma
Prajnantaka
Prajnantakavajra
Prajnapani
Prajna-Paramita
Prajnaparamita (fo-mu)
Prajnasimha
Prajna-taka
Prajnavardhani
Prakama-sri-dada-Vaisravana
Pramoha
Pramudita
Pramudita (fo-mu)
Pranapati
Prana-sadhana-Loha-kila-Svayambhu-rajni-Devi
Pranidhanamati
Pranidhana-Paramita
Pranidhana-Vasita
Prasanna-Tara
Prasanta(?)-(Tara)
Prathama-Bhadra
Prathamacittopadasamsayacche-dika(?)
Prathama-Jaya
Prathama-Nanda
Prathama-Purna
Prathama-Sunya
Pratibhanakakuta-Lokesvara
Pratibhanakuta
Pratibhana-Pratisamvita
Pratisamvita
Pratisara
Pratisara (fo-mu)
Pratyalidha-Bhairavavajra
Pratyangira
Pravira(?)-Tara
Pravira(?)-Tara (fo-mu)
Pretaloka
Pre-ta-pu-ri-La-phyi-gangs
Pretasantarpita-Lokesvara
Prithivi
Prithivi (devi)
Priyadarsana
P'u-ch'ih-chin-kang
P'u-hsien
P'u-hsien p'u-sa
Pu-hsu-ch'ao-yueh p'u-sa
Pu-hui-chi-hsiang-lun fo
P'u-hui fo
P'u-hui Hung-kuang fo
P'u-hui P'i-lu fo
Pu-ka-hsi fo-mu
Pukkase
Pukkasi (fo-mu)
P'u-kuang fo-mu
Pu-k'ung-chuan-so tzu-tsai Kuan-shih-yin p'u-sa
Pu-lun tsu-shih
Punarvasu
Pundarika
Punyavarada-(Tara)
Punyesvari
Pupala-Lokesvara
Purakali
Purana-Kasayapa
Purnabadr-a
Purnabhadra
Purnamati-stotrasadhana-kirtita-Manjughosa
Pu-sa
Pushpema
Puspa
Puspa (fo-mu)
Puspa-Garuda

Puspatara
Pu-ta-ch'a-ka fo
Pu-tai Ho-shang
Pu-tang-fo
Pu-ta-t'ien
Pu-t'ien Chiu-tu fo-mu
Putra-dkar-po
Pu-tra-lcam-dral
Putra-nag-po
Pu-tra-rdo-rje
Pu-tung-chin-kang
Pu-tung-chin-kang pi-mi-fo
Pu-tung fo
Pu-tung fo-mu
Pu-tung-hsing fo
P'yag-na-rdo-rje

- Q -

Qabur-un okin tngri
Qamsang
Qamug-aca geyigul-un jokiyagci
Qamugha sain
Qar-a ayimag-un ejen
Qar-a bagr-a
Qarabtur koke hayangriv-a
Qarabtur ulagan hayagriv-a
Qar-a garudi
Qar-a jambhala
Qar-a manjusri
Qar-a raksa eke
Qar-a simnus-un qagan
Qara tagurg-a-tu
Qar-a tagurg-a-tu
Qar-a yaksa
Qondur vcir-bani
Qongsim-bodhisattva
Qormusda
Qormusda indra
Quan-am
Qubilgan bey-e-tu ayusi
Quricaqu ugei-yin kobegun

- R -

Rab-brtan-ma
Rab-bzad-ma
Rab-sbas-ma
Rab-tu-dpah-bahi-sgrol-ma
Rab-zhi-ma
Raga
Raga-Bhairavavajra
Raganisudana-Tara
Rag-augha-vegavarta-sosani
Ragavajra
Ragi raja
Rahu
Rahua (deva)
Rahula
Rahula-nag-po
Raja-chen-po
Raja-dmar-po
Raja-gang-gi-klu-btsan
Raja-gos-sngon-gyi-klu-btsan
Rajalila-Manjusri
Rajalila-Manjusri (Bodhisattva)
Raja-shel-ging-dkar-po
Raja-shing-bya-dkar-po
Raja-zla-ba
Raksa-Dakini
Raksadkala
Raksa eke
Raksa-glog-'phreng
Raksa-mthu-bo-che
Raksasa
Rakta-Acala
Rakta-Aditya
Rakta-Alpacanda-Vajrapani
Rakta-Bhairavavajra Buddha
Raktadhusaravajra
Rakta-Hayagriva
Rakta-Kamaraja
Rakta-Karma-Yama
Rakta-Kartaridhara-Makahala daksina-pascima
Rakta-krsna-Hayagriva
Rakta-Lokesvara
Rakta-Mahakala
Raktapa=Heruka
Rakta-Parnasabari
Rakta-Sarasvati
Rakta-Sarasvati (fo-mu)
Raktashula-Vaishravana
Rakta-Simhasya
Rakta-Simhavaktra
Raktasula-Vaisravana
Rakta-Vahari
Rakta-Vasudhara

Rakta-Yamantaka
Rakta-Yamaraja
Rakta-Yamari
Ralchigma
Ral-gCig-ma
Ral-gcig-ma-ekajati
Ral-gri-'jigs-byed
Ral-pa-tshar-dgu
Ral-pa-tshar-dgu-can
Rama
Ram-a
Ran-byun-rgyal-mo
Ran-Deng
Ran-Deng-Fo
Rang-byung-lHa-mo
Rangcungm-a
Raqu
Raqula
Rasavajra
Ras-chun-lugs-bsrun-bahi-mkhar-Canda-maharosana-Vajrapani
Rasiian usnir-tu
Rasmisamudgatasrikutaraja
Ratna-Amitayus
Ratnacandra
Ratnacandra Buddha
Ratna-candra-padma-pratimandita
Ratnacandrapadmapratimanditapandita(?) tejahsvaraghosaraja (Buddha)
Ratnacandraprabha Buddha
Ratnacchattrodgata (Buddha)
Ratnacchattrodgataprabha Buddha
Ratnacuda
Ratnadaka
Ratna-Dakini
Ratn-a-dakini
Ratnadala-Lokesvara
Ratnadhara
Ratna-Garuda
Ratn-a garudi
Ratnagni
Ratnagni Buddha
Ratna-Heruka
Ratnakila
Ratna-krodha
Ratna Krotishaurima
Ratnamukuta
Ratnangadyuti Buddha
Ratnangavyuhadyuti (Buddha)
Ratnapadma Buddha
Ratnapadmavikramin
Ratnapadmavikramin Buddha
Ratnapani
Ratnapani-Lokesvara
Ratnaparamita
Ratna-Pita-Jambhala
Ratnaprabhasambhava Buddha
Ratnarcis
Ratnarcis Buddha
Ratna-ruda
Ratnasambhava
Ratnashikhin
Ratnasikhin(?) (Buddha)
Ratna-simhasya
Ratn-a singq-a muka
Ratnavajri
Ratnavajri (fo-mu)
Ratnavijaya
Ratnesvari(?)
Ratnolka
Ratnosnisa
Raudra-krsna-Vaisravana
Raudrantaka-Mahakala
Raudra-Vaisravana
Raudra-Vajrapani
rBod-ltong-lam-ltar-byad-ma
Rddhi-Vasita
rDo-gling-yul-gangs-chen
rDo-rings-dmar-po'i-gri-btsan
rDo-rje-'bar-ba
rDo-rje-bdag-med-ma
rDo-rje-bdag-med-phyag-gnis-ma
rDo-rje-bdud-'dul
rDo-rje-bdud-'dul-(gsang-sgrub)
rDo-rje-bdud-'dul-(nang-sgrub)
rDo-rje-bdud-'dul-(phyi-sgrub)
rDo-rje-bdud-'dul-(sman-gyi-lha)
rDo-rje-bdud-rci
rDo-rje-bdud-rtsi
rDo-rje-bdud-rtsi-ma
rDo-rje-bgegs-gtso
rDo-rje-bgegs-kyi-gtse
rDo-rje-bgegs-kyi-gtso
rDo-rje-blo-gros
rDo-rje-bod-khams-skyong
rDo-rje-brag-btsan-rDo-rje-dbang-drag-rtsal
rDo-rje-brag-skyes-dongs-pa'i-klu
rDo-rje-bse-byin-chen-mo
rDo-rje-bsrun
rDo-rje-'byung-po
rDo-rje-bzhad-pa
rDo-rje-bzhad-pa-mo

rDo-rje-ca-rciga
rDo-rje-chags-pa
rDo-rje-'chang
rDo-rje-'chi-bdag
rDo-rje-chos
rDo-rje-chos-kyi-sgron-ma
rDo-rje-c'os
rDo-rje-damkima
rDo-rje-dam-tshig-gzi-ldan-'bar
rDo-rje-dban-chen
rDo-rje-dbang-drag-rtsal
rDo-rje-dbang-sdud-ma
rDo-rje-dbyans-can-ma-phyag-drug-ma
rDo-rje-dbyans-can-ma-phyag-gnis-ma
rDo-rje-dbyar-mo
rDo-rje-dbyar-mo-bsil
rDo-rje-dByings
rDo-rje-dbyins-kyi-dban-phyug-ma
rDo-rje-de-byin-chen-mo
rDo-rje-dga'-rab-mo
rDo-rje-dge-bsnyen-ma
rDo-rje-dpal-gyi-yum
rDo-rje-dpal-ldan
rDo-rje-dpal-mo-che
rDo-rje-dpal-mo-long-spyod-yum
rDo-rje-dpa'-rtsal
rDo-rje-drag-mo
rDo-rje-drag-mo-rgyal
rDo-rje-dril-bu-gzugs-legs-ma
rDo-rje-dril-bu-pa
rDo-rje-dril-bu-zu-le-ma
rDo-rje-dril-dkar-dar-thod-can
rDo-rje-dus-'tsams
rDo-rje-gandha-ri
rDo-rje-gar-gyi-dbang-phyug-ma
rDo-rje-gar-mkhan-ma
rDo-rje-gDan-bZhi
rDo-rje-gdan-gyi-sa-bdag
rDo-rje-ging-chen
rDo-rje-gnas-g.yon-(ma)
rDo-rje-gnod-sbyin
rDo-rje-gnod-sbyin-nor-bdag
rDo-rje-grags-ldan
rDo-rje-grags-mo-rgyal
rDo-rje-grags-rgyal-ma
rDo-rje-gro-lod
rDo-rje-gsal-ba-srog-byin-ma
rDo-rje-gshin-rje
rDo-rje-gsung-chen-'od-'bar-ma
rDo-rje-gsung-dbyangs-sgrog-pa-mo
rDo-rje-gur-nas-gsuns-pahi-so-sor-hbran-ma
rDo-rje-gyah-mo-skyon
rDo-rje-g.ya'-ma-skyong
rDo-rje-g.ya'-mo-bsil
rDo-rje-g.ya'-mo-sil
rDo-rje-g.yar-mo-bsil
rDo-rje-gya-sil
rDo-rje-gying-chen
rDo-rje-g.yu-bun
rDo-rje-g.yu-bun-ma
rDo-rje-g.yu-sgron-ma
rDo-rje-gzhon-nu
rDo-rje-gzi-brjid
rDo-rje-gzi-ldan-'bar
rDo-rje-gzugs-legs-ma
rDo-rje-hchan
rDo-rjehi-snin-pos-rab-tu-hjoms-pa
rDo-rje-hkur-chur
rDo-rje-hum-mzad
rDo-rje'i-khyung
rDo-rje-'jigs-byed
rDo-rje-khams-skyon
rDo-rje-khro-'bar
rDo-rje-khros-ma
rDo-rje-khyun
rDo-rje-khyung-btsun-ma
rDo-rje-khyung-lung-ma
rDo-rje-khyung-rgyal
rDo-rje-khyun-khra
rDo-rje-klu-mo
rDo-rje-Kro-ti-shva-ri-ma
rDo-rje-Kun-bzan
rDo-rje-kun-bzang
rDo-rje-kun-bzang-ma
rDo-rje-kun-bzang-mthu-mo-che
rDo-rje-kun-grags
rDo-rje-kun-grags-ma
rDo-rje-kun-'grub-ma
rDo-rje-kun-tu-bzang
rDo-rje-las
rDo-rje-las-mkhan-mo
rDo-rje-lcags-kyu-ma
rDo-rje-lcags-sgrog-ma
rDo-rje-legs-ldan-ma
rDo-rje-legs-pa
rDo-rje-legs-pa-ging-gi-gtso
rDo-rje-ma-bdun-ma
rDo-rje-mdzes-pa
rDo-rje-mi-'gyur-dpal-gyi-yum
rDo-rje-Mi-hKhrugs-pa
rDo-rje-mkha'-'gro-ma
rDo-rje-mkhah-hgro

rDo-rje-mkhah-hgro-ma
rDo-rje-mkha'-lding-gi-rgyal-po-gser-mig-'khyil-pa
rDo-rje-mkhan-ma
rDo-rje-Mohi-bu
rDo-rje-nag-po
rDo-rje-nag-po-chen-po
rDo-rje-ne-ne-gnam-sman-sgron
rDo-rje-phag-mo
(rDo-rje-phag-mo) dbu-bcad-ma
rDo-rje-phyag-byin-chen-mo
rDo-rje-phur-pa
rDo-rje-rab-brtan-ma
rDo-rje-rab-snags-ma
rDo-rje-ral-gcig-ma
rDo-rje-rdzing-btsan
rDo-rje-remati
rDo-rje-rgyal-mchan
rDo-rje-rgyal-po
rDo-rje-rgyu
rDo-rje-rin-chen
rDo-rje-rnal-'byor-ma
rDo-rje-rnam-hjoms
rDo-rje-rnam-hjoms-dkar-po
rDo-rje-rnam-hjoms-ljan-snon
rDo-rje-rnam-hjoms-mthin-kha
rDo-rje-rNam-par-hjoms-pa
rDo-rje-rnon-po
rDo-rje-ro-langs
rDo-rje-Sa-hOg
rDo-rje-sems-dpa'
rDo-rje-sems-dpah
rDo-rje-sems-dpah-ser-po
rDo-rje-sengehi-gdon-can-ma
rDo-rje-sgrol-ma
rDo-rje-sgrol-ma-za-byed-ma
rDo-rje-shog-rgod-rtsal
rDo-rje-shugs-ldan
rDo-rje-shugs-ldan-rta-nag-can
rDo-rjes-Khyun-khra
rDo-rje-sman-gcig
rDo-rje-sman-gcig-ma
rDo-rje-smra-ba
rDo-rje-sna-yon-ma
rDo-rje-snin-po
rDo-rje-spyan-gcig
rDo-rje-spyan-gcig-ma
rDo-rje-spyang-khyi
rDo-rje-srin-po
rDo-rje-sugs
rDo-rje-thog-'bebs
rDo-rje-ya-byin
rDo-rje-ye-shes-chen-mo-ma
rDo-rje-zu-le
rDo-rje-zu-le-sman
rDor-legs
rDor-legs-dkar-po
rDza-yul-gangs
rDzogs-chen-pa'i-gter-bdag
Reg-bya-rdo-rje-ma
Rema-dza
Rema-dzu
Rema-mched-bzhi
Reman-ti
Remati
Remati-mched-gsum
Remati-rdo-rje-gshog-rgod-ma
Re-ma-ti-rdo-rje-gsog-rgod-ma
Re-ste-'gong-nyag
Re-ste-mgo-yag
Revati
rGad-stod-kyi-jo-bo-'gyog-chen
rGan-byang-ma
rGol-ba-hjoms-pahi-sgrol-ma
rGva-lo-(tsa-ba)-hi-lugs-Caturbhuja-(Jnana)-Mahakala
rGva-lo-(tsa-ba)-htshal-lugs-Caturbhuja-(Jnana)-Mahakala
rGyal-ba-byin-chags
rGyal-ba-Chu-lHa
rGyal-ba-Chu-lHahi-lHa
rGyal-ba-dBang-pohi-Tog-gi-rGyal-mTshan
rGyal-ba-dPah-bohi-sDe
rGyal-ba-dPal-bZang
rGyal-ba-dPal-dGyes
rGyal-ba-dPal-sByin
rGyal-ba-Dran-pahi-dPal
rGyal-ba-Dri-ma-Med-pa
rGyal-ba-gTsug-tor-Dri-med
rGyal-ba-gYul-las-rGyal-ba
rGyal-ba-gZi-brJid-mThah-yas
rGyal-ba-hOd-dpag-med
rGyal-ba-hOd-dPal
rGyal-ba-khyu-mchog
rGyal-ba-kLu-dBang-gyi
rGyal-ba-Kun-gzigs
rGyal-ba-Kun-nas-sNang-ba
rGyal-ba-Me-tog-dPal
rGyal-ba-mThong-ba-Don-yod
rGyal-ba-mTshan-dPal-Yongs-sGrags
rGyal-ba-Myang-Ngan-med-pahi-dPal
rGyal-ba-Nor-dPal

rGyal-ba-Pad-mahi-hOd-zer
rGyal-ba-rdo-rje-hchan
rGyal-ba-rDo-rje-sNying-po
rGyal-ba-Ri-dBang-gi-rGyal-po
rGyal-ba-Rin-chen-hOd-hphro
rGyal-ba-rin-chen-me
rGyal-ba-Rin-chen-Pad-ma
rGyal-ba-Rin-chen-Zla-ba
rGyal-ba-Rin-chen-Zla-hOd
rGyal-ba-rNam-par-gNon-pa
rGyal-ba-sen-gehi-na-ro
rGyal-ba-Seng-gehi-Nga-ro
rGyal-ba-Sha-kya-Thub-pa
rGyal-ba-Shin-tu-rNam-par-gNon-pa
rGyal-ba-Sred-med-kyi-Bu
rGyal-ba-thod-dkar
rGyal-ba-Tsan-ldan-dPal
rGyal-ba-Tshangs-pa
rGyal-ba-Tshangs-pahi-hOd-zer
rGyal-ba-Tshang-pa-sByin
rGyal-ba-Tshe-dpag-med
rGyal-chab-rje
rGyal-chen-bsod-nams-dpal
rGyal-chen-bsod-nams-dpal-'bar
rGyal-chen-mthu-rtsal-ldan
rGyal-chen-phyogs-skyong-bzhi
rGyal-chen-rnam-thos-sras
rGyal-dkah
rGyal-gyi-mkhan-pa-lung
rGyal-kun-mes-po-Kun-tu-bzan
rGyal-mchan-rce-mohi-dpun-rgyan
rGyal-mchog-li-byin-ha-ra
rGyal-mChog-Rin-chen
rGyal-mo-rnam-gsum
rGyal-mtshan-mthar-phyin
rGyal-mTshan-rTse-mohi-dPung-rGyan
rGyal-po-grub-dbang-chen-po
rGyal-po-har-mdzes
rGyal-po'i-bu-mo-dkar-sham
rGyal-po-khyung-chen-klu-'brug
rGyal-po-nyi-sang-sad
rGyal-po-'od-lha-dkar-po
rGyal-po-sku-lnga
rGyal-po-skye-'gro'i-dpal
rGyal-po-tshangs-pa
rGyal-tshab-rJe
rGyal-yum-chen-mo-the-khyim
rGyam-rgyal-rdo-ti-gangs-dkar
rGya-mtsho-rnam-rgyal
rGya-nag-rim-pahi-sGrol-ma
rGyas-pa'i-gshin-rje
rGyas-pa'i-lha-mo
rGyas-pa'i-rgyal-chen
rGyu-skar-nyi-shu-rtsa-brgyad
Ri-bo-bkra-bzang-dpal-'bar-ri
Ri-bo-bya-rog
Ri-bo-dpal-'bar-brag-btsan-rgod
Ri-bo-rtse-lnga
Ri-bo-rtse-lnga-bya-rkang-can
Ri-btsun-smug-ri-bsil-me-rtse
Rici
Ri-dban-gi-rgyal-po
Riddhivasita
Rig-byed-ma
Rig-hdzin
Rig-pahi-lha-mo-gdon-dmar-can
Rig-pa'i-lha-mo-gdong-dmar-ma
Rigs-gsum-mgon-po
Rigs-ldan-ner-la
Rigs-phyug-'phen-ri
Ri-khrod-lo-ma-gyon-ma-dmar-mo
Ri-khrod-lo-ma-gyon-ma-ljan-gu
Ri-khrod-lo-ma-gyon-ma-nag-mo
Ri-khrod-lo-ma-gyon-ma-ser-mo
Ri-khrod-lo-ma-gyon-ma-snon-po
Ri-khrod-ma
Rikshavaktra
Rin-byun
Rin-chen-brtsegs-(dang)-rtse-mo-drug
Rin-chen-'byung-ldan
Rin-chen-dban-chen
Rin-chen-gcug-tor-can
Rin-chen-gDugs
Rin-chen-gtsug-tor-can
Rin-chen-hbyun-ldan
Rin-chen-hod-hphros
Rinchen Jungden
Rinchen khado
Rin-chen-khyun
Rin-chen-Kro-ti-shva-ri-ma
Rin-chen-me
Rin-chen-mkha'-'gro-ma
Rin-chen-mkhah-hgro
Rin-chen-mkhah-hgro-ma
Rin-chen-pad-ma
Rin-chen-padmas-rnam-par-gnon-pa
Rin-chen-phyag
Rin-chen-rdo-rje-ma
Rin-chen-sengehi-gdon-can-ma
Rin-chen-shugs-ldan
Rinchen tsugtor chen
Rin-chen-zla-ba

Rin-chen-zla-ba-padmas-brgyan
Rin-chen-zla-hod
Rin-hbyun
Rin-po-che'i-khyung
Rin-po-che'i-mtshar-sdug-can
Ripuchakra-vinasini (Tara)
Ri-rab-chen-po'i-sa-bdag
Ri-sti-mgo-g.yag
Ri-tsi-mi-dmar
rJe-btsun-byams-pa
(rJe-btsun)-Byams-pa-(ni-ri-ti-pahi-lugs)
rJe-btsun-ma-ka-pa-li-ta-ra
rJe-btsun-ma-Rig-ma-chen-mo
rJe-btsun-ma-Thod-pa-rgyan
rJe-dGe-hdun-grub
rJe-dpon-nag-po
rJe-drung-bLo-bzang-dpal-ldan
rJe'i-mgur-lha-bcu-gsum
rJe'i-rgyal-po
rJe-lCang-skya-Rol-pahi-rDo-rje
rJe-nag-dban-blo-bzan-rgya-mcho
rJe-Rin-po-che
rJes-pan-chen-blo-bzan-chos-kyis-rgyal-mchan
rJe-yi-mgur-lha-bcu-gsum
rKang-bzhi-phyugs-kyi-bdag
rKong-btsun-de-mo
rKong-rje-brang-dkar
Rksavaktra
rLung-lHa
rLung-rta-sngon-po
rMa-bya-chen-mo
rMa-chen-spom-ra
rMa-chen-spom-ra'i-sring-gcig
rMad-gnyan-spom-ra
rMa-gnyan-spom-ra
rMa-ri-rab-'byans-drag-mo
rMig-pa
rMi-lam-ston-pahi-sgrol-ma
rMu-ru-sha-ru-tsandan-ri
rMu-yi-rum-rje-btsan-po
rNal-hbyor-nam-mkhah
rNam-gzigs
rNam-par-gnon
rNam-par-gnon-pahi-gsegs-pahi-dpal
rNam-par-rgyal-bahi-sgrol-ma
rNam-par-snag-mdzad
rNam-par-snan-mdzad
rNam-rgyal
rNam-rgyal-thog-du-rje-bo
rNam-snag-shugs-ldan
rNam-snan
rNam-snang
rNam-snang-rta-nag-can
rNam-snan-hjam-rdor
rNam-snan-ma
rNam-snan-mnon-byan
rNam-sras
rNam-sras-che-hphel-dkar-po
rNam-sras-dkar-po-tshe-'dzin
rNam-sras-dkar-po-tshe-hdzin
rNam-sras-dmar-po-gar-mkhan-mchog
rNam-sras-drag-byed
rNam-sras-drag-byed-hkhor-klu-brgyad-bcas
rNam-sras-drag-byed-nag-po
rNam-sras-gar-mkhan-mchog
rNam-sras-gsung-mchog-lus-ngan-po
rNam-sras-gsun-mchog-lus-nan-po
rNam-sras-ljang-gu-seng-zhon-manyaja-na'i-lugs
rNam-sras-ljang-ser-be-con-can
rNam-sras-ljan-gu-sen-zhon-ma-dzna-nahi-lugs
rNam-sras-ljan-ser-be-con-can
rNam-sras-mdun-dmar-can
rNam-sras-mdun-dmar-rta-snon-can
rNam-sras-mdung-dmar-can
rNam-sras-mdung-dmar-rta-sngon-can
rNam-sras-nag-po-rta-sngon-can
rNam-sras-nag-po-rta-snon-can
rNam-sras-rgyal-po
rNam-sras-ser-chen
rNam-sras-ser-chen-lha-dgu
rNam-sras-yang-gsang-phyag,-mtshan-bzhi-pa
rNam-sras-yan-gsan-phyag-mtshan-bzhi-pa
rNams-sNang-mNgon-byang
rNams-snan-skya-sen-ge
rNam-thos-kyi bu
rNam-thos-sras
rNam-thos-sras-ma
rNam-thos-sras-mdung-dmar-can
rNa-nam-gangs
rNa-nyan-phra-ma-zer-ma
rNga-la-stag-rtse
rNo-ba-mtshon-gyi-dgra-lha
rNog-lugs-Ekanta-Panjara-Mahakala
rNon-po
rNye-bo-gangs
Rodi
Rogiri
Rogs-ste-nag-po
Ro-kha-ma
Ro-kri-mi-dmar
Ro-lam-lha

Ro-langs-ma
Ro-lans-ma
Rolging yamsud
Rol-pa'i-mtsho-bdun-sa-bdag
Rong-btsan-gangs
Rong-btsan-kha-ba-dkar-po
Rong-gi-jo-mo-kha-rag
Rong-lha-rgyal-mtshan
Rong-mdo-kha-rag-gzhu-gnyan-rtse
Ro-rdo-rje-ma
Roshana
Ro-so-'byor-rtse-ru-bsam-mtho
Ro-tara-ni-bi
rTa-bdag-brgyad
rTa-go-ba
rTag-tu-nu
rTa-mgo-thog-btsan
rTa-mgrin
rTa-mgrin-dkar-po
rTa-mgrin-dmar-po
rTa-mgrin-dpah-gcig-lhan-skyes-jo-bohi-lugs
rTa-mGrin-gSang-sgrub
rTa-mgrin-kha-che-pan-chen-lugs
rTa-mgrin-khyun-gsog-can-jo-bohi-lugs
rTa-mGrin-lCags-Ral-can
rTa-mgrin-rgyal-po
rTa-mgrin-sKyer-sgan-lugs
rTa-mgrin-sva-na-bzhi-skor-jo-bohi-lugs
rTa-mgrin-yan-gsan-khros-pahi-zhabs
rTam-mgrin-padma-gar-dban
rTa-shod-dpang-mto-rgyal-ri
rTog-'dod-ma
rTsa-klu-bdud-rdo-rje
rTsal-thog-rgyug-gi-gri-btsan
rTsal-thog-rgyug-ging-btsan
rTsang-rtsang-'khor-ba
rTse-dmar-po
rTse-ma-ra
rTsi'u-dmar-po
rTsi-yi-rag-ne-mthon-po
Rudhira-varna-Rakta-Karma-Yama
Rudra-Cakrin
Rudra-rdo-rje-bdud-'dul
Rudrarupa Buddha
Rudra-thar-pa-nag-po
Rula
Ruma(?)-gzug-rnyen(?)-bdud
Rung-ma'i-yul-lha-g.Ya'-spang-brgya-byin
Rupavajra
Rupini
Rva-sgreng-gi-jo-bo-Phying-dkar-ba
Rva-shing-'dzoms-pa'i-dgra-lha
Ryu-ju
Ryuri Kwan-non
Ryuzu Kwan-non

- S -

Sabari (fo-mu)
Sabari-(pada)
Sabari-(Tara)
Sa-bcuhi-mgon-po-Byams-pahi-mtshan
Sa-bdag
Sa-bdag-bdud-'dul-chen-mo
Sa-bdag-'brong-nag-po
Sa-bdag-btsan-'dul-chen-mo
Sa-bdag-bstan-ma-gser-mdog-gser-guyi-bum-pa-can
Sa-bdag-bu-mo-'bum-gyi-gtso-mo
Sa-bdag-bya-dmar-po
Sa-bdag-chen-mo-rDo-rje-ya-byin
Sa-bdag-'dod-chag-khon-ma
Sa-bdag-dur-len
Sa-bdag-gser-nya-bo
Sa-bdag-g.yu-'brug-snyon-po
Sa-bdag-gza'-'dul-chen-mo
Sa-bdag-hal-khyi-nag-po
Sa-bdag-klu-'dul-chen-mo
Sa-bdag-ku-ku
Sa-bdag-mche-ba-can
Sa-bdag-rgan-rgon
Sa-bdag-rgyal-po-'jig-rten-bdag
Sa-bdag-rug-zor-dmar-po
Sa-bdag-rus-sbal-skya-bo
Sa-bdag-se-bdud
Sa-bdag-se'u-rta-khrid
Sa-bdag-stag-skya-bo
Sa-bdag-tsang-kun-khyab-pa
Sa-bdag-zin-'phung-nag-po
Sabdavajra
Sa-bsen-gdug-byed
Sadaksari
Sadaksari-Lokesvara
Sadaprarudita
Sadbhuja-Hayagriva
Sadbhuja-Jambhala
Sadbhuja-Jambhalavajra
Sadbhuja-Jnana-Mahakala
Sadbhuja-Mahakala
Sadbhuja-Parnasabari (fo-mu)

Sadbhuja-Sarasvati (fo-mu)
Sadbhuja-Sitatara
Sadbhuja-sita-Tara
(Sadbhuja-Trimukha)-Mativardhana-(Dhanapala)-Pita-Mahakala
Sadbhuja-Vajrasarasvati
Sadhana-kala-sambaddha-Caturmukha-Sri-Mahakala
Sadhumati
Sadhumati (fo-mu)
Sadyonubhava-Arapacana
Sadyonubhava-Manjusri
Sa-'dzin-lag-pa-chen-po
Sagaii
Sa-ga-li
Sagaramati-Lokesvara
Sagarmati
Sa-ghan-er-khe-hong-si-can-tha'i-ji
Sa-gzhi'i-'gong-po
Sahaja-Go-bzlog
Sahaja-Guhyasamaja
Sahaja-Hevajra
Sahaja-Kalachakra
Sahaja-Samvara
Sahampati-Brahma
Sahasra-bhuja Avalokitesvara
Sahasrapramardani (fo-mu)
Sahi-lha-mo
Sahi-lha-mo-brtan-ma
Sahi-snin-po
Sailendraraja (Buddha)
Sailendravaja Buddha
Sa'i Nyingpo
Sakali
Sakamangala
Sakra
Sakra (deva)
Sakti
Saktidhara(?)
Sakti-Vajravarani
Sakyabuddha-Lokesvara
Sakya-hod
Sakyalig-un gerel-tu
Sakyamuni Buddha
Sakya-Pandita
Sakyaprabha
Sakya-sen-ge
Sakyasimha
Sakyasimha (Buddha)
Sa-kya-thub-pa
Samantabhadra
Samantabhadra-Lokesvara
Samantadarsin (Jina)
Samantadharavajra
Samantamukha
Samantaprabha
Samantaprabha (fo-mu)
Samantavabhasavyuhasri
Samantavabhasavyuhasri Buddha
Samayadakini
Samayi-Dharmaraja
Sambara
Sambhu
Samda-biruv-a
Samdajan-a
Samgramatarini (fo-mu)
Samjneya
Samksipta-Bhairava
Samksipta-Marici
Samkusumita
Samkusumita-Tara
Samsaya-pisaca-bhaya-trana-Tara
Samvara
Samvararaja (Buddha)
Samyaksambuddha-asoka
Sa-nahi-gos-can
Sanakavasin
Sangdu
Sang-dui
Sanggye Chema
Sanggye khado
Sanggye mangyila bedurye ochi gyalpo
Sanggye Menlha
Sanglun
Sangngag Chemmo
Sangs-rgyas-bskyangs
Sangs-rgyas-mka'-'gro
Sangs-rgyas-spyan-ma
Sangs-rgyas-Thod-pa
Sani
Sankara(?)vajra
Sankari(?) (devi)
Sankhambara
Sankhanatha-Lokesvara
Sankhapadma
Sankhapali-Devi
San-mien liu-pei pai Chiu-tu fo-mu
San-mien pa-pei hung Ma-t'ou-chin-kang
San-mien ssu-pei Mi-lo p'u-sa
Sanmukha
Sanmukha-Bhairavavajra
Sanmukha-Bhairavavajra Buddha

San pa-lo
Sans-rgyas-bdud-dan-yid-gnis-kun-hjoms(?)
Sans-rgyas-byan-sems-hdul-ba
Sans-rgyas-khyun
Sans-rgyas-mkhah-hgro
Sans-rgyas-mnon-hphags-rgyal-po
Sans-rgyas-ri-dban-gi-rgyal-po
Sans-rgyas-rin-chen-gdugs-hphags
Sans-rgyas-rin-chen-gzugs-bkod-hod-snan
Sans-rgyas-rin-po-che-dan-zla-ba-dan-padmas-rab-tu-brgyan-pa-mkhas-pa-gzi-brjid-sgra-dbyans-kyi-rgyal-po
Sans-rgyas-rjes-su-spyod-pa
Sans-rgyas-rnam-gcigs
Sans-rgyas-sman-gyi-bla-bai-duryahi-hod-kyi-rgyal-po
Sans-rgyas-spyan-ma
Santamati-Lokesvara
Santa-Sahaja-Guhyapati
Santasi-Lokesvara
Santa-Vajrapani
Santideva
Saptaksara
Saptaksara-Lokesvara
Saptami-Tithi
Saptasatika-Hayagriva
Sarad-devi
Sarad-rajni
Saraha
Sa-ra-ha
Sa-ra-ha'i-mgon-po
Sarasiri(?)-Lokesvara
Sarasvati
Sarasvati (devi)
Sardulavaktra
Sariputra
Saroruhavajra
Sarthavaha Buddha
Sarthavaha-Lokesvara
Sarva-bhaya-trana-Tara
Sarvabuddha-Dakini
Sarvabuddhadharmakosavati
Sarvadakini
Sarva-jina-pitamaha-Samanthabhadra
Sarvakarmavaranavisodhani
Sarvanivaranaviskambhi
Sarvanivaranaviskambhi (devi)
Sarvanivaranaviskambhi-Lokesvara
Sarvanivaranaviskambini
Sarvapayanjaha
Sarvarthasadhana-Tara (fo-mu)
Sarvarthasadhana-Varahi
Sarva-sasanaraksa-pradhana-Vajrapanjara
Sarvasokatamonirghata-Lokesvara
Sarvasokatamonirghatamati
Sarvavid
Sarvavid-Vairocana
Sarvavid-Vairocana (Buddha)
Sarva-vighna-vinayaka-Mahakala
Sasanaraks-pradhana-Parvati
Sasiketu Buddha
Sa-skya-dpal-ri-lhun-po-rgyal
Sa-(skya)-lugs-(Pranasadhana)-Rakta-Jambhala
Sa-(skya)-lugs-Raktapita-Arapacana-Manjughosa
Sa-skya-lugs-Rakta-Tara
Sa-(skya)-lugs-Vajrapani
Sa-skya-Pandita-Kun-dgah-rGyal-mTshan
Sa-skyon
Sa-sman
Sa-srin-dmar-mo
Sa-srin-ma-mo
Sasthi-Tithi
Sastradhara-Hevajra (Buddha)
Satakratu
Sa-thel-nag-po
Sa-the(l)-nag-po
Sa-thil-smug-po
Satrumjayavajra
Sattvavajri
Sattvavajri (fo-mu)
Sauddhodani
Sa-yi-brgya-byin-nag-po
Sa-yi-dgra-lha-mtshan-rtags
Sa-yi-lha-mo
Sa-yi-lha-mo-bstan-ma
Sayin ayalgu-tu eke
Sayin cog-tu
Sayin neretu
Sayin nigurtu eke
Sayin oyutu eke
Sayin yabudal-tu eke
Sa-yi-'phung-bye-nag-mo
Sa-yi-raja
Sa-za-ce-spyan-gdon
sBal-mgo-khrag-mig
sBal-te
sBed-byed
sBed-byed-pa
sBye-ba-rkang-ring
sByin-bzang-ma

sByin-ma
sByi-ring-khri
sByi-ring-khrid
sDang-ba'i-srog-gcod
sDong-grogs-zhal-dkar-gnyan-po
sDug-bsnal-bsregs-pahi-sGrol-ma
Season Goddesses
Se-ba-bla-mkhyen
Se-ba-rang-rta-rgyal-po'i-chibs
Se-byi
Sedkiku-yi barigci
Se-gling-bsil-ri-bsam-gtan-ri
Sei-shi
Sems-ma-rdo-rje-ma
Sems-ma-remati
Sen-gdon-ma
Sen-gdon-ma-dmar-mo
Sen-gdon-ma-snon-mo
Sen-ge
Sen-ge-gdon-can
Sengehi-gdon-can-ma
Sengehi-hjigs-skyobs
Senge-Rab-rten
Senge-sgra
Sen-ge-sgra-sgrogs
Sengge Dongchen
Seng-gdong-ma
Seng-ge'i-gdong-can
Seng-ge-rgyab-bsnol
Seng-ge-sgra-ri
Seng-lDing-Nags-sGrol
Sen-ju Kwan-non
Sen-ldan-nags-kyi-sGrol-ma
Sen-lden-nags-sgrol-ma
Ser-bdag-bco-brgyad
Ser-phyin-phyag-bzhi-ma
Ser-phyin-phyag-gnis-ma
Sersang dime rinchennang
Serthup
Ses-rab-kyi-pha-rol-tu-phyin-pa
Ses-rab-mthar-byed
Ses-rab-pha-rol-tu
Ses-rab-seng-ge
Seva-kala-sambaddha-Caturmukha-Sri-Mahakala
Se-yi-lha
sGam-po-dpal-ri
sGam-po-gangs
sGam-po-pa
sGang-btsan-pa
sGang-drug-gzhi-bdag-bcu-gnyis
sGang-ring-dge-bsnyen-chen-po
sGeg-mo
sGeg-mo-ma
sGegs-pa-rdo-rje
sGo-bdud-chen-po
sGo-khro-gshog-brgyad-dil-mo-brgyad
sGo-lha
sGra-can-hdzin
sGra-dbyans-rgyal-po
sGra-gcan
sGra-gcan-'dzin
sGra-gcan-hdzin
sGra-ma
sGra-rdo-rje-ma
sGrib-pa-rnam-sel
sGrog-chen
sGrol-byed-bdud-kyi-shan-pa
sGrol-byed-dpal-ldan-remadzi
sGrol-dkar
sGrol-dkar-Ba-rihi-lugs
sGrol-dkar-kha-che-pan-chen-lugs
sGrol-dkar-yid-bzhin-gyi-hkhor-lo
sGrol-ging-chen-po-brgyad
sGrol-ging-dbang-bsdud
sGrol-ging-dbang-sdu
sGrol-ging-mthu-chen-ma
sGrol-gin-Yam-sud
sGrol-gying-chen-po-srog-bdag-beg-tse-can
sGrol-ljan
sGrol-ljan-kha-che-pan-chen-lugs
sGrol-ma
sGrol-ma-bde-sgrub-ma
sGrol-ma-bdud-hjoms-ma
sGrol-ma-dkar-phyag-drug-ma
sGrol-ma-dkar-po
sGrol-ma-dmar-mo-sa-lugs
sGrol-ma-dnos-grub-hbyun-ma
sGrol-ma-gser-mdog-ma
sGrol-ma-gzhan-gyis-mi-thub-pa
sGrol-ma-hjigs-pa-brgyad-skyob-ma
sGrol-ma-hum-sgra-sgrogs-ma
sGrol-ma-khros-ma-nag-mo
sGrol-ma-(lha-lna)
sGrol-ma-ljan-gu
sGrol-ma-nin-zhi-mtshan-khro
sGrol-ma-nor-sbyin-ma
sGrol-ma-rab-rgyas-ma
sGrol-ma-rnam-par-rgyal-ma-dkar-mo
sGrol-ma-sdug-bsnal-bsregs-pahi
sGrol-ma-ser-mo
sGrol-ma-smin-byed-ma

sGrol-ma-yons-rdzogs-byed-ma
sGrol-ma-zla-mdan-ma
sGro-snyug-'dzoms-pa'i-dgra-lha
sGyog-chen-gdong-ra
sGyu-hphrul-dra-bahi-rim-pahi-spyan-ras-gzigs
Sha ba ri
Shacha Thupa
Sha-ga-li
Shailadeva-Mahakala
Shakamuni
Shakya-Kulendra
Sha-kya-Rigs-dBang
Sha-kya-Seng-ge
Sha-kya-thub-pa
Shakya Tubpa
Sha-lo-men fo-mu
Sha-med-gangs-dkar-ma
Sha-med-rdo-rje-g.yu-bun-ma
Sha-men fo-mu
Sham-po-Gangs-la-bZhugs-pahi-Gangs-pa
Sham-po-gza'-bdud-mgo-dgu
Sha-na-i
Shan-ch'eng-ming-yang-t'ien p'u-sa
Shang-kyi-yul-lha-ga-byang
Shang-lo-wang fo
Shan-hsien p'u-sa
Shan-hsing Shou-ch'ih-chin-kang fo
Shan-hsing Vajrapani (Buddha)
Shan-hui
Shan-hui fo-mu
Shankha
Shankhapali-Devi
Shan-kuan
Shan-lung p'u-sa
Shan-mieh-cheng-ao fo
Shan-mieh-mo-chang fo
Shan-ming-ch'eng-chi-hsiang-wang-ju-lai
Shan-ming-ch'eng-kung-te fo
Shan-ming-ju-lai fo
Shan-sha-ou-lieh t'ien
Shantarakshita
Shantendriya
Shan-te Yung-pao hu-fa
Shantideva
Shan-t'ien tsu-shih
Shan-ting-ro-zan
Shan-ti-ro-zan-ma
Shan-yu-pu fo
Shan-yu-pu-kung-te fo
Sharad-Rajni
Shar-gyi-rma-chen-spom-ra
Sharmana
Sha-skya-Seng-ge
Shatakratu
Shavaripada
Sha-wa-li
Sha-wa-li fo-mu
Sha-za-ce-spyang-gdong-can
Sha-za'i-ma-mo
Sha-za-khrag-'thung-bdud-kyi-bu
Sha-za-nag-po
She-fu-shih-chien Chiu-tu fo-mu
Shel-bzang-gangs
Shel-bza'-sman-gcig-ma
Shel-ging-dkar-po
Shel-'gying-dkar-po
Shel-'gying-rgyal-po-nyi-pang-sad
She-li-fo
Sheng-fa-ting p'u-sa
Sheng-hui-wang-ju-lai fo
Sheng-ti-chin-kang
Sheng t'ien-mu
Sheng-t'ien tsu-shih
Sheng-ting fo
Sherab Sengge
Sherapchi pharoltu chinpa
Sher-phyin-ma
She-shih Wei-lo-wa-chin-kang
Shes-rab-Seng-ge
She'u-mkha'-ri
Shih-ch'eng fo
Shih-chia-kuang tsu-shih
Shih-chia-man-ni fo
Shih-chia-mou-ni fo
Shih-chia-mu-ni
Shih-chia-shih-tzu fo
Shih-ch'i fo
Shih-erh-pei Chi-kuang fo-mu
Shih-hou fo
Shih-hou Kuan-shih-yin
Shih-hou Kuan-shih-yin p'u-sa
Shih-hsiang t'ien-mu
Shih-hsiang yo-mu
Shih-huo t'ien
Shih-hou Wen-shu
Shih-i-mien Kuan-shih-yin
Shih-i-mien Kuan-shih-yin p'u-sa
Shih-i-mien-ta-pei Kuan-shih-yin
Shih-i-wo-shih-ma-mu
Shih-i yo-mu
Shih-lei-yen t'ien

Shih-liu-pei Kuan-shih-yin p'u-sa (WEC *94*)
Shih-lun-wang fo
Shih-miao-chin-kang
Shih-mien fo-mu
Shih-pa-pei Lien-hua-miao-wu-tzu-tsai Kuan-shih-yin
Shih-pei Chi-kuang fo-mu
Shih-p'o-an-hui p'u-sa
Shih-sheng fo-mu
Shih-tzu-ch'uang-mu
Shih-tzu fo
Shih-wei-chin-kang
Shih-wu-wei p'u-sa
Shikanda
Shing-bya-can
Shing-chen-bzhi'i-gzhi-bdag
Shing-lha
Shinje
Shinje she
Shis-chia-mou-ni
Shis-chia-mu-ni
Sho Kwan-non
Shou-ch'ih-chin-kang
Shou-ch'ih-chin-kang p'u-sa
Shramana
Shrivatsa
Shu-ba-srog-zan-btsan-gyi-rje
Shu-bo-lag-ring
Shud-bud-kyi-jo-mo
Shug-lcam-rgyal-mo
Shug-sgrogs-mgyogs-byed
Shugs-sgal?-mgyogs-byed
Shui-t'ien
Shui-t'ien-chung-t'ien fo
Shui-t'ien fo
Shui-yueh Kuan-shih-yin
Shui-yueh Kuan-shih-yin p'u-sa
Siddhaikavira
Siddhasangha
Siddheshvara-Humkara
Siddhida-Tara
Siddhi-sambhava-Tara
Sigemuni
Sikhi
Sikhimalini
Sikhin
Sila-Paramita
Silwetshul Chemmo
Simha
Simha-bhayatrana-(Avalokitesvara)
Simha-bhaya-trana Tara
Simha Buddha
Simhadhvaja
Simhanada
Simhanada-Avalokitesvara
Simhanada Buddha
Simhanada (Jina)
Simhanada-Lokesvara
Simhanada-Manjughosa
Simhanada-Manjusri
Simhanada-Tara
Simhanatha-Lokesvara
Simhasana-Ganapati-Makahala
Simhasya
Simhasya Deities
Simhavahana-Manjusri (Bodhisattva)
Simhavahana-Taksad
Simhavaktra
Simnus-un ejen
Singgali eke
Singq-a
Sinnga-gling-ma
Sin-tu-bzan-po
Sin-tu-rnam-par-gnon-pahi-dpal
Sir-a erlig qagan
Sir-a jambhala
Siri bajar caara
Siri bajar eke
Siri-Devi
Sirisara(?)-Lokesvara
Sirug modu-tu
Sita-Acala
Sita-Acalavajra
Sita-Ayurvardhana-Vaisravana
Sitabrahma
Sita-Candra
Sita-Chakrasamvara
Sita-Cintamani-Mahakala
Sita-Cunda-Devi
Sita (deva)
Sita-Ganapati
Sita-Hayagriva
Sita-Hayagrivavajra (Buddha)
Sita-Jambhala
Sita-Mahakala
Sita-Manjughosa
Sita-Manjusri (Bodhisattva)
Sita-Nagaraja
Sita-nagavahana-Jambhala
Sita-Nagi
Sitaprajnaparamita
Sita-Samvara

Sita-Samvararaja
Sita-Samvararaja (Buddha)
Sita Sarasvati
Sita-Surya-Candra
Sitatapatra
Sitatapatra-Aparajita
Sitatapatra (Bodhisattva)
Sitatapatra (fo-mu)
Sitatapatrosnisa (Buddha)
Sita-Tara
Sita-Tara (fo-mu)
Sita-Vajrapani
Sita-Vajravidarana
Sita-Varahi
Sita-Varuna
Sitavati
Sitavati (fo-mu)
Sita-Vetali (fo-mu)
Sita-Vijaya-Tara
Sita-Visva (fo-mu)
Sita-Visvamatr
Sita-Yamaraja
Siva-Dakini
Skandha
sKar-mchog-khram-shing-kha-'thor
sKed-btsan-nor-lha-mgar-ba-klu
sKem-byed
sKos-rje-trang-dkar-dmag-gi-dpon
sKos-rje-trang-dkar-dung-gi-dpon
sKrag-med-mun-bral-rgyal-po
sKu-bla-gsang-ba
sKu-bla-g.yu-rtse
sKu-gsum-me-lha
sKuhi-rgyal-po
sKu-kyai-rdor
sKu-la-brag-dmar-mtho-cog
sKu-la-mkha'-ri
sKu-la-zhal-gyi-btsan
sKu-la-zhal-gyi-lha-btsan
sKu-lha
sKu-lna-gryal-po
sKu-mchog
sKu-rgyal-she-ne
sKu-sprul-dran-sron-rig-pahi-ye-ses
sKu-sprul-stobs-rgyal
sKu-yi-mgon-po
sKye-bo-yongs-kyi-dgra-lha
sKye-mthing-g.ya'-ma
sKye-mthing-ma
sKye ri gnyen po
sKyer-sgan-lugs-Hayagriva
sKyes-bu-chen-po
sKyes-bu-gnam-thel-dkar-po
sKyes-bu-lung-btsan-thog-gi-rje
sKyes-bu-(')phrag-lha
sKyes-bu-rang-chas
sKyes-mchog-vajra-thig-le-rtsal
sKyes-pa-srog-'dod
sKyid-kyi-gro-ma-lung
sKyid-shod-rdzong-btsan
sKyid-shod-zhog-lha-phyug-po
sKyi-mthing-ya-ma-skyong
sKyi-rong-ma-ri-khyung-rgyal-rtse
sKyi-shod-rdzong-btsan-znags-khrab-can
sKyog-chen-sdang-ra
sKyom-'dam-klu-shod-'phen-yul-ri
sKyon-btsun-de-mo
sKyu-brla-gsang-ba
sMad-shod-rdo-rje-mu-nam
sMan-bla
sMan-bla'i-bka'-sdod
sMan-dkar-gdong-ma
sMan-gcig-ma
sMan-gyi-bla-bai-dur-ya-hi-hod-kyi-rgyal-po
sMan-gyi-bla-bai-duryahi-hod-kyi-rgyal-po
sMan-gyi-bLa-Be-dur-yahi-hOd-kyi-rGyal-po
sMan-gyi-lHa-mo
sMan-phran-'bum-gyi-gtso-mo
sMar-mo-ngang-rdzongs
Smasha
Smashali
sMe-brtsegs-(dud-kha)
sMog-she-shin-'phrang-go-g.yas
sMon-la-bLo-gros
sMon-pa-'hrub-pa'i-dgra-lha
sMra-ba-lce-mgyogs-dgra-lha
Smrtishri
Smrtisri
Smrtisri Buddha
sMyo-kha-mkhar-chu-sbar-rjes
sNa-chen-ma
sNa-chogs-yum
sNag-gsal-pra-ston-ma
sNag-gsal-pra-yi-bdag
sNags-srun-E-ka-dza-tihi-mtshan
sNang-grags-'brug-ldir
sNang-gsal-ma
sNang-gsal-(s)pra-ston-ma
sNan-gsal-ma
sNang-sel-khrab-gyon
sNang-srid-sde-brgyad-tshogs-kyi-rje-dpon
sNang-va-mthah-yas

sNan-mdzad-rdor-dbyins
sNa-tshogs-gzugs
sNa-Tshogs-mKhah-hgro
sNa-tshogs-rdo-rje-mkaha-hgro
sNa-tshogs-yum-dkar-mo
sNgags-bdag-bco-brgyad
sNgags-bdag-dregs-chen-bco-brgyad
sNgo-la-g.yu-rtse
sNin-po-kyai-rdo-rje
sNom-pa-sna-yi-dgra-lha
sNying-bzan-ma
sNying-thang-'cham-ri
sNyong-kha
So-bdar-ma
Sodasabhuja-Avalokitesvara (Bodhisattva)
Sog-po-sha-zan
Sokanirghatanamati
So-ka-raja
Sokavinodana-Tara
So-ni-lo-(mahayaksasenapati)
So-ni-lo yao-ch'a-ta-chiang
Sor-hbrans-phyag-gnis-ma
Sosor dangmo
So-sor-hbran-ma
So-sor-hbran-ma-lha-lna
So-sor-hbrans-ma
sPang-phung-gangs
Sparsavajra
sPe-dkar
sPen-dkar
sPe-ni-ri-bkra
sPen-pa
Sphotadhara (fo-mu)
Sphotadhara(?)-yo-mu
sPo-bo-chu-dmar
sPom-chen-spom-ra
sPos-ri-ngad-ldan
sPrel-nag-mig-gcig
sPrul-pa'i-ma-mo
sPu-gri-nag-ma
sPu-gri-nag-mo
sPyan-gi-mgo-can
sPyang-ki'i-gdong-pa-can
sPyan-mi-bzan
sPyan-ras-gzigs
sPyan-ras-gzigs-bcu-gcig-zhal-dpal-mohi-lugs
sPyan-ras-gzigs-bhu-kham-dmar-po
sPyan-ras-gzigs-don-yod-lcags-kyu
sPyan-ras-gzigs-don-yod-mchod-pahi-nor-bu
sPyan-ras-gZigs-gSang-grub
sPyan-ras-gzigs-hjigs-pa-brgyad-skyob
sPyan-ras-gzigs-Kha-sar-pa-ni
sPyan-ras-gzigs-padma-dban-hbyed
sPyan-ras-gzigs-padma-gar-dban-phyag-gnis-pa
sPyan-ras-gzigs-padmahi-phyag
sPyan-ras-gzigs-phyag-bzhi-pa
sPyan-ras-gzigs-rdo-rje-chos
sPyan-ras-gzigs-rdo-rjehi-snin-pas-rab-tu-hjoms-pa
sPyan-ras-gzigs-rgyal-ba-rgya-mcho
sPyan-ras-gzigs-sems-nid-nal-gso
sPyan-ras-gzigs-sen-gehi-sgra
sPyan-ras-gzigs-sna-tshogs-dban-po
sPyan-ras-gzigs-su-kha-va-ti
sPyan-ras-gzigs-yid-bzhin-nor-bu
sPyan-ras-gzigs-yi-ge-drug-pa-jo-lugs
sPyan-ras-gzig-yi-ge-phyed-dan-bzhi-pa
sPyi-bdud-dgu-rum-rtse
sPyi-bdud-rgyal-po-gu-ru-ma
sPyid-bdud-rgyal-gu-rum-rtse
sPyid-yi-lha
sPyi-phyir-phur-byed
sPyi-sgrub-ma
sPyi-yi-brag-la-mda'-brug
sPyod-pa'i-dbang-po
sPyod-rGyud-Tshe-dpag-med
Sra-ba-ber-gyi-dgra-lha
Srad-nyi-ma-la-dga'-ba
Sramana (devi)
Sramana (fo-mu)
Sras-gar-mkhan-mchog
Sras-rgyal-ba-khyu-mchog
Sras-smon-pa-don-grub
Sred-med-kyi-bu
Sred-spong
Sresthiputri
Srgala-mukha-Pisaca
Sri-Cakrasamvara
Sri-Candamaharosana
Sridatta Buddha
Sridevi
Srid-gsum-yons-bdag-Ma-mo-che
Srid-pa-chogs-byed-ma
Srid-pa-chags-pa'i-dgra-lha
Srid-pa-chags-pa'i-lha-dgu
Srid-pa'i-lha-chen-gnyan-gyi-gtso
Srid-pa'i-rgyal-mo
Sri-Hevajra
Srikantha
Srimadaryavalokitesvara
Sri-Mahakala

Srimatidevi
Srimati-Parvati-rajni
Srinanda Buddha
Sring-mo-bzhi
Sring-mo-khrag-mig-ma
Srin-mo
Srin-mo-chen-mo
Srin-mo-khrag-gi-ral-pa-can
Srin-mo-ral-gcig-ma
Srin-mo-sbal-mgo-khrag-mig
Srin-mo-spun-dgu
Srin-mo-za-byed-chen-po
Srin-po-gcod-byed-'bar-ba
Srin-po-glog-gi-phreng-ba
Srin-po'i-rgyal-po-gza'-bdud-rahula
Srin-po-'jigs-byed
Srin-po-ma-ru-rtse
Srin-po-mi-rengs
Srin-po-mi-ring
Srin-po-mi-zan
Srin-po-nag-po-glog-'phreng
Sri-pa-chags-pa'i-dgra-lha
Sri-Ucarya-Vajrapani
Srivadirat (Bodhisattva)
Srivajra
Srivajrachakra
Srivasamukhi
Srivasundara
Srnkhala(?)
Srnkhala-Dakini
Srod-bdag-dung-gi-thor-tshugs
Srog-bdag
Srog-bdag-bdud-kyi-bu
Srog-bdag-dkar-po
Srog-bdag-dmar-po
Srog-bdag-dung-gi-thor-tshugs-can
Srog-bdag-hob-se
Srog-bdag-ko-sha
Srog-bdag-ko-'o-sha
Srog-bdag-ko-san
Srog-bdag-ko-shing
Srog-bdag-la-li
Srog-bdag-la-li-pa
Srog-bdag-mo
Srog-bdag-'o-ma-dkar-po
Srog-bdag-rgyal-chen
Srog-bdag-rgyal-po-nyi-pang-sad
Srog-bdag-rgyal-po-snying-sbyin
Srog-bdag-srid-pa('i)-rgyal-po
Srog-bdag-thal-ba
Srog-bdag-tshangs-pa
Srog-bdag-tshangs-pa-dkar-po
Srog-bdud-ma
Srog-gcod-bdud-kyi-bu
Srog-gcod-btsan-rje-srog-zan
Srog-lha
Srog-zan-btsan-rgod-znags-ri-mched-gnyis
Srong-zan-dmar-po
Srstikanta-Lokesvara
Sruta-nama-Nivarana-viskambhin
Ssu-mien pa-pei Ma-t'ou-chin-kang
Ssu-pei Chun-t'i fo-mu
Ssu-pei Feng-t'ien
Ssu-pei-hung-tzu-tsai Kuan-shih-yin
Ssu-pei ju-i-lun Chiu-tu fo-mu
Ssu-pei-ju-i-tzu-tsai Chiu-tu fo-mu
Ssu-pei Kuan-shih-yin
Ssu-pei Kuan-shih-yin p'u-sa
Ssu-pei Mi-lo
Ssu-pei Pan-jo fo-mu
Ssu-pei Pu-tung-chin-kang
Ssu-pei yin-yang Wu-liang-shou fo
Ssu-pei Yung-pao hu-fa
Ssu-tso-chin-kang
sTag-gdon-can
sTag-gdong-khra-bo'i-nang-du-ni
sTag-gi-gdong-pa-can
sTag-lung-dge-bsnyen
sTag-lung-dge-bsnyen-chen-po
sTag-mgo-can
sTag-rtse-ri-mGon-po-ri
sTag-sgo-ti-se-Ma-pham-mtsho
sTag-shar-dpa'-bo'i-sras
sTag-sman-zor-gdong
sTag-srin-zor-ba'i-gdong-can
sTeng-gi-dgra-lha-mu-khri
Sthiracakra
Sthiracakra-Manjughosa
sTobs-po-che
sTon-chen-ma
sTon-chen-mo-rab-tu-hjoms-ma
sTong-btsan-pa
sTong-dpon-dgra-lha
sTong-dpon-dgra-lha-rgyal
sTong-dpon-gong-mo-ri-bkra
sTong-la-chags-pa'i-dgra-lha
sTong-ri-dkar-po
sTong-ri-yi-mtsho-nag
sTon-gyi-lha-mo
sTon-gyi-rgyal-mo
sTsug-tor-hBar-ba
Su-bajar

Subha
Subhaga
Subhamekhala
Sucandra
Su-chi-i-t'ien p'u-sa
Sucisutradhara-Marici
Sudarsana
Sudarsana (Bodhisattva)
Sudhana
Sudhanakumara
Sudurjaya
Sudurjaya (fo-mu)
Sugata-Aparimitayur-jnana
Sugati
Sugatisandarsana
Sugatisandarsana-Lokesvara
Sui-ch'iu fo-mu
Sui-ying fo
Sui-yin-p'a-sa(t'i) fo
Sui-yin-p'u-t'i fo
Sujata
Sukanthi
Sukhada-Tara
Sukha-sadhana-Tara
Sukhavati-Avalokitesvara
Sukhavati-Lokesvara
Sukla-Kurukulla
Sukra
Suladhara
Suma
Sumalini
Sumati
Sumbha
Sumbharaja
Sumerukuta (Bodhisattva)
Sumeruparvataraja Buddha
Sumerusikharadhararaja (Bodhisattva)
Sum-ring-gri-btsan
Sumukhi
Sunaman
Sunamatathagata Buddha
Sundara
Sundari
Sunetra Buddha
Sunggi gyalpo
Sung-tzu
Sung-tzu Kuan-yin
Suparikirtitanamasri
Suparikirtitanamasri Buddha
Suparikirtitanamasriraja
Suradatta
Suradatta Buddha
Suraksini
Surangama
Surasmi Buddha
Suravagrhabhairava (?)
Survana-Matsya
Surya-Candra-Gauri
Surya (deva)
Suryadhara (fo-mu)
Suryagarbha Buddha
Suryahasta
Suryaprabha
Suryaprabha (deva)
Suryavairocana (Bodhisattva)
Sutra-krama-Vajrapani
Suvajra
Suvarna
Suvarnabhadravimalaratnaprabhasa
Suvarnabhadravimalaratnaprabhasavrata
Suvarna-bhadra-vimala-sri
Suvarnaratnaprabhatathagata Buddha
Suvikrantagamin Buddha
Suvikrantasri
Suvikrantasri Buddha
Su-wang fo
Su-yung Chiu-tu fo-mu
Svabha-Prajna
Svamimahapandita-Sumatidharmadhvaja
Svami-Vagisvarasumatisagara
Svapnadesaka-Tara
Svaraghosaraja
Svayambhu-rajni
Swayambhu-Devi
Syama-Krodha-Bhurkumkuta
Syama-nila-Vajravidarana
Syama-Parnasabari
Syamasva-Marici
Syama-Tara
Syama-Tara (fo-mu)
Syama-Vajrapani
Szu-chien-t'o

- T -

Ta-an-lo fo
Ta-chia-yeh
Ta-ch'ien-ts'ui-sui fo-mu
Ta-chi-fen-mu

Ta-ch'ih-chin-kang
Ta-ch'un-ching-kang
Taciyanggui vcir eke
Taditkara
Ta-fa-ting p'u-sa
Tagdongchen
Ta-han-lin fo-mu
Ta-hei-chin-kang
Ta-hei hsiung-wei hu-fa
Ta-hei-hsiung-wei Ts'ai-pao hu-fa
Ta-hei t'ien
Ta-hei-wang
Ta-huan-chin-kang
Ta-huan-chin-kang fo
Ta-huang Ts'ai-pao hu-fa
Ta-hui
Ta-hui chin-se Chiu-tu fo-mu
Ta-hui fo-mu
Ta-hui p'u-sa
Ta-hung Yung-pao hu-fa
Tailikapada
Tai-shih-chih
Ta-jou-shan Chiu-tu fo-mu
Takki-Rah-dzah
Takkiraja
Takki-ra-za
Taksad-Mahakala
Taksad-nag-po
Taksad-senge-zhon-pa
Ta-kuang fo
Ta-k'ung-ch'iao fo-mu
Talahi-bla-ma-skol-bzan-rgya-mcho
Ta-lai-la-ma
Ta-lai-la-ma ka-lo-tsang chia-mu-ts'o
Ta-li-chin-kang
Ta-lieh-ma-ta-tu fo-mu
Ta-lieh-yueh-ta-sha t'ien
Ta-li fo
Talika
Ta-lun Shou-ch'ih-chin-kang
Ta-lun Shou-ch'ih-chin-kang fo
Tamdin
Tamdrin
Tamodghatamati(?) (Bodhisattva)
Tamon
Ta-mo-to-lo
Tamra-Kartaridhara-krsna-cola-Makahala
Tamra-Kartaridhara-Mahakala
Tamra-Kartaridhara-Nagna-Mahakala
Tantra-krama-Sabala-Kalacakra-Garuda
Tan-u
Ta-nu t'ien
T'an Wei-lo-wa-chin-kang
Ta-pao-chin-kang fo-mu
Tao-shih fo
Ta-pai-chu-shou Ts'ai-pao hu-fa
Ta-pai Wen-shu
Ta-pao-chin-kang fo-mu
Ta-pao-ju-i Kuan-shih-yin
Ta-p'eng-chin-kang fo
Ta-p'eng Shang-lo-wang fo
Ta-pien-ts'ai-t'ien nu
Ta-p'eng-chin-kang fo
Tara
Tara (fo-mu)
Tara-Mahacina
Tara of Great China
Tarodbhava-Kurukulla
Ta-shan-ch'iu-yueh Chiu-tu fo-mu
Ta-shan fo
Ta-sheng Ch'u-tu fo-mu
Ta-sheng Pai-san-kai fo-mu
Ta-sheng p'u-sa
Ta-sheng-san-chieh-tzu-tsai Wen-shu
Ta-shih-chih p'u-sa
Tashi tshe ringma
Ta-shou fo
Tathagata
Tathatavasita
Ta-ti-hung-se Kuan-shih-yin
Ta-ti Kuan-shih-yin p'u-sa
Ta-ting fo
Tatthata(?)
Ta-tu-tzu Mi-lo-fu
Ta-tzu-tsai
Ta-tzu-tsai t'ien
T'au Wei-lo-wa-chin-kang
Ta-wei-hung-sheng-chin-kang
Tegus amugulang-tu
Tegus cogtu cing eke
Tegus cogtu cing mudur-tu
Tegus erke-tu
Tegus sayin mudur-tu
Tegus sayin narayani
Tegusugsen uiledugci
Tejausnisa(?) (Buddha)
Tejorasyusnisa
Tejosnisa
Tejo(?)vajra
Te-kuang fo
Te-kuang tsu-shih
Te-lo-pa

Te-lo-pa tsu-shih
Tel-pa
Ten Gods of Direction
Tengwama
Te-nien fo
Tenno
Terigun bayasqulang
Terigun ilagugci
Terigun qogusun
Terigun sayin
Terigun tegusugsen
Te-so
Teyin boged cagan darumtatu
Thab-lha
Thab-lha-g.yu-mo
Thab-sman
Tha-chung-rmu-lcam-thang-mo-sman
Thag-bzang-ris
Thags-bzan-ris
Tha-hog-chos-rgyal-po
Thams-cad-mkhah-hgro
Thams-cad-skyob
Thang-bzang-ring-skyes
Thang-lha
Thang-lha-yab-shur
Thang-lha-yar-bzhugs
Thang-lha-yar-shur
Thang-ra-smu-thang-rje
Thang-thang-gyer-mkhas
Thang-thang-khrol-ba
Tha-'og-chos-rgyal-po
Tha-'og-jo-bo-rgyal-mrshan
Tha-skyes-kyi-gtso-bo
Theb-'mying-pa-rdeg
The-se
The-se-chen-po
The-se-nag-po
The-se-rgyal-po
The-tshom-sa-zahi-hjigs-skyob-Sgrol-ma
The'u-rang-rkang-gcig
Thichen Lozang Tanpa Nyima
Thichen Ngagwang Chogdan
Thingi shal sangma
Tho-ba-gyid-bdag
Tho-ba-'jigs-byed
Thod-pa-kye-rdo-rje
Thod-'phreng-rtsal
Thod-sMyon-bSam-grub
Thog-btsan-pa
Thog-gi-bu-yug
Thog-la-rgom-po
Thog-lha-me-'bar
Thog-'phen-ma
Thogs-med
Thog-tsha-dpa'-bo-stag
Thokchho
Tho-ling-snye-nam-lha-brag
Tho-ri-'bar-ba-brag-dkar-btsan
Tho-ri-rgyal-ba
Thub-dban
Thub-pa-Dam-tshig-gSum-bKod
Thub-pa-dam-tshig-gsum-bkod-(gtso-rkyan)
Thub-pa-me-ru-si-sa
Thub-pa-rdo-rje-gdan-pa-gtso-hkhor-gsum
Thugs-kyai-rdor
Thugs-kyi-mgon-po-gri-gug-can
Thugs-kyi-rgyal-po
Thugs-mchog
Thugs-rje-chen-po-bcu-gcig-zhal
Thugs-rjehi-dban-phyug-Spyan-ras-gzigs
Thugs-sprul-dran-sron-rig-pahi-ye-ses
Thugs-sprul-go-bo
Thun-gyi-rgyal-po
Tian-wang
T'iao-fu-nan-t'iao p'u-sa
T'iao-fu-sheng Shou-ch'ih-chin-kang
T'iao-fu-tu-wu-chin-kang
Ti-chu-yung-ning t'ien-mu
T'ieh-chien Ma-t'ou-chin-kang
T'ieh-kuan Shou-ch'ih-chin-kang
T'ieh-so-mu
T'ien-ch'in tsu-shih
T'ien-jung-mu
T'ien-wang
Tiksna-Manjusri
Tiksna-Manjusri (Bodhisattva)
Tiksnosnisa
Tiksnosnisa (Buddha)
Ti-la-pa
Tilopa
Ting-kuang-fo
Ting-lo t'ien-mu hu-fa
Ting-lo-ting-sman
Tinle gyalpo
Tiryagloka
Ti-se-lha-btsan
Ti-sgro-sman-Mal-gro'i-klu
Ti-shih
Ti-shih t'ien
Ti-t'i a-k'a-cha-mu
Ti-ti-chia
Ti t'ien-mu

Ti-t'i k'a-cha-mu
Ti-t'i na-wa-mu
Ti-t'i sa-pu-ta-mu
Ti-t'i ta-sha-mu
Ti-tsang p'u-sa
Ti-tsang-wang p'u-sa
T'o lo
Tong-chemmo-raptu-joma
Tongyi gyalmo
Tonyer Chema
Tonyo Trup-pa
To Tsun-mu
Tou-chan-sheng fo
Tou-mu
T'ou-pei Ta-lai-la-ma
To-wa-na-ta-sha t'ien
To-wen
Trailokyaraja
Trailokyavasamkara-Avalokitesvara
Trailokyavasamkara-Avalokitesvara (Bodhisattva)
Trailokyavasankara-Lokesvara
Trailokyavasyadhikara-Manjughosa
Trailokyavijaya
Trailokyavijaya (Bodhisattva)
Trailokyavijaya (Buddha)
Trailokyavijaya-Tara
Trailokyavijayavajra
Tra-ksad
Tra-ksad-dmar-po
Trakshad-Mahakala
Trayodasa (deva)
Tribhav-adhipati-Mahamata
Trikal-abhijna-raja
Trilokasandarsana-Lokesvara
Trilokyaksepa
Trimukhacaturbhuja-Maitreya (Bodhisattva)
Trimukha-sadbhuja-Canda
Trimukhasadbhuja-sita-Tara (fo-mu)
Trimukhastabhuja-rakta-Hayagrivavajra
Trisamayavyuha-Muni
Trtiya-Bhadra
Trtiya-Jaya
Trtiya-Nanda
Trtiya-Purna
Trtiya-Sunya
Ts'ai-kung-te fo
Ts'ai-pao hu-fa
Ts'ai-pao t'ien-wang
Ts'ai-po t'ien-mu
Ts'ai-shen
Tsa-lieh-tzu-ka fo-mu
Tsa-men-chih t'ien-mu
Tsamundi
Tsamunti
Tsa-mun-tri
Tsan-chih-ka t'ien-mu hu-fa
Tsan-dan-dpal
Tsandhali
Tsandika
Tsang-kun-lcags-kyi-'khor-lo-can
Tsangpa karpo
Ts'angs-pa-dkar-po
Tsang-tsang-'khor-ba
Tsan-ta-li fo-mu
Tsao-li fo-mu
Tsa-ri-tsa-gong-gnyan-po-rtse
Tsechigma
Ts'e-dpag-med
Tse-la-pa-la-ka fo-mu
Tseng-chang
Tseng-chang t'ien-wang
Tsepame
Tseurima
Tsha-ba'i-brtan-ma-chen-mo
'Tshal-lugs-kyi-ye-shes-mgon-po-phyag-bzhi-pa
Tshang-ma
Tshangs-pa
Tshangs-pa-chen-po
Tshangs-pa-chen-po'i-bka'-nyan-pa
Tshangs-pa-dkar-po
Tshangs-pa-dkar-po-dung-gi-thor-tshugs-can
Tshangs-pa-drag-po
Tshangs-pa-drag-po-srog-bdag-'od-kyi-rgyal-po-li-byin-ha-ra
Tshangs-pa-dung-gi-thor-tshugs-can
Tshangs-pa-li-byin-ha-ra
Tshangs-pa-zhi-ba
Tshans-pa
Tshans-pahi-hod-zer
Tshans-pas-byin
Tsha-ri-gangs
Tshe-bDag-mGon-po
Tshe-bdud-nag-po-khrag-med
Tshe-brtan-ma
Tshe-dpag-med
Tshe-dpag-med-bari-lugs
Tshe-dpag-med-dkar-po-mi-trahi-lugs
Tshe-dpag-med-dkar-po-(phyag-bzhi-pa)
Tshe-dpag-med-lha-dgu
Tshe-dpag-med-sprul-sku

Tshe-'dzin-ma
Tshe-hGugs-lHa-mo
Tshenle-yong-depal
Tshepame
Tshe-ring-mched-lnga
Tshes-gnyan-ro-dgu
Tshe-yi-dbang-phyug-ma
Tshogs-bdag
Tshogs-bdag-dkar-po
Tshogs-bdag-dkar-po-phyag-bzhi-pa-jo-bi'i-lugs
Tshogs-bdag-dkar-po-phyag-bzhi-pa-jo-bohi-lugs
Tshogs-bdag-dmar-chen
Tshogs-bdag-dmar-po-phyag-bzhi-pa
Tshogs-bdag-mgon-po
Tshogs-bdag-mgon-po-seng-ge'i-gdan-can
Tshogs-bdag-ser-po
Tshogs-kyi-phyag-tshangs-chen-mo
Tshon-dpon-bu-mo
Tshong-dpon-nag-po
Tshong-lha-tshogs-bdag-glang-sna
Tsi-dmar-ba
Tsi-ma-ra
Tsi'u-dmar-po
Tson-kha-pa
Tsu-ch'a-pan-t'a-ka tsun-che
Tsugtor nampa gyalma
Tsui-neng-san-lu p'u-sa
Tsui-shang-kung-te fo
Tsui-sheng-mu
Ts'ui-sui-chin-kang
Ts'ui-sui-chin-kang fo-mu
Tsun-che su-yung Chiu-tu fo-mu
Tsun-ch'in hu-fa
Tsun-da
Tsung-k'a-pa
Tsung-k'a-pa tsu-shih
Tsun-sheng
Tsun-sheng fo-mu
Tsun-sheng-mu
Tsun-sheng p'u-sa
Tsun-sheng t'ien-mu
Tsun-sheng-ting fo
Tubpa
Tuidker-i arilgagci
Tuitker-tejin arilghaqci
Tula
Tula (deva)
Tu-la t'ien
T'ung-miao-fa
T'ung-miao-fa t'ien-mu
T'ung-tzu Wen-shu
Tura-vira-(Tara)
Turbel ugei
Tu-sheng fo
T'u-ti
Tu-t'o-shuai-pai Chiu-tu fo-mu
Tu-yen-chin-kang
Twelve Jewel Goddesses
Tzu-chu-lin Chiu-tu fo-mu
Tzu-chu-lin Tara (fo-mu)
Tz'u-niao-mien Yung-pao hu-fa
Tz'u-ti (r. shih) p'u-sa
Tzu-tsai-chih-mu
Tzu-tsai-fa-hsin-mu
Tzu-tsai-fa-mu
Tzu-tsai-hsing-mu
Tzu-tsai-huan-hua-mu
Tzu-tsai-i-mu
Tzu-tsai Kuan-shih-yin p'u-sa
Tzu-tsai-sheng-mu
Tzu-tsai-shou-mu
Tzu-tsai t'ien
Tzu-tsai-yuan-mu

- U -

Ubhayavarahanana
Ubhayavarahanana-Marici
Ucarya
Ucary-a
Ucarya-Vajrapani
Ucchusma-Jambhala
Uddhata-vajra-paksa(?)-Remati
Uddiyana-Kurukulla
Ug-chos-g.ya'-mo-bsil
Ug-chos-g.yar-mo-sil
Ug-chos-ya-ma-bsil
'Ug-mgo-can
'Ug-pa'i-gdong-pa-can
Ugra-Tara
Ujegseger tusatu
Ujjvaladyuti(?)-(Tara)
Ujugurgegci eke
Ukeger-un ejen
Uker terigutu
Ukin tegri
Ulagan adity-a

Ulagan arslan terigutu
Ulagan boru vcir
Ulagan erlig qagan
Ulagan hayangriv-a
Ulagan nidutu
Ulagan yamandaga
Uljeitu sakighulsun
Ulkadhara (fo-mu)
Ulu kudelukci
Uma
Uma-Devi
Umdagan barigci
Unur idegci yaksa
Unur-un eke
Unur-un vcir eke
Upadesa-krama-Sabala-Garuda
Upagupta
Upakesini
Upakesini(?) (devi)
Upananda-Nagaraja
Upanandi luus-un qagan
Upapatti-Vasita
Upasaka-Dharmatala
Upasaka-Hva-san
Upayakausalya-Paramita
Upayaparamita
Urbis terigutu eke
Urdhavapadi-Varahi
Ures-un eke
Urna(?) (fo-mu)
Urtu nasutu eke
Urubila gasib
Uruvilva-Kasyapa
Ushnishacakravartin
Ushnishajvala
Ushnisha
Ushnisha-chakravartin
Ushnishajvala
Ushnishasitapatra
Ushnishasitatapatra
Ushnisha- Tara
Ushnishavijaya
Ushnishavijaya-Tara
Usnisa
Usnisa-bijay-a
Usnisacakravartin
Usnisa chakravarti
Usnisa Deities
Usnisasitapatra
Usnisasitatapatra
Usnisa-Tara
Usnisavijaya
Usnisvijaya-Tara
Usun tngri
Usun tngri-yin tngri
Utnauti(?)-Lokesvara
U-tsharya
Uttamasri (Buddha)

- V -

Vac
Vacirbani
Vacir bariqci
Vadali
Vadi-pramardini-Tara
Vadirad-Manjughosa
Vadirat
Vadisimha Manjughosa
Vadya
Vaga-bajar eke
Vaga-raja
Vag-Hevajra
Vagisvara
Vagraja
Vagvajra
Vaidya Buddha
Vairocana
Vairocana-Bhairavavajra
Vairocanabhisambodhi
Vairocanabhisambodhi (Buddha)
Vairocana-Manjuvajra
Vairocana-Sakyasimha
Vairocani
Vaisravana
Vaisravana (female)
Vajra-Amitayus
Vajrabhairava
Vajrabhasa
Vajrabhaskari
Vajrabhedya Buddha
Vajrabhrkuti (fo-mu)
Vajrabhumi
Vajrabhumi (fo-mu)
Vajrabimba
Vajracakra
Vajracarcika
Vajracarya-Paramita
Vajra-Catuhpitha

Vajradaka
Vajra-Dakini
Vajradanta
Vajradhara
Vajradharma
Vajradharma-Avalokitesvara
Vajradharma (Bodhisattva)
Vajradharma (Buddha)
Vajradharma-Lokesvara
Vajradhatu
Vajradhatu (Buddha)
Vajradhatu-Lokesvara
Vajradhatu-Vairocana
Vajradhatu-Vairocana (Buddha)
Vajradhatvisvari
Vajradhatvisvari-Marici
Vajradvidarana
Vajragandha (fo-mu)
Vajragandhari
Vajragandhari (fo-mu)
Vajragarbha
Vajragarbha Buddha
Vajragarbha-Lokesvara
Vajragarbhapramardin
Vajragarbhapramardin-Avalokitesvara
Vajra-Garuda
Vajragaruda-(sabala)
Vajra-garuda-Samvara
Vajraghanta
Vajra-ging-ka-ra
Vajragra (fo-mu)
Vajrahasa
Vajrahasa (Bodhisattva)
Vajraheruka
Vajrahetu
Vajrahumkara
Vajrahunkara
Vajrahuntika-Lokesvara
Vajrajvalanalarka
Vajrakala
Vajrakarma
Vajrakarmaparamita
Vajraketu
Vajraketu (Bodhisattva)
Vajrakhanda-Lokesvara
Vajrakila
Vajra-krodha
Vajra Krotishaurima
Vajrakshobhya
Vajraksobhya
Vajrakumara
Vajrakundalin
Vajralocani
Vajramrita
Vajramrta
Vajramusti (Bhodisattva)
Vajra-Nairatma
Vajranala
Vajrananga
Vajranatha-Lokesvara
Vajranila
Vajrankusa
Vajrankusi
Vajrapani
?-Vajrapani
Vajrapani-Lokesvara
Vajrapanjara-bhasita-Pratisara
(Vajra) Panjarabhasita-Vajratara
Vajrapasi
Vajrapatala
Vajrapranava
Vajraputtali(?) (fo-mu)
Vajraraga
Vajraraga(?) (fo-mu)
Vajraraja
Vajraraja (Bodhisattva)
Vajraraksa
Vajrarasa
Vajraratna
Vajraraudri
Vajrarupa
Vajrasabda (fo-mu)
Vajrasadhu
Vajrasadhu (Bodhisattva)
Vajrasana-Muni
Vajrasanti (fo-mu)
Vajrasarada
Vajrasarasvati
Vajrasattva
Vajrasattva-Aksobhya
Vajrasattvadhatu-Lokesvara
Vajrasattva-Samvara
Vajrasattvatmika
Vajrasaumya
Vajra-simhasya
Vajrasphota
Vajrasphoti
Vajrasphoti (fo-mu)
Vajra-sringhala
Vajrasrinkhala
Vajrasrinkhala (fo-mu)
Vajrasrnkhala

Vajrasrsta-Lokesvara
Vajrasurya
Vajra-Tara
Vajratejas
Vajratiksna
Vajravalanalarka
Vajravarahi
Vajravega
Vajravetala
Vajravetali
Vajravidarana
Vajravidarani
Vajravina-Sarasvati
Vajra-Vinayaka
Vajrayaksa
Vajrayaksa (Bodhisattva)
Vajrayaksi
Vajrayogini
Vajriputra
Vajrodaka
Vajronisa-Lokesvara
Vajrosnisa
Vajrosnisa (Buddha)
Vajrosnisacakravartiraja
Vak
Vamsa
Vanaratna-krama-Sita-Tara
Vanavasin
Varada-Tara
Varadayaka-Lokesvara
Varahamukhi
Varahi
Varahi (devi)
Varahi eke
Varahi-fo-mu
(Varahi)-Indra-dakini
Varali
Varsa-devi
Varsa-rajni
Varsha-Rajni
Varttali
Varuna
Varuna Buddha
Varuna (deva)
Varunadeva Buddha
Varuna-Nagaraja
Vasamkara-Rakta-Caturmukha-(Sri-Mahakala)
Vasanta-devi
Vasanta-Rajni
Vasisthadeva
Vasitas
Vasubandhu
Vasudhara
Vasumati(?) (devi)
Vasumatisri
Vasusri
Vasyadhikara-Lokesvara
Vasya-Tara
Vatadhara(?)
Vayisiravani
Vayu
Vayu (deva)
Vcir amurlinggui eke
Vcir-a satu-a
Vcir-bani
Vcir-dhar-a
Vcir jiruken-e sagugci
Vcir yaksa eke
Veda
Vemacitrin
Vessavana
Vetali
Vetali-Devi
Vidyadevi
Vidya-Dhara
Vidyapati-Lokesvara
Vidyarajni-Grahamatrka
Vidya-(Tara)
Vidyuddhara (fo-mu)
Vidyujjvalakarali
Vighna
Vighnantaka
Vighnantakavajra
Vighnari
Vijaya (female)
Vijaya (male)
Vijaya (Bodhisattva)
Vijaya (devi)
Vijaya (fo-mu)
Vijaya-Tara
Vijayosnisa (Buddha)
Vikalaratri
Vikrantagamisri
Vikrantagamisri Buddha
Vikrantosnisa (Buddha)
Vimala
Vimala Buddha
Vimala (fo-mu)
Vimalakasa
Vimalaprabhakumara
Vina

Vinadhara (fo-mu)
Vina-Sarasvati
Vipasyanti
Vipasyin
Vipasyin (Buddha)
Viracara
Virakali
Viranandin
Viranandin Buddha
Virasena
Virasena Buddha
Virudhaka
Virulha
Virupa
Virupakha
Virupaksa
Viryaparamita
Vishnu
Vishnu (deva)
Vishnu-Upendra
Vishva-Dakini
Visnucakra-Lokesvara
Visnugupta
Visnukanta-Lokesvara
Visnu nubindar-a
Visnupani-Lokesvara
Visvabhu
Visvabhuta-Lokesvara
Visva(?)daka (Buddha)
Visvadakini
Visvadhara
Visvahana-Lokesvara
Visvamata-Tara
Visvamati
Visvamatr
Visvapani
Visvatara
Visvavajra-Lokesvara
Visvesa-Avalokitesvara
Visvosnisa
Vitana(?)dhara (fo-mu)
Vitaraga-Tathagatas
Vrati-Karmara-Kala
Vrksambara
Vrsa
Vrsabhavaktra
Vrscika (deva)
Vrsnacana-Lokesvara
Vyaghravahana-Mahakala
Vyaghravaktra

- W -

Wa-la-hsi fo-mu
Wa-lieh-hsi t'ien-mu
Wang-chug-mas
Wang-kuang-t'ung-tzu
Wa-shih-ssu-ch'a-t'ien p'u-sa
Wei-chi-chin-kang
Wei-chi fo-mu
Wei-kuang-chin-kang
Wei-kuang-ting fo
Wei-kuang-yun-ting p'u-sa
Wei-lieh san-t'ou liu-pei Shou-ch'ih-chin-kang
Wei-lieh Shou-ch'ih-chin-kang
Wei-lo-wa-chin-kang
Wei-lo-wa-chin-kang fo
Wei-miao-yin p'u-sa
Wei-t'o
Wei-yen-mu
Wen-Shu p'u-sa
Wen-shu-shih-li
We-to
Wer-ti-wer-dgu-ger-mdzo-gnyan
Wo-tzu-lo-sa-tsui
Wu-chih-chin-kang p'u-sa
Wu-chin-chih p'u-sa
Wu-cho tsu-shih
Wu-fo Shang-lo-wang fo
Wu-kou fo
Wu-kou fo-mu
Wu-kou-hsu-k'ung p'u-sa
Wu-kou-kuang-t'ung-tzu
Wu-liang-chu-kuang fo
Wu-liang-kuang fo
Wu-liang-kuang p'u-sa
Wu-liang-shou fo
Wu-ma mu
Wu-ma t'ien-mu
Wu-neng-sheng-fen-nu-chin-kang
Wu-neng-sheng-fen-nu t'ien-mu
Wu-neng-sheng-mu
Wu-pien-sheng-yin p'u-sa
Wu-pei Ta-lai-la-ma
Wu-ti fo-mu
Wu-wei-mieh-ming fo
Wu-wo fo-mu
Wu-yu fo
Wu-yu-ju-lai fo
Wu-yu-sheng-chi-hsiang-ju-lai

Wu-yu-te fo

- Y -

Ya-ba-mgo-dgu
Ya-ba-ti
Yab bdud
Ya-bdud-tshogs-kyi-gtso-bo
Yab-gcig-bdud-rje-nag-po
Yab-gcig-yaksa-dzva-la
Yab-'od-de-gung-rgyal
Yab-rdo-rje-srin-po
Yaksa
Yaksa-demons
Yaksa (deva)
Yaksa-me-dbal
Yaksa-nag-mo
Yaksa-Purnabhadra
Yaksi-Remati
Yaku-shi
Yama
Yama-chidup
Yama-daksad (?)
Yama-daksdi
Yamadanda (?)
Yama-dandi
Ya-ma-dandi
Yamadandin
Yama-dati
Yama-Dharmaraja
Yama-disti
Yamaduti
Yam-a eke
Yama (gsang-sgrub)
Yamajaya (?)
Yama-Nag-dup
Yamangaraka
Yamantaka
Yaman-taka
Yamantakavajra
Yama-(phyi-sgrub)
Yama-Raja
Yamari
Yama Sangdup
Yama-tasti
Yami
Yam-shud-dmar-po
Yamu vcir eke
Yan-dag-rdzogs-pahi-sans-rgyas-mya-nan-med
Yan-dag-ses
Yangchenma
Yang-dag-shes
Yang-dag-thugs-kyi-lha-tshogs
Yang-gha-bza'
Yang-gsang-dpal-mgon-dug-ri-nag-phyag-bzhi-pa
Yang-le-ber
Yang-'u-rang-rgyal-po
Yan-lag-hByung
Yan-lo
Yao-ch'a-ta-chiang
Yao-ch'a t'ien
Yao-shi-fo
Yao-shih-ju-lai fo
Yao-shih-liu-li-kuang-wang-ju-lai
Yao-xi
Yar-'brog-mtsho-bdag-chen-mo
Yargyi gyalmo
Yar-lha-sham-po
Yar-lung-gi-yar-lha-sham-po
Yar-shur-gnyan-gyi-lha
Yar-stod-brag-la-yar-'brog-ri
Yasahketu Buddha
Yasodhara (?)
Yasodhvaja Buddha
Yavadi
Ya-wa-ti
Yayati
Yayisiravani
Yeh-ch'a Hsien-man hu-fa
Yeke gara
Ye-nas-srid-pa'i-dgra-lha
Yen-kuang p'u-sa
Yen-lo-wang
Yen-man-te-kia
Yen-ming fo
Yer-ba-gtsug-ri
Yer-ba'i-rdzong-btsan-mthu-bo-che
Yeru-yi butugegci eke
Yeru-yin vcir eke
(Ye-ses)-mgon-po-phyag-bzhi-pa-grub-chen-zhi-ba-sbas-pahi-lugs
(Ye-ses)-mgon-po-phyag-bzhi-pahi-hkhor-lha-mo-tsandi-ka
(Ye-ses)-mgon-po-phyag-bzhi-pa-rgva-lohi-lugs
Ye-ses-mkhah-hgro
Ye-ses-phyag-drug-Mgon
Ye-ses-sems-dpah-Hjam-pahi-dbyans
Ye-shes-bLa-ma

Ye-shes-dakini
Ye-shes-kyi-ma-mo
Ye-shes-mgon-po-phyag-bzhi-pa
Ye-shes-mgon-po-phyag-bzhi-pa-grub-chen-Zhi-ba-sbas-pa'i-lugs
Ye-shes-mgon-po-phyag-bzhi-pa'i-'khor- lha-mo-tsandika
Ye-shes-mgon-po-phyag-bzhi-pa-rGva- lo'i-ligs
Ye-shes-mkha'-'gro-ma
Yi-dam
Yid-bzhin-rgyal-mo-phyag-bzhi-ma
Yid-hphrog-nor-rgyun-ma
Yid-'prog ma
Yi-ge-drug-ma
(Yig-rnin-lugs)Prajnalokakrtya-Sita-Vahari
Yin-chieh-t'o tsun-che
Yin-kuang-t'ien p'u-sa
Yin-t'o-lo yao-ch'a-ta-chiang
Yi-'phrog-nor-rgyun-ma
Yisun salburagsan
Yo-chu t'ien
Yogambara
Yogambara (Buddha)
Yogini
Yons-su-smin-par-mdzad-pahi-sgrol-ma
Yons-su-rzogs-pahi-sGrol-ma
Yon-tan
Yon-tan-gyi-mgon-po-legs-ldan-nag
Yon-tan-gyi-rgyal-po
Yon-tan-gyi-sprul-pa
Yon-tan-hod
Yon-tan-rgyal-po
Yon-tan-sprul-dran-sron-rig-pahi-ye-ses
Yoryu Kwan-non
Yuan-hsing
Yuan-hsing fo-mu
Yuan Po-lo-mi-mu
Yu-chia-hsu-k'ung fo
Yu-ch'ieh-hsu-k'ung fo
Yuddhajaya
Yuddhajaya Buddha
Yueh-hsiang fo
Yueh-kuang-mu
Yueh-kuang-pien-chao p'u-sa
Yueh-kuang p'u-sa
Yueh t'ien
Yu-hsi
Yu-hsi fo-mu
Yu-hsi-tzu-tsai Wen-shu
Yu-hsi-wang Wen-shu p'u-sa
Yul-di'i-gzhi-bdag-tham-cad
Yul-gyi-lha-gnyan-chen-po
Yul-hkhor-bsrun
Yul-hkhor-srun
Yul-'khor-bsrung
Yulkhorsung
Yul-lha
Yul-lha-chag-sangs-klu-sras
Yul-lha-rgyal-po-gzhon-nu
Yum-bdud-mo-nag-mo-Khrag-'jag-ma
Yum-chen-'bar-ma-glog-phreng-ma
Yum-gcig-klu-mo-klog-khyug-ma
Yum-klu-mo-yakso-nag-mo
Yum-mchog-brgya-byin-sras-mo-gnam-mtsho-sman
Yum-mchog-ekajati
Yum-mchog-sgrol-byed-nag-mo
Yum-rdo-rje-glog-'gyu(ma)
Yu-mu-pa t'ien
Yung-hsing p'u-sa
Yung-lun Wen-shu
Yung-shih-chin-kang fo-mu
Yung-shih fo
Yu-p'o-chu-to
Yu-shua-ha-li-mu
Yu-su-wang fo
Yu t'ien-mu
Yuvarajasvamin
Yu-wang-chin-kang

- Z -

Za-byed-spyang-gryal-nag-mo
Zam-bha-la-dkar-po-hbrug-zhon
Zam-bha-la-nag-po
Zam-bha-la-phyag-drug-pa
Zam-bha-la-ser-po
Zangs-brag-dmar-po'i-mnga'-bdag-po
Zangs-mdog-dpal-ri
Zangs-mig-ma
Zangs-phreng-ma
Zangs-phur-can-pa
Zangs-phur-pa
Zangs-ri-btsan-rgod-mthu-chen-mched-gnyis
Zas-gtsan-sras
Zas-ster-ma-dmar-mo
Ze-ba-can
Zeng Zang
Zhabs-ra-dkar-bo

Zhag-lha
Zhags-pa'i-khyung
Zhags-pa-ma
Zhags-pa-mo
Zhal-bram-gzugs
Zhal-bzhi-pa-las-sbyor-mgon-po
Zhal-gsum-mi-bo-che
Zhal-gsum-stod-kyi-mi-bo-che
Zhal-gyi-dbang-po
Zhal-zas-ma
Zhan-blon
Zhan-blon-rdo-rje-bdud-hdul
Zhan-blon-rdo-rje-bdud-hdul-phyi-sgrub
Zhang-lha
Zhang-po-gnyan-dmar
Zhang-po-klu-rgyal-ghi-ha
Zhang-zhung-gi-srung-ma
Zhe-sdan-me-dpun-tshogs-rnams-rab-zhi-ma
Zhi-ba-chen-mohi-sGrol-ma
Zhi-ba-htsho
Zhi-ba'i-gshin-rje
Zhi-ba'i-lha-mo
Zhi-ba'i-rgyal-chen
Zhi-ba-lha
Zhing-skyong
Zhing-skyong-chen-po-kun-dga'-gzhon nu
Zhing-skyong-lha-ba
Zhing-skyong-sha-za-nag-po
Zi-na-mi-tra
Zla-ba
Zla-ba-bzan
Zla-ba-grags-pa
Zla-bahi-hod
Zla-ba'i-sa-rgyal
Zla-ba-lha
Sla-bas-byin
Zla-ba-seng-ge
Zla-ba-thod-dkar
Zla-btsan-gnyan-po-tshe-bdang-rtsal
Zla-ltar-snan-byed
Zla-pang-sad-kyi-rgyal-po
Zla-shel-ma
Zla-yi-dkar-nag-sum-mdo
Zocho
Zojo
'Zur-'gegs-sel-ba'i-tshogs-bdag-chags-pa-rdo-rje
Zur-phud-lnga-pa
Zur-ra-skyes-(drug)

Postscript

When I first began compiling this iconographic encyclopaedia I wanted a complete, comprehensive work. The longer I toiled, the more complex became the problems, some of which seemed to multiply geometrically. After a number of years I realized that the ideal could not be achieved in the time-frame which was set for me and due to the time constraints of publication requirements; an end had to be drawn. Closure had to be made.

A bulk of the major and minor deities have been included within the purview of this endeavor. Yet, there may be inadvertent omissions. Nonetheless, every possible effort under the parameters given, has been made to include the deities of the major pantheons.

The form of the individual entries had evolved over a long period of time. There most certainly may be others that are equally useful. It is, however, a form which seemed most workable and efficient for my use in this compilation. Workable and efficient, in that it gives maximum information within the minimum amount of space.

I am not unaware that an undertaking of this sort may have its flaws and/or errors. Its strengths and short-comings will appear after its use. The improvement of this work is a future goal. To this end I would urge the users of this iconographic encyclopaedia to send their comments either to the author or to the publisher so that they may be considered in the production of a second edition.

F.W.B.